Morton Hunt

THE STORY OF
PSYCHOLOGY

Morton Hunt has been a freelance writer specializing in the
behavioral sciences since 1949. His articles have appeared in
many national magazines, including *The New Yorker* and
The New York Times, and have won him numerous prizes
including the Westinghouse A.A.A.S. Award for best science
article of the year. He has written twenty-one books, the best
known of which are *The World of the Formerly Married*
(about the lives and psychology of separated and divorced
people), *The Universe Within* (cognitive science), and the
earlier edition of this present book. He lives in Gladwyn,
Pennsylvania, with his wife, writer and psychotherapist
Bernice Hunt.

THE STORY OF
PSYCHOLOGY

THE STORY OF
PSYCHOLOGY

MORTON HUNT

Anchor Books
A Division of Random House, Inc.
New York

SECOND ANCHOR BOOKS EDITION, DECEMBER 2007

Copyright © 1993, 2007 by Morton Hunt

Anchor Books and colophon are registered trademarks of
Random House, Inc.

The Library of Congress has cataloged the previous edition as follows:
Hunt, Morton M., 1920–
The story of psychology / Morton Hunt.
p.   cm.
Includes bibliographical references and index.
1. Psychology—History.   1. Title.
BF81.H86   1993
150'.9—dc20   92-15131

Anchor ISBN: 978-0-307-27807-4

Book design by JoAnne Metsch

www.anchorbooks.com

Printed in the United States of America
10   9   8   7   6   5

To Bernice,

for reasons beyond counting

READER

I here put into thy hands what has been the diversion of some of my idle and heavy hours; if it has the good luck to prove so of any of thine, and thou hast but half so much pleasure in reading as I had in writing it, thou wilt as little think thy money, as I do my pains, ill bestowed.

JOHN LOCKE, "The Epistle to the Reader,"
An Essay Concerning Human Understanding

THE STORY OF
PSYCHOLOGY

PROLOGUE:

Exploring the Universe Within

A Psychological Experiment
in the Seventh Century B.C.

A most unusual man, Psamtik I, King of Egypt. During his long reign, in the latter half of the seventh century B.C., he not only drove out the Assyrians, revived Egyptian art and architecture, and brought about general prosperity, but found time to conceive of and conduct history's first recorded experiment in psychology.

The Egyptians had long believed that they were the most ancient race on earth, and Psamtik, driven by intellectual curiosity, wanted to prove that flattering belief. Like a good psychologist, he began with a hypothesis: If children had no opportunity to learn a language from older people around them, they would spontaneously speak the primal, inborn language of humankind—the natural language of its most ancient people—which, he expected to show, was Egyptian.

To test his hypothesis, Psamtik commandeered two infants of a lower-class mother and turned them over to a herdsman to bring up in a remote area. They were to be kept in a sequestered cottage, properly fed and cared for, but were never to hear anyone speak so much as a word. The Greek historian Herodotus, who tracked the story down and learned what he calls "the real facts" from priests of Hephaestus in Memphis, says that Psamtik's goal "was to know, after the indistinct babblings of infancy were over, what word they would first articulate."

The experiment, he tells us, worked. One day, when the children were two years old, they ran up to the herdsman as he opened the door of their cottage and cried out *"Becos!"* Since this meant nothing to him, he paid no attention, but when it happened repeatedly, he sent word to Psamtik, who at once ordered the children brought to him. When he too heard them say it, Psamtik made inquiries and learned that *becos* was the Phrygian word for bread. He concluded that, disappointingly, the Phrygians were an older race than the Egyptians.[1]

We today may smile condescendingly; we know from modern studies of children brought up under conditions of isolation that there is no innate language and that children who hear no speech never speak. Psamtik's hypothesis rested on an invalid assumption, and he apparently mistook a babbled sound for an actual word. Yet we must admire him for trying to prove his hypothesis and for having had the highly original notion that thoughts arise in the mind through internal processes that can be investigated.

Messages from the Gods

For it had not occurred to anyone until then, nor would it for another several generations, that human beings could study, understand, and predict how their thoughts and feelings arose.

Many other complex natural phenomena had long engaged the interest of both primitive and civilized peoples, who had come more or less to understand and master them. For nearly 800,000 years human beings had known how to make and control fire;[2] for 100,000 years they had been devising and using tools of many kinds; for eight thousand years some of them had understood how to plant and raise crops; and for over a thousand years, at least in Egypt, they had known some of the elements of human anatomy and possessed hundreds of remedies—some of which may even have worked—for a variety of diseases. But until a century after Psamtik's time neither the Egyptians nor anyone else thought about or sought to understand—let alone influence—how their own minds functioned.

And no wonder. They took their thoughts and emotions to be the work of spirits and gods. We have direct and conclusive evidence of this in the form of the testimony of ancient peoples themselves. Mesopotamian cuneiform texts from about 2000 B.C., for instance, refer repeatedly to the "commands" of the gods—literally heard as utterances by the rulers of society—dictating where and how to plant crops, to whom to delegate authority, on whom to make war, and so on. A typical clay cone reads, in part:

> Mesilin King of Kish at the command of his deity Kadi concerning the plantation of that field set up a stele [an inscribed stone column] in that place . . . Ningirsu, the hero of Enlil [another god], by his righteous command, upon Umma war made.[3]

A far more detailed portrait of how early people supposed their thoughts and feelings arose can be found in the *Iliad*, which records the beliefs of Homer in the ninth century B.C., and to some extent those of the eleventh-century Greeks and Trojans he wrote about. Professor Julian Jaynes of Princeton, who exhaustively analyzed the language of the *Iliad* that refers to mental and emotional functions, summed up his findings as follows:

> There is in general no consciousness in the Iliad . . . and in general, therefore, no words for consciousness or mental acts. The words in the Iliad that in a later age come to mean mental things have different meanings, all of them more concrete. The word *psyche*, which later means soul or conscious mind, [signifies] in most instances life-substances, such as blood or breath: a dying warrior bleeds out his *psyche* onto the ground or breathes it out in his last gasp . . . Perhaps most important is the word *noos* which, spelled as *nous* in later Greek, comes to mean conscious mind. Its proper translation in the Iliad would be something like perception or recognition or field of vision. Zeus "holds Odysseus in his *noos*." He keeps watch over him.[4]

The thoughts and feelings of the people in the *Iliad* are put directly into their minds by the gods. The opening lines of the epic make that plain. It begins when, after nine years of besieging Troy, the Greek army is being decimated by plague, and the thought occurs to the great Achilles that they should withdraw from those shores:

> Achilles called the men to gather together, this having been put into his mind by the goddess of the white arms, Hera, who had pity on the Greeks when she saw them dying . . . and he said to them, "I believe that backwards we must make our way home if we are to escape death through fighting and the plague."

Such explanations of both thought and emotion occur time and again, said Professor Jaynes.

> When Agamemnon, king of men, robs Achilles of his mistress, it is a god that grasps Achilles by his yellow hair and warns him not to strike Agamemnon. It is a god . . . who leads the armies into battle, who speaks to each soldier at the turning points, who debates and teaches Hector what he must do.[5]

Other ancient peoples, even centuries later, similarly believed that their thoughts, visions, and dreams were messages from the gods. Herodotus tells us that Cyrus the Great, founder of the Persian Empire, crossed into the land of the hostile Massagetae in 529 B.C. and during his first night there dreamed that he saw Darius, the son of his follower Hystaspes, with wings on his shoulders, one shadowing Asia, the other Europe. When Cyrus awoke, he summoned Hystaspes and said, "Your son is discovered to be plotting against me and my crown. I will tell you how I know it so certainly. The gods watch over my safety, and warn me beforehand of every danger." He recounted the dream and ordered Hystaspes to return to Persia and have the son ready to answer to Cyrus when he came back from defeating the Massagetae.[6] (Cyrus, however, was killed by the Massagetae. Darius did later become king, but not by having plotted against him.)

The ancient Hebrews had comparable beliefs. Throughout the Old Testament, important thoughts are taken to be utterances of God, who appears in person in the earlier writings, or as the voice of God heard within oneself, in the later ones. Three instances:

> After these things the word of the Lord came unto Abram in a vision, saying, Fear not, Abram: I am thy shield, and thy exceeding great reward. (Genesis, 15:1)

> Now after the death of Moses the servant of the Lord it came to pass, that the Lord spake unto Joshua the son of Nun, Moses' minister, saying, Moses my servant is dead; now therefore arise, go over this Jordan, thou, and all this people, unto the land which I do give to them, even to the children of Israel. (Joshua, 1:1–2)

> Now the word of the Lord came unto Jonah the son of Amittai, saying, Arise, go to Nineveh, that great city, and cry against it; for their wickedness is come up before me. (Jonah, 1:1–2)

Disordered thoughts and madness were likewise interpreted as the work of God or of spirits sent by Him. Deuteronomy names insanity as one of the many curses that God will inflict on those who do not obey His commands:

> The Lord shall smite thee with madness, and blindness, and astonishment of heart. (Deut., 28:28)

Saul's psychotic fits, which David allayed by playing the harp, are attributed to an evil spirit sent by the Lord:

> But the spirit of the Lord departed from Saul, and an evil spirit from the Lord troubled him . . . And it came to pass, when the evil spirit from God was upon Saul, that David took an harp, and played with his hand: so Saul was refreshed, and was well, and the evil spirit departed from him. (I Samuel, 16:14–23)

When David's fame as a warrior exceeded Saul's, though, the divinely caused madness raged out of all control:

> And it came to pass on the morrow, that the evil spirit from God came upon Saul, and he prophesied in the midst of the house: and David played with his hand, as at other times: and there was a javelin in Saul's hand. And Saul cast the javelin; for he said, I will smite David even to the wall with it . . . [but David] slipped away out of Saul's presence, and he smote the javelin into the wall. (I Samuel, 18:10–11 and 19:10)

The Discovery of the Mind

But in the sixth century B.C. there appeared hints of a remarkable new development. In India, Buddha attributed human thoughts to our sensations and perceptions, which, he said, gradually and automatically combine into ideas. In China, Confucius stressed the power of thought and decision that lay within each person ("A man can command his principles; principles do not master the man," "Learning, undigested by thought, is labor lost; thought unassisted by learning is perilous").

The signs of change were even stronger in Greece, where poets and sages began to view their thoughts and emotions in wholly new terms.[7]

Sappho, for one, described the inner torment of jealousy in realistic terms rather than as an emotion inflicted on her by a god:

> Peer of gods he seemeth to me, the blissful
> Man who sits and gazes at thee before him,
> Close beside thee sits, and in silence hears thee
>   Silverly speaking,
> Laughing love's low laughter. Oh, this, this only
> Stirs the troubled heart in my breast to tremble!
> For should I but see thee a little moment,
>   Straight is my voice hushed;
> Yea, my tongue is broken, and through and through me
> 'Neath the flesh, impalpable fire runs tingling;
> Nothing see mine eyes, and a voice of roaring
>   Waves in my ears sounds.
>
> —"Ode to Atthis"

Solon, poet and lawgiver, used the word *nous* not in the Homeric sense but to mean something like rational mind. He declared that at about age forty "a man's *nous* is trained in all things" and in the fifties he is "at his best in *nous* and tongue." He or the philosopher Thales— sources differ—sounded a note totally different from that of Homeric times in one of Western civilization's briefest and most famous pieces of advice, inscribed on the Temple of Apollo at Delphi: "Know thyself."

Within a few decades there began a sudden and astonishing efflorescence of Greek thought, science, and art. George Sarton, the historian of science, once estimated that in the Hellenic era, human knowledge increased something like forty-fold in less than three centuries.[8]

One of the most notable aspects of this intellectual outburst was the abrupt appearance and burgeoning of a new area of knowledge, philosophy. In the Greek city-states of the fifth and fourth centuries B.C., a small number of reflective upper-class men, who had neither scientific equipment nor hard data but were driven by a passion to understand the world and themselves, managed by pure speculation and reasoning to conceive of, and offer answers to, many of the enduring questions of cosmogony, cosmology, physics, metaphysics, ethics, aesthetics, and psychology.

The philosophers themselves did not use the term "psychology" (which did not exist until A.D. 1520) or regard it as a distinct area of knowledge, and they were less interested in the subject than in more fundamental ones like the structure of matter and the nature of causality. Nonetheless, they identified and offered hypotheses about nearly all the significant problems of psychology that have concerned scholars and scientists ever since. Among them:

— Is there only one substance, or is "mind" something different from "matter"?
— Do we have souls? Do they exist after the body dies?
— How are mind and body connected? Is mind part of soul, and if so can it exist apart from the body?
— Is human nature the product of inborn tendencies or of experience and upbringing?
— How do we know what we know? Are our ideas built into our minds, or do we develop them from our perceptions and experiences?
— How does perception work? Are our impressions of the world around us true representations of what is out there? How can we know whether they are or not?
— Which is the right road to true knowledge — pure reasoning or data gathered by observation?
— What are the principles of valid thinking?
— What are the causes of invalid thinking?
— Does the mind rule the emotions, or vice versa?

There is scarcely a major topic in today's textbooks of introductory psychology that was not anticipated, at least in rudimentary form, by the Greek philosophers. What is even more impressive, their goal was the same as that of contemporary psychologists: to discover the true causes of human behavior—those unseen processes of the mind which take place in response to external events and other stimuli.

This quest launched the Greek philosophers on an intellectual voyage into the invisible world of the mind—the universe within, one might call it. From their day to ours, explorers of the mind have been pressing ever deeper into its terra incognita and uncharted wilderness. It has been and continues to be a voyage as challenging and enlightening as any expedition across unknown seas or lands, any space mission to far-off planets, any astronomical probe of the rim of the world and the border of time.

What kind of men (and, in recent decades, women) have felt compelled to find out what lies in the vast and invisible cosmos of the mind?

All kinds, as we will see: solitary ascetics and convivial sybarites, feverish mystics and hardheaded realists, reactionaries and liberals, true believers and convinced atheists—the list of antinomies is endless. But they are alike in one way, these Magellans of the mind: All of them, in various ways, are interesting, impressive, even *awesome* human beings. Time and again I felt, after reading the biography and writings of one of these people, that I was fortunate to have come to know him, privileged to have lived with him vicariously, and greatly enriched by having shared his adventures.

The explorations of the interior world conducted by such people have surely been more important to human development than the explorations of the external one. Historians are wont to name technological advances as the great milestones of culture, among them the development of the plow, the discovery of smelting and metalworking, the invention of the clock, printing press, steam power, electric engine, lightbulb, semiconductor, and computer. But possibly even more transforming than any of these was the recognition by Greek philosophers and their intellectual descendants that human beings could examine, comprehend, and eventually even guide or control their own thought processes, emotions, and resulting behavior.

With that realization we became something new and different on earth: the only animal that, by examining its own cerebration and behavior, could alter them. This, surely, was a giant step in evolution. Although we are physically little different from the people of three thousand years ago, we are culturally a different species. We are the psychologizing animal.

This inward voyage of the past twenty-five hundred years, this search for the true causes of behavior, this most liberating of all human inquiries, is the subject of *The Story of Psychology*.

Part One

PRESCIENTIFIC

PSYCHOLOGY

ONE

The
Conjecturers

The Glory That Was Greece

"In all history," the philosopher Bertrand Russell has said, "nothing is so surprising or so difficult to account for as the sudden rise of civilization in Greece."[1]

Until the sixth century B.C., the Greeks borrowed much of their culture from Egypt, Mesopotamia, and neighboring countries, but from the sixth to the fourth centuries they generated a stupendous body of new and distinctive cultural materials.* Among other things, they created sophisticated new forms of literature, art, and architecture, wrote the first real histories (as opposed to mere annals), invented mathematics and science, developed schools and gymnasiums, and originated democratic government. Much of subsequent Western culture has been the lineal descendant of theirs; in particular, much of philosophy and science during the past twenty-five hundred years has been the outgrowth of the Greek philosophers' attempts to understand the nature of the world. Above all, the story of psychology is the narrative of a continuing effort to answer the questions they first asked about the human mind.

It is mystifying that the Greek philosophers so suddenly began to theorize about human mental processes in psychological, or at least quasi-psychological, terms. For while the 150 or so Greek city-states around the Mediterranean had noble temples, elegant statues and fountains,

---

*Throughout this chapter, the dates given are B.C. unless otherwise noted.

and bustling marketplaces, living conditions in them were in many respects primitive and not, one would suppose, conducive to subtle psychological inquiry.

Few people could read or write; those who could had to scratch laboriously on wax tablets or, for permanent records, on strips of papyrus or parchment twenty to thirty feet long wrapped around a stick. Books—actually, hand-copied scrolls—were costly, rare, and awkward to use.

The Greeks, possessing neither clocks nor watches, had but a rudimentary sense of time. Sundials offered only approximations, were not transportable, and were of no help in cloudy weather; the water clocks used to limit oratory in court were merely bowls filled with water that emptied through a hole in about six minutes.

Lighting, such as it was, was provided by flickering oil lamps. A few of the well-to-do had bathrooms with running water, but most people, lacking water to wash with, cleansed themselves by rubbing their bodies with oil and then scraping it off with a crescent-shaped stick. (Fortunately, some three hundred days a year were sunny, and Athenians lived out of doors most of the time.) Few city streets were paved; most were dirt roads, dusty in dry weather and muddy in wet. Transport consisted of pack mules or springless, bone-bruising horse-drawn wagons. News was sometimes conveyed by fire beacons or carrier pigeons, but most often by human runners.

Illustrious Athens, the center of Greek culture, could not feed itself; the surrounding plains had poor soil, the hills and mountains were stony and infertile. The Athenians obtained much of their food through maritime commerce and conquest. (Athens established a number of colonies, and at times dominated the Aegean, receiving tribute from other city-states.) But while their ships had sails, the Athenians knew only how to rig them to be driven by a following wind; to proceed crosswind or into the wind or in a calm, they forced slaves to strain hour after hour at banks of oars, driving the ships at most eight miles per hour. The armies thus borne to far shores to advance Athenian interests fought much like their primitive ancestors, with spears, swords, and bows and arrows.

Slaves also provided most of the power in Greek workshops and silver mines; human muscles, feeble as they are compared to modern machinery, were, aside from beasts of burden, the only source of kinetic energy. Slavery was, in fact, the economic foundation of the Greek city-states; men, women, and children captured abroad by Greek armies made up much of the population of many cities. Even in democratic Athens and the neighboring associated towns of Attica, at least 115,000 of the 315,000 inhabitants were slaves. Of the 200,000 free Athenians only the forty-three thousand men who had been born to two Athenian parents possessed all civil rights, including the right to vote.

All in all, it was not a way of life in which one would expect reflective and searching philosophy, or its subdiscipline, psychology, to flourish.

What, then, accounts for the Greeks' astonishing intellectual accomplishments, and for those of the Athenians in particular? Some have half-seriously suggested the climate; Cicero said that Athens' clear air contributed to the keenness of the Attic mind. Certain present-day analysts have hypothesized that the Athenians' living outdoors much of the time, in constant conversation with one another, induced questioning and thinking. Others have argued that commerce and conquest, bringing Athenians and other Greeks into contact with many other cultures, made them curious about the origin of human differences. Still others have said that the mix of cultural influences in the Greek city-states gave Greek culture a kind of hybrid vigor. Finally, some have pragmatically suggested that when civilization had developed to the point where day-to-day survival did not take up every hour of the day, human beings for the first time had leisure in which to theorize about their motives and thoughts, and those of other people.

None of these explanations is really satisfactory, although perhaps all of them taken together, along with still others, are. Athens reached the zenith of its greatness, its Golden Age (480 to 399), after it and its allies defeated the Persians. Victory, wealth, and the need to rebuild the temples on the Acropolis that the Persian leader Xerxes had burned, in addition to the favorable influences mentioned above, may have produced a kind of cultural critical mass and an explosion of creativity.

The Forerunners

Along with their many other speculations, a number of the Greek philosophers of the sixth and early fifth centuries began proposing naturalistic explanations of human mental processes; these hypotheses and their derivatives have been at the core of Western psychology ever since.

What kinds of persons were they? What caused or at least enabled them to think about human cognition in this radically new fashion? We know their names—Thales, Alcmaeon, Empedocles, Anaxogoras, Hippocrates, Democritus, and others—but about many of them we know little else; about the others what we know consists largely of hagiography and legend.

We read, for instance, that Thales of Miletus (624–546), first of the philosophers, was an absentminded dreamer who, studying the night-time heavens, could be so absorbed in glorious thoughts as to tumble ingloriously into a ditch. We read, too, that he paid no heed to money until, tired of being mocked for his poverty, he used his astrological expertise one winter to foretell a bumper crop of olives, cheaply leased all the oil presses in the area, and later, at harvest time, charged top prices for their use.

Gossipy chroniclers tell us that Empedocles (500?–430), of Acragas in southern Sicily, had such vast scientific knowledge that he could control the winds and once brought back to life a woman who had been dead for thirty days. Believing himself a god, in his old age he leaped into Etna in order to die without leaving a human trace; as some later poet-aster jested, "Great Empedocles, that ardent soul / Leaped into Etna, and was roasted whole." But Etna vomited his brazen slippers back onto the rim of the crater and thereby proclaimed him mortal.

Such details hardly help us fathom the psychophilosophers, if we may so call them. Nor did any of them set down an account—at least, none exists—of how or why they became interested in the workings of the mind. We can only suppose that in the dawn of philosophy, when thoughtful men began to ask all sorts of searching questions about the nature of the world and of humankind, it was natural that they would also ask how their own thoughts about such things arose and where their ideas came from.

One or two did actual research that touched on the physical equip-ment involved in psychological processes. Alcmaeon (fl. 520), a physi-cian of Croton in southern Italy, performed dissections on animals (dissecting the human body was taboo) and discovered the optic nerve, connecting the eye to the brain. Most, however, were neither hands-on investigators nor experimentalists but men of leisure, who, starting with self-evident truths and their own observations of everyday phenomena, sought to deduce the nature of the world and of the mind.

The psychophilosophers most often carried on their reasoning while strolling or sitting with their students in the marketplaces of their cities or courtyards of their academies, endlessly debating the questions that intrigued them. And probably, like Thales gazing at the stars, they also spent periods alone in deep meditation. But little remains of the fruits of their labors; nearly all copies of their writings were lost or destroyed.

Most of what we know of their thinking comes from brief citations in the works of later writers. Yet even these bits and pieces indicate that they asked a number of the major questions—to which they offered some sensible and some outlandish answers—that have concerned psychologists ever since.

We can surmise from the few obscure and tantalizing allusions by later writers to the philosophers' ideas that among the questions they asked themselves concerning *nous* (which they variously identified as soul, mind, or both) were what its nature is (what it is made of), and how so seemingly intangible an entity could be connected to and influence the body.

Thales pondered these matters, although a single sentence in Aristotle's *De Anima* (On the Soul) is the only surviving record of those thoughts: "Judging from the anecdotes related of him [Thales], he conceived soul as a cause of motion, if it be true that he affirmed the lodestone to possess soul because it moves iron."[2] Little as this is to go on, it indicates that Thales considered soul or mind the source of human behavior and its mode of action a kind of physical force inherent in it, a view radically unlike the earlier Greek belief that human behavior was directed by supernatural forces.

Within a century, some philosophers and the physician Alcmaeon suggested that the brain, rather than the heart or other organs, as earlier believed, was where *nous* existed and where thinking goes on. Some thought it was a kind of spirit, others that it was the very stuff of the brain itself, but in neither case did they say anything about how memory, reasoning, or other thought processes take place. They were preoccupied by the more elementary question of whence—since not from the gods—the mind obtains the raw materials of thought.

Alcmaeon

Their general answer was sense experience. Alcmaeon, for one, said that the sense organs send perceptions to the brain, where, by means of thinking, we interpret them and derive ideas from them. What intrigued him and others was how the perceptions get from the sense organs to the brain. Unaware of nerve impulses, even though he had discovered the optic nerve, and believing, on abstract metaphysical grounds, that air was the vital component of mind, he decided that perceptions must travel along air channels from the sense organs to the brain: No matter that he never saw any and that no such channels exist; reason told him it must be so. (Later Greek anatomists would refer to the air, *pneuma*, they thought was in the nerves and brain as "animal spirits," and in one form or another this belief would dominate thinking about the nervous system until the eighteenth century.) Although Alcmaeon's theory was wholly incorrect, his emphasis on perception as the source of knowledge was the beginning of epistemology—the study of how we acquire knowledge—and laid the ground for a debate about that topic that has gone on ever since.

Protagoras

Alcmaeon's ideas were borne around the far-flung Greek cities by travelers; soon, philosophers in many places were devising their own explanations of how perception takes place, and a number of them asserted that it was the basis of all knowledge. But some saw the troubling implications of this view. Protagoras (485–411), best known of the Sophists (a term that then meant not fallacious reasoners but "teachers of wisdom"), unsettled his contemporaries and pupils by pointing out that, since perception was the only source of knowledge, there could be no absolute truth. His famous apothegm, "Man is the measure of all things," meant, he explained, that any given thing is to me what it appears to me to be, and, if it appears different to you, is what it seems to you to be. Each perception is true—for each perceiver. Philosophers were willing to debate the point, but politicians considered it subversive. When Protagoras, visiting Athens, tactlessly applied his theory to religion, saying there was no way for him to know whether the gods exist or not, the outraged Assembly banished him and burned his writings. He fled and drowned at sea en route to Sicily.

Democritus

Others carried on that line of inquiry, devising explanations of how perception takes place and maintaining that, since knowledge is based on perception, all truths are relative and subjective. The most sophisticated of such musings were those of Democritus (460–362) of Abdera, Thrace, the most learned man of his time. Vastly amused by the follies of humankind, he was known as the "laughing philosopher." His main claim to fame, actually, derives not from his psychological reflections but from his extraordinary guess that all matter is composed of invisible particles (atoms) of different shapes linked together in different combinations, a conclusion he came to, without any experimental evidence, by sheer reasoning. Unlike Alcmaeon's air channels, this theory would eventually be proven absolutely correct.

From his theory of atoms Democritus derived an explanation of perception. Every object gives off or imprints on the atoms of the air images of itself, which travel through the air, reach the eye of the beholder, and there interact with its atoms. The product of that interaction passes to the mind and, in turn, interacts with its atoms.[3] He thus anticipated, albeit in largely incorrect detail, today's theory of vision, which holds that photons of light, emanating from an object, travel to the eye, enter it, and stimulate the endings of the optic nerves, which send messages to the brain, where they act on the brain's neurons.

All knowledge, according to Democritus, results from the interaction of the transmitted images with the mind. Like Protagoras, he concluded that this means we have no way of knowing whether our perceptions correctly represent what is outside or whether anyone else's perception is identical with our own. As he put it, "We know nothing for certain, but only the changes produced in our body by the forces that impinge upon it."[4] That issue would vex philosophers and psychologists from then until now, driving many of them to devise elaborate theories in the effort to escape the solipsistic trap and to affirm that there is some way to know what is really true about the world.

Hippocrates

When the early philosopher-psychologists concluded that thought occurs in the mind, it was only natural that they would also wonder why our thoughts are sometimes clear and sometimes muddled, and why most of us are mentally healthy but others are mentally ill.

Unlike their ancestors, who had believed mental dysfunction to be the work of gods or demons, they sought naturalistic answers. The most widely accepted of these was that of Hippocrates (460–377), the Father of Medicine. The son of a physician, he was born on the Greek island of Cos off the coast of what is today Turkey. He studied and practiced there, treating many of the invalids and tourists who came for the island's hot springs and achieving such renown that far-off rulers sought him out. In 430 Athens sent for him when a plague was ravaging the city; observing that blacksmiths seemed immune to it, he ordered fires built in all public squares and, legend says, brought the disease under control. Only a handful of the seventy-odd tracts bearing his name were actually written by him, but the rest, the work of his followers, embody his ideas, which are a mixture of the sound and the absurd. For instance, he stressed diet and exercise rather than drugs, but for many diseases recommended fasting on the grounds that the more we nourish unhealthy bodies, the more we injure them.

His greatest contribution was to divorce medicine from religion and superstition. He maintained that all diseases, rather than being the work of the gods, have natural causes. In this spirit, he taught that most of the physical and mental ills of his patients had a biochemical basis (though the term "biochemical" would have meant nothing to him).

He based this explanation of health and illness on the prevailing theory of matter. Philosophers had held that the primordial stuff of the world was water, fire, air, and so on, but Empedocles concocted a more intellectually satisfying theory, which dominated Greek and later thinking. All things, he said, are made up of four "elements"—earth, air, fire, and water—held together in varying proportions by a force he called "love" or kept asunder by its opposite, "strife."[5] Though the specifics were wholly wrong, many centuries later scientists would find that his core concept—that all matter is composed of elemental substances alone or in combination—was quite right.

Hippocrates borrowed Empedocles' four-element theory and applied it to the body. Good health, he said, is the result of a proper balance of the four bodily fluids, or "humors," which correspond to the four elements—blood corresponding to fire, phlegm to water, black bile to earth, and yellow bile to air. For the next two thousand years physicians would attribute many illnesses to humoral imbalances that they would try to cure by draining off an excess of a humor (as in bloodletting) or by administering medicines supplying one that was lacking. The harm this caused over the centuries, particularly through bloodletting, is incalculable.

Hippocrates used the same theory to explain mental health and illness. If the four humors were in proper balance, consciousness and thought would function well, but if any humor was either in excess or short supply, mental illness of one kind or another would result. As he wrote:

Men ought to know that from the brain, and the brain only, arise our pleasures, joys, laughter, and jests, as well as our sorrows, pains, grief, and tears . . . These things that we suffer all come from the brain when it is not healthy but becomes abnormally hot, cold, moist, or dry . . . Madness comes from its moistness. When the brain is abnormally moist, of necessity it moves, and when it moves, neither sight nor hearing is still, but we see or hear now one thing and now another, and the tongue speaks in accordance with the things seen and heard on any occasion. But when the brain is still, a man is intelligent.

The corruption of the brain is caused not only by phlegm but by bile. You may distinguish them thus: those who are mad through phlegm are quiet, and neither shout nor make a disturbance; those maddened through bile are noisy, evil-doing, and restless . . . The patient suffers from causeless distress and anguish when the brain is chilled and contracted contrary to custom; these effects are caused by phlegm, and it is these very effects that cause loss of memory.[6]

Later, followers of Hippocrates extended his humoral theory to account for differences in temperament. Galen, in the second century A.D., said that a phlegmatic person suffers from an excess of phlegm, a choleric one from an excess of yellow bile, a melancholic one from an excess of black bile, and a sanguine one from an excess of blood. That doctrine persisted in Western psychology until the eighteenth century and remains embedded in our daily speech—we call people "phlegmatic," "bilious," and so on—if not our psychology.

Although the humoral theory of personality and of mental illness now seems as benighted as the belief that the earth is the center of the universe, its premise—that there is a biological basis to, or at least a biological component in, personality traits and mental health or illness—has lately been confirmed beyond all question. A vast amount of recent research by cognitive neuroscientists has identified many of the substances produced by brain cells and shown how these enable thought processes to take place, and myriad other studies have shown that foreign substances such as drugs or toxins distort or interfere with those processes. Hippocrates was close to the mark after all.

One can only marvel at the psychological musings of Hippocrates and the pre-Socratic psychophilosophers. Quite without laboratories, methodology, or empirical evidence—indeed, without anything but open minds and intense curiosity—they recognized and enunciated a number of the salient issues and devised certain of the theories that have remained central in psychology from their time to our own.

The "Midwife of Thought": Socrates

We now come upon a man unlike the shadowy figures we just met, a real and vivid person whose appearance, personal habits, and thoughts are thoroughly documented: Socrates (469–399), the leading philosopher of his time and the proponent of a theory of knowledge that directly contradicted perception-based theory. We know a good deal about him as a person because two of his pupils—Plato and the historian-soldier Xenophon—set down detailed recollections of him. Unfortunately, Socrates himself wrote nothing, and his ideas come to us chiefly through Plato's dialogues, where much of what he says is probably Plato's own thinking put in Socrates' mouth for dramatic reasons. Nonetheless, Socrates' contributions to psychology are clear.

He lived during the first half of Athens' era of greatness (the span from its defeat of the Persians at Salamis in 480 to the death of Alexander in 323), when philosophy and the arts flourished as never before. The son of a sculptor and a midwife, he was fascinated by what he learned of philosophy in his youth from Protagoras, Zeno of Elea, and others. He early decided to make it his life work, but, unlike the Sophists, he took no fees for his teaching; he would talk to anyone who wanted to discuss ideas with him. He occasionally worked as a stonecutter and carver of statues but preferred the luxury of thought and discourse to the comforts money could buy. Content to be poor, he wore one simple shabby robe all year and went barefoot; once, looking about in the marketplace, he exclaimed with pleasure, "How many things there are that I do not want!"

Not that he was an ascetic; he liked good company, sometimes went to banquets given by the wealthy, and freely confessed to feeling a "flame" within him when he peered inside a youth's garment. Uncommonly homely, with a considerable paunch, a bald head, broad snub nose, and thick lips, he looked like a satyr, his friend Alcibiades told him. Unlike a satyr, however, he was a model of moderation and self-control; he seldom drank wine, remained sober when he did, and was chaste even when in love. The beautiful and amoral Alcibiades, slipping into Socrates' bed one night to seduce him, was astonished to be treated as if by a father. "I thought I had been disgraced," he later said, according to Plato's *Symposium*, "and yet I admired the way this man was made, and his temperance and courage."

Socrates kept himself in good physical condition; he fought bravely during the Peloponnesian War, where his ability to withstand cold and hunger amazed his fellow soldiers. After long years of instructing his pupils, he was tried and condemned for his teachings, which Athenian democrats said corrupted youth. The real problem was that he was contemptuous of their democracy and numbered many aristocrats, their political foes, among his followers. He accepted the verdict with equanimity and refused the opportunity to escape, preferring to die with dignity.

Although the Delphic Oracle once declared Socrates the wisest man in the world, he disputed that pronouncement; it was his style to claim that he knew nothing and was wiser than others only in knowing that he knew nothing. He claimed to be a "midwife of thought," one who merely helped others give birth to their ideas. This, of course, was a pose; in reality he had a number of firmly held opinions about certain philosophic matters. But unlike many of his contemporaries, he was uninterested in cosmology, physics, or perception; as he says in Plato's *Apology*, "I have nothing to do with physical speculations." His concern, rather, was with ethics. His goal was to help others lead the virtuous life, which, he said, comes about through knowledge, since no man sins wittingly.

To help his students attain knowledge, Socrates relied not on lectures but on a wholly different educational method. He asked his students questions that seemingly led them step by step to discover the truth for themselves. This technique, known as dialectic, was first used by Zeno, from whom he may have learned it, but it was Socrates who developed and popularized it. In doing so, he promulgated a theory of knowledge that would be the major alternative to perception-based theories from then on.

According to that theory, knowledge is recollection; we learn not from experience but from reasoning, which leads us to discover knowledge that exists within us ("to educate" comes from the Latin meaning "to lead out"). Sometimes Socrates asks for definitions and then leads his partner into contradictions until the definition is reshaped. Sometimes he asks for or offers examples, from which his partner finally makes a generalization. Sometimes he leads him, step by step, to a conclusion that contradicts one he had previously stated, or to a conclusion he had not known was implicit in his beliefs.

Socrates cites geometry as the ideal model of this process. One starts with self-evident axioms and, by hypothesis and deduction, discovers other truths in what one already knew. In the *Meno* dialogue he questions a slave boy about geometrical problems, and the boy's answers supposedly show that he must all along have known the conclusions to which Socrates leads him; he was unaware that he knew them until he recalled them through dialectical reasoning. Similarly, in many another dialogue Socrates, without presenting an argument or offering answers, asks a friend or pupil questions that lead him, inference by inference, to the discovery of some truth about ethics, politics, or epistemology—in each case, knowledge he supposedly had but was unaware of.

We who live in an era of empirical science know that Socratic dialectic, though it can expose fallacies or contradictions in belief systems or lead to new conclusions in such formal systems as mathematics, cannot discover new facts. Until Anton van Leeuwenhoek (1632–1723 A.D.) first saw red corpuscles and bacteria under his lens, no Socratic teacher could have led his pupils or himself to "remember" that such things existed; until astronomers saw evidence of the "red shift" in distant galaxies, no philosopher could, through logical searching, have discovered that he already knew the universe to be expanding at a measurable rate.

Yet Socrates' teachings greatly affected the development of psychology. His view that knowledge exists within us and needs only to be recovered through correct reasoning became part of the psychological theories of persons as diverse as Plato, Saint Thomas Aquinas, Kant, and even, in a sense, those present-day psychologists who maintain that personality and behavior are largely determined by genetics, linguists who say that our minds come equipped with language-comprehending structures, and parapsychologists who believe that each of us has lived before and can be "regressed" to recall our previous lives.

The notion that we have lived before is related to Socrates' other major impact on psychology. He held that the existence of innate knowledge, revealed by the dialectic method of instruction, proves that we possess an immortal soul, an entity that can exist apart from the brain and body. With this, the vague mythical notions of soul that had long existed in Greek and related cultures assumed a new significance and specificity. Soul is mind but is separable from the body; mind does not cease to be at death.

On this ground would be built Platonic and, later, Christian dualism: the division of the world into mind and matter, reality and appearance, ideas and objects, reason and sense perception, the first half of each pair regarded not only as more real than but as morally superior to the second. Although these distinctions may seem chiefly philosophic and religious, they would pervade and affect humankind's search for self-understanding throughout the centuries.

The Idealist:
Plato

He was named Aristocles, but the world knows him as Plato—in Greek, *platon*, or "broad"—the nickname he was given as a young wrestler because of the width of his shoulders. He was born in Athens in 427 to well-to-do aristocratic parents, and in his youth was an accomplished student, a handsome charmer of men and women, and a would-be poet. At twenty, about to submit a poetic drama in a competition, he listened to Socrates speaking in a public place, after which he burned his poetry and became the philosopher's pupil. Perhaps it was the gamelike quality of Socrates' dialectic that captivated the former wrestler; perhaps the subtlety of Socrates' ideas entranced the serious student; perhaps the quiet and serenity of Socrates' philosophy appealed to the son of ancient lineage in that era of political upheaval and betrayal, war and defeat, revolution and terror.

Plato studied with Socrates for eight years. He was a dedicated student and something of a sobersides; one ancient author says that he was never seen to laugh out loud. A few scraps of love poetry attributed to him exist, some of them addressed to men, some to women, all of doubtful authenticity, and there is almost no gossip about his love life and no evidence that he ever married. Still, from the wealth of detail in his dialogues, it is evident that he was an active participant in Athenian social life and a keen observer of behavior and the human condition.

In 404, an oligarchic political faction that included some of his own aristocratic relatives urged him to enter public life under its auspices. The young Plato wisely held back, waiting to see what the group's policy would be, and was repelled by the violence and terror it used as its tools of government. But when democratic forces regained power, he was even more repelled by their trial and conviction of his revered teacher, whom he calls, in the *Apology*, "the wisest, the justest, and best of all men I have ever known." After Socrates' death, in 399, Plato fled Athens, wandered around the Mediterranean meeting and studying with other philosophers, returned to Athens to fight for his city, then again went wandering and studying.

At forty, conversing with Dionysius, the despot of Syracuse, he daringly condemned dictatorship. Dionysius, nettled, said, "Your words are those of an old dotard," to which Plato replied, "Your language is that of a tyrant." Dionysius ordered him seized and sold into slavery, which might have been the end of his philosophizing, but Anniceris, a wealthy admirer, ransomed him, and he returned to Athens. Friends raised three thousand drachmas to reimburse Anniceris, who refused the money. They thereupon used it to buy Plato a suburban estate, where in 387 he founded his Academy. This school of higher learning would be the intellectual center of Greece for nine centuries until, in A.D. 529, the Emperor Justinian, a zealous Christian, shut it down in the best interests of the true faith.

We have almost no details about Plato's activities at the Academy, which he headed for forty-one years, until his death in 347 at eighty or eighty-one. It is believed, however, that he taught his students by a combination of Socratic dialectic and lectures, usually delivered as he and his auditors wandered endlessly to and fro in the garden. (A minor playwright, mocking this custom, has a character say, "I am at my wits' end walking up and down like Plato, and yet have discovered no wise plan but only tired my legs."[7])

Plato's thirty-five or so dialogues—the actual number is uncertain, because at least half a dozen are probably spurious—were not meant for his students' use; they were a popularized, semidramatized version of his ideas, addressed to a larger audience. They deal with metaphysical, moral, and political matters and, here and there, certain aspects of psychology. His influence on philosophy was immense and on psychology, although it was not his main concern, far greater than that of anyone who preceded him and of anyone except Aristotle for the next two thousand years.

Despite the veneration in which Plato is generally held, from a scientific standpoint his effect on the development of psychology was more harmful than helpful. Its most negative aspect was his antipathy to the theory that perception is the source of knowledge; believing that data derived from the senses are shifting and unreliable, he held that true knowledge consists solely of concepts and abstractions arrived at through reasoning. In the *Theaetetus*, he mocks the perception-based theory of knowledge: If each man is the measure of all things, why are not pigs and baboons equally valid measures, since they too perceive? If each man's perception of the world is truth, then any man is as wise as the gods, yet no wiser than a fool. And so on.

More seriously, Plato has Socrates point out that even if we agree that one man's judgment is as true as another's, the wise man's judgment may have better consequences than the ignorant man's. The doctor's forecast of the course of the patient's illness, for instance, is more likely to be correct than the patient's; thus, the wise man is, after all, a better measure of things than the fool.

But how does one become wise? Through touch we perceive hard and soft, but it is not the sense organs that recognize them as opposites, he says; it is the mind that makes that judgment. Through sight we may judge two objects to be about equal in size, but we never see or experience absolute equality; such abstract qualities can be apprehended only by other means. <u>We gain true knowledge—that is, the knowledge of concepts like absolute equality, similarity and difference, existence and nonexistence, honor and dishonor, goodness and badness—through reflection and reason, not through sense impressions</u>.

Here Plato was on the trail of an important psychological function, the process by which the mind derives general principles, categories, and abstractions from particular observations. But his bias against sense data led him to offer a wholly unprovable metaphysical explanation of that process. Like his mentor, he held that conceptual knowledge comes to us by recollection; we inherently have such knowledge and discover it through rational thinking.[8]

But going further than Socrates, he argued that these concepts are more "real" than the objects of our perceptions. The "idea" of a chair—the abstract concept of chairness—is more enduring and real than this or that physical chair. The latter will decay and cease to be; the former will not. Any beautiful individual will eventually grow old and wrinkled, die, and cease to exist, but the concept of beauty is eternal.[9] The idea of a right triangle is perfect and timeless, while any triangle drawn on wax or parchment is imperfect and will someday cease to be; indeed, over the door of the Academy was the inscription "Let no one without geometry enter here."

This is the heart of Plato's Theory of Ideas (or Forms), the metaphysical doctrine that reality consists of ideas or forms that exist eternally in the soul pervading the universe—God—while material objects are transient and illusory.[10] Plato is thus an Idealist, not in the sense of one with high ideals but of one who advocates the superiority of ideas to material objects. Our souls partake of those eternal ideas; we bring them with us when we are born. When we see objects in the material world, we understand what they are and the relationships between them—larger or smaller, and so on—by remembering our ideas and using them as a guide to experience.

Or rather we do if we have been liberated from ignorance by philosophy; if not, we are deluded by our senses and live in error like the prisoners in Plato's famous metaphorical cave. Imagine a cave, he says in the *Republic*, in which prisoners are so bound that they face an inner wall and see only shadows, cast on it by a fire outside, of themselves and of men passing behind them carrying all sorts of vessels, statues, and figures of animals. The prisoners, knowing nothing of what is behind them, take the shadows to be reality. At last one man escapes, sees the actual objects, and understands that he has been deceived. He is like a philosopher who recognizes that material objects are only shadows of reality and that reality is composed of ideal forms.[11] It is his duty to go down into the cave and lead the prisoners up into the light of reality.

Plato may have been led to construct his otherworldly and metaphysical explanation of true knowledge by Socrates' and his own reasoning. But perhaps the military and political chaos of his era made him seek something eternal, unshakable, and absolute in which to believe. Certainly his prescription for an ideal state, spelled out in the *Republic*, aims to achieve stability and permanence through a rigid class system and the totalitarian rule of a small elite of philosopher-kings.

In any case, in Plato's epistemology that which is physical, particular, and mortal is considered illusion and error, while only what is conceptual, abstract, and eternal is real and true. His Theory of Ideas, greatly extending the dualism of Socrates, portrayed the senses as deceptive, the spiritual as the only path to truth; appearances and material things as illusory and transient, ideas as real and eternal; the body as corruptible and corrupting, the soul as incorruptible and pure; desires and hungers as the source of trouble and sin, the ascetic life of philosophy as the way to goodness. These dichotomies sound remarkably like anticipations of the fulminations of the early Fathers of the Church but are Plato's own:

> The body fills us full of loves and lusts and fears and fancies of all kinds . . . We are slaves to [the body's] service. If we would have true knowledge of anything we must be quit of the body—the soul in herself must behold things in themselves; then we shall attain the wisdom we desire, be pure and have converse with the pure . . . And what is purification but the separation of the soul from the body?[12]

Soul, for Plato, is thus not only an incorporeal and immortal entity, as many Greeks had long believed: it is also mind. But he never explained how thinking can take place in an incorporeal essence. Since thinking requires effort and thus uses energy, whence would the energy come to enable the soul to think? Plato says that motion is the essence of the soul and that psychological activities are related to its inner motions, but he is silent about the source of the energy for such motion.

Yet he was a sensible man with wide experience of the world, and some of his psychological conjectures about the soul are down-to-earth and sound almost contemporary. In some of the middle and later dialogues—notably the *Republic*, the *Phaedrus*, and the *Timaeus*—he says that when the soul inhabits a body, it operates on three levels: thought or reason, spirit or will, and appetite or desire. Though he castigated the lusts of the body in the *Phaedo*, now he says that it is as bad for reason wholly to suppress appetite or spirit as for either of those to overpower reason; the Good is achieved when all three aspects of the soul function in harmony. Here too he resorts to metaphor to make his meaning clear: He likens the soul, in the *Phaedrus*, to a team of two steeds, one lively but obedient (spirit), the other violent and unruly (appetite), the two yoked together and driven by a charioteer (reason) who, with considerable effort, makes them cooperate and pull together. Plato came to this conclusion without conducting clinical studies or psychoanalyzing anyone, yet to a surprising extent it anticipates Freud's analysis of character as composed of superego, ego, and id.

Plato also said, without any empirical evidence to go on, that the reason is located in the brain, the spirit in the chest, and the appetites in the abdomen; that they are linked by the marrow of the spine and brain; and that emotions are carried around the body by the blood vessels. These guesses are in part ludicrous, in part prescient of later discoveries. Considering that he was no anatomist, one can only wonder how he arrived at these judgments.

In the *Republic* Plato describes in remarkably modern terms what happens when appetite is ungoverned:

When the reasoning and taming and ruling power of the personality is asleep, the wild beast within us, gorged with meat and drink, starts up and having shaken off sleep goes forth to satisfy his desires; and there is no conceivable folly or crime—not excepting incest or parricide, or the eating of forbidden food—which at such a time, when he has parted company with all shame and sense, a man may not be ready to commit.[13]

And he portrays in almost contemporary terms the condition we call ambivalence, which for him is a conflict between spirit and appetite that reason fails to control. In the *Republic* Socrates offers this example:

> I was once told a story, which I can quite believe, to the effect that Leontius, the son of Aglaion, as he was walking up from the Piraeus and approaching the northern wall from the outside, observed some dead bodies on the ground and the executioner standing by them. He immediately felt a desire to look at them, but at the same time loathing the thought he tried to divert himself from it. For some time he struggled with himself, and covered his eyes, till at length, over-mastered by the desire, he opened his eyes wide with his fingers, and running up to the bodies, exclaimed, "Look, ye wretches, take your fill of the fair sight!"[14]

Yet he also says—and it is the most important message of the charioteer-and-team metaphor—that appetite should not be eliminated but, rather, controlled. Attempting total repression of our desires would be like holding the steeds in check rather than driving them on toward reason's goal.

Two other items of Plato's psychology are worth our noting. One is his concept of Eros, the drive to be united with the loved one. It usually has a sexual or romantic connotation, but in Plato's larger sense it refers to a desire to be united with the Idea or eternal Form that the other person exemplifies. Despite the metaphysical trapping of the concept, it contributed to psychology the idea that our most basic drive is for unity with an undying principle. As Robert I. Watson, a historian of psychology, puts it: "Eros is popularly translated as 'love,' but may often be more meaningfully called 'life force.' This is something akin to the biological will to live, the life energy."[15]

Finally, Plato casually offered a thought about memory that would be used much later to counter his own theory of knowledge. Although he viewed recollection through reasoning as the most important kind of memory, he did admit that we learn and retain much from everyday experience. To explain why some of us remember more of that experience, or remember it more correctly, than others do, and why we often forget much of what we have learned, he resorted in the *Theaetetus* dialogue to a simile likening memory of experiences to writing on wax tablets: just as these surfaces may vary in size, hardness, moistness, and purity, so the minds of different persons vary in capacity, ability to learn, and retentiveness. Plato pursued the thought no further, but much later it would epitomize a theory of knowledge diametrically opposed to his. The seventeenth-century philosopher John Locke and the twentieth-century behaviorist John Watson would base their psychologies on the assumption that everything we know is what experience has written on the blank slate of the newborn mind.

The Realist: Aristotle

Plato's most distinguished pupil, Aristotle, spent twenty years at the Academy, but after leaving it he contradicted so effectively much of what Plato had taught that he had as great an influence on philosophy as his master. More than that, through philosophy he left his mark on areas of knowledge as diverse as logic and astronomy, physics and ethics, religion and aesthetics, biology and rhetoric, politics and psychology. "He, perhaps more than any other thinker," asserts one scholar, Anselm H. Amadio, "has characterized the orientation and content of all that is termed Western civilization."[16] And though psychology was far from Aristotle's main concern, he gave "history's first fully integrated and systematic account" of it, says the psychologist-scholar Daniel N. Robinson, adding, "Directly and indirectly, it has been among the most influential as well. Within the surviving works can be found theories of learning and memory, perception, motivation and emotion, socialization, personality."[17]

One might expect such an intellectual giant to have been a strange person, but almost no peculiarities have been recorded of him. Busts show a handsome bearded man with refined and sensitive features; a malicious contemporary said he had small eyes and spindleshanks, but Aristotle offset these drawbacks with elegant dress and impeccable barbering. Nothing is known of his private life during his years at the Academy, but at thirty-seven he married for love. His wife died early, and in his will he asked that at his own death her bones be laid next to his. He remarried, lived with his second wife the rest of his life, and left her well provided for, "in recognition of the steady affection she has shown me." He was usually kindly and warm, but when sorely tried could be tart. When a long-winded fellow asked him, "Have I bored you to death with my chatter?" he replied, "No, indeed—I wasn't paying attention to you."

Although affluent by birth, Aristotle was an extraordinarily hard worker all his life, sparing himself nothing in his quest for knowledge. When Plato read his *Phaedo* dialogue aloud, wearied auditors tiptoed out one by one, but Aristotle, and he alone, stayed to the end. On his honeymoon he devoted much of his time to collecting seashells, and he labored so assiduously at his research and writing that he completed 170 works in forty years.

Aristotle was born in 384 in Stagira, in northern Greece. His father was court physician to Amyntas II, King of Macedonia, whose son would become Philip II, father of Alexander the Great. Medical knowledge being traditionally passed down from father to son in Greece, Aristotle must have learned a good deal of biology and medicine; this may account for the scientific and empirical outlook that later made him the quintessential Realist, as opposed to Plato's quintessential Idealist.

He came to Plato's Academy at seventeen and stayed until he was thirty-seven; then he left, some say in anger, when Plato died and his nephew, rather than Aristotle, was appointed successor. He spent thirteen years away from Athens, first as philosopher-adviser to Hermeas, tyrant of Assus in Asia Minor; then as head of a philosophic academy at Mytilene on Lesbos, then as tutor to the teenage Alexander at Pella, King Philip's capital. All the while, he was intensely busy reading, observing animal and human behavior, studying the skies, collecting biological specimens, dissecting animals, and writing. Some of his works, cast in dialogue form, were said to have been literary masterpieces, but all of these are lost. The forty-seven that remain, though intellectually profound, are numbingly prosaic and pedantic; they were probably lecture notes and treatises meant only for school use.

At forty-nine, at the height of his powers, Aristotle returned to Athens. Although the presidency of the Academy again became vacant, he was again passed over. He then founded a rival institution, the Lyceum, just outside the city, and there assembled teachers and pupils, a library, and a collection of zoological specimens. He lectured both morning and afternoon while strolling up and down the *peripatos*, the covered walkway of the Lyceum (whence our word "peripatetic"), yet doubled his scholarly output by parceling out areas of research to students, much like today's professors, and marshaling their findings in one work after another.

After thirteen years at the Lyceum, he left Athens when anti-Macedonian agitation broke out and he came under attack because of his Macedonian connections. His reason for moving away, he said, was to save the Athenians from sinning twice against philosophy (the first sin having been the conviction and execution of Socrates). He died the following year (322), at sixty-two or sixty-three, of a stomach illness.

None of this explains the immensity of his accomplishments. One can only suppose that, as with Shakespeare, Bach, and Einstein, Aristotle was a genius of the rarest sort who happened to live in a time and at a place that particularly favored his extraordinary abilities.

To be sure, many of his theories were later overturned or abandoned, and his scientific writings are riddled with myths, folklore, and outright errors. In his impressive *De Generatione Animalium* (History of Animals), for instance, he reported as fact that mice die if they drink in summertime, that eels are generated spontaneously, that human beings have only eight ribs, and that women have fewer teeth than men.

But unlike Plato he had the hunger for empirical data and the love of painstaking observation that have characterized science ever since. Despite the high value he placed on deductive reasoning and formal logic, he continually stressed the importance of inductive reasoning— the derivation of generalizations from observed cases or examples, a fundamental part of scientific method and a way of arriving at knowledge exactly contrary to that advocated by Plato.

For far from regarding sense perceptions as illusory and untrustworthy, Aristotle considered them the essential raw material of knowledge.[18] Extraordinary for one who had studied with Plato, he had, says one Aristotle scholar, "an intense interest in the concrete facts";[19] he regarded the direct observation of real things, except in abstract domains such as mathematics, to be the foundation of understanding. In *De Generatione Animalium*, for instance, after admitting that he does not know how bees procreate, he says:

> The facts have not yet been sufficiently established. If ever they are, then credit must be given to observation rather than to theories, and to theories only insofar as they are confirmed by the observed facts.[20]

Like earlier philosophers, he sought to understand how perception takes place, but having no way to gather hard data on the matter— testing and experimentation were unknown, the dissection of human bodies impermissible—he relied on metaphysical explanations. He theorized that we do not perceive objects as such but their qualities, such as whiteness and roundness, which are nonmaterial "forms" that inhere in matter. When we see them, they are re-created within the eye, and the sensations they arouse are transmitted through the blood vessels to the mind—which, he thought, must be in the heart, since people often recover from injuries to the head while wounds to the heart are invariably fatal. (The brain's function, he thought, was to cool the blood when it became overly warm.) He also discussed the possible existence of an interior sense, the "common" sense, by means of which we recognize that various sensations arriving from different sense organs—say, white and round, warm and soft—come from a single object (in this case, a ball of wool).

If we ignore these absurdities, Aristotle's explanation of how perceptions become knowledge is commonsensical and convincing, and complementary to the perception-based epistemologies of Protagoras and Democritus. Our minds, Aristotle says, recognize the similarities in a series of objects—this is the essence of inductive reasoning—and from those common traits form a "universal," a word or concept signifying not an actual thing but a *sort* of thing or a general principle; this is the route to higher levels of knowledge and wisdom. Reason or intellect thus acts upon sense data; it is an active, organizing force.

Having spent so many years examining biological specimens, Aristotle was of no mind to regard the objects of perception as mere illusions, or to rank generalized concepts as more real than the individual things they summarize. Where Plato said that abstract ideas exist eternally, apart from material things, and are more real than they, his realistic pupil said they were only attributes that could be "predicated" of specific subjects. Though he never totally abandoned the metaphysical trappings of Greek thought, he came close to saying that universals have no existence except in the thinking mind. He thus synthesized the two main streams of Greek thinking about knowledge: the extreme emphasis on sense perception of Protagoras and Democritus and the extreme rationalism of Socrates and Plato.

About the relation of mind to body, at times he is hopelessly opaque, at other times crystal clear. The opacity concerns the nature of "soul," which, waxing metaphysical, he calls the "form" of the body—not its shape but its "essence," its individuality, or perhaps its capacity to live. This muddy concept was to roil the waters of psychology for many centuries.

On the other hand, his comments about that part of the soul where thinking takes place are lucid and sensible. "Certain writers," he says in *De Anima,* "have happily called the soul the place of ideas, but this description applies not to the soul as a whole but merely to the power of thought."[21] Most of the time he calls the part of the soul where thinking takes place the *psyche*, although sometimes he uses that term to mean the entire soul; despite the inconsistency, he is consistent in saying that the thinking part of the soul is a place where ideas are formed, not a place in which they exist before the soul inhabits the body.

Nor is soul, or psyche, an entity that can exist apart from the body. "It is clear," he says, "that the soul is not separable from the body, and the same holds good of particular parts of the soul."[22] He rejects the Platonic doctrine of the imprisoned soul whose highest goal is to escape from the bonds of matter; in contrast to Plato's dualism, his system is essentially monistic. (But this is his mature view. Because his views changed during his lifetime, Christian theologians would be able to find ample material in his early writings to justify their dualism.)

Once he has these matters out of the way, Aristotle gets to his real interest: how the mind uses both deduction and induction to arrive at knowledge. His description constitutes, according to Robert Watson, "the first functional view of mental processes . . . [For him] *psyche* is a *process*; *psyche* is what *psyche* does."[23] Psyche isn't an immaterial essence, nor is it the heart or blood (nor, even if he had located psyche in the brain, would it have been the brain); it is the *steps* taken in thinking—the functionalist concept that today underlies cognitive science, information theory, and artificial intelligence. No wonder those who know Aristotle's psychology stand in awe of him.

His description of thought processes sounds as if he based it on laboratory findings. He had none, of course, but being so diligent a collector of biological specimens, he may well have done something analogous, that is, scrutinized his own experiences and those of others, treating them as the specimens on which he based his generalizations.

The most important of these is that the thinking mind, whether functioning deductively or inductively, uses sense perceptions or remembered perceptions to arrive at general truths. Sensation brings us perceptions of the world, memory permits us to store those perceptions, imagination enables us to re-create from memory mental images corresponding to perceptions, and from accumulated images we derive general ideas. Radically differing with his mentor, Plato, Aristotle did not believe that the soul is born with knowledge. According to Daniel Robinson, he believed that

human beings have a cognitive *capacity* by which the (perceptual) registration of externals leads to their storage in memory, this giving rise to *experience*, and from this—"or from the whole universal that has come to rest in the soul"—a veritable principle of understanding arises (*Post. Anal.* 100 1–10).[24]*

It is an extraordinary vision of what scientific psychology would document twenty-three centuries later.

Because he was a creature of his time, some of his comments about memory seem nonsensical now; he said, for instance, that we remember things best when the memory is moist, worst when it is dry, and that very young persons have poor memories because the surface (of the wax tablet–like memory) changes rapidly through growth. But many of his observations were perceptive and close to the mark. For example, the more often an experience is repeated, the better it is remembered. Another: Events experienced only once but under the influence of strong emotion may be better remembered than others experienced many times. And another: We recall things from memory by relying on various kinds of connections among our ideas—similarity, contrast, and contiguity. To find a lost memory, for instance, we call to mind something we believe or know will lead us to the memory we are after.

> Whenever we try to recollect something, we experience certain of the antecedent movements [i.e., memories] until finally we come to the one after which customarily comes the one we seek. This is why we hunt up the series, having started in thought either from a present intuition or some other, and from something either similar or contrary to what we seek, or else from that which is contiguous to it.[25]

Though this is hardly deathless prose, David J. Murray, a historian of psychology, writes, "The last sentence here is possibly the most influential written in the history of psychology, for it enunciates the belief that we are moved by association from one concept to the next."[26] That belief would, from the seventeenth century on, be the foundation of a major theory of learning and a principal way of accounting for human development and behavior.

In *De Anima* and other works, Aristotle dealt briefly with or touched tangentially on a number of other psychological matters. Though none warrants our close attention, the range and perceptiveness of these com-

---

*All emphases in quotations are those of the quoted writers.

ments are remarkable. Among other things, he offered a theory of motivation in terms of pleasure and pain, touched on the drives producing various kinds of behavior (courage, friendship, temperance, and others), and sketched the theory of catharsis (the vicarious purgation of pity and fear) to explain why we feel rewarded by seeing tragedies in the theater.

We may chuckle at some of his wilder guesses, like a good meal making us sleepy because digestion causes gases and body heat to collect around the heart, where they interfere with the psyche. But, writes Robert Watson, the "study of Aristotle is rewarded by a feeling of wonder at the modernity of much of what he says about psychological matters . . . He was, of course, wrong in many of his 'facts' and he omitted important topics, but his overall framework of growing, sensing, remembering, desiring, reacting, and thinking, with but a few changes, bear[s] more than a resemblance to modern psychology."[27]

The
Scholars

The Long Sleep

If it is difficult to account for the sudden appearance and vigor of psychology in Greece, it is almost as difficult to explain the dormancy that overtook it after Aristotle, a sleep that would last two thousand years. Not until the seventeenth century would psychological questions again fascinate and galvanize thoughtful men as they had during the brief flowering of Greek culture.

Yet "dormancy" and "sleep" are misleading; they imply a lack of awareness that was far from being the case. Throughout the twilight of Greek greatness, the Pax Romana, the transformation of society by Christianity, the disintegration of the Roman Empire, the emergence of feudalism in its ruins, and the renewal of learning during the Renaissance, psychology was neither moribund nor forgotten. During those many centuries and metamorphoses of society, some intellectuals continued to ask the questions posed by the Greek philosophers and to formulate answers to them. But they did so as scholarly commentators, reworking what had already been done, rather than as explorers and innovators; not one of them had a major new idea that significantly advanced psychological knowledge.

Perhaps by the end of Aristotle's life psychology had developed almost as far as speculation and reflection could take it. After his time, those who were interested in psychological phenomena continued to rely on that approach, but the science could not progress without observation, measurement, sampling, testing, experimentation, and other empirical procedures.

There is, however, another and larger explanation of the long sleep: none of the social and religious systems that dominated Western civilization for those two millennia inspired men to explore the psychological unknown. For different reasons, Hellenistic society, Roman society, and Christianity motivated those who thought about psychological matters to do no more than pore over the work of their predecessors and revise it to fit their own belief systems.

Yet what these scholars, compilers, and redacters did deserves our attention for two reasons. For one, in the history of every science there are long periods when its practitioners labor at minor modifications of accepted theory in the effort to make it fit unruly facts. During such periods the science, like a pupa in a cocoon, undergoes changes preparing it to emerge new and altered. What takes place during the dormant phase may be less dramatic than the emergence of the metamorphosed creature but is no less essential to the advance of knowledge.

For another, during the latter half of the dormancy of psychology, Christian scholars who winnowed and modified Greek theories of psychology added to them, on theological grounds, certain nonscientific hypotheses about human nature that live on in popular thinking to this day. A look at how and when these hypotheses were developed will help us understand such contemporary debates as whether consciousness can exist in a disembodied mind (as in, say, out-of-body or back-from-death experiences) or whether it is a concatenation of physical and chemical events occurring in a living brain.

The Commentators

Theophrastus

When Aristotle left Athens in 323 because of political turmoil, he named his longtime friend and colleague Theophrastus head of the Lyceum; he also later bequeathed to him his library and the original manuscripts of all his works. Clearly, Aristotle had the highest regard for him.

Theophrastus (372–287) was indeed a distinguished teacher and scholar. He ran the Lyceum efficiently for many years, and was so eloquent a lecturer that two thousand people at a time would come to hear him. And he was phenomenally industrious, completing during his lifetime 227—some say 400—works on religion, politics, education, rhetoric, mathematics, astronomy, logic, biology, and other subjects, including psychology.

Yet Aristotle, for all his good judgment, could not foresee that almost no one would remember or read any of Theophrastus's works except the most trifling of them, the *Characters*. This was a series of brief satirical portraits of such archetypes as the Flatterer, the Garrulous Man, and the Stupid Man—the original exemplars of a genre of literature that has been popular ever since. The sketches are psychological writing in the broad sense that they report behavioral phenomena, but they add nothing to our understanding of the origins or development of traits or patterns of personality.

Theophrastus's other works have been deservedly forgotten. In them he restated, compiled, commented on, and criticized, but added little to, what others had said before him. This is especially true of *On the Senses*, his treatise on psychology; he says many sensible things, but they are no more than evaluations of, or faultfinding with, the work of his predecessors. This is typical:

> [Democritus] attributes perception, pleasure, and thought to respiration and to the mingling of air with blood. But many animals are either bloodless or do not breathe at all. And were it necessary for the breath to penetrate the entire body and not merely special parts—[a notion] . . . he introduces for the sake of a part of his theory—there would be nothing to prevent all parts of the body from remembering and thinking. But reason does not have its seat in all our members—in our legs and feet, for instance—but in specific parts by means of which, at the proper age, we exercise memory and thought.[*][1]

The Hellenists

Theophrastus's writing about psychology is typical of what one finds in the works of post-Aristotelian philosophers of the Hellenistic period, the two centuries following Alexander's death and the dividing up of his empire by three of his generals. Such commentary broke no new ground, but it did begin the compilation of the defects of Greek psycho-

---

[*]Theophrastus says elsewhere that thinking takes place in the brain.

logical thinking that two millennia later would drive a few inquisitive men to devise new hypotheses and, for the first time, test them scientifically.

What was true of psychology in the Hellenistic era was true of much other intellectual activity. The compilation and criticism of the ideas of thinkers of the preceding centuries flourished as libraries grew, particularly in Alexandria, where Ptolemy I, King of Egypt, established the greatest library of antiquity. Only in certain sciences did new ideas appear: geometry, which Euclid greatly expanded; hydrostatics, in which Archimedes made the epochal discovery that an object submerged in a fluid loses as much weight as the fluid it displaces; and geography, which Eratosthenes greatly furthered by calculating the circumference of the earth and coming respectably close to the correct figure. (He did so by measuring the shadow of an obelisk at noon in Alexandria on the day when the noontime sun shone straight down a deep well in Aswan, and, by geometrical means, determining the curvature of earth that could produce the disparity in the shadows.)

These and other sciences in which progress was made had become partly emancipated from philosophy; their practitioners, ignoring metaphysical issues, sought knowledge not through philosophic speculation but empirically. (Mathematics is nonempirical, but Euclid's approach to it was at least free of the mysticism of the Pythagorean geometers.) Psychology, meanwhile, in which no empirical methodology had been conceived of, remained a branch of philosophy.

Which was in decline. The wars that raged intermittently throughout Macedonia and the Near East, and the gradual decay of the social order in the former Greek city-states, engendered weariness and pessimism. Instead of searching for ultimate truths, philosophers sought solace; they distracted themselves with astrology, Near Eastern religions, and mystical adaptations of Platonism, and they narrowed philosophy to systems of ethics that would teach them how to live wisely in troubled times.

In this milieu, psychology no longer greatly interested philosophers. The Platonists and Aristotelians merely ruminated on and refined the hypotheses of their masters. The adherents of three popular new schools, the Epicureans, Skeptics, and Stoics, limited their psychological discussions largely to Democritus's epistemology (the theory that we know only what the senses tell us, from which we extract ideas and meaning through the use of reason), patching up any flaws they noticed and adding a few notions necessitated by their ethics.

The Epicureans

Epicurus (341–270) based his survival ethics on the simplistic doctrine "Pleasure is the beginning and end of the blessed life."[2] Not that he was a sensualist or libertine; a frail and chronically ailing man, he sought and advocated only tranquil and moderate pleasures and lectured against such intense delights as gluttony, public acclaim, the exercise of power, and sexual intercourse. Of the last he said, "No man was ever better for sexual indulgence, and it is well if he be not worse." He did, however, allow himself a concubine, since he considered sexual pleasure relatively harmless if one did not fall in love.[3]

Ethics being Epicurus's major interest, he paid little attention to psychology except to repeat and quibble with some details of Democritus's theory of knowledge, which suited his pragmatic and mundane philosophy. Yet if he had pursued the psychological significance of one of his own doctrines, he would be a major figure in the story of psychology. According to Diogenes Laertius, "[The Epicureans] say there are two passions, pleasure and pain, which affect everything alive. And that one is natural, and the other foreign to our nature, and that this is the basis on which we judge all things that are to be chosen or to be avoided."[4] This is a clear anticipation of the principle known today as the law of reinforcement, which modern psychologists view as the fundamental mechanism of learning. But Epicurus and his followers developed the metaphysical rather than the psychological implications of the dichotomy.

The Skeptics

The Skeptics based their ethical system on the familiar doctrine that we cannot be sure our senses correctly report reality, which they took farther than their precursors. Pyrrho (360–270), the founder of the school, held that it is not only impossible to know whether our perceptions are truthful but equally impossible to find rational ground for preferring one course of action to any other. Such skepticism was useful in those times; if nothing was provably wrong, one could legitimately accept the customs or religion of whoever was in power.[5] The philosopher Arcesilaus took the final step, carrying Pyrrho's skepticism to the ultimate with his mind-numbing apothegm "Nothing is certain, not even this."[6] The Skeptics, in effect, reduced psychology to the systematic doubt of all thought.

The Stoics

Stoicism, founded by Zeno of Citium (336–264), based its ethical system on a psychological concept long familiar in Greek thought, namely, that one could achieve tranquillity through control of the emotions. The good life, Zeno held, was one in which the mind is in total control, enabling the individual to feel as little emotion as possible and thereby immunizing himself against suffering.[7] Even desire and pleasure were to be avoided, since they render us vulnerable.[8]

His followers stressed that such mastery of the passions requires the exercise of the will; they echoed Plato's view that the will carries out the directives of reason over the urgings of desire. But this created a problem for the Stoics. They believed, with Democritus, that the universe was made of atoms that operated according to inviolate physical laws, a concept that seemed to leave no room for free will. To solve or at least sidestep the difficulty, they argued that God cannot be constrained by the laws of the universe and so must have free will; and since the soul of each human being is a bit of God, it too must possess the power to act freely.[9] This hypothesis, which obviously can be neither proved nor disproved, was to create one of the most intractable problems of psychology.

Roman Borrowers

As the eastern Mediterranean world was sinking into decadence and lethargy, Rome was becoming ever more vital and aggressive. But even as it conquered the eastern Mediterranean, it was itself conquered by Hellenistic culture. The Romans, empire builders but not innovators, administrators but not thinkers, adopted Greek styles of literature, architecture, sculpture, religion, and philosophy. Between the second century B.C. and the second century A.D., Rome expanded until, in Gibbon's words, it "comprehended the fairest part of earth, and the most civilized portion of mankind," but in all that time it remained a cultural parasite of Greece. As Bertrand Russell says in his *History of Western Philosophy*, "The Romans invented no art forms, constructed no original system of philosophy, and made no scientific discoveries. They made good roads, systematic legal codes, and efficient armies; for the rest they looked to Greece."[10]

But in philosophy they copied the Greeks very selectively. Preoccupied with military conquest, the management of subjugated territories, the control of slaves and proletarians, and other practical matters, they had no use for the higher flights of Greek philosophic fancy; all they borrowed from Aristotle, for instance, was his logic. By and large they considered the proper sphere of philosophy to be the promulgation of rules for living wisely amid the uncertainties of life.

Lucretius

Epicureanism, therefore, appealed to certain Romans. Lucretius, a contemporary of Julius Caesar's, expounded the doctrines of Epicurus in his roundup of science, a long poem titled *On the Nature of Things*. The rational and passive ethics he set forth there did not appeal to the avaricious, aggressive rulers of the Republic but it did to Roman aristocrats, most of whom stood apart from the violence of war and politics, and needed a philosophy to help them live calmly within the turmoil of their society.

Lucretius contributed nothing of importance to psychology in *On the Nature of Things*; he merely restated the views of Epicurus and Democritus in a somewhat schoolteacherish manner, adding a few comments designed to patch up weaknesses in each. He is as limited in his outlook as his sources; he says, for instance, that since we feel fears and joys in the "middle region of the breast," that is where the mind or understanding is located, and that the mind and soul (which he says are united) are composed of particularly small, fast-moving atoms. But elsewhere he is eminently sensible and realistic. Here, for instance, is a sample of Lucretius at his best:

> The nature of the mind and soul is bodily . . . [and] mortal. If the soul were immortal and made its way into our body at birth, why would we be unable to remember bygone times and retain no traces of previous actions? If the power of the mind has been so completely changed that all remembrance of past things is lost, I regard that as not differing greatly from death; therefore you must admit that the soul which was before has perished and that which is now has been formed.[11]

While we may admire the common sense of the ancient poet, in him psychology is at a standstill; we need not linger here.

Seneca

Stoicism was more to the taste of the aggressive ruling class of Roman society. From the first century A.D. this doctrine was popular among Roman politicians and military leaders, who led lives of luxury and power but knew that at any moment they might lose everything, including their lives. For them, Stoical dispassion and calmness in the face of personal tragedy was an ideal.

It is epitomized in the behavior of the philosopher Seneca the Younger (3 B.C.–A.D. 65) in the face of death. The poet, dramatist, statesman, and Stoic philosopher was rumored, probably falsely, to be plotting against the Emperor Nero. When the rumor reached Nero, he dispatched a centurion to Seneca's country home to tell him that the Emperor desired his death. On hearing this, Seneca quietly called for tablets on which to write his will. The centurion refused permission for this lengthy task, whereupon Seneca told the weeping friends around him, "Since I cannot reward you for your services, I leave you the best thing I have to leave—the pattern of my life." He calmly opened his veins, lay down in a hot bath, and while dying dictated to his secretaries a letter to the Roman people.[12]

Epictetus

The best-known Stoic philosopher in Rome, Epictetus (60–120)—originally a Greek slave—was, like his Stoic forebears, uninterested in the nature of the universe, matter, or spirit. "What do I care," he said, "whether all existing things are composed of atoms . . . or of fire and earth? Is it not enough to learn the true nature of good and evil?"[13] His central concern was to find a way to endure life. The only heed he paid to psychology was to offer a quasi-Platonic rationalization of how to "endure and renounce":

> Never say about anything, "I have lost it," but only, "I have given it back." Is your child dead? It has been given back. Is your wife dead? She has been returned . . . I must go into exile; does anyone keep me from going with a smile, serene? . . . "I will throw you in prison." It is only my body you imprison. I must die: must I then die complaining? . . . These are the lessons that philosophy ought to rehearse, and write down daily, and practice.[14]

Much the same kind of noble but unenlightening sentiment appears in the famous *Meditations* of the second-century philosopher-emperor Marcus Aurelius.

Galen

The only real contributions to psychology by Roman citizens were made by a Greek and an Egyptian.

The Greek, Galen (130–201), was the most famous physician and anatomist of his time and personal physician to Marcus Aurelius and his successors. The title of one of Galen's tracts sounds promising—*The Diagnosis and Cure of the Soul's Passions*—but it contains only warmed-over Stoic and Platonic notions about the control of emotions through reason. Elsewhere, however, he developed in some detail a classification of emotions that Plato briefly suggested in the *Republic*, namely, that they are either of the "irascible" kind, having to do with anger or frustration, or the "concupiscible" kind, arising from the desire for various pleasures and the satisfaction of bodily needs.[15] Virtually all modern psychologists who have classified the emotions have made a similar distinction.

Galen's major effect on psychology, mentioned earlier, was his theory of personality based on Hippocrates' theory of the four humors. It was a negative contribution, since for many centuries it misled physicians and others as to the causes of personality patterns and psychological disorders. He did, however, recognize and correctly describe one kind of physical symptom produced by the emotions. He noticed one day that a female patient's pulse speeded up when someone happened to mention the name of a male dancer. Galen arranged to have someone enter the room during her next visit and talk about the performance of a different male dancer, and to repeat the experiment on another day with another dancer's name. In neither case did the patient's pulse accelerate. On the fourth day someone mentioned the first dancer's name again, her pulse became rapid, and Galen confidently diagnosed her ailment as love sickness, adding that doctors seem not to realize how bodily health can be affected by the suffering of the psyche.[16] Unfortunately, he went no further with the thought, which was not pursued until the advent of psychosomatic medicine in our own century.

Plotinus

The Egyptian Plotinus (205–270) made a wholly different kind of contribution to psychology. By his time, Roman civilization was decadent, corrupt, and violence-ridden. In that atmosphere, many troubled people were attracted to Plotinus's Neoplatonism, which combined the ethics of Stoicism with the mystical and unworldly components of Plato's beliefs, including the most nonscientific and spiritual components of his psychology.

Plotinus, after studying Greek philosophy in Alexandria, came to Rome in 244, where, although a pagan, he lived like a Christian saint amid the city's luxuries. Regarding the body as the prison of the soul—his biographer and disciple, Porphyry, says Plotinus was actually ashamed that his soul had a body—he took no care of himself physically, was unconcerned about dress and hygienic matters, ate the simplest foods, avoided sexual activity, and refused to sit for his portrait on the grounds that his body was the least important part of him. Despite these austerities, he was a popular lecturer and much sought out for his advice on sundry matters by well-to-do Romans.

Like Plato, whom he revered—usually alluding to him simply as "He"—Plotinus considered the evidence of the senses inferior to that of reasoning. He believed that the highest wisdom, the ultimate access to truth, came when the soul temporarily slipped free of the flesh in a trancelike state and perceived the world beyond. He himself, he wrote, had had a number of such experiences.

> Many times it has happened. Lifted out of the body into myself; becoming external to all other things and self-encentered; beholding a marvelous beauty; then, more than ever, assured of community with the highest order; acquiring identity with the divine, stationing within It* by having attained that activity; poised above whatever in the Intellectual is less than the Supreme: yet, there comes the moment of descent from intellection to reasoning, and after that sojourn in the divine I ask myself how it happens that I can now be descending, and how did the Soul ever enter into my body, the Soul which even within the body is the highest thing it has shown itself to be.[17]

This is hard to follow, to say the least. What Plotinus is saying here and elsewhere is that a tripartite real world exists above the material, physical one. It is made up of One (It); of Spirit or the intellect or mind, a kind of reflection or image of the One; and of Soul, which can look upward toward Spirit or downward toward nature and the world of sense.[18]

*God or the Good or the Supreme.

What has this to do with psychology? Little and much.

Little, because Plotinus is not interested in the study of mental functions; he does not say a great deal about psychology except for taking issue with the psychology of Democritus and other atomists.

Much, because the Neoplatonic view of the relation between body and soul, soul and mind, would become part of Christian doctrine and would shape and constrain psychological inquiry until the rebirth of science fourteen centuries later.

Moreover, the way in which Plotinus arrived at his conceptions of Soul, mind, and It became the model for those who took any interest in mental processes before the emergence of scientific psychology. In part, he sought the truth through his trances. But since such experiences were relatively rare—during the six years in which Porphyry worked with him and observed him, he had only four—Plotinus sought to understand the nature of Soul, mind, and It chiefly by meditative reasoning. In other words, he painstakingly thought up a supernatural structure that seemed to him to explain the relation between the material world and the spiritual one. He did not, of course, test his hypothesis; testing belongs to the material world, not the spiritual one.

The Patrist Adapters

The Patrists

Between the first and fourth centuries A.D., while the Roman Empire reached its zenith and then began disintegrating, Christianity became its dominant religion. In the resultant transformation of Western culture, pagan philosophers were gradually replaced as leaders of thought by a very different breed: the Patrists, or Fathers of the Church.

They were leading bishops and other eminent Christian teachers who, in endless and bitter debate with one another, sought to resolve the many controversial issues involved in the new faith. Their names are familiar to everyone who has any acquaintance with the history of those centuries; among them are Clement of Alexandria, Tertullian, Origen, Gregory Thaumaturgus, Arnobius, Lactantius, Gregory of Nyssa, and, of course, Saint Augustine.

Although pagan philosophy was withering away, its psychology lived on in selected and modified form in the Patrists' "apologetics," or sermons and writings defending Christian beliefs. The Patrists were philosopher-theologians who, though primarily concerned with such central questions of faith as whether Christ was divine or human, were necessarily involved in arguments about such psychological issues as the nature of the soul, its relation to the mind and the body, and the sources of the mind's ideas.

Nearly all of the Church Fathers of the early centuries of the Christian era were middle- or upper-class Roman citizens who, born and reared in Mediterranean cities of the Empire, received the education typical of men of their class. They were therefore acquainted with pagan philosophy, and in their apologetics energetically attacked those philosophic ideas which were incompatible with Christian doctrine, but accepted and adapted those which supported it. They rejected and condemned almost all that was scientific in pagan philosophy and that conflicted with such Christian doctrines as God's ability to intervene directly in the lives of human beings, the earth's centrality in the universe, and the reality of miracles. A great deal of scientific knowledge was forgotten, and, says the historian Daniel Boorstin, "scholarly amnesia afflicted the continent from A.D. 300 to at least 1300."[19]

Psychology, however, was not so much forgotten as picked over and adapted by the Patrists to support their religious beliefs. Whatever was naturalistic in it, such as the view that mental processes are due to the movement of atoms within the brain or heart, they assailed as either inadequate or heretical; whatever in it bolstered the Christian belief in the supremacy of the soul and of transcendental reality, such as the Platonic theory of ideas, they welcomed and tailored to fit Christian doctrine.

One major psychological issue troubling them was whether or not the soul was a part of the godhead and came to the body equipped with innate knowledge, as Platonists held. Christian doctrine indicated otherwise: each soul was newly created at birth, and the mind of the newborn infant was therefore blank. Many Patrists accordingly attacked the doctrine of innate ideas, although they accepted most of the Platonic theory of ideas.

Another difficult issue was how the soul is linked to mind and to body and whether the soul needs a body in order to perceive and have sensations, as Aristotle had said. But according to doctrine the soul of the sinner or nonbeliever burns in hell after death; unless it can perceive when detached from sense organs, how can it sense suffering? *Ergo*, said most Patrists, the soul does not need the sense organs to perceive.

Such were the issues—there were many of them—over which the

Fathers of the Church labored and fought among themselves in their efforts to adjust psychology to the new belief; in this form psychology lived on.

Tertullian

Although the antenicene Fathers—those who lived and wrote before the Council of Nicaea, in 325—differed widely in their views, the work of Tertullian, the greatest of them, exemplifies how pagan psychological concepts were incorporated in early patristic writings. Tertullian (160–230), the son of a Roman centurion, grew up in Carthage, where he received a first-rate education; he then studied law, went to Rome, and there became an eminent jurist. In his mid-thirties, for unknown reasons he became a Christian and renounced pagan pleasures. He married a fellow believer, took priestly orders (priests were not then celibate), and returned to Carthage, where he lived the rest of his life and turned out a steady stream of fiery apologetics and denunciations of sin. He was the first Patrist to write in Latin rather than Greek; it has been said that Christian literature in the West sprang from Tertullian full-grown.

A persistently angry man, he was in a constant state of rage at the sybaritic life of Roman pagans and at their cruelty toward Christians. It was he who coined the celebrated maxim "The blood of the martyrs is the seed of the Church." He relished his own fantasies of the suffering the pagans would undergo after death:

> That last eternal Day of Judgment [will come] when all this old world and its generations shall be consumed in one fire. How vast the spectacle will be on that day! How I shall marvel, laugh, rejoice, and exult, seeing so many kings—supposedly received into heaven—groaning in the depths of darkness!—and magistrates who persecuted the name of Jesus melting in fiercer flames than ever they kindled against the Christians!—and sages and philosophers blushing before their disciples as they blaze together![20]

Although married, Tertullian had as poor an opinion of the physical side of marriage as did Saint Paul, the source of much of his thinking. In his late forties he wrote his wife a long letter about marriage and widowhood—it was meant to instruct other women as well—in which he expressed his contempt for his and her physical desires. Though not a psychological discourse, it is representative of a myriad of patristic writings about sexual desire that had profound effects on the sexuality and emotions of believers for eighteen centuries; the nature and extent of those effects would eventually be revealed when Freud began the practice of psychoanalysis.

Tertullian, addressing his wife as "my best beloved fellow servant in the Lord," directed her not to remarry if he died before she did; second marriage, he said, was tantamount to adultery. She should view widowhood as God's call to sexual abstinence, which He much prefers to married intercourse. Nor should she grieve at her husband's death, since it would only end their enslavement by a disgusting habit that, in any case, they would have to give up to enter heaven.

> To Christians, after their departure from the world, no restoration of marriage is promised in the day of resurrection, translated as they will be into the condition and sanctity of angels . . . There will be at that day no resumption of voluptuous disgrace between us. No such frivolities, no such impurities, does God promise to His servants.[21]

History does not record what his wife thought of the letter.

This hellfire-and-brimstone scourger of the wicked was well versed in psychology as it existed at that time. He preserved a fair amount of it in his works in the form of attacks on those psychological theories which clashed with his religious beliefs and adaptations of those which lent them support. The account in Genesis of God's creation of Adam was, for instance, reason enough for Tertullian to reject Plato's theory that the soul of the individual exists before birth:

> When we acknowledge that the soul originates in the breath of God, it follows that we attribute a beginning to it. Plato refuses to assign this to it; he will have the soul unborn and unmade. We, however, from the very fact of its having had a beginning, as well as from the nature thereof, teach that it had both birth and creation . . . The opinion of the philosopher is overthrown by the authority of prophecy.[22]

But although he believed that after death the soul lives on, he saw no reason to disagree with all those philosophers whom he cited as saying that soul is in some sense corporeal and allied to bodily functions:

The soul certainly sympathizes with the body and shares in its pain whenever it is injured by bruises, and wounds, and sores; the body, too, suffers with the soul and is united with it whenever the soul is afflicted with anxiety, distress, or love, testifying to its shame and fears by its own blushes and paleness. The soul, therefore, is proved to be corporeal from this intercommunion of susceptibility.[23]

Like some of the Greek philosophers, he defined the mind as the thinking part of the soul, but as a Christian he disagreed with Democritus's belief that the soul and the mind were the same thing:

The mind or *animus*, which the Greeks designate *nous*, is taken by us to mean that faculty or apparatus inherent in the soul whereby it acts, acquires knowledge, and is capable of a spontaneity of motion . . . To exercise the senses is to suffer* emotion, because to suffer is to feel. In like manner, to acquire knowledge is to exercise the senses, and to undergo emotion is to exercise the senses; and the whole of this is a state of suffering. But we see that the soul experiences none of these unless the mind is also similarly affected . . . Democritus, however, suppresses all distinction between soul and mind, but how can the two be one?—only if we confuse two substances or eliminate one. We, however, assert that the mind coalesces with the soul, not being distinct from it in substance but being its natural function and agent.[24]

And on doctrinal grounds he revises Plato's views on rationality and irrationality, since he cannot accept the latter as God's handiwork:

Plato divides the soul into two parts—the rational and the irrational. To this we take no exception, but we would not ascribe this twofold distinction to the nature of the soul . . . [For] if we ascribe the irrational element to the nature which our soul has received from God, then the irrational element will be derived from God . . . [But] from the devil proceeds the incentive to sin. All sin, however, is irrational: therefore the irrational proceeds from the devil and is extraneous to God, to whom the irrational is an alien principle.[25]

---

*By "suffer" and "suffering" Tertullian refers not to pain but to being subject to feelings ("passions") rather than having mental control of them.

Saint Augustine

After the Council of Nicaea, Christian doctrine became increasingly standardized and Christianity became the official religion of the Empire. Psychology, already at a halt, was diminished to whatever was acceptable to orthodoxy. Many of the views the antenicene Fathers had held on psychological issues became heresies. (Origen, after his death, was condemned for multiple heresies, one of which was his belief in the pre-existence of souls as taught by Plato.) Psychology was largely preserved from the fourth century to the twelfth in the attenuated form it took in the writings of "the Christian Aristotle"—Saint Augustine, the chief authority of the church before Saint Thomas Aquinas.

Augustine (354–430) was born in Tagaste, a town in the Roman province of Numidia (modern Algeria); his mother, Monica (later sainted), was a Christian, his magistrate father, Patricius, a pagan. The world around Augustine, still one of Roman luxury, was fast rotting away; in his youth barbarians were invading the outlying parts of the Empire, by his middle age Rome itself fell to the Goths, and in his old age the whole Western world was on the verge of collapse.

As a sixteen-year-old student in Carthage, Augustine behaved like a typical Roman voluptuary; "I boiled over in my fornications," he later said of this period in his famous *Confessions*. But the following year, plagued by guilt instilled in him by his mother, he gave up promiscuity by taking a concubine, whom he lived with and was faithful to for more than fifteen years.

An apt and eager student, he was so awed by Plato that he called him a "demigod" and later incorporated much Platonism into Christian doctrine. After completing his studies, he became a professor of rhetoric in Carthage, and later in Rome and Milan. He read widely in the pagan philosophers and the Christian Scripture and became an adherent of Manichaeanism, a heretical Eastern offshoot of Christianity. But he was increasingly influenced by Plato and by Plotinus, whose ascetic and mystical Neoplatonism deeply stirred him. He became ever more troubled by guilt over his way of life and by the decay of his world: the Huns were ravaging the Balkans, the Goths laying waste to Thrace, the Germans surging across the Rhine, while in Italy corruption was worse than ever, taxes higher, and the populace more addicted to gladiatorial combats and circuses.

At the age of thirty-two, Augustine, yielding to his mother's entreaties to marry, sent his beloved concubine away and waited for his fiancée to come of age. One day, "soul-sick and tormented" (as he tells us in *Confessions*), he was sitting in his garden in Milan with a friend when he was seized by a fit of weeping, fled to the end of the garden, and there heard a childlike voice saying, "Take up and read; take up and read." He picked up the copy of the writings of Saint Paul that he had been reading, opened it at random, and came upon the words "Not in rioting and drunkenness, not in chambering and wantonness, not in strife and envying: but put ye on the Lord Jesus Christ, and make not provision for the flesh, in concupiscence." In a moment his soul sickness vanished and he felt joyous and serene. He abandoned his plans to marry, gave himself over to study and preparation for his conversion, and on Easter Sunday 387, with Monica standing proudly by, was baptized by Bishop (later Saint) Ambrose.

He returned to Africa, gave his possessions to the poor, and organized a monastery in Tagaste, where he lived contentedly for a few years in poverty, celibacy, and study. Then he answered the call of Valerian, Bishop of Hippo, a small nearby city, to come aid him in diocesan work. Augustine entered the priesthood, and several years later reluctantly became Bishop of Hippo when the aging Valerian retired. He held that post until his death thirty-four years later, by which time Rome had been sacked by the Goths, the Vandals were at the gates of Hippo, and the total collapse of the western half of the Empire was less than fifty years off.

As Bishop of Hippo, Augustine continued to live monastically. Although small, frail, and troubled by a chronic lung disorder, he was constantly embroiled in religious controversies, debates, and struggles against heresies, but he managed nonetheless to write a vast number of letters, sermons, and major works, including his famous *Confessions*, and labored for thirteen years on his masterpiece, *The City of God*. His major aim in that work was to reconcile reason with the doctrines of the Church, but whenever they conflicted he was guided by his own precept, "Seek not to understand in order to believe, but believe in order to understand."[26]

Augustine became the leading authority within the Catholic Church on doctrinal matters and remained so for many centuries. His jurisdiction extended to whatever he said about psychology, which he had a good deal to say about throughout his writings, though he never treated the subject systematically. His views on it, as on science in general, are a mixture of the informing and the obscurant, for he considers psychology, like all science, good when it serves religious purposes, bad when it disserves them. Knowledge other than that in Scripture is either evil or redundant: "Whatever man may have learned from other sources, if it is hurtful, it is condemned there [i.e., in Scripture]; if it is useful, it is contained therein."[27] Yet in his writings a good deal of psychology is preserved and so was made known to the scholars and "doctors of the Church" of the Dark Ages and early medieval centuries.

Galen, for one, survives in Augustine, who echoes his statements that the soul or mind can be influenced by the condition of the body, and, conversely, that the soul or mind can influence the condition of the body. Too much bile, says Augustine by way of example, can make a person irritable, but a person made irritable by external events may cause his body to create too much bile.[28]

He draws on pagan philosophers cited by earlier Fathers for his account of the structure of the mind, which he describes in terms of the three functions of memory, reason, and will. But at times what he says about these three becomes thoroughly mystical, as when he uses psychology to explain how a trinity could also be a unity:

> Since these three, memory, reason, and will, are not three lives but one life, nor three minds but one mind, it follows that they are not three substances but one substance . . . These three are one, in that they are one life, one mind, one essence. But they are three, in that I remember that I have memory and understanding and will; and I understand that I understand and will and remember; and I will that I will and remember and understand . . . And therefore while each as a whole is equal to each as a whole, and each as a whole to all as wholes, these three are one, one life, one mind, one essence.[29]

Augustine equates mind with soul in the living person but says that the soul is immaterial and indestructible, and that after death it leaves the body and becomes immortal. How does he know that? His argument: The soul, or mind, can conceive of the eternal, a concept it cannot possibly obtain from the senses. Just as to think is to exist, so to think of the higher sphere of existence is to be part of that existence.[30]

But he also often deals with mental life in more naturalistic terms. Sometimes he restates, in his own exalted manner, the views of those pagan philosophers who were most interested in the mechanics of sense perception and memory: "I enter the fields and roomy chamber of memory, wherein are the treasures of countless images imported into it from all manner of things by the senses."[31] In this mood he marvels at how images are deposited in memory by the senses, how memory contains not only images but concepts, and how what takes place in the mind is sometimes a sequence of memories experienced spontaneously and sometimes the result of a conscious search.

Yet like so many of the pagan philosophers, Augustine regards sense-derived knowledge as uncertain and untrustworthy, since we cannot be certain that our perceptions truly represent reality. What is certain, what is beyond any doubt, is the primary experience of self-awareness, for to doubt is to think, to think is to exist; the very act of doubting affirms that we are alive and that we think.[32] Thus does he rebut Skepticism and affirm the Platonic theory of knowledge, relying even more strongly than Plato on introspection as the route to knowledge and truth. Drs. Franz Alexander and Sheldon Selesnick assert in their *History of Psychiatry* that "Augustine was not only the first forerunner of Husserl's phenomenology and of existentialism but also a forerunner of psychoanalysis."[33]

And indeed his use of introspection goes far beyond that of Plato. The remarkable self-revelations in *Confessions* are a first in literature; the lineage from there to Rousseau to Freud is patent. But this is introspection leading to self-knowledge, and Augustine was after still bigger game. In *The City of God* and other of Augustine's theological works we find an account of how introspection can reveal higher truths. Through reason, he says, we can rise above the limitations of the senses to acquire concepts such as "number" and "wisdom," but we achieve the highest levels of understanding only by transcending reason through the introspective contemplation of God. Like Plotinus, Augustine rhapsodizes about the illumination that comes to him when, through such rumination, he feels himself "ascending by degrees unto Him who made me" and coming as close to ultimate truth as man can.[34]

The most important faculty of the mind, for Augustine, is the will, since it offers the only solution to the great theological problem of how to explain the existence of evil. If God is all-powerful, all-wise, and good, He could not have created evil, nor been unaware that it would exist, nor could there be another power as great as He who was responsible for evil. How, then, to explain it? Augustine reasons that for human beings to be good, they must be able to *choose* to do good rather than not-good. (God did not create evil; evil is only the absence of good); God therefore endowed them with free will. But human beings can fail to will to do good, or can even will to do not-good; it is thus that evil comes to be.[35]

Augustine had personally experienced the failure of his own will to choose the good by living wantonly with his concubine. He found the explanation of that wickedness in our legacy of original sin, which gave sexual lust such power over us that we will to do evil rather than good. Or, rather, in the area of sexuality our will is powerless to do good. Even as a man cannot will an erection, he cannot will himself flaccid when lust overcomes him. Sexual pleasure practically paralyzes all power of deliberate thought, and the flesh commands man, defying his will as he defied the will of God.

Yet any truly good person, Augustine says, "would prefer, if this were possible, to beget his children without suffering this passion." Had Adam not sinned, he and Eve—and all their descendants—would have been able to procreate sinlessly and without pleasure. How? This is difficult to envision, he admits, but he does not shrink from the task; his thoughts on the matter are an extraordinary mixture of keen psychological observation and ascetic fantasy:

> In Paradise, generative seed would have been sown by the husband and the wife would have conceived . . . by deliberate choice and not by uncontrollable lust. After all, it is not only our hands and fingers, feet and toes, made up of joints and bones, that we move at will, but we can also control the flexing and stiffening of muscles and nerves . . . [Some persons] can make their ears move, either one at a time or both together . . . [Others] can make musical notes issue from the rear of their anatomy so that you would think they were singing . . . Human organs, without the excitement of lust, could have obeyed human will for all the purposes of parenthood . . . At a time when there was no unruly lust to excite the organs of generation and when all that was needed was done by deliberate choice, the seminal flow could have reached the womb with as little rupture of the hymen and by the same vaginal ducts as is at present the case, in reverse, with the menstrual flux.[36]

Such is Augustine's selection and adaptation of what humankind had learned about the human mind in the first eight centuries of psychology; such are the principal notions that received the imprimatur of his authority and became the only acceptable psychology for the next eight centuries.

The Patrist Reconcilers

The Schoolmen

Few people, in the centuries after Augustine's death, actually gave any thought to these matters. Mighty Rome was repeatedly ravaged and sacked; its people gradually crept away to country towns and fortified villages, until by the sixth century only fifty thousand were living amid the burned ruins and rubble of the once-great city. Its libraries and those of other cities were scattered and destroyed; the scientific learning of the past, along with its hygiene, manners, and art, was lost. Most of western European society came to comprise primitive villages, drafty castles, and walled towns, loosely organized in petty fiefdoms and kingdoms whose illiterate and bellicose leaders constantly raided and laid siege to one another, when not joining forces to fight against invading Normans, Norsemen, Magyars, Saracens, Franks, Goths, and Moors.

Eventually, chaos gave way to the settled order of the feudal system, but feudal lords, preoccupied by knightly jousting, wars, the Crusades, intrigues, witchcraft, and the rituals of courtly love, had no interest in learning. In a world where life was nasty, brutish, and short, psychology was as forgotten a cultural artifact as the geometry of Euclid or the dramas of Sophocles, and as irrelevant.

From the sixth to the thirteenth century, the only people in western Europe who had any opportunity to learn about psychology were clerics, who, in the libraries of a few monasteries, could read about it in the limited form of the Patrists' writings. But the subject had little appeal for most clerics, whose time and energy were pre-empted by matters of faith and the rigors of feudal existence. Only a handful, whose names mean nothing to us today, became familiar with what had been written and themselves wrote books on the soul and mind. None of these works is more than a compilation and iteration of what could be found in the apologetic writings, particularly the works of Augustine.

Change, however, slowly overtook the feudal order. The Crusades brought hordes of semiprimitive western Europeans into contact with Muslim commerce and industry; trade went where the cross had led; Italian merchant fleets and ships out of northern European harbors began carrying Oriental spices, silks, foods, and tapestries to European ports, and, with them, books and ideas. As seaborne commerce started to revive, so did inland transportation. Rude towns grew into cities, and in some of them, starting with Bologna and Paris, universities were founded; philosophy was revived in the form of scholasticism, the painstaking logical examination of the great questions of faith.

At first the scholastics (or Schoolmen) were constrained by unquestioning reverence for the authority of Scripture and of doctrine as set forth in the Creeds and in the writings of Augustine and other Patrists. The scholastics' method of examining philosophic and religious problems was to state a proposition, take a negative position, defend that view with scriptural and patristic quotations, then rebut it with an affirmative proposition, defending that with other scriptural and patristic quotations. As time passed, however, they became aware of other and more stimulating sources of knowledge. In part through writings brought from the Middle East, where learning had never died out, and in larger part through the writings of Arab and Jewish scholars in Spain and Constantinople, especially Avicenna, Averroës, and Moses Maimonides, they rediscovered Greek philosophy and psychology and, above all, Aristotle.

To many scholastics, his rigorous logic, vast knowledge, and relatively realistic outlook were a liberation from the arid, otherworldly musings of the Patrists. Aristotle, rather than Plato or Augustine, became the supreme authority for them. But for many years scholastics were divided into two camps: the mystic-Platonic (mostly Franciscans) and the intellectual-Aristotelian (mostly Dominicans). The mystic-Platonic side saw Aristotle's naturalism and logic as a threat to faith; the Aristotelians, among them Abélard, Peter Lombard, Albertus Magnus, and Thomas Aquinas, saw them as a support to, and a way of proving, the truth of Christian doctrine. After decades of bitter struggles, the Aristotelians won out: Aquinas's philosophy, reconciling Aristotelianism with Christianity and using reason to prove the truth of doctrine, became the official one of the Catholic Church and has remained so.

The Angelic Doctor: Saint Thomas Aquinas

What sort of man was the Angelic Doctor, as he is called by his admirers? Not a man to catch one's attention: a large, quiet lump of a fellow dressed in monk's garb, usually absorbed in his own thoughts, a man whose pious and studious life was virtually without drama except of an intellectual kind.

Aquinas's father, the Count of Aquino, whose castle lay halfway between Rome and Naples, came from the German nobility, and his mother was a descendant of the Norman princes of Sicily. Thomas, born in 1225, grew up thoroughly Teutonic in looks—tall and heavy, broad of face, and fair-haired—and Teutonically stolid; it is said that he became angry only twice in his life, and his nickname, among his fellow students, was "the great dumb ox of Sicily."

As a child of five he was sent by his father to live and study in the Benedictine Abbey at Monte Cassino some miles away. His boyhood there could hardly have been carefree or joyous, and by the time he left at fourteen he was a confirmed scholar and ascetic. After five more years at the University of Naples, he became a Dominican monk, to the great distress of his family; they had expected him, rather than leading a life of poverty in a mendicant order, eventually to assume the prestigious post of abbot at Monte Cassino. At his mother's instigation—his father had died—Aquinas's brothers kidnapped him and imprisoned him for a year at the family castle, hoping he would change his mind. He did not; accepting his lot with saintly calm, he pursued his studies in his prison apartment.

He did lose his temper, however, when his brothers, in an attempt to lure him away from asceticism, slipped a seductive young woman into his chambers. On seeing her, Aquinas seized a flaming brand from the fire, drove her in panic from the room, and burned the sign of the cross on his door; his brothers sent him no more temptresses. Eventually Aquinas's piety won his mother over; she helped him escape, and in 1245 he resumed life as a Dominican in Paris, where he studied theology under Albertus Magnus, the champion of Aristotle.

A prodigious student, Aquinas, thanks to a papal dispensation, was granted his doctorate in theology at thirty-one, three years earlier than regulations allowed. He had such powers of concentration that he could pursue a complex train of thought under the most distracting circumstances. Once, at a banquet in the court of King Louis IX, Aquinas, pondering how to refute the Manichaean heretics, was oblivious of the pomp, jewelry, great personages, and witty conversations all around him. Suddenly he slammed his big hand down on the table and cried out, doubtless alarming the assemblage, "And *that* will settle the Manichaeans!"

Not that he was a forbidding person; he was soft-spoken, easy in conversation, and cheerful, but he had important things on his mind and much to do. From waking to sleeping, his days were filled with study, writing, teaching, and worship. He attended all the hours of prayer, either said one Mass or heard two every day, and prayed before delivering every lecture or sitting down to write.

With so many devotions, the wonder is that he got so much done before his death at forty-nine, in 1274. In less than twenty years, while teaching at the University of Paris and at schools in Italy, he wrote a great many sermons, tracts, hymns, and prayers, a number of lengthy commentaries on the works of the earlier philosophers, and the massive (four-volume) *Summa Contra Gentiles* and the gargantuan (twenty-one-volume) *Summa Theologica*.

The *Summa Contra Gentiles* is aimed at philosophic nonbelievers whose rationalism prevents them from believing. Aquinas seeks to lead them to faith by a route as unlike Augustine's impassioned mysticism as imaginable: he presents them with rigorously logical philosophic arguments intended to engender faith through reason alone. As he writes in a tract addressed to a group of opponents, "Behold our refutation of [your] errors. It is based not on documents of faith but on the reasons and statements of the philosophers themselves."[37]

The *Summa Theologica*, intended for students of theology, expounds and defends the whole body of Catholic doctrine; it comprises thirty-eight treatises on various subjects, including metaphysics, ethics, law, and psychology, and takes up 631 "questions" or topics, to which it presents some ten thousand objections or replies. Throughout, Aquinas uses dialectic to examine each question by step-by-step reasoning; the result is no more stirring than a logic textbook, but as a work of orderly argument it is incomparable.

Perhaps worn out by his exertions, Aquinas felt something strange come over him while saying Mass one morning in December 1273; afterward he could not continue his work on the *Summa*. "I can do no more," he said. "Such things have been revealed to me that all I have written seems as straw, and I now await the end of my life." He died three months later, and in less than fifty years was canonized by Pope John XXII.

Aquinas's theology and metaphysics do not concern us here except as he made psychology harmonize with them. This he did chiefly in three parts of the *Summa Theologica*: "Treatise on Man," "Treatise on Human Acts," and "Treatise on Habits." Little of what he set forth in these sections was new; he was not an explorer but a reconciler of Christian doctrine and Aristotelianism.

His psychology is based largely on Aristotle (though couched in Aquinas's own difficult and abstruse terminology), plus odds and ends of

Galen, Augustine, and a few others. He restored to psychology much that was sensible and realistic, and had been lost in the earlier patristic writings. But he froze the science in its classically speculative and argumentative mode and built into it certain key items of Christian faith, such as the dualism of body and soul or mind, that would cloud psychology to our own day.

In the psychological sections of the *Summa Theologica* one can see, despite the fog of Thomist verbiage, many familiar topics.

On perception, Aquinas discusses the five external senses familiar to earlier writers, plus the "common" sense—Aristotle's notion—by which we recognize that data simultaneously perceived through different senses come from one object.

He subdivides the functions of the psyche, in more or less Aristotelian fashion, into the "vegetative" (its autonomic physical functions), the "sentient" (perception, appetite, locomotion), and the "rational" (memory, imagination, and reason or intellect). But he enlarges significantly a passing suggestion of "the Philosopher" (as he often calls Aristotle) that there are two kinds of intellect. The functions of the first, or "possible intellect," are understanding, judgment, and reasoning concerning our perceptions; the functions of the second, or "agent intellect," are to abstract *ideas* or concepts from our perceptions and to know, through faith, those other truths, such as the mystery of the Trinity, that cannot be known through reason.

Aquinas offers no empirical evidence that two distinct intellects exist; his conclusions are based on a combination of logic and doctrine. For whatever in the soul concerns bodily perceptions, sensations, and emotions—whatever is part of the soul-body unit during life—cannot live on after death. But the soul does live on; doctrine says so. It must therefore be that part of the soul-body unit partakes of higher and eternal knowledge and therefore is immortal; this is the agent intellect.[38]

Aquinas thus reconciles Aristotelian psychology, which did not allow a personal afterlife, with Christian doctrine, which insisted on it. Yet in making the perishable "possible intellect" the mechanism through which we create ideas, he excludes from his own psychology the mystical Platonic doctrine of innate ideas. He takes his stand with Aristotle that the mind of the infant is a tabula rasa with the power to extract ideas from experience. The doctrine of innate ideas will plague psychology in later centuries, but not through Aquinas's doing.

He does, however, differentiate between desires rising from the concupiscible appetite and those from the irascible appetite, a dichotomy he took from Galen, who got it from Plato. Aquinas develops it in more detail than his predecessors, organizing the material by means of definition, deduction, and common sense. His schema: When the concupiscible appetite is aroused by a good thing, we feel such emotions as love, desire, and joy; when repelled by an evil thing, hatred, aversion, and sorrow. When the irascible appetite is aroused by a good thing that is hard to obtain, we feel hope or despair; when by an evil thing, courage, fear, or anger.

This categorization of the emotions, though it may seem artificial and pedantic today, is more systematic and thorough than that of any previous philosopher. More important, Aquinas deserves credit for stressing, almost to a modern degree, that pleasure and pain are the basic substrates of the emotions.

On the subject of the will, Aquinas asserts, as doctrine requires him to, that freedom of the will does exist. But his grounds for saying so are derived from Aristotelian psychology. First he offers abstruse metaphysical reasons for asserting that reason is "more noble and more sublime" in its nature than the will;[39] then, more plainly, he says that reason determines what is good, and the will seeks to gratify the desire for that object. We cannot help desiring the objects of our appetites, and we are free to will what we do about those desires, but the will remains subordinate to intellect, which determines what is to be sought or avoided. (If we will to do something evil, it is through lack of true understanding.) In one case, however, the will is a better judge than reason:

> When the desired object is superior to the soul in which its nature is understood by reason, then the will is superior to reason . . . It is better to love God than merely to know God; and conversely it is better only to understand corporeal things than to love them . . . Through love we cleave to God, who is transcendently raised above the soul; in this instance the will is superior to the reason.[40]

This again exemplifies the reconciliation Aquinas seeks between faith and reason. He aims to use natural reason to prove the truth of the Catholic faith, but mysteries such as the Trinity, the Incarnation, the Last Judgment, and the essence of God cannot be deduced from the evidence of the senses or reason and can be known only through faith.[41] He thus establishes a two-part epistemology: We know some things through experience and reason, other things through revelation. This amalgam of naturalistic psychology with supernatural Christian doctrine would prove comforting to many believers in the centuries to come but would long impede the development of scientific psychology.

Aquinas's impact on psychology was thus both positive and negative. In his description of the senses and reason as the means by which we acquire knowledge, he provided a basis on which psychology could someday gain an empirical and scientific outlook. But in describing the higher functions of the intellect as immortal and in insisting that certain kinds of knowledge can be acquired only through faith, he prolonged the grip of supernaturalism on psychology. So great was his authority, at least among Catholics, that at least two histories of psychology written by Catholics in the twentieth century—one as late as 1945—would maintain that psychology went astray after Aquinas.[42]

The Darkness Before Dawn

For several centuries after the death of Aquinas in 1274, psychology was again at a standstill. The Saint's and the Philosopher's combined authority petrified it, and those few clerics who wrote about psychology had almost nothing new to say. Nor were the times congenial to intellectual endeavors; the Hundred Years' War and the Black Death and other epidemics of the fourteenth century played havoc with the social order. In such a world few were motivated to explore the human psyche scientifically or philosophically. Even the educated turned, in desperation, to astrology, superstition, and demonism. Clerics who in a more benign time might have written yet more commentaries on classic and patristic philosophy instead studied and wrote about the practices of witches and the methods by which inquisitors could prove that accused persons were consorting with the Devil and doing his work.

Delusions and hallucinations in which the Devil or swarms of his demons appeared were widely accepted as authentic experiences; psychotic behavior was interpreted as evidence of possession by a dream or the Devil himself; voices, radiances, visions of angels or the Virgin or Jesus were usually considered actual visitations or communications. Understanding of the mind and emotions, at least in western Europe, was back where it had been several thousand years earlier.

Yet by the fifteenth century certain social changes were bringing about conditions that would foster the first major advances in psychology since the Greeks. The introduction to Europe of gunpowder made castle walls and personal armor obsolete, and thereby outmoded the feudal system. With the dawning of the Renaissance there was an increase in the number of scholars who were not clerics and not bound by doctrinal orthodoxy. The invention of the printing press using moveable type, around 1440, made it possible for them to study outside the Church-dominated universities. The rediscovery of the learning of the past began to liberate people's minds from the confines of medieval thought.

During the sixteenth and seventeenth centuries, scientists in a number of fields made the first significant advances in well over a millennium. Vesalius corrected many of Galen's anatomical errors; Copernicus proved the sun to be the center of the solar system; Galileo discovered that there were mountains on the moon and that the Milky Way is made up of individual stars; Harvey discovered the circulation of the blood; and Agricola made important contributions to mineralogy, Paré to surgery, Mercator to mapmaking, Tycho and Kepler to astronomy, and Columbus and Magellan to geography.

Interest in psychology, too, revived, but at first without producing advances. In the sixteenth century hundreds of works were written, but almost all were routine commentaries on the psychological writings of Aristotle, Theophrastus, Galen, and others, or reworkings of Augustine's and Aquinas's discussions of free will and the nature of the soul. Certain thinkers, among them Machiavelli, Paracelsus, and Melanchthon, made shrewed psychological observations of one kind or another in their writings, but none furthered the science in any systematic fashion.

Three authors, however, are worth passing notice before we move on to the dawn of modern psychology.

One is an obscure Serbo-Croatian writer named Marulic, who seems to have been the first to make written use, in an obscure manuscript dating from about 1520, of a newly coined word, *psychologia*.[43] The term did not soon catch on, though one or two other authors used it. But in 1590 a German encyclopedist named Rudolf Goeckel (Latinized as Goclenius) used it in the title of a book: *Psychologia Hoc Est, de Hominis Perfectione* (Psychology This Is, on the Improvement of Man). In the course of the next century the new word gradually became the recognized name of the science.

The third author is Juan Luis Vives, a sixteenth-century Spanish Catholic philosopher of Jewish origin. After tutoring Princess Mary, elder daughter of England's Henry VIII, and spending some time in prison for opposing Henry's divorce from Catherine of Aragon, he devoted himself to writing. One of his works, a lengthy book titled *De Anima et Vita*, is largely a recapitulation of Aristotle and Augustine but

is notable for one thing: Vives compiled a far longer list than his predecessors of the ways in which images and thoughts can be linked by association in the mind, and was a forerunner, if not the actual inspiration,
of the seventeenth-century associationists. One twentieth-century associationist even called him, with doctrinaire exaggeration, the father of
modern psychology.[44]

But modern psychology, unlike any living creature, had many fathers.

The
Protopsychologists

The Third Visitation

I n *The Advancement of Learning*, Francis Bacon, having summarized the state of knowledge in his time—in 1605 it was still possible for one person to do so—concluded with this bold forecast:

> When I set before me the condition of these times, in which learning hath made her third visitation or circuit, in all the qualities thereof: the excellency and vivacity of the wits of this age; the noble helps and lights which we have by the travails of ancient writers; the art of printing, which communicateth books to men of all fortunes; the openness of the world by navigation, which hath disclosed multitudes of experiments, and a mass of natural history . . . I cannot but be raised to this persuasion, that this third period of time will far surpass that of the Græcian and Roman learning.[1]

Such sweeping predictions usually prove wrong, but not this one. Within the century, knowledge would reach a level not even Bacon could have imagined, thanks to the "new learning" of science fostered by major social developments that had been reshaping European society. The semiprimitive feudal way of life centered about church, castle, and keep had given way to larger national groupings, the revival of city life, and the expansion of trade and industry, and the Reformation had weakened the grip of church-centered traditionalism over men's minds and induced a spirit of questioning and intellectual ferment in Protestant lands and, by a kind of social osmosis, even in Catholic ones.

These developments spurred advances in both utilitarian and pure knowledge. Seventeenth-century businesses, armies, and monetary and taxation systems required new, efficient ways of thinking about and handling data. On the purely intellectual side, many thoughtful men turned from engaging in theological hairsplitting to gathering factual information about the real world. For both reasons, this was the century that produced the decimal system, logarithms, analytic geometry, the calculus, the air pump, the microscope, the barometer, the thermometer, and the telescope.

Not that science was universally welcomed. Renaissance humanism had revived the Platonic tradition, with all its mysticism and scorn of the material world, and many intellectuals, echoing Petrarch, Erasmus, Rabelais, and Vives, disparaged science. Religion offered more dangerous opposition: Throughout the seventeenth century not only Catholics but Lutherans and Calvinists harshly punished heretics, and anyone who publicly espoused a scientific theory in conflict with the doctrines of the established church of his country was risking his good name, social position, fortune, and possibly his life.

Despite such obstacles, science flourished. In every major country of western Europe, inquisitive men peered through microscopes and telescopes, mixed reagents in glass flasks, burrowed into the earth, dissected animal and human cadavers, and calculated the movements of the stars and planets. Among these men were such illuminati, in England, as Wallis, Harvey, Boyle, Hooke, Halley, and Newton; in France, Descartes, Fermat, Mariotte, and Pascal; in Italy, Galileo, Viviani, and Torricelli; in Switzerland, Jacques and Jean Bernoulli; in Germany, Leibniz; and in Holland, Huygens and Leeuwenhoek.

Most of them, deeming themselves to be partners in a great movement, wrote to one another to share their thoughts and results. By mid-century, in Oxford, London, and Paris, scientists and science-minded amateurs were meeting in informal groups—"invisible colleges," they were called—to exchange their findings and debate their theories. In 1662 Charles II conferred a charter on the London group, designating it the Royal Society of London for Improving Natural Knowledge; through its *Philosophical Transactions* and similar journals on the Continent, scientists began to create an information network and subculture of their own.

Although psychology was far slower than the physical sciences to emerge from its philosophic-theological chrysalis, some of the finest minds of the age turned their attention to it and for the first time in two millennia began formulating new answers to the questions first asked by Greek philosophers. Although the seventeenth-century protopsychologists and even their eighteenth-century successors had no way to investigate the mind other than by meditation and reflection, they were aware of the new findings of physicists and physiologists; they produced not mere reworkings of earlier theories but two distinctly new versions of old psychologies.

The Rationalists

Descartes

Everyone with even a smattering of higher education knows that René Descartes was one of the most influential philosophers of the modern era, the inventor of analytic geometry, and a physicist of some accomplishment. Few, however, realize that he was, says the historian of psychology Robert Watson, "the first great psychologist of the modern age." But, adds Watson, "this is not the same as saying that he was the first modern psychologist. Unlike some scientists of his day, he still made metaphysical assumptions, and consequently his psychology was subservient to his philosophy."[2] Nevertheless, he was the first person since Aristotle to create a new psychology.

Descartes was born in Touraine in 1596; he acquired tuberculosis from his mother, who died of it a few days after his birth, and was a sickly infant, a weakling during childhood, and a small and relatively frail adult. His father, a prosperous lawyer, sent him off at eight to the Jesuit college at La Flèche, where he got a thorough grounding in mathematics and philosophy. His teachers, recognizing both his physical weakness and unusual mental ability, permitted him to remain in bed reading long after the usual hour of rising, and it became his lifelong practice to lie abed and cogitate all morning. Fortunately, he inherited enough money from his father to make this regimen feasible.

In his late teens the small and rather homely Descartes tried the social life and casinos of Paris, found them boring, and turned to the solitary study of mathematics and philosophy. But he grew troubled as he realized that so many learned men had arrived at so many different answers to the important philosophic questions. Discouraged and depressed, he decided to seek answers in the real world; he enlisted first in the army of Prince Maurice of Nassau and later that of the Duke of Bavaria. It is unclear whether or not he saw action but clear that he found ordinary men no wiser than scholars. After several years, he returned to the world of private thought.

Even before returning to private life Descartes had a memorable philosophical epiphany. At twenty-three, he spent one cold morning shut up in a "stove"—his word, but probably a small heated room—and had several visions through which he realized that he could ignore the disparate opinions of the "ancients" and use the rigorous reasoning of mathematics to achieve philosophic certainties. Thus was rationalist philosophy founded.

After returning to civilian life, Descartes spent some time traveling, then lived in Paris for some years, all the while studying philosophy and the physical sciences. At thirty-two he moved to Protestant Holland, partly because in Paris friends too often broke in on his quiet meditations, partly because he was afraid that his approach to truth—first, doubt everything—might lead to accusations of heresy. This he deeply feared; he sought to stay on good terms with the Catholic Church, even interrupting his discussion of body and mind in one work to say, typically, "Recalling my insignificance, I affirm nothing, but submit all these opinions to the authority of the Catholic Church, and to the judgment of the more sage."[3]

In Holland he lived mostly in peace, though he was sometimes attacked by Protestant extremists for holding dangerous views; to preserve his quiet and privacy he moved twenty-four times in twenty years. But he was not an ascetic or recluse; he welcomed the visits of fellow savants, had a mistress and a daughter (who died in childhood), and always lived in comfortable surroundings with a retinue of servants.

His most important works, *Discourse on Method* (1637) and *Meditations on First Philosophy* (1642), were written during his years in Holland; much of his psychology is in these works. The rest is in *The World*, written in 1633 but not published until after his death. He was about to give it to the printer when he learned that Galileo had been condemned by the Inquisition for maintaining that the earth moves around the sun, and since his own book espoused that idea, he suppressed it.

Though cautious in such matters, Descartes rashly accepted the invitation of Queen Christina of Sweden in 1649 to teach her philosophy. He was received in Stockholm with high honors but learned to his dismay that the Queen wanted him to tutor her at 5 A.M. He who had always lain in bed until noon had to arise in darkness three times a week and trudge through the bitter cold winter night to her library. In February 1650, he caught cold, developed pneumonia, and, after receiving the last rites, died at the age of fifty-four.

Although Descartes' philosophy is not our concern, we must look at its starting point, since this is the foundation of his psychology. He begins the construction of his philosophic system with the insight that came to him the morning in the "stove":

> [I thought] I ought to reject as absolutely false all opinions in regard to which I could imagine the least ground for doubt, so as to ascertain whether after doing so there remained anything in my belief that was wholly indubitable.[4]

He therefore doubts his senses, since they sometimes deceive; all the reasoning he had previously been convinced by, since men may fall into reasoning errors even in the simplest matters of geometry; and, indeed, all the thoughts that enter his mind when he is awake, since similar thoughts, entering it in sleep, are illusions. This leads him to a second and crucial insight:

> Immediately I noticed that even while I thus wished to think all these things were false, it was absolutely necessary that I, who thought this, was some thing; I observed that this truth—*I think, therefore I am*—was so certain and so evident that no ground of doubt, however extravagant, brought forth by skeptics, could shake it. I concluded that I could without scruple accept it as the first principle of the philosophy I was seeking.

Next, he asks himself what this thinking "I" was that necessarily existed. He could imagine, he says, that he had no body and existed in no specific place, but he could not imagine that he did not exist, since his thinking proved otherwise. From this he makes a dramatic inference:

> I concluded that I was a thing or substance whose whole essence or nature was only to think, and which, to exist, has no need of space or of any material thing or body. Thus it follows that this ego, this mind, this

soul, by which I am what I am, is entirely distinct from the body . . . Even if the body did not exist, the soul would not cease to be all that it now is.[5]

And so, while he doubts whatever the ancients may have said, he re-establishes through his own reasoning the old dualism of body and mind.

But he is a seventeenth-century man surrounded by science and its explorations of the material world, and, unlike the Platonists, he considers the objects of the corporeal world not mere shadows on the wall of the cave but as real as mind, not illusions but what they appear to be. This he bases on faith: since God provided our minds with bodies and senses, and since He is not deceitful, material objects must exist and be very like our perceptions of them.[6]

So far, this is pure rationalism. But as a man of his time, Descartes also had a quasi-empirical bent. He was keenly aware of the findings of the new physiology and himself performed dissections on animals, observing the relationship of the nervous system to the muscles. It seemed to him analogous to the design of certain statues in the royal gardens at St. Germain-en-Laye, which, operated by water conducted through pipes, made lifelike movements and sounds.

He therefore advanced a mechanical-hydraulic theory of much of human behavior. The fluid filling the ventricles or cavities of the brain—we know it today as cerebrospinal fluid—he took to be "animal spirits," a highly purified component of blood, the coarser parts of which he supposed were filtered out by tiny arteries before it reached the brain. (This was his modification of the Greek notion that *pneuma*, air, the essential substance of soul, circulated through the nervous system.) Since the nervous system radiates out from the brain to all parts of the body, the animal spirits must flow from the brain through the nerves (which Descartes, like the Greeks, believed to be hollow; the microscope did not yet exist) and, reaching the muscles, cause them to swell and move.[7]

He imagined that the flow of animal spirits also powers digestion, the circulation of the blood, and respiration, and some psychological functions, like sensory impressions, the appetites and passions, and even memory. The latter, though seemingly a function of mind, he explained in mechanical terms. Much as holes in a linen cloth pierced by needles remain when the needles are removed, so repeated experiences make certain pores in the brain remain more open than others to the flow of the spirits.[8] Descartes thus dispensed with Aquinas's theory (derived from Aristotle) that the soul has "vegetative" and "sentient" as well as rational functions. In Descartes' system it was purely rational; the other functions belong to the body.

Erroneous as his mechanical-hydraulic theory is in its details, it is impressively close to right in one major respect: it attributes the control of the muscles to impulses traveling from the brain through efferent nerves. Even more impressive is another of his guesses. He asked himself what initiates the flow of animal spirits to the muscles and again used the analogy of the royal automata, which were activated by water turned on when a visitor stepped on hidden pedals. In living creatures, he suggested, sensory stimuli play the same part by creating pressure on the sense organs; this pressure, transmitted by the nerves to the brain, opens particular valves, thereby causing bodily action of one kind or another. Descartes was thus the first to describe what would later be called the *reflex*, in which a specific external stimulus causes the organism to respond in a specific way.

But the mechanical-hydraulic theory did not explain consciousness, reasoning, or will. Those higher mental activities, Descartes believed, must be functions of the soul (or mind). Whence does this thinking soul get its information and ideas? He says that when it coexists with the body during life, it acquires some ideas via the body's perceptions, passions, and memory, and it manufactures others—imaginary objects, dreams, and the like—out of remembered sensory impressions. But its most important ideas cannot come from such sources, for while he is aware of his own thinking and therefore knows that his soul exists, he never experiences his soul in a sensory fashion. The idea of the soul must be part of the soul itself. Similarly, such abstract concepts as "perfection," "substance," "quality," "unity," "infinity," and the geometrical axioms seemed to him to be independent of sensory experience and so had to originate in the soul itself; they are innate.[9]

He reasonably added that such innate ideas do not exist full-blown at birth; rather, the soul has a tendency or propensity to develop them in response to experience. They are "primary germs of truth implanted by nature"; sensory impressions cause us to discover them within ourselves. For example, a child cannot understand the general truth "When equals are taken from equals, the remainders are equals," unless you show him examples.[10]

His dualistic conception of body and soul presented one exceedingly difficult problem. When body and soul are locked together during life, they interact. The body's experiences engender passions in the soul, and the soul's thoughts and will direct the flow of animal spirits, producing voluntary movement—but where and how does the interaction take place? How can the incorporeal soul, possessing no solidity and occupying no space, connect with the corporeal body and receive its perceptions and experiences or exert any influence over it?

Earlier dualistic philosophers had ignored this problem; the physiologically aware Descartes could not. From his and others' anatomical studies, he knew that the brain has two identical hemispheres but that deep within it is a tiny gland (the pineal body); because this is single, like the soul itself, and because of its position in the brain, it seemed to him the obvious junction of soul and body. He conjectured that, due to its position in the brain, "its slightest motions can greatly affect the flow of the spirits, and conversely the slightest changes in the flow of the spirits greatly affect the motions of the gland."[11] While he never explained how the corporeal pineal gland and the incorporeal soul could make contact, he felt sure that they did and that it was through the gland that the soul affected the body, and the body the soul:

> The whole action of the mind [i.e., soul] consists in this, that by the simple fact of its willing anything it causes the little gland, to which it is closely joined, to produce the result appropriate to the volition[12] . . . [Conversely,] the movements [of the gland] which are excited in the brain by the nerves affect in diverse ways the soul or mind, which is intimately connected with the brain, according to the diversity of the motions themselves.[13]

The body thus engenders in the soul such passions as love, hatred, fear, and desire. The soul consciously considers each passion and freely wills to act in response to it—or, if it deems the passion undesirable, to ignore it. Why, then, do we ever do wrong? Not because the soul chooses to or is in conflict with itself, said Descartes, but because very intense passions may produce "commotions" of the animal spirits that override the soul's control of the pineal gland, eliciting responses contrary to the soul's judgment and will.

But one of Descartes' major goals in setting forth his psychology was to show how to control the passions through reason and will. He offered much sensible advice, such as when powerful passion is aroused, one should deliberately divert one's attention elsewhere until the agitation calms down, and only then make a judgment as to what to do. Most of what he said about controlling the passions is on this level; it is the least interesting part of his psychology.

He classified the passions, but without giving any illuminating theory as to their origins. There are six primary ones—wonder, love, hate, desire, joy, and sadness—all the rest being varieties or combinations of these. Unlike his dramatic description of his search for a first philosophic principle, his discussion of the passions was definitional and dry as dust. A single example will serve:

> Love is an emotion of the soul, caused by the motion of the spirits, which incites it to unite itself voluntarily to those objects which appear to it to be agreeable. And hatred is an emotion, caused by the spirits, which incites the mind to will to be separated from objects which present themselves to it as harmful.[14]

Although Descartes' explanation of the interaction between body and soul is quite wrong—the pineal gland, which produces melatonin and influences vision and sleep, has no influence on either efferent or afferent nervous impulses—the mechanical details are unimportant. What is important is his theory that body and mind are separate entities, composed of different substances, which interact in a living person, sometimes harmoniously, sometimes competitively, and that this competition is the most crucial aspect of human existence. The theory greatly influenced the human search for self-understanding, but not for the better. Raymond Fancher, a historian of psychology, sums up the weakness and the power of Descartes' dualistic theory:

> On the one hand, he taught that a person was a machine, capable of being studied by the methods of natural science. On the other hand, he taught that the most valuable and unique human attribute, the soul, was beyond the reach of scientific method and could be understood only by rational reflection. And then finally the interaction between body and soul was said to be deducible through a combination of anatomical inference, psychological introspection, and a peculiarly empty logical analysis . . .

Despite the logical difficulties with parts of Descartes' position, most people—at least in the West—continue to think of their minds and their bodies as separate but somehow interacting aspects of themselves. This is a tribute to the power of Descartes' theory. Whatever its faults, his interactive dualism captured the Western imagination to

.such an extent that it became accepted almost as a matter of course. Few theories, in any discipline, can claim equal success.[15]

The Cartesians

Over the next century a number of Descartes' followers, usually referred to as the Cartesians, tried to modify his psychology so as to explain how the soul, an immaterial substance not occupying any space, could act upon the material, three-dimensional pineal gland, or vice versa.

Their chief approach was to suggest that actually there is no causal contact between body and mind; God sees to it that whatever happens in one sphere is accompanied by the appropriate happening in the other. This theory would seem to keep Him continually busy, running two worlds for each living person, but one ingenious Cartesian, Arnold Geulincx (1625–1669), suggested that body and mind are like two clocks that God winds up and sets running in perfect harmony with each other, after which He need do nothing more. Mental events only seem to produce physical responses, physical experiences to produce mental responses, but in fact each train of events merely occurs in perfect synchrony with the other.[16]

Whether "parallelism," as this theory is called, is best thought of as metaphysics, theology, or wonderful nonsense, it is clearly outside the realm of psychology; let us pass it by.

Spinoza

But we must not pass by the work of one other major philosopher who, by purely rationalist means, arrived at very different answers from Descartes to the questions of free will, causality, and the body-mind problem. He was Benedict Spinoza (1632–1677), the gentle, quiet Dutch Sephardic Jew whom Bertrand Russell calls "the noblest and the most lovable of the great philosophers" and whose *Ethics Demonstrated in Geometrical Order* (1677) is the most austerely rationalist, but one of the most exalted, of philosophic works.

His influence on psychology, however, is problematic; some scholars have thought it major, others minor. In part, their opinions vary because the *Ethics*, in which Spinoza discusses psychological matters, is hard to understand, being formidably geometric in presentation (axioms, propositions, demonstrations, and QEDs) and filled with metaphysical terminology. But in larger part appraisals of his contribution vary because some of his ideas about the universe and about psychology seem so modern, others so archaic.

His most modern idea is his definition of God: Spinoza makes Him identical with the universe and all the mind and matter in it, subject to its laws, and hence unable to intervene in the order of events. In consequence, Spinoza was harshly condemned by some as an atheist but praised by others for seeing God in all things. The philosopher Bishop George Berkeley thought him "wicked" and "the great leader of our modern infidels," but the German Romantic poet and dramatist Novalis called him *der gottbetrunkene Mensch*—the God-intoxicated man. It is possible to hold either of two equally diverse views about his psychology.

Spinoza was educated in Jewish learning at the synagogue in Amsterdam, where his family lived. But being of a scholarly and inquiring mind, he mastered Latin in his early twenties, took up the study of philosophy, and absented himself from services at the synagogue. The leaders of the Jewish community feared he would become a Christian and offered him a pension of a thousand florins a year if he would conceal his disbelief and appear now and then in the synagogue. An apocryphal story says that when he refused, they tried to have him assassinated, but the attempt failed. It is historical fact, however, that they excommunicated him and pronounced him cursed with the curses that Joshua had laid upon Jericho and those which Elisha had laid upon a band of children who had mocked him and who, in consequence, were torn to pieces by she-bears. The excommunication and curses, the only dramatic note in Spinoza's biography, had no effect on him; he led a quiet and uneventful life in Amsterdam and later at The Hague, earning a meager income as a lens grinder and tutor, living most of his adult years in a single room, going out but rarely, and dying of tuberculosis at forty-five.

Spinoza was greatly impressed by Descartes' philosophy and, like him, used pure reasoning to deduce the nature of the world, God, and the mind. But he found Descartes' theory about the pineal gland totally unconvincing and lacking in proof,[17] and therefore saw no merit to his explanation of how body and mind interact. Unlike Descartes, who believed in free will, Spinoza saw all mental events, like all events in the physical world, as having causes, which in turn have preceding causes; he was, in short, a complete determinist, as he made clear in the early pages of the *Ethics*:*

---

*For greater ease in reading, Spinoza's interpolated references to axioms and previous propositions have been eliminated and other omissions not indicated.

AXIOM 3: From a given determinate cause an effect necessarily follows; and, on the other hand, if no determinate cause can be given, it is impossible that an effect can follow.

PROP. 29: *In nature there is nothing contingent, but all things are determined from the necessity of the divine nature to exist and act in a certain manner.*

Demonst.: Whatever is, is in God; but God cannot be called a contingent thing, for He exists necessarily and not contingently. Moreover, the modes of the divine nature have followed from it necessarily and not contingently, whether it be considered absolutely or as determined to action in a certain manner.[18]

To decode this difficult language, for "God" substitute "the universe," for "modes of the divine nature" read "mental and physical events," and replace "contingent" with "not caused by something else." It then becomes clear that Spinoza's world, including human mental activity, is wholly subject to natural laws and capable of being understood.

He thus anticipates the fundamental premise of scientific psychology. He also says that the most basic of human motives is self-preservation;[19] again, this anticipates modern psychological theory. Yet his ideas affected the development of psychology only indirectly; his impact on modern thought, say Drs. Franz Alexander and Sheldon Selesnick in their *History of Psychiatry*, "was so pervasive that many of his basic concepts became a part of the general ideological climate" and in that way influenced Freud and others without their knowing it.[20]

Aside from these basic concepts, Spinoza's psychology was limited in scope and had little follow-up. He discussed perception, memory, imagination, the formation of ideas, consciousness, and so on, but said almost nothing new about them. In defining "mind" and "intellect" he grossly oversimplified: "mind" is nothing but an abstract term for the series of perceptions, memories, and other mental states that we experience, "intellect" no more than the sum of one's ideas or volitions.

But these subjects do not much concern him; his interest in psychology has to do with the passions (emotions); specifically, how we can escape from bondage to them by understanding their causes. His analysis of the emotions is largely patterned on Descartes'. There are three basic ones, he says (Descartes said six)—joy, sorrow, and desire—and forty-eight different emotions result from the interplay of these three with the pleasant or unpleasant stimuli of everyday life.

These explanations, though reasonable enough, are purely logical and superficial; they say nothing about unconscious motivations, child-hood development, social influences, or other components of emo-tional behavior as it is understood by modern psychologists. Like the rest of Spinoza's writing on psychology, these passages could have been writ-ten by Aquinas, were it not, again, for Spinoza's pantheism and deter-minism.

In one respect Spinoza's psychology is seriously at odds with modern psychology. Although he was a monist, regarding thought and matter as twin aspects of the same underlying reality, he maintained that there is no interaction of mind and body: "The body cannot determine the mind to thought, neither can the mind determine the body to motion or rest" (*Ethics*, Third Part, Prop. 2). Nor is interaction necessary, since both stem from the same reality. Professor Watson calls Spinoza's doc-trine "monistic parallelism" and sums it up as follows:

> Every bodily event coexists with and is coordinate to a mental event. Body and mind correlate, but they do not cause one another any more than the convex side of a glass causes the concave. Apparent interac-tion arises from ignorance on our part and shows only the coincidence of actions; it is a matter of appearance, not a reflection of reality.[21]

Thus, for all Spinoza's modern cosmology and determinism, his explanation of the relation of mind and body is much like Geulincx's two-clock theory, and just as unreal and fantastic. Spinoza's parallelism influenced some nineteenth-century German psychologists, but it has vanished completely from modern psychology.

None of this is to belittle his ethics, the basic message of which—that through knowledge of ourselves and the causes of our emotions we can escape our bondage to them and live as good people—is as valid and as inspiring as ever. But that is the subject of other works, not this one.

The Empiricists

We have only to cross the English Channel to find a wholly different philosophic milieu and genre of psychology. The English have had their mystics, scholastics, and metaphysicians, but for at least the past four centuries most of their philosophers and psychologists have been realis-tic, pragmatic, and down-to-earth. By the early decades of the seven-teenth century, it was typical of English thinkers to be commonsensical and empirical in their search for knowledge. They relied on experiment, or, where that was impossible, everyday experience and good judgment. The Royal Society urged its members to communicate in "the language of artisans, countrymen, and merchants [rather than] that of wits or scholars." The society's first historian, Bishop Thomas Sprat, proudly asserted that "our climate, the air, the influence of the heaven, the composition of the English blood; as well as the embraces of the ocean . . . render our country a land of experimental knowledge."[22]

Whether those influences or subtler social ones account for the English empirical bent, there is no doubt that it existed then, as it does now. In psychology, it produced a series of protopsychologists who rejected Descartes' doctrine of innate ideas and who, while dutifully mentioning God and the soul, proposed earthly explanations of human mental activities and behavior. They are known as the empiricists, not because they were experimentalists (they were not; unlike the natural scientists, they had no idea how to conduct experiments in psychology) but because they believed that the mind develops by empirical means: ideas are derived from experience. The debate between nativists (believers in innate ideas) and empiricists began in ancient Greece, reappeared in new and sharper form in the seventeenth century, and has continued to this very day, where, couched in contemporary research-based terms, it is at the core of the remarkable developments in psychology to be spelled out later in this history.

Hobbes

The first of the English empirical psychologists was Thomas Hobbes (1588–1679), although he is known primarily as a political philosopher. The son of a vicar, he was born prematurely owing to his mother's terror at hearing of the Spanish Armada. This, he said, accounted for his timid disposition — "Myself and fear were born twins"; and his timidity, or at least the feeling that his fellow human beings were inherently dangerous, underlies the antidemocratic political philosophy for which he is famous.

Hobbes states in the first pages of *Leviathan* (1651), written during the turbulent years of the Civil War and Commonwealth, that all men are by nature the enemy of all other men and can live together in peace and prosperity only by ceding their right of self-determination to an autocratic government, preferably a monarchy. Without the "terror" through which such a ruling power enforces civilized behavior, life is

inevitably "solitary, poor, nasty, brutish, and short." This dour philosophy came not from some sickly, ill-favored misfit but from a tall, handsome man who was lively, friendly, and exceptionally healthy
throughout his long life.

Hobbes had reasons other than misanthropy for his Royalist views.
After being educated at Oxford, he spent many years as tutor to several
sons of the Cavendishes, a noble family (one of his pupils became the
first Earl and another the third Earl of Devonshire), and in Paris he lived
among Royalist émigrés during the Commonwealth and tutored the
future Charles II.

It was fortunate for him that he had such connections. A devotee of
the sciences, he was an outspoken determinist and materialist, and in his
later years a group of bishops accused him in Parliament of atheism,
blasphemy, and profaneness, and recommended that the white-haired,
dignified Hobbes be burned. But the accusation failed to win action, the
House of Lords defeated a bill condemning *Leviathan*, the King gave
Hobbes a pension, and he prudently turned his mind and pen to less
incendiary topics. Though "Hobbist" remained for many years a term of
abuse among the clergy and believers, Hobbes lived quietly, continued
to write and to play tennis in his seventies, translated Homer in his eighties, and died just short of ninety-two.

It is not Hobbes's view of human nature but his empiricist epistemology that earns him a place in the pantheon of psychology. Having visited Galileo and been greatly impressed by his physics, Hobbes
concluded that all events are matter in motion; applying this to psychology, he reasoned that all mental activities must be motions of
atoms in the nervous system and brain reacting to motions of atoms in
the external world.[23] He did not say how the movement of atoms in the
brain could be a thought; he simply asserted that it could. Only today
are psychologists and cognitive neuroscientists beginning to answer
that question.

Hobbes boldly declared that no part of the universe is incorporeal,
that "soul" is only a metaphor for "life," and that all talk of the soul as an
incorporeal substance is "vain philosophy" and "pernicious Aristotelian
nonsense."[24] Naturally, he dismissed the doctrine of innate ideas, since
these were supposedly built into the incorporeal soul. He said that everything in the mind arises from sense experience: Complex thoughts are
derived from simple ones, and simple ones from sensations:

Concerning the thoughts of man . . . singly, they are every one a representation or appearance of some quality or other accident of a body
without us, which is commonly called an *object* . . . The origin of
them all is that which we call *sense*, for there is no conception in a
man's mind which hath not at first, totally, or by parts, been begotten
upon the organs of sense. The rest are derived from that original.[25]

The notion, of course, was not new; it had been advanced in one form
or another by Alcmaeon, Democritus, and Aristotle, among others. But
Hobbes went farther than they, using a principle of physics that would
later be known as Newton's First Law of Motion to explain how sensory
impressions become imagination, memory, and general knowledge:

When a body is once in motion, it moveth, unless something else hinder it, eternally; and whatsoever hindereth it cannot in an instant, but
[only] in time and by degrees, quite extinguish it; and as we see in the
water, though the wind cease, the waves give not over rolling for a long
time after: so also it happeneth in that motion which is made in the
internal parts of a man, then, when he sees, dreams, etc. For after the
object is removed, or the eye shut, we still retain an image of the things
seen, though more obscure than when we see it. And this is it, the
Latins call *imagination* . . . [which] therefore, is nothing but *decaying
sense* . . . When we would express the decay, and signify that the sense
is fading, old, and past, it is called *memory* . . . Much memory, or
memory of many things, is called *experience*.[26]

Hobbes foresaw an objection: we can think of things that we have never
seen. This phenomenon, too, he readily explained:

Imagination being only of those things which have formerly been perceived by sense . . . is *simple* imagination, as when one imagineth a
man, or horse, which he hath seen before. The other is *compounded*;
as when, from the sight of a man at one time and of a horse at another,
we conceive in our mind a centaur.

Hobbes's presentation of empirical psychology, though rudimentary
and based on fictitious physiology, is a landmark. It is the first effort to
explain how sense impressions are transformed into higher mental
processes.

He was a pioneer in a second way: he was the first modern associationist. Aristotle, Augustine, and Vives had all said that memories are recalled through linkages, but Hobbes's contribution, though incomplete and elementary, was clearer and more specific. Although he used the term "train of ideas" rather than "association," he is the earliest figure in the tradition that eventually led to experimental psychology in the nineteenth century and to behaviorism in the twentieth.

"When a man thinketh on anything whatsoever," he stated, "his next thought after is not altogether so casual as it seems to be. Not every thought to every thought succeeds indifferently."[27] Again using physics as a model, he likened the succession of thoughts to the "coherence" of matter, one thought following another "in such manner as water upon a plane table is drawn which way any one part of it is guided by the finger."[28] But laying aside the physical simile, he gave a genuinely psychological account of how associations work. Sometimes, he said, the train of thoughts is "unguided" and without design, at other times "regulated" or voluntary, as when we consciously try to remember something or to solve some problem. He thus anticipated the modern distinction between free association and controlled association.

The examples he gave of coherence leading the mind from one thought to another are as good as any in contemporary psychological literature. This is in *Leviathan:*

> In a discourse of our present civil war, what could seem more impertinent than to ask, as one did, what was the value of a Roman penny? Yet the coherence to me was manifest enough. For the thought of the war introduced the thought of the delivering up of the king to his enemies; the thought of that, brought in the thought of the delivering up of Christ; and that again the thought of the thirty pence, which was the price of that treason; and thence easily followed that malicious question, and all this in a moment of time; for thought is quick.[29]

And in a later work, *Human Nature* (1658), he said that the connection of any two ideas in memory is the result of their coincidental occurrence when first experienced:

> The cause of the *coherence* or consequence of one conception to another, is their first *coherence* or consequence at that *time* when they are produced by a sense: as for example, from St. Andrew the mind runneth to St. Peter, because their names are read together; from St. Peter to a *stone*, for the same cause; from *stone* to *foundation*, to

church, and from church to *people,* and from people to *tumult;* and according to this example the mind may almost run from anything to anything.[30]

It was only the seed of associationist psychology, but it fell on fertile soil.

Locke

Although Hobbes was the first English empiricist in psychology, John Locke (1632–1704), born forty-four years later, developed the nascent theory and is often called "the father of English empiricism." He too was both a political philosopher and a protopsychologist; in the latter role he espoused principles similar to Hobbes's, in the former role, very different ones.

In social polity, he argued brilliantly, contravening Hobbes, certain natural rights, including liberty, are not given up when men move from a state of nature to one of social living. His ideas are embedded in the American Declaration of Independence and the French Revolution's Declaration of the Rights of Man.

Locke's liberalism was due partly to family background, partly to experience. His father was a Puritan attorney, and as a boy Locke knew what it was to be a member of a disfavored minority. But he was later disillusioned by the excesses of the victorious Puritans and eventually became an articulate spokesman for a balance of power between King and Parliament, and an advocate of religious toleration for all in England—well, not quite all; he drew the line, probably for politic reasons, at atheists, Unitarians, and Muslims.

At Oxford he studied philosophy, admired Descartes' writings, but was attracted by experimental science. Staying on at Oxford for a while as a don, he met and worked with the great chemist Robert Boyle and with the eminent medical scientist Thomas Sydenham. This induced him to study medicine, and in 1667 he became personal physician and general adviser to Anthony Ashley Cooper—soon to become the first Earl of Shaftesbury—with whom he remained connected for some years. From then on Locke was involved in politics, and during the reign of William and Mary he held various government posts.

His portrait shows a long-featured and serious face, and we hear that he was, indeed, uncommonly orderly, controlled, parsimonious, and abstemious. But he was also a sociable man, had many good friends, and loved children. Although he never married—neither did Descartes, Spinoza, Hobbes, and a number of other seventeenth-century philosophers, a phenomenon worthy of a dissertation—he had a love affair during his Oxford years which, he said, "robbed me of the use of my reason." When the affair ended, his reason returned; philosophy and psychology were the richer for his never again suffering such a loss.

Of Locke's many works, the one that concerns us is his *Essay Concerning Human Understanding.* In 1670, he and a handful of friends met informally in his quarters at Exeter House (Shaftesbury's home) to discuss the view of a number of Platonists at Cambridge that our ideas of God and morality are innate. Locke tells of that meeting in the "Epistle to the Reader" prefacing the *Essay*:

> Five or six friends, meeting at my chamber, and discoursing on a subject very remote from [human understanding], found themselves quickly at a stand, by the difficulties that arose on every side. After we had awhile puzzled ourselves, without coming any nearer a resolution of those doubts which perplexed us, it came into my thoughts that we took a wrong course; and that, before we set ourselves upon inquiries of that nature, it was necessary to understand our own abilities, and see what *objects* our understandings were, or were not, fitted to deal with. This I proposed to the company, who all readily assented.[31]

Locke guessed that one sheet of paper would be enough to contain the list he would offer, at the next meeting, of the mental processes that the mind itself is capable of understanding. As it turned out, he spent nearly twenty years at the task and filled hundreds of pages with his observations and conclusions.

The *Essay*, which he worked on in England and in exile, in peacetime and during the Glorious Revolution of 1688, was finally published in 1690; it immediately made him famous. It went through four editions in fourteen years, was the topic of drawing room conversation, and altered the course of British philosophy and psychology. It also made him infamous. His rejection of innate ideas and his insistence that the soul was unknowable aroused the wrath of Platonists and of divines who, already displeased with his advocacy of toleration, vociferously attacked him for playing into the hands of atheists. Time handed down the verdict: the *Essay* became part of the mainstream of modern thought; the writings of his attackers ended up on the trash pile of history.

What made Locke's *Essay* historic was his explanation of how we acquire knowledge; the rest of it does not concern us. He set about exploring, differently from his predecessors, how the mind comes by knowledge. First, unlike Descartes and Hobbes, and despite his medical training, he chose not to speculate about the "motions of our spirits, or alteration of our bodies" by which we have sensations, perceptions, or thoughts.[32] Either he realized that physiology was still in a primitive state or that psychological processes can be studied at a macro level, ignoring the micro level, as one can study wave mechanics without considering the movements of the molecules making up the waves.

Nor did he rely on formal deductive reasoning, as had Descartes and Spinoza. Instead, he used as nearly empirical an approach as was then available by examining his own experiences and those of others, including children of different ages, asking himself what events take place, and in what sequence, that result in knowledge. He also conducted at least one famous experiment. After putting one hand in a basin of hot water and the other in a basin of cold water, he moved both to a basin of tepid water, which felt cold to one hand and hot to the other. This demonstrated that despite the objective nature of the cause of a perception, our perception of it is subjective and not a replica of the object's qualities.[33]

Locke's first piece of business in the *Essay* is to attack the doctrine of innate ideas. To Descartes' argument that the idea of God must be innate, since we do not experience Him directly, Locke replies that it cannot be innate, because some peoples have been found who have no such idea. He suggests a pious—but empirical—alternative: we derive our idea of God from "the visible marks of extraordinary wisdom and power . . . in all the works of creation."[34] Nor can there be innate principles of right and wrong; history shows so wide a range of moral judgments that they must be socially acquired. Even if some ideas are universal, they are not innate if some other explanation can be found. And it can. He will show "whence the understanding may get all the ideas it has" and, as evidence, "I shall appeal to every one's own observation and experience."[35]

He then states the great primal doctrine of empirical psychology: "Let us then suppose the mind [at birth] to be, as we say, white paper, void of all characters, without any ideas. How comes it to be furnished? . . . I answer, in one word, from *experience*. In that, all our knowledge is founded, and from that it ultimately derives itself."[36] (It is often said that

Locke spoke of the newborn's mind as a tabula rasa, but he did not use that term; it was Aquinas's translation of a phrase in Aristotle.)

Locke says there are two sources of the mind's "ideas" (the word he uses to refer to everything from perceptions to abstract concepts). They are *sensation* and *reflection* (the mind's own operations on whatever it has acquired; in his words, "all the different actings of our own minds").

Our sense organs transmit sensations to the mind; these he calls "simple ideas." From them the mind gradually forms "ideas of reflection" (its recognition of its own ability to perceive, to think, to will, to distinguish between things, to compare, and so on). From the interaction of these two classes of ideas arise all others, including the most complex and abstruse.

Locke goes on at great length to show how this is all that is needed to account for the most remote and difficult concepts. (He apologizes for his prolixity, but says, "I am now too lazy, or too busy, to make it shorter.") He explains how the mind contemplates simple ideas and puts them together to make complex ones; sees similarities and differences between simple and complex ideas; and uses the recognition of differences to construct still more complex ideas. We derive abstract ideas such as whiteness, for instance, by noticing a quality common to certain different things (a sail, a bone, milk) and consciously excluding their differences. In similar fashion we eventually form abstract ideas such as infinity, identity and diversity, truth and falsity.

All this seems soundly put together and watertight, but there was one serious leak in the system. It was the ancient philosophic problem concerning sense perception: How can we know that what we sense is a true representation of what exists outside the mind? Locke sees no reason to doubt that we have true knowledge of the world around us. He does say, like Descartes, that God would not mislead us, but his comments have the sound not so much of piety as of common sense:

> The infinitely wise contriver of us, and all things about us, hath fitted our senses, faculties, and organs to the conveniences of life, and the business we have to do here. We are able, by our senses, to know and distinguish things; and to examine them so far as to apply them to our uses . . . Such a knowledge as this, which is suited to our present condition, we want not faculties to attain.[37]

In two respects, however, his discussion of perception created problems for later psychologists. (Locke did not distinguish between sensation and perception; the differentiation would not be made for nearly two centuries.)

First, he accepted the distinction, as old as Aquinas and maintained by Descartes, Galileo, and Newton, between "primary" qualities and "secondary" qualities of the objects we perceive. Primary qualities are "inseparable" from their objects, no matter how much they may change; they produce in us the simple ideas of solidity, extension, figure, motion or rest, and number. "Take a grain of wheat," Locke says, "divide it in two parts; each part still has solidity, extension, figure, and mobility." Secondary qualities, such as color, sound, taste, and smell, do not exist in the objects in the form that we perceive them but are sensations that the object's primary qualities cause in us. A violet is not violet in the dark; it is violet only when it causes a sensation of that color in us. Or so Locke reasoned.

Second, if our ideas are all derived from our perceptions, we know what we perceive but not the reality underlying them—nor even that any reality exists. Similarly, we never know the substance that is mind; we know only our experiences of our ideas. Reasonable Locke is undaunted:

> Sensation convinces us that there are solid, extended substances; and reflection, that there are thinking ones; experience assures us of the existence of such beings; and that the one hath a power to move body by impulse, the other by thought; this we cannot doubt of.[38]

But this simple reassurance would not convince certain other philosophers and psychologists. They would try, and fail, to find a way to prove either that our knowledge of the world is accurate or that anything exists other than our perceptions.

Locke was vague about the nature of mind. Because of his own belief or perhaps in order not to be heretical, he said it was a substance but insisted that we cannot know it any more than we can know the substance behind the qualities we perceive in objects. In fact, in a celebrated passage of the *Essay* he gingerly suggests that it is as possible to imagine that mind is matter as that it is a different kind of substance:

> We have the ideas of matter and thinking, but possibly shall never be able to know whether any mere material being thinks or no; it being impossible for us, by the contemplation of our own ideas without revelation, to discover whether Omnipotency has not given to some sys-

tems of matter, fitly disposed, a power to perceive and think, or else joined and fixed to matter, so disposed, a thinking immaterial substance.[39]

This infuriated the orthodox, who accused Locke of secretly being a materialist and of endangering all of Christian theology. Locke's psychology survived their attack, and Christianity survived the Lockean threat.

Locke, justly famous for all the foregoing, is often undeservedly credited with being the prime theorist of associationism. It is true that he coined the phrase "association of ideas"; Hobbes and earlier thinkers who discussed the phenomenon did not use that term. But the chapter in which Locke treats of association was an afterthought, an addendum to the fourth edition of the *Essay*; he had developed his entire system without the concept of association.

He does, to be sure, say that we combine simple ideas to form complex ones, and notes that repetition and pleasure play a part in forming such combinations. But he says nothing about the laws of association and does not treat the topic as one of broad relevance. His interest in it is limited to the unreasonable connections or trains of thought found in certain kinds of illnesses and in some bizarre phenomena of everyday life. He tells of a friend who had a surgical operation (no anesthetic yet existed) and who, though grateful to the surgeon, could never bear to look at him afterward, so powerful was the association of the surgeon's face with pain. He also tells of a man who learned complicated dance steps in a room that had a trunk in it, and later was able to dance well only in a room in which there was a similar trunk.

Yet if Locke's treatment of the association of ideas was limited, it stimulated others to work out the ways in which such connections and sequences of ideas are formed in the mind. Eventually, behaviorism would reduce all mental life to associations, and even after psychology escaped from the domination of behaviorism, association would remain one of its principal themes. Locke's thinking was clouded by leftover metaphysics and traces of theology, but he moved psychology away from philosophy and in the direction of science. He wrote with becoming modesty of the contribution he hoped the *Essay* would make:

Everyone must not hope to be a Boyle or Sydenham; and in an age that produces such masters as the great Huygenius, and the incomparable Mr. Newton . . . it is ambition enough to be employed as an under-

laborer in clearing the ground a little, and removing some of the rub-
bish that lies in the way to knowledge.[40]

In his case, such modesty was as unwarranted as it was becoming.

Locke died in 1704, at the beginning of a century in which the exact
sciences advanced by leaps and bounds. Among its notable strides was
the work of Galvani in physiology, Volta in electricity, Dalton in atomic
theory, Euler and Lagrange in mathematics, Herschel and Laplace in
astronomy, Linnaeus in botany, Jenner in preventive medicine, and,
later, of Cavendish, Priestley, and Rutherford in discovering, respectively, hydrogen, oxygen, and nitrogen.

Psychology made no similar bounds forward, and would not until the
emergence of experimentalism in the nineteenth century. For the most
part, the eighteenth-century protopsychologists were either rationalist-
nativists in the Cartesian tradition or empiricist-associationists in the
Hobbist-Lockean tradition. Still, some of them did advance each of
these basic theories in ways that affected the future of psychology. It is
worth meeting them briefly and glancing at their contributions.

Berkeley

The theory for which the philosopher and protopsychologist George
Berkeley (1685–1753) is famous always amuses undergraduates in his-
tory of philosophy courses and gives professors the opportunity to quote
Cicero: "There is nothing so absurd but some philosopher has said it."
Berkeley's philosophy was absurd, but many remember it; his psychol-
ogy was sound, but nearly everyone has forgotten it.

His place in history rests almost entirely on three books he wrote
before he was twenty-eight. For the rest, his life is of little interest. He
was born in Ireland, studied philosophy at Trinity College, Dublin,
earned a doctorate and was ordained a deacon of the Anglican Church
at twenty-four, traveled and preached for some years, and spent the rest
of his life as Bishop of Cloyne in County Cork, Ireland.

Berkeley was inspired to write his first noteworthy book, *An Essay
Towards a New Theory of Vision* (1709), by a brief passage in Locke that
asked whether a man born blind, who later gains vision, would be able by
sight alone to tell a cube from a sphere. Locke thought not; Berkeley
agreed, but was stimulated to study the problem further, basing his analysis on associationist psychology. Sight alone, he said, gives the newborn

no idea of distance, shape, size, or relative position. It is by means of repeated experiences—touch, reaching, walking—that the child learns to make spatial judgments. We associate the visual clues of distance, size, and shape with what we have learned through the other senses.

The thesis is sound, and a genuine contribution to perception theory. Moreover, his breaking down the seemingly simple experience of depth perception into more basic experiences anticipated or perhaps even led to the "molecular" approach of later psychology—the effort to analyze all experiences into their simplest components.

But if Berkeley was realistic in his psychology of perception, he was unworldly in the philosophic theory for which he is famous. Philosophy had long created problems for psychologists; Berkeley's psychology created a problem that would stump philosophers. It started when, as a youth of twenty-one, he decided that materialistic Newtonian science was endangering religion; he told himself in a diary that if he could only do away with the doctrine of matter, the "monstrous schemes" of "every wretched sect of atheists" would collapse.[41]

For a twenty-one-year-old to dream of doing away with the worldwide belief that matter exists—and to publish a book at twenty-five, *The Principles of Human Knowledge* (1710), expounding that dream—sounds ludicrous, if not insane. (His third important work, published in 1713, was a dialogue restating the argument.) But Berkeley was simply following through to its ultimate conclusion Locke's distinction between primary and secondary qualities. If all knowledge comes from our perceptions, we know nothing of the external world except them; but they are only secondary qualities. How do we know that the matter or substance in which primary qualities are said to reside really exists? In dreams, we see trees, houses, mountains vividly, but they are only illusions; why should we suppose our waking perceptions are better evidence that anything real exists? In Berkeley's words:

> But though it were possible that solid, figured, movable substances may exist without the mind, corresponding to the ideas we have of bodies, yet how is it possible for us to know this? Either we must know it by sense or by reason. As for our senses, by them we have only the knowledge of our sensations . . . [As for reason,] what reason can induce us to believe the existence of bodies without the mind from what we perceive? . . . *It is possible we might be affected with all the ideas we have now, though there were no bodies existing without, resembling them.*[42]

What exists, as far as we can know, is only what we perceive. *Esse est percipi*: to be perceived is to be. What is not perceived may as well not exist, for all the difference it makes to us (a doctrine that will reappear in modern times as phenomenological psychology, an offbeat by-product of existentialism).

Berkeley was no fool; he acknowledged in the Preface to his *Principles* that some passages in it, taken by themselves, might seem to have "absurd consequences." And scoffers have accused him of claiming that there is no real world whatever and that all existence is only in our imagination—that a tree exists when we see it but ceases to when we look away. Berkeley, however, rescued the universe by recourse to God, the Permanent Perceiver, Who sees all things all the time. There may be no material world, but the universe of His perceptions is steady and enduring; even when we do not see a thing, He does, and it therefore does not cease to exist when we cease looking at it. The twentieth-century British theologian Father Ronald Knox admirably summed up Berkeley's view in a famous limerick:

> There was a young man who said "God
> Must think it exceedingly odd
> If he finds that this tree
> Continues to be
> When there's no one about in the Quad."*

Berkeley's theory created a problem for both psychologists and philosophers, who found it unanswerable on its own terms. Many years later Boswell asked Dr. Johnson, as they were strolling one August day in 1763, how he would refute Berkeley's theory. Johnson kicked a large stone forcefully and rebounded from it, saying, "I refute it *thus*." He should have known better; Berkeley could have replied that the solidarity and mass of the stone and Johnson's rebounding from it were only perceptions put into his head by God and no proof that any material thing caused them.

*An anonymous correspondent replied:
> Dear Sir:
>   Your astonishment's odd:
> I am always about in the Quad.
>   And that's why the tree
>   Will continue to be,
> Since observed by
>   Yours faithfully,
>   God

There are subtler and better replies to Berkeley than Johnson's, but none simpler or saner than Hume's: Berkeley's arguments, he said, "admit of no answer and produce no conviction."

Hume

But David Hume (1711–1776) himself created a difficult problem for both philosophers and psychologists in his psychological writing. First, let us meet this brightest star of the Scottish Enlightenment.

In Scotland, as elsewhere in the Western world, the Enlightenment was the prevalent eighteenth-century philosophic movement, characterized by reliance on science and reason, the questioning of traditional religion, and the belief in universal human progress. In childhood, Hume was, on two counts, an unlikely prospect to become a luminary of that movement. He was born in Edinburgh of a well-to-do Presbyterian family and indoctrinated in childhood with Calvinist theology. As a boy he seemed dull (his own mother said he was "a fine, good-natured crater but uncommon weak-minded"), but the dullness was probably a misimpression created by his stolidity and tendency toward overweight; he was bright enough to enter the University of Edinburgh at twelve. As for his Calvinism, at fifteen he was avidly reading the philosophy of his time and by eighteen had become a convert to it, later commenting that "he never had entertained any belief in religion since he began to read Locke and Clarke."*

Hume, the second son in his family, inherited only a trifling portion. He therefore studied law, but so loathed it that he had a breakdown. He found a stint in a merchant's office equally intolerable. At twenty-three he decided to eke out an existence as a philosopher and moved to France to live cheaply. He settled at La Flèche (where Descartes had studied), and, though not enrolled at the college, talked the Jesuits into letting him use its library. In only two years he wrote his two-volume *Treatise of Human Nature: An Attempt to Introduce the Experimental (Newtonian) Method of Reasoning into Moral Subjects* (1738), the work in which he first set forth his psychology.

He expected it to make him famous but was bitterly disappointed when it attracted almost no notice. (Rewritten, later, in simpler form, it did better.) Forced to earn a living, he briefly tutored a young nobleman, then became secretary to General James St. Clair, in which post

*The English philosopher Samuel Clarke (1675–1729).

he earned a good salary, wore a scarlet uniform, ate well, and grew stout. A visitor described him as having a broad fat face "without any expression other than that of imbecility" and a body better suited to an alderman than a refined philosopher. Again appearances were deceptive; fairly soon Hume had saved enough to devote himself to writing, and the works of his mature years in politics, economics, philosophy, history, and religion brought him the fame he sought. In France he was, though vast in girth, the darling of the *salonières* and much admired by Voltaire and Diderot; in London his home became a salon where Adam Smith and other liberal thinkers regularly met for stimulating conversation.

Friends and acquaintances considered him wise, amiable, moderate in controversy, and tolerant; he said the same of himself, adding that he was "a man of great moderation in all my passions." (At twenty-three he had made a young woman pregnant, and at thirty-seven wooed a married countess on his knees, without success. These episodes aside, he seems to have been remarkably moderate in at least one passion.) Though he denounced Spinoza as an atheist, he was himself a doubter to the end. When Boswell asked him, as he lay dying of cancer of the bowel, if he did not now believe in another life, Hume replied that it was "a most unreasonable fancy." He was, all in all, a true man of the Enlightenment.

Hume's main purpose in writing the *Treatise* was to develop a moral philosophy based on "the science of man," meaning psychology. He therefore undertook to construct a theory of the human passions and our ideas of them, and this necessitated his knowing where our ideas come from. He approached the matter as a true empiricist: "As the science of man is the only solid foundation for the other sciences, so the only solid foundation we can give to this science itself must be laid on experience and observation."[43]

Accordingly, while he made ample and critical use of the work of others, he relied in considerable part on introspective observation of his own mind. As a thoroughgoing empiricist, he peremptorily dismissed all questions about the nature of the incorporeal soul—the thinking "I" that had seemed so significant to Descartes—declaring that the nature of soul was an "unintelligible question" not even worth discussing. His own view of the conscious thinking self, based on a scrutiny of his own thought processes, was that the mind was made up entirely of perceptions:

> When I enter most intimately into what I call *myself*, I always stumble
> on some particular perception or other, of heat or cold, light or shade,
> love or hatred, pain or pleasure . . . I may venture to affirm the same of
> the rest of mankind, that they are nothing but a bundle or collection of
> different perceptions.[44]

Hume distinguished between "impressions" (his word for sensations or perceptions) and "ideas" (the same experiences, but in the absence of the object, as in memories, reflections, and dreams). Like Locke, he said that these simple elements are the components of which complex and abstract ideas are formed. But how? Here he went far beyond Locke. There must be a "uniting principle," which, he hypothesized, takes three forms: "The qualities, from which this association arises, and by which the mind is, after this manner, conveyed from one idea to another, are three, viz. *resemblance, contiguity* in time and place, and *cause* and *effect*."[45]

The association or combining of ideas by means of these three characteristics seemed to Hume the fundamental principle of the mind and as central to its operations as gravitation to the motions of the stars; he even called association "a kind of *attraction*" that causes ideas to cohere. He thus made much more of association than had Locke, who relied on it chiefly to explain abnormal connections among ideas but not mental processes in general.

So far, so good. But Hume, though convinced that he had found the fundamental scientific law of the mind, proceeded to undercut the very foundation of the sciences by his interpretation of one of the three forces of association, namely, cause and effect. He did not, as is sometimes claimed, say there is no such thing as cause and effect; he did say, however, that we cannot experience causality directly and therefore cannot know what it is or even prove that it exists. We know only that certain events seem always, or almost always, to be followed by certain others, and we therefore infer that the first causes the second. But this is only expectation based on the association of the two events:

> The idea of cause and effect is derived from *experience*, which informs
> us that such particular objects, in all past instances, have been con-

stantly conjoined with each other . . . All our reasonings concerning causes and effects are derived from nothing but custom.[46]

Causality is only a habit of mind. We do not and cannot experience or perceive it in any fundamental sense; we know only that when one thing happens, the other happens. To predict that this will always be so is to commit a fallacy; we can only infer that when A next occurs, B will probably follow.

Hume concluded that we believe in causality and in the reality of the external world not because we really know that they exist but because the skeptical view that he has set forth is too hard to live with:

> It is impossible, upon any system, to defend either our understanding or our senses . . . As the skeptical doubt arises naturally from a profound and intense reflection on those subjects, it always increases the further we carry our reflections, whether in opposition or conformity to it. Carelessness and inattention alone can afford us any remedy. For this reason I rely entirely upon them, and take it for granted, whatever may be the reader's opinion at this present moment, that an hour hence he will be persuaded there is both an external and internal world.[47]

Hume's devastating assault on the concept of causality is of great importance in the history of science, and nowhere more so than in psychology, which, struggling to become a science, was seeking to discover the laws of mental causation. Some psychologists in Hume's time, and many later on, would therefore maintain that psychology cannot yield causal explanations and should attempt to deal only in correlations— the probabilities that two things will continue to occur together or in sequence. Ironically, the empiricism and associationism that Hume meant to be the foundation of his system of morals lives on; his system of morals, a gentle utilitarianism, is quite forgotten.

The Empiricist-Associationist School

Empiricist-associationist psychology disposed of some of the intractable problems in the theory of mind-body dualism and innate ideas, but in all sciences a new theory that answers old questions usually raises new and different ones. The new psychological theory not only led to subjectivism and cast doubt on the validity of causal explanations but, by reducing the major mental processes to perception and association, was able to say nothing illuminating about such high-level mental phenomena as consciousness, reasoning, speech, unconscious thought, problem solving, and creativity. It would, in fact, eventually prove most useful, in somewhat different form, as a theory of animal psychology.

Its simplistic explanation of how the mind forms abstract ideas worked well enough for concepts derived from perceptions, such as equality, but was unconvincing about those with no perceptual basis, such as virtue, soul, nonbeing, possibility, necessity, or the nondimensionality of a point in geometry.

Furthermore, except for Hobbes's atomistic conjecture about nervous impulses, the new theory ignored the physiology of mental phenomena and could say nothing explanatory about reflexive reactions, let alone all those high-level automatic responses which make up much of everyday human behavior.

From Locke's time on, a series of empiricist-associationists, mostly in Great Britain, sought to solve some of these problems, but with only minor success, if any. Nonetheless, some of their work represents courageous venturing into the unknown; if they crossed no uncharted oceans, some of them at least mapped a few miles of alien coastline.

David Hartley (1705–1757) was one of the latter. A scholarly physician, he was inspired by Locke's work to write at length about associationism in his *Observations on Man* (1749). Although he added nothing original, his treatment of the subject was organized and systematic, and thereby, says the great historian of psychology, Edwin G. Boring, turned it into a "school."[48]

In addition, Hartley, as a doctor, was sharply aware of Locke's omission of physiology; he sought to present a more holistic psychology by discussing each phenomenon first in mental terms and then in physiological ones. An admirable effort; unfortunately, in the mid-eighteenth century the neurophysiology he offered was largely imaginary. From Newtonian physics he derived the idea that external vibrations in matter must cause corresponding vibrations of infinitesimal particles within the nerves. These vibrations produced miniature counterparts or "vibratiuncles . . . the physiological counterpart of ideas,"[49] a pure figment of his imagination, yet a little closer to the truth than Descartes' theory of hollow nerves and animal spirits. It did, furthermore, keep an interest alive among associationists in the physical substrate of mental events.

In Scotland, Thomas Reid (1710–1792), Dugald Stewart (1753–1828), and Thomas Brown (1778–1820), professors at Scottish universities and good Presbyterians all, modified associationism to make it more palatable to believers. They felt that as it was expounded by Locke and Hume, it was mechanistic and degrading to the humanity of man. Moreover, Hume's skepticism about causality and the reality of the external world was contrary to religious dogma. All three men therefore altered and added to associationism in an effort to repair these defects.

Their chief answer to Locke, Berkeley, and Hume was actually remarkably simple: subjectivism and skepticism were belied by common sense. People in all ages and nations have believed in the external world and in causality because common sense tells them to—the very view Dr. Johnson expressed by kicking the stone. It was hardly good science, but at least it did no harm.

Reid also made the very good point that the simple laws of association seemed grossly inadequate as an explanation of complex mental functions. He therefore revived and enlarged the ancient concept of mental faculties—special innate abilities—and named several dozen of them.[50] Later psychologists would struggle to prove, or disprove, the existence of such faculties.

Brown made a smaller but more concrete contribution to associationism: he proposed that there were both primary and secondary laws of "suggestion" (association), and that the latter, under special conditions, altered the operation of the former. Thus, the word "cold" might produce at one time and place the association "dark" but at another time and place the association "hot." This valuable insight, however, was ignored until the advent of the experimental approach to learning nearly a century later.

James Mill (1773–1836), social theorist, Utilitarian philosopher, and journalist, offered his own version of associationism in *Analysis of the Phenomena of the Human Mind* (1829). Instead of enlarging the theory, he drastically simplified it. He said that there were only two classes of mental elements—sensations and ideas—and that all association comes about through one factor, contiguity, the simultaneity or nearness in time of two experiences. Complex ideas were nothing but simpler ones conjoined; the idea "everything" was not an abstraction but a mere heap or accumulation of all of one's simple and complex ideas. Robert Watson says that "this brings association as a doctrine to its nadir in logical, mechanistic, and molecular simplicity."[51] Nonetheless, some leading twentieth-century behaviorists would sound like Mill's intellectual offspring.

John Stuart Mill (1806–1873), James Mill's son, primarily a philosopher, discussed psychology in his *Logic* (1843) and his *Examination of Sir William Hamilton's Philosophy* (1865). He restored to mainstream associationism much of what his father had pruned from it, particularly hypotheses about the formation of complex ideas. Unlike the elder Mill, he envisioned them not as mere assemblages of simple elements but as fusions of those elements, much like chemical compounds that have characteristics unlike those of their component elements. Accordingly, he said, the laws of association cannot tell us how any complex idea comes to be or what it is composed of; we can learn that only from experience and direct experiment. Mill thus helped steer associationism toward experimental psychology.

Alexander Bain (1818–1903), a friend of John Stuart Mill's, lived well into the era of scientific psychology. Some scholars say he was the last of the philosopher-psychologists, others that he was the first real psychologist in that he devoted most of his life to psychology and brought more physiology into it than any of his predecessors. The physiology was not imaginary, like Hartley's; it was gleaned from his visits to nineteenth-century anatomists and his reading of their works. The mechanisms described in his discussion of the senses and of movement came closer to modern theory than those of earlier protopsychologists.

But the physiology of his time could not account for higher mental processes. Bain's psychology was therefore largely mainline associationism. He did, however, point out some of its limitations. He noted that it could not explain novel or innovative ideas. And though he denied that there are innate ideas, he said that the minds of infants are not really blank sheets of paper; they possess reflexes, instincts, and differences in acuteness. No school or great theory is linked with his name, but his work contained a number of germinal ideas that others would soon develop.

German Nativism

While explorers of the mind were adventuring in one direction in Britain and in France (where empiricism caught on among intellectual liberals during the Enlightenment), others in Germany were continuing to pursue the direction taken by Descartes. Something about the German culture and mentality gave its philosophers a bent for murky metaphysics, mind-body dualism, and nativism. Yet that direction, too, yielded something of value, chiefly the theory of mind developed by Immanuel Kant, the greatest philosopher of the idealist school.

Before Kant, the German philosophers, for all their intelligence, had contributed little to humankind's understanding of its mental processes. One, in fact, possibly the most brilliant mind of the seventeenth century, made forays into psychology that accomplished almost nothing; his brand of metaphysics, like a faulty compass, led him astray. Still, he is worth a moment's notice if only because his ideas exemplify the tradition that led to the work of Kant.

Leibniz

Gottfried Wilhelm Leibniz (1646–1716), born in Leipzig, Saxony, was a stooped, bandy-legged genius who earned a doctorate in law at twenty, served as a diplomat to the French and English courts, invented the calculus at the same time as Newton (with whom he became involved in a nasty dispute over who deserved credit for it), and wrote extensively on a variety of philosophic issues. Although many of his ideas are worthy of respect, Leibniz is best known today for two that are preposterous. One is familiar to all who have read Voltaire's *Candide*:

> It follows from the supreme perfection of God, that in creating the universe he has chosen the best possible plan . . . For since all the possibilities in the understanding of God laid claim to existence in proportion to their perfections, the actual world, as the resultant of all these claims, must be the most perfect possible.[52]

These are Leibniz's words, not Voltaire's; this is what Voltaire wickedly satirized in the person of Dr. Pangloss, who endlessly repeats his profound philosophic insight, "All is for the best in this best of all possible worlds."

Leibniz's other outlandish notion was that the universe is made up of an infinite number of "monads"—ultimate components of substance that are a kind of soul, dimensionless, pointlike, and impervious to outside influences. What appears to be matter throughout the universe is actually the way the immaterial monads perceive the arrangement of one another in space.[53] Leibniz thought this up to solve a number of problems in classic metaphysics, including those of mind-body dualism. His theory is difficult to grasp, but since "monadology" began and ended with him, we need not bother trying.

Monadology did, however, lead him to suggest that there are different levels of consciousness, a new idea in psychology. Monads, being infinitesimal, are not individually conscious, but when cumulate, their tiny perceptions add up to complex mental functions, including consciousness; the more complex the aggregation, the more so the mental function. Animals, though they perceive, are not self-aware, but human beings are; that is, there is more than one level of consciousness. That's a long way from what Freud would mean by the unconscious and the preconscious, but it's a beginning.

One aspect of Leibniz's psychology did lead in a useful direction. Seeking to explain the source of consciousness, he postulated a process he called "apperception," which, by means of certain innate patterns or beliefs, enables us to become aware of and to understand our many tiny unconscious perceptions. We know, for instance, without learning it, that "whatever is, is," and that "it is impossible for a thing to be and not to be at the same time." Similarly, the truths of reason—principles of logic—are inherent. These innate ideas are not specific concepts but ways of understanding experience. Kant would transform this notion into a historic theory.

Another aspect of monadology would have led psychology into a cul-de-sac if anyone but Leibniz had taken it seriously. Since monads are impervious to outside influences, how is it that anything ever happens in the world—and that it looks as if things influence each other? Leibniz's answer was that God has arranged for all the changes in the infinity of monads to occur in "pre-established harmony"; nothing interacts with anything else but only seems to. So whatever happens in mind exactly parallels what is happening in body, without any interaction between them: "God has originally created the soul, and every other real unity, in such a way that everything in it must arise from its own nature by a perfect spontancity with regard to itself, yet by a perfect conformity to things without."[54] It is the two-clock theory of Geulincx again, except that now every infinitesimal monad is a clock, keeping time with every other one.

The theory would have made psychology pointless, since it portrays mental events as following a fixed and preordained order and psychological responses to outside stimuli as mere illusion. Which only shows whither a splendid mind can travel when steering by a faulty compass. Fortunately, few others followed his route.

Kant

Immanuel Kant (1724–1804) is considered by many the greatest of modern philosophers; he is certainly one of the most difficult to understand, though that may not be an appropriate criterion. Happily, we are interested only in his psychology, which is comprehensible.

Kant's biography sounds like a parody of the life of the ivory-tower intellectual. Born in Königsberg, Prussia, he entered the university at sixteen, taught there until he was seventy-three, and never traveled more than forty miles from the city. Barely five feet tall and hollow-chested, he led a bachelor life of unvarying routine, ostensibly to preserve his frail health. He was awakened by his manservant at 5 A.M. the year round, devoted two hours of the morning to study and two hours to lecturing, wrote until 1 P.M., and then dined at a restaurant. Precisely at 3:30 P.M. he strolled for an hour, whatever the weather, along a walk of linden trees, breathing only through his nose (he thought it unhealthful to open his mouth outdoors) and refusing to converse with anyone. (He was so punctual that his neighbors, who set their watches by his daily walk, were worried when he failed to appear on time one day. He had been reading Rousseau's *Émile* and was so captivated that he forgot himself.) He spent the remainder of each day reading and preparing for the next day's lecture, and retired between 9 and 10 P.M.

Kant wrote and lectured on many topics: ethics, theology, cosmology, aesthetics, logic, and the theory of knowledge. Liberal in both politics and theology, he sympathized with the French Revolution until the Reign of Terror, and was a believer in democracy and a lover of freedom. He was a disciple of Leibniz's until, in midlife, he read Hume and, he said, "was awakened from my dogmatic slumbers" and became inspired to develop a much more detailed theory of knowledge than Leibniz's.

Kant was convinced by Hume that causality is not self-evident and that we cannot demonstrate it logically, but he felt sure that we do understand the reality around us and do experience the causal relationships among external things and events. How is that possible? He sought the answer by pure cerebration. For twelve years he stared out the window at a nearby church steeple and thought. It then took him only a few months to write what became his most famous work, *The Critique of Pure Reason* (1781), of which he candidly said in his Preface, "I venture to assert there is not a single metaphysical problem that has not been solved here, or to the solution of which the key at least has not been supplied."[55]

Although his prose in the *Critique* and elsewhere is all but unintelligible to most readers—his terminology is difficult and his arguments abstruse—he gives his basic view about the mind clearly enough in the Preface. It is true, he says, that experience furnishes us with only very limited knowledge, but it is far from being the mind's only source of knowledge:

> Experience is by no means the only field to which our understanding can be confined. Experience tells us what *is*, but not that it must be necessarily what it is and not otherwise. It therefore never gives us any really general truths; and our reason, which is particularly anxious for that class of knowledge, is roused by it rather than satisfied. General truths, which at the same time bear the character of an inward necessity, must be independent of experience—clear and certain in themselves.[56]

And such clear and certain truths do exist, mathematics being a case in point. For instance, we believe, and feel perfectly certain of our belief, that two and two will always make four. How do we come by that certainty? Not from experience, which provides us only with probabilities, but from the inherent structure of our minds, from the natural and inevitable manner in which they function. For the human mind is not merely blank paper upon which experience writes, and not a mere bundle of perceptions; it actively organizes and transforms the chaos of experience into sure knowledge.

We start to acquire such knowledge by recognizing the relations of objects and events in space and time—not through experience but through inherent capability; space and time are forms of *Anschauung* ("intuition" or "looking at") or innately determined ways in which we see things.

Then, having organized our sense data in space and time, we make other judgments about them by means of other innate ideas or transcendental principles (Kant's term is "categories"); these are the built-in machinery by which the mind comprehends experience. There are twelve categories, including unity, totality, reality, cause and effect, reciprocity, existence, and necessity. Kant derived them from a painstaking analysis of the forms of the syllogism, but his basic reason for believing they exist in the mind *a priori* is that without them we would have no way of making sense of the chaotic mass of our perceptions.

It is not from experience, for instance, that we learn that every event has a cause; if we lacked the ability to perceive cause and effect, we should never understand anything about the world around us. Therefore it must be that we innately recognize causes and effects.[57] The other categories, similarly, are not innate ideas in the Platonic or Cartesian sense but are principles of ordering that enable us to fathom experience. It is they, not the laws of association, that organize experience into meaningful knowledge.

Kant's view of the mind as process rather than neural action steered German psychology toward the study of consciousness and "phenomenal experience." Dualism persisted, since "mind" was apparently a transcendental—Kant's word—phenomenon, distinct from perceptions and associations.[58] His theory would give rise to other varieties of nativist psychology, particularly in Germany, and would have its modern counterparts, if not descendants, in this country, among them Noam Chomsky's theory of the innate capacity of the child's mind to comprehend the syntax of spoken language.

Kant's nativism led to certain valuable lines of inquiry about the workings of the mind, but in one respect it proved to be a serious hindrance. He held that the mind is a set of processes that take place in time but do not occupy space, and this led him to infer that mental processes cannot be measured (since they occupy no space) and therefore that psychology cannot be an experimental science.*[59] Others in the Kantian tradition would continue to hold that view. While it would later be proven as erroneous as Descartes' belief in animal spirits and hollow nerves, it would retard the development of psychology as a science.

---

*He also argued that all psychological knowledge is derived from subjective experience and has no *a priori* logical or mathematical basis. Hence it can never become a science proper. See Leary, 1978 and 1982.

But only retard. Even as the Catholic Church could delay, but not ultimately prevent, humankind's learning that the sun rather than the earth is the center of the solar system, the authority of the greatest of idealist philosophers could not prevent psychology from becoming a science through experimentation.

Part Two

FOUNDERS

OF A

NEW SCIENCE

FOUR

The
Physicalists

While eighteenth- and nineteenth-century philosophers were sitting in their studies and reasoning about mental phenomena, a number of physicians and physicists were taking a very different route toward the goal of psychological knowledge. Emulating scientists like Harvey, Newton, and Priestley, they were using their hands and instruments to gather information, specifically about the physical causes of neural and mental processes. These pioneers of physicalist psychology are the ancestors of today's cognitive neuroscientists; their outlook led to the present-day specification of the molecular transactions in the neurons that are the components of mental phenomena.

The Magician-Healer: Mesmer

Some physicalists, however, were quasi-scientists at best, and some only pseudo-scientists. Yet even the latter are part of our story, since their theories of certain mental phenomena, though later disproved, led others to seek and discover valid explanations of those phenomena.

Such was the case with Dr. Franz Anton Mesmer (1734–1815).[1] In the 1770s, when German nativists and British associationists were still relying on contemplation to understand psychology, Mesmer, a physician, was applying magnets to patients on the theory that the mind and body can be healed of disorders if the body's magnetic force fields are realigned.

The theory was pure nonsense, yet the treatment based on it had such dramatic success that for a while Mesmer was the rage of Vienna and then of pre-Revolutionary Paris, where we now look in on him. It is 1778; we are in a dimly lit, mirror-hung, baroque salon on the Place Vendôme. A dozen elegantly dressed ladies and gentlemen sit around a large oak tub, each holding one of a number of metal rods protruding from the tub, which is filled with magnetized iron filings and chemicals. From an adjoining room comes the faint keening of music played on a glass harmonica; after a while the sound dies away, the door opens wider, and slowly and majestically there enters an awesome figure in a flowing, full-length purple robe, carrying a scepterlike iron rod in one hand. It is the miracle-working Dr. Mesmer.

The patients are transfixed and thrilled as Mesmer, stern and formidable with his square-jawed face, long slit of a mouth, and beetling eyebrows, stares intently at one man and commands, "*Dormez!*" The man's eyes close and his head sags onto his chest; the other patients gasp. Now Dr. Mesmer looks intently at a woman and slowly points the iron rod at her; she shudders and cries out that tingling sensations are running through her body. As Mesmer proceeds around the circle, the reactions of the patients grow stronger and stronger. Eventually some of them shriek, flail their arms about, and swoon; assistants carry them to an adjoining *chambre de crises*, where they are attended and soothed until they have recovered. After the session, many of those who were present and who had been afflicted by everything from the "vapors" to paralysis feel relieved of their symptoms or even cured. No wonder Mesmer, though his fee is enormous, is besieged by those seeking treatment.

Although today his procedures seem pure flimflam, and he himself was given to sharp practices, most scholars think that he truly believed in what he was doing and in the theory by which he accounted for his results. Mesmer, born in Swabia, came from a family of modest position—his father was a forester, his mother the daughter of a locksmith—but he worked his way through the Bavarian and Austrian educational systems, first meaning to become a priest, then a lawyer, and finally a doctor. At thirty-two he received his medical degree in Vienna; his professors, fortunately for him, were unaware that much of his dissertation, *On the Influence of the Planets*, was plagiarized from a work of a colleague of Isaac Newton's. Despite the title, his dissertation was not about astrology; it proposed that there was a connection between Newton's "universal gravitation" and the condition of the human body and mind. In the part of the dissertation that was Mesmer's own work, he advanced the theory, based on a passing comment by Newton, that the human body is pervaded by an invisible fluid that is responsive to planetary gravitation. Health or illness, Mesmer argued, depends on whether the body's "animal gravitation" is in harmony with, or discord with, that of the planets.

Two years after earning his degree, he married a wealthy Viennese widow much older than himself and thereby gained entrance to Viennese society. Freed from the need to practice more than part-time, he devoted much of his attention to cultural and scientific developments. When Benjamin Franklin invented the glass harmonica, Mesmer, a competent amateur musician, bought one and became a skillful performer on it. Passionate music lovers, he and his wife saw a good deal of Leopold Mozart and his family, and twelve-year-old Wolfgang's first opera, *Bastien und Bastienne,* had its debut in the garden of the Mesmer home.

While enjoying these delights, Mesmer was becoming a medical and psychological pioneer. In 1773 a twenty-seven-year-old woman came to him suffering from symptoms that other doctors had been unable to relieve. Nor was Mesmer able to help her until he recalled a talk he had had with a Jesuit priest named Maximilian Hell, who suggested that magnetism might influence the body. Mesmer bought a set of magnets, and the next time the woman came to see him he gingerly touched the magnets, one after another, to different parts of her body. She began to tremble and shortly went into convulsions—Mesmer decided this was "the crisis"—and, when she had calmed down, declared that her symptoms were much relieved. A series of further treatments cured her completely. (Today, her illness would be considered a hysterical neurosis and her recovery the result of suggestion.)

Mesmer now saw a link between magnetism and his own theory of animal gravitation. He decided that the body is pervaded by a magnetic rather than a gravitational fluid, and that the resulting force field can become misaligned, causing illness; realignment through treatment would restore health. What he had previously called "animal gravitation" he renamed "animal magnetism." The patient's crisis he interpreted as a breakthrough of an obstacle to the flow of the body's magnetic fluid and the consequent restoration of "harmony."

Mesmer began treating other patients, telling them to expect certain reactions, including the crisis. They all obligingly responded as anticipated, and Viennese newspapers soon were full of stories of Mesmer's cures. At some point Maximilian Hell publicly asserted that the idea was his, not Mesmer's, and a nasty dispute ensued. Mesmer boldly asserted that he had proposed the theory years earlier in his dissertation (a distortion of truth), won the dispute, and established himself as the discoverer of the phenomenon.

Riding the wave of his fame, Mesmer gave well-attended lectures and demonstrations in a number of cities. In Vienna, however, the flamboyance with which he publicized his cures offended the city's influential doctors. They were further scandalized in 1777 by his claims concerning one patient, Maria Theresa von Paradies, the blind pianist for whom Mozart wrote his B-flat piano concerto, K.456. She came to Mesmer when she was eighteen, having been blind since the age of three. He claimed that under his care she regained partial vision but was able to see only in his presence and never when another witness was present. It is possible that her blindness was psychosomatic and that he did have an influence on her, but in 1778 her parents stopped the treatment, Viennese doctors denounced Mesmer as a charlatan, and he abruptly left everything behind, including his aging wife, and decamped for Paris.

In that jittery, fad-ridden city, Mesmer, with his talent for self-promotion, swiftly achieved great fame and, in time, notoriety. At first he treated patients individually, but as his practice burgeoned, he found it profitable to treat them en masse by means of his own invention, the *baquet* or oak tub, which dispensed magnetic fluid through the iron bars. Since he could also affect his patients by touch, gestures, or long intense looks, he began to think that neither magnets nor iron filings were essential and that his own body must be unusually magnetic, capable of transmitting invisible magnetic fluid directly.

"Mesmerism," as the treatment was soon called, became the *dernier cri*; people flocked to Mesmer's salon, acolytes studied under him, and his disciples wrote at least two hundred pamphlets and books about his treatment in less than a decade. But the faculty of medicine of the University of Paris and other orthodox medical institutions considered him a fraud and said so. If he had known himself to be a faker, he would surely not have responded as he did. Through his aristocratic connections, in 1784 he induced the King to appoint a special commission composed of distinguished doctors and academicians, including the chemist Lavoisier and the American ambassador, Benjamin Franklin, to investigate his claims.

The commission conducted a careful study, including an experiment of a kind common in modern psychology. They told some subjects that they would be magnetized through a closed door, but then did no magnetizing. The tricked subjects responded exactly as they would have had magnetization been performed. After consideration of all the evidence, the commission reported correctly that Mesmer's magnetic fluid did not exist, incorrectly that the effects of magnetic treatment were nothing but "imagination." With that, the popularity of mesmerism waned and the movement broke up into quarreling groups. Mesmer eventually left the scene of his disgrace and spent most of his last thirty years in Switzerland in relative seclusion.

For half a century, mesmerism remained a quasi-magical and thoroughly misunderstood phenomenon practiced by outright charlatans like Count Alessandro di Cagliostro (the pseudonym of a mountebank named Giuseppe Balsamo), sideshow performers, and a number of adventurous laymen and unorthodox doctors in France, England, and America. Most mesmerists gradually abandoned the use of magnets—Mesmer himself had been moving in that direction—claiming that they were able to transmit magnetic fluid by means of rituals and incantations, eye contact, and other procedures. These did, in fact, provoke trances and "crises" and yield relief from certain symptoms.

In England in the 1840s, mesmerism began to gain some respectability when John Elliotson, a physician, used it to treat neuroses, and W. S. Ward, a surgeon, amputated the leg of a patient anesthetized by mesmerism. James Braid, a Scottish physician, after performing a number of experiments with mesmerism, said that its major effect was due not to magnetism flowing from the mesmerist but, rather, to the susceptibility of the patient; in effect, he identified it as a psychological process. Braid renamed it "neuro-hypnology" (from the Greek *neuron* for "nerve" and *hypnos* for "sleep"), which shortly became, in common use, "hypnosis," as it has been known ever since.

In midcentury, a French country doctor named Auguste Liébeault discarded the remainder of the magical-mystical trappings of hypnotism. He had the patient stare into his eyes while he repeatedly suggested that the patient was growing sleepy. When the patient fell into a trance, the doctor told him that his symptoms would disappear, and in many cases they did. By the mid-1860s Liébeault, who had become a celebrity beyond his native Nancy, wrote a book about his method and its results; from then on, hypnotism, though still suspect and a subject of heated controversy, entered into medical practice.

Its most noted practitioner, late in the century, was Jean Martin Charcot, director of the Salpêtrière, a hospital in Paris. Known as "the Napoleon of the neuroses," he believed that hypnotic phenomena had much in common with hysterical symptoms and, indeed, that only a hysteric could be hypnotized. He hypnotized hysterical patients before groups of students to demonstrate the symptoms of hysteria, but did not consider hypnotism potentially therapeutic and did not use it as a therapy.

Charcot also believed, erroneously, that the trance was achieved only after the patient had passed through two prior stages, lethargy and catalepsy, each having specific symptoms and involving major changes in the functioning of the nervous system.[2] His views were later disproved by the followers of Liébeault, who proved that the trance could be directly induced and that nonhysterics could be hypnotized. Still, it was thanks to Charcot's prestige and his skill at inducing the trance that in 1882 the French Academy of Sciences accepted hypnosis as a neurological phenomenon that had nothing to do with magnetism.

A number of Charcot's gifted students, among them Alfred Binet, Pierre Janet, and Sigmund Freud, went on to offer psychological rather than neurological explanations of the hypnotic state and to use hypnosis in their own ways. In the past century, hypnosis has had a checkered history, partly as a sideshow entertainment and partly as a therapeutic tool useful in pain relief, particularly for persons who cannot tolerate anesthesia. Why it works (and why for many people it doesn't) has been answered on two levels: It does not seem linked to most traits of personality, but some recent studies have linked it to absorption, or the capacity to concentrate totally on material outside oneself.[3] Lately, with the advent of brain scans there has been evidence of a physiological mechanism at work: In highly hypnotizable people "top-down" neural processes, generated in the forebrain, override "bottom-up" processes that take place in the sensory perception areas of the brain, while in nonhypnotizables the opposite is true.[4] Dr. Mesmer, could he know all this, would doubtless be outraged that his theory has been totally discarded but mightily pleased that his therapeutic claims have been vindicated.

The Skull Reader: Gall

Other physicalists, taking a totally different approach, palpated and measured the cranium in the belief that the details of its configuration were directly related to the individual's personality traits and mental abilities.

The idea that external physical characteristics are linked to psychological traits was an ancient one. Physiognomy, the interpretation of character and mental abilities from the shape and size of the facial features, had existed since Greek times. It became popular in the late eighteenth century through the writings of Johann Kaspar Lavater, a Swiss theologian and mystic, whose four-volume *Physiognomical Fragments*, purporting to present the "science of physiognomy," went through fifty-five editions between 1775 and 1810. Darwin later said that he almost missed out on his epochal trip on the *Beagle* because its captain, a disciple of Lavater's, "doubted whether anyone with my nose could possess sufficient energy and determination for the voyage."[5]

Physiognomy had no influence on psychology, but it prepared the way for a related theory that did, namely, phrenology, the doctrine that the contours of the skull are determined by the development of specific areas of the brain and therefore are indicative of character and mental abilities.

The chief proponent of the theory was Franz Joseph Gall (1758–1828), a doctor and neurophysiologist born in Germany and trained in Vienna, where he received his medical degree in 1785.[6] Gall, whose small, petulant features seemed bunched low in his face—his numerous eminent patients apparently did not believe in physiognomy—was a chronic nonconformist, ever on the outs with authority, vehement in controversy, given to blatant womanizing, and so unabashedly greedy that, defying convention, he charged admission to his scientific demonstrations.

For all that, he was a first-rate brain anatomist who, by means of his own technique of dissection, first showed that the two halves of the brain are connected by stalks of white matter (the "commissures"); that the fibers of the spinal cord cross over when connecting to the lower brain (with the result that sensations from one side of the body reach the brain on the opposite side); and that the larger the amount of cortex—gray matter on the surface of the brain—a species possesses, the greater its intelligence.

These contributions by Gall became, and still are, part of standard neurological knowledge, but they deeply displeased the ecclesiastical authorities and Emperor Francis I because they attributed the higher mental processes of human beings to the developed brain rather than to an incorporeal soul or mind. In 1801 the Emperor forbade Gall to give further lectures on the grounds that they led to materialism, immorality, and atheism. After repeatedly appealing to the Emperor to lift the ban, to no avail, in 1807 Gall quit Vienna for Paris, where, though Napoleon sought to restrict his influence and his ideas were rejected by the Institut de France, he remained for the rest of his life.

Gall's contributions to the knowledge of brain structure and its relationship to intelligence should have won him a respected place in the history of psychology, but he is best known for, and usually judged by, the theory he called "cranioscopy," which became popularly known as phrenology.

When Gall first realized that human intelligence is superior to that of animals because of the greater development of the human cortex, it occurred to him that, similarly, differences among human beings in intelligence and personality might be due to measurable differences in individual cortical development. This would explain something that had puzzled him for many years. As a schoolboy, and again as a medical student, he had been irked that some of his schoolfellows, though not as bright as he, got better grades because they were better memorizers— and, mystifyingly, all had large, bulging eyes. Gall now guessed this must mean that the area of cortex just behind the eyes was the seat of verbal memory, and that in people who have excellent memories the area is unusually developed and tends to push the eyes forward.

If so, might not every higher faculty be embodied in a particular area or "organ" of the cerebral cortex? Might there not be an organ, for instance, that generates "combativeness," another that produces "benevolence," and so on? Gall was familiar with the several dozen "mental faculties" propounded by Thomas Reid, the Scottish associationist; perhaps each faculty resided in a particular cortical area that was unusually developed in people who possessed that faculty in unusual degree.

He could hardly open up people's skulls to test his theory, and X-rays had not yet been discovered, but Gall came up with a convenient new hypothesis. Just as the eyes of those with good memories were pushed forward, so the skull probably protruded somewhat over any unusually developed area. And, *mirabile dictu*, when he began looking for the evidence, he found it everywhere. Here is how he first located the "organ of acquisitiveness":

> The errand-boys, and others of that class of people, whom I used to assemble in my house in great numbers, would frequently charge each other with petty larcenies, or, as they called them, *chiperies*. Some of these people showed the utmost abhorrence of thieving, and preferred starving to accepting any part of the bread and fruits their companions had stolen, while the *chipeurs* would ridicule such conduct and think

it very silly. On examining their heads, I was astonished to find that the most inveterate *chipeurs* had a long prominence, extending from the organ of cunning almost as far as the external angle of the superciliary ridge;* and that this region was *flat* in all those who showed a horror of theft.[7]

Gall and a colleague, a young doctor named Johann Christoph Spurzheim, painstakingly examined the heads of hundreds of patients, friends, prisoners, inmates of insane asylums, and others, and mapped out twenty-seven regions of the skull (later expanded by Spurzheim to thirty-seven), each of which represented an underlying organ or cortical area in which a particular faculty was located and which, in those in whom that trait was pronounced, was elevated. (Gall's portrait shows him with both hands spread over a model of a head, fingers deftly feeling bumps.) Among the areas Gall and Spurzheim identified were those of amativeness (just below the back of the skull), benevolence (the center of the upper forehead), combativeness (in back of each ear), reverence (just forward of the crown of the head), mirthfulness (midway up and toward the sides of the forehead), and so on.

Gall described his findings in a series of massive volumes published between 1810 and 1819. Spurzheim co-authored the first two but then went his own way; dynamic and charming, he became a highly successful lecturer and popularizer of phrenology in Europe and in the United States. Through Gall's books and self-promotion and Spurzheim's public appearances, phrenology became immensely popular and remained so for nearly a century. At one time, in Great Britain alone there were twenty-nine phrenological societies and several phrenological journals. In New York City, phrenological "parlors" sprang up on Broadway, and itinerant phrenologists gave readings all over the United States. In its heyday, phrenology was the vogue among ordinary folk, who sought in it answers to life's dilemmas. More surprisingly, many distinguished people and serious intellectuals believed in it: Hegel, Bismarck, Marx, Balzac, the Brontës, George Eliot, Walt Whitman, and others.

But from the first it met with powerful scientific opposition, and for good reason. For one thing, Gall collected and presented cases that fit his theory when he should have measured random samples of people and shown that bumps were correlated with hyperdevelopment of the traits in question and the absence of bumps with normal or less than

*That is, just above and forward of the ears.

normal development of those traits. For another, when an individual with a cranial prominence failed to have the predicted trait, Gall explained it in terms of the "balancing action" of other brain parts that offset the part in question. With so many different faculties to work with, Gall could "prove" whatever he chose, and accordingly most scientists found his proofs worthless.[8]

But definitive refutation of phrenology came from the laboratory. Pierre Flourens (1794–1867), a brilliant young French physiologist, was aghast at Gall's slipshod methodology and set out to discover, by experiment, whether specific psychological functions are, or are not, located in particular areas of the brain.[9] A skilled surgeon, he operated on the brains of birds, rabbits, and dogs, removing small areas and carefully nursing the animals back to health to see how their behavior was altered by the loss of those areas.

He could not, of course, test for such human faculties as verbal memory, but he could test for faculties housed in portions of the brain that Gall himself said were comparable to those in human brains. One such was the "organ of amativeness," supposedly located in the cerebellum (the primitive part of the brain, toward the back and base of the skull). When Flourens removed more and more of a dog's cerebellum in a series of operations, the dog gradually lost the power of orderly movement until it would turn left when it wanted to turn right, fall backward when it wanted to go ahead, and so on. The function of the cerebellum, clearly, was the coordination of purposive movement rather than amativeness.

Similarly, Flourens found that the progressive removal of areas of the cortex in animals reduced their responses to sensory stimulation and their capacity to initiate action. A small lesion produced no specific effect, as it should have if phrenology were correct, but merely decreased the animal's overall responsiveness to visual stimuli and its general level of activity. With more removal of the cortex, the animal would become more inert, until all responsiveness and self-initiated movement were gone; a totally decorticated bird, for instance, would not fly unless thrown into the air. Flourens concluded that perception, judgment, will, and memory were distributed throughout the cerebral cortex. Although he had found a gross localization of function in the brain—the cortex and the cerebellum did serve different purposes—the specific functions of each were apparently evenly distributed within each.

Gall's pseudo-scientific theory thus led to the first experimental studies of the localization of brain functions. Moreover, his theory, though wrong in all its details, survived Flourens's assault, since later cognitive neuroscientists, following Flourens's lead, were able to identify particular areas of the brain as being responsible for visual perception, auditory perception, and motor control. Flourens was right that memory and thinking are distributed throughout the cortex, but a number of lower and even some higher mental processes are indeed localized.

The most striking instance of a high-level function carried out by a local area of the brain is language. In 1861, Leborgne, a fifty-one-year-old patient at the Bicêtre asylum in Paris, was transferred to the surgical ward, suffering from gangrene in his right leg. The surgeon, a young man named Paul Broca, questioned the patient about his ailment, but Leborgne could utter nothing in reply but the meaningless sound "*tan*."[10] He communicated only by gestures and "*tan, tan,*" although if one failed to understand his gestures he could angrily blurt out, "*Sacré nom de Dieu!*" Broca learned that Tan, as he was known in the hospital, had come to the asylum twenty-one years earlier, when he lost the power of speech. He had remained otherwise intellectually normal, but after some years had slowly developed paralysis of the right arm and leg.

Tan died six days after arriving at the surgical ward. Broca performed an autopsy and found that an egg-sized area of the left side of the brain somewhat forward of the middle had been destroyed; there was almost no tissue in the center of the lesion, and around its edges the remaining tissue was softened. Based on Leborgne's history, Broca concluded that the lesion had begun at what was now its center and that while it was still relatively small, it had completely destroyed Leborgne's ability to speak; only later did its spread cause paralysis. Evidently, this small frontal-lobe area of the left hemisphere of the brain was the seat of speech. It has been known ever since as Broca's Area.

A little over a dozen years later, a German physician, Carl Wernicke, similarly discovered that certain patients who spoke fluently but used many peculiar words and had difficulty understanding what was said to them had a lesion of another small area in the left hemisphere a few inches to the rear of Broca's Area. It eventually became clear that Broca's Area governs syntax (the structure of speech) and Wernicke's Area, as the second one is known, semantics (the meaning of words). Both are needed for normal speech; a lesion of Broca's Area impairs the ability to muster words but not understanding, a lesion of Wernicke's

Area leaves the sufferer capable of fluent but nonsensical speech and with impaired comprehension of language.[11]

Still later, two German physiologists, Gustav Fritsch and Eduard Hitzig, identified a special region of the cortex—a strip running up and over the brain from left midbrain to right midbrain—as the site of motor control. Other investigators located areas responsible for vision, touch, and hearing. Toward the end of the century Flourens's belief that there was no localization of function began to seem quite wrong and Gall's view quite right, although totally wrong in detail. But in the twentieth century, further research would show that both theories are correct. Many functions reside in specific areas of the human brain, but learning, intelligence, memory, reasoning, decision making, and other high-level mental processes take place throughout the frontal lobes.

Flourens himself once summed up the approach of every science to truth by means of such to-and-fro swings of theory: "*La science n'est pas,*" he said; "*elle devient*" (Science *is* not; it *becomes*).[12]

What psychology has become is due, in part, to Gall. His discoveries of brain structure have stood the test of time, his absurd theory of phrenology led to the experimental study of the localization of brain functions, and his emphasis on the cortex as the seat of intelligence moved psychology farther than ever from metaphysics and closer than ever to empirical science. He deserves better than to be remembered only for his venture into pseudo-science.

The Mechanists

The mapping of the brain was part of a new and larger movement that sought to explain psychological phenomena in physiological terms. Democritus and a few others, to be sure, had hazarded guesses as to the physical events underlying perception and thought, but throughout the centuries most philosopher-psychologists had theorized about mental events in terms of invisible high-level processes such as association, reason, and will. Knowing next to nothing about the physiology of the nervous system and brain, they ignored the question of whether these processes were made up of physical events.

But, as we have seen, with the emergence of physics and chemistry in the seventeenth century a few daring protopsychologists began suggesting mechanical explanations of mental processes. Lacking actual observational data, they speculated about "animal spirits" coursing through hollow nerves (Descartes), atoms streaming through the nerves (Hobbes), nerves aquiver with "vibratiuncles" (Hartley), and a French philosopher, Julien de La Mettrie, even wrote a book in 1748 titled *L'Homme Machine* (Man a Machine).

During the eighteenth century and the early part of the nineteenth, however, physiologists made a number of discoveries about the nervous system that led them to begin explaining lower-level psychological processes, such as perception, reflexes, and voluntary movements, in terms of physical and chemical events that could actually be observed in the nerves. Among the discoveries that made possible this new physiological psychology:[13]

— Around 1730, Stephen Hales, an English botanist and chemist, decapitated a frog, then pinched it; its legs drew up. He destroyed its spinal cord and pinched it again; this time the legs did not move. Hales thereby established the difference between reflex and voluntary actions, and located the source of the reflex in the spinal cord, not the brain.
— In 1791 the Italian physiologist Luigi Galvani hung a frog's leg, with part of the spinal cord attached, from a brass hook; when he produced an electrical discharge from a nearby Leyden jar, the leg kicked. Galvani concluded that "animal electricity," generated in the muscles and brain, flows through nerves and is responsible for movement.
— Until the early nineteenth century, physiologists supposed that the nervous system was like a network of continuous wires. But in the early years of that century, when it was established that plant tissues are made up of cells, the German physiologist Theodor Schwann advanced the idea that animal tissues, too, consist of cells. He identified one kind of nerve cell, and soon others demonstrated that brain cells consist of nuclei and long branches that reach and contact the branches of other brain cells.
— According to Descartes's animal-spirits theory, impulses could flow in the nerve in either direction. According to the electrical model of nervous activity, current flowed in only one direction. Espousing the latter concept, between 1811 and 1822 Charles Bell, an English anatomist, and François Magendie, a French physiologist, working independently, cut different nerves in animals to see what functions were affected. Both men were able to show that the nervous system consists of sensory nerves in which the current is affer-

ent, flowing toward the spinal cord and brain, and of motor nerves in which it is efferent, flowing from the brain and spinal cord toward the muscles and organs.

These and a number of other discoveries, combined with what was already known of the physics of light and color, produced a nineteenth-century explosion of research in the physiology of the sense organs and perception. This new psychology was a radically different approach from the theistic fantasies of Berkeley and the skepticism of Hume to the question of how the mind perceives the world around it. And although at first it could deal only with lower-level psychological processes, most of the new psychologists hoped that eventually higher-level ones would be explicable in similar terms. Emil Du Bois-Reymond, a German physiologist, wrote to a friend in 1842 that he and a colleague had taken a solemn oath to demonstrate the truth of the following creed:

> No forces other than the common physical-chemical ones are active within the organism. In those cases which cannot at this time be explained by these forces, one must either find the specific ways or form of their action by means of the physical-mathematical method, or assume new forces, equal in dignity to the chemical-physical forces inherent in matter and reducible to the force of attraction and repulsion.[14]

Although the "new psychology," as it became known, appeared in a number of countries, it made its strongest showing in Germany, in whose universities, according to the eminent English historian of psychology Leslie Spencer Hearnshaw, "scientific psychology was born."[15]

Nor, he says, was this any accident. Until 1870, Germany comprised a multitude of kingdoms, duchies, and self-governing cities, and had created many more universities than any other European country. Moreover, after certain educational and social reforms of the early nineteenth century, German universities supplied their scientists and scholars with well-equipped laboratories for research in physics, chemistry, physiology, and other sciences.

In that atmosphere, even philosophers and psychologists in the Kantian tradition rejected Kant's assertion that psychology could never be an experimental science. Others came to believe that even the invisible higher-level mental functions, observable only through volunteers' reactions to stimuli, could be experimentally and validly investigated.

But first we will look at the mechanists—or, rather, since there were many of them, at a few whose work was both particularly important and typical of the movement.

Specific Nerve Energy: Müller

Johannes Müller (1801–1858) began in the philosophic tradition, broke away from it to become the first great modern physiologist, then drifted back to philosophy in an effort to answer questions about the soul that lay beyond his physiology.[16] But the time of philosophic psychology was over; his physiological work had considerable influence on psychology, his philosophic work none.

Müller, born in Coblenz of middle-class parents, was extremely gifted, energetic, and driven by a compulsion to excel. He was also endowed with Byronic looks—tousled hair, a sensitive mouth, and piercing blue eyes. Having earned his medical degree in Berlin when he was twenty-one, he set aside his youthful fascination with the quasi-mystical nature-philosophy of Schelling and did such dazzling work in physiology and anatomy that the University of Bonn made him Professor Extraordinarius* at twenty-four and full professor at twenty-nine.

Müller labored so prodigiously at vivisection and animal experimentation in his early twenties that by the time he was twenty-five he had completed two fat books on the physiology of vision. But he was prey to a manic-depressive tendency, and at twenty-six, soon after becoming a professor and marrying his longtime fiancée, he fell into a severe depression and could neither work nor teach for five months. At thirty-nine, when others forged ahead of him in physiological research, he had a second attack of depression; at forty-seven, when he was at odds with the ideals of the Revolution of 1848, a third attack; and at fifty-seven, in 1858, a fourth attack that ended in his suicide.

Nearly all of Müller's significant achievements in physiological psychology were made in his early years; by thirty-two, when he moved to the University of Berlin, he was losing interest in what he called "knife-happy" experimentation and turning instead toward zoology and comparative anatomy. He no longer believed that experimentation could solve the ultimate questions of life; his monumental *Handbook of Phys-*

---

*The term Professor Extraordinarius referred to an unsalaried or low-salaried appointment, valued largely for its prestige. Sometimes, students attending lectures by a Professor Extraordinarius would pay him fees.

iology, though filled with his and others' experimental findings, contained a philosophic discussion of the soul that could have been written a century earlier. In it, he waffled about whether the soul was simply the brain and nervous system in action or was a separate "vital force" that temporarily inhabits the body.

Of Müller's vast number of discoveries about the nervous system, many of which helped establish physiological psychology, one had an especially profound influence. The early physiological psychologists thought that any sensory nerve could convey any kind of sensory data to the brain, much as a tube will carry whatever substance is pumped through it, but they could not explain why, for example, the optic nerve conveyed only visual images to the brain, and the aural nerves only sounds. Müller offered a persuasive theory. The nerves of each sensory system convey only one kind of data or, as he put it, a "specific energy or quality": the optic nerves always and only sensations of light, the aural nerves always and only sensations of sound, other sense nerves always and only their sensations.

Müller had reached this conclusion through a series of anatomical studies of animals—plus a tiny and seemingly clinching experiment that he performed on himself. When he pressed his own closed eye, the pressure created not sound, smell, or taste but flashes of light. He stated his doctrine in these terms:

> The sensation of sound is the peculiar "energy" or "quality" of the auditory nerve; the sensation of light or colors that of the optic nerve; and so of the other nerves of sense. The nerve of each sense seems capable of one determinate kind of sensation only, and not of those proper to the other organs of sense. Among the well-attested facts of physiology, not one supports the belief that one nerve of sense can assume the functions of another. The exaggeration of the sense of touch in the blind will not in these days be called seeing with the fingers; the accounts of the power of vision by the fingers and epigastrium [abdomen] appear to be mere fables, and instances in which it has purportedly been practiced, cases of deception.[17]

As William James would say more dramatically, "If we could splice the outer extremity of our optic nerves to our ears, and that of our auditory nerves to our eyes, we should hear the lightning and see the thunder."[18]

As positive as Müller sounded about this, he debated with himself whether the specificity of the sensory systems resulted from the special quality of each set of nerves or of the region of the brain to which that set traveled. Possibly the area to which optic impulses were delivered interpreted them visually, the area to which aural nerves went as sound. "It is not known," he wrote in the *Handbook*, "whether the essential cause of the peculiar 'energy' of each nerve of sense is seated in the nerve itself, or in the parts of the brain or spinal cord with which it is connected."[19] But Flourens's view that the brain was completely generalized still dominated physiological thinking, and Müller opted for the theory of "specific nervous energies."

Some of his own students, however, later in the century followed the lead of his honest confession of uncertainty and showed that all nerve transmissions possess the same characteristics and that it is indeed the end-location in the brain that determines the kind of experience created by the transmissions.[20]

Nevertheless, Müller's physiology began to answer one of the great questions that had puzzled philosophers and protopsychologists: How do the realities of the world around us become perceptions in our minds? A detailed picture of how perception works was beginning to emerge. The process starts with the optical properties of the eyeball or the auditory machinery of the ear (both of which Müller investigated in detail), continues with the nerves that convey the stimulation coming from the sensory organs, and concludes with the brain areas that receive and interpret those nerve impulses. As opposed to the ancients' supposition that a tiny replica of whatever is perceived passes through the air and nerves to the brain, Müller showed that what is transmitted to the brain are nerve impulses; our perceptions are not replicas of, but analogues or isomorphs of, the objects around us. As he put it:

> The immediate objects of the perception of our senses are merely particular states induced in the nerves and felt as sensations either by the nerves themselves or by the parts of the brain concerned with sensation. The nerves make known to the brain, by virtue of the changes produced in them by external causes, the changes of condition of external bodies.[21]

But how do we know that what our brains make of the incoming excitations corresponds to reality? This issue, which had so plagued earlier philosophers and psychologists, seemed to him to be readily answerable. The state of our nerves corresponds to that of objects in suitable and regular ways; the image on the retina, for instance, is a reasonably faithful portrayal of what is outside, and that is the stimulus the optic nerves carry to the brain. So, too, with the responses of the other sense organs and the messages they transmit.[22] Müller thus answered the epistemological conundrum posed by Berkeley and Hume and transformed the untestable Kantian categories into testable and observable realities. Wrong in its details, his doctrine of specific energies was right in its most profound implications.

Just Noticeable Differences: Weber

At the University of Leipzig, in the early 1830s, a bearded young professor of physiology was conducting perception research totally unlike Müller's. No scalpel and no laid-open frogs' legs or rabbit skulls for Ernst Heinrich Weber; he chose to work with healthy, intact human volunteers—students, townspeople, friends—and to use such prosaic instruments as little apothecary's weights, lamps, pen and paper, and thick knitting needles.

Knitting needles?

Let us look in on Weber on a typical day. He blackens the tip of a needle with carbon powder and gently lowers it perpendicularly onto the shirtless back of a young man lying prone on a table.[23] It leaves a tiny black dot on the young man's back. Now Weber asks him to try to touch that place with a similarly blackened little pointer. The young man, trying, touches a place a couple of inches away, and Weber carefully measures the distance between the two dots and records it in a workbook.[24] He does this again and again on different parts of the man's back, then his chest, arms, and face.

A year or so later, carrying on this line of inquiry, he opens a draftsman's compass and touches both ends to different places on the body of a blindfolded man. When the legs of the compass are far apart, the volunteer knows he is being touched by two points, but as Weber brings the legs closer together, the subject finds it ever harder to say whether there were two points or one until, at a critical distance, he perceives the two as one. The critical distance, Weber discovers, varies according to the part of the body. On the tip of the tongue, it is less than a twentieth of an inch; on the cheeks, half an inch; and along the backbone, anywhere up to two and a half inches—a more than fifty-fold range of sensitivities and a dramatic indication of the relative number of nerve endings in each area.

All of Weber's many experiments on the sensitivity of the sensory systems were similarly simple—and important in the history of psychology. At a time when most other mechanists were working only with reflexes and nerve transmission, Weber was looking at the entire sensory system: not just organs and the consequent nerve responses but the mind's interpretation of them. Moreover, his were among psychology's first true experiments; that is, he altered one variable at a time—in the two-point threshold test, the area of the body being tested—and observed how much change that caused in a second variable—the critical distance between the two compass points.

To recognize how remarkable it was of Weber to conduct such experiments in the early 1830s, consider the period. James Mill, without budging from his desk, was espousing simplistic associationism; Johann Friedrich Herbart, occupying Kant's chair at Göttingen, was maintaining, as Kant had, that psychology could never be an experimental science; Johann Christoph Spurzheim, at the peak of his popularity, was assuring crowds of enthusiasts that phrenologists could read a person's character from the shape of his skull.

Weber (1795–1878), born in Wittenberg in Saxony, was one of three brothers, all of whom became scientists of distinction and, at times, worked together. Wilhelm, a physicist, aided Weber in his research on touch; Eduard, a physiologist, discovered along with him the paradoxical effect of the vagus nerve, which, when stimulated, slows the heartbeat.[25]

Like many another psychological mechanist, Weber had had medical training and specialized in physiological and anatomical research. Early in his career, he became interested in determining the minimum tactile stimulation necessary to produce a sensation of touch in different parts of the body, but soon moved on to a more complicated and interesting question about perceptual sensitivity. Many years earlier, the Swiss mathematician Daniel Bernoulli had made a psychologically shrewd observation: a poor man who gains a franc feels far more enriched by it than does a wealthy man; the perception of gain produced by any given sum of money depends on one's economic status. This led Weber to formulate an analogous hypothesis: The smallest difference we can perceive between two stimuli—two weights, for instance—is not an objective, fixed amount but is subjective and varies with the weights of the objects.

To test the hypothesis, Weber asked volunteers to heft first one small weight and then a second, and say which was heavier. Using a graduated series of weights, he was able to ascertain the smallest difference—the "just noticeable difference" (j.n.d.)—that his subjects could perceive. As he had correctly surmised, the j.n.d. was not a specific unvarying weight.

The heavier the first weight, the greater the difference had to be before his subjects could perceive it, and the lighter the first weight, the greater their perceptual sensitivity. "The smallest perceptible difference," he later reported, was "that between two weights standing approximately in the relation of 39 to 40: that is, one of which is about a fortieth heavier than the other."[26] If the first weight was an ounce, the j.n.d. of a second weight was a fortieth of an ounce; if ten ounces, a quarter of an ounce.

Weber went on to conduct similar experiments on other sensory systems, determining the j.n.d. between, among other things, the length of two lines, the temperatures of two objects, the brightness of two lights, the pitch of two tones. In every case he found that the magnitude of the j.n.d. varied with the magnitude of the standard stimulus (the one with which a second was being compared) and that the ratio between the two stimuli was constant. Interestingly, the ratio of the j.n.d. to the standard varied widely among the different sensory systems. Vision was the most sensitive, detecting differences as small as a sixtieth in the intensity of light. In the case of pain, the minimum perceivable difference was a thirtieth; of pitch perception, a tenth; of smell, a quarter; and of taste, a third.[27] Weber summed up the rule in a simple formula:

$$\frac{\delta(R)}{R} = k,$$

which says that the ratio between the just noticeable stimulus, $\delta(R)$, and the magnitude of the standard stimulus, R, is a constant, k, for any sensory system. Known as Weber's Law, it is the first statement of its kind—a quantitatively precise relationship between the physical and psychological worlds. It was the prototype of the kind of generalization that experimental psychologists would be looking for from then on.

Neural Physiology: von Helmholtz

In 1845, a handful of young physiologists, most of them former students of Müller's, formed a little club, the Berliner Physikalische Gesellschaft (Berlin Physical Society), to promote their view that all phenomena, including neural and mental processes, could be accounted for in terms of physical principles. It was one of the group, Du Bois-Reymond, who had earlier stated the mechanist doctrine mentioned above, "No forces other than the common physical-chemical ones are active within the organism."

Du Bois-Reymond brought to the club a friend, Hermann Helmholtz (1821–1894), who was surgeon of a regiment stationed in Potsdam.[28] He was a shy, serious young man with a broad forehead and large intense eyes; neither by personality nor position did he seem likely to become the front-runner for the society's radical theory. But within a few years he was just that. His research on nerve transmission, color vision, hearing, and space perception clearly showed that the neurological processes underlying mental functions are material and can be experimentally investigated.

Helmholtz never thought of himself as a psychologist; his major interest was physics. Although the first twenty years of his career were devoted largely to physiology, his goal during that period was to explain perception in terms of the physics of the sense organs and nervous system; in so doing, he exerted a major influence on experimental psychology. Ironically, in his own time Helmholtz's best-known scientific achievement was one that took him only eight days and that he himself considered minor — the invention of the ophthalmoscope, with which doctors could for the first time view the living retina.

Although Helmholtz became one of the leading scientists of his century — his achievements earned him elevation to the nobility (hence the "von") — he was totally unlike the scientist he most admired, the ferociously competitive, dour, reclusive Isaac Newton. Toward fellow scientists he was courteous and generous, if rather formal, and in private life he was a remarkably normal middle-class Herr Professor; his biography offers no *frissons*. He got a good grounding in the classics and philosophy from his father, a poorly paid teacher of philosophy and literature at the Potsdam gymnasium; went through medical training, wrote his dissertation under Müller, and served five years as a regimental surgeon; married when he received his first academic appointment and had two children; was widowed, married again, and had three more children. His career consisted of ever-better posts at ever-better universities, constant research and writing, and growing status and acclaim. He engaged in no priority fights and only one scientific controversy, and his only recorded indulgences were classical music and mountaineering.

Helmholtz began his research career during his obligatory service in the military. Since it was peacetime, he had plenty of leisure, and he built a small laboratory in his barracks and conducted experiments on frogs with the aim of supporting a mechanistic view of behavior. He measured the energy and heat produced by the frog's body and was able to account for it entirely in terms of the oxidation of the food the frog ingested. Today this sounds hardly revolutionary, but in 1845 many physiologists were "vitalists," who believed that the processes of life were in part powered by an immaterial and imperceptible "vital force," a sort of latter-day version of soul (though said to exist in all living things).

Helmholtz, firmly opposed to this quasi-mystical view, wrote a paper titled "The Conservation of Force," based on his frog data and his knowledge of physics, and presented it before the Berlin Physical Society in 1847. His thesis was that all machines obey the law of conservation of energy; therefore, perpetual motion is impossible. He then argued that this is true of organic processes, too, and that vital force, having no source of energy, would violate that law and hence did not exist. In short, he put physiology on a firmly Newtonian footing. The paper won him such respect that the Prussian government excused him from further military service, made him a lecturer on anatomy at the Berlin Academy of Arts, and a year later appointed him professor of physiology at the University of Königsberg.

For the next two decades, Helmholtz devoted himself largely to studies of the physiology of sensation and perception. (From then on, he concerned himself chiefly with physics, at the University of Berlin.)

His historic first research achievement was to measure the speed with which the nerve impulse travels along the nerve fiber. His mentor, Müller, like most other physiologists of the time, had taken Galvani's discovery of the electrical nature of the nerve impulse to mean that the nervous system was somewhat like a set of continuous wires through which the current flowed at extremely high speed—roughly the speed of light, according to one reckoning. But Helmholtz's friend Du Bois-Reymond had chemically analyzed nerve fibers and suggested that the impulse might be not purely electrical but electrochemical; if so, it would be relatively slow.

In his laboratory at Königsberg, Helmholtz undertook to measure the speed of the impulse in a frog's motor nerve. Since the high-speed chronoscope was not yet generally available—the first one was then in development—he ingeniously rigged a galvanometer to a frog's leg (with the motor nerve attached) in such a way that a needle drawing a line on a revolving drum would show the time elapsed between the instant a current was applied to the upper end of the nerve and the subsequent kick of the foot. Knowing the distance between stimulus and the foot muscle, Helmholtz could then calculate the speed of the nerve impulse; it proved to be remarkably slow, about ninety feet per second.

He also measured the speed of the nerve impulse in human subjects, asking volunteers to signal with a hand as soon as they felt a tiny current he applied either to toe or thigh. These experiments yielded figures ranging from 165 to 330 feet per second, but Helmholtz considered them less reliable than those based on the frog's leg; something about the testing of humans made for wide variability.

At first his results, published in 1850, were not widely accepted; they were too hard to believe. Physiologists were still wedded to the notion that either immaterial animal spirits or electricity flowed through the nervous system, and Helmholtz's data supported a different theory, namely, that the nerve impulse consisted of the complex movements of particles. Moreover, his findings contradicted common experience. We seem to feel a touch on finger or toe the instant the contact is made; we seem to move a finger or toe the instant we mean to.

Yet his evidence could not be gainsaid, and after initial resistance, his theory won general acceptance. Had he done nothing else, this alone would have made him one of the immortals of psychology, since it prepared the way, says Edwin Boring, "for all the later work of experimental psychology on the chronometry of mental acts and reaction times . . . It brought the soul to time, as it were, measured what had been ineffable, actually captured the essential agent of mind in the toils of natural science."[29]

Here we make a brief detour, looking ahead eighteen years to view a significant offshoot of Helmholtz's study: the first attempt to measure the speed of higher mental processes.

A Dutch ophthalmologist named Franciscus Cornelius Donders (1818–1889) with no background in psychology was intrigued by Helmholtz's research on the speed of the neural impulse and speculated that because nerve impulses take time, higher mental processes probably do so, too.[30] The lag between stimulus and voluntary response, he hypothesized, was due in part to nerve transmission and in part to the time taken by thought processes.

In 1868, Donders devised and conducted an imaginative experiment to test his hypothesis and measure the mental processes at work. He asked subjects to respond to a nonsense sound, like *ki*, by repeating it as quickly as possible. A pointer making a track on a revolving drum would jiggle in response to the vibration of both *ki*s, and the distance between jiggles would be a measure of the time lag.

In the simplest case, the subject knew what the sound would be and what the right response would be; the lag between stimulus and response was therefore simple reaction time. But what if subjects had to do mental work of some kind? What if the experimenter uttered any one of several sounds, such as *ki, ko,* or *ku,* and subjects had to imitate the sound as quickly as possible? If this took longer than simple reaction, Donders reasoned, the difference must be a measure of two mental processes: discrimination (among the sounds heard) and choice (of the correct response).

Donders also thought of a way to disentangle these two mental processes and obtain a measure for each. If he told subjects that they might hear *ki, ko,* or *ku* but were to imitate only *ki* and remain silent in response to the others, they would, by not repeating *ko* or *ku,* be discriminating among the sounds but not choosing a response. By subtracting the discrimination time from the discrimination-plus-choice time, Donders would get a measure of choice time.

The results were striking. On the average, discrimination took thirty-nine milliseconds more than simple reaction time, and discrimination-plus-choice seventy-five milliseconds longer than simple reaction time. Choice thus apparently accounted for thirty-six milliseconds.

Donders optimistically created a number of more complicated procedures in the belief that the time each mental process took would add to the time the other processes had taken, and that each could be measured by the subtraction. But it did not work out well; the differences in times proved to be unreliable and only sometimes additive. Later psychologists would greatly modify Donders's methods.

Still, he had shown beyond doubt that some of the time taken by responses involving cognitive activity was spent by that activity. Far more important, he had used elapsed time as a way to investigate unseen psychological processes; according to one recent appraisal of his work, "With Donders's discovery of a means of apparently measuring the higher mental processes, a new era had begun."[31]

We retrace our steps to 1852 and to Helmholtz. Soon after establishing the speed of the nerve impulse and inventing the ophthalmoscope, he became interested in the problem of color vision. Ever since Newton's discovery in 1672 that the white light of the sun was a mixture of light of all visible colors, physiologists and psychologists had tried to figure out how the eye and mind perceive colors. What was most puzzling was that we see white when light of all colors is mixed, but also when two complementary colors, such as a particular shade of red and one of blue-green, are mixed; similarly, we see orange when exposed to pure orange light, but also when red and yellow light are mixed.

As a physicist, Helmholtz knew that three specific colors—particular hues of red, blue-violet, and green—could, mixed in the proper proportions, reproduce any other color; these are the *primary* colors.* He reasoned that this meant human vision can detect those three colors and hypothesized that the retina must have three different kinds of receptor cells, each furnished with a chemical sensitive to one of the primary colors. Relying on Müller's doctrine of specific nerve energies, he suggested that the nerves leading from each receptor to the brain conveyed not just visual messages but specific color messages.

An English scientist, Thomas Young, had advanced somewhat the same theory in 1802, but without experimental evidence; it had been generally ignored. Helmholtz, however, amassed a variety of supportive evidence, including that of the colors we experience when lights of different hues are mixed, the afterimage of a complementary color that we see after staring at a strong color for a while, the kinds of color blindness that exist in some people and animals, the influence of particular brain lesions on color vision, and so on. He generously acknowledged Young's priority, and his account of color vision has been known ever since as the Young-Helmholtz theory (or the trichromatic theory).

The color theory, a testable mechanistic explanation of how the mind perceives colors, was a stunning achievement. Link by link, from the outside world to the receptive area of the brain, Helmholtz had forged a chain of causal events that replaced the guesses and fantasies of philosophers and physiologists. It is still the reigning theory of color vision, though in more complex form and stripped of the notion that the nerves from each kind of receptor carried different kinds of energy.

As for the profoundly troubling question about perception asked by Democritus, Berkeley, Hume, and others—whether what we see is a true representation of what is out there—Helmholtz, far more mechanistic than Müller, dismissed it as being without meaning or value:

> In my opinion, there can be no possible sense in speaking of any other truth of our ideas except a *practical* truth. Our ideas of things *cannot*

---

*The so-called primary colors of pigments are red, blue, and yellow (or, more precisely, magenta, cyan, and yellow). Pigments absorb as well as reflect light, and the results of mixing them are therefore different from those of mixing lights.

be anything but symbols, natural signs for things that we learn how to use in order to regulate our movements and actions. Having learned how to read those symbols correctly, we are able by their help to adjust our actions so as to bring about the desired result; that is, so that the expected new sensations will arise . . . Hence there is no sense in asking whether vermilion [mercuric sulfide], as we see it, is really red or whether this is simply an illusion of the senses. The sensation of red is the normal reaction of normally formed eyes to light reflected from vermilion . . . The statement that the waves of light reflected from vermilion have a certain length is something different; that is true entirely without reference to the special nature of our eye.[32]

Thus the mechanist physiologist was, after all, a philosopher of psychology, and one to reckon with.

Helmholtz's color vision research was only one facet of a comprehensive inquiry into visual perception that he carried on for a number of years. The fruits of this labor, his *Handbook of Physiological Optics* (1856–1867), ran to half a million words and covered all previous research in the field as well as his own; for several generations it remained the standard authority on the optical and neural properties of the eye. He also performed a similar service for hearing in another, not quite so massive, work.

In *Optics* Helmholtz dealt chiefly with the physics and physiology of vision and made some keen observations about the psychological processes by which the mind interprets messages from the optic nerves. He drew an invaluable distinction that had eluded earlier psychologists between *sensation* (the excitation of the retina's rods by light of whatever color, and the resultant impulses of the optic nerves) and *perception* (the meaningful interpretations the mind makes of the arriving impulses). He made the same differentiation about the input of other sensory systems.

The distinction was central to Helmholtz's epistemology. He agreed with Kant that sensations are interpreted and given meaning by the mind, but disagreed that the mind innately possesses "categories" and "intuitions" that supply those meanings. Rather, he said, the mind learns to interpret sensations by means of trial and error—by learning which reactions to a visual sensation produce an expected result and which do not.

Space perception is a case in point. Kant said that the mind innately intuits spatial relationships; Helmholtz argued that we learn about space by means of *unconscious inference*. As infants, we learn little by little that such visual clues as size, direction, and intensity of hue are related to whether objects are closer or farther, to one side or the other of us, above or below us; through experience we gradually come to make correct judgments about spatial relations. (Every parent who has watched a three-month-old trying to grasp an object knows the process intimately.)

The British empiricist-associationists had said much the same thing but lacked experimental evidence to back it up; Helmholtz, an experimentalist through and through, supported his theory with research findings.

It occurred to him that if he could distort the spatial sensations reaching a subject's brain—and if his theory was correct—the subject should adapt to the distorted vision and learn to interpret it correctly. He therefore constructed eyeglasses with prismatic lenses that shifted the apparent position of objects to the right of where they actually were. When subjects wearing the glasses tried to touch objects in front of them, they missed—they reached toward the apparent rather than the real position of the objects.

Next, for some minutes he had them reach for and handle the objects while wearing the lenses; at first they had to consciously reach to the left of where they saw the object, but soon they began to reach for objects where they actually were without having to think about it. They had made a perceptual adaptation; their minds had reinterpreted the messages arriving from the optic nerves and they now saw the objects in the context of reality.

Finally, when they took off the spectacles and reached for the objects, they missed again, this time erring to the left of the real position; it took a little while for their normal space orientation to reassert itself.

Helmholtz did agree with Kant about one innate capacity, the ability to interpret cause-and-effect relationships. For the rest, he maintained that virtually all knowledge and ideas are the result of the mind's interpretation of sensory experience, and that these interpretations, particularly those having to do with spatial perception, are largely the product of unconscious inference.

This view was strongly opposed by psychologists who held that the mind is innately equipped to interpret its perceptions. A key function they explained in innate terms was the combining of the two images coming from the eyes to form a single three-dimensional image. Some said that each point on the retina receives exactly the same bit of information as the corresponding point on the other retina and that the two optic nerves thus combine their images into one. One opponent of Helmholtz's ideas said that each retina is endowed with innate "signs" that distinguish height, right-left orientation, and depth and that enable the nervous system to fuse the images before they reach the brain.

Helmholtz brusquely dismissed these notions. Nativist theory, he wrote, was "an unnecessary hypothesis"; it relied on unprovable assumptions and added nothing to the demonstrable facts of empiricist theory.[33] His strongest evidence that experience is what enables us to perceive paired images as a single one came from the stereoscope. Through this instrument, invented by Charles Wheatstone in 1833, the viewer sees not two identical images but two slightly different ones taken from slightly different angles. The images cast on the retinas therefore do not match point for point, yet after a novice viewer looks through the stereoscope for a little while, he or she suddenly sees a single image—in three dimensions. The fusion of two nonidentical images yields a result different from either one; the result comes from experience and takes place in the brain.

In the end, Helmholtz did not completely vanquish his opponents; nativism survived in one guise or another, including Gestalt psychology and, more recently, genetic psychology, studies of temperament, and, still more recently, evolutionary psychology. But the mainstream of psychology from Helmholtz's time on has been largely empiricist and experimental. He, who did not consider himself a psychologist, would have been surprised to learn that he had a more profound and lasting influence on psychology than on physics or physiology.

Psychophysics: Fechner

While sensible, normal young Helmholtz was beginning to amass evidence for his mechanistic view of neural and psychic events, a visionary, neurotic middle-aged professor at the University of Leipzig was seeking to demonstrate that every person, animal, and plant in the universe is composed of both matter and soul. Gustav Theodor Fechner (1801–1887) failed in that aim, but in gathering data to show the mathematical relationship between stimuli (the world of matter) and the resulting sensations (the world of mind or soul)—which, he thought, confirmed his panpsychic philosophy—he developed research methods that have been used ever since by experimental psychologists to advance the materialist psychology he meant to invalidate.[34]

Fechner, born in a village in southeastern Germany, was the son of the local pastor. The father combined religious faith with a hard-headed belief in science, as would his son. He preached the word of the Lord but shocked the villagers by installing a lightning rod on the church, a precaution that in those days was seen as a lack of faith in God's care of His own.

Fechner studied medicine at the University of Leipzig, but in 1822, after receiving his degree, switched his attention to physics and mathematics. For several years he supported himself by translating into German a number of French manuals on physics and chemistry—nine thousand pages' worth of them in a few years—and from 1824 lectured on physics at the university, conducted a heavy research program on electrical currents, and wrote numerous technical articles. The hectic pace made his reputation in physics, but at a cost: he began suffering from headaches and spells of inability to control his thoughts, which would obsessively go around and around on matters of no importance.

Although only in his early thirties and prospering—he was able to marry by 1833 and was made a full professor in 1834—his condition continued to deteriorate. "I could not sleep and suffered from attacks of total exhaustion which robbed me of the ability to think and caused me to lose all interest in life," he later said of this period.[35] He sought relief in spas, but to no avail. He then distracted himself by studying afterimages—his first foray into experimental psychology—in the course of which he stared at the sun through tinted glasses for long periods. His research on afterimages was well received—Helmholtz, as we know, made use of the data—but as a result of it Fechner suffered severe photophobia and total emotional collapse.

Virtually blind, he immured himself in a darkened room, where he was tormented by pain, emotional distress, intolerable boredom, and severe digestive problems. (He resigned from the university but was granted a pension, although he had been teaching only half a dozen years.) At the nadir of three years of invalidism, he had his room painted black, remained in it day and night, and saw no one. Not laxatives, steam treatments, mesmerism, nor two kinds of shock treatments did any good. He continued to be troubled by repetitive thinking about minor matters; in addition he was torn between an exalted sense that he was close to discovering the secret of the world and a troubling feeling that he would have to demonstrate the truth of that secret by scientific methods.

At last he began spontaneously to improve and after a while could see without pain and talk to people. When he walked in the garden for the first time in many months, the flowers looked brighter, more intensely colored, and more beautiful than ever; he perceived an inner light in them, the significance of which he instantly grasped:

> I had no doubt that I had discovered the soul of the flower, and thought in my strangely enchanted mood: this is the garden that lies behind the boards of this world. The whole earth and its very body is merely a fence around this garden for those who still wait on the outside.[36]

He soon wrote a book about the mental life of plants and for the rest of his many years sought to promote his panpsychist theory that consciousness coexists with matter throughout the world.

It was this mystical belief that led Fechner to his historic work in experimental psychology. Lying in bed on the morning of October 22, 1850, pondering how to prove to the mechanists that mind and body were two aspects of a fundamental unity, he had a flash of insight: If he could show a consistent mathematical relationship between the force of stimuli and the intensity of the sensations they produced, he would have shown the identity of body and mind.[37]

Or so it seemed to him; the logic of the reasoning may escape the nonmystic. But he had asked a valid and important question about the accuracy with which the mind perceives the outer world: Is there a consistent mathematical relationship between the magnitude of a stimulus and the magnitude of the sensation it creates? Intuitively, it might seem so: the brighter a light, the brighter it looks to us. But if you double the light, do you double the intensity of sensation? Or does some other, less verisimilar relationship prevail?

Fechner, trained in both physics and mathematics, sensed that as the intensity of a stimulus increased, it would require ever larger differences (in absolute terms) to produce increases of constant size in sensation. In mathematical terminology: Geometrical increases in the strength of the stimulus would produce arithmetical increases in the strength of the sensation. A contemporary illustration: In terms of energy delivered to the ear, an average clap of thunder is many times as powerful as ordinary conversation; in terms of decibels—a decibel is the smallest difference in loudness the human ear can recognize—it is only twice as loud.

To confirm his intuition experimentally, Fechner would have to solve a seemingly insoluble problem: He could easily measure stimulus intensity, but sensations are subjective and incapable of being measured. He reasoned, however, that though he could not observe and measure sensation directly, he could do so indirectly by using *sensitivity* as a guide. He could determine the smallest increase in stimulus strength at any level that would be just barely noticeable to the perceiver. Since "just barely noticeable" meant the same thing at any level, that would be a unit of measurement of sensation he could compare with the increase in stimulus necessary to produce that awareness.

Fechner later said that he did not get this idea from Weber, his former teacher, whose work on j.n.d.'s had been published a few years earlier. But he soon realized that he would be using and extending Weber's Law. Weber had found that the ratio between two just noticeably different stimuli remains the same, whatever the magnitude of those stimuli; Fechner was saying that although the absolute difference between two stimuli increases as the magnitude of the stimuli does, the perceiver's sensation of a just noticeable difference remains the same.

Imagine (Fechner later wrote) that you look at the sky through a tinted glass and pick out a cloud that is just noticeably different from the sky background. Now you use a much darker glass; the cloud does not vanish but is still just barely visible—because although the absolute levels of intensity are much lower through the darker glass, the ratio of intensities between cloud and sky has not changed.[38]

To express the relationship between stimulus intensity and sensation intensity, Fechner mathematically transformed Weber's Law, integrating it and making it:

$$S = k \log R,$$

which means, in English, that stepwise increases in sensation intensity are the result of doublings of stimulus intensity (multiplied by some ratio or factor). Bending over backward to give credit to his former teacher, Fechner called this Weber's Law—it was he who gave the name to Weber's formula and his own—but later psychologists, giving credit where credit is due, have called the reformulation Fechner's Law.

Fechner spent the next nine years in plodding experimentation, collecting data to confirm the law. Despite the mystical and poetic aspects of his personality, in the laboratory he was the very model of a compulsive and rigorous researcher. He tirelessly had subjects lift weights, look at lights, listen to noises and tones, look at color samples, and so on, and pronounce them either different or the same. Over those years he experimented with a wide range of intensities of each kind of stimulus, using three methods of measuring such judgments. With just one of those methods he tabulated and computed no fewer than 24,576 judgments.[39] He considered this first systematic exploration of the quantitative relationship between the physical and psychological realms a new scientific specialty and named it "psychophysics."

Of the three methods of experimental measurement that he used, he had borrowed two from predecessors and perfected them, and invented the third himself. Until then, no one had ever used such careful, quantitative, and precisely controllable methods to explore psychological responses. His methods were soon widely adopted, and are in constant use today in every laboratory of psychophysical research.

One is the method of limits, which Fechner called the "method of just noticeable differences." To determine the threshold of a stimulus, the experimenter presents stimuli one at a time, starting with the most minimal and increasing the magnitude until the subject can perceive them. To determine the j.n.d., the experimenter presents a "standard" stimulus and a "comparison" stimulus, increasing the difference by small steps until the subject says it is perceptible.

A second is the method of constant stimuli, which Fechner called the "method of right and wrong cases." The experimenter presents identical stimuli time and again—either single ones at the threshold, or pairs of stimuli that are very similar. The subject replies "Yes" (meaning that he perceives it, or that the two are different), or "No" (he does not perceive it, or the two are not different). The subject's responses yield averages, and these indicate how likely it is that, at any given stimulus level or difference between stimuli, the subject will perceive the stimulus or the difference between two stimuli.

The third, Fechner's original contribution, is called the method of adjustment, which he called the "method of average error." Either the experimenter or the subject adjusts the comparison stimulus until it seems (to the subject) identical with the standard stimulus. There is always some error, however minuscule, to one side or the other. Every error is recorded, and after many trials the average error is computed; it, too, is a measure of the j.n.d. This method established the useful principle that measuring the variability of data can be as informative as measuring the central tendency.

In 1860, Fechner published the fruits of his work in the two-volume *Elements of Psychophysics.* He was fifty-nine, an age at which scientists rarely produce their most original work; *Elements,* however, was truly original and had an immediate impact. Interest was intense and widespread—not in the panpsychism it espoused but in its experimental and quantitative methodology. As Boring once said of Fechner's failure and triumph, "He attacked the ramparts of materialism and was decorated for measuring sensation."[40] Some psychologists, to be sure, regarded psychophysical methodology as a dreary topic. Years later the great William James wrote:

> It would be terrible if even such a dear old man as this could saddle our science forever with his patient whimsies, and, in a world so full of more nutritious objects of attention, compel all future students to plough through the difficulties, not only of his own works, but of the still drier ones written in his refutation.[41]

But many others did not share this view. Even though debate raged over the validity of Fechner's assumption that all j.n.d.'s are equal, his methods were generally considered a genuine breakthrough. The time was ripe for quantitative research on the relation between stimulus and response; almost at once many psychologists began using Fechner's three methods, which firmly linked the body's physical mechanisms to the subjective experiences they aroused.[42] (Fechner himself, though he continued to write in defense of psychophysics, devoted most of the rest of his long life to aesthetics, paranormal phenomena, statistics, and panpsychic philosophy.)

Later psychologists have found fault with or even disproven every one of his findings, yet his methods are not only still useful but fundamental to sensory measurement. Boring sums up Fechner's paradoxical achievement:

> Without Fechner . . . there might still have been an experimental psychology . . . There would, however, have been little of the breath of science in the experimental body, for we hardly recognize a subject as scientific if measurement is not one of its tools. Fechner, because of what he did and the time at which he did it, set experimental quantitative psychology off upon the course which it has followed. One may call him the "founder" of experimental psychology, or one may assign that title to Wundt. It does not matter. Fechner had a fertile idea which grew and brought forth fruit abundantly.[43]

First Among Equals:
Wundt

As Good a Birth Date as Any

According to most authorities, psychology was born on a December day in 1879. All that had gone before, from Thales to Fechner, had been the evolution of its ancestors.

The birth, a quiet affair, went unheralded. At the University of Leipzig that day, in a small room on the third floor of a shabby building called Konvikt ("hostel" or "retreat"), a middle-aged professor and two younger men were setting up apparatus for an experiment. On a table they positioned a chronoscope (a brass clocklike mechanism with a hanging weight and two dials), a "sounder" (a metal stand with an elevated arm from which a ball would fall onto a platform), and a telegrapher's key, battery, and rheostat. They then wired together the five pieces of apparatus, the circuitry being no more complicated than that of a present-day beginning electric train set.[1]

The three were Professor Wilhelm Wundt, a long-faced, austere, densely bearded man of forty-seven, and two young students of his, Max Friedrich, a German, and G. Stanley Hall, an American. The set-up was for Friedrich's benefit; with it he was going to collect data for a Ph.D. dissertation on "the duration of apperception"—the time lag between the subject's recognition that he has heard the ball hit the platform and his pressing of the telegraph key.[2] It is not on record who made the ball drop that day and who sat at the key, but with the first *clack* of the ball on the platform, the click of the key, and the registration of elapsed time on the chronoscope, the modern era of psychology had begun.

One could argue, of course, that it began in the 1830s, with Weber's work on just noticeable differences, or in 1850, with Helmholtz's measurement of the speed of nerve transmission and Fechner's first psychophysical experiment, or in 1868, with Donders's reaction-time studies. Or even, as Robert Watson has suggested, in 1875, since in that year the University of Leipzig granted Wundt the use of the room in Konvikt to store and demonstrate his apparatus, and Harvard University made a small room in Lawrence Hall available to William James for his experiments.[3]

But 1879 is the year recognized by most authorities, and for good reason. That was when the first experiment was conducted in the room in Konvikt that Wundt thenceforth called his "private institute."[4] (In German universities, a formally organized laboratory is called an institute.) Within a few years the laboratory had become a mecca for would-be psychologists and was considerably enlarged and designated the university's official Psychologisches Institut.

Largely because of the institute, Wundt is considered not just one of the founders but the principal founder of modern psychology. It was there that he conducted his own psychological research and trained many graduate students in his laboratory methods and theories, and from there that he sent forth cadres of new psychologists — he personally supervised nearly two hundred dissertations — to the universities of Europe and America. In addition, he wrote a number of scholarly articles and massive tomes that established psychology as a field of science with an identity of its own. He himself was the first scientist who can be properly called a psychologist rather than a physiologist, physicist, or philosopher with an interest in psychology.

Perhaps most important, Wundt restored the study of conscious mental processes to psychology. They had been its core from the time of the Greek philosophers, and still were for the English associationists, who, like all their predecessors, explored them through the traditional method of introspection. But the German mechanists, seeking to make psychology scientific, had rejected introspection on the grounds that it was subjective and dealt with unobservable phenomena. A scientific approach to psychological phenomena, they held, dealt only with the physical aspects of neural responses and, in the words of one of them, was a "psychology without a soul."[5]

It is true that long before the first experiment in Wundt's laboratory both Fechner and Donders had used experimental means to measure certain mental responses. But it was Wundt who fully developed the methods that would be used by the next two generations of psychologists, and it was he who became the leading proponent of the view that mental processes could be experimentally studied. He had, in fact, begun espousing this view as early as 1862, in the introduction to his *Contributions to the Theory of Sense Perception:*

> The importance that experimentation will eventually have in psychology can hardly be visualized to its full extent as yet. It has often been held that the area of sensation and perception is the only one in which the use of the experimental method is possible . . . [but] surely this is a prejudice. As soon as the psyche is viewed as a natural phenomenon, and psychology as a natural science, the experimental methods must also be capable of full application to this science.

He drew an analogy between psychology and chemistry. Just as the chemist learns from experiments not only how a substance is affected by others but also what its own chemical nature is,

> in precisely the same way in psychology . . . it would be quite wrong to say that the experiment determines only the action of [stimuli] on the psyche. The behavior of the psyche in response to the external influences is determined as well, and by varying those external influences we arrive at the laws to which the psychic life as such is subject. The sensory stimuli are, for us, only *experimental tools,* to put it succinctly. By creating manifold changes in the sensory stimuli while continually studying the psychic phenomena, we apply the principle that is the essence of the experimental method; as [Francis] Bacon put it, "We change the circumstances in which the phenomena occur."[6]

As many as a dozen years before the first experiment in his laboratory, Wundt was known as a bridge builder who sought to link physiology and mental processes. Word of his views had even reached America, where in 1867 the young William James wrote to a friend:

> It seems to me that perhaps the time has come for psychology to begin to be a science—some measurements have already been made in the region lying between the physical changes in the nerves and the appearance of consciousness (in the shape of sense perceptions) . . .

Helmholtz and a man named Wundt at Heidelberg are working on it, and I hope . . . to go to them in the summer.[7]

(James did not manage to meet Wundt that summer but did so many years later, by which time he himself was a leading figure in psychology.)

Some contemporary historians, critical of the Great Man approach to history, would say that the new science of psychology was created not by Wundt but by the general social and intellectual milieu of the mid-nineteenth century and by the state of development of the behavioral and social sciences. The animal psychology included in Darwin's *On the Origin of Species* (and later in his *Expression of the Emotions in Man and Animals*), the sociological studies of Auguste Comte, the growing number of reports by anthropologists on the life, language, and ideas of preliterate peoples, and other related factors had created an atmosphere in which it was possible to think that human nature could be scientifically studied.

It is true that no Wundt could have arisen to launch experimental psychology in Tertullian's time or Aquinas's or even Descartes'; there were no batteries, telegraph keys, and chronoscopes, much less a view of human behavior as a set of phenomena that could be investigated by experiment. Yet in any field of knowledge, even at the right time and place there spring up not a thousand great men, and not a hundred, but a very few. Or even one: one Galileo, one Newton, one Darwin, inspiring thousands of lesser men (and, later, women) who learn from them and are able to push farther on. And one Wundt, who had the genius and drive to become the guiding light of the new psychology in Europe and the United States.

Yet today he seems a strange and paradoxical figure. Despite the immense reputation and influence he long had, his name is now all but unknown except to psychologists and scholars; most laypersons who can easily identify Freud, Pavlov, and Piaget have no idea who Wundt was. Even people who do know his place in history cannot agree on what his main ideas were; summaries of his system by various scholars seem to summarize different Wundts. And while for some time most psychologists have felt that Wundt's psychology was narrow in scope, a few historians of the field have recently re-evaluated his work and pronounced him a psychologist of great vision and breadth.[8] (It may be indicative that his *Outlines of Psychology* was still being republished as late as 1998.) To some degree, what makes him an enigma is that he was the epitome of the nineteenth-century German scholar: encyclopedic, dogged, authoritarian, and, in his own eyes, all but infallible — an ideal and a personality hard to comprehend today.

The Making of the First Psychologist

As puzzling as anything about Wundt is how the child could have become the man. In his boyhood and youth he seemed utterly lacking in the drive or intellectual capacity to become even modestly successful, let alone an outstanding figure in science and the world of higher education. He appeared, in fact, to be a dolt.

Born in 1832 in Neckarau, near Mannheim, in southwestern Germany, Wundt came from a family of intellectual achievers. His father was a village Lutheran pastor, but among his forebears were university presidents, physicians, and scholars.[9] For many years Wundt showed no trace of intellectual gifts and had no interest in learning; when he was a child, his only close friend was a retarded boy, and in school he was a habitual daydreamer. One day when Wundt was in first grade, his father visited the school as an observer and was so infuriated by his son's wool-gathering that he slapped his face in front of his classmates. Wundt never forgot the incident, but it did nothing to change him; even at thirteen, attending a Catholic gymnasium at Bruchsal, he was still such a dreamer that his homeroom teacher would publicly slap him, and another teacher would mock him in front of the other students — mostly ignorant farm boys who were themselves no models of scholarship. The teachers' punishments did no good; he failed the year and disgraced himself.

Wundt's parents then sent him to the Lyceum in Heidelberg. There, among students whom he found more congenial, he gained control over his daydreaming and progressed through the school years, though he never became more than an average student. When he graduated, he had no idea what he wanted to do, but since his father had died and his mother had only a meager pension, he had to prepare for a profession in which he could earn a decent living. He chose medicine and enrolled at the University of Tübingen; out of his mother's sight, he played and idled a year away, learning almost nothing.

But when he came home at the end of the year and realized that there was barely enough money to get him through the next three years, he underwent an astonishing change. He started medical training over again in the fall at the University of Heidelberg, threw himself into his studies with such dedication and zeal that he completed his training in three years, and ranked first in the medical state board examinations in 1855.

Along the way, however, he had discovered that clinical practice did not appeal to him but that he was fascinated by the science courses in the curriculum. After receiving his M.D. *summa cum laude* in 1855, he spent a semester at the University of Berlin under Johannes Müller and Emil Du Bois-Reymond, and in 1857 was appointed lecturer in physiology at Heidelberg. The following year, when the illustrious Hermann Helmholtz went there to establish a physiology institute, Wundt applied for the job of his laboratory assistant and got it. His work for Helmholtz further focused his interest on physiological psychology.

Still in his mid-twenties and still single, Wundt had become a thorough workaholic. In addition to his laboratory duties, he lectured, wrote textbooks to augment his income, carried on his own research on sense perception, and began drafting a major book on that subject, the *Contributions*, published in 1862. In it, Wundt, at only thirty, threw down the gauntlet to senior philosophers and mechanist physiologists by asserting that psychology could be a science only if it was based on experimental findings, and that the mind could indeed be experimentally investigated.

In 1864, Wundt was promoted to associate professor and resigned as Helmholtz's assistant to concentrate on his own interests. No longer having access to Helmholtz's laboratory, he created one at home, where he collected and fabricated the necessary apparatus and conducted his own psychological experiments. He continued to teach experimental physiology, but his courses came to contain more and more psychological material. Not until his late thirties did he stray from his work long enough to court a young woman and become engaged to her, although for financial reasons they had to postpone their marriage.

Helmholtz left Heidelberg in 1871. Wundt seemed the logical successor to his chair, but while the university assigned him to many of Helmholtz's duties, it appointed him only Professor Extraordinarius at a quarter of Helmholtz's pay. The promotion enabled Wundt and his fiancée to marry, but he now worked longer and harder than ever on his book, *Principles of Physiological Psychology*, hoping that it would enable him to escape from Heidelberg.

It did. In Part One—it appeared in two parts, in 1873 and 1874—Wundt immodestly wrote, "The work I here present to the public is an attempt to mark out a new domain of science." It brought him the acclaim he sought, the offer of a chair of philosophy at the University of Zürich, and a year later the offer of a much better chair at the University of Leipzig.

Wundt went to Leipzig in 1875, wangled the use of the room in Konvikt for storage and demonstrations, and four years later began using it as his private institute. His lectures became so popular, and his reputation and that of his laboratory drew so many acolytes to Leipzig that in 1883 the university increased his salary, granted his institute official status, and gave him additional space to turn the laboratory into a seven-room suite.[10]

He himself spent relatively little of his time in the laboratory and most of it in lecturing, running the institute, and writing and revising weighty books on psychological subjects and, later, on logic, ethics, and philosophy. His day was as rigidly structured as Immanuel Kant's. He wrote during much of the morning and then had a consultation hour, visited the laboratory in the afternoon, went for a walk during which he thought over his next lecture, delivered it, and then briefly dropped in again at the laboratory. His evenings were quiet; he avoided public functions except for concerts and almost never traveled, but he and his wife often entertained his senior students, and on most Sundays they had his assistants in to dinner.

At home he was genial, if formal, but at the university dogmatic and pedantic; he acted like, and saw himself as, an eminence. At his lectures—the most popular in the university—he waited until everyone was seated and his assistants had filed in and taken front seats. Then the door swung open and in he strode, impressive in his black academic robe, looking neither to right nor left as he marched down the aisle and up the steps of the platform, where he took his time arranging his chalk and papers, and at last faced his expectant audience, leaned on the lectern, and began talking.

He spoke fluently and fervently, without looking at his notes, and although on paper he was often turgid, ponderous, and obscure, when lecturing he could be entertaining in a heavy-footed academic way, as in his lecture on the mental powers of dogs:

I spent a great deal of time trying to discover some positive indication in the actions of my own poodle of the presence or absence of general experiential concepts. I taught the dog to close an open door in the usual way by pressing with the forefeet when the command "Shut the door" was given. He learned the trick first of all on a particular door in my study. One day I wished him to repeat it on another door in the same room, but he looked at me in astonishment and did nothing. It was with considerable trouble that I persuaded him to repeat his trick under the altered circumstances. But after that he obeyed the word of command without hesitation at any other door which was like these two . . . [However, although] the association of particular ideas had developed into a true similarity-association, there was not the slightest indication of the presence in his mind of the principal characteristic of the formation of concepts—the consciousness that the particular object vicariously represents a whole category of objects. When I ordered him to shut a door which opened from the outside, he made just the same movement—opened the door, that is, instead of closing it, and though I impatiently repeated the command, he could not be brought to do anything else, although he was obviously very unhappy at the ill success of his efforts.[11]

That is as far as Wundt ever unbent; even the admiring Edward Titchener, one of Wundt's most devoted disciples, found him usually "humorless, indefatigable, and aggressive."[12] Being possessed of encyclopedic erudition, he saw himself as the Authority. As William James caustically wrote to a friend,

Since there must be professors in the world, Wundt is the most praiseworthy and never-too-much-to-be-respected type of the species. He isn't a genius, he's a professor—a being whose duty is to know everything, and have his own opinion about everything, connected with his [specialty].[13]

With his graduate students, Wundt was helpful, concerned, kindly—and authoritarian. At the beginning of the academic year, he would order the students in his graduate research seminar to assemble at the institute; they would stand before him in a row and he would read a list of the research projects he wanted to see carried out that year, assigning the first topic to the first student in the row, the second to the second, and so on. According to Raymond Fancher,

No one dared to question these assignments, and the students went dutifully off to conduct their research—which in most cases became their doctoral theses . . . [Wundt] supervised the writing of the report[s] for publication. Though he occasionally permitted students to express their own views in their reports, he often exercised his blue pencil. One of his last American students reported that "Wundt exhibited the well-known German trait of guarding zealously the fundamental principles of his standpoint. About one-third of my thesis failed to support the Wundtian doctrine of assimilation, and so received elimination."[14]

It is only fair to add that in his later years Wundt became relatively mellow and grandfatherly. He enjoyed playing host, in his study, to younger people after his lectures and reminiscing about his early experiences. He taught, wrote, and supervised psychological research until his retirement at eighty-five in 1917, and thereafter was busy at his writing until eight days before his death, at eighty-eight, in 1920.

The Curious Goings-on at Konvikt

If we visit Wundt's laboratory in imagination, either in its one-room or later embodiments, and watch experiments being conducted, we will think them curiously trivial, or at least limited to what look like trivial mental phenomena; they explore none of what we usually consider the more intriguing areas of human psychology—learning, thinking, language skills, the emotions, and interpersonal relations.

We see Wundt's students and occasionally Wundt himself spending hours listening to a metronome; they run it at speeds ranging from the very slow to the very fast, sometimes stopping it after only a few beats, sometimes letting it run for many minutes. Each time, the listeners examine their sensations closely and then report their conscious reactions. They find that some conditions are pleasant and some unpleasant, that rapid beats create a touch of excitement and slow beats a mood of relaxation, and that they experience a faint sense of tension before each click and a faint sense of relief afterward.[15]

This seemingly insignificant exercise is serious business; it is training in what Wundt calls introspection. He means by it something very different from the introspection practiced by philosophers from Socrates to Hume, which consisted of thinking about their thoughts and feelings. Wundtian introspection is precise, circumscribed, and controlled; it is confined to what Wundt calls the "elements" of psychic life—the immediate, simple perceptions and feelings aroused by sounds, lights, colors, and other stimuli. The experimenter provides these stimuli and observes the subject's visible reactions, while the subject focuses his attention on the perceptions and feelings the stimuli generate in him.*

Such introspection is a crucial part of many experiments in Wundt's laboratory, the most common being reaction-time research. Like Donders, Wundt and his students often measure the time needed to respond to different kinds of stimuli, in the effort to discern the components of psychic processes and the connections among them.

Many of the experiments we see taking place are somewhat like the very first one in that laboratory, Max Friedrich's. Hour after hour, day after day, an observer causes the ball to drop to the platform, making a sharp noise and closing a contact that starts the chronoscope. As soon as the subject hears the noise, he presses the telegrapher's key, stopping the chronoscope. Such experiments usually come in at least two forms. In one, the subject is told to press the key as soon as he is clearly aware of his perception of the sound; in a second form, he is told to press the key as soon as possible when the sound occurs. In the first case, the instructions focus his attention on his own perception; in the second case, on the sound itself.

The casual onlooker might see little difference between the two cases, but the researchers, after a great many trials and chronoscope readings, find that the first kind of reaction, involving awareness of one's perception of the sound followed by a conscious voluntary response, usually takes about two tenths of a second; the second kind, involving a purely muscular or reflexive response, takes only about one tenth of a second.[16]

These findings seem like mere crumbs of psychology, but there are other differences, more revealing than duration, between the two forms of the experiment. The subjects, having been trained in introspection, report that when their attention is focused on their awareness of hearing the sound, they experience a clear, though fluctuating, mental image of what they expect to hear, a minor, wavering sense of strain, mild surprise when they hear the sound, and a strong motivation to press the key. In the reflexive form of the experiment, on the other hand, they experience a feeble mental image of the expected sound, a considerable sense of strain, strong surprise when the ball drops, and an impulse to press the key almost without consciously willing to. Thus the experiment measures not only the different times taken by conscious volition and reflex-

---

*I use "his" and "him" here because for many years Wundt had no female graduate students. —M.H.

ive volition but identifies the conscious processes that take place in the self-aware version of this simple act.[17]

Despite the focus on conscious mental processes, the researchers look only at the basic components of those processes. Wundt had boldly proclaimed years earlier that experiments could explore the psyche, but now he feels that they can do so only for sensations or perceptions and feelings—the elemental materials of consciousness—and the connections among them. He says that higher mental processes, including complex thoughts, are "of too variable a character to be the subjects of objective observation."[18] He argues that language, concept formation, and other high-level cognitive functions can be studied only by observation, particularly of general trends among groups of people.[19]

Wundt defines a scientific psychological experiment as one in which a known, controlled physiological stimulus—the "antecedent variable," he calls it—is applied and the individual's responses observed and measured. Helmholtz and others had already done that but confined their observations to the individual's visible reactions; Wundt's great contribution is the use of his kind of introspection to gain quantitative information about the subject's conscious inner reactions, though he limits these to the simplest feeling states.

During the laboratory's first two decades, about a hundred major experimental research studies and numerous minor ones were conducted there. Many dealt with sensation and perception, and were generally along the same lines as the work of Weber, Helmholtz, and Fechner. But the laboratory's most original and important findings came from its studies of "mental chronometry," the measuring of the time required by particular mental processes and the interactions among them.

Still others introduced a number of complications in order to invoke and measure a variety of mental processes. For instance, by having several possible stimuli and responses—a stimulus might come in any of four different colors, each calling for a different kind of response—the experimenter could extend the inquiry to include discrimination and choice.[20]

Other studies concerned the boundary between perception and apperception. In a notable one, the experimenter flashed a group of letters or words very briefly through a slit in a revolving drum; the subject "perceived" them (saw them at the periphery of awareness, without having time to recognize them) but in the next instant "apperceived" (consciously remembered and recognized) some of what he had seen. The major finding was the size of the attention span: most subjects could apperceive and name four to six letters or words after having seen them too briefly to identify them.

A smaller group of studies explored association—not the high-level kind discussed by the English associationists, but the elemental building blocks of association. In a typical study the assistant would call out single-syllable words and the subject would press a key the instant he identified each; this measured "apperception time." Then the assistant would utter similar words and the subject would press the key as soon as each word awakened an associated idea. This took longer. Subtracting the apperception time from the total time yielded a measure of what Wundt called "association time"—how long it took the mind to locate a word associated with a heard and recognized word—which, for the average person, is about three quarters of a second.[21]

As the British physicist Lord Kelvin, a contemporary of Wundt's, used to say, "When you can measure what you are speaking about, and express it in numbers, you know something about it; but when you cannot measure it, when you cannot express it in numbers, your knowledge is of a meager and unsatisfactory kind." The data generated in Wundt's laboratory definitely met this criterion of knowledge, at least concerning the elementary components of mental processes.

Wundtian Psychology

Wundt saw himself as much more than an experimentalist. In his books and articles he assumed the role of the systematist of psychology and architect of its master plan. But his system has proven difficult to explicate, and summaries of it differ widely as to its main features.

One reason, according to Boring, is that Wundt's system is a classification scheme that cannot be experimentally proved or disproved.[22] Rather than being the outgrowth of a testable grand theory, it is an orderly pedagogical arrangement of topics based on middle-range theories, many of which could not be explored by the methods used in the Leipzig laboratory.

An even greater obstacle to summarizing Wundt's system is that he constantly revised it and added to it, so that it is not one thing but many. Indeed, in his time critics could hardly find fault with any part of the system before he either changed it in a new edition of one of his works or moved on to some other topic. William James, though he admired

Wundt's laboratory work, complained that his profusion of writings and viewpoints made him unassailable as a theorist:

> Whilst [other psychologists] make mincemeat of some of his views by their criticisms, he is meanwhile writing another book on an entirely different subject. Cut him up like a worm, and each fragment crawls; there is no *noeud vital* in his mental medulla oblongata, so that you can't kill him all at once.[23]

Yet if no central theme is visible in Wundt's psychology, it is possible to name some of its recurring themes.

One is psychic parallelism. Although Wundt has often been labeled a dualist, he did not believe that anything called mind existed apart from the body. He did say that the phenomena of consciousness parallel the processes of the nervous system, but he considered the former to be based on combinations of actual neural events.[24]

Another theme is his view of psychology as a science. At first he proclaimed that it was, or could be, a *Naturwissenschaft* (natural science), but later said that it was largely a *Geisteswissenschaft* (science of the spirit—spirit not in the sense of incorporeal soul but of higher mental activity). He said that only the experimental study of immediate experience was a *Naturwissenschaft*; the rest was *Geisteswissenschaft*. He wrote at length about individual and social psychology and related social sciences, but descriptively and without admitting or even recognizing that rigorous experimental methods could be developed in these fields.[25]

The most nearly central doctrine of Wundtian psychology is that conscious mental processes are composed of basic elements—the sensations and feelings of immediate experience.[26] In his early writings Wundt says that these elements automatically combine to become mental processes, somewhat as chemical elements form chemical compounds. But later he says that the chemical analogy is inaccurate and that the compounding takes place not as in chemistry but by means of attention, volition, and creativity.

Although immediate experience has its rules of causality—particular stimuli cause particular elemental experiences—mental life has its own kind of causality: The mind develops, and ideas follow each other, according to specific laws. Wundt had special names for these laws, but essentially they were his reformulations of association, judgment, creativity, and memory.[27]

Another major theme in his psychology, especially in his later writings, is that "volitional activities" are central to all conscious actions and mental processes; those processes are products of an apperceiving agent that actively *chooses* to think, speak, and act in certain ways. Even simple, unthinking acts are volitional, in his view, although he calls them *impulsive*. Acts resulting from more complex mental processes are volitional and *voluntary*.[28] Although this theory did not survive in psychology, it was an effort on Wundt's part to move beyond the automatism of mechanist psychology and toward a more holistic model.

In sum, Wundt had a broader and more inclusive view of psychology than he is often given credit for. Nonetheless, on balance he was restrictive and confining, leaving out or proscribing many areas that today are commonly accepted as essential parts of the field:[29]

— He was unalterably opposed to practical applications of psychology; when one of his gifted students, Ernst Meumann, turned to educational psychology, Wundt looked at it as desertion to the enemy.

— He was equally opposed to the use of introspection in any way but his own. He scathingly criticized the work of certain researchers— members of the Würzburg School, of whom we will hear more in a moment—who asked their subjects about everything that had gone on in their minds during an experiment. Such procedures, Wundt said, were "mock" experiments, neither experimental nor introspective.

— He rejected out of hand the beginnings of child psychology on the grounds that the conditions of study could not be adequately controlled, so the results were not real psychology.

— He considered animal psychology a fit subject for ruminations, philosophizing, and informal experiments (such as those with his poodle) but allowed no work with animals to be performed in his laboratory because no data based on introspection could be obtained.

— He dismissed contemporaneous French work in psychology that relied largely on hypnotism and suggestion. Since this research lacked exact introspection, he said it was not true psychological experimentation.

— Finally, he was particularly scornful of the psychology of William James, which was far more holistic, insightful, and personally relevant than his own. After reading James's *The Principles of Psychology*—which was greeted enthusiastically by psychologists throughout the world—Wundt sourly commented, "It is literature, it is beautiful, but it is not psychology."[30]

Sic Transit

Nothing about Wilhelm Wundt is as curious as his influence on psychology—paradoxically vast and yet very minor.

Vast:
— He was the encyclopedist and systematist of the field; he drew the intellectual map of the territory and defined it as a new domain of science.
— He personally trained many of the people who became the leading psychologists in Germany and the United States during the first decades of the new science.
— He assembled from the scattered beginnings of physiological psychology a distinct methodology for experimental psychology. His laboratory and its methods were the model for many of those established during the next half century.
— Through his immensely authoritative textbooks, he influenced most of the first two generations of American psychologists and their students. During the early part of the twentieth century, the majority of American students of psychology could trace their historical lineage back to Wundt.[31]

And yet very minor:
Wundt's ideas play little part in contemporary psychological theory. The principal reasons:

— Wundt wrote on every imaginable branch of psychology, including many not amenable to his own experimental methods, such as psychic causality, hypnosis, and mediumship. As a result, certain young psychologists saw him as something of a dualist and metaphysician, and thereupon adopted even more rigorously positivist criteria for those psychological phenomena which could be investigated scientifically.[32] Their views would be embodied in behaviorism, which would regard introspection, even of the Wundtian kind, as unscientific and valueless.

— Many other psychologists, however, reacted against what they saw as the excessive narrowness and rigidity of Wundtian psychology. They were drawn to areas of research with practical applications, among them child psychology, educational psychology, psychological testing, and clinical psychology. All these fields, though beyond the Wundtian pale, grew and prospered.

— Certain new schools of research psychology emerged during Wundt's later years as protests against characteristics of his system. These schools had in common the view that experimental psychology should not be limited to the elemental components of immediate experience but should explore higher mental processes.

Such as memory. At the University of Berlin, Hermann Ebbinghaus (1850–1909) invented a method of investigating memory processes that eliminated subjectivity and the effects of the individual's previous experiences. He created twenty-three hundred nonsense syllables—meaningless combinations of two consonants separated by a vowel, such as *bap, tox, muk,* and *rif*—and used them in a series of memory experiments.

He would read a list of the syllables, for instance, then recall as many as he could. By varying the conditions—the length of the list, the speed at which he read it, the number of times he read it—he rigorously explored such issues as how the number of items is related to the speed with which they can be memorized (the difficulty of memorizing the list increases far faster than its length), how forgetting is related to the time lapse between learning and recall, the effect on learning and forgetting of repetition and review.[33]

So dedicated was Ebbinghaus to his research that he subjected himself to almost incredible labors. In an effort to determine how the number of repetitions affects retention, for instance, he rehearsed 420 lists of 16 syllables 34 times each, a total of 14,280 trials—an Edmond Dantès of psychology, scratching his way through the walls of a Château d'If of research. His method, dreadful as it sounds, was so successful that it has been a staple of the armamentarium of experimental psychology ever since. (In recent decades, to be sure, the predictions he derived from his work have dwindled in importance; the emphasis on memory research in recent decades has been on meaningful rather than meaningless learning.)[34]

George Elias Müller (1850–1934), at the University of Göttingen, added introspection to Ebbinghaus's method in order to examine the mental processes behind the statistical findings. Müller found that the recall of nonsense syllables, far from being related solely to the length of the list, the number of repetitions, and similar factors, was in considerable part contingent on his subjects' active use of stratagems of their own, such as the groupings, rhythms, and even consciously contrived meanings they had imposed on the nonsense syllables. Learning, in short, is not a passive process but an active and creative one.[35] These findings, too, helped free psychology from the limits imposed on it at Leipzig.

Certain other psychologists, including some of Wundt's students, developed even more radical methods of experimental research. Oswald Külpe (1862–1915), though he took his degree under Wundt and was his assistant for eight years, came to think that not only memory but many other thought processes could be studied in the laboratory. In 1896, he founded a psychological laboratory at the University of Würzburg that soon was second in prestige only to Wundt's, and he and his students became known as the Würzburg School. Their distinctive contribution was the use of "systematic experimental introspection," in which the subject reports not just sensations and feelings but all the thoughts he had while performing a mental task.

Külpe used this method to test Donders's hypothesis that complex mental processes consist of simple ones linked together; it revealed that the addition of mental steps to a reaction-time experiment often changed the nature of the thought process altogether, yielding a reaction time different from the simple addition of all the steps involved.[36]

The work of others in the Würzburg School—Karl Marbe, Narziss Ach, and Karl Bühler—made its name synonymous with the experimental study of human thought.[37] In a typical Würzburg experiment, a subject might have been given a stimulus word and asked to produce an associated word that was more comprehensive, or else an associated word that was more specific. If the stimulus was, say, "bird," a "superordinate" (more comprehensive) association might be "animal," a "subordinate" (more specific) one "canary." Afterward the subject recounted everything that had gone on in his mind during the few seconds it had taken him to perform the task—his recognition of the stimulus word, his reaction to the task, the appearance of mental images aroused by the stimulus word, the search for the appropriate response, and the appearance of the appropriate word.[38] These recollections, written down, were analyzed for clues as to how memory works.

(In recent years this very method has been used by artificial intelligence specialists to create "expert systems"—computer programs that simulate human problem-solving activities such as medical diagnosis by replicating, in computer language, the steps of reasoning used by human experts.)

A curious discovery made by members of the Würzburg School was that subjects sometimes found no trace of mental imagery in their introspection. Adding or subtracting numbers, for instance, or making a judgment as to whether a statement was true or false, might involve no images. The researchers called this phenomenon "imageless thought"; it showed that, contrary to Wundtian theory, some thought processes are not composed of elemental sensations and perceptions.[39]

A researcher named Henry Watt made another of the Würzburg School's valuable discoveries. He found that if he told a subject what the task was—perhaps "Find a superordinate word"—before giving him the stimulus word, introspection would show that the subject had not searched for the superordinate word but that it simply appeared of itself. Watt had discovered the effect of a "determining tendency" or, as it came to be more generally known, "mental set"—the mind's preparedness to perform a task by unconscious means.[40]

In these and other ways the Würzburg School expanded experimental psychology far beyond Wundtian boundaries and led the move toward a more holistic psychology.

By the 1920s Wundtian psychology was fading from the scene. Professor Ludy T. Benjamin, a leading historian of the field, sums up what became of it:

> In the end, Wundt's psychology, and that of his contemporaries, was replaced by newer psychological approaches. Although parts of this psychological system exist in modern psychology . . . we continue to remember him principally for his vision in seeing the promise of a science of psychology and then taking the giant steps required in the nineteenth century to establish the discipline.[41]

But, he adds, recent scholarship has shown that Wundt had "a depth of understanding and breadth of interest (e.g., his writings on culture, law, art, language, history, and religion)" that have long been overlooked.

For all that, Boring's evaluation of Wundt, first made over seventy-five years ago and repeated in 1950, seems unassailable:

> Ebbinghaus and not Wundt . . . had the flash of genius about how to investigate learning. So too with the other great problems of emotion, thought, will, intelligence, and personality, which were to be successfully attacked sometime and for which the Wundtian laboratory was not yet ready. We need not, however, despise our heritage because, with its help, we have in time advanced far beyond it.[42]

The Psychologist *Malgré Lui:*
William James

"This Is No Science"

What is one to make of a distinguished professor of the new science of psychology who denies that it is a science? Who praises the findings of experimental psychologists but loathes performing experiments and does as few as possible? Who is said to be the greatest American psychologist of his time (the late nineteenth century) but never took a course in psychology and sometimes even disavows the label of psychologist?

Listen to this maverick, William James:

To a poet friend he writes, in sarcastic allusion to the New Psychology of the German mechanists, "The only Psyche now recognized by science is a decapitated frog whose writhings express deeper truths than your weak-minded poets ever dreamed."[1] In a letter to his brother, the novelist Henry James, he refers to psychology as a "nasty little subject" that excludes everything one would want to know.[2] Only two years after completing his huge and magisterial *Principles of Psychology* he writes:

It is indeed strange to hear people talk triumphantly of "the New Psychology," and write "Histories of Psychology," when into the real elements and forces which the word covers not the first glimpse of clear insight exists. A string of raw facts; a little gossip and wrangle about opinions; a little classification and generalization on the mere descriptive level; a strong prejudice that we *have* states of mind, and that our brain conditions them: but not a single law in the sense in which

physics shows us laws, not a single proposition from which any consequence can causally be deduced. This is no science, it is only the hope
of a science.[3]

Yet this outspoken recusant is not scornful of psychology but has great
expectations of it. He sees its goal as the discovery of the connection
between each physiological "brain state" and the corresponding state of
mind; a genuine understanding of that connection would be "*the* scientific achievement, before which all past achievements would pale."[4] But
he says psychology is not ready for that; its state is like that of physics
before Galileo enunciated the laws of motion, chemistry before
Lavoisier stated the law of the preservation of mass. The best it can do
until its Galileo and Lavoisier come is to explain the laws of conscious
mental life, but "come they some day surely will."

Adorable Genius

The informality and unpretentiousness of James's remarks tell us that
we are in the presence of a man very unlike Wundt; no wonder they did
not appreciate each other's work. James, a short, slender man, lightly
bearded and blue-eyed, with fine features and a noble forehead, chose
to dress in what was, for that time, informal garb for a professor—Nor-
folk jacket, bright shirt, flowing tie. Friendly, charming, and outgoing,
he often walked across Harvard Yard with students, animatedly talking
to them, a spectacle to make a Herr Professor's flesh creep. As a lecturer,
he was so vivacious and humorous that one day a student interrupted
and asked him to be serious for a moment.

Despite his ready smile and boyish, even impish, manner, he was a
complex personality: strong yet intermittently frail, hardworking yet
sociable, joyous but given to spells of melancholy, frivolous but profoundly serious, kind to students and loving to his family but easily
bored and exasperated, especially by nitpicking chores like proofreading
(about which he once wrote, "Send me no proofs! I will return them
unopened and never speak to you again"[5]). Although he had the manners of a gentleman and was thoroughly civil in his behavior, he could
be wickedly derogatory, as in the remarks about Wundt quoted earlier,
but usually he made such comments only in personal letters, and in his
published work was gentle and courteous even when critical.

He wrote with a fluency, informality, and intimacy that no other psychologist of his time, certainly no German, would have dreamed of using. Of the differing codes governing the several social selves of a man he said, "You must not lie in general, but you may lie as much as you please if asked about your relations with a lady; you must accept a challenge from an equal, but if challenged by an inferior you may laugh him to scorn."[6] To illustrate the difficulty of paying attention to a subject one dislikes he offered this case (probably himself):

> One snatches at any and every passing pretext, no matter how trivial or external, to escape from the odiousness of the matter at hand. I know a person, for example, who will poke the fire, pick dust-specks from the floor, arrange his table, snatch up the newspaper, take down any book which catches his eye, trim his nails, waste the morning *anyhow*, in short, and all without premeditation,—simply because the only thing he *ought* to attend to is the preparation of a noonday lesson in formal logic which he detests. Anything but *that!*[7]

He sometimes salted his serious writing with humorous stories and jokes. Describing how Helmholtz and Wundt felt about a psychologist who had recently misapplied their principle of unconscious inference, he wrote, "It would be natural [for them] to feel towards him as the sailor in the story felt towards the horse who got his foot into the stirrup,—'If you're going to get on, I must get off.' "[8]

And he could be wonderfully sensitive and empathetic. He visited Helen Keller when she was a young girl and brought her a gift he thought she could particularly appreciate, and which in fact she never forgot—an ostrich feather.

No wonder the philosopher Alfred North Whitehead summed him up as "that adorable genius, William James."

Born in New York City in 1842, William James was a child of privilege and by all odds should have become a playboy or, at best, a dilettante.[9]

His Scotch-Irish grandfather, who had come from Ireland, was a shrewd, hardworking businessman and a promoter of the Erie Canal who amassed several million dollars. In consequence, his son Henry (William's father) had no need to work. Henry went to divinity school for two years, but found its stern Presbyterian doctrines repugnant and quit; he continued, however, to be concerned with religious and philosophic questions all his life. At thirty-three, he had an acute emotional crisis. After dinner, while idly staring at the fire, he was suddenly over-whelmed by a nameless fear—"a perfectly insane and abject terror, without ostensible cause,"[10] he later said—that lasted for only ten sec-onds but left him badly shaken and prey to recurring anxiety for two years. Physicians, trips, and other distractions were no help, but at last he found relief in the philosophy of the Swedish mystic Emanuel Sweden-borg, who himself had suffered just such anxiety attacks.

After regaining his health, Henry devoted himself in part to writing works of theology and social reform (he styled himself "a philosopher and seeker of truth"), and in part to the education of his children. Dis-satisfied with American schools, he alternately took his family— William James was the eldest of five children—to Europe to broaden their education and experience, and brought them back to their house on Washington Square in New York to keep in touch with their own cul-ture.

As a result, William James attended schools in the United States, England, France, Switzerland, and Germany, and was also privately tutored; became familiar with the major museums and galleries in every city the family visited; acquired fluency in five languages; met, listened to, and talked to such frequenters of the James household as Thoreau, Emerson, Greeley, Hawthorne, Carlyle, Tennyson, and J. S. Mill; and through his father's influence became widely read and well versed in philosophy. Not that Henry James, Sr., was a taskmaster or disciplinar-ian; for his time, he was an unusually permissive and loving father, who encouraged dinner table arguments by the children about every kind of issue and, to his friends' horror, allowed his children to attend theater.

But a loving and permissive father can wield distressing influence over a child. At seventeen William James wanted to become a painter, but Henry James, Sr., who wanted him to seek a career in the sciences or philosophy, disapproved and took the family to Europe for a year as a dis-traction. Only because William persisted was he reluctantly allowed to study with an artist in Newport. After half a year William decided he was not gifted, perhaps more because of guilt feelings than a lack of talent, and, obeying his father's wishes, entered Harvard and began the study of chemistry.

But the detailed laboratory work tried his patience and he soon switched to physiology, then the vogue, what with the pioneering work in Europe of Müller, Helmholtz, and Du Bois-Reymond. After a while, however, because the family fortune was dwindling and William real-ized he would someday have to earn his own living, he switched to Harvard Medical School. Medicine, too, failed to arouse his enthusiasm, and he took off much of a year to travel to the Amazon with Louis Agassiz, the eminent Harvard naturalist, hoping that natural history might be his true love. It proved not to be; he hated collecting specimens.

He resumed medical school but was beset by assorted ailments—back pain, weak vision, digestive disorders, and thoughts of suicide—some or most of which were exacerbated by his indecision about his future. Seeking relief, he went to France and Germany for nearly two years, took the baths, studied under Helmholtz and other leading physiologists, and became thoroughly conversant with the New Psychology.

Finally he returned and at twenty-seven completed medical school. He made no effort to practice because of his poor health, but spent his time studying psychology, sunk in gloom about his prospects and troubled by the profound differences between his scientific views of the mind and the world and his father's mystical and spiritual ones. In 1870, at twenty-eight, after nearly a year in these doldrums, he had an abrupt emotional crisis very much like his father's. Many years later he described it in *Varieties of Religious Experience* in the guise of a memoir given him by an anonymous Frenchman:

> I went one evening into a dressing-room in the twilight to procure some article that was there; when suddenly there fell upon me without warning, just as if it came out of the darkness, a horrible fear of my own existence. Simultaneously there arose in my mind the image of an epileptic patient whom I had seen in the asylum, a black-haired youth with greenish skin, entirely idiotic, who used to sit all day on one of the benches, or rather shelves against the wall, with his knees drawn up against his chin. *That shape am I*, I felt, potentially. I became a mass of quivering fear. After this the universe was changed for me altogether. I awoke morning after morning with a horrible dread at the pit of my stomach, and with a sense of the insecurity of life that I never knew before, and that I have never felt since.[11]

In his mature years William diagnosed his father's crisis as an outbreak of long-repressed hostile feelings against his tyrannical father, but never suggested an explanation of his own crisis. Jacques Barzun has offered a hypothesis: "One may plausibly surmise that it was the intolerable pressure of not being able to rebel against a father who exerted no tyranny but that of love."[12]

The attack left James incapacitated for many months. During this period he was particularly troubled by the German physiologists' mechanistic vision of the world, the scientific equivalent of the Calvinistic determinism his own father had rebelled against. If mechanism gave a true picture of the mind, then all his thoughts, desires, and volitions were no more than the predetermined interactions of physical particles; he was as helpless to determine his actions as the epileptic patient in the asylum.

Finally, like his father, he was freed from his depression by reading—not Swedenborg but an essay on free will by Charles Renouvier, a French philosopher. As James wrote in his diary:

[I] see no reason why his definition of free will—"the sustaining of a thought *because I choose to* when I might have other thoughts"—need be the definition of an illusion. At any rate, I will assume for the present—until next year—that it is no illusion. My first act of free will shall be to believe in free will. I will go a step further with my will, not only act with it, but believe as well; believe in my individual reality and creative power.[13]

His will to believe in free will worked; he slowly began to recover, although all his life his health remained fragile and he continued to have minor bouts of depression. He spent the next two years reading widely in physiological and philosophical psychology and regaining his mental health. In 1872, nearing thirty, he was still financially dependent on his father and had no plans for his future when Harvard's president, Charles Eliot, a neighbor—the James family had been living in Cambridge for some time—invited him to teach physiology at Harvard. He accepted, and remained there for the next thirty-five years.

But not as a professor of physiology. Within three years he began offering courses in physiological psychology and performing demonstrations for students in his little laboratory in Lawrence Hall. He continued to read omnivorously, forming his own lofty conception of psychology, and during the next three years presented some of his ideas so brilliantly in articles and book reviews that the publisher Henry Holt offered him a contract for a textbook of the new scientific psychology. James signed, apologizing that he would need two years. He took twelve, completing the task in 1890, but he produced a work that was successful far beyond the publisher's hopes.

The year James began the book, 1878, was a landmark in another way. At thirty-six, he married. Despite his belief in free will, he seems to have been something less than a free agent in his choice of mate. Two years earlier his father had come home from a meeting of the Radical Club in Boston and announced that he had met William's future wife, Alice Gibbens, a Boston schoolteacher and accomplished pianist. Although William dragged his feet about meeting her, once he did so the die was cast. After a prolonged courtship, Alice became his dutiful, strong wife and helpmeet, mother of his five children, amanuensis, and lifelong intellectual companion. She appreciated his genius and understood his emotional needs and temperamental volatility, and despite many a spell of tension and many a battle, particularly before William's long trips—he needed periods of apartness—they were a devoted and loving couple.

Once he was married, James's remaining nervous and physical symptoms diminished; although his health was always imperfect, he went at life with a zest and energy he had never shown before. He was at last an independent man with his own identity, home, and income, free to pursue his own goals. Two years later Harvard recognized his special interests and abilities by making him an assistant professor of philosophy (his larger view of psychology fit more comfortably in that department than in the department of physiology), and in 1889 changed his title, finally, to professor of psychology.

Founding Father

There were no professors of psychology in American universities before James began teaching the subject in 1875. The only forms of psychology then taught in the United States were phrenology and Scottish mental philosophy, an offshoot of associationism used chiefly as a defense of revealed religion. James himself had never taken a course in the New Psychology because none was available; as he once jested, "The first lecture in psychology that I ever heard was the first I ever gave."

But within two decades at least two dozen American universities were offering instruction in psychology, three psychology journals were being published, and a professional psychology society had been founded. There were several reasons for the efflorescence: the desire of many university presidents to emulate the success of the German psychological institutes, the arrival in America of psychologists trained by Wundt, and, most of all, James's influence, exerted through his teaching, his dozens of well-received articles, and his masterwork, *Principles of Psychology*.

James introduced experimental psychology to America. He began giving laboratory demonstrations to students at least as early as Wundt, and he and his students started performing laboratory experiments about the same time as Wundt and his students, if not earlier. Ironically, while James made much of the value of experimentation, he himself found it boring and intellectually confining. He usually spent no more than two hours a day in the laboratory, told a friend that "I naturally hate experimental work," and said of the Leipzig style of laboratory work, "The thought of psycho-physical experimentation and altogether of brass-instrument and algebraic-formula psychology fills me with horror."[14]

Yet he believed in it and had his students perform a broad array of experiments. They whirled frogs around to explore the function of the inner ear; did the same to human deaf mutes to test James's hypothesis that, since their semicircular canals were damaged, they should be less subject to dizziness than normal people (he was right); carried out reflex experiments on frogs' legs, and reaction-time and speed of nerve-conduction experiments on human subjects; and, venturing far beyond Wundtian physiological psychology, did studies of hypnosis and automatic writing.

Although James hated to do experiments, he forced himself to when it was the best way to prove or disprove a theory. While writing the chapter on memory for *Principles*, he wanted to test the ancient belief still held by "faculty" psychologists that memory, like a muscle, can be strengthened by exercise, and that memorizing anything would therefore improve the memory not just for the memorized kind of material but for every kind. James was skeptical and used himself as his experimental subject. Over an eight-day span he memorized 158 lines of "Satyr," a poem by Victor Hugo, taking an average of fifty seconds a line to do so. Next, working twenty minutes daily for thirty-eight days, he memorized the entire first book (798 lines) of Milton's *Paradise Lost*. If the exercise theory were correct, this prolonged effort should have greatly strengthened his memory. He then went back to "Satyr" and memorized another 158 lines—and found that it took him seven seconds longer per line than the first time. Exercise hadn't increased the strength of his memory; it had diminished it, at least temporarily.[15] (He had several associates repeat the experiment, with roughly similar results.) A psychological theory accepted for two thousand years, and believed today by many laypeople, had been disproven.

But James's own experiments were only one source, and a minor one, of his ideas about psychology. He drew upon all his reading in both philosophical and physiological psychology; spent half a year in Europe in 1882–1883 visiting universities, attending laboratory sessions and lectures, and meeting and talking to dozens of leading psychologists and other scientists; corresponded regularly with many of them; and gathered reports and clinical studies of abnormal minds, and of normal ones under hypnosis, drugs, or stress.

He derived many of his major insights and hypotheses from another and very different source: introspection, of a kind quite unlike that practiced by Wundt and his students. In James's opinion, any effort to seize and isolate individual elements of a thought process by means of Wundtian introspection would be doomed to failure:

> As a snow-flake crystal caught in the warm hand is no longer a crystal but a drop, so, instead of catching the feeling of a relation moving to its term, we find we have caught some substantive thing, usually the last word we were pronouncing, statically taken, and with its function, tendency, and particular meaning in the sentence quite evaporated. The attempt at introspective analysis in these cases is in fact like seizing a spinning top to catch its motion, or trying to turn up the gas quickly enough to see how the darkness looks.[16]

But he felt that a naturalistic kind of introspection—an effort to observe our own thoughts and feelings as they actually seem to us—could tell us much about our mental life. This was, for him, the most important of investigative methods; he defined it as "looking into our own minds and reporting what we there discover."[17] (He was referring to the introspection of conscious mental processes; at the time, neither he nor most other psychologists were aware of how large a part of our mental processes takes place outside consciousness.)

Such introspection required both concentration and practice, because inner states follow each other rapidly and often are blended and difficult to distinguish from one another. Yet it was feasible, James said, likening it to sense perception. Just as with practice one can notice, carefully observe, name, and classify objects outside oneself, one can do so with inner events.

There was, to be sure, a classic question about how this was possible. The conscious mind can observe external objects, but how can it observe itself? Was there a second consciousness that could watch the first one? How could we know that such a second consciousness existed—could we observe it, too? And how? James had an answer to such perplexities: introspection is, in reality, immediate retrospection; the conscious mind looks back and reports what it has just experienced.

He admitted that introspection is difficult and prone to error. Who could be sure of the exact order of feelings when they were excessively rapid? Of the comparative strengths of feelings when they were very much alike? Or which is longer when both occupied but an instant of time? Who could enumerate all the ingredients of such a complicated feeling as anger?

But he said that the validity of some kinds of introspective reports could be tested and verified by at least half a dozen kinds of well-established experimentation. The duration of simple mental processes, for one, could be estimated introspectively and then verified by reaction-time experiments; the introspective report of how many digits or letters one could simultaneously keep in mind, for another, could be verified by apperception experiments.

And while introspective reports of the more complex and subtle mental states might be impossible to verify experimentally, James maintained that since those acts are introspectively observable, any straightforward account of them can be regarded as literal. In any event, "introspective observation is what we have to rely on first and foremost and always."[18]

One other source of James's psychological ideas—possibly the most important of all—was personal and nonscientific: his naturalistic, perceptive, and wise interpretation of human behavior, based on his own experience and understanding. Many of his major insights came from "psychologizing," says the distinguished psychologist Ernest Hilgard in his authoritative *Psychology in America*:

> To "psychologize" is to reflect on ordinary observations and then to offer a plausible interpretation of the relevant experience and behavior. Once expressed, such interpretations are often so plausible that detailed proof would seem irrelevant—or at least too tedious to be worth the effort. Shakespeare was such a "psychologizer" without making any pretense of being a psychologist. Among psychologists, James is the preeminent psychologizer. The consequence is that he encouraged a full-bodied, warm-hearted psychology that is impatient with the trivial—a robust and vital psychology facing courageously psychology's most puzzling problems.[19]

After twelve years of research, introspection, psychologizing, and writing, James completed *Principles*, which had been an almost intolerable burden to him. It was a huge work—nearly fourteen hundred pages in two volumes—and unsuitable for textbook use after all. Within two years, however, he turned out an abridged textbook version. (The full-length version became known as "James" and the abridged version as "Jimmy.") *Principles* was an immediate and resounding success, and had a lasting effect on the development of American psychology. Nearly sixty years later Ralph Barton Perry, professor of philosophy at Harvard, would say of it, "No work in psychology has met with such an enthusiastic reception . . . nor has any other work enjoyed such enduring popularity."[20]

By 1892, when James completed Jimmy, he had been teaching and writing about psychology for seventeen years, and grown weary of it. From then on he turned his creative efforts toward other things: education (he lectured on the applications of psychology in the classroom and published *Talks to Teachers* in 1899); the practical results of different kinds of religious experience (*The Varieties of Religious Experience* appeared in 1902); and philosophy (*Pragmatism*, published in 1907, established him as a leading American thinker).

He did, however, continue to write popular treatments of some of the ideas he had advanced in *Principles* and to keep up with psychological developments. In 1894 he was the first American to call attention to the work of the then obscure Viennese physician Sigmund Freud, and in 1909, though ailing, he went to Clark University to meet Freud on his only visit to the United States and to hear him speak.

Ever the nonconformist, James was willing to explore forms of psychology outside accepted scientific bounds. He took a keen interest in spiritualism and "psychical" phenomena, considering them an extension of abnormal psychology; closely followed the efforts of psychical researchers; attended séances; and in 1884 founded the American Society for Psychical Research. He once made a pact with a dying friend to sit outside his room after his death and wait for a communication from the Beyond; none came. James coupled an open-minded attitude toward such subjects with an insistence on solid scientific evidence; late in life he concluded, "I find myself believing that there is 'something in' these never ending reports of psychical phenomena, although I haven't yet the least positive notion of the something . . . Theoretically, I am no further than I was at the beginning."[21]

From 1898 on, James had a personal reason to be interested in the afterlife. That year, at fifty-six, he overtaxed his heart while climbing in the Adirondacks, and thereafter had chronic heart trouble. His health gradually worsened; he resigned from Harvard in 1907, wrote two of his most important works of philosophy in the next three years, and died in 1910, at sixty-eight. John Dewey said of him at that time, "By common consent he was far and away the greatest of American psychologists. Were it not for the unreasoned admiration of men and things German, there would be no question, I think, that he was the greatest psychologist of his time in any country—perhaps of any time."[22]

Ideas of the Pre-eminent Psychologizer

James had something to say about every topic within psychology, as known in his day, but his chief influence was due to the following handful of his concepts:

Functionalism: This is the label usually applied to Jamesian psychology. Unlike the New Psychologists, who maintained that higher mental processes are assembled in each individual from simple elements, James held that the higher processes were developed over the ages by evolution because of their adaptive value. He was seventeen when Darwin's *Origin of Species* appeared (1859), twenty-nine when *The Descent of Man* was published (1871), and was impressed by both. It seemed clear to him that the mind's complex processes had evolved because of their life-preserving functions, and that to understand those processes one had to ask what functions they perform.

Functionalism is a handy label, and accurate enough, except that it applies only to some parts of James's psychology. He had no actual system and deliberately avoided presenting his ideas as a coherent whole because he felt that it was far too early in the development of psychology for an all-embracing grand theory. As Ralph Barton Perry said, James was an explorer, not a mapmaker. In *Principles* he presented material and theories about every psychological phenomenon from the simplest sensations to reasoning without trying to force everything into a unified framework.

Yet he did have a strong viewpoint. The physiological psychologists of Germany said that mental states were nothing but physiological states of the brain and nervous system; James termed this "an unwarrantable impertinence in the present state of psychology."[23] He viewed mental life as real, and the physiological view that mind was nothing but physical reactions to outside stimuli as unworthy of belief or even debate:

> All people unhesitatingly believe that they feel themselves thinking, and that they distinguish the mental state as an inward activity or passion, from all the objects with which it may cognitively deal. *I regard this belief as the most fundamental of all the postulates of Psychology*, and shall discard all curious inquiries about its certainty as too metaphysical for the scope of this book.[24]

The proper subject of psychology was, therefore, the introspective analysis of the "states of mind" that we are conscious of in daily life and of the functions they perform for the organism.

(We will pass by what James had to say about physiological psychology in *Principles*, since there is little in those chapters that is distinctively Jamesian except for the lucid and often poetic prose.)

The nature of mind: Although James rejected the materialism of physiological psychology, he could not accept the alternative of classic dualism, the theory that mind is a separate entity or substance parallel to and independent of the body. Not only was this wholly unprovable, but Fechner and Donders, among others, had already shown that certain physiological responses to stimuli caused certain states of mind.[25]

James examined every major solution to the mind-body problem, found fault with each, and finally settled for a dualism of perspective. There are external objects, and our knowledge of those objects; there is a material world, and a set of mind states relating to them.[26] The latter are not mere brain states caused by external things; they are *mental* states that can interact with one another and, within the realm of mind, obey their own causal laws.

Whatever the ultimate nature of mental states, James said, psychologists should lay aside the whole mind-body question. Psychology was in no way ready or able to spell out the connections between physiological states and mental states, and its proper concern, for the present, was the description and explanation of such processes as reasoning, attention, will, imagination, memory, and feelings. From James's time on, this would be the dominant view within many branches of American psychology—the study of personality and individual differences, educational psychology, abnormal psychology, child development studies, social psychology; everything, indeed, except experimental psychology, much of which would be behaviorist and anti-"mentalist" for many decades.

The stream of thought: Using introspective analysis as the major approach to investigating the conscious mind, James asserted that the reality most immediately perceived by that method is the unbroken flow of complex conscious thought:

> Most books start with sensations, as the simplest mental facts, and proceed synthetically, constructing each higher stage from those below it. But this is abandoning the empirical method of investigation. No one ever had a simple sensation by itself. Consciousness, from our natal day, is of a teeming multiplicity of objects and relations. The only thing which psychology has a right to postulate at the outset is the fact of thinking itself. *The first fact for us, then, as psychologists is that thinking of some sort goes on.* I use the word thinking for every form of consciousness indiscriminately. If we could say in English "it thinks," as we say "it rains" or "it blows," we should be stating the fact most simply and with the minimum of assumption. As we cannot, we must simply say that *thought goes on.*[27]

James considered consciousness not a *thing* but a process or *function.* Just as breathing is what the lungs do, conducting conscious mental life is what the brain does. Why does it? "For the sake of steering a nervous system grown too complex to regulate itself."[28] Consciousness allows the organism to consider past, present, and future states of affairs, and, with the predictive power thus achieved, to plan ahead and adapt its behavior to the circumstances.[29] Consciousness is "a fighter for ends, of which many, but for its presence, would not be ends at all."[30] The chief one is survival; that is its function.

On further introspection, we notice that consciousness has certain characteristics. Of the five James named, the most interesting—because it contradicted traditional Aristotelian conceptions of thinking—is that each person's consciousness is a continuum, not a series of linked experiences or thoughts:

> Consciousness, then, does not appear to itself chopped in bits. Such words as "chain" or "train" do not describe it fitly as it presents itself in the first instance. It is nothing jointed; it flows. A "river" or a "stream" is the metaphor by which it is most naturally described. *In talking of it*

hereafter, let us call it the stream of thought, of consciousness, or of subjective life.[31]

While the objects of our thoughts or perceptions may seem distinct and separate, our consciousness of them is itself a continuous flow; they are like things floating in a stream.

The concept of the stream of thought (or, as it is better known, the stream of consciousness) struck a responsive chord among psychologists and became useful and important in both research and clinical work. It also was immediately taken up by a number of authors who sought to write in a stream-of-consciousness style, among them Marcel Proust, James Joyce, Virginia Woolf, and Gertrude Stein. (Stein actually studied under James at Harvard.)

The self: Even breaks in consciousness, such as those occurring in sleep, do not interrupt the continuity of the stream; when we awaken, we have no difficulty making the connection with our own stream of consciousness, with who we were and are. But that is because of another major characteristic of consciousness: its *personal* nature. Thoughts are not merely thoughts; they are *my* thoughts or *your* thoughts. There is a personal self that separates one's consciousness from that of others and that knows, from moment to moment and day to day, that I am the same I who I was a moment ago, a day, decade, or lifetime ago.[32]

From the beginnings of psychology, thinkers had struggled with the problem of who or what knows that I am I and that my experiences have all happened to the same Me. What substance or entity, what watcher or monitor, accounts for the sense of selfhood and of continuous identity? James called this "the most puzzling puzzle with which psychology has to deal."[33]

The classic answer was the soul or transcendental self. But a century earlier both Hume and Kant had shown that we can have no empirical knowledge of such a self.[34] Philosophers might still speculate about it, but psychologists could not observe or study it. Accordingly, the experimental psychologists of the nineteenth century did not even discuss the self, and the British associationists sloughed it off as no more than the connected chain of passing thoughts.

James, however, felt that "the belief in a distinct principle of selfhood" was an integral part of the "common sense of mankind,"[35] and found a way to restore to psychology a meaningful—and researchable—concept of self. We are all conscious of our individual identity, we think of certain things as *me* and *mine*; these *feelings* and the *acts* associated with them can be investigated and thus are the "empirical self."

The empirical self has several components: the material self (our body, clothing, possessions, family, home); the social self or selves (who we are and how we behave in relation to the different people in our lives—an anticipation of social psychology, which would not emerge as a specialty for decades); and the spiritual self, a person's inner or subjective being, his entire collection of psychic faculties or dispositions. All these can be explored by introspection and observation; the empirical self is, after all, researchable.

But this still leaves unsolved that most puzzling puzzle of all. What accounts for the sense of me-ness, selfhood, and identity, the sure knowledge that I am who I was a while ago? James identified such thoughts as belonging to the "pure Ego," a wholly subjective phenomenon, and suggested that its perception of continuing personal identity arises from the continuity of the stream of consciousness: "Resemblance among the parts of a continuum of feelings (especially bodily feelings) . . . constitutes the real and verifiable 'personal identity' which we feel."[36]

This being so, James said, psychology need not postulate a watcher or soul that observes the knowing mind and maintains a sense of identity: "[The soul] is at all events needless for expressing the actual subjective phenomena of consciousness as they appear."[37] He stated this powerful conclusion even more forcefully in Jimmy:

> The states of consciousness are all that psychology needs to do her work with. Metaphysics or theology may prove the Soul to exist; but for psychology the hypothesis of such a substantial principle of unity is superfluous.[38]

Will: Some commentators say that James's most valuable contribution to psychology was his theory of the will, the conscious process that directs voluntary movements.[39]

Much of James's discussion of the will in *Principles* was neurophysiological, dealing with how the will generates the nerve impulses that produce the desired muscular movements. But the far more interesting question he took up was how we come to will any act in the first place. The key factor, in his view, was a supply of information and experience about our ability to achieve a desired end:

We desire to feel, to have, to do, all sorts of things which at the moment are not felt, had, or done. If with the desire there goes a sense that attainment is not possible, we simply *wish*; but if we believe that the end is in our power, we *will* that the desired feeling, having, or doing shall be real; and real it presently becomes, either immediately upon the willing or after certain preliminaries have been fulfilled.[40]

How do we sense that the end is in our power? Through experience; through the knowledge of what different actions of ours would achieve: "A supply of ideas of the various movements that are possible, left in the memory by experiences of their involuntary performance, is thus the first prerequisite of the voluntary life."[41] Infants trying to grasp a toy make numerous random movements of their arms and hands, and sooner or later connect with the toy; they eventually become capable of willing the proper movement. In analogous fashion, adults accumulate a vast repertoire of ideas of different actions and their probable consequences; we walk, talk, eat, and perform myriad other activities by willing the appropriate actions and achieving the desired ends.

Much of the time we will our routine actions unhesitatingly, because we feel no conflict about what we want to do. But at other times conflicting notions exist in our mind: we want to do A but we also want to do B, its contrary. In such cases, what determines which action we will? James's answer: we weigh the possibilities against each other, decide to ignore all but one, and thereby let that one become the reality. When we have made the choice, the will takes over; or perhaps one could say, Choosing which idea to ignore and which to attend to *is* the act of willing.[42]

James gave one of his inimitably personal examples. He is lying abed of a chilly morning, he says, knowing how late he will be if he does not get up and what duties will remain undone, but hating the way getting up will feel and preferring the way staying in bed feels. At last he deliberately inhibits all thoughts except that of what he must do that day — and lo and behold, the thought, made the center of his attention, produces the appropriate movements and he is up and out of bed.[43] "The essential achievement of the will, in short, when it is most 'voluntary,' is to ATTEND to a difficult object and hold it fast before the mind . . . Effort of attention is thus the essential phenomenon of will."[44]

Sometimes making the choice is instant and simple, sometimes protracted and the result of deliberation, reasoning, and decision making. Whatever the process, in every case the mind is a cause of behavior, an intervenor in cause-and-effect relationships, and not an automaton responding passively to outside influences. Voluntary action implies *freedom* of the will.

James himself, as we know, had come to believe in free will during his emotional crisis; that belief had enabled him to climb out of his Slough of Despond. But he still had to reconcile that belief with the basic tenet of scientific psychology: All behavior is, or ultimately will be, explicable, and every act has its causes. If every act is the result of determinable causes, how can there be any freedom for us to choose one of several possible, not wholly determined, futures? Yet we all experience what feels like freedom of will every time we make a decision to do, or not to do, anything, however trifling or however weighty.

James was utterly candid: "My own belief is that the question of free-will is insoluble on strictly psychologic grounds." The psychologist wants to build a science, and a science is a system of fixed relations, but free will is not a fixed and calculable relationship; it is beyond science and so is best left to metaphysics. Psychology will be psychology, whether free will is real or not.[45]

But he insisted that a belief in free will is pragmatically sensible and necessary. He developed his philosophy of pragmatism after turning away from psychology, but its seeds exist in *Principles*. James's pragmatism does not say, as crude oversimplifications of it aver, that "truth is what works"; it does say that if we compare the implications of opposed solutions to a problem, we can choose which one to believe in and act on.[46] To believe in total determinism would make us passive and impotent; to believe in free will allows us to consider alternatives, to plan, and to act on our plans. It is thus practical and realistic:

> The brain is an instrument of possibilities, but of no certainties. But the consciousness, with its own ends present to it, and knowing also well which possibilities lead thereto and which away, will, if endowed with causal efficacy, reinforce the favorable possibilities and repress the unfavorable or indifferent ones . . . If [consciousness] is useful, it must be so through its causal efficaciousness, and the automaton-theory must succumb to the theory of common-sense.[47]

As solid and enduring as these observations are, some parts of James's discussion of will sound curiously old-fashioned today. In his discussions of "unhealthiness of will," the "exaggerated impulsion" of the alcoholic or the drug user, or the "obstructed will" of the immobilized person, one hears genuine compassion for people in a diseased state—and overtones of moralistic disapproval:

> No class of [persons] have better sentiments or feel more constantly the difference between the higher and the lower path in life than the hopeless failures, the sentimentalists, the drunkards, the schemers, the "dead-beats," whose life is one long contradiction between knowledge and action, and who, with full command of theory, never get to holding their limp characters erect.[48]

James's psychology of will was an important feature of American psychology for some years, but during the long reign of behaviorism—from about 1920 to the 1960s—the topic all but disappeared from American psychology; there was no place in that deterministic system for any behavior initiated by the organism itself. Nor has will come back into fashion since then, at least not under that name; the word does not even appear in the index of many a contemporary psychology textbook.

Yet James's psychology of will is, in fact, part of the mainstream of modern psychology under other names: "purposive behavior," "intentionality," "decision making," "self-control," "choices," "self-efficacy," and so on. Modern psychologists, especially clinicians, believe that behavior is, or eventually will be, wholly explicable, yet that human beings can to some degree direct their own behavior. If psychologists have not yet been able to answer how both these notions can be true at the same time, they often settle for William James's own conclusion: the belief that we cannot affect our own behavior produces disastrous results; the belief that we can, produces beneficial results.

The unconscious: James's psychology was concerned almost entirely with conscious mental life; in some parts of *Principles* one gets the impression that there are no unconscious mental states and that whatever takes place in the mind is, by definition, conscious. But in a number of places James took a different view of the matter.

In discussing voluntary acts, he carefully distinguished between those which we perform by consciously commanding muscular movements and those others—the great bulk of voluntary acts—which, long performed and practiced, immediately and automatically follow the mental choice as if of themselves. We walk, climb stairs, put on or take off our clothing, without thinking of the movements that are necessary: "It is a general principle in Psychology that consciousness deserts all processes where it can no longer be of use."[49] In many kinds of familiar activity, we actually do better when not thinking about the movements required:

> We pitch or catch, we shoot or chop the better the less tactile and muscular (the less resident), and the more exclusively optical (the more remote), our consciousness is. Keep your *eye* on the place aimed at, and your hand will fetch it; think of your hand, and you will very likely miss your aim.[50]

James thus anticipated modern learning research, which has shown that with practice, complex voluntary movements such as those of piano playing, driving, or playing tennis become "overlearned" and are largely carried out unconsciously as soon as the conscious mind issues a general order.

He also recognized that when we do not attend to experiences, we may remain mostly unconscious of them even though they have their normal effect on our sense organs: "Our insensibility to habitual noises, etc., whilst awake, proves that we can neglect to attend to that which we nevertheless feel."[51]

James was well aware of the role of the unconscious in particular phenomena of abnormal psychology, citing, among other examples, cases of hysterical blindness reported by the French psychologist Alfred Binet: "M. Binet has found the hand of his patients unconsciously writing down words which their eyes were vainly endeavoring to 'see.' "[52] But with his focus on conscious mental life, James could not conceive of knowledge as ever being entirely unconscious; he felt that somehow, somewhere, all knowledge was conscious. He followed another French contemporary, Pierre Janet, in holding that such seemingly unconscious knowledge was the result of a split personality; what the primary personality was unconscious of was "consciously" known to the split-off secondary personality.[53]

James explained certain aspects of the hypnotic state the same way, in particular post-hypnotic suggestion, in which the patient, given an instruction during the trance, carries it out after being awakened but remains completely unaware of having been told to do so.[54] The split-personality hypothesis was awkward, limited, and unverified by empirical evidence, but in presenting it, James was at least recognizing, well before the unconscious was generally accepted as a reality, that certain mental states occur outside primary consciousness.

In the years after the publication of *Principles*, James expanded his view of the unconscious, relying on it to account for dreams, automatic writing, "demoniacal possession," and many of the mystical experiences reported in *The Varieties of Religious Experience*. Unlike Freud, who was beginning to publish his own views about the unconscious, James did not consider the unconscious a source of motivation or the mind's way of banishing impermissible sexual wishes from awareness.[55] Yet as early as 1896 James spoke of the possible usefulness of Freudian discoveries for the relief of hysterical symptoms, and after hearing Freud's Clark University lectures in 1909 he said, "I hope that Freud and his pupils will push their ideas to their utmost limits . . . They can't fail to throw light on human nature."[56]

Emotion: One minor theory advanced by James became more famous and led to far more research than any of the foregoing large-scale theories. This was his theory of emotion, which was as simple as it was revolutionary. The emotion we feel is not what causes such bodily symptoms as a racing heart or sweaty palms; rather, the nervous system, reacting to an external stimulus, produces those physical symptoms, and our perception of them is what we call an emotion. This statement is so intriguing and persuasive that it deserves to be quoted at length:

> Our natural way of thinking . . . is that the mental perception of some fact excites the mental affection called the emotion, and that this latter state of mind gives rise to the bodily expression. My theory, on the contrary, is that *the bodily changes follow directly the perception of the exciting fact, and that our feeling of the same changes as they occur* IS *the emotion*. Common-sense says, we lose our fortune, are sorry and weep; we meet a bear, are frightened and run; we are insulted by a rival, are angry and strike. The hypothesis here to be defended says that this order of sequence is incorrect, that the one mental state is not immediately induced by the other, that the bodily manifestations must first be interposed between, and that the more rational statement is that we feel sorry because we cry, angry because we strike, afraid because we tremble.[57]

He based this on introspection; one had only to look searchingly within to perceive that one's emotions develop their power from their physical manifestations:

> Without the bodily states following on the perception, the latter would

be purely cognitive in form, pale, colorless, destitute of emotional warmth. We might then see the bear, and judge it best to run, receive the insult and deem it right to strike, but we should not actually *feel* afraid or angry.[58]

Virtually the same theory was advanced at about the same time by a Danish physiologist, Carl Lange, whose work James acknowledged. Although he and Lange did not collaborate on the theory, it soon became known as the James-Lange theory, and is discussed, under that name, in today's textbooks.

The theory has had a curious history. It immediately provoked much controversy and research, and eventually was shown to be faulty in a number of ways. Walter Cannon, a Harvard physiologist, demonstrated in 1927 that certain dissimilar emotions are accompanied by generally similar bodily reactions; the physical responses are not specific enough to account for the different emotions. Both anger and fear, for instance, are marked by a speeded-up heart rate and an elevated blood pressure. Moreover, said Cannon, visceral reaction times are slow but emotional reactions are often immediate; physical changes thus cannot always precede the emotion.[59] Cannon concluded that an emotional stimulus activates the thalamus (more recent research has, instead, pinpointed the hypothalamus and limbic system); from the brain, messages go out both to the autonomic nervous system, generating visceral changes, and to the cerebral cortex, creating the subjective feelings of the emotion.

Yet the James-Lange theory is still highly regarded by psychologists. It was correct in postulating that emotions have physical causes, although more recent and more complex explanations are based on physiological research with animals and psychological research with humans; evidence from these studies indicates that the arousing stimulus activates autonomic nervous processes in the brain, sending signals both to the body and to the mind, while other evidence shows that the experience of emotion is often the joint result of physiological arousal and cognitive appraisal based on experience and the situation.[60] Despite the James-Lange theory's shortcomings, it has practical applications. To the degree that we control a physiological response to a stimulus, we govern the associated emotion. We count to ten to control rage, whistle to keep up courage, go running or play tennis to shake off depression. Many contemporary psychotherapists teach their patients to perform relaxation exercises to reduce anxiety or fear and to practice standing, walking, and talking in a confident manner to engender a feeling of confidence in themselves. In the 1980s the psychologist Paul Ekman and his colleagues at the University of California School of Medicine, San Francisco, showed that when volunteers consciously make facial expressions associated with certain emotions—surprise, disgust, sadness, anger, fear, happiness—they affect their heart rates and skin temperatures and induce in themselves a modicum of the appropriate emotion.[61] The physical expression of the emotion arouses a degree of the emotion; the James-Lange theory was partly correct after all.

Jamesian Paradoxes

Anyone who reads James's psychological writings is bound to be frequently puzzled: James is always clear and persuasive, but often equally so on opposing sides of an issue. He is chronically self-contradictory, not out of muddleheadedness but because he is intellectually too expansive to be confined within a closed or consistent system of thought. Gordon Allport, a leading psychological researcher and theorist of several decades ago, summed up James's chameleonlike qualities:

> In the *Principles* alone, we find brilliant, baffling, unashamed contradictions. He is, for example, both a positivist and a phenomenologist. On Tuesdays, Thursdays, and Saturdays, he points in the direction of behaviorism and positivism, although he seems more exuberantly natural on Mondays, Wednesdays, Fridays, and Sundays, when he writes about the stream of consciousness, the varieties of religious experience, and the moral equivalent for war.[62]

Allport, however, found this inconsistency a virtue. He spoke of James's "productive paradoxes"; seeing both sides of a question often laid open the kernel of a problem and left it ready for others to work on.[63]

But the result was that James's influence on psychology, though great, was fragmented; though pervasive, was never dominant. James avoided creating a system, founded no school, trained few graduate students, and had no band of followers. Remarkably, however, a number of his ideas became part of mainstream psychology, particularly in America. Wundt won out over James as far as laboratory methods and experimentation were concerned; James's psychology, with its richness, realism, and pragmatism, won out over the Wundtian system.[64] As Raymond Fancher has said:

James transformed psychology from a somewhat recondite and abstract science that some students avoided because of the difficulty of introspective methodology, into a discipline that spoke directly to personal interests and concerns. James's characterization of psychology as a "nasty little subject" that excludes all one would want to know is nowhere more clearly belied than in his own textbooks on psychology.[65]

Outside the mainstream, James influenced psychology in two other respects, both of them practical. One: His suggested applications of psychological principles to teaching became the core of educational psychology. The other: In 1909, James, as an executive committee member of the National Committee for Mental Hygiene, was largely responsible for getting the Rockefeller Foundation and similar groups to allocate millions of dollars to the mental hygiene movement, the development of mental hospitals, and the training of mental health professionals.

When the American Psychological Association celebrated its seventy-fifth anniversary in 1977, the opening speaker, David Krech, spoke of William James as "our father who begat us." Referring to the past three quarters of a century of work on questions James had raised, Krech said, "Even if I were to total up all advances in gains and achievements and multiply them by a factor of hope, the total would still not suffice as an adequate tribute to lay at James's feet."[66]

SEVEN

Explorer of the Depths: Sigmund Freud

The Truth About Freud

More than any other figure in the annals of psychology, Sigmund Freud has been both extravagantly praised and savagely castigated for his theories, venerated and condemned as a person, and regarded as a great scientist, a cult leader, and a fraud. His admirers and critics agree that his impact on psychology, the psychotherapies, and the way human beings in Western society think about themselves has been larger than that of anyone else in the history of the science; for the rest, they seem to be talking about different people and different bodies of knowledge.

The sociologist and Freud scholar Philip Rieff said in 1959 that "the greatness of the man is beyond question, complementing the greatness of his mind," and rated his writing "perhaps the most important body of thought committed to paper in the twentieth century." But several years later a well-known scholar and humanities professor, Erich Heller, asserted in the *Times Literary Supplement* that Freud was one of the most overrated figures of our time, and Nobel Laureate Sir Peter Medawar called psychoanalytic theory "the most stupendous intellectual confidence trick of the century."

The political scientist Paul Roazen judged Freud to be "unquestionably one of the greatest psychologists of history" and "a great thinker," and the theologian Paul Tillich considered him "the most profound of all the depth psychologists." But an English scholar, E. M. Thornton, gathered up bits of evidence that, in her opinion, prove "that [Freud's] central postulate, the 'unconscious mind,' does not exist, that his theories were baseless and aberrational," that he formulated them while under the influence of cocaine, and that he was "a false and faithless prophet."

Freud's admirers, including the historian Peter Gay, author of a massive 1988 biography, see him as a brave and heroic fighter for truth. His detractors see him as a neurotic and ambitious egotist who sought notice by propounding fantastic theories. In two lengthy diatribes in *The New York Review of Books* in 1993 and 1994, and later in other writings, Frederick Crews, a professor of English literature, established himself as perhaps the most savage of the many Freud bashers, saying that as a therapy psychoanalysis is "indifferently successful" and "vastly inefficient"; that as an empirical approach to scientific knowledge it is "fatally contaminated" by assuming, in dialogue with patients, the very ideas it seeks to corroborate; that Freud himself was "indifferent to his patients' suffering" and that they achieved only mediocre or negative therapeutic results; that he often sought to "nail" the patient "with hastily conceived interpretations which he then drove home unabatingly"; and so on and on.

Most historians of psychology credit Freud with a long string of influential discoveries, the most noteworthy being that of the dynamic unconscious. But Frank Sulloway, a historian of science, has learnedly argued that Freud's concepts were largely "creative transformations" of ideas already extant in neurology and biology, and the scholar Henri Ellenberger has painstakingly made the case that Freud's discovery of the dynamic unconscious merely crystallized and gave shape to diffuse ideas that had already been put forward by many of his predecessors and contemporaries.

Freud saw himself, and most of his biographers have seen him, as an outsider—an isolated Jew in anti-Semitic Vienna—courageously battling medical conservatives to bring humanity the benefit of his discoveries. His disparagers say that he exaggerated the anti-Semitism around him in order to present himself as an embattled hero and that in any case he got many of his ideas from his friend Wilhelm Fliess but passed them off as his own.

What is one to make of such contradictions?

But, then, what is one to make of a man who was himself a bundle of contradictions?[1] Radical in his theories about human nature and a militant atheist, Freud was, except in his early years, a political conservative. He espoused liberated attitudes toward sexuality but was himself a model of decorum and sexual restraint. He claimed that he rid himself of his own neuroses through his famous self-analysis, but throughout his life suffered from assorted neurotic symptoms, among them migraine headaches, urinary and bowel problems, an almost morbid dislike of the telephone, a tendency to faint at times of intense interpersonal stress, and a pathological addiction to cigars. (He smoked twenty a day and could not stop even after he developed cancer of the jaw as a result.) He hated Vienna and was never part of its easygoing café society but could not bring himself to leave it for any more congenial place until 1938, when he moved to London after the Nazi takeover of Austria.

At times, he was unabashedly egotistical; he likened himself to Copernicus and Darwin, and told an admirer of one of his later works, "This is my worst book, the book of an old man. The genuine Freud was really a great man."[2] At other times he was unassuming and modest; late in life, in "An Autobiographical Study," he wrote:

> Looking back, then, over the patchwork of my life's labors, I can say that I have made many beginnings and thrown out many suggestions. Something will come of them in the future, though I cannot myself tell whether it will be much or little. I can, however, express a hope that I have opened up a pathway for an important advance in our knowledge.[3]

He was surrounded by a large and loving family and a circle of devoted followers but over the years fought with a number of his closest friends and disciples. In his seventies he ruefully wrote:

> I cannot count on the love of many people. I have not pleased, comforted, edified them. Nor was this my intention; I only wanted to explore, solve riddles, uncover a little of the truth.[4]

In photographs, Freud invariably looks formal and grave — impeccably dressed, neatly barbered, somber and unsmiling — yet his own writings and the reminiscences of those who knew him well attest that he was uncommonly witty and that he loved telling funny stories with a psychological point to them. An example from his study of humor, *Jokes and Their Relation to the Unconscious*:

> If [a doctor] enquires from a youthful patient whether he has ever had anything to do with masturbation, the answer is sure to be: "O, *na,*

nie!" [German for "Oh, no, never"—but in German *Onanie* means "masturbation"].[5]

And a longer joke, of the kind Freud enjoying telling and told well:

The *Schadchen* [Jewish marriage broker] was defending the girl he had proposed against the young man's protests. "I don't care for the mother-in-law," said the latter. "She's a disagreeable, stupid person."— "But after all you're not marrying the mother-in-law. What you want is her daughter."—"Yes, but she's not young any longer, and she's not precisely a beauty."—"No matter. If she's neither young nor beautiful she'll be all the more faithful to you."—"And she hasn't much money."—"Who's talking about money? Are you marrying money then? After all it's a wife that you want."—"But she's got a hunchback too."—"Well, what *do* you want? Isn't she to have a single fault?"[6]

Evidently, the truth about Freud is, to say the least, no simple matter. But let us see what we can see.

The Would-Be Neuroscientist

One thing about Freud is obvious and indisputable: unlike the majority of noted psychologists of his time, he came from far outside the mainstream of his culture and in terms of background was most unlikely to become a towering figure in the discipline.

He was born in 1856 in Freiberg, a small town in Moravia (then part of the Austro-Hungarian Empire), the son of an impoverished itinerant Jewish trader in woolens, cloth, hides, and raw foodstuffs. At home, as a boy, he heard nothing of science, let alone modern psychology, and none of his ancestors had ever attended a university or even a gymnasium; by all odds, he should have become a small-time merchant like his father, Jacob.

For his first several years, he, his middle-aged father—who had been married before and raised another family—and his young mother lived in a single rented room that was soon further crowded by a baby sister. When Sigmund was four the family moved to Vienna, where, though his father's business gradually improved, the family's growth—eventually there were seven children—made for many hard years.

Freud thus had reason for his lifelong anxiety about money. And about his place in society; although by the 1860s legal reforms in the empire had freed Jews to live outside the ghetto and to attend gymnasia and universities, they remained social outcasts and were barred from practicing most professions or holding high public office.

Freud was doubly an outsider. His father had thrown off the Orthodox faith of his forebears and become a freethinker, possibly in the futile hope of being assimilated into Gentile society, and although Freud always considered himself a Jew and consorted mainly with fellow Jews, he was, he once told a Protestant friend, "a totally Godless Jew," belonging to no congregation and taking no part in the life of the Jewish community. It is not surprising that he would later seek from psychology answers to questions so unlike those asked by Helmholtz, Wundt, and James, the outstanding psychologists of his youth. In their separate ways they asked, "How does the mind work?" while Freud would ask, "What am I and what made me that way?" But he would do so only after many years of trying to become a scientist in the mold of Helmholtz.

At Freud's birth, a peasant woman had prophesied to his mother that he would become a great man, and his parents often told him the story during his boyhood. Whether for that reason or others, he early became extremely ambitious and diligent in his studies and was first in his class in the gymnasium for seven years. Law and medicine were the two professions then open to Jews, and in his final year at the gymnasium, after reading an inspiring essay by Goethe on Nature, he decided to spend his life in science. In 1873 he enrolled in the medical school at the University of Vienna; there, despite his exclusion from the fellowship of his anti-Semitic classmates—or perhaps because of it—he excelled as a student.

But medicine, he discovered, had little intellectual appeal for him, and as for actual practice, he found the prospect repellent. Partway through medical training he came under the spell of Ernst Brücke, professor of physiology and a co-founder, with Emil Du Bois-Reymond, of the Berlin Physical Society, the nucleus of the mechanist-physiological school that had dominated psychology for a generation. Freud was impressed by Brücke's presentation of physiological psychology and charmed by his warm and fatherly demeanor. Brücke, nearly forty years older than Freud—as was Freud's own father—took a personal interest in his brilliant young student and became both scientific mentor and father-figure to him. Freud later said that Brücke "carried more weight with me than anyone else in my whole life,"[7] a remarkable statement for one who spent nearly fifty years developing a subjective, introspective psychology totally unlike Brücke's.

But Freud's concern with introspection would come later. As a serious, hardworking medical student, he had no time for and no interest in inward-looking psychology; indeed, he was so taken by the physiological approach to psychology that he delayed the completion of his medical studies to do research in Brücke's Physiological Institute. There, the person one always envisions as sitting unseen behind a couch listening to the ruminations of neurotic patients spent much of his six-year stay at laboratory tables, dissecting fish and crayfish, tracing their nerve pathways, and peering at nerve cells through a microscope.

Intellectually committed to physiological psychology, he hoped to become a physiologist and do pure research. But Brücke advised against this. Freud had no money—he still lived at home and was supported by his father—and at that time a career in pure science was impossible for a person without an independent income unless he could count on achieving a high academic position, which a Jew could not. Freud gave up the dream, reluctantly completed his medical studies, and received his M.D. in 1881.

He hung on briefly at the institute but the next year met and fell in love with a friend of one of his sisters, an attractive young woman named Martha Bernays, and soon proposed marriage. She was entranced by the darkly handsome young doctor and accepted the offer, though they would not be able to marry until he could support a wife and family. The most feasible way for him to do so was to enter private practice, but he needed clinical experience and training in a specialty he could tolerate. Neurology being the specialty closest to neuroscience, he left Brücke's institute and joined the Vienna General Hospital, where he studied under Theodor Meynert, then the world's leading brain anatomist, and over the next three years became expert at diagnosing different kinds of brain damage and disease.

(During this time, as nearly everyone knows, Freud briefly experimented with cocaine. He used it himself and touted it in medical circles as a valuable analgesic and antidepressant until, seeing its destructive effects on a friend who became addicted to it, he abandoned it. By then, however, he had made himself suspect in the Viennese medical community.)

His years of hard work at the General Hospital were lonely and dispiriting; Martha Bernays lived with her mother in Hamburg, and Freud saw his fiancée only at long intervals and then for brief periods. He wrote to her and she to him almost daily; in his chatty, loving letters, he envisioned himself as Dr. Sigmund Freud, Neurologist in Private Practice, earning a good living, happily married to his beloved Martha, and raising a family. Only rarely did he write of some inner turmoil (for instance: "I have been so caught up in myself, and then I have days on end — they invariably follow one another, it is like a recurring sickness — when my spirits decline for no apparent reason"[8]), but there is no hint in the letters that he would someday search his psyche in an effort to understand his distress, no premonition that deep-probing psychology would drive neurology out of his mind and life.

The Hypnotherapist

Freud's move toward his unique career was initiated by his friendship and collaboration with Josef Breuer, a successful physician and physiologist fourteen years his senior whom he had met through Brücke. Despite the gap in age and status, Breuer and Freud became close friends, and Freud was a frequent visitor in the Breuer home. The friendship grew particularly close as Freud gained medical experience at the General Hospital and was able to discuss cases with Breuer.

In November 1882, Breuer told Freud about one of his patients, a young woman suffering from hysteria whom he had treated for a year and a half. Known to history by the case-study pseudonym Anna O., she was Bertha Pappenheim, a pampered, overprotected daughter of wealthy Jewish parents and a friend of Martha Bernays's. Freud was fascinated by the case, got Breuer to go over it with him in great detail, and a dozen years later co-authored with Breuer a report that is often called the first case of psychoanalysis, although in actuality it was only the seed from which psychoanalysis sprouted and grew.[9]

Bertha Pappenheim, an attractive, intellectual woman of twenty-one, was deeply attached to her father and had nursed him during his illness until she became bedridden with severe hysterical symptoms, including loss of appetite, muscular weakness, paralysis of the right arm, and a severe nervous cough. Her father died two months later, and she then became much worse. She suffered from hallucinations of black snakes and skeletons, speech difficulties (at times she was unable to speak in her native German, though she could speak in English, French, or Italian), the inability to drink even when painfully thirsty, and periods of "absence" or somnolent confusion that she called "time missing."

Breuer told Freud that he had visited her regularly but could not help her until he accidentally stumbled on a curious method of doing so.

During her "absences," she would mutter words that arose from a train of thought, and Breuer found that by lightly hypnotizing her, he could get her to use these words as a starting point to reproduce for him the images and fantasies in her mind—after which, strangely, she would be free of mental confusion for a number of hours. The next day she might relapse into another absence, but Breuer could again dispel it by another light hypnosis. She called it "the talking cure" or sometimes "chimney sweeping."

Breuer also told Freud that the talking cure could do much more than temporarily relieve her mental confusion; if he could get her to remember under hypnosis when, and in what connection, a particular symptom first appeared, the symptom would disappear. In one session, for instance, she traced her inability to drink water back to a time when she saw a little dog drink from a water glass and was disgusted by the sight; when she came out of the trance she was able to drink and the symptom never returned. Similarly, the talking cure rid her of the paralysis in her right arm after she recalled that one time, while tending her father, that arm was draped over the back of the chair and became numb, at which point she had had a dream of a black snake approaching and of being unable to use her arm to fend it off.

By this method Breuer tackled her symptoms one by one and brought them all under control. But one evening, he told Freud, he found her confused again and writhing with abdominal cramps. He asked her what was the matter. "Now comes Dr. B.'s child," she said.[10] He realized with alarm that she was undergoing a hysterical pregnancy stemming from fantasies about him. He abruptly referred her to a colleague, went on vacation with his wife, and treated Bertha Pappenheim no more.

She had not, in fact, been cured by the catharsis of the talking cure but only temporarily relieved of her symptoms. It remained for Freud to discover years later that such patients needed to do more than remember the events that triggered each symptom; they had to search for their hidden meanings. In most cases, he would find, these were sexual, as in the episode of "Dr. B.'s child." But Breuer was uncomfortable with the topic of sexuality, and though at the moment of the hysterical pregnancy he had "had the key in his hand" (as Freud later wrote to a friend), "he dropped it . . . [and] in conventional horror took to flight."[11]

(Bertha Pappenheim spent some time in a sanatorium, where she eventually recovered. She went on to have a successful career, first as housemother in an orphanage, then as head of an institution for unwed mothers and young prostitutes, and the leader of a long-term campaign to protect "endangered girls." She never married and had no recorded love life; the sexual problems underlying her hysteria were not cured but sublimated—a process Freud would later elucidate—in good works for fallen women.[12])

In 1886, four years after Breuer told him about that case, Freud, then thirty-one, opened an office (and later that year married Martha) and began private practice as a specialist in neurological and brain disorders, which he treated with such physical therapies as were then available. But few patients arrived, and he was glad to get Breuer's referrals of patients suffering from hysteria. Freud had recently taken special training in that subject; he had gone to Paris for several months on a small grant from Brücke's Neurological Institute to study under Jean Martin Charcot, the noted neuropathologist and director of the Salpêtrière hospital. Charcot was, among other things, the discoverer of the phenomenon of hysteria. He was also a skilled hypnotist, but he hypnotized hysterics only to get them to display the symptoms of hysteria to his students. He believed that hysteria, though it may have been triggered by some traumatic event, such as a railroad accident, resulted from a hereditarily weak neurological system, and he considered the disease progressive and irreversible.

Impressed by Charcot's views, Freud at first treated his own hysterical patients as if the neurosis were indeed a neurological disorder. For the most part he used "electrotherapy," a method in vogue at the time; he applied electrodes to the affected part of the body and delivered a mild electric current that produced a tingling or muscular twitch. He had some initial success with the method, but his familiarity with hypnosis led him to suspect that the benefits were due less to the electric current than to suggestion—his assurance to the patient that the treatment would dispel the symptom.

With this in mind, he began the more direct use of hypnotic suggestion, although this was disapproved of in Viennese medical circles and considered close to quackery. Freud knew that members of the "Nancy School" in France, followers of the medical hypnotist Auguste Liébeault, of whom we heard earlier, were treating hysteria by posthypnotic suggestion. They would hypnotize their patients and tell them that the symptom would disappear when they awoke from the trance. Freud adopted the technique and was delighted by the results. In December 1887 he wrote to Wilhelm Fliess, a Berlin ear, nose, and throat specialist he had met that year and with whom he had struck up a close friendship, "During the last few weeks I have plunged into hypnotism, and have had all sorts of small but peculiar successes."[13]

But all too soon he found to his sorrow that the relief was usually partial and temporary, so he took a different tack, using hypnosis as Breuer had with Bertha Pappenheim. For several years Freud hypnotized hysterics and asked them to recall and talk about the "traumatic event" that first brought about a particular symptom. He had fairly good results with some, but, disappointingly, either the improvement was temporary or the banished symptom was replaced by a different one. Moreover, the technique was inapplicable to the many patients who could not be hypnotized.

Despite these limitations, in the course of half a dozen years Breuer and he discussed a series of cases—Bertha Pappenheim and Freud's more recent patients—and gradually worked out a theory of hysteria that, unlike Charcot's, was wholly psychological. They concluded that "hysterics suffer from reminiscences"—memories of emotionally painful experiences—that have somehow been excluded from consciousness. As long as such memories remain forgotten, the emotion associated with them is "strangulated" or bottled up and converted into physical energy, taking the form of a physical symptom. When the memory is recovered through hypnosis, the emotion can be felt and expressed, and the symptom disappears.

This was the gist of a brief paper that Breuer and Freud published in 1893[14] and of a lengthy, detailed work published in 1895, *Studies on Hysteria*, which reported on Breuer's one case and four of Freud's, presented their theory of hysteria, and discussed the relief of symptoms by hypnotic catharsis—and by a better method Freud had discovered that abandoned hypnosis altogether and brought about not temporary relief but actual cure.

The Invention of Psychoanalysis

No historical or sociological account of scientific progress can adequately explain the sudden appearance of psychoanalysis and its discoveries of unconscious psychological processes. In the latter part of the nineteenth century many men reared in Vienna or other leading European cities were trained in medicine and steeped in the tradition of physiological psychology, but Freud alone went on to practice neurology, then to use hypnotherapy with hysterics, and finally to invent psychoanalysis. The evolution of his thinking was nurtured in part by the social conditions and state of scientific knowledge in his era, but in part by his genius and the personal problems that made him sensitive to similar problems in others.

Freud took his first small step toward the invention of psychoanalysis not by design but in response to a demand made by one of his patients. She was Baroness Fanny Moser, a forty-year-old widow whom he called Frau Emmy von N. in *Studies on Hysteria*. She sent for Freud in 1889 when she was suffering from facial tics, hallucinations of writhing snakes and dead rats, fearful dreams of vultures and fierce wild animals, frequent interruptions of her speech by a spastic clacking or popping noise that she made with her mouth, a fear of socializing, and a hatred of strangers.

Over a period of time Freud rid her of many of her symptoms by the cathartic Breuer method—she was the first patient with whom he used it—and also by the Nancy method of post-hypnotic suggestion. As he later reported in *Studies:*

> The therapeutic success on the whole was considerable; but it was not a lasting one. The patient's tendency to fall ill in a similar way under the impact of fresh traumas was not got rid of. Anyone who wanted to undertake the definitive cure of a case of hysteria such as this would have to enter more thoroughly into the complex of phenomena than I attempted to do.[15]

From Frau Emmy, however, he learned something of great importance. When he asked her to recall the traumatic episode that had initiated some symptom, she would often ramble on tediously and repetitiously without relating anything pertinent. One day Freud asked her why she had gastric pains and what they came from:

> Her answer, which she gave rather grudgingly, was that she did not know. I requested her to remember by tomorrow. She then said in a definitely grumbling tone that I was not to keep on asking her where this or that came from, but to let her tell me what she had to say.[16]

To his credit, Freud sensed that this was an important request and let her proceed as she wished. She began talking of her husband's death and wandered on from there, eventually speaking of the slander circulated by his relatives and by a "shady journalist" to the effect that she had poisoned him. Although this had nothing to do with her gastric pains, it revealed to Freud why she was so isolated and unsociable, and why she hated strangers; previous urging had not elicited the significant thoughts, but allowing her to ramble freely had. He realized that, wearisome as it might be, allowing the patient to say whatever came into her mind was a more effective route to hidden memories than prodding and probing; this eventually led him to the use of the technique, critically important to both therapy and research, of "free association."

Freud recognized, too, that the technique might spare him the attempt at hypnosis with patients who could not be hypnotized. He asked them—and, after a while, all his patients—to lie down on a couch in his office, close their eyes, concentrate on remembering, and say whatever came to mind. Often they would go blank; nothing would come to mind, or what came was irrelevant, and for good reason: Freud had already noticed that forgotten memories that were retrieved only with great difficulty were those one would prefer to forget—memories involving shame, self-reproach, "psychical pain," or actual harm. Patients who could not remember traumatic episodes were unconsciously defending themselves from pain.

Freud called this inability to retrieve painful memories "resistance" and invented a way to break through it. He first used the technique in 1892 with a young woman who could not be hypnotized and who was unable to produce useful memories. He pressed her forehead with his hand, assuring her that this would infallibly produce such memories. And it did. What came to her mind that first time was the recollection of a night when she returned home from a party and stood beside her father's sickbed. From that she went on, slowly and meanderingly, to related thoughts, and after a while to the recognition that she had felt guilty for enjoying herself while her father lay critically ill. At last, and with much effort, Freud got her to recognize that one of her symptoms, severe pain in her legs, was her way of fending off guilt-producing pleasures. She later made a complete recovery and married.[17]

The essential aspect of the process, however, was not what Freud did with his hand but what the patient agreed to do. As he later explained:

> I assure [the patient] that, all the time the pressure lasts, he will see before him a recollection in the form of a picture or will have it in his thoughts in the form of an idea occurring to him; and I pledge him to

communicate this picture or idea to me, whatever it may be. He is not to keep it to himself because he may happen to think it is not what is wanted, not the right thing, or because it would be too disagreeable for him to say it. There is to be no criticism of it, no reticence, either for emotional reasons or because it is judged unimportant. Only in this manner can we find what we are in search of, but in this manner we shall find it infallibly.[18]

What came forth was very rarely a forgotten painful memory but usually a link in a chain of associations that, if pursued, slowly led to the pathogenic idea and to its hidden meaning. In *Studies* Freud called this process "analysis," and the next year, 1896, began using the term "psychoanalysis."

Freud soon concluded that the pressure technique, which was only another form of suggestion, was inadvisable, because it was reminiscent of hypnosis and also made the doctor too vivid a presence at a time when the patient was trying to focus on memories. He abandoned it by 1900, relying thereafter on verbal suggestion.[19]

Thus, by 1900 the basic elements of the method consisted of relaxation on the couch,* the therapist's repeated suggestion that free association would yield useful ideas, the patient's agreeing to say whatever came to mind without any holding back or self-censorship, and the unconscious associations this process revealed in the patient's memories and ideas. The method proved applicable not only to hysteria but to other neuroses. Freud tinkered with the technique for decades, but its fundamentals, aimed at achieving curative insight by looking into the psychodynamic unconscious, had all been established within a dozen years of the time he first treated a patient without using hypnosis.

There is, of course, a great deal more to psychoanalytic technique than this, much of it arcane and complex. Since we are concerned primarily with the development of psychological science and only to a limited extent with the treatment of mental disorders, we need not linger here over the details of psychoanalytic therapy or the variants devised by followers of Freud who came to disagree with his theories and therapeutic methods. But we must take note of two other elements of psychoana-

*Freud felt that the use of the couch helped focus the patient's attention on his own ideas, not on the analyst, but he also admitted having a personal motive: "I cannot put up with being stared at by other people for eight hours a day (or more)" (*On Beginning the Treatment* [1913], S.E. XII: 134).

lytic therapy that Freud worked out, since they are central not only to his treatment of patients but to his use of psychoanalysis as the investigative method by which he made his major psychological discoveries.

The first is the phenomenon of *transference*. Freud had mentioned this briefly and in a limited sense in *Studies*, but five years later, in 1900, a failed treatment led him to make much more of it. At that time he began treating an eighteen-year-old girl identified in his case report as Dora. He and she traced her hysterical symptoms back to a sexual approach made to her by Herr K., a neighbor, and to her conflicting feelings of repulsion and sexual attraction to him. But Dora broke off treatment after only three months, just as she was making good progress. Freud, stunned, pondered long and deeply about why she might have done so. Re-examining a dream of hers about leaving treatment—an analogue of her fleeing Herr K.'s house at the time of the sexual advance—he concluded that he himself, a heavy smoker whose breath smelled of tobacco smoke, had reminded Dora of Herr K., also a smoker, and that she may have begun to transfer the feelings she had for Herr K. to Freud. Not noticing this, he had failed to deal with it constructively. His conclusion:

I ought to have listened to the warning myself. "Now," I ought to have said to her, "it is from Herr K. that you have made a transference onto me. Have you noticed anything that leads you to suspect me of evil intentions similar (whether openly or in some sublimated form) to Herr K.'s? Or have you been struck by anything about me or got to know anything about me which has caught your fancy, as happened previously with Herr K.?"[20]

This, he said, would have enabled Dora to clear up her feelings about Freud, remain in treatment, and look still deeper into herself for other memories.

Transference, Freud concluded, cannot be avoided; dealing with it is by far the hardest part of the task but is an essential step in breaking through resistance and bringing the unconscious to light:

It is only after the transference has been resolved that a patient arrives at a sense of conviction of the validity of the connections which have been established during the analysis . . . [In treatment] all the patient's tendencies, including hostile ones, are aroused; they are then turned to account for the purposes of the analysis by being made conscious . . . Transference, which seems ordained to be the greatest obstacle to psychoanalysis, becomes its most powerful ally, if its presence can be detected each time and explained to the patient.[21]

Seen from the viewpoint of therapy, the analysis of transference is a corrective experience that reveals and repairs the trauma. Had Freud acted in time, Dora would have seen that, unlike Herr K., he (and presumably many other men) could be trusted and that she did not have to fear their feelings about her or hers about them. Seen from the viewpoint of psychology, the analysis of transference is a way of investigating and verifying hypotheses about the unconscious motivations behind inexplicable behavior.

The second element of analytic technique that became a principal method of psychological investigation for Freud is *dream interpretation*. Despite his failure to recognize Dora's dream as a signal of her transference to him, he had been fruitfully using patients' dreams for five years to get at unconscious material; he later called dream interpretation "the royal road to the knowledge of the unconscious in mental life."[22]

Freud was far from the first psychologist to be interested in dreams; in *The Interpretation of Dreams* (1900), he cited 115 references to earlier discussions of the subject. But most psychologists had viewed dreams as degraded, absurd, and meaningless thoughts that originated not in any psychic process but in some bodily process that was disturbing sleep. Freud, conceiving of the unconscious as not merely ideas and memories outside of awareness but as the repository of painful feelings and events that have been forcibly forgotten, saw dreams as significant hidden material breaking into view while the protective conscious self is off duty.

He hypothesized that dreams fulfill wishes that would otherwise wake us and that their basic purpose is to enable us to continue sleeping. Some dreams fulfill simple bodily needs. In *Interpretation* Freud said that whenever he had eaten salty food, he became thirsty during the night and dreamed of drinking in great gulps. He also cited the dream of a young medical colleague who liked to sleep late and whose landlady called through the door one morning, "Wake up, Herr Pepi! It's time to go to the hospital!" That morning Pepi particularly wanted to stay in bed, and dreamed that he was a patient in bed in the hospital, at which point he said to himself, "As I'm already *in* the hospital, there's no need for me to go there," and went on sleeping.[23]

But the wish fulfillment of many dreams is far subtler and more recondite. Often, wishes that have been hidden in the unconscious threaten to break through into consciousness during the relaxed condition of sleep; if they did, they would produce distress sufficient to awaken the sleeper. To protect sleep, Freud supposed, the unconscious mind disguises disturbing elements, transforming them into relatively innocuous ones; the dream is mysterious precisely because what it seems to be about is not what it is really about. But by free-associating to what we remember of dreams, we may be able to recognize the real content behind the disguise and so peer into our unconscious mind.

Freud arrived at this view after he first analyzed a dream of his own. In July 1895, he dreamed about "Irma," a young woman he was then treating. The dream is complicated and Freud's analysis of it very long (over eleven pages). In brief, he meets Irma in a large hall where guests are arriving and learns from her that she has been having choking pains in her throat, stomach, and abdomen; fears that he has incompetently overlooked some organic trouble; and after many other details, discovers that his friend Otto, a physician, had given Irma an injection with an unclean syringe and that this was the source of her trouble.

Pursuing the real meanings of the many components of the dream through free association, Freud recalled that the previous day he had met his friend Oscar Rie, a pediatrician who knew Irma, and who had said to him, "She's better, but not quite well." Freud had felt annoyed; he had taken this to be veiled criticism, meaning that he had been treating Irma with only partial success. In the dream, he disguised the truth by turning Oscar Rie into Otto, changing Irma's remaining neurotic symptoms into physical ones, and making Otto responsible for her condition—unlike himself, who was always scrupulous about the cleanliness of needles he used. Freud's conclusions:

> Otto had in fact annoyed me by his remarks about Irma's incomplete cure, and the dream gave me my revenge by throwing the reproach back on to him. The dream acquitted me of responsibility for Irma's condition by showing that it was due to other factors . . . The dream represented a particular state of affairs as I should have wished it to be. *Thus its content was the fulfillment of a wish and its motive was a wish.*[24]

Through ruthless self-examination of his own less than creditable motives in the dream, Freud had discovered a technique of incomparable value. Within the next five years he analyzed over a thousand dreams of his patients and reported in *Interpretation* that the method was one of the most useful tools of psychoanalytic treatment and of research on the workings of the unconscious mind.

The use of psychoanalytic procedures for research purposes has been much criticized as methodologically unsound. Free association leads the patient and analyst to an interpretation of a dream, but how can one prove that the interpretation is correct? In a few cases there may be historical evidence that a trauma, reconstructed from a dream symbol, did in fact occur, but in most cases, as in Freud's Irma dream, there is no way to prove objectively that the interpretation has revealed the real dream content.

Yet as anyone knows who has ever interpreted his or her dreams in therapy, there comes a moment in the effort when one feels a shock of recognition, an epiphany, a sense of having stumbled on emotional truth. In the end, dream analysis is authenticated by the analysand's own response—"Yes! This must be the true meaning of it because it *feels* true"—and because that response enables him or her to begin grappling with the problem that generated the dream.

In Freud's case, free association and dream analysis led him to just such experiences of illumination and rescued him from a serious scientific error. Very early in his practice of psychotherapy, he suspected that sexual difficulties were at the basis of many or most neurotic disorders. He might have got that idea from the *Zeitgeist*. Although Viennese society was still thoroughly prudish and hypocritical about sexuality, in medical and scientific circles it had become a matter of much interest. Dr. Richard von Krafft-Ebing had published a lengthy account of sexual deviations, and anthropologists were reporting the sexual customs of peoples around the world.

But these works dealt with adult sexuality; children were thought to be innocent, pure, and untouched by sexual desires or experiences. Freud, however, had repeatedly heard patients recall, after much effort, that they had had sexual feelings in childhood and, astonishingly, that they had been sexually molested by adults, their experiences having ranged from being fondled to being raped. Hysteria was one outcome;

obsessional neuroses, phobias, and paranoia were others. The guilty adults were nursemaids, governesses, domestic servants, teachers, older brothers—and, most shockingly, in the case of female patients, fathers.[25]

Freud was amazed, and thought he had made a major discovery. By 1896, after half a dozen years of hypnotherapeutic and analytic experience, he announced his so-called seduction theory in a published paper and in a lecture before the local Society for Psychiatry and Neurology presided over by the great Krafft-Ebing.[26] The lecture was received icily, and Krafft-Ebing told him, "It sounds like a scientific fairy tale."[27] In the weeks and months after the lecture Freud felt shunned by the medical community and totally isolated, and referrals of patients fell off alarmingly. But although he clung to his belief in his discovery for a while, eventually he too reluctantly began to doubt its validity.

For one thing, he was having only partial success treating patients who had unearthed recollections of molestation; some, in fact, who he thought were doing best, broke off treatment before being cured. For another, he was finding it ever harder to believe that perverse acts by fathers against their daughters were so widespread. Since there was no unarguable indication of reality in the unconscious, these recollections of seduction might actually be fictitious.[28] This was a depressing thought; what he had considered a major discovery and "the solution of a thousands-[of-]years-old problem" might be an error.

Although he had recently been able to move his growing family to a spacious apartment at Berggasse 19 and was doing well enough to indulge in his keenest pleasure, an annual trip to Italy, he had many other reasons for being depressed and anxious. His father's death, in October 1896, had affected Freud far more deeply than he had anticipated (he felt "torn up by the roots"); his long friendship with Breuer, who had been so helpful to him but who would not accept his increasingly radical ideas about neurosis and therapy, was disintegrating; and although he had held the unpaid but prestigious position of *Privatdozent* (lecturer) in neuropathology at the university for nearly a dozen years, he still had not been appointed a professor, a far more prestigious status that would have aided his career. For all these reasons, Freud's neurotic symptoms became exacerbated, particularly his worries about money, fears of heart disease, obsession with thoughts of death, and a travel phobia that made it impossible for him to visit Rome, which he desperately wanted to do but the thought of which filled him with inexplicable fear.

In the summer of 1897 the forty-one-year-old Freud began to psychoanalyze himself in an effort to understand and combat his own neurosis.[29] To a degree, he had already been doing this by analyzing some of his dreams, but now he subjected himself daily to his own scrutiny in a rigorous, systematic fashion. Descartes, Kant, and James—even, perhaps, Socrates—had examined their conscious minds, but only Freud sought to unlock the secrets of his unconscious mind.

Self-analysis may seem a contradiction in terms. How can one be guide and guided, analyst and analysand, at the same time? How can one be the patient and also the therapist onto whom the patient transfers feelings that he then analyzes? But no one else was trained or able to serve as Freud's analyst, and he had to do it himself. To some extent, however, he made Wilhelm Fliess, to whom he was developing a powerful attachment, a surrogate analyst. Fliess, although an ear, nose, and throat specialist, had many interests, including psychology, about which he formulated a number of theories, some brilliant and others mystical and absurd. Freud wrote regularly and often to Fliess, telling him what was happening in his research and self-analysis, and met him from time to time for what Freud called "congresses"—two or three days of intense discussion about his and Fliess's work and theories. Fliess's letters in response to Freud's do not exist nor is there any record of what he said in their congresses, but it is generally believed that he helped in the self-analysis or at least that Freud clarified his own thinking in the course of telling the results of self-analysis to a trusted confidant.

Every day, for several years, Freud used free association and the examination of each night's dreams to seek hidden memories, early experiences, and the concealed motives behind his daily wishes, emotions, slips of the tongue, and little memory lapses; he sought to understand himself and, through himself, psychological phenomena common to humankind. "This analysis is harder than any other," he wrote to Fliess early in the process. "But I believe it has got to be done and is a necessary stage in my work."[30] Time and again he thought he was finished, only to discover otherwise; time and again he came to a standstill, fought to make progress—and made it, as a later letter tells:

I am now experiencing in myself all the things that as a third party I have witnessed going on in my patients—days when I slink about depressed because I have understood nothing of the day's dreams, fantasies, or mood, and other days when a flash of lightning brings coherence into the picture, and what has gone before is revealed as preparation for the present.[31]

No wonder it was hard work. He was unearthing from his "dung heap," as he called it, memories that had been deeply hidden because they were repellent and guilt-producing, such as his childish jealousy of a younger brother (who died in infancy, leaving a permanent residue of guilt in Freud), his conflicting feelings of love and hate for his father, and particularly a time when, at two and a half, he saw his mother nude and was sexually aroused.[32]

Ernest Jones, in his monumental biography of Freud, said that the self-analysis produced no magical results and that Freud's neurotic symptoms and dependence on Fliess actually became more pronounced in the first year or so as disturbing material came to light. But by 1899 Freud's symptoms were much improved and he felt far more normal than four or five years earlier. By 1900 the task was largely complete, although for the rest of his life he continued to spend the last half hour of every day analyzing his moods and experiences.

The self-analysis, imperfect though it was, had considerable personal benefit but yielded a far greater one, according to most Freud scholars. Through it Freud arrived at a number of his theories about human nature or confirmed theories he had been deriving from his experience with patients.

The most important of these was that children, even in their early years, do have powerful sexual feelings, which are particularly apt to involve sexual attraction toward a parent, usually of the opposite sex. But children sense that these desires and fantasies are so wicked in the eyes of their parents and other adults that they thrust them into the unconscious and forget that they have ever had them.

Now at last Freud understood why so many of his patients had told of being seduced in childhood. The "memories" they had unearthed were of childish fantasies, not of actual seductions.[33] He had been on the right track; he simply hadn't gone far enough to reach the psychic truth. Jeffrey Masson, an apostate psychoanalyst and ferocious Freud critic, has alleged that Freud gave up his seduction theory because it offended his fellow physicians and was bad for business, but in fact Freud's contemporaries found his new theory of infant sexuality and incestuous desires even more repugnant than the seduction theory. Yet Freud, despite his money worries, sense of isolation, and desire to be publicly recognized, felt compelled to publish the truth, and did so, partly in 1900 and more fully in 1905.

By 1900, he had done much more than invent a new therapy for neuroses and discover childhood sexuality. He had developed a number of

highly consequential theories about human psychology, both normal
and abnormal. While he drew on the latest findings and ideas of certain
psychologists (the French psychologist Pierre Janet would even accuse
Freud of plagiarizing his ideas about the "subconscious," as he called it),
what was original in Freud's work—and much of it was—was based on
what he had gleaned from his own mind and his patients' by a form of
exploration without precedent in the history of psychology.

Dynamic Psychology:
Early Formulations

The theories that would make Freud famous and would profoundly
affect Western culture describe mental processes in purely psychological terms. Freud had begun as an adherent of the mechanist-
physiologist school, in which all mental events supposedly were, or
someday would be, explicable in physiological terms. Not until he gave
up that view did he make his major discoveries.

Freud had clung to the physiological doctrine for some time after
turning to hypnotherapy and psychoanalysis. In 1895, the very year in
which Breuer and he published *Studies on Hysteria*, a predominantly
psychological approach to that subject, he wrote an eighty-page rough
draft of a "Project for a Scientific Psychology" in which he ambitiously
sought to explain mental processes in terms of the physiological events
taking place in the brain.[34] While the "Project" contained a number of
his budding psychological theories, it accounted for them in such physical terms as the laws of motion, the quantity of nervous excitation in
neurons, the inertia or discharge of that energy, the pathways of discharge, and the principle of the conservation of energy.

Freud sent the draft to Fliess, but he himself criticized it harshly and
left it unfinished. Neuroscience, he found, was not yet advanced
enough for such an approach; like William James, he felt that for the
time being psychology would have to deal with thoughts and emotions
solely in psychological terms. Freud wrote to Fliess, a month after sending him "Project," "I no longer understand the state of mind in which I
hatched [it] out . . . It seems pure balderdash."[35] A few years later he
added:

> I have no desire at all to leave psychology hanging in the air with no
> organic basis. But, beyond a feeling of conviction [that there must be

such a basis], I have nothing, either theoretical or therapeutic, to work on, and so I must behave as if I were confronted by psychological factors only.[36]

Although he abandoned the attempt at a unified theory, Freud in no way reverted to the traditional dualist view that mind is a substance separate and distinct from body. He often used the word *Seele*, which is translated in the Standard Edition of his writings as "soul," but the German word has many meanings and the psychoanalyst Bruno Bettelheim has persuasively argued that Freud meant by it *psyche*, the mental and emotional aspects of the individual, or, simply, the entire apparatus of mind and emotions.[37] All his life Freud was firmly convinced that no aspect of mind existed apart from the brain and that physical processes in its neurons are the materials of the phenomena of mind. Also, as a scientist he was a thorough determinist; he believed that every mental event has its causes, and that free will is only an illusion.[38]

After Freud gave up the effort to construct a physiologically based theory of mental events, he made a series of great leaps forward. In only five years (1895 to 1900), he invented a new psychotherapy and formulated a number of revolutionary theories of human psychology. In the years to come he would amplify, alter, and add to them, but had he done nothing after 1900, he would have added a whole new dimension to psychology. His theory of the mind, as strewn in bits and pieces throughout his writings of that period, has the following main components:

The dynamic unconscious:[39] Nearly all the previous research and theorizing of psychologists had dealt with conscious mental processes, such as perception, memory, judgment, and learning. What Freud added to psychology and to Western culture was a set of theories of the unconscious and its crucial role in human behavior. Ernest Jones says this is generally held to be his greatest contribution to science.[40]

Freud, to be sure, did not discover the unconscious, as is often said. For two centuries thinkers had speculated about it—everyone from the rationalist Leibniz to the nineteenth-century hypnotherapists and from the poets and philosophers of the Romantic movement to Helmholtz, the members of the Würzburg School, and William James. By and large, though, they had all considered the unconscious merely a repository, a warehouse of experiences and information waiting to be called to use. Freud would label this relatively inert but accessible area of mental life the "preconscious" and conceive of it as quite distinct from the unconscious.

There had been, however, many clues in the work of Freud's predecessors and contemporaries, especially the hypnotherapists, that the unconscious played an active role in mental life; some even applied the term "dynamic" to it. Freud adopted and transformed this idea on the basis of his clinical experience and self-analysis.

He envisioned the mind as having three levels of functioning: the conscious, the preconscious, and the unconscious. The last was the largest and most influential part; far from being a warehouse of inactive material, it was an area of highly active and powerful primitive drives and forbidden wishes that constantly generated pressure on the conscious mind, in disguised or altered form, thereby motivating and determining much of our behavior.

This had become apparent to Freud from his clinical work. The thinking and behavior of his neurotic patients before analysis were controlled by forces they knew nothing of and could not master. The goal of psychoanalysis was to give the patient's ego "freedom to decide."[41] This did not imply free will but an awareness of one's unconscious motives and the attainment of a state in which choices were determined by conscious ones.

Freud came to believe that what was true of neurotics was equally true of normal people. The latter, however, developed in such a way that their unacceptable desires, hidden from awareness, were converted into acceptable ways of acting. Thus, healthy behavior, like pathological behavior, was motivated and directed largely by the forces of the unconscious.

Primary and secondary processes:[42] The unconscious mind, in Freud's view, is not merely a place in which we sequester the intolerable ideas and desires of the primitive and infantile part of the mind. He termed the mental processes that take place in it "primary"; they seek the uninhibited fulfillment of wishes either through actions or, when these are blocked by real-world forces, fantasies like those of childhood seduction, or dreams. The content of the unconscious, though not derived from the real world, is the *psychic reality* that motivates us.

As we grow up we learn that we cannot behave according to these untamed primary-process urges; we learn what is acceptable and successful in the real world and what is not. Our conscious mind operates according to "secondary processes"—the thinking, knowing, and problem-solving mental activities needed to conceive of and carry out ways of satisfying our desires that are socially acceptable.

The pleasure principle:[43] Many philosophers and psychologists had theorized that human behavior is largely governed by the quest for pleasure and the avoidance of pain. Freud incorporated this doctrine into his theory of the unconscious but altered its focus. The fundamental motive force for the entire psychic apparatus, he said, is a wish arising from any unfulfilled want or excitation—a wish to relieve the resulting *Unlust* (unpleasure), thus dissipating the tension and yielding pleasure. In the early period, Freud called it the "unpleasure principle," but later renamed it the "pleasure principle," the label by which it became a part of the psychological vocabulary.

"The pleasure-unpleasure principle is fundamental in Freud's psychology," Jones says. "It automatically regulates all the processes of cathexis."[44] "Cathexis," a critically important term in Freud's writing, is a word coined by James Strachey, translator of the Standard Edition, to approximate Freud's use of *Besetzung*, the German word meaning "occupation" or "filling" that Freud used to signify "charge of psychical energy,"[45] or, in lay terms, "emotional investment."

Hunger is a typical wish. When primary-process thinking (imagining food, dreaming of food) fails to relieve unpleasure, secondary-process thinking takes over; the cathexis or psychic energy is transferred to real-world activities, such as buying food and cooking, that will, after a while, alleviate the hunger and bring about the pleasure of relief.

Primary processes therefore operate according to the pleasure principle, secondary processes according to the *reality principle*. But as Freud would later add:

> The substitution of the reality principle for the pleasure principle implies no deposing of the pleasure principle, but only a safeguarding of it. A momentary pleasure, uncertain in its results [i.e., those of the wish], is given up, but only in order to gain along the new path an assured pleasure at a later time.[46]

Sexuality; the Oedipus complex:[47] Although Freud's ideas about sexuality would not assume their mature form or significance in his system until somewhat later, we have seen that even before 1900 he had come to believe that the sexual drive is one of the most powerful, exists even in

childhood, and plays a major role in the development of both the normal and the neurotic personality.

The most important aspect of this drive, he held, was that in young
children it is usually directed by primary processes toward the parent of
the opposite sex. As everyone knows, Freud called these wishes Oedipal,
because Oedipus, in the Greek myth, unknowingly kills his father and
marries his mother. In the young boy, the sexual wish directed toward
the mother is accompanied by hatred of the rival, the father, and by the
hostile wish to be rid of him. But through realistic secondary-process
thinking the child recognizes that his father is far stronger than he and
would certainly win any struggle between them, and that the Oedipal
wish involves grave danger.

The resulting conflict between wish and fear causes intolerable anxiety. Not until 1910 would Freud label this the "Oedipus complex,"[48] but
in letters to Fliess in the late 1890s he had begun drawing the analogy to
the Oedipus myth, and he publicly stated the theory in brief form in
1900 in *The Interpretation of Dreams*. He saw the Oedipus complex as
an inevitable part of human experience: "It is the fate of all of us, perhaps"—soon he would drop the "perhaps"—"to direct our first sexual
impulse toward our mother and our first hatred and our first murderous
wish against our father. Our dreams convince us that this is so." Later,
he would theorize about a different but analogous phenomenon in
female children.

Repression:[49] To survive the anxiety of the Oedipus complex, the child
represses the Oedipal wishes, hiding them away in the unconscious.
Repression is a central and essential mechanism of the mind, the psyche's basic way of defending itself against a highly anxiety-producing
conflict produced by a primitive wish and fear of harm in the real world.
Jones says that it "may certainly be counted as one of Freud's most
important and original contributions."

In the years to come, Freud would extend the theory of the Oedipus
complex and its resolution through repression to make it the core of a
theory of child development.

Principle of constancy:[50] Although Freud had given up the attempt to
explain psychological processes in physiological terms, he continued to
believe that Helmholtz's principle of the conservation of energy—that
the sum of forces in any isolated system remains constant—applied to
psychic phenomena. As Breuer and he had stated in *Studies on Hyste-*

ria, "There exists in the organism a tendency to keep intracerebral excitation constant."[51]

When some event induces surplus excitation, as in an occurrence that makes us angry, we tend to discharge the anger one way or another in order to preserve our normal balance of excitation. How we do so is the outcome of primary-process thinking governed by—or sometimes breaking through—the constraints of secondary-process thinking. Breuer and Freud gave an example: "When Bismarck had to suppress his angry feelings in the King's presence, he relieved himself afterward by smashing a valuable vase on the floor."[52]

The principle of constancy is a basic tenet of Freud's psychology; it is an essential part of his explanation both of the neuroses as well as certain other phenomena, most notably displacement. Since the total amount of psychic excitation remains constant, if it is diminished in one idea, it is increased in a related idea; it is "displaced." As we know, Freud relied on this concept to account for neurotic symptoms and dreams, in both of which the energy of impermissible wishes is displaced onto permissible activities. Later, he would apply the concept to account for "sublimation"—constructive acts that use the energy of unfulfilled or repressed desires in positive ways. Hostile impulses, for example, can be redirected into competitive striving for success; the energy of self-love achieves satisfaction through love of another. Freud, always skilled at finding an appropriate quotation or literary example, here quoted a poem in which Heine imagines God explaining Creation:

> *Illness was no doubt the final cause*
> *Of the whole urge to create;*
> *By creating, I could recover;*
> *By creating, I became healthy.*[53]

Success

In 1900, despite the completion of his self-analysis, Freud, at forty-four, had reason to feel discouraged and depressed. He had had high hopes that *The Interpretation of Dreams*, which he considered his most important work, would be a major success. Later, he remarked, "Insight such as this falls to one's lot but once in a lifetime."[54] Yet on publication, in November 1899, it received a few flattering but muddled reviews in

Vienna and little notice elsewhere, and commercially was an abysmal failure, selling only 351 copies in six years.

Freud felt more ignored and isolated than ever. His practice, which he had hoped the book would increase, fluctuated erratically, and he continued to be plagued by the fear of poverty. His friendship with Breuer was long over and his intensely close and dependent reliance on Fliess as confidant, supporter, co-worker, and idol was crumbling. During his self-analysis Freud had scrutinized his near-worship of Fliess, finding in it neurotic tendencies and a disguised homoerotic component; as the analysis freed Freud from emotional dependence on Fliess, Fliess became testy and critical. At a congress in August 1900, they attacked each other's ideas fiercely, and Fliess told Freud he doubted the value of Freud's psychoanalytic researches. They never held another meeting, and the warmth disappeared from their correspondence. The friendship abruptly ended a few years later when Fliess accused Freud of divulging his unpublished theory of universal inherent bisexuality to the philosopher Otto Weininger (who then used it in print) without identifying it as Fliess's idea.[55]

Freud must also have felt isolated in his private life. Although he had a solid relationship with Martha, the intensity and intimacy of the years before marriage were long since gone, and he never discussed his ideas with her. He and she had suspended conjugal relations when he was only thirty-seven in order to give her some relief from childbearing, and although they later resumed their sexual connection, by 1900 he told Fliess that he considered himself "done begetting."[56]

From that year on, however, Freud's life began to improve. In 1902 he was at last promoted to Professor Extraordinarius at the University of Vienna and for the rest of his life was generally known as Professor Freud. The honor came late, but was both symbolically and practically of great value to him.

That same year, Wilhelm Stekel, a Viennese physician whom Freud had successfully treated for impotence, suggested that Freud hold weekly evening meetings with a handful of colleagues who were interested in his work. Freud liked the idea and sent invitations to three other physicians. In the fall of 1902 the five, calling themselves the Wednesday Psychological Society, began regular meetings in Freud's office. One member would present a paper, after which, over coffee and cake, the group would discuss it and relevant aspects of psychoanalytic theory and therapy. In the group's first years, according to one member, "there was an atmosphere of the foundation of a religion in that room. Freud himself was its new prophet who made the heretofore prevailing methods of psychological investigation appear superficial."[57]

The group grew gradually; its early members included Otto Rank, Alfred Adler, Sandor Ferenczi, and Ernest Jones, all destined to become important in the psychoanalytic movement. By 1906 there were seventeen, and two years later the expanding group, now factional and acrimonious, became the Vienna Psychoanalytic Society. Many such societies sprang up in other cities in Europe and America, and by 1910, at a congress in Nuremberg, the International Psychoanalytic Association was founded.

Freud's professorship and the formation of the Wednesday Psychological Society brought an increase in his practice and income. In his office suite, completely separate from the family's spacious living quarters, he began collecting the Roman and Greek statuettes and other antiquities that he loved, arranging them on a table in his line of vision where he sat behind the head of the patients' couch. He also could now afford more luxurious vacations to more remote areas. It was his custom to work extremely hard for nine months of the year and then take a three-month summer break. He would spend the first part of the vacation in the mountains with his large family—Martha, their six children, and Martha's unmarried sister, Minna. Although in photographs he always looks stern, even severe—he is said to have had a piercing gaze and a commanding air—in private life he could be warm, relaxed, and informal, and on vacation would put on a backpack, hiking clothes, and boots and take his older children walking in the forest, climbing, hunting mushrooms, and fishing.

After some weeks of this, he would leave the family and go to Italy, where, as a result of his self-analysis, he was now able to visit Rome. Martha did not accompany him; Freud was very much a conservative, middle-class Viennese paterfamilias whose wife was the chatelaine of the household, her only purpose in life being, she said, to serve "our dear chief." She maintained peace and order, relieving Freud of all mundane concerns, laid out his clothes for him each day, and even put toothpaste on his toothbrush.[58] With such support, it is not surprising that Freud, a compulsive worker, could accomplish so much. Although he saw patients eight or nine hours a day, he wrote prolifically in the evening and on weekends, and his lifetime output of psychological writings fills twenty-three good-sized volumes.

Among the many works, both short and long, that Freud completed in the early years of the new century were two that are particularly important, one because it added greatly to his renown, the other because it added greatly to his notoriety.

The first, published in 1901, was *The Psychopathology of Everyday Life*. It dealt with such topics as forgetfulness, slips of the tongue, and bungled actions, which Freud viewed not as mere accidents but as having significant unconscious causes. Although the purpose of the work was serious, it was filled with entertaining anecdotes from Freud's own life, from his patients' lives, and from the newspapers and other sources. One example is a favorite of Freud's, which he used again in several later writings. The President of the Lower House of the Austrian Parliament, expecting a particular session to yield little good and secretly wishing it were already over, formally opened it with the announcement, "Gentlemen, I take notice that a full quorum of members is present and herewith declare the sitting closed!"[59] *The Psychopathology of Everyday Life* became Freud's most widely read book; it went through eleven editions and was translated into twelve languages in his lifetime.

The second notable work, which appeared in 1905, was *Three Essays on the Theory of Sexuality*; it went much further than his previous work in picturing sexuality as a fundamental force in human behavior. The first essay dealt with sexual aberrations, picturing them as the consequences of incomplete or distorted development. The second dealt with infantile sexuality, enlarging Freud's earlier views of the subject and maintaining that all human beings are innately perverse but that in healthy development the perversity is mastered. The third essay dealt with the development of sexuality in puberty and the differentiation of male and female personalities as a consequence of anatomical differences.

The explicit details in *Three Essays* and its theoretical ideas about infantile sexuality outraged the straitlaced burghers of middle-class Europe and America. Freud was called a dirty-minded pansexualist and "Viennese libertine," and the book was labeled "pornography" and a befouling of the purity of childhood. According to Jones, writing in 1955, "It was this publication that brought the maximum of odium on his name; much of it still remains, especially among the uneducated. The book was felt to be a calumny on the innocence of the nursery."[60] But the book struck a responsive note. It was widely discussed in psychological and psychiatric circles, reissued a number of times, and translated into nine languages. James Strachey says that it and *The Interpretation of Dreams* are Freud's "most momentous and original contributions to human knowledge."[61]

Three years later Freud received an invitation to be a key speaker at the psychology conference that would be part of Clark University's twentieth-anniversary celebration. It was the first international recognition of the man and his work. He accepted, went to Worcester, Massachusetts, accompanied by two colleagues, Sandor Ferenczi and Carl Jung, and delivered five lectures before an audience of leading psychologists and psychiatrists on the history of psychoanalysis, its major theories, and its therapeutic technique. A few listeners found the material offensive (Weir Mitchell, an eminent physician, called Freud a "dirty, filthy man," and a Canadian dean said that Freud seemed to advocate "a relapse into savagery"[62]), but most listeners, including William James, were impressed. The lectures were favorably discussed in the daily papers and in *The Nation*, were published in the *American Journal of Psychology*, and greatly widened the impact of Freud's ideas. By the time Freud returned from the conference, he was famous.

Not that this brought him tranquillity. Proud, sensitive, stubborn, and egotistical, like many other great pioneers, Freud became deeply embroiled in the politics of the movement he had started, and he struggled to control the disputes arising within it over theory and therapeutic methods. He seems to have felt that the Vienna Psychoanalytic Society should be run not as a democracy but as a hierarchy, an attitude perhaps natural to one who lived in a monarchy. But his view may also have been reasonable in one who had made important discoveries and wanted to preserve them from distortion or contamination. The resulting wrangles over theory and practice, and the bitter schisms, became a recurring pattern in the psychoanalytic movement.

To some extent the pattern may have been only an institutionalized version of a trait in its founder's personality. Freud had been very close to Breuer and then to Fliess, and in each case the friendship cooled and ended in bitterness when they developed views differing from his. Similar breaches occurred over the years in Freud's friendships with three of his closest followers and colleagues.

Alfred Adler came to believe that the main factors affecting the child's development had to do with his or her position in the family and the parents' child-rearing practices. When these were pathogenic, they created in the child an "inferiority complex," leading to behavior that sought to compensate for it. Adler was critical of Freud's ideas about the role of sexuality in character development and the neuroses, arguing, for instance, that women's character is shaped not by the lack of a penis so much as by envy of men's social position and privileges, and that the boy's conflicts at around age five stem less from Oedipal desires than from the conflict between his competitive urges and his feeling of powerlessness. After a prolonged struggle with Freud, who tried unsuccessfully to harmonize Adler's views with his own, Adler and a group of his followers resigned from the Vienna society in 1911 and formed one of their own.

Carl Jung, a Swiss psychiatrist and psychoanalyst, disagreed with Freud's central doctrine of the sexual origin of the neuroses. He interpreted them as manifestations of current maladjustment, not as disorders arising from traumas in infancy or childhood. Jung also held religious and mystical convictions, and a belief in the "collective unconscious," a psyche common to all individuals; these doctrines were a source of contention between him and Freud. After having been an enthusiastic follower, Jung gradually drew away from Freud, and in 1914 he formally broke with the Freudian movement and founded his own.

Otto Rank, a faithful disciple and close associate of Freud's for many years, slowly developed a theory of his own in which the chief source of anxiety is the trauma of birth, and the male sexual urge is a desire to return to the mother's womb. Efforts by Freud to reconcile Rank's views with his own failed; the relationship grew strained and finally ended in 1926.

Once, when the subject came up at dinner in the Freud home of his inability to hold on to his followers, an aunt of Freud's spoke up: "The trouble with you, Sigi," she said, "is that you just don't understand people."[63]

Remarkably, Freud remained immensely productive through all these stressful developments, the deprivations and social disruptions of World War I, which caused his practice to dwindle alarmingly, and the postwar inflation, which wiped out his life savings.

He continued to develop psychoanalytic theory through his clinical work with patients and to share ideas with a number of fellow analysts by letter and at conferences, although he never again collaborated with anyone as he had with Breuer and Fliess. Until his later years he did not cease extending and adding to his body of psychological theories in an outpouring of articles, case histories, and books.

Freudian psychology is, of course, only a part of human psychology, as Freud himself recognized.[64] It has little to say about all those conscious processes of learning, reasoning, problem solving, and creativity which seem the peak achievements of evolution and culture, and nothing whatever about behaviorism, the strictly external approach to psychological research that swept through university psychology departments in the United States by the 1920s and that Freud dismissed in a footnote.[65]

Freud's psychology was and remained entirely inward-looking and seemingly timeless, in contrast to so much that was happening in the world around him. Electricity, internal combustion engines, the automobile and airplane, the telephone and radio, were radically altering daily life and social patterns; wars and revolutions were dismantling empires and breeding new democracies and dictatorships; class structures and the Victorian foundations of family life were eroding and yielding to widened suffrage, social mobility, women's rights, and divorce. Amid all this, Freud remained focused on primal and eternal inner verities: sexual and other instincts, inner conflicts between them and the demands of the outer world, and the events of childhood and their influence on the development of personality and the emotions.

Yet perhaps the speed of social change, the disintegration of traditions, and the emergence of a bewildering array of social options made Freud's psychology particularly appealing, especially in America (except in academic, behaviorist circles). In a time of rapid change, it spoke of unchanging aspects of human nature; in a time of tremendous emphasis on material goods and the physical sciences, it stressed humanistic phenomena—desires, frustrations, conscience, moral values; to a culture of individualism and optimism, it spoke of the personal determinants of behavior, and offered theory and therapy supportive of the hope that people can change themselves for the better. In 2004, the neuropsychologist Mark Solms wrote, "For the first half of the 1900s, the ideas of Sigmund Freud dominated explanations of how the human mind works," and the historian Eli Zaretsky credits Freud with having created the *"first great theory and practice of 'personal life'* . . . the experience of having an identity distinct from one's place in the family, in society, and in the social division of labor."[66]

Whatever the reasons for the success of psychoanalysis as a therapy and a psychology, Freud's fame grew from 1909 on and reached a peak between the two world wars. His name indeed became a household word. Though relatively few people had read any of his works, every reasonably well-read person knew who he was. He was likened to Einstein in his influence on modern thought, and many noted intellectuals wrote to him or sought him out and lionized him. Media bigwigs attempted to capitalize on his name and fame. In 1924, at the time of the Leopold and Loeb murder trial, Colonel Robert McCormick, publisher of the *Chicago Tribune*, offered Freud $25,000 to come to Chicago and analyze the two young killers; Freud declined. Samuel Goldwyn offered Freud $100,000 to assist in making a film portraying famous love stories of history; Freud's reply earned him a *New York Times* headline: "FREUD REBUFFS GOLDWYN. Viennese Psychoanalyst Is Not Interested in Motion Picture Offer."[67] Freud was unimpressed by these indications of his fame, but when he was awarded the Goethe Prize in 1930, he called it "the climax of my life as a citizen."[68]

In 1923, at sixty-seven, Freud developed cancer of the upper jaw from his lifelong heavy cigar smoking and underwent the first of what would be thirty operations over the next sixteen years to remove recurrent precancerous or cancerous tissue. He had to wear a prosthesis—a kind of large denture—to separate his mouth from his nasal cavity; it made talking and eating difficult, and had to be removed regularly, a painful procedure, so that the affected area could be cleaned.

His final years were darkened by the rise of the Nazis in Germany, who began burning his books in 1933. As the danger grew that the movement would overwhelm Austria, friends and family tried to get him to leave, but he adamantly refused. Only when Germany took over Austria in March 1938 and the Nazis confiscated his passport did the fragile, aged Freud, nearing eighty-two, recognize his peril and agree to leave if he could. Partly through the intervention of President Franklin Delano Roosevelt and his ambassador to France, William C. Bullitt, the Nazis were induced to let him go, and late that year he and the faithful Martha moved to London. Although his cancer had become inoperable, he was still of perfect mind and continued to write and to see a few patients. At last, in intolerable pain, he asked his physician to end his suffering by an overdose of morphine; he died on September 23, 1939, three weeks after the outbreak of World War II.

Dynamic Psychology: Extensions and Revisions

Between 1900 and 1923 Freud expanded and altered his theories of psychology but thereafter, he said, he made "no further decisive contributions to psychoanalysis."[69] He did produce three major works between 1923 and 1939, but they deal with issues reaching beyond the bounds of psychology and are not our concern.*

He also further elaborated his ideas about psychoanalytic technique in a number of papers, but the fundamentals remained unchanged. In truth, Freud was not much interested in therapeutic technique except as a means to two ends—earning a living and, more important, exploring human nature and adding to the science of the mind.[70] "Psychoanalysis," he said late in life, "which was originally no more than an attempt at explaining pathological mental phenomena . . . [has] developed into a psychology of normal mental life."[71]

As a method of investigating mental life, psychoanalytic therapy sees the world in a grain of sand. Freud derived some of his largest and most daring theoretical ideas from tiny details—an image or name in a patient's dream, a slip of the tongue, a joke, an odd symptom, a remembered scene of childhood, a facial expression. In a lecture on the "parapraxes" (little slips and mistakes), Freud told his listeners he knew they might regard these as too trivial to merit study, but, he explained in his inimitably charming manner, they are clues to hidden psychological realities:

> The material for [psychoanalytic] observations is usually provided by the inconsiderable events which have been put aside by the other sciences as being too unimportant—the dregs, one might say, of the world of phenomena . . . [But] are there not very important things which can only reveal themselves, under certain conditions and at certain times, by quite feeble indications? . . . If you are a young man, for instance, will it not be from small pointers that you will conclude that you have won a girl's favor? Would you wait for an express declaration of love or a passionate embrace? Or would not a glance, scarcely noticed by other people, be enough? a slight movement, the lengthening by a second of the pressure of a hand? And if you were a detective engaged in tracing a murder, would you expect to find that the murderer had left his photo-

*The three works: *The Future of an Illusion,* 1927 (on the origins of religion); *Civilization and Its Discontents,* 1930 (on the control of human desires that makes society possible); and *Moses and Monotheism,* 1939 (on the origins of monotheism).

graph behind at the place of the crime, with his address attached? or would you not necessarily have to be satisfied with comparatively slight and obscure traces of the person you were in search of?[72]

It was from patient attention to endless trivia that Freud pieced together the main elements of his psychology. The chief extensions and revisions of his early discoveries are as follows:

Infantile sexuality:[73] Although Freud had early recognized sexuality as a powerful force in childhood, not until 1905, in *Three Essays*, did he state the far more radical conclusion that the sexual drive is present even in infancy. What convinced Freud was his own accumulating clinical evidence plus confirming observations reported in the medical literature. His conclusion: "A child has its sexual instincts and activities from the first; it comes into the world with them."[74]

But what he meant by sexuality in infancy and childhood is a broader and more pervasive impulse than the sexuality of adulthood; although Freud called it sexuality or libido, he was speaking of the general desire for *sensuous* pleasure of any kind. Gentle stimulation of any part of the infant's body yields such pleasure; the infant is, in Freud's term, *polymorphous perverse*. At first, the mouth is the major site of sensuous pleasure, obtained initially by sucking, then by mouthing and eating; when the child is between one and a half and three, the anal region becomes a chief source of sensuous pleasure as he or she begins to control and be aware of the expulsion or the willful retention of feces; and between the ages of three and six the child derives pleasure from self-stimulation of the genitals.

Parents, however, exert a powerful restraining influence on these elemental gratifications, mostly through toilet training and the disapproval or punishment of masturbation. The originally polymorphous sexual instinct becomes narrowed and channeled so that in adulthood it will be focused on genital sexuality with a partner.

Faulty child rearing—undue emphasis on eating or toilet training, or the failure to inhibit taboo impulses—can block the child's development toward genital sexuality. The child remains fixated at an early level of development; the fixation can appear in adult life as a preference for exclusively oral sex or anal sex, but more commonly takes the form of traits of character. The child overindulged at the oral stage may in adulthood be obsessed with eating, drinking, and smoking; the child deprived or insufficiently gratified in the oral stage may grow up passively dependent on others for feelings of self-esteem. Similarly, difficulties of adjustment during the anal stage may result, in adult life, in compulsive neatness, stinginess (retentiveness), and stubbornness.

The later stages of sexual development:[75] The most crucial psychological event of the child's life takes place at the "phallic" stage of development (Freud applied that term to both sexes), in the age range of three to six. The child's sexuality, though chiefly autoerotic, is potentially responsive to persons of either sex, but by the phallic stage the child has divined from many clues the sort of person who might appropriately provide gratification of his or her sexual urges. The ideal model—and the closest at hand—is the parent of the opposite sex.

This, Freud had said earlier, leads directly to the Oedipus complex, which he had portrayed as a critical stage. Now, going further, he envisioned its resolution as central to character development. Freud theorized that the boy's rivalry with his father causes him to fear that the powerful father will conquer him by castrating him (rather than killing him), and he reacts to that fear not only by totally repressing his sexual feelings toward his mother and replacing them with feelings of affection but by transforming his hostility and rivalry toward his father into identification with him and his role in life.

Things take a somewhat different course with the girl, who, in Freud's later view of female development, imagines she has already been castrated. She suffers "penis envy"; her love of her mother turns into hostility (she fantasizes that her mother allowed her to be born without a penis or to be castrated); she dreams of making up for the loss by having a child by her father. But the dream proves impossible; eventually she gives it up and rids herself of her anxiety-producing hostility toward her mother by identifying with her. Since, however, she has no penis, her fear of harm is less powerful than the boy's. Throughout life her feeling of having been deprived of a penis negatively influences her personality, her goals in life, her moral sense, and her self-esteem. As Gay puts it, "By the early 1920s, Freud seemed to have adopted the position that the little girl is a failed boy, the grown woman a kind of castrated man."*[76]

*Freud's theory of female psychology has come to be widely considered parochial and culture-bound, and thoroughly disproven by the changes of the past four decades in the status of women and the nature of femininity. Freud himself admitted that his understanding of feminine psychology was "incomplete and fragmentary" and once said, "The great question that has never been answered and which I have not yet been able to answer, despite my thirty years of research into the feminine soul, is 'What does woman want?'" (Jones, 1955: 421).

Both boys and girls, at about the age of five, having undergone repression of their sexuality, enter the "latency" stage of life, during which they are largely freed of the concerns and anxieties caused by the sexual instinct and turn their attention and energy toward schooling and growing up. But the repressed sexual impulses have been only locked away, not eliminated, and they continually try to break through. They find indirect and disguised outlet in the form of dreams and, in those children who have not adequately resolved the Oedipal complex, pathological symptoms.

Finally, when the child is around twelve, the hormonal changes of puberty awaken the sleeping sexual impulse, and the repressed feelings begin to be directed outward, in socially approved fashion, toward people of the opposite sex outside the family. In this final "genital" phase of development, the sexual urge is transformed into "object love"—acceptable fulfillment of sexual and emotional desires through the love of another person, often one who is in some way similar to the forbidden object of sexual love, the opposite-sex parent.

Thus Freud's theory of psychosexual development, often narrowly misconstrued as concerned only with sexual desire and behavior, actually deals with far larger issues: the basic, inevitable conflicts between childishness and maturity, instinctive desires and societal norms, and wishes and reality, the resolutions of which are crucial to character development and social life.

The structure of the psyche:[77] Freud had at first pictured the psychic apparatus as made up of the unconscious, the preconscious, and the conscious, but as he worked out his theory of psychosexual development he found this a too-simple formulation. He depicted instead a tripartite psyche comprising id, ego, and superego; these are not entities in any physical or metaphysical sense but merely names of groups or clusters of mental processes that serve different functions.

In the newborn, all mental processes are id processes, unconscious and primary. There is nothing akin to logical reasoning in the id; it is a cauldron of instinctual demands for the satisfaction of primitive desires having to do with self-preservation (hunger, thirst, and the like), sexuality, and aggression. The demands of the id operate in accordance with the pleasure principle; they seek the relief of tension without any consideration of social rules or the practical consequences of relief-seeking acts.

Since social life would be impossible if the id directed behavior, child rearing and socialization are aimed at controlling the forces of the id and directing them into acceptable activities. In part this is achieved through training and education of the conscious mind, which understands, reasons, and functions according to secondary-process thinking; this is the ego, or self, which develops and becomes differentiated from the id as the child grows. The ego is not sharply separated from the id but somewhat overlaps and merges with it. However, ideas and emotions in the id that enter the ego and create anxiety, such as the Oedipal impulse, are thrust back by repression and walled off so that they cannot re-enter consciousness.

Many other impulses, in contrast, are consciously controlled by the ego. The child learns, among other things, that one does not take another's property, strike another without just cause, or masturbate in public; we teach our children that such actions are not acceptable and will have dire consequences. Although in part we train them, as we do animals, by simple reward and punishment, in larger part we rear them by telling them how they should behave and why. The ego, absorbing these lessons, becomes capable of self-criticism and self-control.

Much of the ego, however, is not conscious. Many of its processes are preconscious—not repressed but not in the spotlight of attention. We do a good deal of our problem solving, for example, outside of consciousness, continuing to consider information we have gathered and ways of achieving our goal without consciously thinking about the matter. When a solution pops into mind seemingly from nowhere, it is because we were working on it all along. Similarly, the preconscious operates many of our well-learned skills, freeing the conscious mind to use its limited attention elsewhere. The trained musician's fingers automatically strike the right notes as he reads music; he does not have to think about them.

In contrast, the superego, which monitors and censors the ego, is unconscious and critically important to the governing of social behavior. It develops within the ego as a result of the Oedipus complex, at which time the child, coming to identify with the same-sex parent, absorbs the parent's injunctions and beliefs and makes them part of himself or herself. Perceived commands like "you must not" or "you should" are transformed by identification into "I must not" and "I should." This mechanism turns all sorts of moral values into internalized and self-imposed rules; collectively, they form the "ego ideal" or superego, what we usually call conscience. Moral issues are consciously weighed by the ego; the superego evokes a compelling sense of *ought* or *ought not.* The ego of a person adrift in a life raft might reason that to give food and water to a dying companion would be wasteful and result in the death of both of them; the superego might override the ego and insist on sharing what remained.

Earlier, Freud had held that the development of the superego takes place in girls in a fashion exactly analogous to that in boys. Later, he came to think that the girl, lacking castration anxiety, has a less intense Oedipal crisis and therefore a less developed superego and moral sense throughout life.[78] (Curiously, the paper in which he stated these patriarchal views was, at his request, read on his behalf at the 1925 International Psycho-Analytical Congress by his beloved daughter, the psychoanalyst Anna Freud.)

The individual's behavior is thus the outcome of an interplay among the three agencies of the psyche. The id seeks immediate gratification of its desires; the ego, using reality-principle thinking, seeks to restrain the impulse and find acceptable forms of gratification; and the superego exerts control by means of parental values absorbed into the unconscious. When the id is too strong for the ego and superego, the person's behavior is either pathological or criminal; when the superego is too strong for the ego, the person is guilt-ridden and frustrated or moralistic and persecutory of others.[79] In the healthy individual, the ego controls the system, finding ways to permit sufficient gratification of the id but not at the cost of bringing about overwhelming guilt feelings from the outraged superego.

Instinct theory:[80] By "instinct" Freud did not mean what biologists mean: specific forms of behavior coded into the genes—web spinning by spiders, nest building by birds—forms of behavior he referred to by the German word *Instinkt*. But the German word translated in the Standard Edition as "instinct" is *Trieb*, which denotes "impulse," "moving force," or "drive."[81]

In his early work Freud had assumed that the sexual instincts associated with the mouth, anus, and sex organs made up the sum total of psychic energy. But his later research on "repetition compulsions" (tendencies to repeat self-defeating or painful acts) plus the horrendous events of World War I broadened his thinking; he became convinced that there is also an instinct to destroy. When directed outward, it takes the form of aggression, but if blocked, it may turn inward, as seen in repetition compulsions.

He thus propounded a two-instinct theory: The life instinct, or Eros, comprises all life-preserving impulses, among them the sexual drive; and the death instinct, or Thanatos, embraces all impulses toward hostility, sadism, and aggression—and even, he tentatively suggested, a mysterious drive toward one's own death.

Anxiety, symptoms, defenses:[82] Originally Freud held that neurotic anxiety and its symptoms—as distinguished from the realistic anxiety one feels when facing a real-world danger—arise from the blocked energy of the repressed sexual instinct: unrelieved sexual tension generates anxiety. But as he accumulated clinical data, he developed the more sophisticated explanation on which he based the theory of the Oedipus complex and its resolution, and extended it to account for other forms of neurotic anxiety. An instinctual desire reaching consciousness either as a fantasy or overt action creates an anticipation of harm. This causes the child to feel intolerable anxiety; the ego, to defend itself, represses the instinctual desire, whereupon the anxiety disappears.

But what does the psyche do with the bottled-up energy, the tension-producing unpleasure of the unfulfilled instinctual demand? How does the psyche keep it from breaking through into consciousness? One solution—the defective, pathogenic one Freud saw in his neurotic patients—was the formation of symptoms:

> A symptom arises from an instinctual impulse which has been detrimentally affected by repression . . . The instinctual impulse has found a substitute in spite of repression, but a substitute which is very much reduced, displaced, and inhibited and which is no longer recognizable as a satisfaction. And when the substitutive impulse is carried out there is no sensation of pleasure; its carrying-out has, instead, the quality of a compulsion.[83]

He illustrated the process by citing one of his most famous case histories, that of Little Hans.[84] At the Oedipal stage of childhood the boy developed a phobia that prevented him from going out to the street; he was afraid of horses (the streets were full of them in that era), which he thought would bite him. His inability to go out was, Freud says, "a restriction which his ego had imposed on itself so as not to arouse the anxiety-symptom." But where had the fear of being bitten by horses come from? Analysis traced it back to Little Hans's Oedipal desires, his wish to do away with his father, and the resultant fear that his father

would harm him. Instead of resolving it in a healthy fashion, he had displaced it to horses (significantly, his father used to play the part of the
horse and let Hans ride on him) and transformed his fear of castration
into a fear of being bitten.

In short, an impermissible wish, repressed but maladaptively dealt
with, becomes a neurotic symptom. The symptom is costly to the sufferer, but not as costly as the anxiety it allays:

> An agoraphobic patient may start his illness with an attack of anxiety in
> the street. This would be repeated every time he went into the street
> again. He will now develop the symptom of agoraphobia; this may also
> be described as an inhibition, a restriction of the ego's functioning,
> and by means of it he spares himself anxiety attacks. We can witness
> the converse of this if we interfere in the formation of symptoms, as is
> possible, for instance, with obsessions. If we prevent a patient from car-
> rying out a washing ceremonial, he falls into a state of anxiety which
> he finds hard to tolerate and from which he had evidently been pro-
> tected by his symptom.[85]

Repression is thus the fundamental defense against all anxiety-
producing wishes, memories, or feelings, and the very bedrock of the
psychological structure.[86] It works unconsciously; the child who has
repressed the wish that a little sibling would die does not know that he
harbors such a wish and will react with scorn or rage to any suggestion
that he does. (Suppression, a different mental act, is the conscious control of an impermissible desire; one wills oneself to avoid acting on the
desire, but this does not get rid of the anxiety.)

As with the Oedipal conflict, repression can result in neurosis but
normally does not; the psyche finds adaptive ways to handle the
repressed material. It does so by means of a number of other defenses—
again, all unconscious—that transmute the unacceptable into the
acceptable. Freud named several and referred readers to a more complete treatment of the defense mechanisms by his daughter, Anna
Freud.[87] Among the more commonly used defenses named by Freud or
discussed by Anna Freud are these:

Denial is a relatively primitive defense in which the individual simply
fails to perceive or acknowledge an anxiety-producing reality. A woman
who is forced to care for a dying husband may tell herself (contrary to all
the evidence) that he will recover shortly, or she may say, "I want to keep

him alive as long as possible," when unconsciously she wishes the ordeal were over.

Rationalization is a more sophisticated version of denial. The individual acts out of one motive but justifies the act in terms of another that is more acceptable. A battered woman whose low self-esteem makes her too dependent to be alone tells herself that she stays with her abusive lover or husband because she loves him.

Reaction formation goes a step further, exaggerating and displaying for all to see a trait exactly opposite to the repressed one. The man repressing homosexual wishes may behave in a macho fashion or physically assault gays. The would-be sybarite may become a born-again Christian or an implacable foe of erotic art and literature.

Displacement directs repressed feelings toward an acceptable substitute. A woman with an unduly strong attachment to her father may choose a man his age as a husband. A man who has buried his fierce anger at his controlling father may become a chronic rebel, fighting with all sorts of authority figures.

Intellectualization fends off anxiety by taking an ostensibly intellectual interest in an impermissible desire, a painful loss, or the like. A person with repressed sadistic impulses may become a social scientist specializing in the study of sadists or torturers. Freud's contemporary Havelock Ellis, though sexually inhibited during most of his life, wrote a mass of scholarly studies of normal and abnormal forms of sexual behavior.

Projection, a very common defense mechanism, is the attributing of one's own unacceptable impulses to the object of those impulses. People who deny feeling racial hatred may believe that persons of the other race hate them, or attribute to the others the impulses they deny in themselves, as in the case of Ku Klux Klan members who see blacks as vicious and sexually animalistic.

Sublimation, finally, is the most prosocial of the defense mechanisms; by means of it, superego and ego transmute the instinctual demand into some socially valuable related activity. Painting is often a sublimation of the childish impulse to smear or handle feces; writing or performing, sublimations of the impulse to exhibit oneself; surgery, a noble transformation of the urge to do harm; and most athletic games (and such nonathletic ones as chess), acceptable and enjoyable sublimations of aggression.

But Is It Scientific?

Ever since Freud began publishing his ideas, his psychology has been fiercely attacked on one ground or another. At first and for some decades many physicians and psychologists called it dirty and perverted; by the 1930s communist theorists were castigating it as decadent and bourgeois; and in the same decade the Nazis condemned it as Jewish filth and burned Freud's books.

Psychoanalysis outlived these assaults, but for many years it has been under attack of a more thoughtful kind: A number of psychologists and philosophers of science have asserted that it is not scientific. Their chief argument is that psychoanalytic research is not experimental; the psychoanalyst does not construct a situation in which he or she can control variables and manipulate them one at a time to measure their impact and so establish causal connections.

Experimentation, however, is not the only way to do science; induction from observation is another. Having perceived a pattern in a mass of data, the scientist hypothesizes about its cause, then tests the supposition by looking at more examples. If they too fit the hypothesis, it is strengthened; if they fail to, it is weakened. It is this method that is the basis of psychoanalytic research.

But the evidence so gathered, says the philosopher Adolf Grünbaum, is weak. For one thing, the observations that reveal a pattern have a "shared contaminant"—the analyst's influence. After the analyst offers an interpretation of some piece of behavior, for instance, the patient may dutifully come up with a confirming memory (which may in fact be imaginary).[88] For another, when free association is used to investigate such different areas as neurotic symptoms, dreams, and parapraxes, the agreement among the data may be the result of using a single method to explore different phenomena rather than a genuine concurrence of the findings.

Grünbaum says that this does not warrant the conclusion that psychoanalysis is unverifiable; rather, it indicates that verification of its theories must come from well-designed *extra*clinical studies, either epidemiological or even experimental.[89]

Many efforts toward that end have, in fact, been made. Some have involved laboratory experiments in which volunteers are subjected to a stimulus that, according to Freudian theory, should yield a particular result. Others, relying on tests to measure certain character traits among which there is supposed to be a psychodynamic connection, have sought the statistical correlations among those traits that would support the supposition. Still others have taken a developmental approach, observing and measuring the personality traits and behavior of children as they grow up to see whether character development proceeds according to Freudian theory or requires other explanations.

By now a large body of such studies has accumulated. They vary greatly in methodological soundness, and range widely in scope, testing everything from overarching theory to small and specialized subtheories. This makes it difficult to weigh the cumulative outcome, but a few hardy scholars have sought to do so.

One review of such studies, made some years ago by the psychologists Seymour Fisher and Roger P. Greenberg, focused more on results than on methodological adequacy, and rendered a split decision. Fisher and Greenberg named the following Freudian theories as being well supported: his concepts of the oral and anal character; the etiology of male homosexuality (Freud postulated that a hostile, rejecting father and a close, binding mother so intensify Oedipal rivalry as to inhibit the choice of a female partner); the origin of paranoia as a defense against homosexual impulses; several aspects of Oedipal theory; and as much of dream theory as concerns the dream's function as an outlet for psychological tension.

They cited as those found faulty the thesis that the dream is a camouflaged unconscious wish, the claim that psychoanalysis is superior to other therapies in the treatment of neurosis, some parts of the Oedipal theory, and many of Freud's ideas about the female character.

Their summation:

When we add up the totals resulting from our search, balancing the positive against the negative, we find that Freud has fared rather well. But like all theorists, he has proved in the long run to have far from a perfect score. He seems to have been right about a respectable number of issues, but he was also wrong about some important things. If one considers only his formulations concerning men and if, further, one considers only his theoretical propositions . . . , his record of correct hits is excellent.[90]

A later review of such studies, the 1981 edition of Paul Kline's *Fact and Fantasy in Freudian Theory*, was more inclusive than Fisher and Greenberg's and, according to Kline, more discriminating, because he drew conclusions only from research with the soundest methodology. Making no effort to appraise such larger Freudian theories as the death instinct and the pleasure principle, which are "metapsychological"— essentially philosophic, and so untestable—Kline found that no fewer than sixteen Freudian concepts have been verified. He summed up as follows:

> The objective evidence [provides] some confirmation of a tripartite division of mental activity into ego, super-ego, and id. Developmental theory is supported in that oral erotism [the erotic component in the infant's oral pleasure], Oedipus and castration complexes appear to occur. Furthermore adult personality patterns like the oral and anal character can be generally observed. There seems no doubt that the defence mechanism repression is commonly used and other defences have been observed. Sexual symbolism is a verified phenomenon both within and outside dreams . . . [In sum] many of the Freudian concepts most important to psychoanalytic theory have been supported.[91]

Decline and Fall—and Revival

But by the time these partial confirmations had appeared, the prestige and influence of Freudian psychology and the popularity of psychoanalysis—always limited, to be sure, by its cost, if nothing else—were waning.

Throughout the 1960s, 1970s, and 1980s, a congeries of pervasive social changes and important developments within the behavioral sciences undercut the status of the theory and the elitist appeal of analytic therapy.[92]

The social developments and protest movements of those decades turned public attention toward broader and more external issues, the women's movement generated bitter vocal opposition to Freud's ideas about women, and spokespersons of the homosexual revolution fiercely assailed Freud's ideas about homosexuality.

In academic psychology, new and empirically based research was demonstrating many influences on child development other than those Freud had posited; in clinical psychology, there gushed forth an unending stream of briefer and more practical adaptations of psychoanalysis and of nonanalytic therapies; in psychiatry, in the 1950s and 1960s, tranquilizers and antipsychotic medications were beginning to empty mental hospitals of deeply depressed and moderately schizophrenic patients, and outside the hospitals medication appeared to be far more efficient and quicker than insight-oriented talk therapy.

Psychoanalytic organizations had sought to cast psychoanalysis as a specialty within medicine,* but the American Psychiatric Association rejected or radically revised in its *Diagnostic and Statistical Manual III* (1980) and *IV* (1994) many Freudian-based diagnoses of mental illness. And as mentioned earlier, by the 1980s and 1990s a number of penetrating (but often tendentious) attacks on Freud's scientific methodology and his personality appeared.

No wonder *Time* magazine's cover of November 29, 1993, was a portrait of Freud alongside the boldfaced question "Is Freud Dead?"—the answer apparently being self-evident.

Guess again.

Despite all the valid and invalid attacks on Freudian theory, many of Freud's ideas have permanently perfused and modified our culture. "The world's history is the world's judgment," said Schiller, and this is surely true in Freud's case. After all the assaults on his character, the philosophic arguments about his theories, and the laborious efforts to validate or invalidate them, the measure of the man and his ideas is their impact on the history of psychology and on Western civilization. Today, Freud's enemies and admirers agree, his ideas have permeated Western culture, spawning a host of variant psychotherapies and, more important, profoundly influencing the way artists and writers, legislators, teachers, parents, advertisers, and the majority of literate people think about human nature and themselves. As Fisher and Greenberg said in 1977, "Freud's theories are now a basic part of our cultural substance,"[93] and by any number of objective criteria, that is still undoubtedly so. But we all intuitively know it to be so. We have only to reflect for a moment on how often, and how naturally, we think in terms of Freudian psychology: the sexual symbolism of various objects, the secret (or at least half-secret) hostility of much humor, the unconscious reasons for mistakes and slips of the tongue, the hidden motives in risk taking and self-

---

*A personal note: I remember being astonished when in the early 1950s I visited the psychiatrist Dr. Karl Menninger to interview him about suicidal patients and found him wearing a white coat.

defeating behavior, the parental role in homosexual development, the everyday effort to look for the "real" reason someone has said or done something we find hard to understand, and on and on. Such ways of thinking pervade everyday life.

These and similar beliefs are based on a larger one: the existence of the dynamic unconscious. It is this which Freud was alluding to when, late in life, he told an admirer, "I am not a great man—I made a great discovery."[94]

His great discovery, opening up what had been a vast unexplored area of the mind, permanently enlarged the dimensions and changed the direction of modern psychology, according to the British historian of the field, L. S. Hearnshaw:

> [Freud] brought psychologists face to face with the whole range of human problems, with the central questions that had been treated by great thinkers, artists and writers from ancient times, but had been almost excluded from the arid abstractions of the academic schools— with problems of love and hate, of happiness and misery; with the turmoil of social discontent and violence, as well as the trifling errors and slips of everyday existence; with the towering edifices of religious belief as well as the petty, but tragic, tensions of family life.[95]

Raymond Fancher went even further:

> His demonstration of the importance and pervasiveness of unconscious mental factors was so effective that this once revolutionary idea is almost taken for granted today. The best art and literature of our time portrays human beings as creatures in conflict with themselves, subject to forces beyond their personal conscious control, and unaware of their own identities . . . Sigmund Freud was among the small handful of individuals whose work vitally affected not just a single field of specialization, but also an entire intellectual climate.[96]

The central component of that climate remains as real today, many psychologists and psychiatrists feel, as when Fancher made that statement in 1979. As Jonathan Lear, a philosopher and psychiatrist at the University of Chicago says, Freud's reputation rests on the "core idea" that human life is "essentially conflicted," but that the conflict is hidden from us because it stems from wishes and instincts that are actively repressed because we cannot tolerate recognizing them consciously.[97]

Yet others, even though they prize certain central concepts of Freudian psychology, fear that with the decline and fall of psychoanalysis those concepts are in danger of being forgotten. Eli Zaretsky, for one, feels less than optimistic that we will preserve the profound understandings Freud and psychoanalysis brought us. "Can [those understandings] survive the decline of psychoanalysis? Have the global speedup, the near collapse of the boundary between the public and the private, and computerization, which reduces the psychology of meaning to the transfer of information, eviscerated intrapsychic experience? Do our new insights into race, nations, and gender obviate the need for individuals to understand their own unique individuality?"[98]

Offsetting this rather gloomy view, there has been, lately, a surprising development: a resurgence of interest in psychoanalysis—both as therapy and as psychology. (*Newsweek*'s March 27, 2006, cover, heralding a long and deeply researched article,[99] consisted of Freud's portrait and the headline FREUD IS NOT DEAD.)

In part, the revival represents a renewed interest in modern and greatly modified forms of analytic therapy. The American Psychoanalytic Association has actually grown a little in the past half-dozen years and now has 3,400 members, and a rival group, the National Association for the Advancement of Psychoanalysis, has 1,500.

But in part—and far more important—a number of elements in Freudian psychology have recently been validated by contemporary neuroscience, making real his 1905 fantasy that psychological phenomena would someday be explicable in physical terms. In a review of this evidence in *Scientific American*, Professor Mark Solms of the University of Cape Town says:

> For decades, Freudian concepts such as ego, id, and repressed desires dominated psychology and psychiatry's attempts to cure mental illnesses. But better understanding of brain chemistry gradually replaced this model with a biological explanation of how the mind arises from neuronal activity. The latest attempts to piece together diverse neurological findings, however, are leading to a chemical framework of mind that validates the general sketch Freud made almost a century ago. A growing group of scientists are eager to reconcile neurology and psychiatry into a unified theory.[100]

Solms goes on to list several ways that neuroscience has validated Freudian ideas, among them the following:

— Neuroscience has shown that the major brain structures essential for forming conscious memories are not functional during the first two years of life, accounting for what Freud called infantile amnesia. As Freud supposed, it is not that we forget our earliest memories; we simply cannot recall them to consciousness. But this does not prevent them from affecting adult feelings and behavior. "It is becoming increasingly clear," writes Solms, "that a good deal of our mental activity is unconsciously motivated."

— Neuroscientists have identified unconscious memory systems that account for some irrational phobias. Joseph LeDoux of New York University has shown that under the conscious cortex a neuronal pathway, bypassing the hippocampus—which generates conscious memories—sends perceptual information to the primitive brain structures that generate fear responses. The result: Current events often trigger unconscious memories of emotionally important past events, resulting in irrational conscious fear.

— Even if much of our behavior is unconsciously driven, this does not prove Freud's claim that we actively repress unpalatable information. But neurological case studies supporting the concept of repression are beginning to accumulate. Vilayanur Ramachandran of the University of California at San Diego reported a study, now famous, of a woman whose left arm was paralyzed by a stroke but who remained completely unaware of it for days, until Ramachandran artificially stimulated the right hemisphere of her brain; she then recognized that her arm was paralyzed and that she had unconsciously ignored the defect for eight days. But after the effects of stimulation wore off, she reverted to the belief that her arm was all right—and even forgot the part of an interview in which she had recognized the paralysis. Ramachandran, impressed, wrote: "The remarkable theoretical implication of those observations is that memories can indeed be selectively repressed . . . Seeing [this patient] convinced me, for the first time, of the reality of the repression phenomena that form the cornerstone of classical psychoanalytic theory."[101]

— Dreams, which many anti-Freudians explained in terms devoid of Freudian meanings, do, after all, have meaning. Although some dreaming is driven by brain chemistry and reflects random cortical activity, brain scans and other evidence show that dreaming is generated by a network of structures centered on the forebrain's instinctual-motivational circuitry; this has given rise to a number of theories about dreaming similar to Freud's. Solms and others have also found that dreaming stops completely when certain fibers deep in the frontal lobe have been severed (as by an accident or brain surgery)—a symptom that coincides with a general reduction in motivated behavior.

Solms's conclusion: "It appears that Freud's broad brushstroke organization of the mind is destined to play a role similar to the one Darwin's theory of evolution served for molecular genetics—a template on which emerging details can be coherently arranged . . . It is gratifying to find that we can build on the foundations he laid, instead of having to start all over."

In the end, we have to disagree with Freud's modest statement that he was not a great man but had made a great discovery. Only a great man could have done so.

EIGHT

The
Measurers

"Whenever You Can, Count":
Francis Galton

At the 1884 International Health Exhibition in London, a small fenced-off area of the hall, only six by thirty-six feet, was grandly designated the Anthropometric Laboratory. In it, on a long table staffed by three attendants, were a number of pieces of simple apparatus, among them a pendulum and a response key, a handgrip and dial, a photometer with which to compare small patches of color, and a long tube that emitted a whistle when an assistant blew through it and whose pitch he raised by turning a calibrated screw plug at the end until the visitor could no longer hear it. For threepence, the visitor could be tested and measured for thirteen characteristics: reaction time, keenness of sight and hearing, color discrimination, ability to judge length, strength of pull and squeeze, strength of blow, height, weight, arm span, breathing power, and breathing capacity.[1]

Why anyone thought it worth even threepence to obtain these data is hard to say, but during the run of the exhibition, 9,337 persons did so. Perhaps the activity seemed meritorious in itself; it was a time when precise measurement was becoming the hallmark of science and had great cachet even if one had no specific purpose in mind.

If the visitors to the Anthropometric Laboratory had no specific purpose in mind, its proprietor did. He was Francis Galton, a tiny bald man with white sideburns whose penetrating blue eyes, jutting nose, and slit of a mouth gave him an air of authority a larger man might envy. Galton, an amateur psychologist, was convinced that the differences in intelligence among individuals were largely hereditary, and hence that society could advance the evolution of the human race by offering the most intelligent people rewards for procreating. But how were they to be identified? He believed that a number of hereditary physical traits or abilities, particularly acuity of the senses and reaction time, were related to intelligence and therefore were gauges of it. (Among his reasons for thinking so were two of his own observations: first, that mental retardates had poor sensory discrimination; second, that work requiring sensory acuity, such as piano tuning, wine tasting, or wool sorting, was always done by men, who, he took for granted, were far more intelligent than women.)[2]

Galton's lineage may have predisposed him to his view of intelligence. On one side, he was a grandson of the eminent physician and botanist Erasmus Darwin (Charles Darwin, another grandson, was Galton's cousin), and on the other side the grandson and son of successful bankers. But he had additional grounds. Earlier, he had collected genealogies of a large number of illustrious men and shown that eminence—which he equated with intelligence—runs in families.

It was to run trials of tests measuring physical characteristics allied to intelligence and to collect the results that Galton, at his own expense, set up the Anthropometric Laboratory at the exhibition. In so doing, he initiated a form of psychological research wholly unlike the experimentation Wundt was even then conducting in Leipzig, the introspection James was practicing at Harvard, and the "talking cure" Freud was discussing with Breuer in Vienna and would shortly start using in his office.

Whatever one may think of Galton's views, he was no well-to-do, idle, Victorian chauvinist but a scientist of extraordinary mental gifts, enthusiasm, curiosity, and dedication to work. A genuine polymath, he was a successful inventor, award-winning geographer, authoritative travel writer, meteorologist, developer of the first workable system of identifying fingerprints, pioneer in the use of twin studies to tease apart the influences of heredity and environment, and inventor of correlation analysis, one of the most valuable research tools of psychology and other sciences.

Above all, Galton was the first to use mental tests, thereby inaugurating a new form of psychological research and a new field of study: individual differences. Other psychologists, Wundtians in particular, were looking for universal psychological principles such as the difference between how long it takes to respond to a sound reflexively and how long consciously. Galton was looking at the differences in individuals' characteristics (such as response times) and the relationship of those differences to their other traits and abilities.

Galton's interest in individual differences reflected the status of psychology in Britain in his time. Unlike the German universities, the British universities gave psychology no support and established no laboratories or departments of psychology; those who were interested in the field pursued it not as a subspecialty of physiology or of psychotherapy but according to their own interests and as a hobby. In a German university, Galton might well have been guided into physiological psychology; in Britain, he was free to ask what had made him a gifted person and how society could increase the number of people like himself.

Galton was born in Birmingham in 1822, well before Wundt and James and long before Freud, though his contributions to psychology, made in his middle and late middle years, were roughly contemporaneous with theirs.[3] The precocious youngest of seven children in an intellectual middle-class family, he began to read at two and a half, and before five could read almost anything in English, knew a good deal of Latin and some French, and could solve most basic arithmetic problems. At six, when he went to a local school, he was scornful of the other boys because they had never heard of *Marmion* or the *Iliad*, and at seven he was reading Shakespeare and Pope for pleasure.

This promising start was blighted in boarding school, where rote learning was stressed and natural curiosity and independence were suppressed by floggings, sermons, and punitive homework assignments. Nor did he fare well when he went to Cambridge: feeling himself under pressure to excel, he was obsessed by examinations and by his academic standing relative to other students. In his third year, failing to rank at the very top of the list and seeing no possibility of becoming a Wrangler (an honors student in mathematics), he developed palpitations, dizziness, and an inability to concentrate. "A mill seemed to be working inside my head," he recalled late in life. "I could not banish obsessing ideas; at times I could hardly read a book, and found it painful even to look at a printed page." In the throes of breakdown, he left school and returned home. Only after deciding not to compete for an honors degree but to settle for a pass degree was he able to return and complete his studies. His obsession with tests and the ranking of intellectual ability, though, remained for the rest of his life.

After Cambridge, Galton completed medical training (which he had begun earlier), but when his father died, in 1844, leaving him well-to-do at twenty-two, he dropped the idea of practicing medicine and for several years lived the life of a gentleman, riding, shooting, attending parties, and traveling. However, the life of pleasure proved to be thin gruel for his restless mind, and in his late twenties, after consulting the Royal Geographical Society, he led a two-year expedition, at his own expense, to the interior of southwest Africa. He brought back a wealth of cartographic information on what had been a blank area of the map and at thirty-one was awarded the society's gold medal and recognized as a leading explorer.

In that same year, 1853, he married and thenceforth limited his traveling, keeping up his interest in exploration by writing travel books and helping to plan major expeditions. But these activities could not long content him, and he turned to invention, producing a number of useful devices, among them a printing telegraph (forerunner of the teletype), an improved oil lamp, a device for picking locks, a rotary steam engine, and a periscope to enable him to see over taller people in crowded places.

By his forties, in need of a new challenge, he took up meteorology. It had occurred to him that he could collect simultaneous weather data from many places by means of the recently developed telegraph, plot them on a map, and see whether significant patterns became apparent. When he did so and drew lines connecting points having the same barometric pressure, he discovered that they described roughly circular low-pressure and high-pressure systems ("cyclones" and "anticyclones") whose movements across the surface of the earth were a basis for predicting weather.

At about the same time, Galton finally came upon the principal interest of his life, the inheritance of intelligence. In 1859 Charles Darwin had published his epochal *On the Origin of Species*, which vastly impressed Galton. One of Darwin's basic assumptions was that among the members of any species there are small inheritable variations or differences and that evolution occurs through the natural selection of the fittest members. Although *Origin* was concerned chiefly with animal species, Galton applied its conclusions to humankind; he reasoned that the evolution of the human species must take place by means of the natural selection of those with better minds and the transmission of their innate mental superiority to their offspring.

This accorded with the impression he had had at Cambridge that many men winning high honors had fathers and brothers who also were honors winners. Galton now conceived of and carried out a valuable, if laborious, research project: he examined and tabulated by family, over the past forty-one years, the top-scoring students in classics and mathematics at Cambridge.[4] As he had expected, top honors had been disproportionately won by men in certain families. He published his findings in 1865; from then on, the hereditary nature of mental ability and the improvement of the human race by selective breeding dominated his life and work. Galton must have found it a cruel trick of fate that he and his wife never had any children; a Freudian might suggest that his fixation on the subject was compensation for his failure to reproduce.

Although Galton had been unable to win mathematics honors at Cambridge, his research method was mathematical; like Demosthenes, determined to become an orator despite a speech defect, Galton made his weakness into his greatest strength. His approach to the study of intelligence, or indeed any problem that interested him, was to find something to count so that he could calculate proportions, compare averages, and draw conclusions. In Africa he measured the figures of native women (from a judicious distance) and found them impressive compared with those of Englishwomen. Back home, in cities he visited he kept track of whether every girl he passed on the street was pretty, average, or ugly, and found that the incidence of pretty girls was highest in London, lowest in Aberdeen. At scientific meetings he counted the number of fidgets per minute in a sample of fifty members of the audience and reckoned that fidgeting decreased by more than half when the presentation interested the audience.

Galton's plan in *Hereditary Genius* (1869), the first and most influential of his four books on the inheritance of mental ability, was to select a number of unusually gifted people and see how common talent was in their families as compared with the general population. His criterion of unusual mental ability was, at this point, public reputation:

> I look upon social and professional life as a continuous examination. All are candidates for the good opinions of others, and for success in their several professions, and they achieve success in proportion as the general estimate is large of their aggregate merits.[5]

To establish how frequent such reputation (and thus mental ability) is, he counted the obituaries in the London *Times* for 1868 and some earlier years, and found that those who merited obituaries totaled about 250 per million of the population beyond middle age, or one in four thousand.

He then undertook to compare to this the proportion of eminent persons in the families of a number of illustrious men: English judges since the Reformation, premiers of the past century, and a sampling of famous military commanders, literary men, scientists, poets, painters, musicians, and Protestant divines. These men, he calculated, were far rarer than one in four thousand; he estimated their frequency as one in one million. If genius was hereditary, he should find among their relatives a far greater proportion of eminent persons than one per million or even one per four thousand.

Galton based his estimate of the rarity of genius on the "law of deviation from an average." That law had been worked out early in the century by mathematicians to express the distribution of errors in astronomic observations and of cards or numbers in games of chance. But it also applied to variations in human traits. In 1835 the Belgian astronomer Adolphe Quételet, using information about French conscripts, reported that a few men were very tall, a few very short, and the rest in between, with by far the largest number being average or close to it. The data, when plotted on a graph, yielded a bell-shaped curve, with most individuals in the center. The farther to either side of the midline one went, the fewer there were. The concept of the "curve of normal distribution" of human traits is so familiar today that it is hard to believe that in Quételet's time it was a revelation.

Galton assumed that what was true of height must be true of other bodily characteristics, like brain weight, number of nerve fibers, sensory acuity—and, hence, mental capacity. If so, the mental ability of individuals followed a normal curve of distribution. He divided the curve of human intelligence into sixteen equal segments—eight above average, eight below—and from the shape of the curve calculated the proportion of the population in each segment. The two highest segments, he reckoned, would total only 248 people per million, which tallied with the figure of one in four thousand for obituary-based eminence. But a very small number were even farther out at the high end of the curve. They were the one in one million who were truly illustrious and who, he hoped to show, were born that way, not made or self-made:

I have no patience with the hypothesis . . . that babies are born pretty much alike, and that the sole agencies in creating differences between boy and boy, and man and man, are steady application and moral effort. It is in the most unqualified manner that I object to pretensions of natural equality. The experiences of the nursery, the school, the university, and of professional careers, are a chain of proofs to the contrary.[6]

Galton felt certain that in a "progressive" society (his term) such as Victorian England, innate ability was sure to be rewarded by success: "If a man is gifted with vast intellectual ability, eagerness to work, and power of working, I cannot comprehend how such a man should be repressed . . . [Rather,] he is sure to be welcomed with universal acclamation."[7]

Heroic labor at his genealogical research yielded Galton the finding that of the 286 judges in his sample, about one in nine was the father, son, or brother of another judge; in addition, the judges numbered among their relatives many bishops, admirals, generals, novelists, poets, and physicians. The incidence of eminence in these families was hundreds of times greater than in the general population; the same was true of the other categories of eminent persons.

Summing up the data for all his categories of illustrious people, he reported that 31 percent had eminent fathers, 41 percent eminent brothers, and 48 percent eminent sons. Moreover, the closer the relationship between an eminent person and a relative, the greater the likelihood that the relative was eminent. Galton was satisfied that he had thoroughly proved his hypothesis—"that a man's natural abilities are derived from inheritance, under exactly the same limitations as are the form and physical features of the whole organic world."[8]

Contemporary psychologists can point to a number of naïve shortcomings in Galton's methodology, in particular his failure to evaluate the environments in which the illustrious grew up; if most of them had been reared in strongly favorable circumstances, the data might point to environmental influence as much as to hereditary influence. But whatever the limitations of Galton's technique, he had established the hereditary aspect of intelligence as a valid subject for psychological research, and it has remained so ever since.

Galton's name, however, has been tarnished by the recommendations for social policy that he based on his findings and by the meanings history has given to them. It was he who coined the term "eugenics" and who argued, from his first book about hereditary genius in 1869 until his death in 1911, that society would be improved if it encouraged and rewarded the breeding of superior people:

> [Eugenics is] the science of improving stock, which . . . takes cognisance of all influences that tend in however remote a degree to give to the more suitable races or strains of blood a better chance of prevailing speedily over the less suitable than they otherwise would have had.[9]

This view came to seem horrendous in the wake of Nazi efforts to encourage the procreation of pure "Aryans" and to exterminate Jews, Gypsies, and other groups they considered human vermin. Galton himself, according to his biographers, seemed a gentle and decent human being, and certainly not an advocate of genocide, but some of his comments about the proper treatment of undesirable people tread close to the line:

> I do not see why any insolence of caste should prevent the gifted class, when they had the power, from treating their compatriots with all kindness, so long as they maintained celibacy. But if these continue to procreate children, inferior in moral, intellectual and physical qualities, it is easy to believe that the time may come when such persons would be considered as enemies to the State, and to have forfeited all claims to kindness.[10]

One might expect a man with such views to have been a racist who saw all human groups other than his own as subhuman, but Galton was not. Although he estimated the average intelligence of blacks as two levels below the English, he rated the English as two levels below the ancient Athenians; he also said that he would have liked to investigate Italians and Jews, "both of whom appear to be rich in families of high intellectual breeds."

While Galton's ideas about eugenics are no part of present-day psychology, they led him to invent some of the field's most valuable methods of research. The genealogical study of the inheritability of psychological traits is only one of them. Another and even more useful one was inspired by criticisms of *Hereditary Genius* that pointed to evidence of the influence of environment on intelligence, particularly the statistical findings of the Swiss botanist Alphonse de Candolle, showing that great scientists tend to come from countries with moderate climates, religious tolerance, democratic government, and healthy commercial interests— all environmental influences.

This spurred Galton on to an effort to distinguish the influences of heredity and environment in the achievement of eminence, specifically in science. In 1874, in *English Men of Science,* he stated the problem very fairly, using a shorthand expression for genetic and environmental influences on development that immediately entered the language:

> The phrase "nature and nurture" is a convenient jingle of words, for it separates under two distinct heads the innumerable elements of which personality is composed. Nature is all that a man brings with him into the world; nurture is every influence that affects him after his birth. The distinction is clear: the one produces the infant such as it actually is, including its latent faculties of growth and mind; the other affords the environment amid which the growth takes place, by which natural tendencies may be strengthened or thwarted, or wholly new ones implanted.[11]

To learn about the part played by nature and by nurture in scientific eminence, Galton invented another new research tool: the self-questionnaire. He drew up a set of questions about the respondent's racial, religious, social, and political background, traits of character, and even hair color and hat size, and sent copies to two hundred members of the Royal Society. Among the crucial questions were: "How far do your scientific tastes appear to have been innate? Were they largely determined by events after you reached manhood, and by what events?"

Despite the questionnaire's "alarming" length—Galton's own rueful term—most of the subjects completed and returned it. (It was the first such questionnaire in history; today a researcher might get no such compliance.) When Galton tabulated the responses, he found that a majority believed their taste for science was innate; on the other hand, most respondents had a lot to say about how their education had either helped or hindered them. Galton felt obliged to admit that environmental factors, education in particular, could enhance or inhibit the development of scientific aptitude, and that its inheritance did not inevitably lead to success. Nonetheless, he maintained that hereditary aptitude had been shown to be the essential factor in scientific achievement.

Much later, as research methodology developed, it would become apparent that Galton's questionnaire and his analysis of the data had serious weaknesses. For one thing, many of the questions, particularly those about the reasons for the respondents' success, yielded purely subjective answers; for another, Galton had not given the questionnaire to noneminent scientists and nonscientists to see whether their answers were any different from those of eminent scientists; for a third, he had no way (though later he would invent one) to mathematically measure the relation between any two factors so as to judge whether it was accidental or significant. All the same, Galton's use of the questionnaire and analysis of the data were innovations of immense value and have been important weapons in the armamentarium of psychological research ever since.

During the next decade Galton, now middle-aged, worked harder than ever at studies of individual psychological differences. In 1883 he published his observations on some thirty miscellaneous topics in an *omnium gatherum* titled *Inquiries into Human Faculty and Its Development*, a curious mixture of science and speculation, data and conjecture, statistics and anecdotes. Some of it purported to be science but was little more than Victorian male prejudice. In the chapter on "character," for instance, Galton asserted without offering evidence that "one notable peculiarity in the character of the woman is that she is capricious and coy, and has less straightforwardness than the man." He approved of this on evolutionary grounds: in courtship, were there no female hesitancy and male competition, "the race would degenerate through the absence of that sexual selection for which the protracted preliminaries of love-making give opportunity."

But a good deal of *Inquiries* consisted of highly original scientific studies. One dealt with the ability to summon up mental images. Many nonscientists, Galton found, think in vivid images, many scientists in purely abstract terms, and he speculated that the ability to summon up sharp mental images hinders thinking in highly generalized and abstract terms. In another study he reported his invention of the word-association test; he drew up a list of seventy-five stimulus words and exposed them to his own view one by one, jotting down his first two or three associations to each. Most of what he learned was unremarkable, such as that, on repeating the test, he came up with the same associations. But there was genuine value to his observation that many of his associations sprang from his own experiences and that other people would be unlikely to have his associations. The result was that word-association tests became a leading way of studying individual personality traits.

Another noteworthy study was a report of one more Galton innovation. Still grappling with the problem of how to demonstrate the relative influences of nature and nurture on the development of the mind and personality, he had the brilliant idea of examining "the after-history of those twins who had been closely alike as children, and were afterwards parted, or who had been originally unlike and afterwards reared together." He knew that twins came in two kinds: those who were physically almost identical and those who were no more alike than any other two siblings. If twins who were originally very similar became less so as they went through life, it could only be nurture that made them so; if twins who were originally dissimilar and were reared identically remained dissimilar, it could only be nature that kept them so.

It was a dazzling hypothesis, though Galton had only crude means of proving it. He sent a questionnaire to twins or relatives of twins he knew; he also asked them to give him the names of other twins. Eventually he had replies from ninety-four cases, eighty of which were of "close similarity" (probably identicals) and thirty-five of which provided enough details to be useful.

His report of the twin study is largely anecdotal; it tells of identicals who played tricks on people, or were both paddled by a schoolmaster who could not tell which one deserved punishment, of one who sometimes courted his brother's fiancée, and so on. But when Galton sorted through his cases in search of identicals who became dissimilar in character, he found that, for some, "the resemblance of body and mind continued unaltered up to old age, notwithstanding very different conditions of life." Others did exhibit differences, but in every case it was because an illness or accident had affected only one of the pair. In contrast, twins who had been dissimilar in childhood (probably fraternals), even if reared together and identically, did not become more alike over the years.[12]

Not one given to caution, Galton proclaimed, "There is no escape from the conclusion that nature prevails enormously over nurture when the differences of nurture do not exceed what is commonly to be found among persons of the same rank of society and in the same country." From a contemporary perspective, the study was simplistic, imprecise, and far from conclusive. Still, it was a notable first, and the twin study method has been an important research strategy ever since and the most nearly definitive way of assessing the influences of heredity and environment on intelligence, personality traits, and other psychological characteristics.

Finally, Galton discussed in *Inquiries* his development of a number of mental tests in order quickly and simply to identify persons of superior intelligence, as part of his grand dream of improving the human race through eugenics. The year after *Inquiries* appeared, he began his trials of the tests at the International Health Exhibition, and when the fair closed down, he got permission from the South Kensington Museum to continue operating the laboratory there for a number of years. During that time he devised a number of new mental tests, among them a bar with a variable distance on it to test the ability to estimate extension, a rotating disk to test the ability to judge perpendicularity, sets of weights to be arranged in order of heaviness, and sets of bottles that contained aromatic material to be arranged according to intensity of odor.[13]

Galton was in his late sixties, far beyond the age at which scientists usually make their important discoveries, when he made his most important one. Appropriately, it involved his lifelong obsession, counting. Each kind of measurement made in the Anthropometric Laboratory had yielded a bell-shaped probability curve, but Galton sensed that he might glean other and highly significant information if he could discover how the different sets of measurements were related to one another. Some of the relationships were obvious—taller people, for instance, tended to weigh more—but what was the relationship between other sets of measurements? Which of them varied together and in the same degree? What did it mean if they did not vary in the same degree? Only by knowing how the data were related and which measures had little connection with the others would he be able to design an ideal battery of tests indicative of intelligence.

Galton had been led to consider this problem by an odd finding in his studies of hereditary genius: the children of unusual parents were generally less unusual. In terms of physical traits, for instance, the children of tall parents tended to be less tall, though still above average, and the children of short parents not as short, though still below average, a tendency Galton called "regression towards mediocrity" (later, the term became "regression towards the mean"). He wanted to know what it indicated about the strength of heredity and how he could express it mathematically. On the face of it, this seemed a purely intellectual puzzle; as it turned out, the solution to the problem would become one of the most useful research tools in psychology and many other sciences.

After pondering the matter for a long while, Galton set down a "scatter plot" of the heights of some three hundred children. First he created a grid, the horizontal dimension of which was children's heights and the vertical dimension of which was parents' heights (actually, the heights of "mid-parents"—the average of each parental pair). Then, in each cell of the grid (each intersection of a particular children's height and a particular parental height) he wrote down the number of children who fit that category. The scatter plot looked like this:

Mid-parents		ADULT CHILDREN Heights and deviations from 68 1/4 inches									
Heights in inches	Deviation in inches	64	65	66	67	68	69	70	71	72	73
		−4	−3	−2	−1	0	1	2	3	4	
72	3						1	2	2	2	1
71	2				2	4	5	5	4	3	1
70	1	1	2	3	5	8	9	9	8	5	3
69	0	2	3	6	10	12	12	2	10	6	3
68	−1	3	7	11	13	14	13	10	7	3	1
67	−2	3	6	8	11	11	8	6	3	1	
66		2	3	4	6	4	3	2			

For a time, it revealed nothing to him; then one morning, poring over it while waiting for a train, he suddenly saw a regularity in the numbers. If he drew a line connecting any set of approximately equal values, it would describe a tipped-over ellipse whose center point was the midpoint of the scatter plot (the averages for both parents and children). When he did so and then drew lines across the ellipse connecting its extreme horizontal and vertical points, they passed through the average height of children in each vertical column and the average height of parents in each horizontal row. It looked like this:

Mid-parents		ADULT CHILDREN their heights and deviations from 68 1/4 inches									
Heights in inches	Deviation in inches	64	65	66	67	68	69	70	71	72	73
		-4	-3	-2	-1	0	1	2	3	4	
72	3					1	2	2	2	1	
71	2				2	4	5	5	4	3	1
70	1	1	2	3	5	8	9	9	8	5	3
69	0	2	3	6	10	12	12		10	6	3
68	-1	3	7	11	13	14	13	10	7	3	1
67	-2	3	6	8	11	11	8	6	3	1	
66		2	3	4	6	4	3	2			

Overlaid on the diagram: Minor axis, Major axis, Locus of vertical tangential points, Locus of horizontal tangential points, tangential points, and points labeled Y, N, M, X.

The ellipse and the lines crossing it revealed the relationship he had been looking for. At any given parental height ("Locus of horizontal tangential points"), the average height of the children was only about two-thirds as far from the mean (average) as that of the parents; that is, the children had "regressed" a third of the way toward the mean.[14] Conversely, for any children's height ("Locus of vertical tangential points"), parents were somewhat closer to the mean (that is, parents of unusual children were less unusual than their children).

Galton had discovered the analytical device of the "regression line." If the children's heights had been exactly the same as the parents', the two regression lines would have coincided; if the children's heights had no relation whatever to the parents', the regression lines would have been perpendicular to each other. As it was, they were fairly close, meaning that the relation between the two variables in this case—their *correlation*—was about midway between total and nil.

That was in 1886. Ten years later the British biometrician Karl Pearson, a Galton disciple and later his biographer, worked out a mathematical means of calculating the "coefficient of correlation"—which he called r, for regression—without any need to create scatter plots. For any two sets of data, it would show a correlation ranging from 1 (a perfect one-to-one covariation) to 0 (no relationship whatever) and to –1 (a totally inverse relationship). The Pearsonian method has been the standard way of evaluating correlation to this day. In the case of parents and children, r turned out to be .47 (somewhat different from Galton's first calculations): that is, children averaged about half as far from the population's average as their parents.[15]

The importance of Galton's discovery of correlation analysis can hardly be overestimated. It meant that whenever two variables change in the same direction (or the opposite direction), even though not to the same degree, they are correlated, and the strength of the correlation indicates how meaningful the relationship between them is. The stronger the relationship, the less likely it is happenstance and the more likely the connection is causal. One variable may be the cause (or a contributing cause) of the other, or vice versa, or they may be the concurrent and linked effects of some other cause. In either case, a strong correlation suggests an explanation of the phenomenon under study. In the numbers are, if not answers, at least clues.

(Even a strong correlation, to be sure, may be "spurious"—an artificial result of some other cause. In men, for instance, the degree of baldness correlates with length of marriage—not because one has any connection with the other but because age is related to each. Later techniques of analysis have been able to screen out such misleading correlations.)

The psychologist George Miller, appraising the value of Galton's discovery, writes:

Covariation is a central concept, not only for genetics and psychology, but for all scientific inquiry. A scientist searches for the causes of events; all he ever finds are correlations between antecedent and consequent conditions . . . Galton's insight has been, and continues to be, essential for vast stretches of modern social and behavioral science, and is useful in countless ways to engineers and natural scientists as well.[16]

Add to that his many other important methodological contributions and one can see why, although Galton was not a profound thinker, Raymond Fancher says that "few men have had greater impact on modern psychology."[17]

Galtonian Paradoxes

The outcome of Galton's work is a paradox. Although several of his methodological inventions are of vital importance in contemporary psychological research, his name means little to most psychologists and is all but unknown to the public. Working alone outside a university setting, he created no school of psychology, supervised no doctoral dissertations, and had few followers. Moreover, his chief contributions were research methods rather than illuminating theories, but the world remembers the latter, even though ingenious research methods are often the route to great insights.

And there is another and larger paradox. The measuring of individual differences in intelligence, a prominent goal of Galton's life, has had a great impact on Western society since the early part of the present century—but not by means of his method. Although he conceived of and originated mental testing, his name is not linked with any of the tests used today or in the past ninety years; except in histories of psychology, he is remembered, if at all, as the originator not of mental testing but of eugenics.

In Great Britain, Galton was the founder of a "new psychology" of individual differences, but almost no British psychologists thought of themselves as Galtonians.[18] In the latter part of the nineteenth century most British experimental psychologists went to Germany for training and brought Wundtian procedures and theory back with them. They adopted many of Galton's ideas and methodological inventions but considered themselves Wundtians. The new German psychology was held in much greater esteem than the British; it was the product of the university system and was "pure," while Galton's was the product of a gifted amateur and was intended to serve practical purposes.

Galton's effect was greatest in America, but again not in the form of a school of psychology. Before the turn of the century, many American psychologists were structuralists (Wundtians), who had no interest in the measurement of individual differences. By 1905 the functionalists (Jamesians) were dominant, but though they were sympathetic to many of Galton's ideas, they defined themselves in grander theoretical terms than those of his psychology. Like William James, many leading figures in American psychology, including John Dewey, James Rowland Angell, George H. Mead, James McKeen Cattell, Edward Lee Thorndike, and Robert S. Woodworth, based their theories on the evolutionary selection of the mentally fittest and its social equivalent, the struggle to get ahead. None called himself a Galtonian, but they shared a utilitarian outlook and all of them, therefore, valued Galton's methods of measuring individual differences because the methods were so practical.[19]

The most enthusiastic advocate of anthropometric measurement was James McKeen Cattell (1860–1944).[20] Born in Easton, Pennsylvania, and educated there at Lafayette College, he went to Leipzig in 1883 and studied with Wundt until 1886. His main research interest was the study of reaction times, but he was a fiercely independent young man and dared to differ with the great Wundt on a key methodological issue: Cattell doubted that anyone could really introspect in the manner called for by Wundt, namely, by subdividing reaction time into perception, choice, and so on. As a consequence, Cattell, though he was Wundt's laboratory assistant, had to carry out some of his work in his own quarters, because Wundt would not allow in the laboratory research by those who could not or would not follow his introspection method.

Cattell was intrigued by the differences in reaction time among the people he tested, and discussed it as a matter of "special interest" in an 1885 paper.[21] After earning his doctorate the following year, he went to London, met Galton, and, despite nearly a forty-year gap in their ages, found him a kindred spirit. Deeply impressed by Galton—many years later Cattell called him "the greatest man whom I have known"—he worked for him off and on for two years in the Anthropometric Laboratory at the South Kensington Museum and became thoroughly conversant with the tests performed there.

In 1888, at only twenty-eight, Cattell became a professor of psychology at the University of Pennsylvania (probably the first person in the world to hold that title; James, at Harvard, was not designated a professor of psychology until the following year). Cattell assembled a set of fifty tests, some Galtonian and some adapted from Fechner, Wundt, and other sources, and administered ten of them to his students to measure individual differences in intelligence. He supposed, as Galton had, that the chiefly physical characteristics measured by the tests were related to intelligence: strength of grip, speed of arm movement, reaction time to sound, just noticeable differences in weight, memory span for letters, and five others. In 1890, he described his work in a paper, in the journal *Mind*, called, "Mental Tests and Measurements"; it was the first use of that term and launched the mental-testing movement.

In 1891 Cattell moved to Columbia University as professor of psychology and head of the department. He expanded his battery of tests and each year gave them to fifty volunteers from among the entering freshmen. His admirable aim was to prove that the tests measured intelligence by showing a relationship between the test results and the students' grades; toward that end, he collected test data and student grades for close to a decade. Meanwhile the same method of testing intelligence was demonstrated at the Chicago World's Fair of 1893, where Joseph Jastrow, a leader of the American Psychological Association, created a virtual replica of Galton's Anthropometric Laboratory. Visiting psychologists undoubtedly found it interesting and impressive; during the 1890s such testing was begun in a number of laboratories in America and Europe.

By 1901 Cattell had collected enough data for a definitive study, and Clark Wissler, one of his students, performed a Galton-Pearson correlation analysis of them. His findings astonished and dismayed Cattell: there were no significant correlations between the students' grades and any of the anthropometric tests. If grades and academic standing were indications of intellectual ability, the anthropometric tests were not.[22] Furthermore, the tests were so little correlated with one another that it seemed plain they were not measuring a common attribute, as intelligence was presumed to be. Thus by yet another paradox, it was Galton's discovery, correlation analysis, that invalidated his own method of intelligence testing.

But that was not the end of the story for Cattell or for mental testing. Cattell, undaunted, developed a number of other tests, particularly in the field of value judgments, edited two science magazines, founded the Psychological Corporation to do applied psychology as a business, and became the prime exemplar of the hustling, practical, commercial side of psychology.

Although Galton's anthropometric approach to mental testing died out rapidly, intelligence testing of a different sort shortly took its place and soon made the study of individual differences the leading area of American psychology. By 1917, well over half of all research reported at meetings of the American Psychological Association dealt with individual differences.[23] Galton's assessment of the value of mental testing came to dominate American psychology, and intelligence testing became the means by which his hereditarian views influenced the schooling offered to students, the assignments given men in the military service, and the immigration policies of the nation.

A final paradox is that none of these results was the intent of the man who developed the intelligence tests that supplanted Galton's. Alfred Binet's tests won out over Galton's; Galton's views won out over Binet's.

The Mental Age Approach:
Alfred Binet

Alfred Binet, whose name every undergraduate learns in Introductory Psychology, was not a great psychologist; he formulated no important theory, made no brilliant discoveries, and was not a charismatic teacher. But he had one original and relatively simple idea, on the basis of which he and his collaborator, Théodore Simon, fashioned a mental test that has profoundly affected the lives of millions of people.

Binet was born in Nice, France, in 1857; his father was a physician and his mother a woman of some artistic talent.[24] His parents separated when he was young and he was raised by his mother; whether due to that circumstance, unusual in his time, or to his being an only child or to a constitutional bent, he grew up an introverted man who made few friends and was most comfortable working and studying alone.

Seeking to find his proper métier, Binet made many false starts. In his student years, he earned a law degree, but then decided that science was more interesting and began the study of medicine. However, having an independent income and not faced with the need to earn a living, he dropped out of medical school to study psychology, to which he had felt drawn for years. He unwisely chose not to pursue psychological training in a formal way but immersed himself in solitary reading in the library (where, among other works, he studied Galton's *Hereditary Genius*).

His self-education might have led nowhere, but in 1883 an old classmate, Joseph Babinski (who would later discover the infant reflex that bears his name), introduced him to Charles Féré, a staff member at the Salpêtrière, who in turn introduced him to Jean Martin Charcot, its director. Though Binet had no degree in medicine or psychology, Charcot was impressed by his intelligence, knowledge, and interest in hypnosis, and offered him a position at the Salpêtrière clinic of neurology and hypnosis.

After some productive years there, Binet took another wrong turn. He and Féré conducted some poorly controlled experiments in hypnosis, imagined that they had discovered a previously unknown phenomenon in hysterical patients, and made public their findings. By the use of magnets, they said, they had been able to shift any action the patient performed under hypnosis, such as lifting an arm, from one side of the body to the other. Even more remarkable, they had been able, also by means of magnets, to transform any of the patient's emotions or perceptions into the opposite—the fear of snakes, for instance, into a fondness for snakes.

Their report of this hocus-pocus, which would have looked suspect even in Mesmer's time, brought immediate criticism. Auguste Liébeault and his followers, the Nancy School of hypnotism, said that the effects were produced by suggestion; they proved it by eliciting the very same responses in nonhysterical persons by suggestion alone, without any use of magnets. Binet, who had staked his reputation on the results of the work, had to admit publicly that the results had been brought about by inadvertent experimenter suggestion and were worthless. (Afterward he would often say, "Tell me what you are looking for and I will tell you what you will find," a succinct statement of what came to be known among psychologists as "experimenter expectancy effects.")

The shattering experience led to Binet's resignation from the clinic and his withdrawal from contact with other psychologists. In virtual isolation for about two years, he wrote and produced several plays with themes of terror, murder, and mental illness. Happily, he also spent much time observing the thought processes of his two children, Madeleine and Alice, who were then four and a half and two and a half. To study the nature of thinking at their ages, he devised a number of simple tests: In one he asked them to name the uses of certain everyday objects; in another he asked them to judge which of two piles of coins or beans contained more items; in a third he removed a group of objects from view and then put them back one by one, asking whether any remained unreturned. When the girls were older, he gave them little problems to solve in order to study the growth of reasoning processes. These studies, which he described in three papers, foreshadowed the achievements of Jean Piaget, the developmental psychologist, and were the first step toward the work that would make Binet famous.

Another step in that direction was his return, at thirty-five, to professional life. In 1892, on a train platform, he happened to meet Henri Beaunis, director of the Laboratory of Physiological Psychology at the Sorbonne, and fell into a friendly argument with him about hypnosis. The upshot was that Beaunis invited Binet to become his assistant, and two years later, on Beaunis's retirement, Binet succeeded him as director. At the laboratory he conducted his own research studies, directed those of many students, and at thirty-seven belatedly earned a doctorate. The degree was in natural science, not psychology, but by this time, thanks to his position and publications, he was a recognized figure in French psychology; and, what with his twirled, pointed mustache, pince-nez, and hair swirled artfully across his forehead in the mode of the god Pan, he looked the part. But his dearest wish, to become a professor of psychology, never came true; to members of the establishment, his notorious work on hypnotism, his unorthodox education, and his wrong kind of doctorate stood against him.

Besides, there was his latest bizarre enthusiasm: an effort to prove that intelligence was directly linked to brain size and could be gauged through "craniometry" (skull measurement). He had read and been convinced by Paul Broca's (and possibly also by Galton's) views to this effect. Binet reviewed previous craniometric studies, made a number of skull measurements on his own, and between 1898 and 1901 published nine papers on the subject in *L'Année Psychologique*, a journal that he had founded and of which he was the editor.

Once again he had taken a wrong trail. Early in the series he had said it was "incontestable" that head size was correlated with intelligence,[25] but later he measured the skulls of a number of schoolchildren identified by their teachers as the most intelligent in their classes and others as the least intelligent, and found that the differences in head size were insignificant. After much remeasuring and reconsideration of his data, he concluded that there were indeed regular but quite small differences in head size, but only between the five brightest and five dullest students in each group. He abandoned craniometry as an approach to the measurement of intelligence.

One could hardly have guessed, at this point, that Binet, in middle age, would shortly produce a work of solid scholarship that would have a considerable effect on the world.

Still interested in the measurement of intelligence, he went back to the method he had used to study his daughters' thinking. Conceiving of intelligence not as Galton had, in terms of sensory and motor abilities, but as a combination of cognitive abilities, Binet and a co-worker at the laboratory, Victor Henri, began trying out on Parisian schoolchildren a number of tests of those abilities—memory tests (for words, musical notes, colors, and digits), word-association tests, sentence-completion tests, and so on. Their findings suggested that a battery of such tests might measure intelligence if one knew how to weigh the data.

A propitious turn of events spurred Binet to develop this promising lead. Mandatory universal education of children had been instituted in France in 1881, and in 1899 the Free Society for the Psychological

Study of the Child, a professional group of which Binet was a member, began urging the Ministry of Public Instruction to do something about retarded children who had to go to school but were unable to cope with standard classroom work. In 1904, the ministry appointed a commission, of which Binet was a member, to study the problem. The commission unanimously recommended that children who had been identified by an examination as retarded should be placed in special classes or schools where they could get education suitable to their condition, but it said nothing about what the examination should consist of.

Binet and his former colleague in craniometry, Théodore Simon, took it on themselves to create such an examination. First they assembled a number of tests, some drawn from studies made earlier at the Salpêtrière, others from the work of Binet and Henri at the Sorbonne laboratory, and still others that they formulated. They then visited some primary schools and tried their tests on children ranging from three to twelve who were considered normal by their teachers, and on others who were considered subnormal. They also tested a number of children institutionalized at the Salpêtrière who were classified as idiots, imbeciles, and *débiles.* *

After laboriously administering the examination to hundreds of children and omitting or modifying those tests which proved unfeasible, Binet and Simon fashioned what they called a "measuring scale of intelligence." They described it in *L'Année Psychologique* in 1905 as "a series of tests of increasing difficulty, starting from the lowest intellectual level that can be observed, and ending with that of normal intelligence. Each group [of tests] in the series corresponds to a different mental level."[26]

It was not yet an intelligence test, since it provided no method of scoring the results; it was only a first effort to suggest how one could be constructed. The first of the thirty tests in the battery was extremely simple. The experimenter moved a lighted match back and forth before the eyes of the subject to see whether there existed the coordination of head and eyes associated with vision. The later tests were increasingly difficult, involving such tasks as the ability to judge which of two lines was longer, to repeat three numbers, to repeat a sentence fifteen words long, to draw from memory a design that had been displayed, to say how a folded and refolded paper, out of which a small piece was cut, would look when unfolded, and finally and most difficult, to define abstract terms ("What difference is there between esteem and affection? What difference is

---

*Literally, "weaklings." Later, the term came to be translated as "morons," a word that did not yet exist.

there between weariness and sadness?").[27] At each age, normal children could answer questions and accomplish tasks satisfactorily up to a point; the older they were, the farther they could go through the series. The scale was indeed a measuring device of sorts.

While Binet and Simon were testing some children who were identified as normal and others considered retarded, they had a brilliant insight: the retarded children's intelligence was not of a different kind from that of the normal children; it was simply not as developed as it should have been by their age. By and large, they responded in the same way as normal children younger than themselves. Thus, intelligence could be measured by comparing the performance of a child with the average performance of normal children of the same age. As Binet and Simon put it:

> We shall therefore be able to know . . . if one [child] rises above the average level of other individuals considered normal, or if he remains below. Understanding the normal progress of intellectual development among normals, we shall be able to determine how many years such an individual is advanced or retarded. In a word we shall be able to determine to what degrees of the scale idiocy, imbecility, and *débilité* correspond.[28]

Defining intelligence in terms of age and assembling a set of cognitive tasks that measured the mental age of a child replaced Galton's anthropometric testing and became the foundation of the intelligence-testing movement.

After publishing their study, Binet and Simon took into account shortcomings they had discovered and criticisms offered by others and revised the scale extensively in 1908 and again in 1911. These revisions were supplied with scoring information—a set of standards as to the questions and tasks a child of any age should be able to answer and perform. (If 60 to 90 percent of the children at any given age could pass a particular test, Binet and Simon considered it normal for that age.) Here are some of the items in the 1911 scale:[29]

Three years:
    Points to nose, eyes, and mouth.
    Repeats two digits.
    Enumerates objects in a picture.
    Gives family name.
    Repeats a sentence of six syllables.

Six years:
    Distinguishes morning and evening.
    Defines words by use (e.g., "A fork is to eat with").
    Copies a diamond shape.
    Counts thirteen pennies.
    Distinguishes drawings of ugly and pretty faces.
Nine years:
    Gives change out of twenty sous.
    Defines words in a form superior to use (e.g., "A fork is an instru-
        ment for eating").
    Recognizes the value of nine pieces of money.
    Names the months in order.
    Answers easy "comprehension questions" (e.g., Q: "When one has
        missed the train what must one do?" A: "Wait for another
        train").
Twelve years:
    Resists suggestion. (The child is shown four pairs of lines of
        different length and asked which is longer in each case; in the
        last case the lines are the same length.)
    Composes a sentence using three given words.
    Names sixty words in three minutes.
    Defines three abstract words (charity, justice, goodness).
    Makes sense out of a disarranged sentence.

The 1908 scale included tests for age thirteen and the 1911 scale for
adults; as later researchers would show, the growth of intelligence continues to early adulthood and then ceases.

    The 1908 and 1911 revisions were the first functional tests of intelli-
gence validated against classroom performance and "normed" (provided with scores representing the normal level of response at every
age). For the first time, psychologists could determine how far, in years,
a child's mental development was behind normal or ahead of it. Binet
and Simon said that if the child's mental age was two or more years
below his or her chronological age, the child was likely to require special education. They also defined three levels of retardation in terms of
mental ages. The idiot, they said, had a mental age of two or less; the
imbecile, between two and seven; and the *débile* above seven but significantly lower than his or her chronological age.

    The weakness in these ratings was that they were fixed mental ages,
while nearly all retarded children continue to develop mentally,

although at a slower pace than normal. A child of four with a mental age of two is an idiot, but at age eight or ten, though still an idiot, his mental age will probably have reached the four- or five-year-old level.

In 1912 a German psychologist, William Stern, solved the problem by suggesting that if the child's mental age is divided by its chronological age, the result will be its "mental quotient"[30] (soon renamed "intelligence quotient," or IQ), a ratio that expressed the child's relative degree of retardation or advancement. The IQ of a child of four with a mental age of two is 50 (the ratio is multiplied by a hundred to get rid of the decimal place), and at ten, with a mental age of five, is still 50. Similarly, a child of five with a mental age of eight, or of ten with a mental age of sixteen, has a genius-level IQ of 160. The IQ is thus a useful way of expressing test results and offers a basis for predicting a child's potential development.

Although Binet and Simon, in their choice of test material, sought to measure "natural intelligence"—innate ability—rather than rote learning,[31] Binet was not a rigid hereditarian like Galton. He explicitly stated that the scale said nothing about the child's past or future but was an appraisal only of his present state.[32] Binet warned that the test results, if interpreted rigidly, might label and condemn to an inferior life some children who, with special help and training, could raise their intelligence level, and in a late work he cited with pride the increases in intelligence that had been obtained in special classes for subnormal children in an experimental school that he had founded.[33]

The 1908 scale was a remarkable success. By 1914 over 250 articles and books had been published commenting on or making use of it, and by 1916 the 1908 or 1911 revisions were being used throughout much of the United States, Canada, England, Australia, New Zealand, South Africa, Germany, Switzerland, Italy, Russia, and China, and had been translated into Japanese and Turkish. The need for such a measuring device clearly had become great in industrial societies. The psychologist Henry H. Goddard, who introduced the scale to American psychologists in 1910, wrote in 1916 that it was hardly an exaggeration to say that "the world is talking of the Binet-Simon Scale."[34] And that was only the beginning.

Binet, who died in 1911 at the age of fifty-four, did not live to see his triumph, but if he had, he might have been saddened to note that his scale, widely adopted in other countries, was neither appreciated nor used in France. It came into use there only in the 1920s, when a French social worker brought it back from America. Binet himself was little esteemed in his own country until 1971, when at last a ceremony honoring him and Simon was held at the school where he had instituted experimental methods of teaching the retarded.

The Testing Mania

Nowhere was intelligence testing as swiftly and enthusiastically adopted as in the United States. And for good reason. In a country with a fluid social structure, a rapidly expanding need for workers who could master complex technological jobs, a growing underclass of the poor, delinquent, and criminal, and an influx of millions of ill-educated and seemingly semiprimitive immigrants, a scientific way of evaluating the mental capacity of individuals offered the leaders of society a way to make social order out of chaos.[35]

But while Binet had believed that the intelligence of mental defectives, especially those close to normal, could be increased by special training, most of the early advocates of intelligence testing in the United States took Galton's position that heredity was the largest determinant of mental development and that the individual's intelligence was therefore unchangeable. They saw mental measurement as a means by which society could channel its members into the kinds of schools and jobs their innate capacity fitted them for and as a diagnostic device with which to identify those individuals who should be restrained from reproducing and passing on their defectiveness.

Henry Goddard was one of the leading exponents of this view. Goddard (1865–1957), a forceful and dynamic man, had been trained at Clark University, where G. Stanley Hall (one of Wundt's early students), a convinced hereditarian, was the head of the psychology department. Goddard absorbed the hereditarian view, and when, in 1906, he became the director of the research laboratory of the Vineland, New Jersey, Training School for the Feeble-minded, it seemed to him that he saw it amply confirmed all around him; many of the feeble-minded not only behaved, but looked, innately flawed. Goddard even hypothesized that mental defectiveness was due to a single recessive gene.[36]

He did recognize, however, that the children at Vineland were not all defective to the same degree, and that to determine what kind of training would be best for each one, he needed a way of measuring individual levels of mental ability. For a while he tried using Cattell's anthropometric tests, but with no success. Then, during a trip to France, he learned about the 1908 Binet-Simon scale, recognized its merits, and immediately translated it into English, making no changes except to replace a few French cultural references with American equivalents.

Goddard was the first to use the Binet-Simon scale for mass testing; he administered it to four hundred children at the training school and two thousand children in the New Jersey public schools. His results showed a broad range of intelligence scores among the feeble-minded children and also, surprisingly, among public school pupils, an alarming number of whom tested below their age norms.[37]

This motivated him to begin a campaign for intelligence testing in the public schools to locate below-normal children and shunt them into special classes; he also began offering courses for teachers in the use of the Binet-Simon scale and distributed thousands of copies to colleagues across the United States. Within half a dozen years the Binet-Simon scale was being used in many public schools, where it played an important part in the decisions teachers made about the education of students. It was also in use at a number of institutions for "mental defectives," reform schools, and juvenile and police courts, where it influenced the treatment accorded inmates and offenders.[38]

Goddard argued that low intelligence was a serious societal problem that had to be vigorously attacked. Idiots and imbeciles were no threat to society, he said, since they usually do not propagate their kind, but "high-grade defectives" or morons (a word Goddard invented) were very likely, he claimed, not only to become social misfits or criminals but to beget offspring who were equally likely to become antisocial. He also viewed the matter the other way around, saying that many criminals, most alcoholics and prostitutes, and "all persons who are incapable of adapting themselves to their environment and living up to the conventions of society or acting sensibly" were hereditarily mentally inferior.[39]

These assertions were based both on his use of the Binet-Simon scale and on his study of the descendants of a soldier in the American Revolution, one Martin Kallikak (a pseudonym), who sired a son by a feeble-minded barmaid and later married a Quaker woman and had children by her. Goddard traced Kallikak's many hundreds of descendants by both women down the generations to the early years of the twentieth century, and reported that a majority of those on the barmaid's side were feeble-minded, immoral, or criminal, and nearly all of those on the Quaker woman's side were upstanding members of society.

We now know that the study was grievously flawed. Among other things, few family members were or could be tested, and most were rated as to intelligence by looks alone or secondhand reports and hearsay. Also, Goddard said that the environments in which descendants of both sides were raised were basically the same, but existing information (such as infant mortality in the two lines) clearly showed the opposite. But at the time (1912) and for many years, *The Kallikak Family* was taken by many psychologists and the reading public to be dramatic proof of the genetic transmission of intellectual ability—Goddard actually spoke of "good blood" and "bad blood"[40]—and of its social consequences.

Goddard's Binet-Simon data and his findings about the Kallikak family led him to take a position far more severe than Galton's: "It is perfectly clear that no feeble-minded person should ever be allowed to marry or become a parent. It is obvious that if this rule is to be carried out the intelligent part of society must enforce it."[41] In pursuit of this goal, he served as an expert witness to two national committees advocating the sterilization of "mentally defective" people, and one of which sweepingly extended the recommendation to paupers, criminals, epileptics, the insane, and the congenitally handicapped.

Legislators were impressed by Goddard's testimony and that of other psychologists. By 1931 twenty-seven states had laws authorizing eugenic sterilizations, and thousands of mentally and socially "defective" people were sterilized during the next three decades—nearly ten thousand in California alone. By the 1960s, however, both because the compulsory sterilization of the unfit seemed akin to Nazi policies and because an environmental view of mental and social disability had become dominant, state legislatures began repealing the laws in favor of statutes authorizing sterilization of the mentally retarded on a voluntary basis.

Goddard made an equally consequential social application of the Binet-Simon scale to the immigration question. Since the turn of the century, immigrants had been pouring into the country. Many were illiterate and socially backward, raising fears that the nation was being swamped by social and mental defectives. Congress had passed a law forbidding entry to lunatics and idiots, and immigration inspectors rejected about 10 percent of the thousands arriving each day, but it was thought that many others were slipping through. In 1913 the United States commissioner of immigration asked Goddard to study the screening procedures at Ellis Island and offer his advice. For a week, Goddard and several assistants picked out immigrants whose appearance they considered suggestive of mental defectiveness and, through interpreters, gave them the Binet-Simon. Most scored in the defective range—hardly surprising, in view of their fatigue, fear, lack of education, and the difficulties of interpretation—and Goddard thereupon recommended that immigration inspectors henceforth use brief "psychological methods" based on Binet-Simon testing. In 1913 deportations of ostensibly feeble-minded immigrants rose by 350 percent, and in 1914 half again as much.[42]

Goddard continued his work at Ellis Island for some months in 1914; the testing of a sample of arriving immigrants showed that about four fifths of the Jews, Hungarians, Italians, and Russians were feeble-minded. Even Goddard was incredulous; he reviewed the data, tinkered with the results, and lowered the figures, but only to the 40 to 50 percent range. These findings, along with evidence offered by other psychologists of like mind, influenced Congress in its drafting of the severely restrictive immigration law of 1924, which reduced total quotas for southern and eastern Europe to less than a fifth of that for northern and western Europe.[43]

Despite the acceptance of Goddard's translation of the Binet-Simon scale, Lewis M. Terman, a professor of psychology at Stanford University, saw certain flaws in it, and felt that he could correct them and make the scale more accurate. Like Goddard and many others who subscribed to the hereditarian view of intelligence, Terman believed there was a social need for such an instrument. He also saw a scientific need for it: although he was a hereditarian, he said that the relative influences of heredity and environment would not be known until perfected intelligence tests were widely used,[44] and he undertook a major revision of the Binet-Simon scale, known as the Stanford-Binet scale.

Terman himself had no personal reason to believe in the inheritance of intelligence; he was the twelfth of fourteen children of an Indiana farm family, none of whose members and none of whose ancestors on either side had ever belonged to a profession or gone to college.[45] But when he was ten, an itinerant book peddler, while selling Terman's parents a book on phrenology, felt the boy's head and proclaimed that he had unusual abilities. The incident may have given Terman his bent toward the innatist view, and his subsequent history seemed to confirm it. He was able to work his way up, despite serious financial odds, from a country school to normal school, thence to college, and finally, by means of a fellowship, to Clark University, where he earned a doctorate in psychology in 1905. By that time he was a convinced hereditarian and admirer of Galton's.

At Stanford University he spent several years in the education department and then became head of the psychology department. In the course of a long and distinguished career he made the department a leading graduate and research center, conducted a respected long-term study of gifted children, and carried out a classic study of the psychological factors in marital happiness. But his main claim to fame, major contribution to psychology, and chief influence on American life was the Stanford-Binet scale.

Terman's experience with the Binet-Simon scale, even in its 1911 revision, had led him to believe that it had too few tests at the upper mental levels, that many tests at both the low end and the high end were misplaced in the sequence, and that the correct procedures for giving and interpreting the test were inadequately defined. With the help of eight collaborators and many public school teachers, he tried out the old tests and forty new ones (twenty-seven of which, and nine others taken from other sources, were added to the final series) on seventeen hundred normal children, two hundred retarded and superior children, and over four hundred adults. In its final form, the Stanford-Binet scale comprised ninety tests; those applicable to children between the ages of three and five took about half an hour to administer, and those to older groups longer and longer; the adult level required from an hour to an hour and a half.[46]

How well children of any age did with each test was compared with how well they did on others; those tests which were too easy for children of a given age were shifted to an earlier place in the sequence, those which were too hard, to a later one. To balance the scale, additional tests were added at the lower and upper ends. The results of the testing were compared with teachers' estimates of the same children's intelligence by the Pearsonian correlation method; the overall correlation was .48, or moderately high, thereby validating the scale. The correlation would have been still higher had not teachers, in estimating childrens' intelligence, sometimes failed to take into account that some of the children were either younger or older than most of their classmates.

The most valuable aspect of the revision was that the entire scale was far more thoroughly "standardized" than Binet-Simon or Goddard-Binet-Simon; that is, the scores were based on results achieved with a large standard sample of normal, retarded, and superior children and adults. On this basis, a child or adult who scored 100 was average; one who scored 130 or better was more intelligent than 99 percent of the population at large; and one who scored 70 or below was less intelligent than 99 percent of the population. Terman classified the grades of intelligence as follows:

140 and up .... "Near" genius or genius
120–140 .... Very superior intelligence
110–120 .... Superior intelligence
90–110 .... Normal or average intelligence
80–90 .... Dullness, rarely classifiable as feeble-mindedness
70–80 .... Border-line deficiency, sometimes classifiable as
                        dullness, often as feeble-mindedness
Below 70 .... Definite feeble-mindedness

Terman, a mild-mannered and kindly man, voiced benign hopes for the use of the new scale:

When we have learned the lessons which intelligence tests have to teach, we shall no longer blame mentally defective workmen for their industrial inefficiency, punish weak-minded children because of their inability to learn, or imprison and hang mentally defective criminals because they lacked the intelligence to appreciate the ordinary codes of social conduct.[47]

If the Stanford-Binet did not exactly make those sentiments a reality, neither did it, fortunately, make a reality of Terman's vision of its use in eugenics:

It is safe to predict that in the near future intelligence tests will bring tens of thousands of . . . high-grade defectives under the surveillance and protection of society. This will ultimately result in curtailing the reproduction of feeble-mindedness, and in the elimination of an enormous amount of crime, pauperism, and industrial inefficiency.[48]

The Stanford-Binet, published in 1916, swiftly became the standard test for measuring intelligence and remained so for over two decades. It was soon being used in a number of schools, preschools, colleges, and institutions for the feeble-minded. But its influence was both broader and more profound than that; the Stanford-Binet scale (and, later, its 1937 revision) became the standard for virtually all IQ tests that followed it. What Binet, Simon, and Terman took to be the attributes making up intelligence became the model for nearly all later intelligence tests; these components included memory, language comprehension, size of vocabulary, eye-hand coordination, knowledge of familiar things, judgment, likenesses and differences, arithmetical reasoning, ability to detect absurdities, speed and richness of association of ideas, and several others.[49]

A subsequent test using Stanford-Binet components revolutionized the field of intelligence testing.

All versions of the Binet scale—eventually there were dozens—have to be given by a psychologist or trained technician to one person at a time. But group testing, in which subjects read questions to themselves and check off multiple-choice answers or make appropriate marks on the form, would be far quicker, simpler, and very much less expensive.

This breakthrough in mental measurement came about as a result of the entry of the United States into the First World War. Within two weeks of President Woodrow Wilson's signing of the declaration of war, on April 6, 1917, the American Psychological Association appointed a committee to see what role psychology could play in the war effort. The committee reported that the most useful contribution of the profession would be the development of psychological examinations that could be quickly given to large numbers of military personnel so as to eliminate the mentally incompetent, classify individuals according to their abilities, and select the most competent for special training and responsible positions.

A group of psychologists—among them Terman, Goddard, and Robert Yerkes, a Harvard professor—met at Vineland and began planning the tests. In August, Yerkes was commissioned a major in the Army and was ordered to carry out the plans. He assembled a staff of forty psychologists who, in two months, produced the Army Alpha, a written test of intelligence, and the Army Beta, a pictorial test for the 40 percent of inductees who were functionally illiterate (the instructions for Beta were read aloud by an assistant). The widely used Alpha looks, from today's perspective, like a curious mixture of scientific information, folk wisdom, and morality, as can be seen by these questions:

1. If plants are dying for lack of rain, you should
   —water them,
   —ask a florist's advice,
   —put fertilizer around them.

8. It is better to fight than to run, because
   — cowards are shot,
   — it is more honorable,
   — if you run you may get shot in the back.
11. The cause of echoes is
   — the reflection of sound waves,
   — the presence of electricity in the air,
   — the presence of moisture in the air.

Yerkes' team began giving the tests in four camps, but within weeks the surgeon general decided to extend the program to the entire Army; by the time the war ended, in November 1918, more than 1.7 million men had taken the tests and some three hundred psychologists under Yerkes had graded each man and suggested a suitable military assignment for him.[50] Although Yerkes' psychological corps met resistance and noncompliance from professional officers, the tests resulted in the discharge of about eight thousand men as unfit and the assignment of about ten thousand of a low level of intelligence to labor battalions and similar services. Of greater importance, the Alpha was a factor in the selection of two thirds of the 200,000 men who became commissioned officers during the war.[51]

The Army Testing Program, however, had far greater impact outside the military than within it. It made America more conscious than ever of the practical applications of psychology, specifically those derived from mental measurement. (James McKeen Cattell said that the war had put psychology "on the map," and G. Stanley Hall that it had given psychology an invaluable redirection toward the practical rather than the "pure.")

The Alpha, in particular, led to an explosive expansion of intelligence testing, which rapidly became a multimillion-dollar industry. Within a few years of the war's end, a number of Alpha-type paper-and-pencil intelligence tests were being marketed to school administrators throughout the country. One of the most successful, appearing in 1923, was put together by Terman, Yerkes, and three co-workers, under the auspices of the National Research Council, which advertised it as "the direct result of the application of the army testing methods to school needs." By the end of the decade it had been given to seven million American schoolchildren.[52] Another major success was the Scholastic Aptitude Test, developed by Carl C. Brigham, a colleague of Yerkes', from Army models. Testing became prevalent in schools, colleges, the military services, institutions of all sorts, and various segments of industry.

The widespread use of intelligence testing was given further impetus by statistical evidence that the tests measured not just a series of separate mental aptitudes but an innate core of mental ability or "general intelligence." Charles Spearman, an English psychologist and statistician, had shown that many mental abilities are correlated. (A person who does well in vocabulary, for instance, is likely to do well in arithmetic and other subtests.) He took this to indicate that an inherent general intelligence, which he called *g*, underlay all the specific abilities. Even if intelligence tests relied in part on learning, the correlations implied the existence of an innate ability to learn.

This provided additional justification for intelligence testing in the schools, which by the 1930s, both in the United States and in Great Britain, were classifying pupils early in the educational process and assigning them to broad programs preparatory for higher education or to narrow "vocational" or "technical" programs readying them for blue-collar jobs. In America this was called "tracking" and in Great Britain "streaming."[53]

The growth of testing was not limited to the measurement of intelligence. During the 1920s and 1930s many other scales were developed to measure musical, mechanical, figural, verbal, mathematical, and other abilities, and a number of vocational aptitudes. Even though intelligence testing itself came under attack as early as the 1920s, Binet's approach to mental testing had opened up a vast new area of psychological research, and the Army Alpha had transformed his cumbersome and costly procedure into one that was easy and inexpensive enough to be the psychological equivalent of the assembly line.

The IQ Controversy

Intelligence testing did not long maintain its unquestioned status. From 1921 on, when Yerkes edited a massive report of the findings of the Army Testing Program, intelligence testing came under attack by various advocates and spokespersons of the underprivileged, who claimed that it measured not innate intelligence but acquired knowledge and cultural values and therefore was biased in favor of the dominant white middle class and against the lower classes and immigrants.

The Alpha, they charged, measured not native intelligence but the kinds of knowledge possessed by men with schooling and a degree of sophistication. Here, for instance, is a typical example of the culturally biased kind of question:

> The Knight engine is used in the
> —Packard,
> —Stearns,
> —Lozier,
> —Pierce Arrow.

The Beta was similarly far from impartial: in it, illiterates had to complete certain pictures such as a face without a mouth—fair enough—but others, such as a lightbulb without a filament or a tennis court without a net, made many lower-class men and immigrants seem stupid.[54]

The same criticism was made, and rightly so, as far as the Stanford-Binet scale was concerned. Many or most of the items in it measure a combination of inherent ability and acquired information or skills, but a person who has had little chance to acquire the information or skills will do poorly with the questions, no matter what his or her inherent mental power.

At the twelve-year-old level, for instance, the Stanford-Binet asked for definitions of "charity" and "justice." If a Mexican-American child from a rural southwestern shanty town gave inadequate answers, did that indicate a lack of innate intelligence or the child's failure to learn the meanings of those concepts in white, middle-class America? Again, at the eight-year-old level Stanford-Binet asked, "What's the thing for you to do when you have broken something which belongs to someone else?" If the eight-year-old lived in a city slum where children struggled to survive, was his or her answer a gauge of innate intelligence or of the mores and folkways of the slum subculture?

Binet had left moot the extent to which mental development, measured by his scale, was due to heredity and to experience. But the tenor of Terman's comments in *The Measurement of Intelligence* (the Stanford-Binet instruction manual), despite the disclaimer quoted above, was that intelligence is largely hereditary and that poor scores reveal mental deficiency—which, he said, was a genetic and a racial trait:

> [Low intelligence] is very, very common among Spanish-Indian and Mexican families of the Southwest and also among negroes. Their dullness seems to be racial, or at least inherent in the family stocks

from which they come . . . The writer predicts that . . . there will be discovered enormously significant racial differences in general intelligence, differences which cannot be wiped out by any scheme of mental culture.[55]

In 1922, the respected columnist and pundit Walter Lippmann launched a critical attack in *The New Republic* on Terman, Yerkes, and others who claimed that intelligence testing measured innate mental ability. Lippmann sounded the theme, repeated from that time until now, that such testing stamped a permanent label of inferiority on children, especially the underprivileged, and served the purposes of the prejudiced and the powerful.[56]

He and others who shared his views had even stronger grounds for objecting to the Army Alpha and Beta than to the Stanford-Binet, and for disputing Yerkes' claim that tests modeled on the Alpha "measure native intellectual ability." The answers to many Alpha questions clearly required learned information rather that intelligence, as Stephen Jay Gould later made plain in his polemical study, *The Mismeasure of Man*, in which he cited these examples:[57]

Washington is to Adams as first is to . . .
Crisco is a: patent medicine, disinfectant, toothpaste, food product.
The number of a Kaffir's legs is: 2, 4, 6, 8.
Christy Mathewson is famous as a: writer, artist, baseball player,
    comedian.

Beta, for illiterate subjects, in the choice of pictures to be completed was similarly unfair, as already mentioned.

The result was to give a distorted assessment of the population and the effects on it of immigration. The Army Testing Program, as presented by Yerkes in his 1921 report, portrayed a society whose population was being degraded by increases in poor genetic stock. According to the Alpha and Beta, the average mental age of white American males was only thirteen, just above the level of moronity, although Terman had previously put the figure at sixteen. Gould said that this shocking datum lent power to xenophobic, racist, and elitist elements in America:

The new figure became a rallying point for eugenicists who predicted doom and lamented our declining intelligence, caused by the unconstrained breeding of the poor and feeble-minded, the spread of Negro blood through miscegenation, and the swamping of an intelligent native stock by the immigrating dregs of southern and eastern Europe.[58]

Yerkes also lent support to Goddard's Ellis Island data by reporting that the Alpha and Beta showed the peoples of southern Europe and the Slavs of eastern Europe to be less intelligent than the peoples of northern and western Europe; these "findings" helped bring about the 1924 immigration law.

As the IQ controversy grew more heated, however, intelligence testing began to lose favor among psychologists during the 1930s and still more in the 1940s. By then, too, the belief in general intelligence had waned; new research using advanced statistical methods had found all sorts of "factors" or clusters of special correlations among the traits and cast doubts on the meaningfulness or usefulness of Spearman's g. Still, tests measuring a number of mental abilities and yielding a composite score, called intelligence, continued to be used by educators, business heads, and others.

By the 1960s, however, with protest movements of the disenfranchised and the discriminated-against gaining power, a protracted IQ war got under way. According to a study the author of this book made in 1999:

Militant minority groups and their white sympathizers [in the civil rights movement] succeeded in getting the boards of education in several major cities to stop IQ testing in the public schools. Public demonstrations and mass protests by activist groups died down by the late 1970s, but efforts to stop IQ testing continued by means of court cases and pressures on state legislators.

And with considerable success. By the 1990s, in schools throughout California, and in many school systems in other states, laws had been passed that forbade giving standardized tests of intelligence and academic aptitude to minority black and Hispanic children who had scholastic problems. In other cases school administrators who were not legally forbidden to do such testing avoided it in response to the wishes of parents . . . Nationally, between a third and a half of all public school districts administered no group intelligence or aptitude tests K to 12, and of those that did, according to a survey of eastern states, about half made little or no use of the results to tailor programs to students' abilities.[59]

Some psychologists went so far as to deny that there was such a thing as intelligence. Professor Martin Deutsch of New York University asserted, "It's a convenient label for certain kinds of behavior, but I suspect that, in actual fact, the thing itself doesn't really exist." Other psychologists and educators preferred to state, as Boring had done earlier, that one cannot say what intelligence is but only that it is what intelligence tests measure.

To meet the criticisms of existing IQ tests, in 1958 the psychologist David Wechsler developed two new ones, the Wechsler Intelligence Scale for Children (known as WISC) and the Wechsler Adult Intelligence Scale (WAIS). WISC and WAIS have two major parts: a verbal subtest assesses vocabulary, comprehension, and other aspects of verbal ability, and a performance subtest is made up of nonverbal tasks such as arranging pictures in an order that tells a story, or spotting the missing elements in a picture. Over the years intelligence researchers have modified and improved them as well as the Stanford-Binet Intelligence Scale to better measure the abilities of test takers from diverse cultural and linguistic backgrounds, and have developed more sophisticated and fairer ways of administering and interpreting the tests.[60]

Accordingly, despite the long history of opposition to intelligence tests, WISC and WAIS have continued to be widely used in their latest versions (WISC III and WAIS III), and for good reason.

For one thing, in those school systems that use them they predict rather well how children will perform in school and which children should be given special attention or be enrolled in enrichment programs.

For another, a number of recent, statistically sophisticated studies of fraternal twins and identical twins, particularly pairs who were separated shortly after birth and reared in dissimilar homes, have established, far better than Galton could, that mental abilities are in considerable part due to genetic makeup, and therefore that intelligence testing does indeed test innate ability as well as acquired knowledge.[61]

This graph clearly shows the two influences of genetics and environment on IQ.

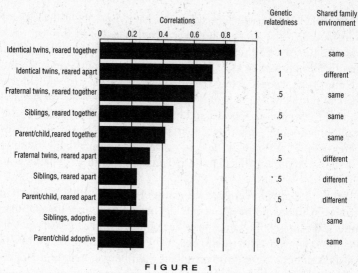

FIGURE 1

IQ and genetic relationship

Each bar shows how closely the IQ scores of the individuals listed are related. For instance, the top bar indicates that if identical twins are reared together—genetics and environment being the same—their IQs will have a greater than 0.8 correlation (or in informal terms, are very likely to be the same or nearly so.) In contrast, the bar for siblings reared apart—with only half the same genes and different environments— shows that their IQs are likely to be rather different.

(Data of this kind are often mislabeled "heritability," which is a quite different matter. Heritability refers to how much of the range of differences in a given trait, within a group of people, results from genetics. If the heritability of intelligence were found to be zero, no part of the range from nearly zero to 200 would be of genetic origin; if it were 100 percent, all of the variance would be of genetic origin. Recent reviews of a variety of studies of heritability of IQ conclude that roughly half of the variance in IQ scores is due to genetic makeup.[62] But how genetic makeup interacts with culture and which contributes how much of the result in any individual is a complex issue, only now being studied in new and illuminating ways—an area of contemporary psychology that we will see more of later in this history.)

One reason test designers have had to keep tinkering with the IQ tests is bizarre: in Western society, IQ scores have risen about three points every decade. The average IQ today would be 115 if the tests were scored as they were 50 years ago. To correct for this, scoring methods are periodically adjusted to keep the mean at 100.[63] Several explanations of the improving average scores have been offered: one, that daily life has become more challenging and thereby increased people's coping ability; two, that nutrition is better and has increased height—and, possibly, brain functioning; and three, that perhaps there has been no real increase in IQ but only in the kind of reasoning ability that is useful in test taking. At present, the definite explanation for rising IQ scores is not known.[64]

A more serious challenge to the status of IQ tests is the development of more complex portrayals of intelligence. Rather than the summary entity g, a number of theories have been offered in recent years that distinguish among kinds of intelligence. The two that currently command the most attention are those of Robert Sternberg of Yale and Howard Gardner of Harvard. Sternberg distinguishes between analytical intelligence (such as one uses in solving anagrams), creative intelligence (called upon in problem solving), and practical intelligence (used in the management of everyday affairs).[65] Gardner's view is more complex: He identifies (and offers evidence for) eight intelligences, some of which are promoted by Western society, others by other societies.[66] Here—and we will spare ourselves the details—are his eight:

- Logical-mathematical
- Linguistic
- Naturalist
- Musical
- Spatial
- Bodily kinesthetic
- Interpersonal
- Intrapersonal

His evidence is persuasive—and indeed nearly everyone has known people who are particularly gifted in one or more of these areas but all too average, or even deficient, in some of the others.

Yet despite these and other challenges and oppositions to standard IQ testing, it continues to be "one of psychology's greatest successes," writes Etienne Benson, a staff member of *Monitor on Psychology*, an online publication of the American Psychological Association. "It is certainly one of the field's most persistent and widely used inventions."[67] Many of the biases identified by critics of intelligence testing have been reduced, she says, and since the 1970s the field has acquired more sophisticated methods of interpretation, more advanced statistics, and new, methodologically more sophisticated, tests.[68]

In addition to all the uses made of IQ testing, it also is an essential tool for various kind of neurological research. Psychologists have long wondered whether the brains of highly intelligent people differ, physically, from those of average people. A new study initiated by the National Institute of Mental Health, relying on brain scans by magnetic resonance imaging over a period of seventeen years, has shown that the cortex—the outer sheet of neurons covering the brain that is the seat of many higher mental processes—grows thicker than average in highly intelligent children as they age and then thins out later, ending up even thinner than average. "This is the first time that anyone has shown that the brain grows differently in extremely intelligent children," says Paul M. Thompson, a brain-imaging expert at the University of California at Los Angeles. Apparently, the brains of the highly intelligent children are rewiring themselves, developing fruitful connections among the neurons and later pruning out redundant ones, thus operating more effectively during childhood and remaining more effective in adulthood. And here's the point: All the data on the different growth of these children's brains would tell us nothing about intelligence were it not for the IQ tests and scores taken along with the scans.[69]

The IQ controversy has raged, died down, and raged again; politics beclouds science, and science is used for political ends. The struggle continues and shows no signs of ending, but lineal descendants of the early intelligence tests, now greatly modified and more nearly "culture-fair" than the early tests, are widely used in schools, institutions, the military, industry, and elsewhere.

Whatever one calls them, and whatever one's stance on intelligence testing, the fact remains that mental measurement is useful, is beneficial to society (though not in the way Goddard and Terman had in mind), and remains one of psychology's major contributions to modern life in America and most other developed nations.

The
Behaviorists

A New Answer to Old Questions

By the late 1890s, humankind, after some twenty-four centuries of speculation about how the mind works, seemed on the verge of understanding it. The followers of Wundt and James were, in their different ways, introspectively examining their conscious sensations and thoughts; Freud was peering into the murky depths of his own unconscious and that of his patients; and Binet was preparing to measure the growth of the intellect throughout childhood.

Why, then, were a number of psychologists and physiologists playing little tricks on animals that could tell nothing about their inner experiences, and calling it psychological research?

How could it advance the understanding of the human mind to offer a baby chick two kinds of caterpillars, one of which presumably tasted bitter? ("Presumably" because it appears that the researcher himself never tasted it.) Or to soak some kernels of corn in quinine, others in sugar water, dye them different colors, and strew them before chickens? The baby chicks pecked at both kinds of caterpillar and shortly began to avoid the bitter ones, and the chickens soon ate only the sweetened kernels of corn, but what did any of that have to do with human learning?[1]

How could any of the great questions of psychology be answered by putting a hungry cat in a slatted "puzzle box" from which it could escape only by stepping on a treadle that opened a door? After placing the cat inside and latching the door, the researcher set a scrap of fish outside. The cat, galvanized by the sight and smell of the fish, pressed its nose into the space between the slats, thrust its paws through, then backed away and scrambled wildly around the cage for two and a half minutes until it happened to step on the treadle, causing the door to fall open. Out popped the cat to eat the bit of fish—only to be put back in the box for another try. It did better the second time (forty seconds to escape), worse the third time (ninety seconds), and only after over twenty trials promptly released the door each time.[2] A tiny addition to knowledge, no doubt—knowledge about cats. But what did that have to do with people?

How could it enlighten human beings about their own minds to harness a dog in a box, start a metronome ticking for fifteen seconds, then drop some meat powder in a bowl inside the box, and repeat this process until at the sound of the metronome saliva would drip from the dog's mouth even though the meat powder had not yet been delivered? Many psychologists, when they first heard about this experiment, said that it represented a type of association that accounted for only simple forms of behavior in animals; the researcher, however, believed that the principle he had discovered would explain even the most advanced and complex forms of behavior in human beings.[3]

These experiments and many like them were part of a bold attempt, beginning at the end of the nineteenth century, to answer—actually, to eliminate from discussion—the most perplexing and intractable problems of psychology: those having to do with the nature of mind. Among them:

— What is it within us that sees, feels, and thinks, every moment we are awake, vanishes temporarily when we sleep (or, if we dream, seems to leave the body and travel elsewhere), and disappears permanently the instant we die? Is it identical with, or a part of, the soul? Or is it something else equally nonmaterial?
— In either case, how could a nonmaterial essence—not even a vapor, not even a shadow—exert any influence on the material body it inhabits, and how could it feel the body's sensations?
— Does it endure after the body dies—and if so, where? And lacking any connection with sense organs and nerves after death, how can it perceive anything of whatever realm it inhabits?

These were but a few of the questions about the nature of mind, mental states, and the processes of thinking that philosophers, theologians, and protopsychologists had long sought to answer, though their efforts created more puzzles than they solved.

There was, however, another and totally different answer to such questions, though it was abhorrent to most philosophers and psychologists. Mind is an illusion; there is no incorporeal self within us; our mental experiences, including consciousness, awareness of self, and thinking, are only physiological events taking place in the nervous system in response to stimuli.

Over the centuries a few materialist philosophers suggested this alternative in vague and unconvincing terms, but as the physical and physiological sciences developed, the hypothesis became increasingly specific and plausible. By the latter half of the nineteenth century, Helmholtz and a number of other physiologists were linking simple sensations to electrochemical events in the sensory nerves, and followers of Wundt were beginning their effort to construct a whole psychology out of the elemental components of sensation and perception.

Toward the end of the century the rejection of "mentalism" (the belief in mind as a separate essence) gained support from a quite different quarter—animal psychology, a field in which interest had been sparked by Darwin's demonstration of the link between humankind and the other species. At first some biologists and psychologists had assumed that animals possess thought processes similar to, though simpler than, our own; in the 1880s, George Romanes, an English biologist, explored animal psychology through "introspection by analogy"; he asked himself what he would do were he the animal in any given situation. But in 1894 the zoologist C. Lloyd Morgan—the researcher who offered two kinds of caterpillars to chicks and two colors of corn kernels to chickens—sliced this approach to the bone with a version of Ockham's Razor:*

> In no case may we interpret an action as the outcome of the exercise of a higher psychical faculty if it can be interpreted as the exercise of one which stands lower in the psychological scale.[4]

Even the intricate tricks performed by pet dogs, Morgan said, could be explained in terms of reflexes and simple associative learning; there was

---

*William of Ockham, a fourteenth-century Franciscan, is supposed to have said, "Entities are not to be multiplied without necessity," although some sources claim that what he actually said was "It is vain to do with more what can be done with fewer." In either case, the message is that the best explanation is the simplest one.

no need to assume the existence in the animals of higher mental functions.

Jacques Loeb, a German-born biologist, went even further. During the 1890s, when he was teaching in the United States, he argued on the basis of wide-ranging evidence that a good deal of animal behavior consists of "tropisms," a term he used for all involuntary responses of worms, insects, and even higher animals to stimuli. In his view, much or most animal behavior consists of such tropisms, the creature being no more than a stimulus-driven automaton.[5]

The implication of all this seemed clear to a growing number of psychologists: if human beings are related to animals, and if animal behavior can be explained without mentalist concepts, then part of human behavior—perhaps even all of it—can be, too. The answer to the intractable questions about the nature and operations of the mind might be utterly simple: mind does not exist, or if it does, it can be ignored, since it is not only unobservable but unnecessary to the explanation of behavior.

Behavior—overt, visible, indisputable action—*that* is the real subject of psychology, rather than memory, reasoning, will, and all the other unseen processes imagined by mentalist psychologists. Not conjectures and hypotheses about invisible functions, but *laws* derived from observable phenomena, such as the cat's learning to escape from the puzzle box, could be the substance of a thoroughly objective and rigorously scientific psychology. Such was the thinking of many psychologists in the 1890s and the early 1900s, long before the word "behaviorism" had been coined or the theory's tenets set forth.

Two Discoverers of the Laws of Behaviorism: Thorndike and Pavlov

The animal experiments mentioned above exemplify two different principles of behaviorism: the laws of natural learning (the chickens' associating a particular color with the reward of the sweet-tasting corn, the cat's associating a step on the treadle with escape and food), and the laws of conditioning (the dog's salivating at the sound of the metronome, a stimulus artificially linked to the salivary reflex). These laws were discovered by two men of dissimilar backgrounds, training, and personality, one a brilliant and dedicated psychologist, the other a physiologist who was scornful of psychology and doubted that it could be regarded as a science.

The first was Edward Lee Thorndike (1874–1947), a psychologist of such catholic and diverse interests that some historians have classified him as a functionalist, others as a behaviorist, and he himself as neither.[6] Except for one year, he spent all of his long career in psychology at Teachers College, Columbia University, where he researched and wrote fifty books and 450 articles dealing with educational psychology, learning theory, tests and measurements, industrial psychology, language acquisition, and social psychology. For good measure he produced such unusual items as a teachers' list of the twenty thousand words students most often encountered in general reading, a rating of American cities according to how desirable they were to live in, and a highly popular dictionary. Our interest in Thorndike, however, is focused on his work as a graduate student, when, notwithstanding his later demurral, he was very much a behaviorist.

Born in Massachusetts, Thorndike, the son of a Methodist minister, was a homely, lonely, and painfully shy child who found satisfaction in his studies. Exceptionally gifted, he ranked first or second in all his high school courses and graduated from Wesleyan University in 1895 with the highest average achieved there in fifty years. He found the basic undergraduate psychology course dull but James's *Principles of Psychology* entrancing. He went on to Harvard for graduate work, planning to study English, philosophy, and psychology, but after two courses with James he was fully committed to the last of these.

Despite his admiration for James, he chose to do graduate research on a very un-Jamesian topic, "the instinctive and intelligent behavior of chickens." Later in life he said that his motive had been "chiefly to satisfy requirements for courses and degrees . . . I certainly had no special interest in animals."[7] Perhaps, but no doubt a shy person (as he still was at the time) would find animals easier to work with than people. James approved the project and Thorndike bought a batch of chicks, which, for lack of laboratory space, he housed in his room until his outraged landlady ordered him to get rid of them. When he told James of his problem, James, going far beyond the bounds of professorial duty, allowed Thorndike to install them in the cellar of his house.

There, using stacked books, Thorndike built a maze with three blind alleys and a fourth leading to an adjoining enclosure in which were food, water, and other chicks. When he put a chick in the maze, it raced in and out of the blind alleys, peeping loudly, until it blundered to the exit; when he put it back in again and again, it slowly got better at finding its way out. Clearly, there was no intelligence at work but something much simpler. In Thorndike's words:

> The chick, when confronted by loneliness and confining walls, responds by those acts which in similar situations in nature would be likely to free him. Some one of these acts leads him to the successful act, and the re-sulting pleasure stamps it in. Absence of pleasure stamps all others out.[8]

Those sentences contained the seed of behaviorist theory.

The following year, after being rejected by a young woman he had proposed to, Thorndike felt it necessary to flee from Cambridge. He transferred to Columbia University to complete work for his Ph.D. under James McKeen Cattell, who was then in the middle of his effort to measure intelligence by anthropometric tests. Though Thorndike too would later do research in mental testing, for his dissertation he continued his animal-learning studies. From fruit and vegetable crates he built fifteen puzzle boxes of various designs, and in the attic of an old university building began studying the ability of cats (plus a few dogs) to learn how to escape.

In some boxes his cats could escape by performing a single action: stepping on a treadle, pushing a button, or pulling on a loop of string. In others, escape required multiple actions such as pulling on the loop and then moving a stick, and in one experiment Thorndike released the door only if the cat licked or scratched itself. Driven by fierce ambition—Thorndike meant to (and did) reach the top of his profession in five years—he worked so hard in the attic with his animals that in less than a year he had arrived at several findings that leaders in the field at once recognized as being of major importance. The New York Academy of Sciences invited him to talk about his results at a meeting in January 1898; in June, *Science* published a paper by him on his work; his thesis appeared as a monograph supplement to *Psychological Review* late in the year; and the American Psychological Association had him make a presentation at its annual meeting in December.

Thorndike's findings, though simple, had significant implications.

First, the cats had not learned to escape by means of reasoning or insight; rather, by trial and error they slowly eliminated useless movements and made the connection between the appropriate action and the desired goal. They learned nothing from seeing how an experienced cat escaped, or from having Thorndike manipulate their paws to release the door of the box. All the cats learned to escape when only a single response was required, but more than half of them never learned to escape when two responses were required.

From all this, Thorndike formulated a theory of "connectionism," expressed in two laws of learning.

One he called the Law of Effect. The puzzle box was a stimulus that elicited a number of responses; the effects of most were "annoyers" (failures to escape or to reach the food), but one was a "satisfier," which yielded both escape and food. Annoyers and satisfiers selectively "stamp in" (or, as Thorndike later said, "reinforce") certain stimulus-response connections and weaken or eliminate others. The effect of any action thus determines whether it becomes the response to a given stimulus or not.

The second law he called the Law of Exercise. Other things being equal, "a response will be more strongly connected to a stimulus in proportion to the number of times it has been connected with that situation and to the average vigor and duration of the connection."

Thorndike's monograph had an immediate effect on psychological thinking. It lent new, research-based meaning to old philosophic notions of associationism; it provided convincing support for C. Lloyd Morgan's dictum against assuming higher mental functions if lower ones could explain behavior; and it established animal experimentation as the pattern for most learning research for the next half century.

While later researchers (and Thorndike himself) would somewhat modify the Law of Effect and greatly qualify the Law of Exercise, the two laws became the basis of behaviorist psychology, human as well as animal. For although human behavior is vastly more sophisticated than that of cats, behaviorists argued that it is explicable by the same principles; the difference, Thorndike said, is simply that "the number, delicacy, and complexity of cell structures" in the human brain make for a corresponding "number, delicacy, and complexity of associations."[9] He even held that the reason human culture develops so slowly is that it is the result of trial-and-error learning with accidental success, the same method by which animals acquire associations.

Ivan Pavlov (1849–1936), a very different breed of scientist, was a research physiologist who spent the first half of his career investigating the digestive process. It was in the course of this work that he noticed the odd phenomenon of the salivating dog, and he spent the second half of his career studying what he called "conditioned reflexes."[10] From first to last he considered conditioning a physiological rather than a psychological process, and although the laws of conditioning became as basic to behaviorism as the laws of learning and effect, he had so poor an opinion of psychology that he threatened to fire anyone in his laboratory who used psychological terminology. To his dying day he insisted that he was not a psychologist but a physiologist studying brain reflexes.

Pavlov was born in a central Russian farming village. His father was the local Orthodox priest, his mother the daughter of a priest, and Pavlov planned to follow in the family tradition. Czar Alexander II had recently made free education available to gifted but poor students; Pavlov qualified on both counts, and was educated in a primary school and a seminary. But while he was at the seminary he read Darwin's *Origin of Species* and the Russian physiologist Ivan Sechenov's *Reflexes of the Brain,* and underwent something akin to a conversion. Abandoning his plans for the priesthood, he quit the seminary to study natural science at the University of Saint Petersburg (again thanks to the Czar's largesse), where Sechenov was a professor of physiology.

Pavlov graduated in 1875 with a brilliant record and went on to study medicine, but his goal was research, not practice, and he had to support himself—and, after 1881, a wife—on ill-paid assistantships. At that time, Russia offered far fewer opportunities to young scientists than did the Western countries, and despite Pavlov's extraordinary talent and his impressive research studies in physiology, he could eke out only a marginal existence for many years.

He was too absorbed in his work, however, to be concerned about the exigencies of daily living; he was the embodiment of the impractical intellectual. During his engagement, he spent what little money he had on luxuries for his fiancée and only once bought her something practical: a pair of shoes that she urgently needed for a trip. But when she got to her destination and opened her luggage, she found only one shoe. She wrote to ask what had happened, and he replied, "Don't look for your shoe. I took it as a remembrance of you and have put it on my desk."

When they were married and living in near poverty, he often forgot to pick up his monthly salary until his wife reminded him. One winter, when he could afford little fuel for their apartment, a batch of butterflies he kept at home to study metamorphosis succumbed to the cold. When his wife complained about their poverty, he answered, exasperated, "Oh, leave me alone, please. A real misfortune has occurred. All my butterflies have died, and you are worrying about some silly trifle."

But in the laboratory, Pavlov was practical, perfectionist, and systematic. He expected his assistants to live up to his standards, and castigated or fired those who fell short in any way, whatever the reason. During the Revolution (with which, for many years, he had no sympathy, though eventually he became a supporter of the system), one of his employees arrived late. When Pavlov upbraided him, the man said there had been street fighting en route and he had been in danger of losing his life, but Pavlov angrily replied that that was no excuse and that devotion to science should supersede all other motives. According to some accounts, he sacked the man.

That was long after Pavlov had become successful. In 1891, at the age of forty-two, he was at last appointed professor at the St. Petersburg Military Academy, and a few years later professor at St. Petersburg University. With this solid footing, he was able to organize the Institute of Experimental Medicine, the laboratory in which he conducted his research for forty years. His work during the 1890s was on digestion, which he studied by surgically creating in the stomach of laboratory dogs a little pouch or separate compartment with a fistula implanted in it. This enabled him to observe the gastric reflex (the secretion of gastric juices when the dog began to eat) without the contaminating presence of food. His findings won him a Nobel Prize in medicine in 1904, and in 1907 he reached the height of scientific prestige in Russia when he became an academician, or full member, of the Academy of Sciences.

Sometime between 1897 and 1900, in the course of his gastric-reflex research, Pavlov became aware of an odd and annoying phenomenon: the dogs would secrete gastric juices and saliva at times other than feedings—for instance, when they saw or heard their keeper shortly before a regular mealtime. At first Pavlov regarded this as a nuisance, since it interfered with the data on the quantities of digestive secretions. But he recognized that there must be an explanation for the production of such fluids when there was no food in the dog's mouth or even nearby. An obvious one was that the dog "realized" that mealtime was near and these thoughts produced the secretions, but the resolutely antipsycho-

logical Pavlov would have nothing to do with such subjective speculations.

Though reluctant to do research on the matter, he finally decided he
could look into it, since in his opinion it was an entirely physiological
phenomenon—a "psychical secretion" due to a reflex in the brain
caused by the stimulus of the sight or sound of the person who usually
brought food. In 1902 he began to study how and when such a stimulus,
inherently unconnected to the glandular response, was capable of causing it, and he spent the rest of his life investigating the phenomenon.

Although Pavlov was an expert surgeon, he spared himself the labor of
creating stomach pouches for this research. Since the dogs produced
saliva as well as gastric juices at the sight of their keepers, it was enough
to implant a simple fistula in one of the salivary glands and hook this up
to a collecting and recording device. The dogs were trained to stand still
on a table, and were praised, petted, and fed for doing so. Eager to
please, they would jump onto the table without being told to and
patiently remain there, loosely harnessed in place and attached to
equipment. The harness was necessary to prevent disruption of the
apparatus, a rubber tube connecting the fistula to a collecting vessel and
a recording drum. The dogs faced a wall with a window in it; directly in
front of them, inside the experimental chamber, was a bowl into which
food could be mechanically dropped.

As soon as a dog had food in its mouth, its saliva began to flow; since
this was a response that required no training, Pavlov called the food an
"unconditioned stimulus" and the salivary response an "unconditioned
reflex." The matter to be studied, however, was the link between a neutral stimulus and the same reflex. Typically, the experimenter, out of
sight so as not to be a signal to the dog, would make a sound—ring a
bell, buzz a buzzer—and would cause food to drop into the bowl anywhere from five to thirty seconds later. At first, the sound of the bell or
buzzer would produce only a normal reflex—the pricking-up of the
dog's ears—but no salivary response. But after a number of these
sequences, the sound alone would cause the dog's saliva to start flowing.
In Pavlov's terms, the sound had become a "conditioned stimulus" to
salivation, which had become a "conditioned reflex" to the sound.

Pavlov and his assistants ran many variations of this experiment.
Instead of a sound, they would flash a light or rotate an object the dog
could see through the window, manipulate apparatus that touched the
dog or tugged on a part of its harness, change the length of time between
the neutral stimulus and the delivery of food, and so on. In all cases,

neutral stimuli could be made into conditioned ones, but with varying degrees of ease; a neutral odor (not of food) might require twenty or more pairings to become a conditioned stimulus, while the rotation of an object in the dog's view might take only five pairings, the sounding of a loud buzzer only one.[11]

A psychologist would have called the conditioning process associative learning, but Pavlov explained it in physiological terms. Acknowledging indebtedness to his mentor, Sechenov, and to Descartes, the first to offer a reflex theory, he theorized that an unconditioned response, such as salivating on taking food into the mouth, was a brain reflex: A direct connection existed between the sensory and motor nerves in the spine or lower brain centers. In contrast, a conditioned response, such as salivating at the sound of a bell or other formerly neutral stimulus, was the result of new reflexive pathways created by the conditioning process in the cortex of the brain.

Pavlov developed this theory of localized brain reflexes in great detail to fit his findings about conditioning. But it was largely ignored except in the Soviet Union, and in America was soon conclusively disproven by the psychologist Karl Lashley, who removed different areas and amounts of cortex from rats, then had them learn mazes, and found that their loss of ability to learn was related not to the destruction of any particular cortical area but to the total amount destroyed.[12]

The fate of Pavlov's physiological theory, however, in no way diminished the enthusiastic acceptance of his laboratory data and laws of conditioning as a major addition to psychological knowledge. These were some of his more noteworthy findings:

Timing: The sequence of the stimuli is critical. Only if the neutral stimulus precedes the unconditioned reflex does it become a conditioned stimulus, capable of eliciting the reflex. In one experiment, an assistant gave a dog food and five to ten seconds later turned on a loud buzzer; even after 374 such pairings, the buzzer alone did not bring about salivation. When he sounded the buzzer *before* giving the dog food, a single pairing was enough to make it a conditioned stimulus.[13]

Extinction: Unlike an unconditioned reflex to an unconditioned stimulus, the connection between a conditioned stimulus and a conditioned reflex is impermanent. If the conditioned stimulus is repeatedly presented without reinforcement (food), the salivary response weakens and eventually disappears.

Generalization: If a dog was presented with a stimulus similar to, but somewhat different from, a stimulus it had become conditioned to—for instance, a tone higher or lower than the one paired with food—the dog would salivate, but less strongly than in response to the conditioned tone. The greater the difference between tones, or between any conditioned stimulus and a related stimulus, the weaker the response. The dog was, in effect, generalizing from its experience and expecting similar experiences to yield similar results.

Differentiation: After a dog had been conditioned to salivate on hearing a given tone and also on hearing another tone some notes lower, if the first tone was then always reinforced by food but the second one never was, the dog would gradually cease to salivate in response to the second tone. The dog had learned to "differentiate"—the term more often used by English and American psychologists is "discriminate"—between the stimuli.

Experimental neurosis: In seeking to determine the limits of his dogs' ability to discriminate, Pavlov unexpectedly precipitated in them something resembling a nervous breakdown. In one historic study, a dog learned to discriminate between a circle flashed on a screen, always followed by food, and an elongated ellipse flashed on the screen, never followed by food. When the dog's salivating at the sight of the circle and failure to salivate at the sight of the ellipse were well established, the assistant began changing the shape of the ellipse, making it ever more nearly circular. The dog kept learning to discriminate between the circle and the rounder ellipses until the ratio of the axes of the ellipse was 7:8. The assistant then tried an even rounder ellipse whose axes had a ratio of 8:9, but at that point, Pavlov later wrote,

> the hitherto quiet dog began to squeal in its stand, kept wriggling about, tore off with its teeth the apparatus for mechanical stimulation of the skin, and bit through the tubes connecting the animal's room with the observer, a behavior which never happened before. [Later,] on being taken into the experimental room the dog barked violently, which was also contrary to its usual custom; in short, it presented all the symptoms of a condition of acute neurosis.[14]

Only after long rest and careful treatment did the dog recover enough to tolerate experiments in easier differentiations.

Pavlov believed that he had identified the fundamental unit of learning in animals and human beings. All learned behavior, he said, whether acquired in school or outside it, was nothing but "a long chain of conditioned reflexes" whose acquisition, maintenance, and extinction were governed by the laws he and his assistants had discovered. His ideas profoundly influenced Russian psychology from early in the century until the 1950s, but in the West remained largely unknown for some years, even though Pavlov had mentioned conditioning in his 1904 Nobel award address.

In 1908 Robert Yerkes (who would later direct the development of the Army Alpha and Beta) and a colleague learned about Pavlov's work from German journals, corresponded with him, and published a brief article in the *Psychological Bulletin* describing his method and main findings. They emphasized the usefulness of his research methods but failed to predict the effect the concept of the conditioned reflex would have on American psychology.[15]

But in 1916 John B. Watson—whom we are about to meet—began to spell out how Pavlovian conditioning enlarged the behaviorist theory of psychology, and a few years later he termed the conditioned reflex "the keystone of the arch" of behaviorist theory and methodology.[16] In 1927 Pavlov's book, *Conditioned Reflexes*, appeared in English, and from then on behaviorist psychologists rapidly absorbed his ideas and borrowed his research methods. The number of articles on Pavlovian conditioning published in psychological and medical journals increased geometrically from the mid-1920s on, totaling nearly a thousand by 1943.[17] In 1951, Professor Henry Garrett of Columbia University summed up the impact of Pavlovian ideas on experimental psychology, which had been largely behaviorist for more than three decades:

> There is perhaps no subject in experimental psychology upon which more time and effort have been expended than upon the conditioned reflex. The acquisition of conditioned reflexes by animals, children, and adults; the relative ease of conditioning of various reflexes; the stability of conditioned reflexes, their extinction and reappearance; the relation of school learning to ease of formation of conditioned reflexes . . . [have all] been subjected to experimental attack . . . Many psychologists hoped—and the strict objectivists believed—that the conditioned reflex would prove to be the unit or element out of which all habits are built.[18]

Mr. Behaviorism: John B. Watson

No one did more to sell behaviorism to American psychologists than Professor John B. Watson of Johns Hopkins University. A gifted huckster, he energetically and skillfully peddled himself and his ideas to his colleagues, rose swiftly to the top of his profession while launching the behaviorist movement, and later, having been expelled from academia because of a sexual scandal, had a second and financially lucrative career as psychological adviser to a major advertising firm.[19]

Like the fictional traveling salesman, Watson exuded self-assurance, stated his views flamboyantly and with certainty, and was a lifelong womanizer. Behind the facade, however, he was insecure, afraid of the dark, and emotionally frozen. He could be sociable and charming in company, but if the conversation turned to deeper feelings he would leave the room and busy himself with chores. He was loving to animals but almost incapable of expressing affection to the people in his life. (He never kissed or held his children; at bedtime he shook hands with them.) After the untimely death of his second wife, whom he seems to have cared for deeply, he never spoke of her to their two sons, one of whom later bitterly recalled, "It was almost as if she had never existed."[20] No wonder he was the champion of a psychology that rejected introspection and self-revelation, dealt only with external acts, and as experimental subjects preferred rats to human beings.

Watson's success story was as remarkable as any by Horatio Alger. Born in 1878 near Greenville, South Carolina, he was the son of a petty farmer of violent nature and unsavory reputation, and an upright, devout Baptist woman. Torn between these dissimilar models of adulthood, Watson was a shiftless, indolent small-town boy. When he was thirteen, his father abandoned the family and ran off with another woman, and his mother sold the farm and moved to Greenville. There Watson, teased by classmates for his country ways and upset by his father's abandonment, did poorly in school. "I was lazy," he later recalled, "somewhat insubordinate, and, so far as I know, never made above a passing grade." Like his vanished father, he had a penchant for violence: He often boxed with a friend until one or both were bloody, was much addicted to what he called "nigger fighting" (beating up blacks), and was arrested twice, once for racial brawling and once for firing a gun within city limits.

Despite his redneck attitudes and habits, he somehow developed the desire to make something of himself and had either the courage or effrontery to request a personal interview with the president of Furman College, a small Baptist institution in Greenville; he was granted the interview and made a good enough impression to be accepted as a student. He had intended to study for the Baptist ministry—his mother's wish—but, always rebellious, turned against religion. He was never at ease with his fellow students, but when he grew into a strikingly handsome youth with sharp, clean-cut features, a strong chin, and dark wavy hair, he began a lifelong series of affairs. He was serious enough about his ambition, however, to work hard and do well academically, and he particularly liked those philosophy courses which included psychological subjects.

After graduation, Watson taught in a one-room school for a year, but his favorite philosophy professor, George Moore, who had moved to the University of Chicago, urged him to go there as a graduate student. Again Watson was brash enough to go directly to the top. He wrote a boldly self-promoting letter to William Rainey Harper, president of the university, telling him that he was poor but earnest, and entreating him either to waive tuition or let Watson pay it off later. He also persuaded the president of Furman College to write an extraordinarily strong letter on his behalf. President Harper accepted him—on what financial basis is not clear—and off Watson went. He arrived in Chicago with $50 to his name, completely on his own (his mother had died, his father had never been heard from) but ready for anything.

At first he majored in philosophy, but soon realized that it was psychology he cared about, and switched. He worked hard at his studies and supported himself by holding several odd jobs: he waited on table at his boarding house, served as a janitor in the psychology department, and took care of rats in an animal laboratory. At one point, overwhelmed by anxiety and sleeplessness, he suffered a breakdown and had to spend a month recuperating in the country. Another man, after such an experience, might have become self-searching and interested in introspective psychology; Watson did his doctoral research in the winter of 1901–1902 on how the level of brain development of young rats was related to their ability to learn mazes and open doors to get food. In part, he was simply falling in with the latest trend in psychology (Thorndike had announced his puzzle box findings four years earlier), but in part he was choosing the kind of psychology he found congenial:

At Chicago, I first began a tentative formulation of my later point of view. I never wanted to use human subjects. I hated to serve as a subject. I didn't like the stuffy, artificial instructions given to subjects. I always was uncomfortable and acted unnaturally. With animals I was at home. I felt that, in studying them, I was keeping close to biology with my feet on the ground. More and more the thought presented itself: Can't I find out by watching their behavior everything that the other students are finding out by using O's?[*][21]

Watson did such excellent work at Chicago that when he graduated, the department offered him an assistantship in experimental psychology. After only two years he was promoted to instructor, after two more to assistant professor-elect, and a year later, at thirty, was offered the chair of psychology at Johns Hopkins University at what was then (1908) a munificent salary, $3,500.

His swift rise had been, in part, the consequence of carefully cultivated contacts but, in larger part, of splendid experimental work in animal learning. He taught rats to make their way through a miniature replica of the maze at Hampton Court, Henry VIII's royal retreat outside London. At first the rats needed as much as half an hour to find their way, but after thirty trials they could race through in ten seconds. By what means had they learned the route? To find out, Watson deprived them of first one sensory cue, then another, to see which one was crucial to maze learning. He blinded some of the trained rats; their performance dropped off but rapidly returned to what it had been before. He washed the maze to remove odor cues, but trained rats did as well as ever. He surgically destroyed the sense of smell of some untrained rats, but they learned the maze as readily as intact rats. Hearing, similarly, proved to play no part in their learning. Watson concluded that kinesthetic cues—muscle sensations—were the key element in the rat's learning process.[22]

From such research and from his knowledge of the work of Thorndike and other objectivists, Watson, rejecting all conjectures about invisible mental processes, began to formulate a new psychology based entirely on observable behavior. He first voiced these views at psychological meetings in 1908 and 1912 (in the latter year he and James R. Angell independently coined the term "behaviorist"), and in 1913 wrote an article, published in the *Psychological Review* and often called "the behaviorist manifesto," that formally inaugurated the era of behaviorism in psychology.[23]

---

[*]Observers (of their own conscious processes).

The manifesto, "Psychology As the Behaviorist Views It," started off with a declaration of independence from all schools of psychology that dealt with mental processes:

> Psychology as the behaviorist views it is a purely objective experimental branch of natural science. Its theoretical goal is the prediction and control of behavior. Introspection forms no essential part of its methods, nor is the scientific value of its data dependent on the readiness with which they lend themselves to interpretation in terms of consciousness.

In three sentences, he had proclaimed three revolutionary principles: first, the content of psychology should be behavior, not consciousness; second, its method should be objective rather than introspective; and third, its purpose should be "prediction and control of behavior" rather than fundamental understanding of mental events.

Watson charged that psychology had failed to become an undisputed natural science because it was concerned with conscious processes that were invisible, subjective, and incapable of precise definition. He jettisoned the psychologizing of the Greek philosophers, the medieval scholars, the rationalists and the empiricists, and such greats as Kant, Hume, Wundt, James, and Freud, all of whom had been, in his view, misguided.

> The time seems to have come when psychology must discard all reference to consciousness; when it need no longer delude itself into thinking that it is making mental states the object of observation. We have become so enmeshed in speculative questions concerning the elements of mind, the nature of conscious content . . . that I, as an experimental student, feel that something is wrong with our premises and the types of problems which develop from them.

As some wit said later, "Psychology, having first lost its soul to Darwin, now lost its mind to Watson."

His assault on introspection as a method of research was based on its failure to yield objective data. It so often led to endless debates about subjective and undecidable issues, like the number of sensations, their intensity, or what any individual meant by his report of what he was experiencing, that the method itself had to be judged defective and a hindrance to progress.

For good measure, Watson also dismissed all dualist discussions of mind and body, whether couched in metaphysical terms or modern ones. These concepts, "time-honored relics of philosophic speculation," were of no use either as guides to psychological problems worth studying or as solutions of those problems; he himself would prefer, he said, to bring up his students in total ignorance of such hypotheses.

In place of the psychology he junked, he proposed a new one free of all such terms as "consciousness," "mental states," and "mind." Its sole subject matter would be behavior. Based on the premise that all organisms adjust to their environment and that certain stimuli lead them to make the necessary responses, psychology would study the connections between stimuli and responses, that is, the ways in which rewarding responses are learned and unrewarding ones are not. Since consciousness would be ignored, much of this study could be carried on with animals; indeed, "the behavior of man and the behavior of animals must be considered on the same plane as being equally essential to the study of behavior."

Watson's manifesto was actually less original than it seemed; it presented ideas that had been germinating for fifteen years. But it did so in an audacious, forceful, and crystallizing way; it was, in short, a sales pitch. Watson's ideas did not sweep the field overnight, but over the next half-dozen years behaviorism became an important topic at meetings and a formative influence on the thinking of psychologists. By the 1920s it had begun to dominate psychology, and was the ruling paradigm in American psychology and an important one in Europe for well over four decades.

Popular accounts of Watson's life say that the manifesto catapulted Watson to the presidency of the American Psychological Association in 1915, but a careful review of the evidence by the social psychologist Franz Samelson finds it more likely that he was elected because he was highly visible as the editor of the *Psychological Review*, was well known to and on good terms with the three members of the nominating committee, and was a representative of the new generation of genuinely experimental psychologists.[24]

Whatever the reason, he was flying high, but he knew that he had not yet suggested a specific method by which behaviorists could pursue research, and in his presidential address to the APA he addressed this problem.[25] He now had something to offer: the conditioned reflex method. Though he knew only the bare outlines of Pavlov's work, he presented it as a model for behaviorist experimentation not only with animals but with humans. He noted that his student Karl Lashley (who had disproven Pavlov's physiological theory), had already made a removable fistula that could be installed inside the human cheek; with it, he had successfully measured both unconditioned and conditioned salivary reflexes in human volunteers.

Watson himself began to study conditioned reflexes in human beings, although, not surprisingly, he did so with infants rather than adults. The psychiatrist Adolf Meyer, head of the Phipps Psychiatric Clinic at Johns Hopkins, had invited him to set up a laboratory there, and in 1916 Watson began observing infants from birth through much of their first year. World War I interrupted the work, but he got back to it in late 1918.

Watson first sought to discover what unconditioned reflexes infants possess, that is, what stimuli would produce reflexes without any learning process. From simple experiments with infants in the clinic he concluded that there are only a few instinctive reflexes in humans, among them sucking, reaching, and grasping. (A famous photograph shows Watson holding a rod from which a newborn is hanging by one hand like a little monkey.) He also found that infants have three innate emotional responses to certain stimuli: fear at hearing a loud sound or at suddenly being dropped (the infant catches its breath, puckers its lips, and then cries); rage when its arm or head movements are forcibly restrained (it stiffens its body, makes thrashing arm movements, holds its breath, and turns red in the face); and love when stroked, rocked, gently patted, and the like (it gurgles, coos, or smiles).[26]

But since these, in his opinion, made up the sum total of innate human responses—later research would find otherwise—his larger aim was to show how virtually all other human behaviors and emotional reactions were built up of conditioned reflexes. He began by enunciating a Pavlovian hypothesis about emotional responses:

> When an emotionally exciting object stimulates the subject simultaneously with one not emotionally exciting, the latter may in time (often after one such joint stimulation) arouse the same emotional reaction as the former.[27]

To verify this hypothesis, in the winter of 1919–1920 Watson and a student of his, Rosalie Rayner, conducted what became one of the most famous experiments in the history of psychology, an attempt to produce a conditioned fear response in an eleven-month-old boy they called, in their report of the work, Albert B.[28] When Albert was nine months old,

they placed a white rat near him, and he showed no fear; he did, however, react with fear when a steel bar was banged with a hammer just
behind his head. Allowing two months to pass so that the experiences
would fade, Watson and Rayner then began the experiment. A rat was
put down in front of Albert, who reached for it with his left hand; just as
he touched it, the steel bar was struck behind him, and he jumped violently, fell forward, and buried his face in the mattress. On a second
trial, Albert reached for the rat with his right hand, and as he touched it
the bar was struck again; this time Albert jumped and fell forward and
began to whimper.

Watson and Rayner delayed further trials for a week "in order not to
disturb the child too seriously," as they wrote—a curious comment,
since they intended to and did disturb him seriously when they continued. In the course of half a dozen more pairings in which the rat was
placed close to Albert and the bar hit behind his head, Albert developed
a full-fledged conditioned fear response to the sight of the rat:

> The instant the rat was shown the baby began to cry. Almost instantly
> he turned sharply to the left, fell over on his left side, raised himself on
> all fours and began to crawl away so rapidly that he was caught with dif-
> ficulty before reaching the edge of the table.

Still more experiments showed that Albert had generalized his fear to
other furry things: a rabbit, a dog, a seal coat, cotton wool, and Watson
sporting a Santa Claus mask. After a month's layoff, Albert was tested
again, and, as Watson and Rayner reported with apparent gratification,
he cried and was afraid of a rat and a number of furry stimuli shown him
without any accompanying clanging of the steel bar.

Shockingly—by today's ethical standards of research—Watson and
Rayner made no effort to decondition Albert, who left the clinic several
days after the final tests. They did say in their report that "had the opportunity been at hand we should have tried out several methods [of decon-
ditioning]," which they outlined. They then jested that twenty years
hence some Freudian analyst might extract from Albert a pseudo-
memory of having tried to play with his mother's pubic hair at age three
and been violently scolded for it.

Watson paid a high price for what he had done in the course of the
collaboration, though not what he had done to Albert. He developed a
mad passion for beautiful young Rosalie Rayner and began an affair
with her. He was seen around town with her, was away from home a

great deal, and carelessly (or perhaps by unconscious design) left in a pocket a passionate note from Rosalie that his wife, Mary, found. He had been unfaithful on previous occasions and Mary had known about some of the episodes and weathered them, but this involvement was far more threatening to her and she felt compelled to take action.

She thought up a way to get damning evidence of his involvement, hoping to use it to force him to give up Rosalie instead of risking a scandal that would cost him his professorship. The Watsons dined at the home of Rosalie's parents one evening, in the course of which Mary said she had a headache and would like to lie down for a while in Rosalie's room. Alone and with the door shut, she searched the room and found and made off with a batch of love letters from Watson, who had been uncharacteristically expressive in them and rather explicit about his and Rosalie's lovemaking.

But when she confronted Watson and threatened to expose him, he refused to break off with Rosalie. Mary decided to sue for divorce, and either she or her brother, to whom she had lent the letters and who had made copies of them, sent them to Frank Goodnow, president of the university. At that time and in that place, such conduct by a professor was utterly impermissible. In late September 1920, Goodnow summoned Watson to his office and demanded his resignation; Watson hotly defended himself but had no choice except to comply. When he left the office, he went home, packed a bag, and headed for New York, his dazzling career in psychology abruptly and permanently ended just as the movement he had spearheaded was succeeding.

Watson later married Rosalie and had two sons with her. He landed a job in New York, which eventually earned him a very large salary, as resident psychologist to the J. Walter Thompson advertising agency. There he combined his knowledge of psychology and his gift of salesmanship to conceive some of the firm's most successful campaigns for deodorants, cold cream, Camel cigarettes, and other products. Among his triumphs: a campaign for Pond's Cold and Vanishing Creams using testimonials from the Queens of Spain and Romania, one for Johnson & Johnson convincing mothers that it was important to use baby powder after every diaper change, and one for Maxwell House that helped to make the "coffee break" an American custom in offices, factories, and homes.

During the first decade of his banishment from the academic world, Watson continued to write books and magazine articles about behaviorism and child rearing. (He advocated strict behaviorist methods, with all emotionality and affection banned.) But he did no more psychological research and no longer played a role in the field, although his expanded thoughts about behaviorism, presented in his books, were adopted by some of his former colleagues and entered behaviorist thinking.

And popular thinking. Watson's psychology, attributing almost all human behavior to stimulus-response conditioning, was a simple, convenient rebuttal of the hereditarian views of Galton's followers and appealed broadly to liberals and egalitarians—an irony, since Watson was politically conservative. In his popular writings, he waxed messianic: behaviorism could create a better world by scientifically engineering the development of personality. In 1924, in *Behaviorism*, he made what is probably his most famous and often-quoted statement:

> Give me a dozen healthy infants, well-formed, and my own specified world to bring them up in and I'll guarantee to take any one at random and train him to become any type of specialist I might select—doctor, lawyer, artist, merchant-chief and, yes, even beggar-man and thief, regardless of his talents, penchants, tendencies, abilities, vocations, and race of his ancestors.[29]

From 1930 on, Watson had nothing to do with psychology except as it applied to advertising. He and Rosalie settled into the good life on a large estate in Connecticut, where in his leisure hours he played gentleman farmer. But after some tranquil years tragedy struck: Rosalie contracted dysentery, grew steadily worse despite treatment, and died in her mid-thirties. Watson, fifty-eight, was shattered. He continued to work in advertising (he had recently moved to the William Esty agency), but his only real interest lay in puttering about on his farm. There were always women in his life, but he never came close to marrying again. As he aged, he became careless about himself, dressed poorly, grew fat, and was something of a solitary.

In 1957, when Watson was nearly eighty, the American Psychological Association notified him that it was awarding him its gold medal for his contributions to psychology. Astonished and pleased, he went to New York with his sons to receive the award, but at the last moment, afraid that after almost forty years of exile he would burst into tears at the ceremony, he sent one of his sons to stand in for him. The citation accompanying the medal read:

> To John B. Watson, whose work has been one of the vital determinants

of the form and substance of modern psychology. He initiated a revolution in psychological thought and his writings have been the point of departure for continuing lines of fruitful research.

It was a gracious tribute. But in fact Watson had oversimplified or overstated many issues, and other behaviorists later had to elaborate on and qualify them. Almost no one today holds as extreme an environmental position as he did, nor does anyone now recommend withholding affection from children and rearing them by frigid behavioral rules. The Pavlovian conditioning that he made the keystone of his system proved not to be the only significant kind; later behaviorists added to it another major model called "operant" conditioning. Most important, at the very time that Watson received the gold medal it was becoming clear that chains of S-R units (series of linked conditioned stimulus-response connections), no matter how long, could not adequately explain complex and sophisticated kinds of behavior.

For all that, Watson was the first and most important spokesman of a radical theory and practice that dominated American psychology for nearly half a century. Raymond Fancher, in his *Pioneers of Psychology*, writes that although many of the developments of behaviorism might have happened without Watson, "he certainly hastened their occurrence, and lent a vitality and power to the objective psychology movement that it might otherwise have lacked."[30]

Watson died in 1958, the year after he received the gold medal. To the end, he believed that the revolution he had started, and which had so long been the leading school of psychology in America, was also the psychology of the future. He was wrong. But we'll come to that.

The Triumph of Behaviorism

After a slow start, behaviorism rapidly gained favor among psychologists in the 1920s, particularly in America; it soon became the ruling view and, after a while, almost the only acceptable one, at least in academic circles.

The main reason for its popularity was its claim to be the first truly scientific psychology. Until the nineteenth century, psychology had consisted largely of philosophic speculation, not science. In the nineteenth century, adherents of the New Psychology had sought to turn psychology into a natural science but got no further than explaining a few simple reflexes and perceptions in physiological terms—and even to achieve that much, they had had to rely on unverifiable introspections.

Behaviorists, in contrast, said they could construct a psychology entirely from visible, measurable events—the causally connected stimulus-response units of which, they maintained, the whole range of animal and human behavior was assembled. Such a psychology would be based on reactions as specific and unvarying as those of chemistry or physics, and should enable the psychologist, in Watson's words, "given the stimulus, to predict the response—or, seeing the reaction take place, to state what the stimulus is that has called out the reaction."[31]

Another reason so many psychologists found behaviorism appealing was that by limiting themselves to visible behavior they could dispose of all those intractable questions about the mind that philosophers and psychologists had labored over for more than twenty-four hundred years. Behaviorists said that we not only cannot know what goes on in the mind, we don't need to know in order to explain behavior. They often likened the mind to a black box containing unknown circuitry; if we know that when we push a particular button on it, the box will emit a specific signal or action, what is inside is of no consequence. Nor should what goes on in the mind even be discussed, since all talk about mental processes is tantamount to believing in some bodiless entity that runs the brain's machinery—"the ghost in the machine," as the English behaviorist philosopher Sir Gilbert Ryle derisively called it. (Equally derisive was the statement of an antibehaviorist: "The mere mention of the word 'mentalism' offends the sensibilities of a behaviorist in much the same way the word 'masturbation' offends polite company."[32])

There were, moreover, deep-seated social and cultural reasons for the success of behaviorism. It appealed to the twentieth-century personality, especially in America, because it was practical; it sought not ultimate explanations but commonsense knowledge that could be put to use.

At least one historian of behaviorism, David Bakan, has also linked its rise to the urbanization and industrialization of America; these social developments, he says, created an urge to master the incomprehensible and worrisome strangers all around us—exactly what behaviorism promised to help us do.[33]

Bakan adds two other societal reasons for the success of behaviorism. First, World War I evoked hostility to German psychology, and behaviorism served as an up-to-date and available replacement. Second, behaviorism fit in with the endemic anti-intellectualism of America; it justified ignorance of the subtleties of mentalist psychology on the grounds that mental phenomena, being either illusions or unknowable, were not worth one's time and effort.

From the 1920s to the 1960s, behaviorism (or the more complex versions of it known as neobehaviorism) was the regnant force in American psychology and the model that it exported to the rest of the psychological world. Some psychologists still clung to older schools of thought, and a number of others, among them Freudians, developers of mental testing, child development psychologists, and Gestaltists, were concerned with mental processes, but on most campuses such people had to adapt their work and language to the behaviorist paradigm. Gregory Kimble, a historian of behaviorism, says, exaggerating only a little, "In midcentury American psychology, it would have cost a career to publish on mind, consciousness, volition, or even imagery," since to use such terms signified that one was a mentalist who believed in outdated, subjective, and mystical concepts.[34]

In consequence, much of the research conducted between 1920 and the 1960s dealt with minute, undeniably objective but not very enlightening topics. A few representative titles from the *Psychological Bulletin* and the *American Journal of Psychology* in 1935 were:

"Influence of Hunger on the Pecking Responses of Chickens"
"Comparison of the Rat's First and Second Explorations of a
    Maze Unit"
"The Use of Maze-Trained Rats to Study the Effect on the Central
    Nervous System of Morphine and Related Substances"
"Differential Errors in Animal Mazes"
"Circuits Now Available for the Measurement of Electrodermal
    Responses"

Even when human beings were the experimental subjects, the topics and methods were constrained by behaviorist doctrine. Some typical titles from the *American Journal of Psychology* in 1935 were:

"The Reliability of the pH of Human Mixed Saliva as an Indicator of
    Physiological Changes Accompanying Behavior"
"A Comparison of the Conditioning of Muscular Responses Which
    Vary in Their Degree of Voluntary Control"
"Experimental Extinction of Higher Order Responses"

"The Galvanic Skin Reflex as Related to Overt Emotional Expression"
"Over-Compensation in Time Relationships of Bilateral Movements
  of the Fingers"

The authors of these and similar studies were not really interested in
the pecking behavior of chickens or the pH of human saliva but in
learning—the acquisition of behavioral responses to different kinds of
stimuli. Learning was the central concern of American psychology during the behaviorist era, the assumption being that almost all behavior
could be explained by S-R learning principles.[35] An equally important
assumption was that these principles held true of all sentient creatures,
much as the principles of valence are true of all elements in chemical
compounds. What one learned from chickens, cats, dogs, and especially
rats applied to human beings.

Rats were the favorite experimental animal because they were relatively cheap, small, easy to handle, and fast-maturing. Countless thousands of them served the cause of research by learning to run mazes,
operate levers or push buttons to get food, jump at doors of different colors, depress a bar to turn off an electric current that was making their
feet tingle, and a host of other tasks. There was nothing frivolous about
these experiments; they were aimed at the discovery of important universal laws of behavior. A few examples:[36]

—A rat is placed at the start of a simple maze that includes six choice
  points (each choice point is a T, one branch being a blind alley, the
  other an alley that continues) and ends at the goal box. The rat
  begins exploring and sniffing about, and runs a little; it goes into a
  blind alley, turns back and runs the other way, and after making
  three wrong choices and three right ones reaches the goal box—
  and is lifted out and, after a brief rest, put back in the start box. On
  its seventh run it finds a food pellet at the goal; the rat sniffs it, then
  bolts it down. Another rat gets the same training but without any
  food reward, not even on the final run.

  For a week both rats get the same training every day. By the end
  of the week the first rat knows the route perfectly and races through
  the maze, making no mistakes; the second rat still makes as many
  errors as ever. But finally the second rat gets a food reward at the
  end of its run—and, remarkably, on the next trial makes no errors.
  It learned as much from one rewarded trial as the other rat learned
  in a week. The experiment demonstrates the operation of two prin-

ciples: *reward produces learning,* exemplified by the first rat's behavior; and *lacking reward, there may be latent learning,* exemplified by the second rat's behavior. (Learning takes place in some sense when there is no reward but becomes activated as soon as a reward is associated with the "right" behavior.)

What has this got to do with human behavior? Any teacher can tell you. A child practicing drawing or any other skill may make little progress until the teacher has a moment to say something encouraging or complimentary; then, suddenly, the child shows improvement. Similarly, a novice at flying may make a dozen bumpy landings, finally "grease one in" half by accident, winning praise from his instructor, and from then on make landings as if he had at last "got the idea."

—One at a time, a number of rats are put in the start box of a simple T-shaped maze. At the end of the right-hand branch is a white door behind which is a bit of cheese; at the end of the left-hand branch is a black door behind which is a metal grid floor that gives the rat's feet a mild but unpleasant shock. The rats learn, after a while, to turn right and push through the white door. But once they've learned, the experimenter switches the situation. Now the white door and food are at the end of the left branch, the black door and electrified grid at the end of the right branch. The rats turn right, get shocked, and soon learn to turn to the left.

Once again the diabolic experimenter reverses things, but now the rats learn almost immediately; they have come to associate reward and punishment with the colors of the doors, not their direction. The experiment revalidates Pavlov's principle of *discrimination,* the determination of the rewarding cue in a two-cue situation.

Does this apply to humans? Of course. A novice at gardening gets only a meager crop of tomatoes but sees that his neighbor, who plants a different variety in a sunnier location, gets a bumper crop. The novice tries the neighbor's variety the next year; still no luck. He realizes that the number of hours of sunshine must be the critical factor, fells some trees to get more sunshine, and is successful.

—Another T-maze in which rats learn to turn to the right. This time there is no punishment for choosing the left branch but merely a lack of reward. Some rats are lucky; they find a reward every time they choose the right side. Others are unlucky; they find food there only once every four times. The unlucky rats learn far more slowly than the lucky rats to choose the right-hand branch. The experiment demonstrates that *partial reinforcement* is less effective in learning than is continual reinforcement.

But now the experimenter changes things; there is no reward at either branch for either group. What happens? Oddly, the rats who had previously been lucky lose their conditioning rapidly and begin to alternate their choices, while the ones who were rewarded only every fourth time continue to choose the right branch for a long while. The experiment has demonstrated the *partial reinforcement effect*: the higher the creatures' expectations, the more disruptive a change in the situation; with lower expectations, their learned behavior is more stable when change occurs.

A human analogue: A highly efficient employee has had a generous raise every year; in a year of poor income for the company, he gets only a modest raise, loses his drive, starts taking longer lunches, leaves promptly at 5:00 P.M., and calls in sick now and then. A less capable employee, who has only occasionally gotten a raise bigger than a cost-of-living adjustment, gets only a COLA in the poor year; his commitment to his job is unaffected, because, not expecting much, he does not interpret the lack of bonus as a change in the system.

Two Great Neobehaviorists: Hull and Skinner

As the above experiments show, behaviorists were enlarging their theory and methodology far beyond Watson's formulations. He had described behavior in simplistic terms as "the total striped and unstriped muscular and glandular changes which follow upon a given stimulus,"[37] a view later dubbed "muscle-twitch psychology." For a while, his followers stuck to this view; as one of them, Walter Hunter, wrote in 1928, "All behavior seems to be a combination, more or less complex, of the relatively simple activities of muscles and glands."[38]

Yet to say anything meaningful about complex forms of behavior, it was necessary to see them intact, as acts with an *identity* and *meaning*. A bird building a nest is not just an organism responding to X number of stimuli with X number of reflexes; it is also a bird building a nest—an intricate kind of behavior with a *goal*. As one behaviorist, Edwin Holt, said in 1931, behavior is "what the organism is doing"—hunting, courting, and so on—an organized entity, and not merely the string of reflexes of which that entity is constructed, not just "an arithmetical sum, related only by the *and* or *plus* relation."[39]

But Holt refused to attribute *purpose* to the creature itself; that would have implied the influence of a mind that looked ahead to the goal and set out to reach it. Rather, he ascribed the purposiveness of complicated behaviors to the process by which S-R units were combined: the creature's seeking or avoiding, at each step, assembled S-R units in such a way that the assemblage appeared to be purposive behavior. It was a vague and unsatisfying formulation, but it went as far as any orthodox behaviorist could go.

A more important development was the neobehaviorist effort of Clark L. Hull (1884–1952) of Yale University to make behaviorism a quantitatively exact science modeled after Newtonian physics. Hull, who had started out to be a mining engineer, suffered an attack of polio and remained partly crippled. He switched to psychology, since it was less likely to involve heavy physical activity, but the engineering training carried over, and he set out to develop a kind of calculus of behaviorism. As he wrote in his autobiography:

> [I] came to the definite conclusions around 1930 that psychology is a true natural science; that its primary laws are expressible quantitatively by means of a moderate number of ordinary equations; that all the complex behavior of single individuals will ultimately be derivable as secondary laws from (1) these primary laws together with (2) the conditions under which behavior occurs; and that all the behavior of groups as a whole, i.e., strictly social behavior as such, may similarly be derived as quantitative laws from the same primary equations.[40]

Hull's central concept was a familiar one: behavior consists of sets or chains of linked habits, each of which is an S-R connection that developed as a result of reinforcement. This was his version of Thorndike's Law of Effect. What was new about Hull's work was his postulation of a number of factors, each of which, he held, enhances, limits, or inhibits the formation of such habits, and his development of equations by which one could calculate the exact effect of each of those factors.

They included the level of the creature's drive (a hungry rat has a stronger drive to food than a sated rat); the strength of the reinforcement (expressed in such terms as "5 grams of a standard food"); the number of times a stimulus had been followed by reinforcement; the degree of "need reduction" achieved by each reinforcement; the degree of "drive reduction" (drives are fueled by needs) due to fatigue and the length of time between one trial and the next trial; and so on and on. As Edwin Boring later said, with consummate understatement, it was a "ponderous" theory.[41]

An example: By means of the following equation one can calculate the extent to which any given number of repetitions of a reinforced act increases the strength of the learned habit:[42]

$$_S^N H_R = M - Me^{-iN}$$

The equation says that the strength of the learned habit depends on the number of reinforced trials (N), the relationship between the afferent and efferent nerve impulses in the specific act ($_S H_R$), the physiologically maximum strength of that particular habit (M) minus — well, it goes on and on.

Hull's work was a major attempt to model neobehaviorist psychology on the physical sciences and thereby have it achieve intellectual respectability. His calculus of learning, appearing piecemeal during the 1930s and in systematic form in his *Principles of Behavior* (1943), was greatly admired and hugely influential. In the late 1940s and the 1950s thousands of master's theses and doctoral dissertations were based on one or more of his postulates; he became the most frequently cited psychologist in the literature of psychological research and the leading figure in the psychology of learning.[43]

But during the 1960s, the unwieldiness of his theory and the dwindling of behaviorism's status made Hull's name and work fade rapidly from sight. By 1970 he was rarely quoted, and today there is virtually no research based on his theory. When Hull died, in 1952, he seemed assured of scientific immortality; now he is a figure of minor historical interest, and few young psychologists and very few people outside the profession know his name.[44]

B. F. Skinner (1904–1990), another leading neobehaviorist, had a very different fate. He became, and remained until his death at eighty-six, the best-known psychologist in the world,[45] and his ideas are in wide use today in psychological research, education, and psychotherapy.[46]

So he must have been one of the great contributors to humankind's quest for self-understanding, right?

Far from it.

Human self-understanding, at least as sought by philosophers and psychologists for so many centuries, was no part of Skinner's aim or contribution. Throughout his long life he held fast to his extreme behaviorist view that "subjective entities" such as mind, thought, memory, and reasoning do not exist but are only "verbal constructs, grammatical traps into which the human race in the development of language has fallen," "explanatory entities" that themselves are unexplainable.[47] Skinner's goal was not to understand the human psyche but to determine how behavior is created by external causes. He had no doubt about the correctness of his views; as he wrote in a short autobiography—he also wrote a three-volume one—"[Behaviorism] may need to be clarified, but it does not need to be argued."[48]

Nor did he add much to psychological theory; he considered theories of learning unnecessary and claimed not to have one. Such theory as he did hold can be summed up in the statement that everything we do and are is determined by our history of rewards and punishments; the details of the theory, as he developed them through research, consisted of such principles as the partial reinforcement effect described above, concerning the circumstances that cause behavior to be acquired and those that cause it to be extinguished.

What, then, made him so well known?

Like Watson he was by nature a controversial man, a provocateur, and a superb publicist. On his very first TV appearance he posed a dilemma originally propounded by Montaigne—"Would you, if you had to choose, burn your children or your books?"—and said that he himself would burn his children, since his contribution to the future would be greater through his work than through his genes.[49] Predictably, he elicited outrage—and many invitations for further appearances.

At other times he seemed to take pleasure in offending thoughtful people by deriding the terms in which they talked about and comprehended human behavior:

> Behavior . . . is still attributed to human nature, and there is an extensive "psychology of individual differences" in which people are compared and described in terms of traits of character, capacities, and abilities. Almost everyone who is concerned with human affairs . . . continues to talk about human behavior in this prescientific way.[50]

He consistently pooh-poohed the effort to understand the inner person:

> We do not need to try to discover what personalities, states of mind, feelings, traits of character, plans, purposes, intentions, or other perquisites of autonomous man really are in order to get on with a scientific analysis of behavior . . . Thinking is behaving. The mistake is in allocating the behavior to the mind.[51]

All we need to know or can know, he said, are the external causes of behavior and the observable results of that behavior; these will yield "a comprehensive picture of the organism as a behaving system."

Consonant with that view, he was a rigorous determinist: "We are what we are because of our history. We like to believe we can choose, we can act . . . [but] I don't believe a person is either free or responsible." The "autonomous" human being is an illusion; the good person is one who has been conditioned to behave that way, and the good society would be one based on "behavioral engineering" — the scientific control of behavior through methods of positive reinforcement.[52]

Skinner was a deft showman and popularizer; he was fluent, lucid, unabashedly egotistic, and charming. To demonstrate the power of his own technique of conditioning, he taught a pigeon to peck out a tune on a toy piano, and a pair of pigeons to play a kind of table tennis in which they rolled a ball back and forth with their beaks; millions who have seen these performances on TV documentaries think of Skinner as a Svengali, at least of animals. He presented his vision of the ideal, scientifically controlled society in the form of a utopian novel, *Walden Two* (1948), picturing a small society in which, from birth onward, children are rigorously conditioned by rewards (positive reinforcement) to be cooperative and sociable; all behavior is controlled, but for the good and the happiness of all. Despite wooden dialogue and a labored plot, it became a cult book and perennial favorite with undergraduates, and has sold well over two million copies.

But his fame with the public was greater than his standing with fellow professionals. As one admirer, the psychologist Norman Guttman, wrote in *The American Psychologist* some years ago:

> [Skinner is] the leading figure in a myth . . . [the] scientist-hero, the Promethean fire-bringer, the master technologist . . . [the] chief iconoclast, the image-breaker who liberates our thoughts from ancient restrictions.[53]

Skinner was born in 1904 in a small Pennsylvania railroad town, where his father was a lawyer. As a boy, he had a great aptitude for building Rube Goldberg contraptions; later, as a psychologist, he would invent and build remarkably effective apparatuses for animal experimentation. In school and college he aspired to become a writer, and after college spent a year, much of it in Greenwich Village, trying to write. Although he closely observed the manifold forms of human behavior all around him, he discovered after a while that he had nothing to say about what he saw and, deeply dejected, gave up the effort.

But he soon found another and, for him, more practicable way to understand human behavior. In his reading he came across discussions of Watson's and Pavlov's work, read books by each of them, and decided that his future lay in a scientific approach to human behavior, particularly the study of conditioning. "I was very bitter about my failure in literature," he told an interviewer in 1977, "and I was sure that writers never really understood anything. And that was why I turned to psychology."[54]

He proceeded to Harvard. Introspective psychology reigned there, but he was no longer interested in what he called "the inside story," and quietly went his own way, doing behaviorist research with rats. In his autobiography he recalls with pleasure having been something of a bad boy: "They may have thought that someone in psychology was keeping an eye on me, but the fact was that I was doing exactly as I pleased."[55] Despite the teachings of his professors, he became ever more thoroughly behaviorist, and at his dissertation examination, when asked to name some objections to behaviorism, he could not think of one.

Making good use of his mechanical aptitude, he constructed a puzzle box that was a great improvement over the Thorndike model; widely used ever since, it is known as the Skinner box. In its basic form—it has many models—it is a cage, large enough to comfortably accommodate a white rat, with a horizontal bar on one wall just above a little food tray and a water spout. When the rat, prowling about the cage, happens to rest its forepaws on the bar, pressing it down, a food pellet automatically drops into the tray. Connected equipment outside the cage automatically records the behavior by drawing a line showing the cumulative number of bar pressings minute by minute. This was a much more efficient way of gathering data than Thorndike's puzzle box procedure, since the experimenter did not have to observe the rat or deliver the food when it pressed the bar but merely look at the record.

The box also yielded more objective data on the acquisition or extinction of behavior than anyone had gathered thus far. The rat, and it alone, determined how much time elapsed between one pressing of the bar and the next. Skinner could base his findings of learning principles on the "response rate"—the rate at which the animal's behavior changed in response to reinforcement—uncontaminated by the experimenter's actions.

Moreover, Skinner could program the box in ways that approximated many circumstances in the real world that either reinforce or fail to reinforce behavior. He could, for instance, study the learning of a response when it is regularly rewarded; the extinction of a learned response when the reward is abruptly discontinued; the effects on learning and on extinction when rewards are delivered intermittently at regular intervals (say, every fourth bar pressing); the effects when rewards are delivered intermittently at irregular intervals; the effects of mixed results of bar pressing (such as a reward coupled with an electric shock); and so on. In each case, the data yielded a curve showing the rate of acquisition or extinction of a behavior under those particular circumstances.

From these curves, Skinner formulated a number of principles that cast light on the behavior of rats—and human beings. An example is his discovery of an important variation of the partial reinforcement effect. After rats had been trained on a schedule in which food pellets were delivered only once in a while and at irregular intervals, the rats would persist in their bar pressing even if the food-dispensing apparatus was turned off altogether. Their learned behavior was more resistant to extinction than that of rats trained to intermittent but regular reinforcement.[56] This has been likened by some to the behavior of a slot machine player in a casino: neither the rat nor the gambler has any way of predicting when the next reinforcement is to come, but, being accustomed to occasional rewards, will hang on in the hope of getting one on the next try.[57]

Skinner's most important contribution, however, was his concept of "operant conditioning"; for this alone he merits a permanent place in the Hall of Fame of psychology.

In "classical" (Pavlov's) conditioning, the animal's unconditioned response (salivating) to food is made into a conditioned response to a formerly neutral stimulus (the sound of the metronome or bell); the crucial element in the behavior change is the new stimulus.

In "instrumental" (Thorndike's) conditioning, the crucial element in behavior change is the response, not the stimulus. A neutral response— the accidental stepping on the treadle during random efforts to get to the food — is rewarded and becomes a learned bit of behavior serving an end it formerly did not have.

Skinner's operant conditioning is an important development in instrumental conditioning. Any random movement the animal makes, for whatever reason, can be thought of as "operating" on the environment in some way and therefore, in Skinner's terms, is an "operant"; rewarding the movement produces operant conditioning. By rewarding a series of little random movements, one by one, the experimenter can "shape" the behavior of the animal until it acts in ways that were not part of its original or natural repertoire.

Here is how Skinner shaped the behavior of a pigeon to peck at a small colored plastic disk set flush in one wall of the Skinner box:

> We first give the bird food when it turns slightly in the direction of the spot [i.e., the disk] from any part of the cage. This increases the frequency of such behavior. We then withhold reinforcement until a slight movement is made toward the spot. This again alters the general distribution of behavior without producing a new unit. We continue by reinforcing positions successively closer to the spot, then by reinforcing only when the head is moved slightly forward, and finally only when the beak actually makes contact with the spot.
>
> In this way we can build complicated operants which would never appear in the repertoire of the organism otherwise. By reinforcing a series of successive approximations, we bring a rare response to a very high probability in a short time . . . The total act of turning toward the spot from any point in the box, walking toward it, raising the head, and striking the spot may seem to be a functionally coherent unit of behavior, but it is constructed by a continual process of differential reinforcement from undifferentiated behavior.[58]

(Other experimenters, using Skinner's technique, have constructed far more peculiar behaviors. One taught a rabbit to pick up a coin in its mouth and drop it into a piggy bank; another taught a pig named Priscilla to turn on a TV set, pick up dirty clothes and put them in a hamper, and run a vacuum cleaner over the floor.[59])

Skinner likened the operant training of his pigeons to a child's learning to talk, sing, dance, play games, and in time acquire the entire repertoire of adult behavior. All, in his view, is due to the assembling of long chains of behavior out of tiny links of simple behaviors by operant conditioning. One might call it an Erector-set view of the human being

(*Homo erectorus?*)—a mindless robot assembled by operant conditioning from a multitude of meaningless bits.

Skinner was more or less ignored by the psychological establishment for a long while but slowly acquired a number of devotees—enough, finally, to result in the publication of four journals of Skinner behaviorist research and theory and the creation of a special section of Skinner-type studies within the American Psychological Association (Division 25, Experimental Analysis of Behavior, since renamed Behavior Analysis). Skinner boxes and the techniques of operant conditioning have long been widely used by experimental psychologists. In recent years Skinner's name and work have been cited in hundreds of behavioral science publications each year (though far less often than Freud's).[60]

Still, it was outside of mainstream psychology that Skinner had his major impact.

During a visit to his daughter's fourth-grade class in 1953, it occurred to him that operant techniques similar to those by which he had taught pigeons to play the piano would make for more efficient teaching than traditional methods. Complicated subjects could be broken down into simple steps in a logical sequence; the students would be presented with questions, and immediately told whether their answers were correct. Two principles would be at work here: the knowledge that one has answered correctly is a powerful reinforcer (reward) of behavior; and immediate reinforcement works better than delayed reinforcement. The result is known as "programmed instruction."

But since one teacher cannot simultaneously provide reinforcement to a roomful of children, new textbooks would have to be written in which questions and answers were presented one by one, each taking a short step toward mastery of the subject and each permitting children to reward themselves immediately by uncovering the answer. Skinner also developed teaching machines for operant self-instruction by comparable means; the mechanical models were a fad for a time, then dropped out of use, but today, computer-based self-instruction with immediate reinforcement is widely used by schools, businesses, and elder-care centers, among others.

For some years the programmed learning movement had a major influence on teaching; courses and course materials designed to teach through operant conditioning were in use in a large proportion of grade schools and colleges in America, and in many schools in dozens of other countries. But eventually educators recognized that the atomistic methods of programmed instruction provide only part of what human beings need; they also need holistic, hierarchical thought structures. And later research showed that in human beings delayed reinforcement often has better results than immediate reinforcement; thinking about one's responses may lead to more learning than quickly responding and getting an answer.[61] Finally, the observation of other people's behavior, a highly effective form of learning for humans, even if not for cats, involves no immediate reinforcement. Still and all, Skinner's doctrine of immediate reinforcement has proven useful, is familiar to most teachers, and is incorporated into many curricula and grade school textbooks.

Skinner also had a measurable effect on the treatment of mental and emotional disorders. It occurred to him that a system of tiny rewards for tiny changes from sick acts toward healthy ones might reshape the patient's behavior. Beginning in the late 1940s, he and two of his graduate students made the first experimental trials of what came to be known as behavior modification. They set up lever-pressing stations at a state mental hospital near Boston; psychotic patients received candy or cigarettes for operating the machines in an orderly fashion. Once that worked, the therapists gave tokens to patients for appropriate behavior, such as voluntarily attending meals, grooming themselves, and helping with housekeeping tasks. The tokens could be exchanged for candy, cigarettes, or privileges like choosing a dining companion, talking to a physician, or watching TV.[62]

The rewarding of desired behavior in deeply disturbed people often worked. One depressed woman would not eat and was in danger of dying of starvation, but she seemed to enjoy visitors and the TV set, radio, books and magazines, and flowers in her room. The therapists moved her into a room devoid of all these comforts, and put a light meal in front of her; if she ate anything at all, one of the comforts was temporarily restored. The therapists gradually withheld the rewards unless she ate more and more. Her eating improved, she gained weight, and within two months she was released from the hospital. A follow-up eighteen months later found her leading a normal life.[63]

The behavior modification movement spread to a number of mental hospitals and reform schools. Psychiatrists and psychologists now consider it a useful component of their therapies for severely disordered patients, though a costly one in terms of time and staff effort. Behavior modification is also used by many psychotherapists in the treatment of less severe problems, like smoking, obesity, shyness, tics, and speech problems. It is a specialized technique within the field of behavior therapy, most of which is based on Pavlov-type conditioning rather than on Skinner's behavior modification.

Skinner's best-known work, *Walden Two*, has not remade American society or even part of it, but it undoubtedly has influenced the thinking and social concepts of its millions of readers. Only one effort has been made to create an actual utopia on the *Walden Two* model: Twin Oaks Community in Louisa, Virginia, a commune founded by eight people in 1967. After surviving many rocky years, it has grown to a population of eighty-five adults and fifteen children. While still modeled administratively on *Walden Two*, the commune long ago gave up the effort to define ideal behavior and to shape one another's behavior through methods of Skinner reinforcement.[64]

Skinner was sometimes self-deprecating about his impact on the world. "In general," he once said, "my effects on other people have been far less important than my effects on rats and pigeons—or on people as experimental subjects." That was probably not meant to be taken seriously. What he did mean seriously was the following remark: "I was never in any doubt as to [my work's] importance." And he added, on a characteristically perverse note: "When it began to attract attention, I was wary of the effect rather than pleased. Many notes in my files comment on the fact that I have been frightened or depressed by so-called honors. I forgo honors which would take time away from my work or unduly reinforce specific aspects of it."[65]

The Impending Paradigm Shift

As behaviorist research accumulated, it became evident to all but the most dedicated adherents of the theory that rats and other laboratory animals frequently acted in ways that the theory could not explain.

For one thing, their behavior often failed to conform to supposedly universal principles of conditioning. "Pigeon, rat, monkey, which is which? It doesn't matter," Skinner had written[66]—but it did matter. Researchers could easily train a pigeon to peck at a disk or a key for food but found it almost impossible to train the bird to flap its wings for the same reward. They could easily teach a rat to press a bar for food but could get a cat to do so only with great difficulty. A rat given sour blue water to drink, followed by a nauseating drug, would thereafter shun sour water but willingly drink blue water; a quail, given the same treatment, would shun blue water but drink sour water. These and scores of comparable findings forced behaviorists to admit that each species has its own built-in circuitry that enables it to learn some things easily and instinctively, others with difficulty, and still others not at all. The laws of learning were far from universally applicable.[67]

A more serious flaw in behaviorist psychology was that experimental animals kept acting in ways that could not be explained by the neat rate-of-response curves. Many researchers had found, for instance, that at the beginning of an extinction trial an animal would respond to the stimulus with greater vigor than it had during a long series of reinforcements. A rat that had been getting a food pellet each time it pressed a bar would, if no pellet emerged, press the bar with extra force again and again, although according to strict behaviorist theory the absence of the reward should have weakened the response, not strengthened it.[68]

But of course human beings do the same thing. When a vending machine fails to deliver, the customer pulls or pushes the lever harder a few times, or even hits or kicks the machine, either expressing frustration or acting on the thought that something is jammed and needs an extra jolt. There was no place in behaviorist theory for such internal processes, particularly not for thinking about a problem, yet a number of behaviorists noticed that their rats sometimes behaved as if they were indeed doing rudimentary purposive thinking.

One leading researcher who was aware of this was Edward Chace Tolman (1886–1959), an eminent contemporary of Hull's and a leading neobehaviorist of the 1930s and 1940s. He observed that after a rat had run a maze a few times, it would pause at a point of decision, look this way and that, take a few steps, and perhaps turn back, all before making its choice and going on. In his presidential address to the APA in 1938, Tolman said it seemed clear that the rat was performing "vicarious trial and error" in its head. "Anthropomorphically speaking," he added, "it appears to be a 'looking before you leap' sort of affair."[69]

That was only one of many bits of rat behavior that Tolman concluded could be explained solely in terms of processes going on in the rat's head. Years earlier, he and a colleague had built a simple maze with three routes to the goal box. The shortest was a straight path from the start box to the goal box; the second, a little longer, made a short loop to the left, then rejoined the straight path partway toward the goal box; and the third, the longest, made a long loop to the right, then rejoined the straight path close to the goal box. In a series of trials the rat, as behaviorist theory predicted, found its way to the food by all three routes but learned to take the shortest, since that was the most easily established habit.

Tolman then put a barrier across the straight path halfway to the goal so that the rat could reach it only by the longest route. According to theory, when the rat ran down the straight path and came up against the barrier, it should have turned back and tried the next most easily established habit—the medium-length route—but it immediately took the long route. To Tolman this suggested that the rat had built up a sort of mental map of the entire maze and "realized" that the barrier blocked all but the longest route.[70]

Tolman conducted many similar experiments, most of them far more complicated, and all of which supported his belief that "something like a field map of the environment gets established in the rat's brain." Standard behaviorist theory, he said, offered only a partial explanation of maze learning: "We agree . . . that the rat in running a maze is exposed to stimuli and is finally led as a result of these stimuli to the responses which actually occur. We feel, however, that the intervening brain processes are more complicated, more patterned, and often, pragmatically speaking, more autonomous than do the stimulus-response psychologists."[71]

These studies led Tolman to propound a theory he called "purposive behaviorism." Its essence was that rats act not as automata, developing habits solely according to the number and kind of stimuli they experience, but as if, in addition, they are influenced by their own expectations, their knowledge of what leads to what in a given situation, their goals, and other internal processes or states.[72] As one orthodox behaviorist derisively said, Tolman's rats were "buried in thought."[73]

Tolman called these internal factors "intervening variables" (they intervened between stimulus and response) and insisted that they were compatible with behaviorism. "For the behaviorist," he wrote, " 'mental processes' are to be identified and defined in terms of the behaviors to which they lead. [They are] naught but inferred determinants of behavior . . . Behavior and these inferred determinants are both objective, defined types of entity."[74] It was a valiant effort to remain faithful, but Tolman had, willy-nilly, breached the dike of behaviorism and let in a trickle of mind. In time it would be a flood.

If reward and repetition only partly explain rat behavior, they give an even more limited account of the determinants and workings of human behavior. Consider memory, for example. Behaviorists portrayed it in purely mathematical terms: the more trials and reinforcements, the greater the rewards, the closer in time the S and the R, the more certain it is that the S will produce the R. If the stimulus is the question "What comes after five?," the response is "six." If the stimulus is the question "What is your phone number?," the answer is a sequence of seven digits (ten if you include the area code). The first digit is the response to the question but is also the stimulus that produces the response of the second digit, and so on, in a chain of associative links.

But even at the height of the behaviorist era, psychologists knew that human memory was more complicated than that. For one thing, we "chunk" some information: we remember area codes, for instance, as units, not as a series of linked responses. For another thing, we have different kinds of memory: we learn some phone numbers only for a moment—we look them up, hold them in "short-term memory" until we dial, and then instantly forget them, but make others a part of our "long-term memory" (the vast stockpile of stored knowledge we draw on as needed). Some things require inordinate amounts of repetition and reward to become fixed in memory (many people can't seem to remember their own Social Security number, though they've looked it up scores of times); other things (the exorbitant price we paid for dinner at a particular restaurant, our baby's first words) remain indelibly fixed in memory after only a single experience. These and many other characteristics of human memory cannot be explained by the confined and rigid formulas of behaviorism.

Throughout the behaviorist era, some psychologists continued to explore, in broader and deeper terms, not only human memory but a number of the psychological phenomena that behaviorism had ignored, like perception, motivation, personality traits, reasoning, problem solving, creativity, child development, the interplay of hereditary tendencies and experience, and interpersonal relations. Gradually, the new data gathered about these subjects, and the questions those data raised that behaviorism could not answer, prepared the way for what Thomas Kuhn, in his famous analysis of scientific revolutions, called a "paradigm shift"—a relatively abrupt switch to a new theory encompassing and making sense of a large accumulation of data that could be accounted for only with difficulty, if at all, by the reigning theory.[75]

Meanwhile, research in a number of other fields was beginning to cast new light on the workings of the mind. From anthropology came studies of how preliterate peoples think; from psycholinguistics came accounts of how human beings acquire and use language; and from computer science came a wholly new way to conceive of thinking—as information processing, proceeding step by step like a computer program.

The convergence of all these forces achieved intellectual critical mass during the 1960s, resulting in a knowledge explosion and a new conception of psychology. The former cognitive specialties within psychology regained their status, and cognitive science became the hot new interdisciplinary specialty or, more accurately, aggregation of specialties. It was a mind-based science relying on experimental methods by means of which reasonable inferences could be made about mental processes. By the 1980s, cognitive science studies were going on in the psychology departments of nearly every American university, and a handful of universities had created semi-independent institutes of cognitive science. We'll look at this more closely later in this history.

With the advent of the paradigm shift, behaviorism rapidly lost its commanding position in psychology and its claim to be a sufficient explanation of all behavior. Gregory Kimble of Duke University sums up the disenchantment of psychologists with behaviorism:

> Although the classical theories were formulated and tested in terms of simple learning, behind the scenes there was always the presumption that these theories could be applied to all behavior . . . [and] that most of the basic laws of learning had already been discovered and all that remained was the minor problem of resolving the few systematic issues that separated the main theorists . . . [But] by the middle of the century it had become clear that the classic theories of learning were limited in scope and that the stature of our scientific knowledge was pre-Galilean rather than post-Newtonian, as Hull and others had thought.[76]

Curiously, it was only when behaviorism was in its decline that its offshoot, behavior therapy, became a widely used and reasonably successful form of treatment for a limited range of psychological disorders.

What is true of behavior therapy—its usefulness but limited applicability—is similar to what has proved true of its parent, behaviorism. A number of its findings have been put to practical use, an example being taste-aversion learning: To inhibit coyotes from killing sheep, researchers put toxic lamb burgers, wrapped in sheep fur, on the perimeters of fenced areas of sheep ranches; coyotes that eat this bait get sick, vomit, and develop an instant aversion to lamb meat and to sheep.[77] Other conditioning mechanisms have been used to counter the aversion cancer patients develop to food if mealtime comes just before painful chemotherapy (the simple answer: separate mealtime widely from treatment).[78] Behavior modification methods have been used in programs with mentally retarded children and adults, psychiatric patients, and prisoners: They earn "tokens" for good behavior that can be traded for privileges. Secondary reinforcement methods have proved useful in the workplace in such applications as giving employees bonus vouchers for getting to work on time.[79] Phobias of various kinds, including extreme fear of snakes, have been successfully treated by step-by-step conditioning of the phobic person to thoughts of, the sight of, and eventually the handling of, snakes.[80]

More generally, behaviorism yielded a legacy often taken for granted but considered essential in most areas of psychology: the need for rigorous experimentation and carefully defined variables. Behavior analysis continues to attract some psychologists as a field of research and application; in addition to the 4,500 members of the Association for Behavior Analysis, another 5,000 or more psychologists are members of local chapters of ABA. But their interest in it is apparently more as an adjunct to other areas of research than a primary identification, an indication being the membership of Division 25 of APA, which peaked at some 1,600 members in the early 1970s, then slid steeply downhill to a little over 600 in the last half dozen years, about 7 percent of APA membership.

In any case, the kinds of studies being performed within the field of behavior analysis these days seem strangulated to cognitivists. Here, for instance, are the titles of typical articles in the January 2006 issue of the *Journal of the Experimental Analysis of Behavior*:

"The influence of prior choices on current choice."
"Resistance to extinction following variable-interval reinforcement:
     Reinforcer rate and amount."
"Second-order schedules of token reinforcement with pigeons:
     Implications for unit price."

And here is a brief excerpt exemplifying much of the work being done by contemporary behaviorists:

Rats obtained food-pellet reinforcers by nose poking a lighted key. Experiment 1 examined resistance to extinction following single-schedule training with different variable-interval schedules, ranging from a mean interval of 16 min to 0.25 min. That is, for each schedule, the rats received 24 consecutive daily baseline sessions and then a session of extinction (i.e., no reinforcers). Resistance to extinction (decline in response rate relative to baseline) was negatively related to the rate of reinforcers obtained during baseline, a relation analogous to the partial-reinforcement-extinction effect. A positive relation between these variables emerged, however, when the unit of extinction was taken as the mean interreinforcer interval that had been in effect during training (i.e., as an omitted reinforcer during extinction) . . .[81]

It is time for us to move on to something more easily recognizable as psychology.

The
Gestaltists

A Visual Illusion Gives
Rise to a New Psychology

On a train speeding through central Germany late in the summer of 1910, a young psychologist named Max Wertheimer stared at the landscape, intrigued by an illusion millions have taken for granted but that he felt, at that moment, required an explanation. Distant telegraph poles, houses, and hilltops, though stationary, seemed to be speeding along with the train. Why?[1]

The puzzle led him to think about another illusory motion—that produced by the stroboscope, a toy employing the same principle as motion pictures, which were just becoming popular. In both cases, the rapid exposure to the eye of a series of photographs taken at split-second intervals, or drawings showing the smallest of changes, created the impression of continuous motion.

The phenomenon, known for decades, had never been satisfactorily explained. Thomas Edison and others who had developed motion pictures in the 1890s were content to achieve the effect without understanding what caused it. But on the train that day Wertheimer had a sudden intuition about the answer. He had taken his doctorate at Würzburg, where, in defiance of Wundtian principles, a handful of psychologists had been using introspection to explore conscious thinking. It now occurred to him that the illusion of motion might be due to something happening not in the retina, as many psychologists thought, but in the mind, where some higher-level mental process supplied transitions between the successive pictures, thereby creating the perception of movement. He promptly lost interest in the problem of the moving landscape and never returned to it.

At the time, Wertheimer, who had been doing research at the University of Vienna on the inability to read, was on his way to the Rhineland for a vacation. But his idea so excited him that he got off the train at Frankfurt to consult Professor Friedrich Schumann, an expert on perception with whom he had studied at the University of Berlin before going to Würzburg, and who had recently moved to the University of Frankfurt.

In town, Wertheimer bought a stroboscope at a toy store and spent the evening working with it in his hotel room. (A stroboscope is a scientific instrument for seeing moving parts, as in machinery, slowed down or stationary, but in the nineteenth century and early in the twentieth the term referred to a popular toy that created the impression of motion.) The stroboscope came with pictures of a horse and boy; at the right speed of operation the horse appeared to trot and the boy to walk. Wertheimer replaced the pictures with pieces of paper on which he alternately drew lines in two locations, parallel to each other. He found that at one speed of operation he saw first one line and then the other in their different places; at another, both lines side by side; and at yet another, a single line *moving* from one position to another. He had a historic experiment and a theory of psychology in the making.

The next day Wertheimer called on Schumann at the university, told him what he had observed and what he guessed was the explanation, and asked his opinion. Schumann could cast no light on the matter but offered Wertheimer the use of his laboratory and equipment, including a new tachistoscope of his own design. With it a researcher, by regulating the speed of rotation of a wheel with slits in it, could expose a visual stimulus to the viewer for brief durations, and by using wheels with differently located slits and a prism could present the viewer with alternating images. The tachistoscope did with precision and control what the stroboscope did crudely.

Because Wertheimer would need volunteers to serve as experimental subjects, Schumann introduced him to one of his two assistants, Wolfgang Köhler, who shortly brought in the other assistant, Kurt Koffka.[2] They were somewhat younger than Wertheimer (he was thirty, Köhler twenty-two, and Koffka twenty-four), but all three were interested in the higher-level mental phenomena that the New Psychology of the physiologists and the followers of Wundt ignored, and they hit it off at once. They were to be friends and co-workers for their entire lives.

Wertheimer, single and possessed of an independent income—his father had been director of a successful commercial school in Prague—could do as he pleased; what he pleased was to abandon his vacation plans and remain in Frankfurt for nearly half a year conducting a series of experiments, with Köhler, Koffka, and Koffka's wife serving as his subjects.

In his basic experiment, adapted from the hotel room try-out, Wertheimer alternately projected a three-centimeter horizontal line and another one about two centimeters below it. At a low rate of exposure, his volunteers (who did not know until much later what he was doing) all saw first one line and then the other; at a high rate of exposure, both lines simultaneously; and at intermediate rates, a single line smoothly moving from the upper to the lower position and back again.[3]

In a variation, Wertheimer used a vertical line and a horizontal line. At the right speed his subjects saw one line rotating back and forth through 90 degrees. In another variation he used lights; these, at the critical speed, appeared to be a single light moving. In still others he used multiple lines, different colors, and different shapes, and in every case was able to produce the illusion of motion. Even after he told his three subjects what was happening, they could not make themselves *not* see the motion. Through still other variations, Wertheimer ruled out any possibility that the phenomenon was due to eye movements or retinal afterimages.

The illusion, he concluded, was a "psychic state of affairs," which he called the φ phenomenon. The letter *phi*, he said, "designates something that exists outside the perceptions of *a* and *b*," resulting from a "psychological short-circuit" in the brain.[4] The φ phenomenon, he suggested, resulted from "a psychological short-circuit" in the brain between the two areas stimulated by the nerve impulses coming from the retinal areas stimulated by *a* and *b*.

This physiological hypothesis did not stand up in later research; what did was Wertheimer's theory that the illusion of motion takes place not at the level of sensation, in the retina, but of perception, in the mind, where incoming discrete sensations are seen as an organized unity with a meaning of its own. Wertheimer called such an overall perception a *Gestalt*, a German word that means form, shape, or configuration but that he used to mean a set of sensations perceived as a meaningful whole.

Seemingly, he had spent months of work to explain a trivial illusion. In actuality, he and his co-workers had sown the seed of the Gestalt school of psychology, a movement that would enrich and broaden psychology both in Germany and the United States.*

The Rediscovery of the Mind

Wertheimer's theory that the mind adds structure and meaning to incoming sensations was distinctly out of step with the antimentalist psychology that had been dominant in Germany for nearly half a century and in America for a generation.

His theory was also out of step with the *Zeitgeist* of 1910, which centered on the transformation of life and thought by the physical sciences and technology. The electric light was radically altering nighttime in cities and even remote towns, the automobile was changing the habits of nations, airplanes were becoming capable of sustained flight (Louis Blériot had flown across the English Channel), Marie Curie had just isolated radium and polonium, Rutherford was working out his theory of atomic structure, Zeppelin passenger service had recently begun, and Lee De Forest had lately patented the radio tube. The New Psychology was in harmony with such developments; mentalist psychology seemed more than ever metaphysical, unscientific, and passé.

But for some years a number of psychologists had considered Wundtian psychology barren and confining because it did not deal with complex forms of experience such as emotions, thinking, learning, and creativity—the most important aspects of human life. James, Galton, Binet, Freud, and the members of the Würzburg School, though they had dissimilar concerns, were all interested in and had been investigating phenomena that could be explained only in terms of higher mental processes.

In addition, other researchers had been turning up bits of evidence that perceptions are not identical with the sensations received by the retina or other sense organs but are the mind's interpretation of the data in those sensations.

As far back as 1890, Christian von Ehrenfels, an Austrian psycholo-

---

*Gestalt psychology is often confused with Gestalt therapy. The former is a theory of psychology; the latter, a technique of psychotherapy that uses a few key concepts borrowed from the psychology, but greatly altered in meaning, plus notions drawn from depth psychologies and existentialism.

gist, pointed out that when a melody is transposed, every note is changed, yet we hear the very same melody. He explained that we recognize the sameness of relations among the parts of the whole—what he called the melody's *Gestaltqualität* or "form quality," a crucial characteristic perceived by the mind, rather than the ears.

Ernst Mach, a physicist with an interest in psychology, noted in 1897 that when we see a circle at different angles, it seems circular to us even though it looks ellipsoidal to a camera, and that when we see a table from different angles, the image on the retina changes but the inner experience of seeing a table does not. The mind interprets the sensations to mean what it knows the object to be.

In 1906 Vittorio Benussi, experimenting with the famous Müller-Lyer illusion, in which two lines (the horizontal ones in the following

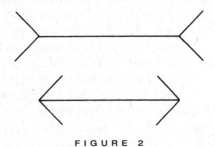

FIGURE 2

The Müller-Lyer illusion

illustration) look different in length although they are exactly the same, found that even when he told his subjects to concentrate on the horizontal lines, they could not make themselves ignore the whole figure; they could reduce the illusion but not eliminate it.

And while Wertheimer was conducting his first experiment in Frankfurt, David Katz, a psychologist at Göttingen, was exploring the phenomena of "brightness constancy" and "color constancy." When we see an object in shadow, he found, we perceive it as having the same brightness and color as when we see it in sunlight, even though objectively it is darker and its color different. We see it, that is, within a known context.

Wertheimer, Koffka, and Köhler had all been exposed to such findings and concepts in their training, and had all been influenced at Berlin by Carl Stumpf, who had imported phenomenology from philosophy into psychology. (In phenomenological psychology, the primary materials of research are everyday real-life experiences, not elemental sensations and feelings.) Wertheimer and Koffka had also studied at Würzburg, where the research emphasis was on thought processes. All three, moreover, had done research involving higher mental functions: Wertheimer on the thinking of feeble-minded children and patients with reading disorders, Koffka in his dissertation on rhythmic Gestalten,* Köhler in his on the psychology of acoustics.

Still, they were a distinctly dissimilar threesome, and hardly looked like an intellectual attack force capable of assaulting and defeating Wundtian psychology.

Wertheimer, reared in Prague, was a Jew. Boyish of feature but balding, he sported a huge, martial, Bismarckian mustache but was poetic, musically gifted, warm, humorous, and cheerful. He was an exciting and fluent speaker; his ideas brimmed and bubbled over. But reining in his thoughts to set them down on paper was so difficult and painful for him that he was genuinely phobic about writing.

Koffka, a Berliner, was half Jewish. Small and frail, with a long, thin face and a somber look, he was introverted, sensitive, and insecure; inexplicably, these traits, though they made him an uninspiring lecturer, endeared him to his female students. Ill at ease at the rostrum, he was comfortable at the writing table and produced systematic, scholarly expositions of the Gestalt psychology.

Köhler, a Gentile born in Estonia and reared in Wolfenbüttel, Germany, was hawk-featured, with a short, stiff thatch of hair parted in the middle. He was the most painstaking experimenter of the three, and later became a strong institute administrator. Arrogant, stiff, and formal in person—he had to know someone socially for ten years before he would use the personal *du* instead of the formal *Sie*—in his writing he could be surprisingly relaxed and charming.

In the end, the differences among the three produced an advantageous specialization of function. As one history of the Gestalt movement puts it, Wertheimer was "the intellectual father, thinker, and innovator," Koffka "the salesman of the group," and Köhler "the inside man, the doer."[5]

But only one of the three ever held a major position in the psychological establishment. Wertheimer, his way impeded by anti-Semitism and his limited output of publications, was for years merely a lecturer, and

---

*Plural form of Gestalt; used more often in psychological writing than the Anglicized "gestalts."

later a Professor Extraordinarius at the University of Berlin. Not until 1929, when he was forty-nine, did he finally become a full professor (at Frankfurt), only to have to flee abruptly four years later when the Nazis came to power. He emigrated to the United States, where he taught at the New School for Social Research but never held a major chair in psychology.

In Germany, Koffka rose only to the rank of Professor Extraordinarius at the University of Giessen. He gave a series of lectures in America and in 1927 obtained a full professorship at Smith College—not a center of psychological research—and remained there for the rest of his life.

Köhler alone achieved major status in Germany. After several years of teaching and over six years of brilliant experimental work in the Canary Islands, in 1921 he was appointed head of the Psychological Institute at the University of Berlin—the premier post in German psychology—at the age of thirty-four, and made it a center of Gestalt studies. But he held the post only fourteen years; in 1935, after courageously but vainly struggling to keep Nazi influence out of the institute, he resigned, came to America, and spent the rest of his career at Swarthmore College.

Yet even before Köhler rose to his high position at Berlin, the three young men, in only ten years, breached the defenses of Wundtian psychology and established the legitimacy of their new mentalism—a psychology of the mind based on demonstrations and experimental evidence rather than on rationalist arguments and metaphysical speculations.

Although they published relatively little in that time (partly because of the disruptions of World War I), it was enough to show that Gestalt theory offered a better explanation than earlier cognitive psychologies of both perception and higher mental functions. Their evidence was so striking and their arguments so plausible that by 1921 Gestalt psychology had begun to supplant Wundtian psychology, as evidenced by Köhler's appointment.[6]

Until the mid-1930s, Gestaltism was a major force in German psychology and a growing one in many other countries. It had only limited effect on American psychology before the arrival of the triumvirate between 1927 and 1935. Then, although none of the men held a leading position in the American psychological establishment, their ideas infiltrated psychological thinking and slowly began to expand it beyond the confines of behaviorism.

The Laws of Gestalten

From the outset, Wertheimer saw Gestalt theory as far more than an explanation of perception; he believed it would prove to be the key to learning, motivation, and thinking.

He based this view not only on the odds and ends of evidence offered by the predecessors of Gestalt theory but on some early research of his own. Shortly after his Frankfurt work on the illusion of motion, he was asked by the director of the children's clinic at the Psychiatric Institute of Vienna to find ways of teaching deaf-mute children. One method he experimented with consisted of his building a simple bridge with three wooden blocks while a deaf-mute child watched, and then dismantling it. The child would then try it, and usually, after one or two mistakes, would catch on and successfully build a number of bridges of different shapes and sizes. The child's thinking, it appeared to Wertheimer, was based not on the number and size of the items used in the demonstration but on the perception of a stable configuration—a Gestalt—in which both uprights are of the same length and are positioned toward the ends of the horizontal piece.[7]

Wertheimer also read anthropological reports of numerical thinking by primitive peoples and wrote a paper on it in 1912. Speakers of certain South Sea languages, he learned, have different ways of counting fruit, money, animals, and men; each way represented a Gestalt appropriate to the item. He also discovered that people who lack our abstract system of grouping and numbering use natural groupings as numerical thinking. A primitive man about to build a hut might not count the number of vertical posts needed but would know without counting what the hut's framework should look like and, thus, how many posts to seek.[8]

Using these data plus his experiments at Frankfurt, Wertheimer drew up the outlines of a new psychology in a 1913 series of lectures. The central doctrine was that our mental operations consist chiefly of Gestalten rather than strings of associated sensations and impressions, as followers of Wundt and associationists believed. A Gestalt, he said, was not a mere accumulation of associated bits but a structure with an identity; it was different from and more than the sum of its parts. The acquisition of knowledge often took place through a process of "centering" or structuring and thereby seeing things as an orderly whole.[9]

Although Wertheimer envisioned Gestalt theory as the basis of an entire psychology, much of his research and more than half the research of all Gestalt psychologists in the early years dealt with perception.*[10] Within a dozen years the three leading Gestaltists, their students, and several other Gestalt-oriented psychologists had discovered a number of principles of perception, or "laws of Gestalten." Wertheimer, drawing on his and others' findings, named and discussed a handful of the major laws in one of his rare papers in 1923,[11] and as time went on he, his colleagues, and their students discovered many others. (Eventually 114 laws of Gestalten were named.[12]) Here are a few of the more important ones:

Proximity: When we see a number of similar objects, we tend to perceive them as groups or sets of those which are close to each other. Wertheimer's simple demonstration:

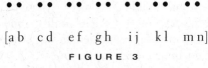

FIGURE 3

The Law of Proximity: a simple case

People shown the line of dots, he found, spontaneously see it as pairs of dots close to each other (ab/cd/ . . .), and while it could also be construed as pairs of widely spaced dots with little room between the pairs (a/bc/de/ . . .), no one sees it that way, and most people cannot even make themselves do so. A more striking example:

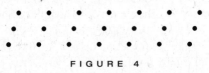

FIGURE 4

The Law of Proximity: a more extreme case

Here one sees lines made up of three closely spaced dots, tilted slightly to the right of the vertical; one does not see, and can see only with difficulty, an alternative structure—lines made up of three widely spaced dots, tilted far to the left of the vertical.

*Wertheimer wrote up few of his experiments, but most of them are briefly noted in Koffka's *Principles of Gestalt Psychology* (1935).

Similarity: When similar and dissimilar objects are mingled, we see the similar ones as groups:

○ ○ ● ● ○ ○ ● ● ○ ○ ● ● ○ ○ ● ● ○ ○ ● ●

FIGURE 5

The Law of Similarity: a simple example

The similarity factor can, in fact, overcome the proximity factor. In the left-hand box below, we tend to see four groups of closely spaced objects; in the right-hand box, two sets of dispersed but similar objects.

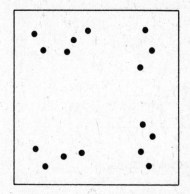 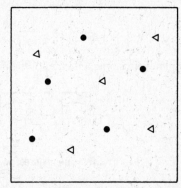

FIGURE 6

The Law of Similarity: a more complex example

Continuation or direction: In many patterns, we tend to see lines that have a coherent continuation or direction; this is why we are able to pick out a meaningful shape from a bewildering background, as we do in "hidden figure" puzzles. Such a line or shape is a "good Gestalt"—one with inner coherence or inner necessity. In this pattern, for instance,

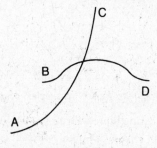

FIGURE 7

The Law of Continuation: two curves or two pointed shapes?

we can force ourselves to see two curved pointed figures, AB and CD, but what we tend to see is the more natural Gestalt of two intersecting curves, AC and BD. The factor of continuation can be astonishingly powerful. Consider these figures —

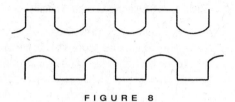

FIGURE 8

Two figures, easily seen as distinct

and now this one, a merger of the previous two:

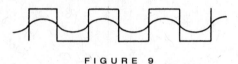

FIGURE 9

The same figures, now visually inseparable

It is virtually impossible to see the originals in the merged figure because of the dominance of the continuous wavy line.

Prägnanz: The related English word "pregnancy" does not convey Wertheimer's meaning, which is "the tendency to see the simplest shape." Much as physical laws cause a soap bubble to assume the simplest possible shape, so the mind tends to see the simplest Gestalten in complex patterns. This figure

FIGURE 10

The Law of *Prägnanz:* We see the simplest possible shapes.

could be interpreted as an ellipse with a right-angled segment cut out of the right side of it touching a rectangle with a curved chunk cut out of the left side of it. But that is not what we see; we see the far simpler image of a whole ellipse and a whole rectangle overlapping.

Closure: This is a special and important case of the Law of *Prägnanz*. When we see a familiar or coherent pattern with some missing parts, we fill them in and perceive the simplest and best Gestalt. We see this as a star

FIGURE 11

The Law of Closure: We supply what is missing.

instead of the five V's that make it up.

In the 1920s, the Gestalt psychologist Kurt Lewin noticed that a waiter could easily remember the details of a customer's bill if it had not yet been paid, but as soon as it was paid he forgot the details. It occurred to him that this was an instance of closure in the area of memory and motivation. As long as the transaction was incomplete, it lacked closure and generated tension, maintaining memory, but as soon as closure was achieved, the tension and the memory disappeared.[13]

A student of Lewin's, a Russian psychologist named Bluma Zeigarnik, put his conjecture to the test in a well-known experiment. She assigned a number of volunteers a series of simple tasks—making clay figures, solving arithmetic problems—allowing them to complete some of the tasks but interrupting them during others on a pretext and not letting them finish the work. A few hours later, when she asked them to recall the tasks, they remembered the uncompleted ones about twice as well as the completed ones, confirming Lewin's guess.[14] The study made her famous, in a small way; to this day, psychologists writing about motivation refer to the "Zeigarnik effect."

Figure-ground perception: When we pay attention to an object, we see little or nothing of the background; we see the face we are looking at, not the room or landscape beyond it. In 1915 Edgar Rubin, a psycholo-

gist at the University of Göttingen, explored this "figure-ground" phenomenon—the mind's ability to focus attention on a meaningful pattern and ignore the rest of the data. He used a number of test patterns,
one of which, the so-called Rubin vase, is familiar to almost everyone:

FIGURE 12
The Rubin vase: Pottery or profiles?

If you look at the vase, you do not see the background; if you look at the
background—two faces in profile—you do not see the vase. Moreover,
you can *will* yourself to see whichever you choose; will apparently does
exist, in spite of the New Psychologists and the behaviorists.

Size constancy: An object of known size, when far off, projects a tiny
image on the retina, yet we sense its real size. How do we manage that?
Associationists said that we learn from experience that remote objects
look small and pale, and we associate these clues with distance.
Gestaltists found this explanation simplistic and contrary to new evidence. Very young chicks were trained to peck only at larger grains of
feed. When the habit was firmly established, the larger grains were put
at a distance, where they looked smaller than the nearby small grains,
but the chicks unhesitatingly went for the larger ones. An eleven-
month-old baby girl was trained (by means of a reward) to choose the
larger of two side-by-side boxes. The larger box was then moved far

enough away for its retinal image to be only ⅕₅ the area of the smaller box, but she still chose it.[15]

We sense that distant objects are as large as when they are near because of the mind's organization of data in terms of relationships—to adjoining known objects, for instance, or to perspective-giving features.[16] The two illustrations in Figure 13, from a relatively recent textbook of perception, make the point:

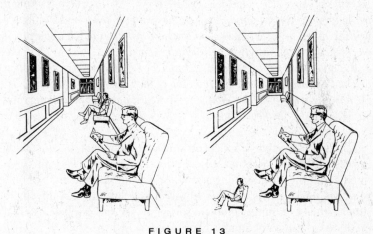

FIGURE 13
Perspective gives clues to size.

In the left-hand panel, the relationship of the farther man to things near him and to the hallway enables us to perceive him as being as large as the nearer man. Yet on one's retina the image of the farther man is very much smaller, as the right-hand panel shows.

Out-of-Reach Bananas and Other Problems

Sultan, a male chimpanzee living in an anthropoid research center, has had nothing to eat all morning and he is hungry. His keeper lets him into a room where a bunch of bananas is hanging from the ceiling, out of reach. Sultan jumps toward the bananas a few times but comes nowhere near them. He then prowls around the cage, making discontented sounds. Some distance from where the bananas are hanging he comes upon a short stick and a large wooden box. He picks up the stick and tries to knock the bananas down, but they are too high. For a while, he bounces around, upset and angry; then, he suddenly rushes to the box, pulls it under the bananas, climbs up on it, and with a little jump seizes his prize.

Days later: The situation is the same except that now the bananas are hanging considerably higher. This time there is no stick, but there are two boxes, one larger than the other. Sultan knows what to do, or thinks he does. He drags the larger box under the bananas, climbs up, and crouches, as if to jump. But after looking up, he does not; the bananas are well beyond his range. He leaps down, seizes the smaller box, and, pulling it behind him, gallops around the room, shrieking in anger and kicking the walls. Plainly, he seized the second box not with the thought of putting it on the first one but merely to help vent his anger.

But all at once he stops shrieking, pulls the smaller box over to the other one, with some difficulty hoists it on top of the larger one, and climbs up. He has solved the problem. Wolfgang Köhler, watching and making copious notes, is deeply pleased.[17]

Köhler conducted a series of studies of chimpanzee mentality between 1914 and 1920 that became almost as famous as Pavlov's experiments with the salivating dog and Watson's with little Albert. Not only were Köhler's findings valuable in themselves but they led directly to similar studies of human problem solving by Gestalt psychologists that produced a number of significant discoveries.

The nature of the thinking involved in problem solving had interested philosophers and psychologists for much of the previous twenty-four centuries, but in Germany the subject had been out of fashion for some time. Like all higher-level mental processes, it lay outside the boundaries of scientific psychology as defined by the physiological psychologists and the Wundtians. In America, although William James and John Dewey had written about problem solving, Thorndike's puzzle box experiments with cats had led many psychologists to regard it as the result of trial-and-error activity, even in human beings, rather than of conscious planning and problem solving.

Wertheimer, who in his formative years had read and admired Spinoza, took a different view: he believed in the power of the thinking mind. He was impressed, too, by the statements of Galileo and other great discoverers indicating that their breakthroughs often came from a new view of the problem that produced a sudden insight.

To illustrate how such a perception can produce a solution, Wertheimer liked to tell a little anecdote about Karl Gauss, the famous mathematician. When Gauss was six years old, his teacher asked the class who could first give the total of $1 + 2 + 3 + 4 + 5 + 6 + 7 + 8 + 9 + 10$. In seconds young Gauss raised his hand. "How did you get it so quickly?" the teacher asked. Gauss said, "If I had to add one and two and three, and so on, it would have taken a long time, but one and ten are eleven, two and nine are eleven, three and eight are eleven, and so on — five elevens in all. The answer is fifty-five." He had seen a structure that led instantly to a solution of the problem.[18]

Wertheimer was interested all his life in reasoning and problem solving, and in his last years wrote *Productive Thinking* (1945), a general discussion of the subject as seen by Gestalt psychology. But other Gestaltists, Köhler leading the way, did the bulk of the experimental work on the matter.

Köhler, after working with Wertheimer on the motion-illusion experiments, had stayed on at Frankfurt for another three years; then, at twenty-six, he was offered the post of director of the Prussian Academy of Sciences' anthropoid research station on Tenerife, one of the Canary Islands, a Spanish possession off the coast of northwest Africa. Köhler shipped out in 1913, never imagining that a world war and chaotic postwar conditions in Germany would trap him there for over six years.

But he put the time to good use. He had been profoundly impressed by Wertheimer's ideas and, as he later recalled, "had a feeling that his work might transform psychology, which was hardly a fascinating affair at the time, into a most lively study of basic human issues."[19] During his years on Tenerife these ideas were often on his mind, and his primate studies, although not formally couched in Gestalt terms, strikingly confirmed Gestalt theory as applied to problem solving. He pursued the investigation, with numerous variations and replications, for a number of years. Several British intelligence agents were convinced that he was a German spy, since no scientist would have spent so much time studying how apes get hard-to-reach bananas.[20]

(Ronald Ley, a psychologist at the State University of New York at Albany, recently spent nearly fifteen years trying to determine whether Köhler had been a spy. He gathered gossip and rumors from elderly Tenerifans, but neither on the island nor in Germany did he find any hard evidence bearing on the matter. Ley thinks Köhler may well have been a spy; other scholars doubt it.)

Köhler created a number of different problems for his apes to solve. The simplest were detour problems, in which the chimpanzees had to get to the bananas by a roundabout route; that gave them no trouble. More complicated were problems in which the chimpanzees had to use "tools" to reach bananas hanging out of reach—sticks with which they could knock them down, ladders they could lean against a wall (they never did figure out how to prop the ladders securely but always stood them sideways to the wall), and boxes.

Some of the chimpanzees took a long time to see that the boxes could be used to reach the bananas, and they never did use them well. Some would do ineffective things like piling up boxes where they happened to be rather than under the bananas, or stacking them so poorly that they toppled over when the chimpanzees tried to climb on them. Others, clearly smarter, did better, learning to stack boxes in a more secure fashion even when it took more than two boxes for them to reach the bananas. Grande, a female, actually was able, albeit with difficulty, to build a stack of four boxes when necessary.

Time and again, an ape would seem to suddenly see a solution at some juncture; Köhler interpreted this as a restructuring of the ape's view of the situation. He called the sudden discovery "insight," and defined it as "the appearance of a complete solution with reference to the whole layout of the problem,"[21] obviously quite a different process from the trial-and-error learning of Thorndike's cats.

Köhler thought the cats might have exhibited insight in a different kind of situation, but the puzzle box was a problem they could not solve through intelligence because it contained mechanical elements they could not see. But he did determine that insight thinking does not take place in simpler animals. He set up a fence at right angles to the wall of a house, with a segment at a right angle to its outer end, making an L. When he put a chicken inside the L and food outside, the chicken rushed back and forth along the fence, unable to recognize that by momentarily turning away from the food it could get around the end of the barrier. A dog, however, quickly sized up the situation and ran around to the food. A one-year-old girl, put inside the L and seeing her favorite doll on the other side, first tried to push through the fence but then laughed joyfully and toddled around the corner to it.[22]

With chimpanzees, some of the most dramatic instances of insight were elicited by another problem. Köhler would put an ape in a cage and a bunch of bananas outside, out of reach. In the cage would be several sticks; a chimpanzee might not realize for some time that it could reach the bananas with a stick but then all at once see that it could. A female chimpanzee, Tschego, first tried to reach the bananas with her hands and after half an hour got discouraged and lay down. But when a few other chimpanzees came into view outside the cage, she leaped to her feet, seized a stick, and deftly pulled the bananas within reach. Apparently the sight of other apes nearing the food served as motivation and produced the click of insight.

In another stick problem, the moment of illumination was even more dramatic. Köhler's account of it:

> Sultan cannot reach the fruit, which lies outside, by means of his only available short stick. A longer stick is deposited outside the bars. [It] cannot be grasped with the hand, but it can be pulled within reach by means of the small stick. Sultan tries to reach the fruit with the smaller of the two sticks. Not succeeding, he tears at a piece of wire that projects from the netting of his cage, but that too is in vain. Then he gazes about him (there are always in the course of these tests some long pauses, during which the animals scrutinize the whole visible area). He suddenly picks up the little stick once more, goes up to the bars directly opposite the long stick, scratches it toward him with the "auxiliary," seizes it, and goes with it to the point opposite the objective, which he secures.[23]

In an even more complicated problem, the bananas lay beyond reach with either of two available sticks; one of them, however, was thinner than the other and could be pushed into the thick one to combine their lengths. Even clever Sultan did not quickly see this solution. He spent about an hour trying to reach the fruit, to no avail; Köhler gave him a hint by sticking one of his own fingers into the end of a stick, but Sultan did not get the idea. Then:

> Sultan squats indifferently on a box, which has been left standing a little back from the bars; then he gets up, picks up the two sticks, sits down again on the box, and plays carelessly with them. While doing this it happens that he finds himself holding one rod in either hand in such a way that they lie in a straight line. He pushes the thinner one a little way into the opening of the thicker, jumps up and is already on a run toward the bars, to which he had up to now half turned his back, and begins to draw a banana toward him with the double stick.[24]

One of Köhler's most important findings, with sweeping implications for the psychology of learning, was that insight learning does not depend on rewards, as did the stimulus-response learning of Thorndike's cats. The chimpanzees were, of course, seeking a reward, but their learning was not brought about by the reward; they solved the problem before eating the fruit.[25]

Another important finding was that when animals achieved an insight, they learned more than the solution to that particular problem; they were able to generalize and apply the solution in modified form to different problems.[26] In psychological terms, insight learning is capable of "positive transfer"; in lay terms, the chimpanzees became test-wise.

Köhler reported his findings in a monograph in 1917 and in a book, *The Mentality of Apes*, in 1921. Both monograph and book made a considerable impression in the world of psychology, and not only as a study of animal problem solving; Köhler's observations prepared the way for Gestaltist studies, using the same techniques, of human problem solving.

In 1928, a psychologist at Teachers College, Columbia University, used Köhler-type situations with children ranging in age from a year and a half to four years. Instead of bananas, the desirable objects were toys, which she placed out of reach, either outside the bars of a playpen or on a shelf. Sticks were available in the playpen experiment, and a chair and a box for the shelf. Sometimes the children showed immediate insight, and sometimes saw the solution only after a certain amount of fumbling around. The process was remarkably similar to what had taken place in the apes' minds, although, not surprisingly, even these immature human beings were more insightful than the mature chimpanzees.[27]

Similar experiments with eight still younger children, ranging in age from eight to thirteen months, were conducted a little later by a young German psychologist, Karl Duncker, who had studied with both Wertheimer and Köhler at Berlin. He used a simple problem situation. The children sat at a table on which an attractive toy lay beyond reach; a stick was at hand. Only two children had insight almost at once; five others played with the stick until they either deliberately or accidentally moved it close to the toy, at which point they abruptly perceived the stick as a retrieval implement. The youngest child never solved the problem.[28]

Duncker's more important work involved a series of problem-solving studies conducted between 1926 and 1935 with adult subjects. One of his research methods was to present a problem and ask the subject to think out loud as he tried to solve it; Duncker recorded what was said and then analyzed his "protocol" or written record to see how the subject formulated the problem and searched for a solution. This was one of the two problems:

Given a human being with an inoperable stomach tumor, and rays which destroy organic tissue at sufficient intensity, by what procedure can one free him of the tumor by these rays and at the same time avoid destroying the healthy tissue which surrounds it?[29]

A typical subject's protocol (excerpted and much abbreviated here) read like this:

> Send rays through the esophagus.
> Expose the tumor by operating.
> One ought to decrease the intensity of the rays on their way; for example — would this work? — turn the rays on at full strength only after the tumor has been reached.
> Either the rays must enter the body or the tumor must come out. Perhaps one could alter the location of the tumor — but how? Through pressure? No.
> The intensity ought to be variable.
> Adapt the healthy tissues by previous weak application of the rays.
> I see no more than two possibilities: either to protect the body or to make the rays harmless.
> (Experimenter: How could one decrease the intensity of the rays en route [as you suggested earlier]?)
> Somehow divert . . . diffuse rays . . . disperse . . . stop! Send a broad and weak bundle of rays through a lens in such a way that the tumor lies at the focal point and thus receives intensive radiation.[30]

This protocol and others showed that when faced with such a problem, people use a number of different heuristic (exploratory) techniques. Most often they start with mechanical or routine heuristics, such as trying random possibilities based on the most immediate or obvious characteristics of the problem; such heuristics usually yield poor solutions or none. In the above protocol, sending rays through the esophagus or exposing the tumor by operating are efforts of this kind.

Eventually, after reaching a number of dead ends, many subjects get around to more productive "functional" heuristics (a few others use them from the outset), such as trying to identify the essential properties of the problem. They ask themselves, for instance, what the fundamental goal is, and only then do they look for a specific solution. In the above protocol, the subject began thinking this way when he said, "One ought to decrease the intensity of the rays on their way." He then reverted to the first kind of thinking ("Perhaps one could alter the location of the tumor"), but after the experimenter reminded him of his more basic heuristic he suddenly had his dramatic insight into a feasible solution. The mechanical heuristics are analogous to the chicken's running back and forth along the fence, the functional heuristics to looking at the situation in broad perspective and seeing a less direct but effective way of reaching the goal.

Duncker's other principal research method was to bring a subject into a room where a jumbled array of objects and materials lay on a table and then ask him to perform a task for which none of the objects seemed suitable. The goal was to see under what conditions the subject would weigh other possible uses of one or more of the available objects and under what conditions such restructuring was inhibited.

In one situation, for instance, the subject was asked to mount three small candles on the door at eye level, ostensibly for "visual experiments." On the table were some candles, a few tacks, paper clips, pieces of paper, string, pencils, and some other objects, including the crucial ones: three small empty cardboard boxes. After fumbling around, every subject eventually restructured his view of the things at hand and saw that the boxes could be tacked to the door and used as little platforms to mount the candles on.

But in another version of the problem, the three boxes were filled, one with little candles, the second with tacks, and the third with matches. This time, fewer than half of Duncker's subjects solved the problem. They had seen the boxes being used for a specific purpose, and that made it harder to see them as usable in an unboxlike way.[31] Duncker called this common and serious impediment to problem solving "functional fixedness"; when a problem solver sees an object as having a specific function, it is far more difficult for him to see it as serving any other function.

This was a noteworthy discovery. It explains why so often the very people who know most about any subject are the least likely to find a good solution to a new problem in their field. Education creates expertise but also functional fixedness. An expert sees the tools he has at hand in terms of the functions he knows they serve; a neophyte may, while coming up with uninformed and even absurd suggestions, see them more creatively. It is no accident that scientists generally make their most original and important contributions early in life.

Duncker, thought by many to have been the most brilliant of the Gestalt group in the 1930s, might have gone much farther with his investigation of problem solving had he not died tragically early. A political liberal, he fled from Germany in 1935 and went first to England and, in 1938, to the United States to teach at Swarthmore. In 1940, at thirty-seven, deeply depressed by the outbreak of war, he committed suicide.

The studies of problem solving by Köhler, Duncker, and other Gestalt psychologists look relatively simple but their implications were profound. They demonstrated that problem solving in human beings (and to some extent in animals) is not limited to trial and error and to conditioned responses but often involves certain kinds of higher-level thinking that produce new vision, thoughts, and solutions. The studies of problem solving were one of the most important ways in which the Gestaltists restored mind as the central concern of psychology.

Learning

For many centuries the study of how knowledge is acquired had been one of the chief interests of psychologist-philosophers and psychologists. But with the advent of the physiologist-psychologists and Wundt, most of it was stored in the attic of culture with other obsolete mentalist topics.

What little the physiologists and followers of Wundt said about learning was mostly secondhand associationism; they saw it as merely the linking or joining of bits of experience. The behaviorists made learning the central topic of their research—but only the mindless learning of S-R conditioning; the higher-level mental processes involved in much human learning were ignored in favor of such calculations as the relationship between the number of reinforced trials and the strength of the established habit.

Among the contributions of the Gestaltists, and perhaps their greatest, was the restoration of meaning and thought to the study of learning. Although the Gestalt movement flourished only briefly in Germany and did not replace behaviorism in the United States, it revived and renovated the cognitive tradition and prepared the way for the cognitive revolution of the 1960s.

It was not the human mind, however, but the mind of the hen that provided the first solid evidence that associationist and S-R theories of

340 The Story of Psychology

learning were seriously inadequate. Köhler, during his stay on Tenerife, conducted a tedious but enlightening experiment with four chickens. He allowed two of them to peck at grain scattered on a light gray square of paper but shooed them away whenever they tried to peck at grain on a darker gray square of paper. He gave the other two chickens the opposite treatment. Chickens are notoriously stupid, but after four hundred to six hundred trials the first two would peck only at grain on the lighter paper and the second two only at grain on the darker paper.

Köhler then altered both situations. He kept the background color the chickens had been trained to eat from but replaced the other one, substituting a still lighter paper in the first case, a still darker one in the second. Associationist and S-R theory would predict that since the chickens had learned to associate eating with a particular shade of gray, they would continue to do so, but in 70 percent of the trials they pecked at grain on the new backgrounds rather than the old ones. The pair that had been trained to eat from the lighter of two backgrounds now mostly chose the new, still lighter background; the two who had been trained to peck at the darker of two backgrounds now mostly chose the new, still darker background. Gestalt theory offered an answer: The chickens had learned to associate food not with a specific color but with a *relationship*—in one case the lighter, in the other case the darker, of two backgrounds.[32]

Köhler repeated the experiment with chimpanzees and with a three-year-old child. He presented each with two boxes, one of a dull color, the other of a bright color. When a chimpanzee was the subject, the bright-colored box had a bit of food in it; when the child was the subject, a bit of candy. After the chimpanzee and the child learned that the bright box contained the reward, Köhler eliminated the dull box and substituted a new one, even brighter than the reward box. This time he put a reward in both boxes so that there was no incentive for the subjects to choose either except its color relationship to the other—and in fact the chimpanzees and the child usually chose the new, brighter box.

Behaviorists and Wundt's followers had known that an animal can be trained to choose one of two different-colored objects, but had refused to believe that what the animal learned was the relationship between the colors. To these "elementalist" psychologists, a relationship could not be a primary psychological fact. As Solomon Asch, a student of Wertheimer's, observed, "This premise was sufficiently potent to blot out the ceaseless evidence of experience."[33]

But Köhler's experiment showed conclusively that the relationship between the colors was indeed the primary fact the animals had learned, since they *transposed* it to a different situation.[34] It was an example of the general rule, said Asch, that animals and humans perceive and learn nearly everything in terms of relationships. This object stands on top of that one, is between two others, is bigger than, smaller than, earlier or later than another, and so on. Relations are the key to perception, learning, and memory. That truth had been excluded from psychology but was reinstated by the Gestaltists.

Wertheimer, Köhler, Koffka, and many of their students did research on learning, but much of the credit for promulgating their cognitive view of it goes to Koffka. That shy, self-doubting, homely little man with his odd, high-pitched voice was at his best when assembling facts and theory on paper; in print he could be masterful and scathing.

Koffka himself conducted no noteworthy research on learning; nearly all his experimental work was on the perception of depth, color, and motion. But because his English was excellent, the editor of the *Psychological Bulletin*, Robert M. Ogden (who had studied with Koffka at Würzburg), invited him to prepare the first account in English of Gestalt psychology. It appeared in 1922; from then on Koffka was the unofficial spokesman of the movement. Largely through his journal articles and two books, the research findings and ideas of the Gestaltists about learning became known to the profession.

In one of those books, *The Growth of the Mind*, published in German in 1921 and English in 1924, Koffka reviewed existing knowledge about mental development from a Gestaltist viewpoint. Of the many new ideas and interpretations he offered, two stand out.

The first: Instinctive behavior is not a chain of reflexive responses mechanically triggered by a stimulus; rather, it is a group or pattern of reflexes—a Gestalt imposed by the creature on its own actions—aimed at achieving a particular goal. A young chick pecks at certain things that it "knows" are edible, but the instinct is goal-oriented, driven by hunger, not a mechanical and automatic response to the sight of food.[35] The chick does not peck when sated, despite the sight of food and the existence of the reflex.

The second: Against the behaviorist doctrine that all learning consists of chains of associations created by rewards, Koffka argued that much learning takes place through the processes of organization and reorganization in the mind in advance of reward; he offered as proof Köhler's studies of problem solving by apes and comparable data on problem solving by children. But the exact cause of those organizing processes, he admitted, was not yet known.

Fourteen years later, in *Principles of Gestalt Psychology* (1935), a heroic attempt to review all existing knowledge of psychology from a Gestaltist viewpoint, Koffka was ready to offer a theory as to the cause of the organization and reorganization in the mind. The theory, elaborated from one originally proposed by Köhler, was that "psychophysical" forces inherent in the brain—neuronal energy fields—act like the force fields elsewhere in nature that always seek the simplest or best-fitting configuration (as in, again, the bubble, or the lines of force in a magnetic field). Hence the mind's tendency to construct and reconstruct information in the form of "good Gestalten."[36]

But are those good Gestalten faithful representations of the outside world? Koffka gave a resounding affirmative to this ancient question. He offered the theory, suggested by Wertheimer and developed by Köhler, that our thoughts about the world are *isomorphic* with the world itself— they are brain events that are, in some way, similar in structure to the external things they represent. If we see two separate lights, there are two separate areas of brain excitation; if we see movement, there is a corresponding movement in the field of arousal in the brain.[37] The contents of the mind are not something wholly unlike the outside world but a neural simulacrum of it.

This solved the classic problem of how thought, a different kind of phenomenon from the material world, could represent that world. Or so it seemed to Koffka and his colleagues. But in the 1950s Karl Lashley and other neurophysiologists conducted experiments designed to interrupt the supposed electrical fields of isomorphic theory. They implanted mica plates in the visual cortex of some animals and in others placed silver foil on the surface of the brain, short-circuiting the different electrical potentials that were supposed to simulate the perceived world. In neither case did the animals respond differently to visual experiences; isomorphism and force field theory was effectively scuttled.[38]

Yet if force field theory is viewed not as a physiological reality but as an illuminating metaphor, it has genuine value. It says that in a manner analogous to the operation of force fields, we group, categorize, and reorganize our experiences, always seeking the simplest and most meaningful constructs of the contents of our mind. As a guiding image, this comes closer than associationism, conditioning, or any earlier epistemological theory to describing how we perceive, learn, store, and utilize information. Field theory was not the ultimate truth, but it was a better approximation of the truth than earlier theories, and the basis of better approximations yet to come.

Memory is an aspect of epistemology about which Gestalt psychology offered some particularly useful and illuminating ideas.

One was the hypothesis, presented in some detail by Koffka, that the physiological basis of memory is the formation of "traces" in the central nervous system—permanent neural changes induced by experience. It was an acute guess; decades later, neurophysiologists would begin to discover the actual cellular and molecular changes that constitute traces.

Another keen guess dealt with the psychological basis of memory. Previously laid-down memory traces, Koffka said, influence how new experiences are perceived and remembered. Unlike associationism, which said that new experiences are merely added to old ones, Koffka said that new experiences interact with traces, traces with new experience, in ways not available to the mind early in life, and that this interaction is the cause of mental development.[39] His idea would be borne out by a wealth of observational data that the Swiss child psychologist Jean Piaget was even then gathering.

Koffka marshaled a mass of experimental evidence to show that memory is not a mere sticking-together or aggregation of experiences, as in association theory, but a weaving together by means of the *meaningful* connections. Among the evidence he adduced was that of Ebbinghaus and his followers, that it is much harder to learn a string of nonsense syllables than a series of words connected by meaning. Koffka gave a simple and persuasive example: If every connection between items were merely one of association, these two lines would be equally easy to learn:

> pud sol dap rus mik nom
> A thing of beauty is a joy for ever.

Koffka's comment: "It is not easy for association theory to explain why the second line is learned and retained so much more easily than the first, a difficulty which, as far as I know, was never explicitly mentioned by the associationists."[40]

Like much else about Gestalt psychology, the truth illustrated by those two lines seems so obvious that one wonders why it needed to be rediscovered. But psychology has not moved in a steady course from ignorance toward knowledge; its progress has been more like that of an explorer of an unknown land who tentatively advances toward a distant goal by this valley or that, this river or that, and often must pursue a roundabout route or double back on his tracks when the chosen route proves a poor one. The followers of Wundt and the behaviorists made important headway toward the remote goal but went off into dead ends; the Gestaltists put psychology back on a truer course.

Boring made this point with a different metaphor in his magisterial history of psychology: "It appears that orthodoxy had been led astray along the straight and narrow path of sensory analysis. It is the wide gate and the broad way of phenomenology that lead to life."[41] Although the Gestalt psychologists were not the first or the only ones to make this discovery, it was they who made it in a form so convincing that it was amalgamated into the structure of scientific psychology.

Failure and Success

In Germany, as we saw, Gestalt psychology became a leading school in the 1920s but virtually disappeared in the mid-thirties after its three founders and many of their former students left Germany.

In the United States, after the publication of Koffka's introductory article in 1922, Gestalt psychology met at first with great interest and even enthusiasm.[42] Koffka and Köhler were asked to give seminars and colloquia at nearly all the important American research centers; Köhler was a visiting professor at Clark University in 1925; and Harvard later offered him a visiting professorship, which he had to decline.

But behaviorism was even then rapidly becoming the ruling brand of psychology in America, and there was no room in it for Gestaltist ideas. Most behaviorists saw Gestalt psychology as a regression to a discredited, unscientific nativism. To the extent that nativism means a belief in innate ideas, this was simply untrue. To the extent that nativism means a belief that the mind, by its very nature, imposes certain kinds of order on experience, it was correct. Gestalt theory was, in a way, a modern version of Kantian epistemology.[43]

Decades later this central tenet of Gestalt psychology would be strikingly confirmed by several forms of research. Studies of language acquisition, for instance, showed that children sense the grammatical structure of sentences and begin speaking in grammatical sentences long before they are taught anything about grammar. Even more remarkably, a study of deaf children who had not been taught any sign language found that when they were three or four years of age, they communicated by making up strings of gestures—quasi-sentences—that distinguished between agent, action, and object, just as verbal language does.[44]

The antipathy of behaviorists toward Gestalt psychology was reciprocated: Koffka, Köhler, and Wertheimer all were dismissive of behaviorism (and other psychologies) and presented their own approach as the only valid one, thereby offending many American psychologists. Reviewing the reception of Gestalt psychology in America, the psychologist Michael Sokal writes:

> American psychologists were especially bothered by the attitude of the Gestaltists . . . Recently the term "Mandarin" has been used to characterize the attitudes and behavior of many of the German university professors of the period. In some ways the entire Gestalt movement represented a revolt against traditional German university culture, but in other, deeper ways the Gestaltists shared many traits typical of the faculties of German universities.[45]

The result was that by the early 1930s, Gestalt psychology, though it had become a definite part of the American psychological scene, remained a subordinate part; like the structuralists, functionalists, Freudians, and others, Gestaltists were a minority in a behaviorist-dominated establishment.[46] Nevertheless, they had an influence on the development of psychology out of all proportion to their numbers and position.

Wertheimer, a warm and impassioned teacher, had a loyal but small following at the New School for Social Research, but no physical research facilities to speak of. Yet according to his distinguished student Abraham S. Luchins, during Wertheimer's decade in America (he died in 1943) he was a "conspicuous and disquieting figure" in the behaviorist milieu.[47]

Koffka, though dry and overly theoretical as a teacher, was adored by the girls he taught at Smith. However, because the college's emphasis was on undergraduate education, he supervised only one Ph.D. in his years there. But he did have an extensive effect on the psychological community through his writings, particularly the encyclopedic *Principles of Gestalt Psychology*, and he would undoubtedly have produced other influential works had his life not been cut short in 1941, at the age of fifty-five, by heart disease.

Köhler, despite his Germanic stiffness, was best able of the three to fit into the traditional academic framework. He created a center of psychological research and scholarship at Swarthmore that attracted a number of top-notch doctoral candidates, among them David Krech, Richard Crutchfield, Jacob Nachmias, and Ulric Neisser. Köhler retired in 1958 but remained active in research until his death at eighty, nine years later. After his retirement, he received the highest accolade of American psychology, election to the presidency of the American Psychological Association, an acknowledgment both of his personal achievements and of the contributions of the Gestalt movement to psychology.

For paradoxically, even though by midcentury the movement had lost its identity and was fading from view, its most important ideas had become part of the mainstream of psychology. Indeed, they remain a significant part of it today, although a number of Gestaltist ideas are now so taken for granted that they are rarely even identified as such when cited in textbooks of psychology.

The central Gestaltist doctrine, that the whole—the *Gestalt*—is greater than the sum of its parts and that it dominates our perceptions has stood the test of time and testing. In one recent experiment, psychologist David Navon measured the time it took observers to identify large and small letters in a display like this:

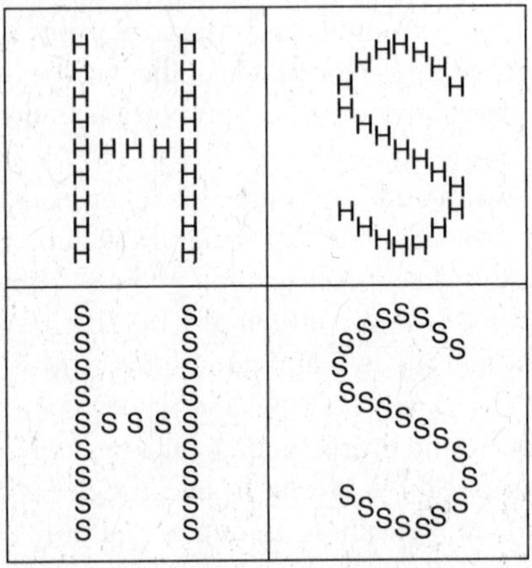

FIGURE 14

The "Forest Before Trees" Effect: It takes longer to identify the tiny letters than the bigger ones they make up.

Observers were able to name the large letters more swiftly than the small ones, whether or not the small ones were the same as the large ones they made up; in contrast, it took them longer to name the small letters when they were different from large ones made up of them.[48] Evidently, the whole was recognized more easily than the parts it was made of.

Prägnanz, the tendency to see the simplest shape in complex patterns (see Figure 10, page 328), has held up as a valid perceptual principle. So has grouping (the Laws of Proximity and of Similarity, illustrated above on pages 326 and 327), although later research has extended and somewhat modified it.[49]

As for problem solving, although the reward-based, trial-and-error model espoused by behaviorism remains valid for many simpler animals, research with more intelligent animals and human beings has followed the direction taken by Köhler, Duncker, and Wertheimer. Newer models, based on information-processing theory, do not contradict Gestalt problem-solving theory so much as provide detailed programs of the step-by-step reasoning and searching for which Gestalt psychology had only such vague terms as "restructuring."[50]

Gestalt psychology also significantly deepened the study of memory. The work of Ebbinghaus and his followers with nonsense syllables revealed certain of its principles, but only within the narrow confines of the meaningless. Gestalt psychology restored a perspective in which the broader aspects of memory could be investigated—the web of meanings into which we weave new material and through which we locate and recall desired information.[51] Recent work on memory has gone far beyond Gestalt explanations but along the same lines.

Most important, the Gestaltists restored consciousness and meaning to psychology; they did not discredit the findings of Wundt's followers or the behaviorists so much as radically enlarge the scope and dimensions of scientific psychology, re-establishing within it mind and all its processes—including, according to Koffka, meaning, significance, and value. As he said:

> Far from being compelled to banish concepts like meaning and value from psychology and science in general, we must use these concepts for a full understanding of the mind and the world.[52]

In 1950, when Gestalt psychology was losing visibility as a distinct school, Edwin Boring summed up its fate in terms that have not been improved on:

> Schools can fail, but they can also die of success. Sometimes success leads to later failure. [Gestalt psychology] has produced much important new research, but it is no longer profitable to label it as Gestalt psychology. Gestalt psychology has already passed its peak and is now dying of its success by being absorbed into what is Psychology.[53]

Forty years later, that valuation was reiterated by two perception researchers, Irvin Rock and Stephen Palmer, who were extending and revising Gestalt theories of perception in cognitive science terms:

> The list of major perceptual phenomena [the Gestaltists] elucidated is impressive. In addition, they were victorious over the Behaviorists in their clash regarding the nature of learning, thinking and social psychology. Although behavioral methods are adhered to by modern psychologists, Behaviorist theory has been abandoned in favor of a cognitive approach more in line with Gestalt thinking. The theoretical problems they raised about perceptual organization, insight, learning and human rationality remain among the deepest and most complex in psychology. The remarkable surge of interest in neural-network models attests to the fact that Gestalt theories are very much alive today and that their part in psychological history is assured.[54]

Part Three

SPECIALIZATION

AND SYNTHESIS

Introduction:
The Fissioning of Psychology—
and the Fusion of the
Psychological Sciences

We have come a long way.

We have seen philosophers progress from metaphysical speculations and fancies about the mind to a quasi-scientific understanding of some of its processes, and at last, aided by physiologists, extract psychology from philosophy and establish it as an independent science.

We have seen, too, that like other immature sciences, in its early decades as an independent field of knowledge psychology developed no truly unifying theory but only a number of special theories, each of which explained particular phenomena. The theories were the work of great men—men like Wundt, James, Freud, Watson, and Wertheimer—but great though they were, none was the Newton of psychology.

Their followers, however, thought otherwise. The early decades of scientific psychology were "the era of the schools"—there were at least seven in the 1930s[1]—and the adherents of each claimed that *their* school's theory could make a coherent science out of the chaotic mass of findings and mini-theories that had been accumulating since the time of Helmholtz. But by the middle of the last century, many psychologists had begun to think that none of the existing theories had or could become the unifying paradigm of psychology. Neither Wundtian theory nor behaviorism, for instance, had anything useful to say about such matters as problem solving or decision making; Freudian theory cast no light on such matters as perceptual processes or learning; Gestalt theory was unenlightening about child development. As Nevitt Sanford, then of Stanford University, said in 1963, "The great difficulty for general psychology is that the 'general' laws so much admired and so eagerly sought are never very general. On the contrary, they are usually quite specific."[2]

This could mean that psychology was simply not advanced enough to permit anyone to conceive an overarching theory. But it could mean something quite different: that psychology is not a science in the same sense as physics, chemistry, or biology; that it is a cluster of scientific fields that, though related, are too disparate to fit into the framework of a single theory. Two decades ago, in a summing-up of the condition of psychology, William Kessen, a distinguished developmental psychologist, and his co-author, Emily D. Cahan, wrote in *American Scientist*:

> Lying at the deepest level is the conviction (for some of us, no more than a suspicion) that psychology is not susceptible to unifying ontological and epistemological premises any more than it is susceptible to definition by a particular content, a particular method, or a particular functional process . . . In the extreme version of this view, psychology has no core problem; rather than elevating perception or learning or problem-solving into a model for all psychology, we must recognize that psychology is as wide as the human mind and as rich in variety.[3]

The story of psychology since the end of the era of the schools seemed for several decades to prove that conviction (or suspicion) correct. A number of new theories had appeared, but they pertained to specific fields of psychology, not all or even most of the discipline. No school claiming jurisdiction over the whole territory had been founded, and in fact the field of psychology burst apart and became a number of autonomous fields of specialization. By 1990 the American Psychological Association had recognized fifty-eight fields of psychology and had forty-five "divisions" (membership subgroups) representing those fields—the fission products of the split-up. And on it goes: Today APA recognizes some seventy fields of psychology and has fifty-six divisions.

Michael Gazzaniga, president of the Association for Psychological Science (APS, formerly the American Psychological Society), recalled in a recent article that some years ago Leon Festinger epitomized the problem when telling him why he was quitting psychology for archaeology: "I realized I was learning more and more about less and less."[4]

Today, Gazzaniga said in the article, "every psychology department carries this curse, as does every field of human endeavor. We split, titrate, and specialize as a way of becoming experts on at least something. We then protect that turf as if it were life itself. We frown on the integrative and feel it is sort of for lightweights." But in fact he himself has recently moved from Dartmouth to the University of California, Santa Barbara, where he now heads an interdisciplinary institute attracting "collaborators from philosophy, biology, psychology, anthropology, computer science, and the humanities . . . in the hunt for a better understanding of mind."

That, in a nutshell, is what has been happening to psychology. Ever since the decline and fall of behaviorism, psychology has been fissioning into specialties—and yet in recent decades, especially in the past two, a stunning and invaluable reaction has been taking place. Under the pressure of developments in other behavioral sciences, as well as neurobiology and computer science, a number of psychology departments and special institutes within universities have created interdisciplinary programs aimed at a larger and deeper understanding of the human mind. Fission is being countered by intellectual fusion.

From here on, accordingly, we will not follow a single chronological story but will look at what has happened in each of six principal fields of psychology and in the psychotherapies. We will see and appreciate the specialization that has advanced their work—and threatened to choke them—and the synthesis that is currently making psychology an extraordinarily exciting and illuminating science, a true science of the mind. Whether this course will result in a new grand theory, a unified theory of mind, or only several interlocking theories remains to be seen.

Finally, in chapters 18 and 19, we will briefly look at a number of other aspects of contemporary psychology that could not be given fuller treatment without unduly fatiguing the reader as well as the author.

ELEVEN

The Personality Psychologists

"The Secrets of the Hearts of Other Men"

The nature and origin of personality has long been an issue of paramount importance to psychologists. For them the question, central to understanding human nature, is: What accounts for the differences in the characteristics of individuals and in their behavior? The same issue is of the greatest interest to laypersons. For them the question, of crucial importance in everyday life, is: How can one best judge other people's characters and know what to expect of them?

Clearly, what people say is not a reliable source of information; human beings, alone among living species, are able to lie, and often do. Nor can one depend on their gestures and expressions; people can dissemble, some expertly. Not even their deeds always reveal the truth; people can practice deception until at some critical juncture they reveal the real self. Yet whoever the other person is—the one we are thinking of marrying, the potential buyer of our house, the leader of an enemy nation (or our own)—nothing could be more valuable than to be able to make a sound judgment as to what that person is really like and how he or she is apt to behave.

For such reasons, the study of personality has been a leading interest of both the philosopher and Everyman throughout recorded history and one of the most important fields of modern psychology for the past seven decades.

The earliest known efforts to appraise personality relied on the pseudo-science of astrology. From the tenth century B.C. on, Babylonian astrologers had predicted wars and natural disasters on the basis of the positions of the planets, and by the fifth century B.C. Greek astrologers were using these data to interpret the personality and forecast the future of individual clients. The notion that the positions of the planets at the time of one's birth influence one's personality and fate had great appeal in that scientifically naïve time; oddly, it still does, even though modern astronomy and the behavioral sciences show it to be a baseless superstition.

Physiognomy, mentioned earlier, was another fictive system for spying out the hidden terrain of personality. Unlike astrology, the idea that facial traits are clues to the inner person has some psychological validity; how we look surely plays a part in how we feel about ourselves. But Hippocrates, Pythagoras, and other physiognomists did not perceive this relationship; instead, they compiled lists of fanciful connections between particular facial characteristics and traits of character. Even the great Aristotle asserted that "persons who have a large forehead are sluggish, those who have a small one, fickle; those who have a broad one are excitable, those who have a bulging one, quick-tempered."[1]

Like astrology, physiognomy has endured. The sophisticated Romans believed in it: Cicero asserted, "The face is the image of the soul" and Julius Caesar said, "I am not much in fear of these fat, sleek fellows, but rather of those pale, thin ones." (Caesar's view is best known in Shakespeare's version: "Let me have men about me that are fat; / Sleek-headed men and such as sleep o' nights; / Yond Cassius hath a lean and hungry look; / He thinks too much: such men are dangerous.") Jesus' actual looks are unknown (the earliest "portraits" in Roman catacombs were painted two or three centuries after his death), but from the second century A.D. to the present he has been shown as having refined and delicate features. The physiognomic tradition lives on; most of us, on seeing or meeting people we do not know, make guesses about their personality on the basis of their looks.

Another approach to divining character from visible traits was phrenology, the pseudo-science of skull reading that was the rage in the nineteenth century. Although it died out in the twentieth, many people still assume that a person with a high bulging forehead is "brainy" and sensitive, one with a low flat forehead stupid and unfeeling.

The best-known ancient effort to link personality to physical characteristics was Galen's humoral theory of temperament—his belief that an excess of phlegm makes one phlegmatic; of yellow bile, choleric; of black bile, melancholic; and of blood, sanguine. The doctrine survived until the eighteenth century; its successors take the form of nutrition fads, chelation, steam-room sweating, and other quasi-scientific efforts to modify body chemistry with the aim of enhancing mental and physical well-being.

In contrast, an approach that sounds remarkably modern was proposed three centuries ago by Christian Thomasius (1655–1728), a German philosopher and jurist, and the founder of the University of Halle. Thomasius worked out a scheme for measuring personality by assigning numerical scores to various traits of character; his method, though crude, remarkably foreshadowed the current personality-assessment technique known as the "rating scale." Equally noteworthy is the title he gave his book: *New Discovery of a Solid Science, Most Necessary for the Community, for Discerning the Secrets of the Heart[s] of Other Men from Daily Conversation, Even Against Their Will.*[2] A bit long for modern taste, no doubt, but as up-to-date in spirit as any contemporary how-to-succeed best seller.

Throughout the ages the discussion of personality has often centered on one of the basic, much-debated issues in psychology: Is human nature determined from within or from without? Are our minds and behavior the products of inner forces, or are we shaped and prodded into thought and action by the stimuli of the environment?

The debate began when Plato and his followers maintained that the contents of the mind exist in it from before birth and need only to be remembered; Protagoras and Democritus countered that all knowledge arises from perception. In the seventeenth and eighteenth centuries the dispute was more alive than ever, Descartes and other rationalists arguing that the mind's ideas are innate, Locke and other empiricists claiming that the newborn's mind is a blank slate on which experience writes its messages.

When psychology became a science, the hereditarians—Galton, Goddard, Terman, and others—presented survey data to support their view, while the behaviorists—Pavlov, Watson, Skinner, and others—produced experimental evidence to back theirs. The argument has continued ever since, with the "dispositionists" or "innatists" (to use contemporary terminology) interpreting personality and behavior in terms of internal (dispositional) forces, the "situationists" or "environmentalists" interpreting personality and behavior in terms of the situations the individual experiences.

The two views lead to opposite conclusions about child rearing, educational methods, psychotherapy, public policy toward minority groups, the treatment of criminals, the status and rights of women and of homosexuals, immigration policy, and many other personal and social issues. Accordingly, the question has dominated personality psychology in recent decades.[3] One longs for a definitive scientific answer; let us see what researchers and theoreticians on both sides have been learning and whether such an answer is emerging.

The Fundamental Units of Personality

Early in this century the chief contributions to personality theory were made by the psychoanalysts. Freud developed an account of adult personality as the outcome of the ego's efforts to control instinctual drives and channel them into acceptable forms of behavior. Adler was more interested in the effects of social forces on personality, such as the birth position of the middle child as a cause of inferiority feelings. Jung portrayed personality as shaped largely by the interplay of the opposing inherent tendencies toward assertiveness and passivity, introversion and extraversion, and the conflict between experience and "the collective unconscious" (concepts, myths, and symbols that he believed were inherited, unlearned, by each person from earlier generations).

While psychodynamic concepts thus suggested how personality develops, they did not provide psychologists with a way to measure personality quickly and precisely, as had become possible with intelligence. The lineaments of personality revealed by psychoanalysis appeared only after scores or even hundreds of clinical sessions; even then, the process yielded impressionistic evaluations, not quantitative measurements. As Raymond Cattell, one of the great names in personality measurement, said, the clinical method was "nothing more than a reconnaissance" and what psychology needed was a "quantitative taxonomy."[4]

The first such taxonomy was a product of World War I. When the United States entered the conflict in 1917, Robert S. Woodworth (1869–1962), an eminent experimental psychologist and professor at Columbia University, was commissioned to devise a quick, simple way to identify emotionally disturbed recruits. With no time to spare, he threw together one of the first tests of personality, the Personal Data Sheet, a questionnaire that asked the respondent a number of unsubtle questions about symptoms, such as, "Did you ever walk in your sleep?" and "Do you feel like jumping off when you are on high places?" The score was arrived at by adding up the number of symptoms admitted to.[5]

As personality assessment, the Personal Data Sheet was primitive and limited; it gathered only such information or misinformation as the subject offered and only about neurotic symptoms. Yet it had "face validity"—one intuitively felt that its questions did distinguish between normal and neurotic people. And, in fact, a later effort to validate the test found that diagnosed neurotics averaged thirty-six unfavorable ("Yes") answers, normal people only ten.[6]

Woodworth's pioneer effort set a pattern; after the war, many psychologists developed other questionnaires that similarly asked subjects to evaluate themselves. But these soon went beyond symptoms to include questions about a few general personality traits. The best known of the early tests, developed in 1931 by the psychologist Robert Bernreuter, asked 125 questions and scored the answer to each for four traits: dominance, self-sufficiency, introversion, and neuroticism. If, for instance, a respondent answered "?" ("Don't know" or "Can't say") to the question "Do you often feel just miserable?" he or she got three points on introversion, one on dominance, zero on neuroticism, and zero on self-sufficiency. These scores were only educated guesses—Bernreuter had no empirical evidence for each answer's relation to the four characteristics—but such was the national fascination with psychological testing that over a million copies of the Bernreuter Personality Inventory, and large quantities of similar tests, were marketed and used during the 1930s.[7]

By then personality was a distinct field of psychology and was dominated by trait theory, a scientific version of the commonsense view that each person has a recognizable set of characteristics and usual ways of behaving in particular situations. Traits describe the elements of a given personality, though they say nothing about underlying psychodynamic structure or how that personality developed.[8] The Bernreuter and other early personality tests were efforts to measure some of those elements.

An important study that appeared in 1928 and 1929 seemed to cut the ground out from under trait theory. The Reverend Hugh Hartshorne, a religious educator at Union Theological Seminary, and Mark May, a psychologist who had formerly been at Union, studied the effectiveness of adult efforts such as the Boy Scout movement to inculcate moral behavior in children. Hartshorne and May had a number of children take paper-and-pencil tests of attitudes toward cheating, stealing, and lying. Then they had the children take part in activities like party games and the self-grading of tests, in which they had the opportunity to cheat, steal, and lie without, seemingly, being found out, although in fact the researchers could tell exactly what they had done.

The results were disconcerting. Not only was there little relation between what the children said on the paper-and-pencil tests and how they actually behaved, but remarkably little consistency between how honest or dishonest any child was in one situation and how honest or dishonest in a different one. Hartshorne and May concluded that if traits existed, they did not cause individuals to behave similarly in different situations.

> [We] are quite ready to recognize the existence of some common factors which tend to make individuals differ from one another . . . Our contention, however, is that this common factor is not an inner entity operating independently of the situations in which the individual is placed but is a function of the situation.[9]

This contradicted everyday experience. We all feel that some of the people we know are honest and others dishonest, some reserved and others outgoing, some painstaking and others slapdash. Gordon Allport (1897–1967), a leading light of the psychology department at Harvard, came to the rescue with a series of studies and a book, *Personality: A Psychological Interpretation* (1937). Allport, a mild-mannered, hardworking man with plain doughy features, had many research interests, among them prejudice, communication, and values, but personality, and in particular trait theory, was the central concern of his life. It was in part thanks to his own personality that he was the ideal person to counter Hartshorne-May situationism with scientific proof of commonsense dispositionism.[10]

Allport was the youngest of four sons of a country doctor in Indiana. His father's family had come from England several generations earlier, his mother was of German and Scottish descent, and Allport home life, he recalled many years later, "was marked by plain Protestant piety and hard work." There being no hospital facilities in the area, for years the Allport household included patients and nurses, and young Allport did his fair share of tending the office, washing bottles, and caring for patients. He absorbed his father's humanitarian outlook and values, and in later years liked to quote his father's favorite dictum: "If every person worked as hard as he could and took only the minimum financial return required by his family's needs, then there would be just enough wealth to go around."

At Harvard Allport found time, even with his studies, to do a good deal of volunteer work in social services. This satisfied a deep-seated need to help people with problems and, he said in an autobiographical sketch, "gave me a feeling of competence (to offset a generalized inferiority feeling)." His two interests, psychology and social service, merged when he became convinced that "to do effective social service, one needed a sound conception of human personality."

For Allport the study of personality was always a commonsense matter; he was interested in the conscious and easily accessible rather than the murky depths of the unconscious. He often told of his only meeting with Freud, an episode that profoundly affected him. As a brash youth of twenty-two, he had written to Freud while visiting Vienna to say that he was in town and would like to meet him. Freud graciously received him but sat in silence, waiting for him to speak. Trying to think of something to say, Allport mentioned that in the tram on the way to Freud's office he had heard a four-year-old boy talking to his mother about wanting to avoid things that were dirty; he was displaying a genuine dirt phobia. Allport described the mother as a well-starched, domineering *Hausfrau*, and thought the connection was plain, but, as he recalled, "Freud fixed his kindly therapeutic eyes upon me and said, 'And was that little boy you?' " Flabbergasted, Allport changed the subject; the experience, he later concluded, "taught me that depth psychology, for all its merits, may plunge too deeply and that psychologists would do well to give full recognition to manifest motives before probing the unconscious."[11]

(He was equally disenchanted with behaviorism, which, he said, portrayed the human being as a purely "reactive" organism—acting only in response to external prodding—when in fact human beings are "proactive" and driven largely by their own goals, purposes, intentions, plans, and moral values.[12])

During his graduate years Allport began devising his own paper-and-pencil tests of personality traits. He and his older brother, Floyd, a psychologist, created a test that was more objective than the Bernreuter and other early efforts. In order to measure what they called "ascendance-submission," they asked respondents not how ascendant or submissive they were but how they would behave in specific situations involving that trait dimension. An example:[13]

Someone tries to push ahead of you in line. You have been waiting for some time, and can't wait much longer. Suppose the intruder is the same sex as yourself, do you usually

— remonstrate with the intruder   . . . . .
— "look daggers" at the intruder or make clearly audible
  comments to your neighbor   . . . . .
— decide not to wait, and go away   . . . . .
— do nothing   . . . . .

After trying the test on a number of volunteers, the Allports concluded that people who gave either an ascendant or a submissive answer to any one challenging situation were very likely to give the same kind of answer to other such situations. "People by and large," they wrote, "do tend consistently to occupy a given spot on the continuum from high ascendance to low submission." This seemed to them to establish the reality of traits and of the similarity of a person's behavior in similar situations. As Allport later put it:

> If it can be proved that one kind of activity is usually associated with another kind of activity, there is evidence that something underlies the two activities, viz., a trait . . . [i.e.,] *a neuropsychic structure having the capacity to render many stimuli functionally equivalent, and to initiate and guide equivalent (meaningfully consistent) forms of adaptive and expressive behavior.*[14]

Then why did the children tested by Hartshorne and May behave inconsistently? Allport found an answer in Gestalt theory. Each individual's traits are assembled in a unique configuration with a hierarchical structure: at the top is the person's master quality or *cardinal* trait; below it are a handful of *central* traits, the ordinary foci of the individual's life (the kind of qualities, said Allport, that we are likely to mention when writing a letter of recommendation); and finally below these are a large number of *secondary* traits, each aroused by a few specific stimuli.[15] So a person's behavior could be inconsistent in specific ways but consistent—Allport preferred "congruent"—in larger ones.

For example, he said, if you observe a man strolling and see him later hurrying to take a book back to the library, you might judge him inconsistent because in one situation he ambles, in the other hurries. But that is trait behavior at the secondary level. A more central trait is *flexibility*.

If you asked him to write large on a blackboard and small on a paper and he did so, you could judge him flexible—as he is, too, in his walking. His behavior in both activities exhibits flexibility and thus is congruent, though not consistent.[16]

This was also Allport's solution to the question: Why is it so common for a person to exhibit traits that seem incompatible or to behave in different situations in ways that seem inconsistent? Transient moods or "states" often make for what looks like inconsistency; an alarming situation may create a temporary state of anxiety in anyone, even a person who is usually placid.

Although Allport modified his theory of personality over the years, he always considered traits the fundamental and relatively stable units of personality. His trait research earned him acclaim and honors in his time; he would be gratified to know that despite the advent of genetic, neurological, cultural, sociological, and other factors affecting personality, many psychologists still regard personality psychology as all but synonymous with the study of traits.[17]

Measuring Personality

Since traits are neither visible objects nor specific actions but personal qualities, the central problem for researchers is how to measure them.

First they have to decide exactly what it is they mean to measure. Early personality researchers chose a handful of intuitively obvious traits such as introversion, dominance, and self-sufficiency. But soon they began looking farther afield and attempted to measure many others, so many, indeed, that the field rapidly became chaotic.

For there are all too many possibilities. The hardworking Allport and a colleague once counted all the words in the dictionary that designate distinctive kinds of human behavior or qualities; the total was about eighteen thousand. Not all refer to traits: some are the observer's reactions to another person rather than that person's traits ("adorable," "boring"); some describe temporary states rather than enduring traits ("abashed," "frantic"); and some are only metaphors ("alive," "prolific"). But that still left four to five thousand terms denoting traits.[18] And even after nearly seven decades of research had winnowed out most of these as unfruitful, a relatively brief review article in 2001 still listed forty-one topics as just "some" of the significant traits or manifestations of personality:

The ability to delay gratification, the ability to process social information, aggressiveness, agreeableness, behavioral inhibition, carelessness, coercive behavior, conformity, conscientiousness, criminal behavior, curiosity, distractibility, driving while intoxicated, emotional expressiveness, extraversion, fearfulness, impulsiveness, industriousness, irritability, job satisfaction, leadership ability, moodiness, narcissism, neuroticism, openness, political attitudes, religious attitudes, restlessness, self-confidence, self-control, self-directedness, shyness, sociability, social potency, social responsibility, spouse abuse, submissiveness, substance use, the tendency to feel mistreated or deceived by others, the tendency to have temper tantrums, and the tendency to seek or avoid danger.[19]

Many of these and hundreds of Allport's list have been explored by means ranging from subjective impressions to laboratory experiments and from psychoanalytic interpretations to behavioral data. These are some of the major methods:

Personal documents and histories: Letters, memoirs, autobiographies, diaries, and the like are full of information—and misinformation—about the personality of their subject, since a self-portrayal meant to be read by others is apt to present a dressed-up self rather than naked reality. (Pepys' diary, full of licentious episodes and shameful thoughts, was meant only for his own eyes and was written in code.) Certain celebrated interpretations of famous personalities have been based on personal documents, but tastes and theories change from generation to generation, and the same sources can yield widely differing portraits of the writer. Analyses of personality based on such sources are sometimes good literature but rarely, if ever, good science.

The interview: This is perhaps the most common method of personality assessment but one of the least effective. Some employment interviewers, college admissions personnel, and psychotherapists can glean a good deal about a person from an interview, but many others cannot. Even skilled interviewers, studies have shown, may evaluate the same person quite differently. Moreover, interviews yield descriptions and interpretations but not quantitative measurements of traits. The interview is best suited to the identification of distinct mental or emotional disorders, but with normal people it is most useful as a source of personal data, attitudes, recollections, and other details that throw light on the more objective data gathered about that person by other methods.[20]

Ratings by observers: Researchers often ask an individual's friends or acquaintances to rate him or her on a number of specified traits. To achieve precision, the researchers direct respondents to weigh each trait on a scale that runs from zero to five or perhaps one to ten—essentially what Thomasius suggested in 1692. But the method has many difficulties. Raters have their own styles of rating (some avoid extremes, others favor them); subjects are not necessarily consistent when asked the same questions at different times; and ratings are subject to the "halo effect" (a subject rated high for one trait tends to be rated high for others).[21]

In general, then, ratings are considered neither especially reliable nor especially valid. (A *reliable* method yields consistent answers time after time; a *valid* method measures what it is supposed to be measuring.) Still, under certain conditions ratings *can* be both reliable and valid. Raymond Cattell, a leading trait researcher who relied on them in his own work, used only data from raters who saw the subject under many circumstances and over a long time (a year, if possible) and gathered ratings on only one trait at a time to reduce the halo effect. Such conditions improve both reliability and validity but make the method prohibitively costly, time-consuming, and nearly impossible to use anywhere except in an institution, where the population is relatively fixed and always visible.[22]

The questionnaire: This is by far the most commonly used tool for personality assessment. As we have seen, the method quickly expanded beyond simple self-evaluation to quasi-objective techniques, such as presenting real-life situations and asking respondents how they would most likely behave in them. Other early tests continued to present questions about the respondent's attitudes and feelings rather than probable behavior but were worded in ways that made the respondent less likely to prettify his self-portrait than did the questions in the Personal Data Sheet. Most offered as possible answers "yes-no" or "true-false" options, but some included a "don't know" middle ground.

The famous Minnesota Multiphasic Personality Inventory (MMPI), developed in the late 1930s by Starke Hathaway, a psychologist, and J. C. McKinley, a psychiatrist, both of the University of Minnesota, is of the latter type. It contained 550 statements, among them:

I am happy most of the time.
I enjoy social gatherings just to be with people.
I am certainly lacking in self-confidence.
I believe I am a condemned person.

The respondent answers "yes," "no," or "?" (uncertain) to each question. The questions were grouped into ten scales that measured hypochondriasis, depression, hysteria, psychopathic deviancy, masculinity-femininity, paranoia, psychasthenia, schizophrenia, hypomania, and social introversion. These names convey the impression that the MMPI was concerned chiefly with mental illness; it did measure mental illness but also traits of normal personality. Those who, for instance, answered "false" to "I am happy most of the time" and most other questions in the same scale were said to be shrewd, guarded, and worrisome; those who answered "true" to "I enjoy social gatherings just to be with people" and related questions were rated sociable, colorful, and ambitious; and those who answered "false" were rated modest, shy, and self-effacing.[23]

Such interpretations were based not on intuition or common sense but on empirical evidence. In constructing the MMPI, Hathaway and McKinley tried a large number of questions on people hospitalized with neurosis or mental illness and on the presumably normal people who came to visit them; the MMPI was made up only of those items which differentiated the two groups. The depression scale of the MMPI, for instance, consisted of questions that were answered differently by depressed and not-depressed people.

Although the MMPI has been the single most widely used personality questionnaire for more than a half century, it has limitations and flaws. For one thing, it is very long. For another, respondents feel that many items, if answered honestly, are embarrassingly revealing ("Bad words, often terrible words, come into my mind and I cannot get rid of them," "I am very strongly attracted by members of my own sex"). For a third, other items are so obviously aimed at pathology as to strike many normal people as either funny or insulting. Some time ago the humorist Art Buchwald lampooned the MMPI by suggesting additional questionnaire items like:

A wide necktie is a sign of disease.
When I was younger, I used to tease vegetables.
I use shoe polish to excess.[24]

In 1949, a small group of personality psychologists got a grant from the Rockefeller Foundation to set up within the University of California at Berkeley a new research unit, the Institute for Personality Assessment and Research. Its original purpose was to develop better methods of personality assessment.* Over the next forty years it produced a phenomenal number of studies and new psychological tests; but the best known and most widely used of them to this day, the California Psychological Inventory (CPI), was completed within the organization's first two years.

The CPI was the work of Dr. Harrison Gough, an institute member and Berkeley professor, who set out to improve on the MMPI by using material appropriate to a normal population. As raw material, he assembled a pool of a thousand items, some taken from the MMPI, others written by him and some of his colleagues. With the help of associates and collaborators, he tested the items, first on eighty graduate students, then on eighty medical school seniors, and, over the years, on a total of thirteen thousand males and females of various ages and socioeconomic status. To assess the validity of the items—or, rather, of the answers they elicited—Gough and his colleagues had a sample of respondents rated by friends, and then compared the ratings with the subjects' own answers, weeding out those items which proved untrustworthy.

The final form of the CPI included 480 items (the 1987 revision had 462), such as:

> *People often expect too much of me.*
> *It is hard for me just to sit still and relax.*
> *I like parties and socials.*

The respondent answered "true" or "false" to each; the answers yielded scores on fifteen personality traits ranging from dominance and self-acceptance to self-control and empathy.† By every measure—sales, number of versions in other languages (thirty-six, including Arabic, Mandarin, Chinese, Romanian, and Urdu), a research bibliography of more than two thousand entries, and importance ascribed to it by

---

*It is now called the Institute of Personality and Social Research, and its goals have become much broader.
†In a still later version, the CPI has twenty-eight scales. They measure dominance, capacity for status, sociability, social presence, self-acceptance, independence, empathy, responsibility, socialization, self-control, good impression, communality, well-being, tolerance, achievement via conformance, achievement via independence, intellectual efficiency, psychological-mindedness, flexibility, detachment, norm favoring, realization, managerial potential, work orientation, anxiety, and three measures of masculinity-femininity.

experts in assessment—it is among the top five personality tests in use today, five decades after it was developed.[25]

Many other personality tests offer the respondent a wider choice of answers to questions than the MMPI or CPI, as in these three examples:[26]

Most policemen are really friendly.

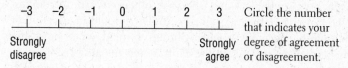

Falling in love can be more trouble than it's worth.

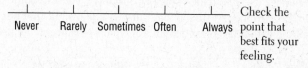

My anger at people usually is:

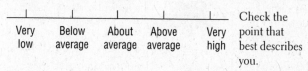

Responses scaled in this fashion yield more precise measurements of attitudes and feelings than "yes-no" responses.

Over the years, hundreds of personality inventories have been devised by psychologists and published by research institutes and commercial publishers; some embody good scientific practice, others do not, but many of each kind are good business properties. The sales figures for the CPI, for instance—guidebook, reusable test books, answer sheets, and other items—though a secret, can be assumed to be fairly large.

Projective tests: From the early 1930s on, a growing number of psychologists accepted the psychoanalytic doctrine that unconscious processes are major determinants of personality and, *pace* Gordon Allport, sought ways of testing that would measure those processes as well as the traits they generated. The most feasible way to do so was to present the respondent with ambiguous stimuli—vague or suggestive shapes or pictures—and ask him or her to describe them; presumably, the answers would reveal partially or completely unconscious fantasies, fears, wishes, and motives.[27]

The best-known such test had been developed many years earlier—between 1912 and 1922—by a Swiss psychiatrist, Hermann Rorschach. He created a number of inkblots and asked patients to say what each looked like; after years of experimentation he had narrowed down the test to ten blots, some black-and-white and others colored. In administering the Rorschach, the tester shows a card to the subject, asks him or her what the blot may be or what it brings to mind, writes down the response and, after showing all the cards, scores the answers. Scoring, which requires careful training and the use of a manual, is based on such criteria as whether the subject responds to the whole blot or only part of it, what part of the blot is attended to, and whether the answer deals with the blot itself or the shape of the background.[28] Here are some blots similar to those in the test (the actual Rorschach blots may not be reproduced), along with brief interpretations of typical responses:*

Response	Inkblot	Nature of Interpretation
This is a butterfly. Here are the wings, feelers, and legs.		Using the whole blot in this way is considered to reflect the subject's ability to organize and relate materials.
This is part of a chicken's leg.		Referring to only a part of this inkblot is interpreted usually as indicative of an interest in the concrete.
This could be a face.		The use of an unusual or tiny portion of this blot may suggest pedantic trends.
Looks somewhat like a spinning top.		Persons who reverse figure and ground in this manner often are observed as oppositional, negative, and stubborn.

FIGURE 15

Rorschach-type blots and typical interpretations

(from Kleinmuntz, 1980, by permission)

*If these were actual Rorschach blots, each would be on a separate card.

The Rorschach test became extremely popular among psycholo-gists in the United States in the 1930s and was used widely. For several decades it was the leading topic of Ph.D. dissertations in clinical psychology, and thousands of research papers have been written about it, but the net verdict is mixed. Some have found the prescribed interpretations reliable and valid, others have not.[29] Nonetheless, it remains one of the tests most often used by clinical psychologists and psychiatrists.

Another well-known projective test is the Thematic Apperception Test (TAT), created by the psychologist Henry Murray and an assistant, Christiana Morgan.

Murray, coolly patrician in appearance but driven by some demon, had traveled a tortuous road before finding himself. He began as a history major, went through medical training, specialized in surgery, and then spent five years in physiological chemistry. Still searching, he visited Jung in Zürich and for three weeks had daily sessions and long weekends of psychotherapy with him, from which "explosive experience," as he calls it, he "emerged a reborn man."[30] Freed of hitherto incurable stuttering and immensely attracted to psychology, he turned to the study of that subject, became a psychoanalyst, and eventually found his calling as a psychoanalytically oriented researcher at the Harvard Psychological Clinic. He briefly collaborated with Allport, but thereafter his psychodynamic view of personality kept them, according to Allport, "in a state of friendly separation."

Murray's most significant contribution to personality research was a three-year project that he and some two dozen other psychologists conducted at the clinic. They intensively studied the personalities of fifty-one men of college age by an assortment of evaluation techniques, including depth interviews, frustration tests (such as a jigsaw puzzle that could not be solved), the measurement of finger tremor when the experimenter uttered provocative words like "cheating" and "homosexual," and projective tests, of which the TAT was the most revealing. (It is remarkable that Murray was able to carry on and complete this major project despite falling madly in love with co-worker Christiana Morgan, and flagrantly conducting a somewhat perverse affair with her for many years.[31])

In administering the TAT, which Murray and Morgan developed in 1935 for the research project, the tester shows the subject nineteen black-and-white pictures in which it is not clear what is going on or why, and asks him to make up a story for each, giving his imagination free rein and spending about five minutes per story. The psychological interpretations of the stories are based largely on a list of thirty-five personality "needs" or motives compiled by the project research team, among them the needs for achievement, dominance, and order, and the need to be succoring.[32]

Murray and Morgan, in a report describing their development of the TAT, printed several pictures as examples. In one, a middle-aged woman is seen in profile facing to the left, and near her, closer to the viewer, and turned partly away from her, is a decently dressed young man, his head slightly bowed, a faint frown on his face. (The description will have to suffice; the publisher of the test does not allow reproduction of the pictures.) This is the story that Murray and Morgan said one subject made up about the picture:

> Mother and boy were living happily. She had no husband. Her son was her only support. Then the boy got in bad company and participated in a gang robbery, playing a minor part. He was found out and sentenced to five years in prison. Picture represents him parting with his mother. Mother is sad, feeling ashamed of him. Boy is very much ashamed. He cares more about the harm he did his mother than going to prison.[33]

The boy (the story goes on) gets out for good behavior; his mother dies; he falls in love but drifts back into crime; he goes to prison again; and he emerges as an old man and spends his remaining years repentant and wretched.

Murray and Morgan interpreted the story as indicating the narrator's perception of the dominance of bad external influences over one's behavior; it also revealed several deep needs, among them to be nurturing (to his mother), to acquire money, and to suffer abasement. The example, said Murray and Morgan, illustrates the special value of the TAT:

> The test is based upon the well-recognized fact that when a person interprets an ambiguous social situation he is apt to expose his own personality as much as the phenomenon to which he is attending. Absorbed in his attempt to explain the objective occurrence, he becomes naively unconscious of himself and of the scrutiny of others

and, therefore, defensively less vigilant . . . The subject reveals some of his innermost fantasies without being aware that he is doing so.[34]

Despite its value, the TAT is cumbersome to use, and with some people yields lengthy stories and too much information but with others barren stories and too little. Still, it has proven to be a reliable and valid tool for measuring personality traits, and has been shown to have predictive power. Fifty-seven Harvard graduates who took the TAT in 1952, when they were about thirty years old, were studied fifteen years later; those whom the 1952 tests showed as having high motivation for intimacy were significantly better adjusted in their marriages, work, and other areas of interaction.[35] The TAT, despite some trenchant criticisms, has continued to be widely used, though less often than the Rorschach, and has spawned many similar tests.

A large number of projective tests have been created in recent decades, and many are in current use. They include the Blacky Test, a set of picture stories about a little dog (the child makes up a story to fit each picture); word association tests (in some tests, the subject, on hearing or reading a word, mentions the first word that comes to mind; in others, uses the given word in a sentence); sentence completion tests ("I only wish my mother had _____," "The thing that bothers me most is _____." and so on); drawing tests (in one, the subject is asked to draw a house, a tree, and a person; the drawings are interpreted psychodynamically, a dead tree, for example, suggesting emotional emptiness, a leafy tree liveliness, a spiky tree aggressiveness).[36]

Conduct sampling or performance testing: In this category of assessment, a trained psychologist observes the individual in particular situations and measures or rates his or her behavior. Through a one-way mirror, an observer may watch children in a classroom working together on a project, playing, or responding to a contrived stimulus, like cries for help from an adjoining room. Or the unseen observer may watch a group of individuals in a special situation, like attempting to solve a problem that requires cooperation.

In another form of performance testing, the psychologist, face to face with the individual, subjects him or her to problematic or stressful situations and rates the person according to the resulting behavior. Candidates for Air Corps flight training in World War II went through a battery of tests, one of which consisted of the subject's trying to hold a thin metal rod steady inside a tube (whenever it touched the tube, a light flashed) while the tester made unpleasant or belittling remarks or suddenly snarled at him.

Also during World War II the Office of Strategic Services took candidates for secret service assignments to an isolated estate and there put them through a three-day series of trials. In addition to undergoing the usual interviews and questionnaires, the men faced a sequence of difficult tasks: assembling a hut without proper instructions, scaling a high wall, fording a stream, and keeping their wits under the influence of alcohol. Psychologists rated them on leadership ability, the capacity to withstand stress and frustration, and so on. The method sounded promising, but the team members, in their final report, admitted that they had received almost no feedback from overseas and therefore had little idea how accurate or useful their evaluations had been.[37] In any event, as a way to assess individual personality it is too costly, difficult, and demanding for general use.*

Other more practical performance tests have been devised, but because most of them require a tester for each tested individual and many must be performed in a laboratory, they too are unsuited to such large-scale applications as personality testing in schools, industry, clinics and institutions, and the military. A few examples:

— The subject has to trace four printed mazes, each in less than fifteen seconds, without letting the pencil's track touch the sides. Success is thought to indicate an assertive ego.
— The subject reads a story aloud normally and then backward; the greater the difference in the elapsed times, the stronger the presumption that the subject is rigid and inflexible.
— A group of subjects takes a test of attitudes on some controversial issue; each is then privately informed that his or her view is different from that of the majority. (For test purposes this need not be true.) Somewhat later the subjects are retested; the degree of change in an individual's stated attitudes is taken as a measure of

---

*The original goal of the Institute for Personality Assessment and Research at Berkeley was to further develop and test the OSS assessment method. That goal was abandoned after a time.

his or her vulnerability to pressure to conform, or, in some versions, of adaptability.

— The subject sits in a chair and waits for a scheduled event to occur, but it is delayed. Unknown to him or her, the chair is a "fidgetometer" that records all movements; those who do a lot of fidgeting are considered nervous or easily frustrated.[38]

This is only a small sampling; graduate students in pursuit of a degree and psychologists in search of a marketable product have concocted hundreds of others. They may also have a nonmaterial motive for developing such products: in order for the results to be trustworthy, the real purpose of the tests must be hidden from the subject, and constructing one therefore has some of the quality of playing a game or devising a practical joke. It may be that some of the psychologists who design such assessments find this particularly appealing.

Making Order out of Chaos

Early in the history of personality research, it became evident that the vast amount of data gathered about traits was only raw material. A set of miscellaneous trait scores of an individual did not add up to a picture of his or her personality, and compilations of scores from large samples of people yielded no insights about personality in general.

Allport put his finger on the problem: "It seems clear that the units we seek in personality and in motivation are relatively complex structures, not molecular."[39] But trait measurements are molecular, and it was not apparent how to see a structure in a mass of findings like the twenty-six trait scores produced by the MMPI, much less in the hundreds of scores that could be gathered from a battery of different tests.

A number of psychologists suggested making order out of chaos by grouping allied traits into larger tendencies or syndromes such as "general activity," "sense of well-being," and "emotional stability," or into such psychodynamic syndromes as aggressiveness and oral or anal tendencies. Others recommended sorting personalities into bimodal categories or types, like Jung's division of people into the extraverted and the introverted.

But such terms were vague catchalls; researchers wanted rigorous evidence that traits cohered in clear-cut, identifiable clusters. And a way to gather such evidence did exist. Galton had discovered correlation analysis, the statistical procedure for measuring co-variance (the degree to which one variable, like a trait, increases or decreases when another does). Then the English psychologist and statistician Charles Spearman had developed the more sophisticated technique known as factor analysis to measure, simultaneously, the correlations among a whole group of variables—exactly what was needed to make sense of trait data. The method is complicated but its basic concept is simple. If a number of traits all co-vary—that is, if a higher or lower score in any trait is accompanied by somewhat higher or lower scores in the others—it is reasonable to suppose that they are all influenced by an underlying general tendency or factor.

An intriguing application of factor analysis to personality was made during the 1940s by Hans J. Eysenck (1916–1997), a German-born psychologist who, though not Jewish, left Germany after it came under Nazi domination and became a British citizen. Adopting Jung's two-part typology, Eysenck hypothesized that a number of traits such as rigidity and shyness would be strongly correlated in introverted people and that opposite traits would be as strongly correlated in extraverted people. To this he added another two-part typology of his own, the dimension of neuroticism, with highly stable personalities at one extreme and highly unstable ones at the other; again, he expected certain traits to be associated with each.

When he put his suppositions to the statistical test, using trait data yielded by the MMPI and a personality test of his own devising, he found them confirmed: there were indeed correlations among the traits he thought should be clustered in introverts and in extraverts, and comparable correlations among those he expected to find clustered in neurotics and in mentally healthy people. When he plotted out these four factors, they bore an astonishing resemblance to the four temperaments of Galen's ancient humoral theory. Eysenck, normally an outspoken maverick, was untypically cautious about this coincidence:

> It is easy to read into historical writings what one wishes to see, and particularly to interpret ancient terms in line with modern connotations. Nevertheless, there do appear to be certain similarities between these early speculators and the more modern work [of others and of Eysenck himself].[40]

With this caveat, he offered the following diagram:[41]

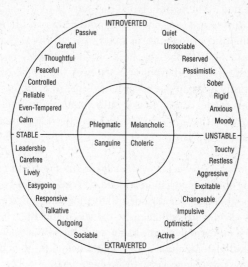

FIGURE 16

Eysenck's fourfold personality table

As fascinating as the coincidence was, most users of the MMPI found Eysenck's fourfold typology too general; they hoped to extract more specific and detailed diagnoses from the many scores the test yielded. Such diagnoses were made possible by a different use of factor analysis developed over several decades of unremitting work by the English-born psychologist, Raymond B. Cattell (1905–1998), mentioned earlier. Cattell was far more cautious and methodical than Eysenck; instead of beginning with hypothesized conclusions, as Eysenck had, he let factor analysis lead the way. He computed the correlations among a large number of variables, assembled lists of those which showed significant correlations, and gave them the names of factors. It was an onerous task, even with the help of computers; to calculate all the possible correlations of a hundred variables, for instance, one would need to calculate 4,950 relationships.

An example of Cattell's work: In an early stage, he found that a strong tendency to admit common faults was somewhat correlated with a high tendency to agree, and that both of these tendencies were correlated with emotionality, susceptibility to annoyance, critical severity, and certain other traits, plus such physical criteria as high heart rate. To Cattell the web of correlations among these "surface traits" suggested an under-lying "source trait" that he designated "anxiety."

Such research sounds austere and remote from real life, but Cattell, though urbane and aristocratic of mien, was no dry-as-dust pedant.[42] The son of an English engineer, he thought—probably because of his father's profession—that the physical sciences should be his field, and studied chemistry and physics at the University of London. But he was an omnivorous reader and an eager participant in the intellectual and political ferment of the times (the 1920s), and these activities eventually brought about an epiphany:

> My laboratory bench began to seem small and the world's problems vast. Yet, like someone in a railroad station, watching trains depart and knowing they are not his, I declined all the standard remedies by polit-ical parties or religious affiliations. Gradually I concluded that to get beyond human irrationality one had to study the workings of the mind itself . . . From that moment, a few months before my science degree, I realized that psychology was to be my life interest.[43]

Cattell plunged into graduate work in psychology, studying under Spearman at the university and acquiring expertise in factor analysis. Unfortunately, at the time he received his Ph.D. psychology had gained only a bare toehold in English universities, and for fifteen years he had to earn his living as a school psychologist and clinician. Doing so had its costs—the heavy workload and meager income wrecked his first mar-riage—and its rewards: it greatly added to his understanding of the com-plexity and richness of personality. But his real goal was to do the kind of research he believed in, factor analysis:

> It was plain to me, as John Stuart Mill had stated it, that the only proof of structure and causal relation lies in covariation, and that correlation and the new tool of factor analysis which Spearman had created could now be advantageously applied on a wide front—to personality structure and to the difficult problem of finding the dynamic roots of behavior.

Cattell came to the United States in 1937, briefly held positions at several leading universities, remarried happily, and began to carry out factor analysis of personality traits. In 1945 his work went into high gear when he became director of the Laboratory of Personality Assessment at the University of Illinois. There, for twenty-seven years, and later at the

University of Hawaii, he pushed ahead, doing ever more advanced factor analysis and deriving ever higher-level personality factors.

In the early years he was able to group 171 surface traits into sixty-two
clusters. He found, however, that these clusters overlapped—correlated
with one another—and later was able to consolidate them into thirty-
five.[44] Still later he and others—in his autobiography he generously
credits some eighty associates—pressed the analysis still further, eventually concluding that sixteen source traits or factors were, in his words,
"necessary and adequate to cover all kinds of individual differences of
personality [i.e., surface traits] found in common speech and psychological literature. They leave out no important aspect of total personality."[45]

Each of the sixteen personality factors is bipolar. Emotional stability, for
instance, ranges from "affected by feelings" at one extreme to "emotionally stable" at the other, and suspiciousness from "trusting" at one end to
"suspicious" at the other. Through procedures outlined in a manual,
testers can draw a personality profile of a tested individual or of a category
of individuals. The differences in such profiles are striking and illuminating. Here, for instance, are the profiles of three kinds of professional persons; such profiles became an important tool of career counseling.

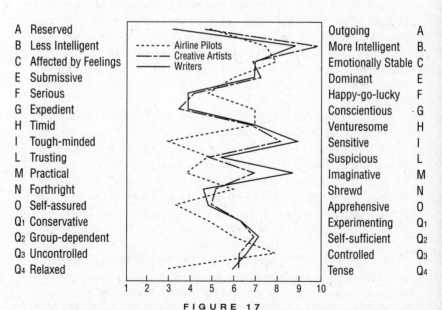

FIGURE 17

Three personality profiles, according to Cattell's sixteen-factor system

Cattell's 16 Personality Factor Questionnaire was in wide use for some time; in recent years it has largely been supplanted by less complex analyses, many of which are its intellectual offspring.

Learned Personality

No, not "learnéd" but "learned." Behaviorist theory, quite unlike either psychodynamic theory or trait theory, sees personality as nothing but a set of learned (conditioned) responses to stimuli. Psychodynamic and trait theories, in their different ways, see personality as inherent qualities of the individual that determine behavior; behaviorists have dismissed such talk as "mysticism," which deserves no place in scientific psychology. Skinner, in his characteristically immoderate way, called personality or the self merely "an explanatory fiction . . . a device for representing *a functionally unified system of responses.*" A trait, he said, is only a group of similar responses that lead to similar reinforcements in various situations; it does not cause behavior but is a label for a set of similarly conditioned responses.[46]

But the strict behaviorist view proved to be an inadequate explanation of much human behavior—and even of some animal behavior. Tolman, though a behaviorist, saw his rats acting at right-left choice points in a maze as if they were remembering, weighing information, and making decisions; and even before midcentury he and other behaviorists were trying to include internal mental processes in the stimulus-response paradigm.

An important effort of this kind was made by two Yale scientists, the sociologist John Dollard and the psychologist Neal Miller, who in the 1940s jointly worked out a theory of "social learning" as an expansion of behaviorism. Under certain conditions, they noted, rats—contrary to Thorndike's experience with cats—will imitate each other, evidently learning not by means of S-R conditioning but by means of cognitive processes. In human beings, said Dollard and Miller, much learning is social and takes place through high-level cognitive processes as well as drives and needs that underlie motivation.[47]

From the 1950s on, a number of other behaviorists further developed social learning theory, particularly its cognitive aspects. Central to all versions of the theory is the concept that human personality and behavior are shaped not only by rewarded actions but by the individuals' predictions or expectations, based on what they have observed, that specific ways of behaving will yield certain rewards. Although this view is much more cognitive than strictly behaviorist, it differs from both trait theory and psychoanalytic theory in that it still sees experiences and situations—external influences—as the major determinants of personality and behavior.

But in the 1950s, a trait-like modification of the social learning view of personality was made by Julian Rotter (1916–1987), then a professor in his mid-thirties at Ohio State University. Rotter was both a psychotherapist and an experimentalist, and although a behaviorist in the laboratory, his experience as a therapist gave him a respect for cognitive processes and emotions that researchers who are best acquainted with mice and rats often lack. Like most other clinicians, Rotter had found that often his patients' basic attitudes toward life had been formed by critical experiences, some good and others bad. Recasting this in behavioral terms, he theorized that when particular acts are either rewarded or not rewarded, people develop "generalized expectancies" about which kinds of circumstances and behaviors will or will not be rewarding.[48] A student who studies diligently and gets good grades, wins praise, and feels good about himself may come to expect that hard work in other situations will be similarly rewarding; a student who studies hard but fails to get good grades and their associated benefits may come to expect that in general hard work does not pay off.

Rotter and his graduate students conducted a series of experiments that demonstrated the pervasive influence of such generalized expectations. In a typical study, he or his collaborator would tell the volunteers—undergraduate men and women at OSU—that they were being tested for ESP. (This was a cover story to camouflage what they were really doing.) The experimenter would hold up, with its back toward the volunteer, a card on which there was either a square or a circle, the volunteer would guess which it was, and the experimenter would say he or she was either right or wrong. After a set of ten, he'd ask the volunteer to estimate how many he or she would get right of the next ten. Some students regularly estimated that they would do worse the next time because, as they later revealed in questionnaires and interviews, they ascribed their right guesses to luck. Others estimated that they would do better the next time because they attributed their right guesses to their skill at ESP, which they expected would increase with practice.

At about the same time, Rotter was supervising a psychotherapist in training, E. Jerry Phares, one of whose patients was a single man in his twenties who complained of having no social life. Phares urged him to

attend a free dance held on campus. He did so, and several girls danced
with him, but he told Phares, "It was just lucky—it would never happen
again." When Phares reported this to Rotter, it crystallized an idea he
had been forming. Reminiscing some thirty years later, he recalled that
moment:

> I realized there were always some subjects in our experiments whose
> expectancies, like this patient's, never went up even after successes.
> My graduate students and I had run various experiments in which we
> rigged the volunteers' success or failure—we did so in the ESP series,
> and also in an angle-matching test in which we could control the num-
> ber of supposedly "right" or "wrong" responses because the angles
> were so close that they looked alike and the volunteers would believe
> whatever we told them. Some volunteers, whether we told them they
> were right or wrong most of the time, didn't change their expectation
> that they'd get most of them wrong on the next set. Others, whatever
> we told them, thought they'd do better the next time.
>
> At that point I put together the two sides of my work—as practitioner
> and as scientist—and hypothesized that some people feel that what
> happens to them is governed by external forces of one kind or another,
> while others feel that what happens to them is governed largely by
> their own efforts and skills. Phares and I then worked out a test to meas-
> ure the degree to which any individual perceives reward or the lack of
> reward as the result of his own behavior or as having nothing to do with
> it.[49]

Rotter called this crucial attitude—the major discovery of his career—
"locus of control." The test he and Phares developed to measure it, the
Internal-External (I-E) Locus of Control Scale, is made up of twenty-
nine items, each of which comprises two statements; the person taking
the test says which of each pair of statements seems more true to him.
Some typical items:[50]

2. a. Many of the unhappy things in people's lives are partly due to
   bad luck.
   b. People's misfortunes result from the mistakes they make.
4. a. In the long run people get the respect they deserve in this
   world.
   b. Unfortunately, an individual's worth often passes unrecog-
   nized no matter how hard he tries.

11. a. Becoming a success is a matter of hard work; luck has little or nothing to do with it.
     b. Getting a good job depends mainly on being in the right place at the right time.
25. a. Many times I feel that I have little influence over the things that happen to me.
     b. It is impossible for me to believe that chance or luck plays an important part in my life.

Choices 2a, 4b, 11b, and 25a indicate that the respondent feels he or she has little control over events, the others that the respondent feels in charge of his or her own life. People who score high on external locus of control tend to attribute their successes and failures to fate, luck, or the power of other people; people who score high on internal locus of control attribute their successes and failures to their own intelligence, hard work, or other personal traits. Locus of control, a generalized attitude affecting many aspects of personality and behavior, is thus like a "central trait" in Allport's scheme and a "source trait" in Cattell's.

The concept of locus of control and the I-E scale struck a responsive chord among personality psychologists. Since the scale appeared in 1966, some two thousand studies using it have been published, and for at least two decades it remained one of the more popular personality tests. Then it was largely supplanted by other and more sophisticated tests, but the locus of control concept has remained a staple in personality assessment.[51] Many of the research studies using the I-E Scale showed how locus-of-control expectations affect behavior. For instance, elementary school students who scored as Internals got higher grades, on the average, than Externals; "helpless" children (Externals) did worse after failing a test containing difficult problems, "mastery-oriented" children (Internals) tried harder and did better. In experiments where volunteers were confronted with a dilemma, Internals were more likely to seek useful information, Externals to rely on others to help them. Among people hospitalized with TB, Internals knew more about their illness and asked more questions of their doctors than Externals. Internals brushed and flossed their teeth more than Externals. Internals were more likely than Externals to use seat belts in automobiles, get preventive shots, engage in physical fitness activities, and practice effective birth control.[52]

On the negative side, some studies have found that Internals are less likely than Externals to sympathize with people in need of help, since

Internals believe that needy people brought their troubles on themselves. And although Internals feel proud when they succeed, they feel ashamed or guilty when they fail; Externals, in contrast, feel less strongly about either success or failure. (Normal and healthy personalities, some researchers believe, are balanced between Internal and External and explain their lives to themselves in a self-protective, if inaccurate, way: they tell themselves, the social psychologist Fritz Heider has said, "I caused the good things; the bad things were forced upon me.")[53]

Social learning theory and locus-of-control research led to some notable developments in personality theory and clinical psychology. One was a growing recognition that conscious attitudes and ideas, not just unconscious ones, account in considerable part for the individual's traits and actions. What the psychologist George Kelly called "personal constructs" — sets of conscious ideas about one's own abilities and character, the behavior other people expect of us in various situations, how others are likely to behave in response to us, what they mean by the things they say, and so on — are important determinants of personality and behavior.[54]

Research based on this view has produced such interesting findings as the laboratory demonstration in 1978, by Edward E. Jones and Steven Berglas, of the ego-protecting tactic they labeled "self-handicapping."[55] Self-handicappers, faced with a situation in which they fear they may fail, protect their self-esteem by arranging things so that other people will attribute their failure to forces they could not control. A mediocre tennis player may choose only partners distinctly better than he so that losing will do him no discredit; a student about to take a final exam may burden himself with campus duties when he should be studying so as to have an ego-defending excuse if he performs poorly. The self-handicapper defeats himself in the effort to protect himself.

A particularly noteworthy byproduct of locus-of-control theory was the elucidation of a disabling phenomenon known as "learned helplessness." We have all known people who, hopeless and passive, are unable to make the effort to cope with their problems even though they possess sufficient abilities and resources. Many clinicians had offered conjectures about the cause of such passivity, but in 1967 Martin Seligman, a twenty-one-year-old graduate student at the University of Pennsylvania, had a flash of insight that led, after many years of work, to valuable understanding of such passivity.

Seligman had just gone to his professor's laboratory for the first time and found him and his graduate assistants deeply troubled. Their experimental dogs wouldn't perform. The dogs had been conditioned by tone and shock given together until they associated the tone with the shock. Now they were in a "shuttlebox," a large cage with a low fence dividing it into two compartments, where they were being subjected only to the tone. When dogs are put in such a box and given a shock in one compartment but not the other, they rapidly learn to leap the fence to escape the shock; the experiment was intended to find out whether they would do the same when they heard the tone without the shock. But at the tone, these dogs lay still and whimpered. No one could understand it, but young Seligman had a sudden thought. While the dogs were being conditioned to tone and shock, they couldn't escape the shock; they had learned that nothing they did mattered. Now, in a situation where they could have escaped the shock, they still acted as if nothing they did would help.[56]

With a fellow student, Steven Maier, and later with another colleague, H. Bruce Overmier, Seligman conducted a series of experiments in the creation of learned helplessness. A central experiment had the dogs placed, one at a time, in a cage where, harnessed and unable to escape, they received a series of electric shocks to their feet through the metal floor. Then each dog, and a number of others that had not had the shock treatment, were put in a shuttlebox where, from time to time, a light would go on in the compartment the dog was in, followed in ten seconds by a shock. All the animals quickly associated the light with an imminent shock; when it went on, the untreated dogs scrambled about wildly and soon found that they could escape the shock by jumping over the fence into the other chamber, but the dogs that had been subjected to unavoidable shock stayed put and let themselves be shocked without making any effort to escape. They had developed the expectation that nothing they could do would avoid the shock; they had learned to be helpless.[57]

That seemed to explain learned helplessness in human beings as well as dogs. But Overmier and Seligman went further. Depression in human beings, they boldly suggested, might often be due less to actual inability to cope with problems or sorrows than to learned helplessness—the feeling or belief that there is nothing to be done. This theory was immediately rebutted by psychologists and psychiatrists, who pointed out that some people never become helpless when bad things happen to them; some do but bounce back rapidly; some become help-less not only in the given situation but in new and different ones; some blame themselves and some blame others for their misfortunes.

Seligman, in collaboration with one of his critics, a British psychologist named John Teasdale, and another colleague, set out to find a better explanation of human depression. They worked out a new hypothesis combining learned helpless and locus of control. When human beings have painful experiences they can do nothing about, they either interpret them as the result of external forces or blame themselves, and the erroneous latter interpretation induces depression.[58] The team tested the hypothesis by means of a complicated locus-of-control questionnaire; the information supported the hypothesis, and after their study was published in 1978, a rash of similar and confirmatory studies — more than three hundred in the next twenty years — with dogs, rats, and people confirmed and extended it.[59]

One such study, for instance, rated a group of pregnant women, on the basis of personality testing, as either Internalists or Externalists, and found a markedly higher rate of postpartum depression among the Internalists. These women blamed the difficulties of the period on their personal attributes; the Externalists blamed them on the situation and, though feeling helpless, were not particularly depressed.[60]

Later, Seligman broadened his theory into what he called "explanatory style." It accounts for the basic aspect of personality that appears as overall optimism or general pessimism. In Seligman's words:

Take a bad event such as a defeat in business or love, for instance. Pessimists attribute it to causes that are long-lasting or permanent, that affect everything they do, and that are their own fault. Optimists regard the causes of a defeat as temporary, limited to the present case, and the result of circumstances, bad luck, or the actions of other people.

Optimism leads to higher achievement than pessimism. Optimistic life insurance agents, we found, sell more insurance and stay at it longer than pessimistic agents. Optimistic Olympic-level swimmers, when they're defeated, get faster; pessimistic swimmers, when they're defeated, get slower. Optimistic professional baseball and basketball teams do better, particularly after they're defeated, than pessimistic teams.[61]

On this basis, Seligman developed his own distinctive approach to personality: helplessness or pessimism could be learned (as the dogs had learned it)—but so could the opposite, optimism; one could learn mental skills that would change one's view of life in a positive and self-directing fashion. "Learned optimism" became the basis of what he views as a new discipline, Positive Psychology, which studies positive emotion, positive character traits, and therapeutic methods of achieving them. Since 2000 this has been Seligman's main interest, and at the University of Pennsylvania he now heads a training and research facility known as the Positive Psychology Center.[62]

One other issue on which social learning theory cast new light is that of the differences between male and female personalities. Ostensibly wise persons have had a lot to say about this subject throughout the ages, most of them men, who have spoken well of their own sex and ill of the other. Their views have ranged from Plato's mild denigration of woman ("The gifts of nature are alike diffused in both [sexes], but in all of them a woman is inferior to a man") to Clement of Alexandria's tirade against woman's sinful nature ("You are the gate of hell, the unsealer of that forbidden tree, the first deserter of the divine law") to Lord Chesterfield's genteel sneer at woman's mind and personality:

> Women are only children of a larger growth; they have an entertaining tattle, and sometimes wit; but for solid, reasoning good sense, I never in my life knew one that had it . . . A man of sense only trifles with them, plays with them, humors them, and flatters them, as he does with a sprightly, forward child.

A number of traditionally female traits—emotionality, timidity, vanity, nurturance, perceptiveness, deviousness, and so on—have always been assumed to be innate. In the early decades of psychology, most psychologists, Freud among them, believed that these traits were the inescapable outcome of women's hormonal and biological endowments and of the special experiences these brought about. As late as 1936, Lewis Terman and a colleague, C. C. Miles, published a well-received and influential study of male and female personalities, *Sex and Personality*, based on the results of a test they had constructed. Many of the answers were scored on the basis of traditional beliefs about gender differences. In the word-association section of the test, for instance, if the respondent's association to "tender" was "meat," the answer was scored as masculine, if "kind" or "loving," feminine. Reading detective stories and liking chemistry were scored as masculine; reading poetry and liking dramatics, feminine.[63]

Extraordinary though it may seem today, the Terman and Miles test was used for many years before such assumptions were questioned. But as women's social position changed in recent decades, so did many aspects of female personality; moreover, a mass of research findings by social-learning theorists and others challenged many of the traditional assumptions. A few examples of the hundreds in the research literature:

— Girls are indeed more fearful than boys of mice, snakes, and spiders — but largely because they learn early that it is more permissible for them than for boys to express fear.
— Girls spontaneously play with dolls more than boys do, a fact long taken as evidence that girls are innately more nurturing and helpful. But girls are more often *given* dolls to play with, a form of social training. Girls' greater nurturance is at least partly learned.
— Elementary school girls appear to be more compassionate than boys, as judged by such criteria as their greater willingness to write letters to hospitalized children; boys, however, are very ready to be helpful when the activity called for is one they have been taught to think of as properly masculine. At the adult level, women seem readier to help people in distress than men, but chiefly in situations traditionally thought of as calling for female ministrations, such as tending a hurt child; males are readier to help in risky or strenuous situations. In sum, sex differences in helping behavior are partly or largely attributable to social learning.[64]

For a while, some feminists took the extreme position that virtually all personality and intellectual differences between the sexes are the result of social inequities, pressures, and conditioning. But as research evidence accumulated, it became clear that certain cognitive and personality differences are indeed influenced by biology. For instance:

— Women have become somewhat more aggressive in sports, business, and in experimental laboratory situations. But in social life most of them continue to be much less aggressive than men. The latter commit by far the larger share of family violence, rapes, homicides, and crime in general. The greater aggressiveness of males appears very early in life, well before most social influences come to bear; the findings strongly suggest that social learning, while it plays a large part, acts on and accentuates biologically built-in differences.

— Girls and women have the edge on boys and men in verbal ability, on the average, but are slightly inferior in spatial visualizing ability. The verbal difference appears early and the spatial difference before adolescence, when social influences become most influential; both, therefore, point to some degree of difference in the structure of the brain. A recent review of studies of the brain lists a number of minor differences between the female and the male brain—one such difference, a stronger linking between the two hemispheres in females, has been thought to account for females' verbal edge over males—but the net conclusion is that "few data are available linking structural differences [in the brain] to functional sex differences."

— Women are better than men at sensing the meaning of such non-verbal cues to emotion as posture, body movements, and facial expressions. In part this is probably an acquired skill, but some evidence, such as the appearance of these differences in early childhood, points to a biological predisposition produced by evolution. It may have been more important to the survival of the weaker sex to read body language.

— In a painstaking survey of recent data, Melissa Hines, a leading British neuroendocrinologist, reports that there are dramatic differences in "core gender identity" (the sense of oneself as male or female), but that other much-researched differences are quite small. She listed 3-D rotation ability (mental rotation of pictures of objects to see if they are the same as other objects), math ability, verbal fluency, spatial perception, and even rough-and-tumble play and physical aggressiveness. Some of these criteria favored males, some females, but in all cases the differences were small compared to the average sex difference in height. In any case, Hines concludes, "Variation within each sex is great, with both males and females near the top and the bottom of the distributions for every characteristic.[65]

The upshot is that while the radical feminist view is not justified by the findings, many traditional beliefs about innate differences in male and female personality have been disproved. Most male-female differences are now ascribed to social learning or to the interplay of social forces and biological factors, but some do appear to be innate. Kay Deaux, a psychologist at the City University of New York, concluded a review of research in the field with this comment:

What one may wish as a feminist is not necessarily what one sees as a scientist . . . Attempts to "disprove" the existence of sex differences have given way to arguments, both at the scientific and popular level, that differences do exist. Acknowledgment of the existence of differences should not, however, serve as a cap on efforts to understand the processes by which sex and gender have become influential in human behavior.[66]

But that temperate summary did nothing to quiet the long-running debate. Over the past two decades, many other studies of gender differences in personality have been published, some concluding that there are only trifling differences, others that there are significant differences, some holding that such differences as exist are culturally acquired, others that they are largely of genetic or biological origin. It would be tedious to exhibit examples of all this, but the distinguished researcher Stephen Kosslyn and co-author Robert Rosenberg recently summarized what has been learned:[67]

In general, personality differences between females and males are not very great, especially when compared with the large differences among people within each sex. For example, there are no notable sex differences in social anxiety, locus of control, impulsiveness, or reflectiveness.

Nonetheless, some consistent differences have been found. Women tend to score higher on traits reflecting *social connectedness*, which is a focus on the importance of relationships, men on traits reflecting *individuality* and *autonomy*. Women tend to be more empathic than men and report more nurturing tendencies [and] are better at spotting when their partners are deceiving them.

Males and females also differ in their degree of neuroticism, with men scoring lower. However, women generally score lower on anger and aggression.

The fact that a difference exists doesn't tell us *why* it exists—what might be the role of biological or cultural factors. In spite of the evidence that culture and context shape gender differences, we must also note that there are biological explanations for these differences.

Which nicely illustrates a general truth about psychology that will become ever more apparent as our story proceeds: to some degree,

opposed and seemingly incompatible theories about many a psychological phenomenon, pitted against each other for two and a half millennia, are both proving in the light of accumulating knowledge to be right.

Body, Genes, and Personality

The theory that male-female trait differences are biologically determined is part of the larger one that personality is innate. There are two
related versions of this theory: one, the characteristics of an individual's
body influence personality; and two, personality is determined by specific genes or the interactions of certain genes.

The first version is nearly as old as psychology itself. Galen's humoral
theory of personality was one form it took in antiquity. Another was physiognomy, the view held from Greek times to today that the shape of the
features and configuration of the body are accompanied by related personality traits. One example, of thousands: In *The Canterbury Tales*
Chaucer pictures the sober, studious Clerk (scholar) as "not right fat"
but "hollow," the earthy, much-married Wife of Bath as "bold" of face,
"red of hue," and "gat-tothed" (gaps between the teeth, according to
physiognomists, denote boldness and amorousness), and the vulgar
Miller as stout, brawny, big-boned, and possessed of a gross nose with
wide black nostrils.

In the early years of this century, body-personality theory took on the
look of science when Ernst Kretschmer (1888–1964), a German psychiatrist who worked in several mental hospitals in southern Germany,
claimed he had found a relation between patients' physiques and their
personalities and mental states. Patients who were short-limbed, round
of face, and thickset, he said, tended to have mood fluctuations and to
be either very elated or very depressed; they were manic depressives.
Those who were long-limbed, thin-faced, and slender tended to be
introverted, shy, cold, and antisocial; they were schizophrenics. Those
who had balanced physiques and muscle development were energetic,
aggressive, and cheerful; they had other mental ailments.[68]

Kretschmer believed that both the body shapes and the personality
types or mental states were produced by hormonal secretions. His theory, advanced in 1921 in *Körperbau und Charakter* (the English edition
is called *Physique and Character*), attracted much favorable attention
because it seemed to lend scientific support to ancient tradition. But

other scientists poked holes in Kretschmer's theory. Many people, they noted, do not fit neatly into any of the three categories—short, fat people often have personalities that should go with being tall and thin, and tall, thin people often behave like athletic types. Moreover, Kretschmer's sample was skewed. Hospitalized schizophrenics are younger, on the average, than hospitalized manic depressives, and this alone might account for much of the difference he found in the distribution of body fat.[69]

But the body-type idea was appealing and soon had a new and more scientifically rigorous champion, William H. Sheldon (1899–1977), a physician and psychologist at Harvard. Shortly after Kretschmer's book appeared in English, Sheldon began a study of "somatotypes" (body types) and over several decades collected data on the physical dimensions and personalities of normal people. (Late in life, he extended his studies to mental patients and delinquent boys.)

As a researcher, Sheldon spared himself no pains: he photographed no fewer than four thousand male college students in the nude and recorded their key physical measurements. From this mass of data he concluded that there are three basic body types much resembling Kretschmer's: the *endomorph*, soft, rounded, and plump; the *mesomorph*, hard, square, big-boned, and muscular; and the *ectomorph*, tall, thin, and large of skull. These types, he believed, represent the special development of one or another of the three layers of cells that first differentiate in the embryo: the endoderm, from which arise the digestive tract and internal organs; the mesoderm, from which come bones and muscles; and the ectoderm, from which develops the nervous system.

To show the relation of personality traits to these somatotypes, Sheldon administered personality tests to two hundred of his subjects, and over the years gathered a wealth of other trait data from extensive interviews and his own observations of behavior. He found, as he had expected to, that a characteristic personality pattern was associated with each somatotype. The short, plump endomorph is usually social, relaxed, talkative, and sybaritic; the well-balanced mesomorph is energetic, assertive, courageous, optimistic, and sports-loving; and the tall, thin ectomorph is introverted, shy, intellectual, inhibited, and unsociable. Sheldon hypothesized that the genes determine which somatotype prevails as the fetus develops and thus which personality pattern the person manifests.[70]

His major publications, appearing in the 1940s, aroused much public and professional interest. But most psychologists found Sheldon's typology simplistic and his research methods faulty: he paid little attention to the socio-economic background of his subjects, although a child of poverty is hardly likely to grow up a fat, jolly endomorph or a child of wealth and advantage a shy, cerebral ectomorph. Psychologists were particularly leery of the extremely high correlations—+.79 to +.83— Sheldon reported between the three somatotypes and their associated personality types. Correlations of that magnitude are so unusual in psychology, where most phenomena have multiple causes, as to suggest a fundamental flaw in research design. And indeed there was one. To quote one eminent authority, Gardner Lindzey:

> There are a number of factors that would have to be considered in a full discussion of why so much co-variation is observed, but for most psychologists the explanation has seemed to lie in the fact that Sheldon himself executed both sets of ratings. Consequently, one may reason that implicitly Sheldon's prior convictions or expectations in this area led him to rate both physique and temperament in a consistent manner, whatever may have existed in reality.[71]

Supporters of Sheldon's views sought to repair this shortcoming in later studies; they had the somatotype ratings made from photographs by raters who never met the individuals, and the personality evaluations made by other raters from questionnaire data rather than interviews. These studies confirmed Sheldon's connections between body type and personality, but with considerably smaller correlations.[72] Even these data, however, might not prove a direct link between somatotypes and personality; the link could be indirect and social. Because people expect strong muscular mesomorphs to be leaders, weak skinny ectomorphs to avoid physical competition and rely on their minds, children, sensing what people expect of them, may come to behave accordingly.[73]

Although the somatotype theory attracted attention and sparked much research during the 1950s, the trenchant criticisms of it, and the fact that the theory was hereditarian and thus out of tune with the prevailing liberalism of the time, caused it to fade in influence. By the 1960s, according to the distinguished historian of American psychology Ernest Hilgard, it had almost vanished from the scene. But stronger evidence of the innateness of personality, or of at least a predisposition toward one pattern or another, has continued to crop up.

In the 1940s, Alexander Thomas and Stella Chess, psychiatrists at the New York University Medical Center, began studying individual temperamental differences in infants and young children. ("Temperament," a part of personality, is the individual's characteristic way of reacting emotionally to stimuli and situations.) Thomas and Chess collected data on babies' behavior starting at birth, partly by personal observation and partly by asking parents specific questions, such as how the infant reacted to the first bath or the first mouthful of cereal. They found good evidence of what every mother of more than one child knows, namely, that infants are temperamentally different from one another from their first hours on.

After years of study, Thomas and Chess specified nine differences that are manifest from the beginning of life. Some babies are more active than others; some have regular rhythms of eating, sleeping, and defecating while others are irregular and unpredictable; some like everything new (they gobble up the first spoonful of new food) while others do not (they spit it out); some adapt quickly to change, while others are distressed by any alteration of their schedules; some react to stimuli strongly, either laughing or howling, while others only smile or whimper; some are happy most of the time, others unhappy; some seem aware of every sight, sound, and touch, while others respond only to some stimuli and ignore others; some can be easily distracted if they are uncomfortable, but others are more single-minded; and some have a good attention span and will play with one toy for a long time, while others shift quickly from one activity to the next.

Summing up, Thomas and Chess found that about two thirds of all babies show a characteristic temperament early in infancy. Four out of ten are "easy" (placid and adaptable), one out of ten is "difficult" (irritable and hard to pacify), and one out of six is "slow to warm up" (moderately fussy or apprehensive but able to get used to things and people).[74]

As Thomas and Chess watched some of the children develop to near adulthood, they were initially impressed by how often the temperament of a baby remained substantially unchanged in childhood and adolescence. Later, their more detailed findings led them to a more qualified conclusion. Frequently, some or many aspects of the basic temperament were modified by such major events as a serious accident or illness, or such changes in the environment as the death of a parent or a dramatic alteration in the family's economic status. But when there were no such events or changes in the environment, the temperamental style of the first days of life was likely to be the temperamental style of the grown person.[75]

Even more impressive evidence that personality is partly innate has come from research in behavior genetics. This specialty, formerly somewhat outside mainstream psychology but now becoming more central to it, deals with genetic influences on psychological characteristics. Its major method of inquiry, originated by Galton, is to see to what extent people related to each other in differing degrees have similar mental abilities, personality, and achievements. First cousins have an eighth of their 25,000 to 30,000 genes in common, siblings a half, and identical twins all. If genes exert an influence on psychological development, the closer the genetic relationship between two people, the more psychologically alike they should be.

A vast amount of research conducted over the past half century has shown this to be the case. Some studies have shown that the closer the genetic relationship, the more alike the people are in mental health or illness.[76] Others have found the same to be true of general intelligence and of specific mental abilities.[77] And in the past three decades a number of geneticists and psychologists have found that the closer the genetic relationship, the more alike the personalities of the individuals.

Some of the personality research is based on analyses of the correlations in the traits of fraternal twins and of identical twins; consistently, the identicals are much more alike than the fraternals. Still, if they have been reared together in the same home, the evidence is less than perfect; they have had the same or very similar environmental influences all along (and identical twins, in particular, are even treated alike by their parents). For that reason, the best data—but the hardest to gather because instances are so rare—come from studies of identical twins separated at or soon after birth and raised in different homes and areas, where the environments are at least somewhat dissimilar.

Consider the case of Jim Lewis and Jim Springer, identical twins who were separated a month after their birth in 1940 and reared forty-five miles apart in different families in Ohio. They were totally unaware of each other's existence until 1979, when they were thirty-nine. In that year they met, but not by accident. They had been tracked down by Professor Thomas Bouchard, director of the Minnesota Center for Twin and Adoption Research at the University of Minnesota, who was conducting a study of fraternals and identicals reared apart. Jim Lewis and Jim Springer, except for their clothing, were physically indistinguishable, as are almost all pairs of identicals. Remarkable as this always seems, what was far more remarkable were other similarities. Both men had wives named Betty, were heavy smokers of Salems, drove Chevrolets, bit their fingernails, and had dogs named Toy.

This sounds as if it had been concocted by a writer for one of those supermarket tabloids filled with accounts of such wonders as babies borne by eighty-year-olds. But the story was not concocted. Of course, some of the peculiar coincidences may have been due to the twins' living in the same part of the country, others to chance. What was more important was the evidence adduced by psychological testing. Bouchard and his research team put the twins through a battery of personality tests and found their responses and trait scores nearly identical.[78]

From 1979 to 1990, Bouchard and his researchers tracked down nearly eighty pairs of identicals and thirty-three pairs of fraternals reared apart (out of some eight thousand pairs in their files), and put each twin through about fifty hours of intensive tests and interviews. For comparative purposes, they did the same with a number of identical and fraternal twins reared together. Statistical analysis of all the correlations within the twin pairs and among these various groups led the team to conclude that about 50 percent of variance in personality is due to heredity.[79] (They reported similarly remarkable findings for many other psychological variables, including general intelligence, language ability, social attitudes, homosexuality, substance abuse, and even religious interests.)

Some other studies in behavior genetics, however, have yielded more modest estimates. John C. Loehlin, of the University of Texas, Austin, recently reviewed a large number of twin studies and found that on the whole the evidence indicated that heredity accounts for about 40 percent of the variance in personality.[80] Several studies comparing adopted children to their adoptive mothers and to their biological mothers found only 25 percent of the variance attributable to heredity (although, interestingly, the adopted children resemble their biological mothers more than those who reared them in personality).[81]

Clarifying the matter, in 2003 Bouchard and a colleague, Matt McGue, performed a comprehensive review of Bouchard's and other researchers' twin, family, and adoption research. Sophisticated mathematical analysis produced cumulative evidence that "genetic influence on personality trait variation is in the 40%–55% range" and that "common (shared) family influence on personality traits is very close to zero." Nonshared—that is, different—environmental influences account for much or most of the other personality variations, but have been extremely difficult to identify.[82]

The figures do not mean that 40 to 55 percent of any individual's personality results from hereditary influences. Variance refers to the range of differences among people in any trait or set of traits. Data from Bouchard's center show, for example, that if a group of adults range in height from, say, four feet to seven feet, 90 percent of that span of differences is due to heredity, 10 percent to environment. Similarly, the twin studies mean that 40 to 55 percent of the range of personality differences among any group of people are of hereditary origin. This may explain why Americans have so many more variations in personality than the members of a more genetically homogeneous population, like the Japanese.

The findings of behavior genetics yield new understanding on a theoretical level—a level very different from that which interests most personality psychologists, namely, insight into the emotions and social relations involved in personality, and ways of testing and influencing them. It is even possible to see behavior genetics as diminishing the hope that psychology can improve the quality of human life, since to the degree that personality is hereditary in origin, it is not amenable to parental or social influence, therapy, or any other potentially controllable environmental factor. Many psychologists, therefore, including those in the field of personality, consider the findings of behavior genetics valuable as science but of no benefit in practice. What matters to them is the rest of variance in personality—the extent to which it can be influenced for better or worse.

Late Word from the Personality Front

Personality is no longer the most prominent field of psychology, not because it has shrunk in size but because by a generation ago certain newer fields had expanded and become the foci of attention. Also, as in any mature field of science, many personality researchers now churn out overspecialized studies of minutiae; happily, some others are still doing expansive and exciting work.

Among the more interesting developments in the field has been the study of the influence of personality on "well-being" (the general sense of contentment) in the middle and later years. Paul T. Costa and Robert R. McCrae, working with people enrolled in the Baltimore Longitudinal Study of Aging, a long-running research project of the National Institute on Aging, found that extraverts, who score high on such traits as sociability, general activity, and "ascendance" (similar to dominance), were happier in midlife and beyond than most introverts. They also found that people who score low on neuroticism adapted better to the changes of middle age and old age than people who score high on neuroticism (measured by such traits as chronic anxiety, hostility, self-consciousness, and impulsiveness). The latter were likely to see the problems of middle age as a crisis, worry about their health, be frustrated and disappointed by retirement, and be at risk for depression and despair.[83]

What can one do to counteract such personality handicaps? Costa and McCrae suggested that psychotherapy could help, but to a limited extent, since the data of the Baltimore and other studies indicated that personality traits are relatively stable in adult life. Still, they said that even a modest improvement in well-being is as worthwhile as a modest improvement in the control of a serious physical disease.

Physical diseases of many kinds, according to much recent research, originate in or are exacerbated by certain traits of personality. Two important studies, appearing in 1975 and 1980, produced survey evidence that people with the so-called Type A personality (competitive, striving, hostile, and driven) are likely to develop coronary heart disease. Many later studies of the matter somewhat qualified but did not negate the finding.[84]

More generally, Martin Seligman and his colleagues Christopher Peterson and George Vaillant offered evidence in 1988 that one's explanatory style affects one's health. On the basis of data yielded by a thirty-five-year longitudinal study of Harvard graduates, they concluded that people who customarily have a pessimistic or negative interpretation of life fall ill more often than optimists and have shorter life expectancies. They saw psychotherapy—particularly short-term cognitive therapy—as a useful antidote. As we have already seen, Seligman has gone on to develop the doctrine that cognitive training can convert a negative explanatory style to a positive one, with beneficial effects on physical and mental health, this being the core of his present system of Positive Psychology.[85]

Hans Eysenck, reviewing the results of a number of personality and health studies, including some he himself conducted, said that the "dramatic results . . . point to a very strong connection between certain personalities and specific diseases." He noted that many physicians have associated cancer-proneness with the inability to express anger, fear, or anxiety, and with feelings of hopelessness, helplessness, and depression, and that longitudinal studies show many of the same traits to be associated with heart disease. On the basis of these data, Eysenck and a collaborator, a Yugoslavian psychologist named Ronald Grossarth-Maticek,

conducted an experiment in preventive medicine, with the following
extraordinary results:

> [We] tried to use behavior therapy to teach cancer- and heart
> disease–prone people to express their emotions more readily, to cope
> with stress, to wean them of their emotional dependencies, and to
> make them more self-reliant. In other words, we taught them to
> behave more like the healthier personality types.
>
> 100 people with cancer-prone personalities were divided into two
> groups: 50 who received no therapy and 50 who did receive it. After 13
> years, 45 people who got therapy were still alive. Only 19 were alive in
> the no-therapy group.
>
> We tried a similar experiment with 92 heart disease-prone people,
> divided into therapy and no-therapy groups. Here too there were
> marked differences 13 years later, with 37 people surviving with ther-
> apy and 17 surviving without it.[86]

One can only wonder why these experiments have not been replicated or emulated.

Trait theory, still the guiding view in personality research, has continued
to mature, chiefly in the form of the "Big Five model" of trait theory.

For many years a number of researchers sought to look even deeper
into factorial structure than Cattell did and to identify a smaller, more
comprehensible, and more fundamental set of factors than his sixteen.
Three decades ago, some of them, reworking Cattell's correlation data,
said they could find evidence of five superfactors. Over the years others
have found one or more of the same five, in assorted guises, when they
put other widely used personality inventories through the statistical
wringer. By the 1990s, most personality psychologists had come to agree
that the Big Five are the basic dimensions of personality.[87] Since then,
different researchers have modified some of the factor names, but the
Big Five are the basis of current trait theory. They are:

— Extraversion, the factor some personality inventories list under
  such related labels as sociability, activity, and interpersonal
  involvement.
— Neuroticism, or, in the terminology of other studies, emotionality,
  emotional stability, and adjustment.

— Openness to Experience, also identified as inquiring intellect, intelligence, and "intellectance" (an unnecessary neologism that, fortunately, has not caught on).
— Agreeableness, also appearing as likability, altruism, trust, sociability, and so on.
— Conscientiousness, or dependability, superego strength, and restrained self-discipline, among other aliases.

These, according to present thinking, are the crucial and governing personality factors; the multitude of specific traits that account for the richness and variety of human personality are branches and twigs of these five trunks. Although these superfactors blur rather than focus the vision—imagine Hamlet, Lady Macbeth, or Lear described in terms of the Big Five—they offer researchers and clinical psychologists a set of proven dimensions along which to construct personality research designs and organize the data of whatever personality tests they use clinically.[88]

Another aspect of the field's maturing is the resolution of the "consistency paradox": although individuals have measurable traits and recognizable personalities, the behavior of any individual in a particular situation is a far from certain indication of how he or she will behave in others. The man who is brave under enemy fire may be cowardly in conflict with his wife; the woman who is a pillar of her church may, in her role as a company treasurer, plunder company funds to support a lover; the model family man and Little League dad may have a second wife elsewhere or be a closet public-lavatory homosexual.

Because of such cross-situational inconsistency, for years some psychologists attacked trait theory as having little validity. But more precise recent research data have led to a sensible resolution of the argument: the more similar the situations, the more consistent a person's behavior; the less similar, the less consistent. As Walter Mischel of Columbia University, a leading personality researcher and former critic of trait theory, has written:

The data . . . do not suggest that useful predictions cannot be made. They also do not imply that different people will not act differently with some consistency in different types of situations . . . The particular classes of conditions or equivalence units have to be taken into account much more carefully and seem to be considerably narrower and more local than traditional trait theories assumed.[89]

The latest word on consistency and the prediction of behavior strikes a different note, but one that is good news: personality traits do tend to change over the life course—most of them for the better. Using a six-factor variant of the Big Five, a meta-analysis (a pooling of the mean changes reported in ninety-two studies of a total of 50,120 people) showed that on average, there is improvement in four of the six "trait domains" throughout middle and old age. These are the findings in graph form (the vertical dimension measures *d* values, a statistic expressing average differences from the norm):[90]

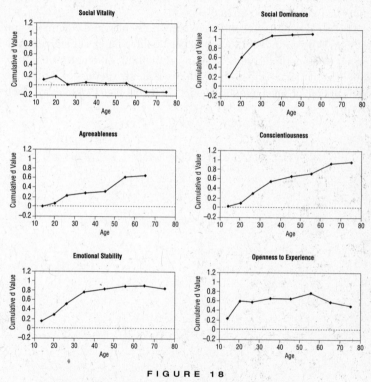

F I G U R E   1 8

Cumulative *d* scores for each trait domain across the life course

(adapted from Brent W. Roberts et al., "Patterns of Mean-Level Change in Personality," *Psychol. Bull. 132,* Jan. 2006: 15, by permission)

Still another late development of the field is the winding down of the old quarrel between situationists and dispositionists. Most psychologists are now inclined toward the interactionist view that any given piece of behavior results from the interaction of the situation with the individual's personality. Similarly, the ancient debate as to whether personality is innate or learned is yielding to the interactionist view. Some psychologists still talk as if parents, peers, social class, and other environmental influences are the only significant determinants of personality; some as if our behavior, like that of most other animals, is largely programmed by our genes. But increasingly, psychologists see the personality and behavior of the individual at every point in life as the outcome of the interaction between his or her innate temperament and all the experiences he or she has had up to that point.

This is a complex concept. Hereditary influences and environmental influences do not merely add up in personality but, like chemicals joining in a compound, interact to form something different from either, which then interacts differently with subsequent experiences. This is the core concept of development, the field of psychological studies to which we turn next.

TWELVE

The
Developmentalists

"Great Oaks from Little Acorns Grow"
—English proverb

Many people, when they think of a scientist at work, picture a stereotype: the aproned chemist pouring a fuming liquid into a flask, the cell biologist peering through a microscope, the khaki-clad paleontologist brushing away earth to reveal an ancient bone. But no such image exists of the psychologist at work; psychology is an aggregation of sciences, each with its own mise-en-scène. Even the specific fields within psychology are highly diversified, and none more so than developmental psychology. For instance:[1]

— A white-coated technician holds the head of an unhappy laboratory rat while an assistant deftly pries apart the lids of its left eye and inserts a tiny opaque contact lens.
— A young woman, very pregnant, lies on a table; a few inches above her abdomen is a loudspeaker through which her own voice, previously recorded, recites a two-minute poem.
— A four-month-old baby is propped up and facing a flashing light; a researcher covertly watches the baby's face. The light flashes regularly for a while, then flashes less often.
— An eight-month-old boy sits before a miniature stage; a researcher, hidden behind it, pushes a toy dog into view and just as the baby is about to reach for it draws a curtain, hiding the dog.

— A man kneels down next to a five-year-old boy playing with marbles and says, "I used to play a lot but now I've quite forgotten how. I'd like to play again. Let's play together. You teach me the rules and I'll play with you."

— A young mother, on the floor next to her year-old daughter, suddenly pretends she has hurt herself. "Oh! *Ooo!* It hurts!" she cries out, clutching her knee. The little girl reaches out as if to pat her, then bursts into tears and hides her face in a pillow.

— In a small office, a psychologist holds up a green poker chip and says to the ten-year-old girl seated on the other side of the desk, "Either the chip in my hand is red or it is not yellow. True or false?" She promptly says, "False." Later that day he does the same with a fifteen-year-old girl; she thinks a moment, then says, "True."

— A woman researcher plays a tape-recorded scene for a dental student. In it, a Mrs. Harrington, new in town, goes to a dentist for the first time. He says that some of her expensive crowns are defective and cannot be repaired, and that she has advanced periodontal disease, which her previous dentist did nothing about. Mrs. Harrington is upset and disbelieving. The researcher stops the tape and asks the student to assume the role of the dentist and deal with the situation.

In their diverse activities, these people have a common quest: the discovery of the processes by which the psychological acorn becomes a psychological oak. Specifically:

— After inserting the opaque lens, the experimenters trained the rat to run a maze, then sacrificed it and examined its brain under a microscope. Their aim was to find out, by comparing its right and left visual cortexes, the extent to which experience increased the number of dendritic branches in the neurons. (Because the left eye was obscured, the right visual cortex did not receive messages during the maze training.)

— The heartbeat of the pregnant woman's fetus was being monitored, and proved to be more rapid than when the same poem was read above her abdomen by a stranger. The unborn child evidently recognized its mother's voice.

— The four-month-old seeing the blinking light showed surprise when the flashing became less frequent; even at that age, an infant is aware of regularity in temporal intervals.

— The researcher who drew the curtain, hiding the toy dog, was exploring the development of infant memory—in this case, the awareness that a hidden object still exists.
— The man asking to be taught how to play marbles—Jean Piaget, in the 1920s—was studying the development of moral reasoning in young children.
— The mother simulating pain was collaborating with researchers in seeking to pinpoint the earliest appearance of empathy in children.
— The researcher asking the odd questions about a green poker chip was examining the growth of logical reasoning in children.
— The woman asking the dental student how he would handle a difficult situation was investigating the development of moral reasoning at the adult level.

These are only a few examples of the multiform activities and interests of contemporary developmental psychologists. Their field is a very broad specialty, and in a way the quintessential one: It deals with all that makes us become what we are and with the ways in which we can influence those processes.

Until the seventeenth century, there was little interest in this vast subject. Until then, according to the historian Philippe Ariès, the dominant view in much of Europe was that children were miniature adults, with small-scale adult traits, virtues, and vices. They were cared for until about the age of six, when they could care for themselves. Thereafter they were dressed like adults, put to work alongside them, punished like them for wrong deeds or disobedience to authority, and even hanged for thievery.

That attitude toward childhood began to change when Locke asserted that the infant's mind was a blank slate. But his theory of what turns it into an adult mind was rudimentary and grossly incomplete; development was believed to be due simply to the accumulation of experiences and associations.

Two centuries later, Darwinian theory gave rise to a more sophisticated conception offered by several early psychologists. Much as evolution proceeds from simple homogeneous forms of life to complex and highly differentiated ones, they said, psychological development moves from homogeneity and simplicity to complexity and specialization of mental functions, in an inevitable upward progress from infancy to maturity.[2]

Today this seems naïve; modern psychologists more realistically see development pursuing any of various routes, some distinctly undesirable. Racists, crack-addicted prostitutes, psychopathic killers, professional torturers, child abusers, genocidal religious fanatics, and the like are all end products of development. Moreover, developmental psychologists now consider that their subject extends to the later decades of life, when mental abilities wane and the incidence of the dementias of old-age illnesses rises. In dealing with so far-reaching a domain, they draw upon virtually every specialty of psychology, and with pardonable hubris consider theirs the most authentic approach to psychological knowledge. As the developmentalist Rochel Gelman put it some years ago, "We will not understand the end product unless we watch its evolution."[3] A bold statement; let us look at the evidence.

Grand Theory and Nontheory

"It is characteristic of a science in its earlier stages," said the philosopher Alfred North Whitehead, "to be both ambitiously profound in its aims and trivial in its handling of details."[4]

That was certainly the case with developmental psychology. In the late nineteenth and early twentieth centuries, the leading theory in the field scanted details and hard data in favor of a bold and sweeping concept. The Englishman George Romanes, the Russian Ivan Sechenov, and the Americans James Mark Baldwin and G. Stanley Hall all in various ways likened the developmental changes taking place during childhood to the stages of evolution from lower creatures to humankind. But this seemingly brilliant analogy was only an intellectual conceit, not an empirical finding, and it was soon swept away by the rising tide of research data that could not be contained within it. (Only psychoanalytic theory survived from this era, but unlike the evolutionary theories it did not attempt to be comprehensive; it dealt with character structure and personality, but had little or nothing to say about the growth of intellectual and social skills.)

Hall, however, made a seminal contribution to developmental psychology. He steered what was then known as the "child study movement" toward experimentation and data gathering. Himself a diligent researcher, for many years he conducted questionnaire studies of the thinking of schoolchildren and published his data; this, rather than his effort at grand theory, set the direction of the nascent field of child psychology.

By the 1920s, child psychology—the term "developmental psychology" came into vogue only thirty years later—was thoroughly research-oriented and largely atheoretical. This was consonant with the vogue for mental testing then sweeping the country. Much as Binet and Terman had measured intellectual achievement at each year of childhood without explaining how and why the mind grew, child psychologists from the 1920s through the 1950s concentrated on determining norms: the behavior and mental capacities infants "should" exhibit week by week, and children month by month. At Yale, Arnold Gesell compiled precise descriptions of normal behavior at every juncture of the child's life; at Berkeley, Yale, Harvard, and elsewhere, researchers launched major longitudinal studies in which people were tested and retested from infancy to adulthood in order to learn which factors, measured early in life, were predictive (though not explanatory) of what the adult became.

The lack of interest in developmental theory was also due in part to the dominance of the behaviorists, whose research in learning, as we have seen, consisted chiefly of determining the correlations between stimuli and responses. Behaviorist developmental theory, if it deserves that name, is epitomized in Skinner's writing:

> The consequences of behavior may "feed back" into the organism. When they do so, they may change the probability that the behavior which produced them will occur again . . . When changes in behavior extend over longer periods, we speak of the independent variable as the age of the organism. The increase in probability as a function of age is often spoken of as maturation.[5]

Happily, a far more sophisticated approach to developmental research and a correspondingly more profound theory would soon transform the field. These were the work of the man who asked the five-year-old boy to teach him how to play marbles.

A Giant, and a Giant Theory

Jean Piaget (1896–1980), most developmentalists agree, was the greatest child psychologist of the twentieth century; without him, said the distinguished British developmental psychologist Peter Bryant, "child psychology would have been a meager thing."[6] In the 1920s, when Piaget was a young man, his early contributions revolutionized child psychology in France and Switzerland, and thirty years later the products of his mature years did so in America. What made his work so influential was in part the beauty and explanatory power of his theory, and in part the many remarkable discoveries, made through painstaking research, on which he based it.

"Painstaking" is an understatement. From the days when he was a tall, slender young man with bangs on his forehead until his eighties, when he was white-haired, stooped, and portly, Piaget spent a great deal of his time watching children play and playing with them, telling them stories and listening to theirs, asking them innumerable questions about why things work the way they do ("When you go walking, why does the sun move with you?", "When you dream, where is the dream and how do you see it?"), and inventing puzzles and problems for them to solve. Through these activities, Piaget made a number of what the developmental psychologist Jerome Kagan of Harvard has called "amazing discoveries . . . a host of fascinating, hardy phenomena which were under everybody's nose but which few were talented enough to see."[7]

One of them: Piaget would show a baby a toy, then put his beret over it. Until about nine months of age, the baby would forget the toy the moment it disappeared, but at about nine months would realize that it still existed under the beret. Another: Piaget would show a child two identical wide beakers containing equal amounts of water, pour the water from one into a tall thin vessel, and then ask the child which container had more. A child under seven would almost always say the tall thin one, but a child of seven or more would recognize that although the shape had changed, the quantity had not. Piaget made many such discoveries, most of which, despite later modifications, have held up; child psychology, says Kagan, "had never possessed such a covey of sturdy facts."[8]

To account for his findings, Piaget constructed a complex theory made up of his own concepts of cognitive processes plus others from biology, physics, and philosophy. (He also explored but made little use of Freudian and Gestalt psychologies.) His basic message was that the mind, through its interaction with the environment, undergoes a series of metamorphoses. It does not merely accumulate experiences but is changed by them, achieving new and more advanced kinds of thinking, until by about age fifteen it is the sort of mind we think of as characteristically human. And so modern developmental psychology was born.

What was he like, this man who could sit with and listen to children for sixty years but who also had the intellectual might to transform a major area of psychology?[9] The unlikely answer: gentle, dignified, benign, friendly, and warm. His colleagues and co-workers all referred to him affectionately as *le patron* (the boss), he never aroused vicious opposition, he almost always responded mildly to criticism of his work, and none of his close associates ever broke with him. Pictures of Piaget in his later years tell no lie: the genial face, owlish behind horn-rimmed glasses, the flowing white hair escaping on both sides of the inevitable beret, the pipe jutting from the left side of the smiling mouth, all suggest a comfortable man to be with. The worst one can say of him is that he was so serious that he took almost no interest in children's jokes and laughter.

Born in Neuchâtel, Switzerland, Piaget, unlike Freud, was not an outsider who had to claw his way to acceptance; unlike Pavlov, he lived through no period of economic hardship; unlike James, he suffered no breakdown; unlike Wertheimer, he experienced no epiphany. The one singular feature of his relatively uneventful formative years was that he had virtually no childhood—which may be why he spent so much of his adult life with children. His father was a meticulous and critical profes-sor of history, his mother neurotic and, unlike her husband, exceedingly pious. The discrepancies resulted in a troubled family life, to which lit-tle Jean made a bizarre adaptation:

I started to forgo playing for serious work very early; this I obviously did as much to imitate my father as to take refuge in both a private and a non-fictitious world. Indeed, I have always detested any departure from reality, an attitude which I relate to my mother's poor mental health.

No fairy tales, adventure stories, or games for this sober child; by seven he was devoting his free time to studying birds, fossils, sea shells, and internal-combustion mechanics, and before ten he wrote a book on birds of the region.

But his pride in the book evaporated when his father regarded it as a mere compilation. At ten, Piaget "decided to be more serious." Having seen a partly albino sparrow in the park, he wrote a brief scientific report about it and sent it to a natural history journal in Neuchâtel, whose edi-tor, unaware that the author was a boy, published it. This success emboldened Piaget to write to the director of the Neuchâtel natural his-tory museum, asking whether he could study their collection after hours; the director went him one better by inviting him to assist in classifying and labeling his shell collection. Piaget did so twice a week for four years, learning enough to begin publishing scientific articles on mollusks in zoology journals before he was sixteen.

About that time, he spent a long vacation with his godfather, a literary man who considered the youth's interests too narrow and introduced him to philosophy. A larger world opened up before Piaget. He was fascinated by the subject, particularly the problem of epistemology, and by the end of the vacation decided "to consecrate my life to the biological explanation of knowledge." He still considered himself, however, a natural scientist, not a psychologist, and at the University of Neuchâtel went through undergraduate studies and on to a doctorate, which he received at twenty-two, in the natural sciences.

Only then did he turn to his real interest. He worked briefly in two psychological laboratories in Zürich, went to Paris and took some courses at the Sorbonne, and was recommended to Théodore Simon (Binet's collaborator), who put him to work standardizing certain tests of reasoning on five- to eight-year-old Parisian children. For two years Piaget did that—and much more. What interested him was not just determining the age at which children could give the right answer to each reasoning problem, but why, at earlier ages, they all made similar mistakes. He engaged the children in conversations, asking them questions about the world around them, listening carefully to their explanations, and inviting them to solve little puzzles of his own invention, all of which became the core of his lifelong method of investigation. In his autobiography he jubilantly says, "At last I had found my field of research."

At that point, his goal for the next five years—it turned out to be closer to sixty—was to discover "a sort of embryology of intelligence." Piaget meant it metaphorically; he did not attribute the growth of intelligence to the maturation of the nervous system but to the mind's acquisition of experience and the transformations that this forced it to undergo.

From then on he occupied a succession of important academic and research posts. In his twenties he was director of research at the Rousseau Institute in Geneva for five years; for the next five, professor of philosophy at the University of Neuchâtel; then back to Geneva as co-director, and later director, of the Rousseau Institute and professor at the university; later still, professor at the Sorbonne; and from 1956 on, director of the newly formed Center for Genetic Epistemology at the University of Geneva. ("Genetic epistemology," a term of his, has nothing to do with genetics; it means intellectual development.)

In all these posts as well as on sidewalks, in parks, and in his own home with his three children—he had married one of his students at the Rousseau Institute—Piaget conducted endless research, focusing now on one age, then on another, until eventually he had pieced together a complete picture of mental development from the first weeks of life to adolescence. In a steady outpouring of articles and books (couched, unfortunately, in exceptionally ponderous prose) he presented the world of psychology with a plethora of remarkable discoveries, a mass of valuable data, and the theory that transmuted the field of child study into developmental psychology. He became world famous, was (and still is) cited more often in psychological literature than anyone but Skinner and Freud, received honorary degrees from several great universities, and won the American Psychological Association's award for his distinguished contribution to psychology.

All that, without any systematic training or degree in psychology.

Piaget amplified and modified his theory over the years, but we need look only at the final product.

Behaviorists held that development takes place through conditioning and imitation, hereditarians that it is the automatic result of maturation. Piaget differed with both. He held that mental development requires both experience and maturation but is the result of an ever-changing interaction between organism and environment. In that interaction the mind adapts to an experience, is then able to interact in a different fashion with the environment, and adapts still further, undergoing a series of metamorphoses until it reaches the adult state. An infant's digestive system can at first handle only milk, but later, having developed thanks to the milk, can digest solid food. In similar fashion, the intellect is at first a simple structure that can absorb and utilize only simple experiences but, nourished by them, becomes more advanced, competent, and able to handle more complex ones.

A four-month-old baby, according to Piaget's research, does not recognize that the toy is under Piaget's beret; at that stage of mental development, the mind has only current perceptions, not stored images, and a concealed object is as good as nonexistent. But by the latter part of the first year, after accidentally finding the toy under the beret a few times, the baby has modified the reaction to seeing it covered over.

In another classic experiment, the child who has not yet learned to count says that six buttons spaced out in a line are "more" than six buttons bunched together in a line. When he learns to count, he discovers otherwise and his mind's way of handling such perceptions is transformed.

Both experiments exemplify the two crucial processes of mental development in Piaget's theory: *assimilation* and *accommodation*. The child assimilates the experience of counting the buttons—ingests it, so to speak, as if it were like previous experiences when what looked bigger was indeed bigger. But the new experience produced by counting is discordant with that assumption; the mind, to restore its equilibrium, accommodates (reorganizes) sufficiently to incorporate the new experience, and from then on sees and interprets sets of objects in a way better adapted to reality.[10]

Piaget once recounted the story of a mathematician friend that nicely illustrates how the assimilation of new information leads to accommodation and new thinking. The friend, as a small child, was counting pebbles one day. He lined them up, counted from left to right, and got ten. Then, to see what he would get by counting in the other direction, he recounted them from right to left—and was amazed: he still got ten. Inventively, he then arranged them in a circle and counted them: ten, of course. He recounted, going around the circle the other way: ten! "He discovered here," Piaget commented, "what is known in mathematics as commutativity; that is, the sum is independent of the order."[11]

Such mental development does not take place smoothly and continuously. From time to time, the accumulation of small changes such as the discovery of commutativity brings about a relatively abrupt shift to a different stage of thinking. The notion that the human psyche develops stage by stage was not original with Piaget—it had been suggested earlier by other psychologists—but Piaget was the first to identify and describe the stages on the basis of a wealth of observational and experimental evidence. The four major stages in Piaget's theory (there are many substages) are:

— sensorimotor (birth to 18–24 months),
— preoperational (18–24 months to 7 years),
— concrete operations (7 years to 12 years), and
— formal operations (12 years and up).

The ages are only averages; Piaget was well aware that there are individual differences. But he said that the sequence was invariant; each stage is the necessary foundation of the succeeding one.

This is what takes place in each (some of the following findings have been modified by later research, as we will shortly see):[12]

Sensorimotor (birth to 18–24 months): At first infants are aware only of their sensations and do not connect them with external objects. They do not even connect the images of their hands with the sensations of their hands moving, and only gradually, through trial and error, discover how to make their reaching for a toy coincide with what they see.

Even when their movements become more purposeful and accurate, they have no sense of what the objects around them are like or how those things will respond to their actions. So they experiment: they suck, shake, bang, hit, or throw objects, thereby acquiring new knowledge that leads to more intelligent and purposeful actions.

From such experiences, and with the help of the growing power of memory (in part due to continuing maturation of the brain), children begin to have a store of mental images. This is why they realize, in the latter quarter of the first year, that a hidden object still exists, even though the perception of it is gone. Piaget called this the attainment of "object permanence."

Toward the end of this stage, children begin to use their stored images and information to solve problems involving physical objects; they think about what might happen, instead of relying solely on manipulating things. Piaget, as a young father, proudly reported an episode of such thinking by his daughter Lucienne, who was sixteen months old. While playing with her, he put a watch chain in an empty matchbox, which he carefully left slightly open. He handed the matchbox to Lucienne, who had not been aware of his opening and closing it and had not seen him put the watch chain in it. She had only two "schemes" (learned ways of dealing with the situation): turning the box upside down to dump out its contents, and pushing her fingers in the slit to bring out the chain. She tried the second procedure first, groping to reach the chain, but was unable to. Then came a pause, during which Lucienne did something odd and noteworthy; as Piaget later reported the event:

She looks at the slit with great attention; then, several times in succession, she opens and shuts her mouth, at first slightly, then wider and wider . . . [then] unhesitatingly puts her finger in the slit, and instead of trying as before to reach the chain, she pulls so as to enlarge the opening. She succeeds and grasps the chain.[13]

Children also begin, at this time, to think about how to effect desired social consequences. Again Piaget reports his observation of one of his children:

> At one year, four months, twelve days, Jacqueline has just been wrested from a game she wants to continue and placed in her playpen, from which she wants to get out. She calls, but in vain. Then she clearly expresses a certain need [i.e., to go to the bathroom], although the events of the last ten minutes [attest that] she no longer needs to. No sooner has she left the playpen than she indicates the game she wishes to resume![14]

The child is acquiring a rudimentary ability to imagine or predict the results of certain simple actions and to conduct trial-and-error experiments in the mind. Henceforth, says Piaget, intellectual development proceeds "in the conceptual-symbolic rather than purely sensorimotor arena."[15]

Preoperational (18–24 months to 7 years): Now the child rapidly acquires images, concepts, and words and becomes better able to talk and think about external objects and events in symbolic terms. The two-year-old shoves a wooden block around the floor and makes the sounds of a truck; the three-year-old pretends to drink out of an empty toy cup. At first, the child learning to talk regards things and their names as one and the same (the two-year-old sees a bird and says "Bird!" and if an adult uses the word "bird" the child says, "Where bird?"), but eventually learns that the word is a symbol, detachable from what it stands for. From then on, he or she is able to talk and think about absent things and past or future events.[16]

But the child's internal representation of the world is still primitive, lacking such organizing concepts as causality, quantity, time, reversibility, comparison, and perspective. The child cannot perform mental operations involving these ideas; hence it is the "preoperational" stage. (By "operation" Piaget meant any mental routine that transforms information for some purpose. Classifying, subdividing, recognizing the parts in a whole, and counting are typical operations.) This is why the five-year-old thinks that six buttons spread out are more than six closely bunched, and water transferred to a tall thin glass is more than it was in a wide shallow glass. Even when children learn to count, for some time they do not grasp that 2×3 has to equal 3×2. Shown a bunch of flowers, most of which are yellow, and asked, "Are there more flowers or more yellow flowers?" they answer "Yellow."

The preoperational child is also "egocentric" (as was the sensorimotor child), a term Piaget defined as incapable of imagining how things look from another perspective. Piaget would show four- to six-year-olds a model of three mountains, put a little doll in a particular place amidst the mountains, display a set of photographs of the mountains taken from different positions, and ask the children which one showed what the doll was now seeing. The children always chose the view they themselves saw. Similarly, he reported, preoperational children have trouble imagining what other people are thinking, and often speak without realizing that the other person is unfamiliar with what they are talking about.

Concrete operations (7 to 12 years): By seven or thereabouts, children shift to a distinctly new and more competent level of thinking. Now they can perform such operations as counting and classifying, and can understand and think about relationships. Where the preoperational child knows the word "brother" but cannot say what a brother is and knows what "big" is but cannot say which is the bigger of two big things, the operational child can deal with both.[17] Mentally reversing a procedure is another operation. When a child can imagine pouring water back from the tall thin container into the original one, he acquires the concept of reversibility and with it that of "conservation," the recognition that quantity does not change when shape does.

Children in this stage also become aware that events outside themselves have causes outside themselves. Preoperational children will say it gets dark at night because we go to sleep; concrete-operational children say it is because the sun sets. They are also better able to imagine how things look from another perspective, and how other people think and feel. They can thus mentally manipulate symbols as if they were the things they refer to—but only symbols of physical objects and actions, not abstract ideas or logical processes. Deductive reasoning eludes them. Give them the first two propositions of a syllogism and they are not consistently able, if able at all, to draw the right conclusion.

Nor can they proceed systematically when tackling a problem with several variables. One of Piaget's most productive tests was his pendulum problem. He would show a child a weight hanging from a string and demonstrate how to vary the length of the string, the amount of weight suspended by it, how to release the weight from different heights, and how to push it with different degrees of force. Then he would ask the child to figure out what factor or factors (length, weight, height, and force, singly or together) affected the pendulum's rate of swinging. Pre-operational children made no plan of action; they tried different things at random, often varying several factors at once, making many incorrect observations, and reaching wrong conclusions. Operational children, though more systematic and accurate, still made frequent mistakes owing to illogical thinking. One ten-year-old boy tried changing the length of the string and concluded correctly that a pendulum swings slower when the string is longer. Then he compared the effect of a hundred-gram weight on a long string against that of a fifty-gram weight on a short string and concluded incorrectly that the pendulum also swings slower when the weight is greater.[18]

Formal operations (12 and up): In the final stage of development, children become capable of thinking about abstract relationships, like ratio and probability. They grasp syllogistic reasoning, cope with algebra, and begin to comprehend the elements of scientific thought and methodology. They can formulate hypotheses, concoct theories, and systematically examine the possibilities in a puzzle, mystery, or scientific problem. They play a game like Twenty Questions methodically, starting with broad questions and narrowing down the field of possibilities; until this stage their questions skipped from broad areas to narrow ones and back to broad ones, or overlapped, or were repetitive.

More important, they can now think not only about the concrete world but about possibilities, probabilities, and improbabilities, about the future, about justice, and values. As Piaget and his longtime collaborator, Bärbel Inhelder, say:

> The great novelty of this stage is that by means of a differentiation of form and content the subject becomes capable of reasoning correctly about propositions he does not believe, or at least not yet; that is, propositions he considers pure hypotheses. He becomes capable of drawing the necessary conclusions from truths which are merely possible.[19]

Jerome Kagan has called Piaget's analysis of the fundamentally new cognitive powers of adolescence "one of the most original ideas in any theory of human nature" and the source of "insights about adolescent behavior that challenge traditional explanations." For one thing, it helps us understand the rise in the suicide rate in the teen years: the ability to think about hypothetical situations and know when one has exhausted all solution possibilities enables the adolescent to tell himself (rightly or wrongly) that he has tried or examined all ways of solving some personal problem and that none will work. For another, the ability to perceive inconsistencies within his own beliefs or those he is told to believe helps explain the rebelliousness, anger, and anxiety of the adolescent. Among the common and deeply troubling inconsistencies: conflicting values about teenage sex (it is immoral and risky, yet to abstain may seem "hung up" and abnormal); conflicting perceptions of the teenager's relation to his parents (he wants and needs their support but also wants to be independent); and so on.[*20]

As opposed to admiration like Kagan's, for several decades there has been a rising tide of revision and modification of Piaget's ideas and findings; thousands of neo-, post-, and anti-Piagetian papers have been published or delivered at seminars. While much of this work has value, most of it is small stuff compared with the work of the giant himself. Isaac Newton once said, with false modesty, "If I have seen farther, it is by standing on the shoulders of giants"; the swarm of psychologists who have been correcting and revising Piaget's theory could say in all truth that they see farther than he because they stand on his shoulders.

Cognitive Development

In the 1920s, Piaget's early publications launched the modern study of cognitive development in Europe and America. But in the United States interest soon waned; behaviorism was becoming supreme and its adherents saw little value in what they considered new wine in the old bottle of mentalism. However, in the 1960s, when cognitivism began to regain favor, Piaget was rediscovered, and intellectual development research in his mode became a booming field.

But the tidy outlines of Piaget's theory became blurred as swarms of doctoral candidates and psychologists, performing hundreds of Piaget-inspired studies, produced findings that often modified and sometimes challenged various aspects of the original. In the course of the past four

*Piaget, early in his career, studied the moral development of the child (Piaget, 1948 [1932]), but this work dealt only with the pre-adolescent years and children's attitudes toward rules, lies, and the like. It is his later work on cognitive development that deals with morals and justice.

decades, the field of cognitive development, though still much influenced by Piaget, has become an overgrown and unweeded garden. Outside it, moreover, researchers in two relatively new and burgeoning fields, cultural psychology and evolutionary psychology, have been vigorously raising a crop of studies that broaden and modify developmental psychology in distinctly non-Piagetian ways. But we will defer looking into these two specialties until we have seen what has been happening in Piagetian-based studies, some of which are sure to enlighten, delight, and occasionally astonish the viewer. Here, with no pretense to completeness or even representativeness, is a small gathering of the flowers and fruits of several decades of this genre of research.

Memory: How is one to investigate the memory of an infant who cannot speak, or, in the case of a newborn, indicate recognition even by facial expressions or hand movements? Researchers have thought up ingenious approaches to the problem. In an experiment conducted in 1959, infants less than a month old were conditioned to turn their heads at a particular sound (they turned them in response to a touch on the cheek and were rewarded by a bottle); a day later they still turned their heads when they heard the sound.[21] The method, used with infants of different ages, yielded data on the growth of memory.

With infants a few months old, the method most frequently used has been the observation of their eye movements. The baby lies on his back looking up; above him is a display area where the experimenter puts two large cards, each containing a design such as a circle, a bull's-eye, or a sketch of a face. The researcher times how long the baby's eyes are directed at one pattern or the other. Since infants look at a new image longer than at a familiar one, the method yields a direct indication of what the infant remembers having seen.

Another technique, used in a 1979 experiment, called for a mobile to be suspended over the crib of an infant; subjects ranged from two to four months. When the baby kicked his legs, the researcher made the mobile move, and the infant soon learned to kick in order to see it move. Then he did not see the mobile again for a week, but when he did, he immediately started kicking. However, if two weeks went by, he did not. Again, the growth of memory was precisely measured.[22]

Such memory (recognition) is different from the more actively employed memory involved in a baby's looking for an object that he has seen being hidden from view. If a baby of eight or nine months has twice retrieved a toy from under one of two similar covers, and if the researcher then puts it under the other cover—while the baby watches—the baby, unless allowed to look for the toy within a few seconds, will look where he previously found the toy. His memory functions at a primitive level. But a few months later he no longer makes that mistake. The advance is due to maturation of certain brain circuits. Monkeys in whom a particular region of prefrontal cortex is surgically destroyed never learn to look under the correct cover.[23]

By five, children effortlessly remember thousands of words, but the longest number they can repeat after hearing it read slowly is four digits long. By six or seven they can remember five digits, and by nine to twelve, six. This increase, however, comes about less from maturation than from the knowledge of how to remember. Before going to school children do not "rehearse" (repeat or review) information or use associative strategies; parents of a first-grader are often puzzled that their child can't remember what went on at school that day. But in school children gradually learn memory strategies and soon know how, for instance, to visualize themselves in class at the beginning of the school day and so recall what happened first, and next, and next.[24]

Sense of self, sense of competence: The young child's explorations of its world are a measure of his sharpening sense of self and growing sense of competence. At nine months, children still mouth and bang objects or aimlessly turn them over and over, but toward the end of their first year they begin to explore actual uses of those objects: they try drinking from a toy cup, "talking" into a toy phone, and so on. They become interested in investigating new territory and will momentarily crawl out of the mother's sight; they turn whatever knobs and dials they can reach; they open closet and cupboard doors and take everything out. Such activities show what many developmentalists call "the attainment of competence." Exploratory behavior, contrary to behaviorist theory, is not the consequence of rewarded acts but is spontaneous and self-initiated; the human infant and child has a need to investigate his own capacity for acting on objects, intervening in events, and widening his horizons.[25]

Another indication of the growth of the sense of competence is the smile of a child nearing two, even if no one is present, on successfully building a tower, putting a final piece in a puzzle, or fitting a dress on a doll. At the same time the child is becoming aware of failure and its meaning about the self. Jerome Kagan and his colleagues have noted that between fifteen and twenty-four months, children show anxiety if an adult demonstrates a form of advanced play and then tells them it is their turn. The play may consist of making a doll cook food in a pan and then have two dolls eat dinner, or making three animals take a walk and then hide under a cloth to avoid getting wet. Faced with the challenge of following such a relatively complicated scenario, children will fuss, cry, or cling to their mother. Kagan has interpreted this as evidence of the child's fear of being unable to remember or to carry out the play in front of the adult, since if no onlooker is present, the child will often try out the modeled act or some part of it.[26]

Language and thought: Piaget believed that language plays only a limited role in the development of thought and that logical thinking is primarily nonlinguistic and derives from actions—first, doing things to the world around one, and later, doing things to one's mental images of those things.[27] Developmentalists in the Soviet Union and America found evidence to the contrary. Although it is true that some thinking is nonlinguistic, language is a set of symbols that give the child extraordinary freedom to manipulate the world mentally and to behave appropriately toward new stimuli without needing to experience them directly ("It's hot—don't touch"). Jerome Bruner, an eminent developmentalist, has long maintained that language is a crucial part of the child's symbol system and "a means, not only for representing experience, but also for transforming it."[28]

A bit of research evidence about the role of language in thought: Prekindergarten children were shown three black squares and told to choose one; if they chose the largest, they were rewarded. Once they had learned to choose the largest, they were shown three new squares, the smallest of which was the same size as the former largest one; again it was the largest that was rewarded. But the children had no mental symbols with which to tell themselves to "always choose the largest" and kept picking the size that had previously been rewarded, even though it now brought no reward. Kindergarten and older children, however, were quickly able to tell themselves to choose "the largest one," regardless of the actual size of the square.[29]

More complex and advanced problems are also easier to solve if words are used to guide thought. A group of nine- and ten-year-olds was instructed to think out loud while trying to solve difficult problems involving moving disks from one circle to another in the fewest moves; another group did not receive these instructions. The group that thought out loud solved the problems faster and more efficiently than the silent group; the deliberate use of words caused them to think of new reasons for trying one method or another and thus helped them find correct solutions.[30]

Language acquisition: Developmentalists and psycholinguists (psychologists interested in language acquisition and use) have spent a great deal of time in recent decades listening to children speak, calculating how rapidly they learn new words, tracking the kinds of mistakes and corrections they make, and so on. Among the findings is that children develop or acquire new forms (word endings, forms of verbs, prepositions) in a relatively uniform sequence. Between two and four their vocabularies increase from a few hundred words to an average of twenty-six hundred. (They acquire fifty or more per month.) They first imitate verb forms they hear, then generalize on verb endings, reasonably (but wrongly) assuming that language has regularities throughout ("I taked a cookie," "I seed the birdie"), and only slowly learn to use irregular verb forms. They stubbornly cling to their grammatical errors, as in this bit of dialogue reported by one psycholinguist:

CHILD: Nobody don't like me.
MOTHER: No, say, "Nobody likes me."
CHILD: Nobody don't like me. (eight repetitions of this interchange)
MOTHER: No, now listen carefully; say, "Nobody likes me."
CHILD: Oh! Nobody don't *likes* me.[31]

They correct their errors by themselves when they are good and ready. Apparently they acquire many elements of grammar that they do not use until, at some moment, they mentally compare what they are saying to some stored knowledge and see the discrepancy.

JAMIE (nearly seven): I figured something you might like out.
MOTHER: What did you say?
JAMIE: I figured out something you might like.[32]

The most significant advance in the study of language acquisition concerns the means by which children understand syntax—the arrangement of words in a sentence that denotes their relationship to one another and thus the meaning of the sentence. In 1957 B. F. Skinner published a book called *Verbal Behavior*, in which he explained the child's acquisition of language entirely in terms of operant conditioning:

when the child uses a word or sentence correctly, the parents or others approve, and that reward conditions the child to use it correctly the next time.

But in the same year Noam Chomsky, a brilliant young psycholinguist, presented a radically different analysis in his *Syntactic Structures*. He asserted that "there must be fundamental processes at work quite independently of 'feedback' from the environment"; the brain must have inborn capacities to make sense of language. As evidence, he pointed out that children produce innumerable sentences they have never heard, which makes imitation through conditioning seem a quite inadequate explanation of sentence formation. Furthermore, children's efforts to make sentences are often ungrammatical but never grossly in violation of syntax. (They never produce backward sentences.) Most important, children understand what is meant even when the form of a sentence is ambiguous; they must have a built-in ability to perceive the "deep structure" of the sentence, whatever its "surface structure." An example Chomsky gave:

John is easy to please.
John is eager to please.

The sentences have the same surface structure, but if you try to paraphrase them in the same fashion, only one makes sense:

It is easy to please John.
It is eager to please John.

No child makes such an error; every child comprehends the deep structure. "John" in the first sentence is the *deep object* of "please," so the paraphrase works; "John" in the second sentence is the *deep subject* of "please," so that any paraphrase has to take the form "John is eager to please (someone)." An understanding of deep structure is not learned from surface structure or from rules of thumb; the ability to perceive it is innate. (Neither Chomsky nor any other psycholinguist, however, says that language itself is innate, but only that the child has an innate predisposition to recognize and interpret the deeper structure of sentences.)

In recent studies of creoles—languages that have evolved from the mixing of existing languages—the linguist Derek Bickerton has found that creoles formed in different parts of the world are more similar to each other in grammatical structure than to long-lived languages. He also has claimed that pidgin—an informal first-generation creole that lacks consistent grammatical rules—tends to become more developed and grammatical when spoken by the children whose parents speak it. Both bodies of evidence, according to Bickerton, are evidence of the brain's built-in sense of grammar.[33]

Intellectual development: Often ploddingly but sometimes inventively, researchers have devised experimental techniques better than Piaget's and, as noted, produced a substantial number of modifications and a few outright rejections of parts of his work. Some examples:

— Heart rhythms of babies as young as four months increase when an object disappears and also when it reappears, indicating surprise. This suggests that, contrary to Piaget's doctrine, babies expect objects to continue to exist.[34] (But it is still true that they seem to forget about an object as soon as it has disappeared.)
— Piaget tested children for "conservation of number" (the ability to recognize that, say, six closely grouped objects are as many as six spaced ones), and concluded that they did not attain it until the stage of concrete operations, at about seven. But later researchers used different experimental methods, such as Rochel Gelman's "magic" procedure, in which one of a small set of toy mice on a plate is surreptitiously removed or an extra one added while the plate is covered. Children of five or even less recognize that there are fewer or more, and say that one has been taken away or added.[35]
— Researchers studying children's ability to take another person's view have used more naturalistic methods than Piaget's mountain experiment. Instead of asking questions about what things look like from a different perspective, they let the children talk to different people about the workings of a toy. Surprisingly, even a four-year-old will use short and simple sentences when talking to a two-year-old but longer and more complex ones when talking to an adult. Indeed, the latest work on "theory of mind"—the child's recognition that other people have their own reasons for what they do, based on their own perspective and experience—shows that children become aware of this quite early in life: They begin to read others' intentions in their first year of life and are good at doing so by the end of the second year. Preschoolers, it is now clear, are far less egocentric and far more capable of taking another person's perspective than Piaget thought. The evidence is derived not only

from observations of children's behavior but from physiological evidence: according to a study published in 2006, fMRI brain scans (to be discussed in Chapter 16) indicate that it is when the right and left temporo-parietal junction and the posterior cingulate areas of the brain develop early in life that children become capable of reasoning about other people's thoughts and beliefs.[36]

— Piaget said that children acquire the concept of causality gradually over a period of years. Later researchers say that he came to this conclusion because he asked children to explain what causes wind and rain, how machines work, and other processes beyond their ken. If, instead, one tests them on things they are familiar with, the results are different. In one such experiment, children saw a ball roll down an incline in a box and disappear, at which point a jack-in-the-box popped up. Then the box, which was actually made in two parts, was pulled apart, and the ball, seen rolling down into one part, obviously could not reach the other part—out of which, nonetheless, the puppet popped up. When it did, children of four and five laughed, giggled, wriggled, and said things like "It's a trick, right?," clearly indicating that they sensed that it should not have happened.[37]

— On the basis of many experiments, a number of psychologists maintain that human intellectual growth is not accomplished in the clear-cut stages depicted by Piaget; there is much more overlapping or gradual change than his model depicts. There is also some evidence that at times children perform—or can be trained to perform—certain mental tasks of an advanced stage before completely mastering the stage they are in; the sequence of steps of mental development is not invariant. Moreover, children can sometimes be trained to think beyond their present stage.

— When psychologists began using Piaget's tasks to study cognitive development in children in other cultures, they often failed to find evidence of the stage of formal operations. In his later years, Piaget himself began to think that what he had characterized as formal relations relied more on the type of science education children received than on a predetermined psychological growth process.[38] This was a foretaste of cultural psychology, one of the two new psychological specialties mentioned earlier that have recently modified and enriched developmental theory far more than all the above-mentioned (and many other) Piagetian-type studies.

Cultural psychology: This minor specialty (also known as cross-cultural psychology) has been bringing a broader and deeper perspective to development theory. We all know, of course, that people in other cultures behave and evidently think and feel anywhere from a bit differently to vastly differently from ourselves ("honor killing" by family members of women in Pakistan who have had an illicit sexual relationship is a "vastly different" example, as is, on a more amiable note, the "wife-lending" of the Inuit of Alaska and the Tupi-Kawahib of central Brazil). But although we are all aware of cultural differences, the great majority of psychological research studies have been conducted with American undergraduates in psychology courses, surely not a representative sample of humanity; generalizations drawn from such studies may be valid for that kind of sample but not necessarily for other people in other countries.[39]

Relatively few psychologists are devoting themselves to this new discipline, but it has made a number of significant contributions to the field of developmental psychology, these being notable examples:

— Children's cognition has been shown to develop in whatever way enables them to perform functions valued in their society; the tasks Piaget had his children perform were those he found appropriate and valuable, but, as one researcher has pointed out, if those same children had been evaluated with respect to their grasp of the cognitive complexities of weaving, they would likely have seemed retarded compared to Mayan children in Guatemala.[40]
— Many Americans never think seriously about their dreams unless they are in therapy or are students of psychology. But in many non-Western cultures, dream interpretation is an important part of cultural life. The male Archur Indians of Ecuador, for instance, sit together every morning and share their dreams from the night before; this ritual is "vital to the life of the Archur," writes a researcher. "It is their belief that each individual dreams not for themselves but for the community as a whole."[41]

The following are a few of the many other subjects on which cultural psychology is influencing the study of human development:[42]

— Do different languages cause people to think differently? Apparently not, but the issue is still undecided.

— Does culture influence the creation of one's sense of self? Apparently yes: The evidence indicates that in an individualistic culture such as our own, the growing and maturing individual develops an independent sense of self—one guided by one's own thoughts, feelings, and actions. In contrast the collectivist cultures in which three quarters of the world's population live, rate the rights and responsibilities of the group higher than those of the individual and tend to generate a collectivist sense of self—one guided by the thoughts, feelings, and actions of others.

— Do genes or culture account for the fact that only 4.1 percent of Chinese children and 10.3 percent of Japanese children score as low in mathematics as the average American child? When researchers asked Asian and U.S. students, teachers, and parents which is more important, "studying hard" or "innate intelligence," Asians stressed hard work, Americans innate ability. Clearly, cultural belief is the key.

— Even within our own county, the culture of people living at an economic hardship level is distinctly different from that of "normal" life. A combination of physical hardship and cultural influences has been shown to result in poorer working memory and lessened cognitive control in adolescents.[43]

In an overview in the APS *Observer*, Alana Conner Snibbe sums up: "Cultural psychologists' efforts have yielded a bevy of intriguing, often controversial cultural differences in psychological processes, including reasoning styles, motivation, perceptions of time, space, and color, relational styles, and emotional experience, regulation, and expression."[44]

Evolutionary psychology: This relatively new field is, according to one of its leading enthusiasts, David M. Buss of the University of Texas at Austin, nothing less than "a revolutionary new science, a true synthesis of modern principles of psychology and evolutionary biology."[45] It came on the scene in the late 1980s, although it had been suggested earlier by William James and other functionalists. But while its early proponents thought natural selection had built specific behaviors into our brains, the new evolutionary psychologists believe that natural selection built into us general cognitive strategies which are expressed in various behaviors suitable to our circumstances.

An example of such an inborn strategy is the use of deception to achieve one's goals. A number of theorists, among them Buss and

Steven Pinker, argue that we lie because those of our ancestors who could do so had an advantage over their nonlying contemporaries and hence were more likely to live and to produce surviving children — who, inheriting the ability, again outproduced nonliars, until eventually the ability to lie became common to our species. But note: Lying is not a specific inherited behavior; it is a cognitive strategy that can take the form of many different behaviors, including lying, all of them deceitful but varying according to the norms of one's culture and the particular situation.[46]

"Wait a moment!" you may be thinking. "The proof of evolution is the record shown by fossils — but what evidence can there be of how the mind worked in prehistoric times? Or that it was evolution that selected cognitive abilities such as the ability to deceive?"

One proof, say the evolutionary psychologists, is cultural universality: If people in all sorts of different and far-removed cultures exhibit certain similar tendencies or behaviors, this is unlikely to be due to cultural transmission, and it is likely that evolution is responsible. Among such cultural universals are not only lying but telling stories, gossiping, using proper names, expressing emotions with the same facial expressions, dancing, giving gifts, making medicines, and so on and on.[47]

A very different source of evidence consists of the actual testing of hypotheses derived from evolutionary theory. Here's an example. First, start with a well-supported observation: Men give higher priority to physical appearance than do women in the selection of a mate. Next, generate an evolutionary hypothesis to account for this: Women's physical appearance was a clue to ancestral man as to fertility. Finally, test the hypothesis: Show male volunteers a variety of pictures of women with varying waist-to-hip ratios and ask their preferences. The result: Men find women with a low waist-to-hip ratio — a known fertility correlate — attractive, apparently a preference built in by evolution.[48]

Another: Sexual jealousy, though common to both sexes, has been shown by studies to be activated in men far more than in women by signs of sexual infidelity rather than emotional infidelity. Evolutionary psychologists see this as an adaptation that originated in ancestral males' uncertainty of parenthood, which was less an issue for ancestral women.[49]

Still another genre of evidence: laboratory tests of built-in fears. In a series of studies, some participants were asked to find such phobia-related images as spiders and snakes embedded in pictures filled with nonfear images such as flowers and mushrooms. Other participants were asked to find nonfear images embedded in pictures filled with phobia-related stimuli. People in the first category found the spiders and snakes significantly faster than people in the second category found the flowers and mushrooms, and the difference held true no matter how confusing the array of images and no matter how many distractions such as noises and interruptions were introduced.[50] As Buss says, "It was as if the snakes and spiders 'popped out' of the visual display and were automatically perceived." Yet objects that are products of modern life and that are as dangerous as snakes do not automatically trigger the same kind of atten-tion: we fear snakes and not electrical outlets, for example, because elec-trical outlets are too recent an invention to have become objects of built-in fear response.[51]

Again: Why is cautiousness and fearfulness far more common than boldness and bravery? Because, according to evolutionary psychology, it's more adaptive: Our cautious ancestors were more likely to survive and procreate than our bold ancestors.

Why do most human beings tend to conform to the beliefs and behav-iors of their own group? Because of a built-in desire to reduce uncer-tainty, which leads us to see ourselves as members of our group (even in an individualistic culture).

Why do men have better spatial ability than women? Because primi-tive males were the hunters, and those of them with superior spatial abil-ity had a better chance of survival and progeny creation; women were not subject to the same selective force.

Why do human beings have an apparently innate need for self-esteem? For several reasons, according to evolutionary psychologists. For one thing, self-esteem derives in part from the esteem and respect in which one is held by others; hence behavior that tied the individual in closely to his or her group—and so improved the group's chances of sur-vival—was selected by evolution and became a human tendency. Again, an accurate level of self-esteem was a guide to one's status and security in the social hierarchy; too low or too high a self-evaluation lessened the individual's chances of survival. Finally, self-esteem was a valuable mechanism in the mate-selection process, success in which was essen-tial to pass on one's genes; the individual with no self-esteem tended to be weeded out by evolution.

And so it goes, on and on. At times, the evolutionary psychologists sound as if their discipline will provide fundamental understandings not just of development but of practically everything within traditional psy-chology. David Buss, for one, sees it as "a scientific revolution that will provide the foundation for psychology in the new millennium . . . the metatheory that seeks to present a unified understanding of the mechanisms of the mind."[52] Steven Pinker of Harvard has said that "in the study of humans, there are major spheres of human experiences—beauty, motherhood, kinship, morality, cooperation, sexuality, violence—in which evolutionary psychology provides the only coherent theory."[53]

To be sure, there are other candidates for a metatheory that will provide a unified mental science; more of that later. Meanwhile, we have gone far afield from development, to which, after a final word about Piaget, we return.

About Piaget: Many developmentalists, while accepting his general conception of human development, now consider his scheme of stages physiologically limited and culturally biased. A number of modified stage theories have been advanced, but it is unclear which one will eventually dominate the field. Whichever one does, however, it will embody Piaget's fundamental concepts but go far beyond them, even as Einstein's physics embodied but went far beyond Newton's.

Maturation

Despite Piaget's training in the natural sciences and his early decision to explore the biological explanation of knowledge, his theory deals almost entirely with development through cognitive processes; he either ignores the role of maturation—the growth processes of the body that automatically cause changes in behavior—or takes it for granted. But for some years many developmentalists have felt that until the part that maturation plays in psychological development is fully spelled out, we cannot know to what extent behavior is innate rather than acquired by means of assimilation and accommodation.

Yet how is one to distinguish between the two influences? From the infants' first day outside the womb they are learning as well as maturing; isolating the results of each process is a scientific problem of the first order. Newborns do, to be sure, possess important reflexes at birth that cannot owe anything to learning, such as turning their head toward a touch on the cheek as if in search of the nipple before they have ever known a nipple. And as most parents know, if you stick out your tongue at infants only one to three weeks old, they reflexively stick out their own tongues, an inherent reaction produced by "mirror neurons" that have recently been identified by brain scans and located as being in the premotor cortex. But in general most changes in behavior or new forms of behavior may come either from maturation or learning or both.

Sometimes, however, nature accidentally provides an experiment that separates the two. Infants begin to babble at three or four months as a preparation for speech — but so do deaf children, obviously not in an effort to imitate heard speech but for some other reason. Babbling is evidently a form of programmed behavior that owes nothing to experience but begins spontaneously when the neural centers that direct it reach a certain stage of development. In normal children, babbling changes through learning, coming more and more to resemble the sounds and intonations of speech; in deaf children it slowly disappears from lack of learning.[54]

Since opportunities to observe behavioral development in the absence of learning are rare, during the early years of the specialty a few developmental psychologists made history by creating the conditions experimentally. In 1932, Myrtle McGraw, then at the Columbia-Presbyterian Medical Center in New York, got a low-income Brooklyn family to lend her their twin boys for an experiment. For two years Johnny and Jimmy, apparently identical twins, spent eight hours a day, five days a week, in McGraw's laboratory. Johnny got extensive training in physical skills; Jimmy remained in his crib "undisturbed" (not even played with) and with only two toys at a time. Johnny, before he was a year old, could climb a steep incline, swim under water, and rollerskate; Jimmy could do none of these (but had become as adept as Johnny at grasping objects, sitting alone, and walking). Photographs taken by McGraw show Johnny, at twenty-one months of age, boldly letting himself down from a five-foot stand, hanging by his hands, and dropping to a mattress; Jimmy, crouched on a much shorter stand, stares down and refuses to budge.[55]

At the end of two years McGraw gave Jimmy intensive training to see whether he could catch up to Johnny; he never fully did. But psychologists who have reviewed her data feel that Johnny's training gave him only a small and largely temporary advantage over Jimmy. McGraw did not agree; many years later — after experiments like hers, which stunt a child's development, had come to be considered gravely unethical — she asserted that although Jimmy had caught up in most ways, even as a young adult he still had less ease and grace of physical movement than Johnny.[56] What this proves, however, is hard to say, since it turned out that the boys were fraternal twins, not identicals. The only safe conclusion is that intensive physical training can push a child to achieve physical skills ahead of schedule and that most of the gain is temporary.

A more drastic experiment was conducted, also beginning in 1932, by Wayne Dennis, then at the University of Virginia. From an indigent Baltimore woman he obtained her fraternal twin girls, Del and Rey, when they were five weeks old, and, with his wife's help, reared them in his home for over a year. His plan was to deprive them of all stimulation and learning to see what forms of behavior arose spontaneously with maturation. In a journal article, Dennis reported, with no qualms or apologies, how he carried out his experiment:

> During the first six months we kept a straight face in the babies' presence, neither smiling nor frowning, and never played with them, petted them, or tickled them, except as these actions reasonably were incorporated into routine experiments . . . To restrict practice which might influence sitting, the infants were kept almost continually on their backs in the cribs.[57]

They were not even allowed toys or the sight of each other for eleven months. (There was a screen between their cribs.)

The results, Dennis claimed, showed that "the infant within the first year will 'grow up' of his own accord," as evidenced in the twins by such behavior as laughing, bringing their feet to their mouths, and crying in response to sounds at about the same ages as children reared normally. But they lagged far behind other children in crawling, sitting, and standing. After fourteen months Dennis gave them a period of training that, he said, quickly brought them up to normal. By his own admission, however, Rey could not walk without holding on until her seventeenth month and Del not until her twenty-sixth month.

The twins spent the rest of their childhood in institutions and the homes of relatives. Although Dennis claimed he had brought them up to par, he later had good reason to doubt it. In Iran he studied orphanage children and found that many of them, neglected and given little attention, were developmentally retarded at two years and remained somewhat so in adolescence. But he never followed up on Del and Rey to see how they turned out; perhaps he did not want to know.

Such experiments, rare seventy years ago, are nonexistent today; after the civilized world learned of the "medical research" conducted by Nazi doctors in concentration camps, legal constraints on research with human subjects became stringent. But developmentalists have pursued their goals in other ways. One is by experimenting with animals. Much as behaviorists sought principles of learning in rats that would be relevant to learning in humans, developmentalists sought principles of maturation in animals that would apply to humans.

In one well-known case, newly hatched goslings, which were thought to trail after their mother instinctively, were taught by the German ethologist and Nobelist Konrad Lorenz to follow him instead. Lorenz arranged to be the only moving creature the goslings saw during their first days. Their instinct being to follow a moving object, they followed him—and having learned to do so, ignored their mother when they later saw her. Lorenz theorized that at a "critical period" of maturation, the image of the creature being followed becomes fixed in the nervous system. Nature meant it to be the mother goose and failed to anticipate the meddling of an ethologist.[58]

Eckhard Hess, an American, built a moving, quacking, decoy mallard, and put mallard ducklings in its presence. If he did so as soon as they were hatched, half of them became attached to it, but if he first did so when they were thirteen to sixteen hours old, over 80 percent became attached to it. What looked like an instinct was a more complex phenomenon: the nervous system of the duckling is wired to respond to moving objects but is most readily "imprinted" on a particular target at a special time slot in the maturation process.[59]

As a result of these findings, in the 1970s some developmentalists and pediatricians came to believe that it is in the first hours after birth that the mother-infant bond can best be formed. They advised mothers to cuddle the newborn against their naked body for a while immediately after delivery instead of having it whisked away to be cleaned up and parked in a bassinet in the hospital nursery. But while some subsequent research showed stronger infant-mother bonding when this was done, it was the mother who was bonded. Much other research has shown that the infant's attachment to the mother (or father or other principal caretaker) develops over a period of four to five months in response to innumerable acts of caretaking and expressive attention.[60]

Much maturation research is concerned with physical skills and physical attributes, and adds little to our knowledge of the growth of the mind. But research on the development of perceptual abilities has been providing solid factual answers, in place of speculation, to the ancient central question of psychology: How much is due to nature and how much to nurture (or, in developmental terms, to maturation and to learning)?

The work has been focused on early infancy, when perceptual abilities evolve rapidly; its aim is to discover when each new ability first appears, the assumption being that at its first appearance, the new ability arises not from learning but from maturation of the optic nervous structures and especially of that part of the brain cortex where visual signals are received and interpreted.

Much has been learned by simply watching infants—noting, for instance, at what age they can fix their gaze on nearby objects. But such observations leave many questions unanswered. What, exactly, do very young infants see? Not much, apparently; their eyes often seem unfocused and do not even track a moving object. On the other hand, mothers know that their infants gaze steadily at them while they nurse. Since we cannot ask them what they see, how can we find out?

In 1961, the psychologist Robert Fantz devised the ingenious method of doing so briefly mentioned earlier. He designed a stand in which, on the bottom level, the baby lies on his back, looking up. A few feet above is a display area where the experimenter puts two large cards, each containing a design—a white circle, a yellow circle, a bull's-eye, a simple sketch of a face. The researcher, peering down through a tiny peephole (so that he is not visible), can watch the movement of the baby's eyes and time how long they are directed at one or the other of each pair of patterns. Fantz found that at two months babies looked twice as long at a bull's-eye as at a circle of solid color, and twice as long at a sketch of a face as at a bull's-eye. Evidently, even a two-month-old can distinguish major differences and direct his gaze toward what he finds more interesting.[61]

Using this technique and others of a related nature, developmental psychologists have learned a great deal about what infants see and when they begin to see it. Some of what the psychologists learned: In the first week infants distinguish light and dark patterns; during the first month they begin to track slowly moving objects; by the second month they begin to have depth perception, coordinate the movement of the two eyes, and differentiate among hues and levels of brightness; by three months they can glance from one object to another, and can distinguish among family members; by four months they focus at varying distances, make increasingly fine distinctions (they look longer at an oblique angle they have not seen before than at an acute angle they have seen a number of times), and begin to recognize the meaning of what they see (they look longer at a normal sketch of a face than at one in which the features have been scrambled and are in unnatural positions); and from four to seven months they achieve stereopsis, recognize that a shape held at different angles is still the same shape, and gain near-adult ability to focus at varying distances.[62]

A mass of comparable studies have been conducted, over the past half century, on the development of hearing, including the emergence of pitch and volume discrimination, discrimination among voices, and recognition of the direction a sound is coming from.

Exactly how maturation and experience interact in the brain tissues to produce such developmental changes is becoming clear from recent and current neuroscience research. Microscopic examination of the brains of infants who have died shows that in the first months of life a profusion of dendrites (branches) grow from its neurons and make contact with each other, as shown in Figure 19 (see page 433). This burgeoning continues apace; during the first two years of life the brain triples in size and the synaptic connections among the neurons reach astronomical numbers. (The rat's brain, it has been estimated, forms a quarter of a million synapses—connections between nerve cells—every *second* during the first month of its life. In the human brain during the first months and years of life the rate of synaptic formation must be very many times greater.)

By the time a human is twelve, the brain has an estimated 164 trillion synapses.[63] Those connections are the wiring plan that establishes the brain's capabilities. Some of the synaptic connections are made automatically by chemical guidance, but others are made by the stimulus of experience during the period of rapid dendrite growth. Lacking such stimulus, the dendrites wither away without forming the needed synapses. Mice reared in the dark develop fewer dendritic spines and synaptic connections in the visual cortex than mice reared in the light, and even when exposed to light never attain normal vision. Kittens reared in a stroboscopic environment, where they see only during flashes of light, fail to develop cortical cells sensitive to movement; when they are grown cats, they see the world as a series of stills. If one eye of a young monkey is kept shut during the critical period, the neurons of that eye never catch up to those of the other eye. Thus, maturation provides—for a limited time—a multitude of potential nerve pathways among which experience makes the choice, "hard-wiring" those circuits needed for perception.[64]

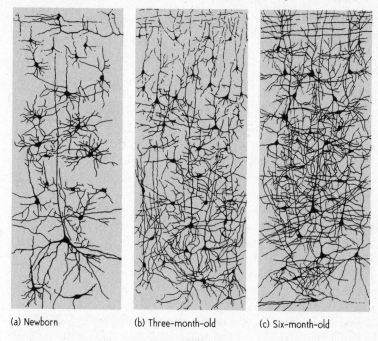

(a) Newborn   (b) Three-month-old   (c) Six-month-old

FIGURE 19

Brain Development: These drawings of neurons in the visual cortex show the
flourishing and development of the human brain in the first half-year of life.

Why should nature have done that? Since we can learn all through
life—and all learning, at any age, involves the creation of new synaptic
connections—why should perceptual development be possible only at a
critical period and not later? Apparently, the developing brain's "use it or
lose it" policy is efficient and economical of resources; the growing neurons are preserved by myelinization (which wraps them in a fatty protective sheath), and those sensory connections that are used are further
myelinized to make them more permanent. Since the essential experiences are almost always available for carrying out this process at the right
time in brain development, the pruning of unused connections fine-tunes
the brain structure and provides far more specific perceptual powers than
would result from genetic control alone of synapse formation.[65]

Here again we see the vague old terms "nature" and "nurture" taking
on more precise meaning; we see mind being constructed not by the
addition of nurture to nature but by the interaction between them, each

affecting and being affected by the other. Mysteries begin to fade away; wonders take their place.

Personality Development

Unlike personality researchers, whose primary interest is measurement, developmentalists are concerned with natural history. They watch personality grow from birth on, and seek to identify the forces that shape it. And in contrast to psychoanalysts, who base their theories of personality development chiefly on what they hear from adult patients, developmentalists base theirs on firsthand evidence.

Part of that evidence adds much detail and meaning to psychoanalytic ideas about mother-infant attachment. This has been a leading topic of developmental research ever since 1952, when the World Health Organization published *Maternal Care and Mental Health* by the English psychoanalyst John Bowlby, who studied children raised in institutions, found them deficient in emotional and personality development, and attributed that to their lack of maternal attachment.

Bowlby theorized that the infant is genetically programmed to behave in certain ways (crying, smiling, making sounds, cooing) that evoke care and hence survival, and that the mother's nurturance engenders attachment in the infant at a "sensitive period" of his or her development. This powerful special bond, which gives the infant a sense of security, is crucial to normal personality development; without it, said Bowlby, the child is likely to develop "an affectionless character" and to be permanently vulnerable to psychopathology.[66]

Bowlby's views aroused great interest—and discomfort—in America, where the rising divorce rate and, a little later, the women's movement caused a growing number of mothers to work, leaving their children with caretakers. Many child psychologists and developmentalists doubted that the sensitive period is as specific and crucial, or the mother as all-important and irreplaceable, as Bowlby said. But most of them agreed that, under normal circumstances, attachment to the mother (or mother substitute) does occur and is a major force in personality development.

Intriguing evidence of the harm done by the lack of attachment was shown in a 1965 study of infant smiling conducted in Israel. It compared babies raised under three conditions: in their own families, in *kibbutzim* (collective settlements) where they are reared in large houses by professional caretakers but often fed by their mothers for the first year, and in institutions. It is rare for one-month-old infants to smile at a strange human face, but with each passing week they do so more and more often, the behavior reaching a peak at about four months and then declining slowly. In the study, all three groups smiled often at strange female faces by the fourth month, but at eighteen months while the family-reared infants were only slightly less responsive than at four months, the kibbutz-reared infants were only about half as much so, and the institution-reared infants less likely to smile than they had been at one month.[67]

But smiling is a byproduct of attachment, not a measure of it. Researchers needed such a measure, and in the late 1960s Mary Ainsworth, a former colleague of Bowlby's who had come to America, devised a relatively easy one. Known as "the Strange Situation," it has been the mainstay of attachment research ever since. In the Strange Situation, the infant and mother are put in an unfamiliar playroom while the researcher watches them through a one-way mirror. Eight different scripts are followed, one at each visit. In one, the mother leaves the room briefly; in another, a stranger comes in while she is there; in a third, when she is not; and so on.

From about eight months to two years, the infant typically cries when the mother leaves the room ("separation anxiety"), and when she returns goes to her and clings to her. (There are, of course, temperamental differences that make one infant more anxious than another; the findings of the Strange Situation are generalizations.) If a stranger enters and does not smile or talk, an infant of seven or eight months will look at the mother and in a little while start to cry ("stranger anxiety"), although at three or four months the same infant probably would have smiled. Stranger anxiety dissipates within a few months, but separation anxiety continues to rise until early in the second year, then declines gradually throughout the year.[68]

There are several explanations for the appearance and disappearance of the two reactions, but the most widely held is that with growing mental capacity, the infant is better able to evaluate the situation. Stranger anxiety wanes as the infant gains the ability to recall pleasant experiences with other strangers, separation anxiety as the infant becomes capable of understanding that the mother will return.[69]

Ainsworth's original aim was to see how infants react when their mothers are absent, but she unexpectedly found that how they react when the mother comes back was even more interesting. Some are glad to see her and go to her to cling or be held; others ignore or avoid her; and still others squirm, hit, or kick her if she tries to hug them. Ainsworth called the first reaction (shown by about 70 percent of one-year-olds) "secure attachment," the second kind (20 percent) "anxious-avoidant attachment," and the third kind (10 percent) "anxious-resistant attachment."

After studying all three kinds in greater depth, Ainsworth and other researchers concluded that avoidant attachment occurs when the mother is emotionally inexpressive, resistant attachment when the mother has been inconsistent in responding to the infant's needs. Still other researchers have ascribed avoidant and resistant attachment to such factors as the mother's personality traits, lack of expressiveness, negative feelings about motherhood, rejection of the infant, and harsh responses to the infant's crying or demands.

Some psychologists later identified variants of Ainsworth's three attachment styles, finding her explanations too pat. Jerome Kagan is one.

A child whose mother has been otherwise attentive and loving, but has successfully encouraged self-reliance and control of fear, is less likely to cry when the mother leaves and, therefore, is less likely to approach her when she returns. This child will be classified as "avoidant" and "insecurely attached." By contrast, the child whose mother has been protective and less insistent that her child "tough it out" is likely to cry, to rush to the mother when she re-enters the room, and to be classified as "securely attached."[70]

In a study of his own, Kagan found that mothers of the ostensibly less securely attached babies had careers outside the home and, while psychologists might regard them as less nurturing, may have tried to make their infants self-reliant and able to cope with separation. The mothers of the more securely attached infants may have been overprotective and prevented them from developing such inner security.[71]

A valuable study conducted in the 1980s used the Strange Situation to measure the attachment of 113 one-year-olds to their mothers and five years later evaluated their behavior and mental health by means of a questionnaire given their mothers and another given their teachers. Of the boys who had been securely attached at one year of age, only 6 percent showed signs of psychopathology; of those who had been insecurely attached, 40 percent did. (Girls, for unknown reasons, showed no such connection between the quality of early attachment and later psychopathology.) The research team cautiously concluded that the results "lend partial support to the hypothesis that the quality of the early mother-infant attachment relationship predicts later social-emotional functioning."[72]

Most research on the development of the emotions has been focused on the first two years of life, and for good reason. According to Michael Lewis and his colleagues at the Institute for the Study of Child Development, University of Medicine and Dentistry of New Jersey, the primary emotions (joy, fear, anger, sadness, disgust, and surprise) appear during the first half year, the secondary or "derived" emotions (embarrassment, empathy, and perhaps envy) in the second half of the second year, and other secondary emotions (pride, shame, and guilt) soon after. Studies of infants' videotaped facial expressions by Carroll Izard and his colleagues and students at the University of Delaware have yielded related findings.[73]

Until a generation ago, developmentalists had no theory of the development of emotions; now they have several. These differ on various issues, the most important being whether the development of the emotions is due chiefly to the maturation of specific neural circuits or to social learning of emotional behaviors and their displays. In both views the emotions are said to assume specific form through learning, but one holds that the major determinant is maturation, and the other, cognitive capacity and training. Consider a piece of the evidence for each side:

First, the maturational view:

A team of researchers at the National Institute of Mental Health set out to pinpoint the earliest appearance of altruism or care giving in children by observing children in play groups and at home. Altruism is a form of behavior based on the emotion of empathy; the team expected to see the first signs of empathy at about age six, as predicted by psychoanalytic theory, but they could see that younger children—as young as three—seemed distressed when another child was in pain or unhappy. Going back still farther, they looked for empathy in toddlers by having mothers simulate pain or a choking cough at home in the presence of their child. Some years ago, Dr. Carolyn Zahn-Waxler, a member of the team, told the author of this book what the team, to its own surprise, found: "Even a one-year-old might look distressed when his mother cried, and in children only a few months older, we'd see unmistakable expressions of concern for the other person." These reactions are almost universal and show up in predictable forms at relatively predictable stages and ages. "That suggests to me," she concluded, "that whatever part experience plays, the organism is hard-wired with a tendency to respond empathetically."*[74] In very recent years she has been proven quite right: Brain scans—a subject we'll come to later—provide abundant evidence that particular brain circuits respond in similar ways to the circuits of others in emotional states, and that this empathy-generating neural architecture develops very early in the infant brain and hence is very likely hard-wired.

Second, the cognitive-developmental view:

A curious bit of methodology, first used with children several decades ago, consists of unobtrusively dabbing rouge on a child's nose and then putting him or her in front of a mirror. Until they are about twenty months old, most children either do nothing or try to touch the rouge spot in the mirror; at twenty months and older, most of them touch the spot of rouge on their noses. This is taken as evidence of the emergence of a sense of self; children realize that the image in the mirror is of them.[75] Michael Lewis and a group of colleagues used the mirror-rouge technique to find out when and why the emotion of embarrassment first appears. Most children who touch the rouged spot, they reported, also looked embarrassed (the criteria: an embarrassed smile, a turning away of the head, and a nervous touching of the body), but most non-touchers did not. The team's conclusion:

> The ability to consider one's self—what has been called self-awareness or referential self—is one of the last features of self to emerge, occurring in the last half of the second year of life . . . [and] is the cognitive capacity that allows for all self-conscious emotions such as embarrassment.[76]

There seems to be good evidence, then, for both the maturational and the cognitive-developmental views; the truth, one suspects, is probably an amalgam of the two.

An influence on personality development that has long been a leading subject of research is parenting style. Researchers have explored it by

---

*Michael Lewis et al. put the appearance of empathy later, but the discrepancy may lie in whether empathy is defined as distress at seeing distress (an early development) or as an attempt to help (a later development).

means of an array of techniques—observation, questionnaires, experiments, correlation analysis—and their findings, which have been quickly picked up by the media, are familiar to most literate people. Here, in brief, ignoring passing fads in parenting, is a handful of enduring findings gathered in recent decades. Bear in mind, however, that both genetic tendencies and external factors exert significant influences on personality development; the connections listed here between parent behavior and child personality are only correlations, and not always strong ones.

Discipline: Power assertion (threats and punishment) and withdrawal of love are forms of external control; they may produce compliance, chiefly while the parents are watching or can carry out sanctions. But discipline by induction (explaining why a certain act is wrong, how it violates a principle, how it makes the other person feel) leads the child to absorb the parents' values and make them part of his or her own standards; it creates self-control.[77]

Child-rearing style: The children of authoritarian (dictatorial) parents tend to be withdrawn, low in vitality, mediocre in social skills, and often prejudiced, and, for boys, low in cognitive skills. The children of permissive parents have more vitality and sunnier moods but poor social and cognitive skills (the latter is true of boys in particular). The children of authoritative (firmly governing but democratic) parents tend to be self-assertive, independent, friendly, and high in both social and cognitive skills.[78]

Modeling: Parents are models for their children's behavior and traits of personality. An aggressive parent tends to produce an aggressive child, a gentle parent a gentle child. When parents preach particular values but themselves behave differently, children will imitate the behavior rather than follow the preachments. Children are especially likely to model themselves on a nurturing or strong parent, less so a cold or weak one.[79]

Parent-child interaction: Children whose parents talk to them a lot develop higher verbal and social skills than those whose parents talk to them little. Children whose parents play with them a lot tend to be popular with other children and good at recognizing and interpreting other children's moods and emotional expressions. The way the parent and child interact is likely to be the model for the child's other relationships.[80]

Sex-role behavior: While many of the behavioral differences between boys and girls have some basis in biology, much sex-typed behavior is learned from the parents. It begins at birth, when parents unconsciously respond differently to boy infants and girl infants. It continues in direct instruction about how to behave and, even more important, in the child's identification with the same-sex parent and imitation of that role model. Macho men tend to have macho sons, seductive women seductive daughters, and so on. The child tends to imitate even non-sex-role traits of the same-sex parent more than those of the other-sex parent.[81]

We could look at dozens of findings about parenting and personality development, but we have tarried long enough. It is time to see what develops when the child goes outside the home.

Social Development

"Go to the ant, thou sluggard; consider her ways and be wise." The formicine activity that Solomon (or whoever wrote Proverbs 6) would like us to emulate concerns gathering and putting by food in good times. But the social cooperation of ants is far more remarkable. From the moment they emerge from the larval stage, they are perfectly socialized, their minuscule nervous systems programmed to respond automatically to the chemical signals and touches of their fellows with appropriate social behaviors—food gathering, housekeeping, defensive combat, and the tending of larvae and the queen. We, in contrast, need fifteen to twenty years to become relatively socialized and even then are not done but must adapt our behavior as our roles change throughout life.

For well over half a century, developmentalists have been using a variety of techniques to gather evidence about the processes of human social development. Clipboard on knee and stopwatch in hand, they have observed babies and toddlers at home and in nurseries, preschoolers and schoolchildren on playgrounds and in classrooms; interviewed parents and plied them with questionnaires; recorded and analyzed volumes of child conversations; told children the beginnings of stories and asked what they thought happened next; designed hundreds of experimental situations to measure the level of social development at different ages; and calculated the correlations between blood hormone levels and sex-typed behavior.

From all this (and much more) they have gleaned a mass of findings. Some lend support to the psychoanalytic view of development, others to the social-learning view, others to the cognitive-developmental view, others to the cultural psychology view, and, finally, still others to the evolutionary psychology perspective. We need not sort them out but merely glance at a sample of the more interesting highlights.

Turn taking: The earliest lessons in social behavior are learned in the family, where in addition to the fundamental one of trusting another human being, infants learn the lesson, crucial to social relationships, of taking turns when communicating. Parents talk to the infant, wait until the infant responds with a sound or smile, and then talk again; the infant senses the pattern and, by the age of toddlerhood, even before uttering a word, will carry on with another toddler in turn-taking fashion. In the following bit of dialogue from a study of this process, Bernie, thirteen months old, has been watching Larry, fifteen months, mouthing a toy. He finally "speaks":

BERNIE: Da . . . da.
LARRY: (Laughs very slightly as he continues to look)
BERNIE: Da.
LARRY: (Laughs more heartily this time)

The same sequence is repeated five more times. Then Larry looks away and offers an adult a toy. Bernie pursues him.

BERNIE: (Waving both hands and looking directly at Larry) Da!
LARRY: (Looks back at Bernie and laughs again)

After nine more such interchanges, Bernie gives up and toddles away.[82]

Play: The developmentalists L. Alan Sroufe and Robert G. Cooper saw play as the "laboratory" where the child learns new skills and practices old ones.[83] Infants cannot play together; that requires emotional and cognitive skills that take two to three years to develop. Two toddlers, put close together, usually just stare at each other, watch each other play, or play side by side. But by three or thereabouts they begin to play together (not necessarily at the same game), and by five they play cooperatively.[84]

In play, toddlers and preschoolers learn the first lessons in self-control. They discover that aggression is not tolerated by adult onlookers, and may cause the other child to retaliate or refuse to be a playmate. They learn sharing, albeit with some difficulty. They develop preferences for certain other playmates which, by four, turn into friendships marked by mutuality and commitment.[85]

By three or four they begin learning rules of play and the rudiments of right and wrong in play with older children: "Three strikes and you're out"—and a tantrum won't get you any more, but may well get you expelled from the game.[86]

At about the same time they become more skillful at lying and concealing any facial expression or tone of voice that would give them away. This, one research team claims, is often a direct result of training by parents ("Remember to thank Grandmother for the sweater even though you wanted a toy").[87]

Role playing: Sroufe and Cooper have also called play the "social workshop" in which children try out roles alone and with other children. They often play Mommy-and-Daddy, Mommy-and-baby, Daddy-and-baby, doctor-and-patient, and victim-and-rescuer games. They particularly like playing the parent and ordering their own parent, in the child role, to eat up everything, or get washed, or go to bed. Whether one interprets role playing psychoanalytically, behavioristically, cognitively, or otherwise, it serves as training for social life. One study even found that the more social fantasy play a preschooler engages in, the greater the child's "social competence," as rated by teachers.[88]

Social competence: The elements of social competence are readiness to engage with peers, ability to sustain give-and-take with them, and popularity with or acceptance by them. Developmentalists measure popularity by such methods as asking the children in a particular play group which of their playmates they "especially like" and which they "don't especially like"; simply by subtracting the negative responses from the positive ones and adding up the scores, they get an index of each child's popularity in the group.

Self and group: In play groups, and even more in classrooms, close contact with other children spurs the development of the sense of psychological self (as distinguished from the physical sense of self of the toddler at the mirror). By eight, children begin to recognize that inwardly as well as outwardly they are different from others and that they are, in fact, unique.[89]

At the same time they become keenly aware and observant of group norms—for instance, the rules of games (choosing sides, taking turns, tossing a coin for first side at bat), and group loyalty ("telling on" a peer to parents or teachers is grounds for ostracism). Even at the elementary school level it is important to children to wear whatever is the fad in their group. As they near adolescence, the need to conform to peer-group norms—tastes in clothing, forms of speech, smoking, music, slang, drug use, sexual behavior—becomes extremely powerful. Adolescent peer-group norms and values differ among ethnic groups and social and economic levels, but the need to conform is omnipresent. After early adolescence, it wanes throughout the teen years.[90]

Sex-typed behavior: Fifty years ago, it was well established that throughout childhood, and particularly with the approach of adolescence, children increasingly exhibit behavior considered appropriate to their sex. In the 1960s, with the emergence of the women's liberation movement, many people believed that most sex-typed behavior would prove to be socially prescribed rather than inherent, and would shortly disappear. Much of it has; but some remains and apparently is likely to continue.

That may be due in part to biology. In the 1970s radioimmunoassay studies showed that hormone levels begin to rise at around seven—long before secondary sex characteristics appear and sex-typed behavior becomes exaggerated.[91] It is probably no coincidence that from seven on, few girls play games as rough as those of boys or get as dirty, and that until adolescence few boys are as conscious of their clothing and hair as most girls.

Yet despite all the changes that the women's movement sought to initiate four decades ago, the preadolescent accentuation of sex-typed behavior continued to reflect social learning of one's probable position as an adult in society. Even in 1990, most girls still saw their future in less optimistic terms than boys; that year, a nationwide poll of three thousand boys and girls in grades four to ten found that although in the elementary school years the self-esteem of girls was only slightly lower than that of boys, by middle school it declined markedly and continued at that level in high school. However, a decade later a meta-analysis of later self-esteem studies totaling forty-eight thousand young Americans showed only a minor advantage in self-esteem for males at all ages, a result its four female researchers said surprised them. They offered a number of explanations, but it may well be that the women's movement had slowly had an effect in our society.[92]

Empathy and altruism: In the 1960s, a number of psychologists became interested in "prosocial behavior"—all those cooperative forms of behavior which make social life possible. Many were social psychologists, but others were developmentalists who were intrigued by one form of prosocial behavior, altruism. Much prosocial behavior is selfishly motivated—we stop at red lights and pay our taxes not out of love of our fellow creatures but out of self-interest—but altruism is motivated by concern for the other person. The question the developmentalists found interesting was how such behavior arises, since it is often in conflict with the strongest of all motivations, self-interest.

In the past four decades hundreds of developmentalists have conducted many hundreds of studies of altruism, using the empirical methods mentioned earlier. The answer to the question "How does altruism develop?" seems to be that it results from a complex interplay of influences: the brain circuitry that tends to cause humans to feel distress at the sight of another human in distress, the model set for children by parental care, cultural values, the growth of the child's ability to imagine another person's feelings, social experience (helping someone else enables the helper to see himself or herself as a good sort of person and to be seen as such a person by others), and judgment based on real-world knowledge of the probable consequences for the person in distress of being helped or not being helped.[93]

A few salient findings:

— At ten months or a year, a child, seeing his mother in pain, will, as noted above, whimper or try to crawl away, but by fourteen months is more likely to pat, hug, or kiss her.
— Beyond eighteen months, a child will make efforts to comfort another child who is crying or will seek adult help.
— At two to four, a child will ask worried questions of another who is hurt or in pain, try to give reassurance or get help, and will seek to protect other children from harm (by warning them, for instance, of some danger).
— By seven, most children will go to the aid of a strange child who appears injured or in some difficulty.
— From seven on, children become more and more willing to give

money or toys to unknown poor children or to help others in trouble even when it means giving up something they want to do.

Developmentalists see a pattern in the data. Altruistic behavior seems to form in a series of fairly distinct stages, but there is no general agreement on how many there are or what they are. In one view there are four, in another five, and a six-stage model has been proposed by the longtime altruism expert Dennis L. Krebs and a colleague, Frank Van Hesteren, of Simon Fraser University, Burnaby, B.C.[94] Krebs and Van Hesteren's six stages are based on (1) obedience to the rules of authorities and the need for personal security and safety, (2) the maximizing of personal gain and quid pro quo decisions, (3) conformity to role and group expectations, and reciprocity and cooperation, (4) a sense of social responsibility, and behaving in accord with internalized values, (5) upholding the rights of other individuals and a willingness to make a sacrifice to benefit another, and (6) the upholding of universal moral values and identification with all humanity.

Moral development: Altruism is only one outcome of the development of the moral sense. Interest in that aspect of psychological development began in 1908, when the distinguished English psychologist William McDougall sketched a theory of the development of the moral sense based on his general knowledge of human psychology. In the 1920s Piaget began empirical investigation of the subject by observing children playing games and by telling them stories of little transgressions and asking their views of the proper punishment. (An example: In the first case, a boy fills his father's inkwell to be helpful but makes an inkblot on the tablecloth. In the second, a boy plays with his father's inkwell and makes an inkblot on the tablecloth. Should the punishment be the same in each case?)

Piaget concluded that moral behavior, within the context of game playing, develops between the ages of four and twelve, in three stages, changing from unquestioning acceptance of the rules handed down by parents or older children to a recognition that rules are made by people and can be changed by mutual agreement. Similarly, the basis on which an act (such as the spilling of ink) is judged right or wrong changes from the damage done to the individual's intentions.[95]

Piaget's *Moral Judgment of the Child,* appearing in English in 1932, inspired a rash of studies of moral development in America, but most were little more than tinkering and nitpicking. The next major advance, a landmark in the study of moral development, came three decades later and was the work of Lawrence Kohlberg of Harvard. He conceived a new method of measuring moral development and over a twenty-five-year span revised it, collected and analyzed data, and propounded a six-stage theory of moral development that became the classic in the field and the model that all others, ever since, have either emulated, modified, or reacted against.

Kohlberg would have made a good clergyman had he not found his calling as a moral-development psychologist. Earnest and thoughtful, warm and gently humorous, talkative and impassioned, he was profoundly concerned about ethical questions and the moral life. Indifferent to externals, he was the very archetype of the intellectual professor, his clothes baggy and rumpled, his hair disheveled, his briefcase badly scuffed and overfull, his glasses shoved up on his forehead and forgotten there.

The son of a well-to-do businessman, Kohlberg was born in 1927 in Bronxville, an affluent suburb of New York.[96] He attended the Phillips Academy in Andover and graduated as World War II ended. Then, instead of proceeding to college, he was driven by his conscience to become a merchant mariner so as to join a project that was smuggling shiploads of refugee European Jews through a British blockade into Palestine. The experience gave Kohlberg a lifelong interest in the question of when one is morally justified in disobeying the law and legitimate authority. It also gave him a lifelong disease: he was captured and briefly interned in a camp in Cyprus from which he soon escaped, but not before acquiring a parasitic intestinal infection that intermittently ravaged him throughout his life.

Kohlberg took his undergraduate and graduate degrees at the University of Chicago; psychology and philosophy (particularly ethics) were his twin passions. He read and admired Piaget's *Moral Judgment of the Child,* but in the spirit of American psychology felt that a sound theory of moral development should be based on data gathered by objective methods rather than Piaget's naturalistic observations. For his doctoral dissertation, therefore, he created a rating system (he later made it into a test) that he modified and used for the rest of his life and from which he derived his cognitive-developmental theory of the stages of moral development. The test consists of nine moral dilemmas, which the researcher presents, one at a time, to a subject. Each is followed by an interview comprising a long series of questions about what the subject considers the right and wrong thing to do in the case.

An example (the "Heinz dilemma"): In a European town, a woman is near death from a special kind of cancer; a new drug, discovered by a druggist in the town, might save her, but he is a profiteer and charges ten times what it costs him to make the medicine. Heinz, the woman's husband, can borrow only half the amount and pleads with the druggist to cut his price, but the druggist refuses. Heinz thinks about breaking in and stealing the drug to save his wife's life. Should he? Why or why not? Does he have a duty or obligation to steal the drug? Should he steal the drug for his wife if he doesn't love her? What if the person dying were a stranger—should Heinz steal the drug for him? It is against the law to steal; does that make it morally wrong? And so on, for a total of twenty-one questions.[97]

Kohlberg's original sample consisted of a cross-section of seventy-two Chicago-area males aged ten, thirteen, and sixteen, whom he tested every two to five years for the next three decades. After the initial testing, the differences in the answers given by the three age groups suggested to Kohlberg that the moral sense develops in distinct stages. Later, when his subjects were all older, he found them advancing through those stages much as he had expected them to. Here, in abbreviated form, and with a simplification of some of Kohlberg's difficult wording, are the stages of the theory and typical responses at each stage both in favor of and against Heinz's stealing the drug:

— Stage 1: Naïve moral realism; action is based on rules, motivation is the avoidance of punishment.
   PRO: If you let your wife die, you will get in trouble.
   CON: You shouldn't steal the drug because you'll be caught and sent to jail.
— Stage 2: Pragmatic morality; action is based on desire to maximize reward or benefit, minimize negative consequences to oneself.
   PRO: If you do get caught, you could give the drug back and you wouldn't get much of a sentence. It wouldn't bother you much to serve a short jail term if you have your wife when you get out.
   CON: If you steal the drug, your wife will probably die before you get out of jail, so it won't do you much good.
— Stage 3: Socially shared perspectives; action is based on anticipated approval or disapproval of others and actual or imagined guilt feelings.
   PRO: No one will think you're bad if you steal the drug, but if you

let your wife die, you'll never be able to look anybody in the face again.

CON: Everyone will think you're a criminal. After you steal it, you won't be able to face anyone again.

— Stage 4: Social system morality; action is based on anticipation of formal dishonor (not just disapproval) and guilt over harm done to others.

PRO: If you have any sense of honor, you won't let your wife die. You'll always feel guilty that you caused her death if you don't do your duty to her.

CON: You're desperate and you may not know you're doing wrong when you steal the drug. But you'll know it when you're sent to jail. You'll always feel guilt for your dishonesty and law-breaking.

— Stage 5: Human rights and social welfare morality; the perspective is that of a rational moral person considering the values and rights that ought to exist in a moral society; action is based on maintaining the respect of the community and one's self-respect.

PRO: You'd lose other people's respect if you don't steal it. If you let your wife die, it would be out of fear, not reasoning it out. You'd lose self-respect, and probably the respect of others.

CON: You'd lose standing and respect in the community and violate the law. You'd lose respect for yourself if you're carried away by emotion and forget the long-range point of view.

— Stage 6: Universal ethical principles; the perspective is the moral view all human beings should take toward one another and oneself; action is determined by equity, fairness, and concern about maintaining one's own moral principles.

PRO: If you don't steal the drug and let your wife die, you'd always condemn yourself for it afterward. You wouldn't be blamed and you would have lived up to the law but not to your own standards of conscience.

CON: If you stole the drug, you wouldn't be blamed by other people but you'd condemn yourself because you wouldn't have lived up to your own conscience and standards of honesty.[98]

Kohlberg had many devoted followers and admirers, particularly in the 1960s and 1970s, when his emphasis on justice and his elevation of Stage 6 decision making over the law made him a favorite with civil rights activists, Vietnam War protesters, and women's liberationists. But his test and theory have been attacked by many developmentalists on a number of grounds. Some say there is evidence that development is not always upward and sequential (some individuals skip stages in their development, others regress). Some say that moral thinking doesn't necessarily lead to moral behavior and that individuals often rank higher on the Kohlberg scale than their behavior warrants.[99] (Kohlberg insisted that most studies show a correlation between the stage of moral judgment and the actual behavior.) Carol Gilligan, an associate of Kohlberg's at Harvard, charged that his scale is biased in favor of men: women are likely to respond to moral dilemmas through caring and personal relationships, men by calling on abstract concepts like justice and equity; women therefore score lower on the Kohlberg scale, as if they were less morally developed than men.[100]

Kohlberg stoically endured these and other criticisms and assaults, some of which he agreed with (and changed his scoring accordingly), and some of which he quietly rebutted with new data and arguments. He also suffered the failure of two dreams he had devoted much time and energy to. One was a pilot project to raise the moral thinking of prisoners to Stage 4 through discussions of moral dilemmas, the other an attempt to do much the same thing with troubled teenagers. (The results were encouraging, but the project failed to spread beyond a few schools in Cambridge and New York.)

Added to these strains and disappointments was a severe recurrence of his chronic parasitic infection, causing him racking stomach and intestinal pain. Kohlberg, nearing sixty, became deeply depressed. He had discussed the moral dilemma of suicide with a close friend, to whom he said that if one had important responsibilities to others, one ought to go on. But the battle became too much for him. On January 17, 1987, his car was found parked beside a tidal marsh of Boston Harbor, and three months later his body washed up at Logan Airport. In a loving memorial tribute in the *Harvard Gazette* of December 15, 1989, three eminent psychologists (Carol Gilligan was one of them) summed up his contribution: "[Larry] almost single-handedly established moral development as a central concern of developmental psychology." He would have been gratified to hear that; what would have gratified him even more was that by the late 1990s, well over a hundred cross-cultural studies had confirmed that the development of moral reasoning in the stages set forth by Kohlberg does appear to be a cultural universal.[101]

Kohlberg revisionists do not disagree with his general theory so much as they modify it to accommodate their own empirical data.* Dennis Krebs is one who has done so. Although Krebs greatly admired Kohlberg, with whom he became acquainted at Harvard, he and colleague Kathy Denton published a study in 1990 demonstrating that whatever moral level people reason at when considering Kohlberg dilemmas, in situations in their own lives they are apt to reason at a lower level.[102]

The study is noteworthy because, unlike most other moral development research, it is based not only on a test but on a real-life situation. Kathy Denton went to bars, nightclubs, and parties and asked drinkers to take part in a study on "the effects of alcohol on judgment." Volunteers—she collected forty in all—were interviewed then and there about two Kohlberg dilemmas, answered questions about the morality of driving when impaired (should you drive at all if impaired? if you are impaired but don't feel drunk? if you take particular care?), and took a Breathalyzer test. In a follow-up session at the university, the same people were interviewed about two other Kohlberg dilemmas, and were asked how they got home the night of the first interview.

Denton and Krebs found that people scored higher in moral development at the university than they had when drinking; in fact, the higher their blood alcohol level at the first interview, the lower their moral judgment score. Worse, when they were sober they judged it morally wrong to drive when impaired and said that they themselves would not do so, but when they were drinking they took a less firm moral stand. Indeed, all but one drove home on the night they were first interviewed, no matter how impaired they were.

This is only one example of Krebs's effort to measure moral development realistically. For some years he and colleagues conducted research projects using everyday dilemmas, rather than Kohlberg's, to assess people's moral judgment. (Two examples: a business dilemma—whether or not to disclose information that would jeopardize selling one's business; a prosocial dilemma—a student with an appointment, coming up within a few minutes, to serve as a subject in a psychology experiment encounters another student having a bad drug trip who wants help.) In

*The evolutionary psychologist David Buss bypasses Kohlberg altogether, explaining the moral emotions as adaptive devices acquired by our ancestors, built into us, and evoked by environment and experience (Buss, 2004: 386–388).

several of the studies, volunteers were also interviewed about moral dilemmas in their own lives.

More recently, Krebs has been conducting research on moral reasoning and behavior, his latest work being a neo-Darwinian explanation of the origin of morality, including altruism.[103] Why would anyone spend so much time and effort in an area of psychology that is uncommonly contentious and, unlike mental testing, consumer psychology, and industrial psychology, offers no practical rewards? Developmentalists who concentrate on moral development have sundry motivations. Some were students in the idealistic 1960s and have been wedded to the study of prosocial behavior ever since; others are interested in morality from a religious viewpoint but find the psychological approach more realistic and productive; a handful of devoted moral development researchers are Holocaust survivors for whom the study of the humane side of humankind has been compensatory and healing.

And then there is Dennis Krebs, whose reasons are very special. Born in Vancouver in 1942, Krebs was the son of a carpenter and inventor of equipment to produce special effects on electric guitars. He was a top student and class president in junior high school and, though tall and skinny, a prize-winning amateur boxer. When he was fourteen, the family moved to the San Francisco area, where there were greater opportunities for his father in the electronic music business. The move was disastrous for young Dennis. In that milieu he rapidly changed from an upstanding youth to a juvenile delinquent. As he told the author of this book:

> I went from a place where I was a Golden Boy to a culture I didn't understand and where I didn't fit in and people made fun of everything about me — my clothing, my accent, my behavior. Having been a very good boxer, I very quickly got into fights and developed a reputation for fights — which generated *more* fights, most of which I won, and as a result of which I became part of a gang.

He drifted into a pattern of skipping school, fighting, and shoplifting. Eventually he was caught and served first one, then a second, term of some months in a juvenile detention home. Released on parole, he stayed out of trouble for a while. But one night, after too little sleep and too much wine, he drove fast and erratically and was stopped by the police. They released him, but he said goodbye with a vulgar curse and roared away. He ignored the police chasing him with flashing lights and sirens, and ended up against a telephone pole. He was unhurt but was sentenced to the county jail. In a spirit of total defiance, he picked the lock on the bars at the window, slid down a rope made of sheets, and hitchhiked his way to Oregon. There he vanished into a remote logging camp, where he worked hard, thought a lot about his life, and made a plan:

> I had gotten out of the context of delinquency and could see that I had to turn my life around. I decided to go back to Vancouver and go to the University of British Columbia. First I worked at a logging camp there for half a year, saving up enough money to start. Then I entered the university. By then I was in my twenties, a few years older than everyone else, and had this nagging sense of being behind, so I was an immensely intense and serious student, carrying extra courses and working part time.
>
> I graduated in 1967, at 25, as the top student in psychology honors. I'd applied to Harvard, where I wanted to go on to a Ph.D., but when I was accepted, it hit me that I'd live in constant fear that somebody would expose me as an escaped convict. So I decided to give myself up. I went back to the San Francisco area and turned myself in—considering what I had become, it was very sensational and made the front pages and all the TV news shows—and the upshot was that I was pardoned.

Krebs went off to Harvard, where he earned his master's in one year and his doctorate in two more—an almost unheard-of feat by that time and all the more remarkable since during part of his graduate years he had a half-time job as head teaching assistant of the introductory course in psychology and social relations at Harvard. He received his Ph.D. in 1970, was immediately hired by Harvard as an assistant professor and head of the undergraduate program, and stayed for four years. Then he moved to Simon Fraser University and has been a full professor there since 1982. At sixty-five, he is still tall, reasonably trim, and relatively youthful-looking; one would never take him for so hardworking a scholar with so strange a history.

Krebs's curriculum vitae has an impressive list of publications, most of them in the field of moral development. He has said of his career, "I think it's no accident that I became so interested in moral development." To which one must add that he has continued his own academic development by abandoning the Kohlberg approach after many years of working with it, devising a rather different model, and, as mentioned above, elaborating his own Darwinian explanation of the matter.

Development from A to Z

The latest trend in developmental psychology was foretold nearly four centuries ago by that most perceptive of lay psychologists, William Shakespeare. Unlike Piaget and his followers, who see development as substantially complete by adolescence or early adulthood, Shakespeare offered a whole-life and less idealized picture in the famous "All the world's a stage" soliloquy in *As You Like It,* in which Jaques sets out the "seven ages" of man, starting with "the infant, / Mewling and puking in the nurse's arms" and ending with "second childishness, and mere oblivion, / Sans teeth, sans eyes, sans taste, sans everything."

As early as the 1920s, some psychologists began to think of development as continuing throughout life; it was then that several major longitudinal studies, described earlier, were begun. But their goal was primarily to measure changes over the years rather than to elucidate the processes that produced those changes. In 1950, however, the psychoanalyst and developmentalist Erik Erikson offered the first detailed process model of development throughout life, based on his analysis of the major psychosocial challenges confronting the individual at each of eight stages of life and the changes those challenges bring about.

Erikson (1902–1994), though he never earned a higher degree, was one of the most highly respected developmentalists in this country for over half a century and held professorships at several illustrious universities.[104] He was born of Danish parents; his Protestant father left his Jewish mother before Erik was born, and she later married a German-Jewish pediatrician. Erik grew up doubly an outsider, scorned as a Jew in school but mocked as a goy in the synagogue because of his blond hair and blue eyes. The experience gave him a special interest in the struggle to achieve identity in the course of development.

In his youth he studied art and for a few years worked as an artist, but during a visit to Rome, poring over the works of Michelangelo and thinking of his own, he suffered such feelings of inferiority and anxiety that he went to Vienna to be psychoanalyzed by Anna Freud. The result was not only relief from the anxiety but a new goal: he studied psychoanalysis and became a lay analyst.

In 1933, when the Nazis achieved power in Germany, Erikson and his wife immigrated first to Denmark and then to America. He practiced psychoanalysis, taught at Harvard, Yale, and the University of Chicago (eventually returning to Harvard), took part in longitudinal research at Berkeley, and spent some time with anthropologists investigating two

Native American cultures. From his own diverse experiences he perceived human development as a lifelong process in which the individual undergoes a series of psychological struggles, each characteristic of a stage of life, and each resolved by the attainment of new knowledge and development of the personality.

The central issue in Stage 1, infancy, is the conflict between the basic attitudes of trust and mistrust. Through the relationship with loving parents the infant resolves the crisis, learning to appreciate interdependence and relatedness, and acquiring trust. In Stage 2, early childhood, the struggle is between the child's need for a sense of autonomy versus a sense of doubt and shame. If allowed experiences of free choice and self-control under proper guidance, the child resolves the crisis by learning the importance of rules and acquiring self-control or will. So it goes, each stage presenting a new crisis, adding to the personality, building ever further, and, if passage through each stage is successful, achieving ever greater integration of the self with society.

Here is Erikson's life-span view in tabular form. Each stage is a higher level of development than the preceding one:[105]

Stage: conflict	Successful resolution
1. Infancy: basic trust vs. basic mistrust	Trust
2. Early childhood: autonomy vs. shame	Will power and independence
3. Play age: initiative vs. guilt	Purpose
4. School age (six to ten or so): industry vs. inferiority	Competency
5. Adolescence: identity vs. role confusion	Sense of self
6. Early adulthood: intimacy vs. isolation	Love
7. Middle adulthood: generativity vs. stagnation	Caring for others; productiveness
8. Old age: ego integrity vs. despair	Wisdom; a sense of integrity strong enough to withstand physical disintegration

Failure to pass through any stage successfully blocks normal healthful development. A neglected or unloved infant, for instance, may never learn to trust anyone, a lack that will interfere with or distort all the later stages of development. A young adolescent whose parents keep him or her too tightly bound to them may fail to pass successfully through Stage 5 and achieve an independent identity; the outcomes are such failures as "Momma's boy," at one extreme, and the rebellious delinquent at the other.

Erikson's theory played a major part in the shift in developmental psychology to the life-span perspective. Another influence in that shift was the mass of life-span data produced by the several major longitudinal studies that had been under way for decades. A third was the passage of the post–World War II "baby boom" generation from childhood to young and middle adulthood, and the concomitant increase in the over-sixty-five segment of the population, both of which forced social scientists and legislators to pay attention to the changes and problems characteristic of middle and old age.

The shift to the life-span view began slowly in the 1950s, picked up in the 1960s, and became a definite trend in the 1970s. In that decade, the psychiatrist Roger L. Gould of the UCLA School of Medicine outlined a theory of adult life-stage development in several articles, the psychoanalyst George E. Vaillant of Dartmouth did likewise in *Adaptation to Life*, the psychologist Daniel J. Levinson of Yale did so in *The Seasons of a Man's Life*; and the writer Gail Sheehy brought the message to a large popular audience with her best-selling *Passages: Predictable Crises of Adult Life*. By 1980, although most research in developmental psychology still dealt with the early years of life, the view that development continues in stages throughout life had become the dominant paradigm of developmental psychology and the common opinion of the literate laity.[106]

Unlike Erikson's view, current life-span developmentalism is pluralistic and deals with all aspects of development, not just the psychosocial. It explains the stage-by-stage changes in personality, social relations, and cognition in terms of biological influences, age-related psychological changes, and the social and environmental influences that are associated with particular ages as well as those which can occur at any age.[107] Moreover, unlike Erikson's optimistic view, in which normal and healthy development is portrayed as ever onward and upward, the prevailing tone of most life-span developmentalism in recent years is empirical and grittily realistic. It sees development beyond the adult stage as a series of changes rather than continuing upward movement, as adaptation to changing realities rather than progress.

Not that today's life-span developmentalism is pessimistic; indeed, some of its findings have been heartening. A few instances:

Adolescence: Many of the new data about the adolescent stage deal with familiar topics: sexual behavior, social development, the struggle to achieve emancipation from parental control, problems with self-esteem and anxiety. But contrary to long-standing opinion that adolescence is a period of intense turmoil, several research programs have found that for the majority of adolescents it is not. One study reported that, while 11 percent of young adolescents have serious chronic difficulties and 32 percent intermittent and probably situational difficulties, 57 percent experience "basically positive, healthy development during early adolescence."[108] And while drug and alcohol use, smoking, and sexual behavior increase during adolescence and create serious difficulties for some adolescents, one research team said that more often these behaviors are "purposive, self-regulating, and aimed at coping with problems of development.[109] A summary of research held that few adolescents experience the turmoil and unpredictable behavior so often ascribed to them.[110]

Adult "crises": The focus of adult development research has been on the strenuous transitions that men and women must make, particularly at about forty to forty-five, when they may see their careers topping out, dreams fading, children distancing themselves from the family, and physical youthfulness slipping away. It was Sheehy, the popularizer, who called them "predictable crises"; most researchers talked instead of painful and strenuous "transitional periods."

One team found that only some men have a midlife crisis, and that most either thrive or muddle through. Others have found that the adult personality is not as rigid and unchanging, and wholly determined by childhood experiences, as had formerly been thought; many adults can adapt sufficiently to make successful transitions to new life circumstances. Paul Mussen and his co-authors said in *Psychological Development: A Life-Span Approach*, "Perhaps the most important result of the research on personality and aging is a renewed appreciation of the potential for personality change at any point in the life span." Another research team has said that most people do cope with the inevitable challenges of the passing years, especially if they have a can-do attitude.[111]

Aging: Developmental change in the elderly has been a recognized field of research for two generations and a major one for at least two decades. Much of it has focused on the psychological changes brought about by declining physical abilities, chronic disease, the slowing down of mental functions, retirement, widowhood, the deaths of friends, and other losses. To such changes, it was widely believed, on the basis of aging studies conducted in Kansas City in the late 1950s, the common and beneficial adaptation was "disengagement"—minimizing stress by abandoning stressful roles and voluntarily withdrawing into a "subculture of aging." But a reanalysis of the Kansas City data by the psychologist Robert J. Havighurst and his colleagues, and a twenty-five-year longitudinal study of aging at Duke University, showed that not to be the case. Some people choose to disengage and others are forced by ill health to do so, but most aging people maintain their social activities and adapt to the loss of friends and mates by expanding their contacts with younger people, particularly family members. Moreover, they are more content and psychologically healthier than those who disengage. This remains the dominant view of successful aging, which is now thought to involve the selection of the most appropriate goals for oneself, the directing of one's efforts to areas of the highest priority, and the active seeking of ways to compensate for the losses that time brings.[112]

In late middle age and beyond, many people complain of failing memory, and recent studies do show a gradual decline in memory in most people after fifty. Although this alarms many of those who experience it, it is normal and does not usually indicate Alzheimer's disease, remains minor until the eighties, and in most cases can be ameliorated by the use of mnemonics and other techniques and by the elimination of overmedication.

Developmental psychology may seem now to be fully mature. It encompasses the entire life of the human being, takes a broad view of the causes of change, and has sound evidence that development proceeds stage by stage.

For all that, the field is in a disorderly condition. There is not one stage theory; there are at least a dozen major and some minor ones. They agree on certain points, disagree on others. Life-span developmental psychology is not actually a theory so much as a way of looking at the subject, an approach in which different theories can be integrated or considered simultaneously. It may never be more than that; as noted more than once during this chapter, developmental psychology is so vast a field that it may require a cluster of theories rather than one encompassing theory.

This is not to discredit developmental psychology; physics, the queen of the natural sciences, suffers the same limitation. Many physicists are convinced that there is a single theory that can account for the four forces of physics (the strong force within atomic nuclei, the weak force holding certain particles together, electromagnetic force, and gravitation), but nobody has been able to formulate one. There may be none. Or perhaps any unifying explanation is beyond the range of the mind's eye even as radio waves are invisible to the eye itself. When psychology was the province of philosophers, theories seemed to explain everything; when it became a science, overarching theories were harder to construct. Certainly, that is the case with developmental psychology.

THIRTEEN

The Social
Psychologists

No Man's Land

Q: What busy and productive field of modern psychology has no clear-cut identity and not even a generally accepted definition?

A: Social psychology. It is less a field than a no man's land between psychology and sociology, overlapping each and also impinging on anthropology, criminology, several other social sciences, and neuroscience. Ever since the emergence of social psychology, its practitioners have had trouble agreeing on what it is. Psychologists define it one way, sociologists another,* and most textbook writers, seeking to accommodate both views and to cover the field's entire gallimaufry of topics, offer nebulous definitions that say everything and nothing. An example: "[Social psychology is] the scientific study of the personal and situational factors that affect individual social behavior." A better definition: "Social psychology is the study of the ways in which thoughts, feelings, perceptions, motives, and behavior are influenced by interactions and transactions between people."[1] Better, but it still leaves one with a multiform and even bewildering impression of the field. As Brenda Major, president in 2006 of the Society for Personality and Social Psychology, admits, "It's hard to pigeonhole social psychology. In cognitive neuroscience you can say, 'I study the brain,' but in social psychology you can't say anything clear-cut like that."

---

*We will concern ourselves only with the psychological version of social psychology.

The problem is that social psychology has no unifying concept; it did not develop from the seed of a theoretical construct (as did behaviorism and Gestalt psychology) but grew like crabgrass in uncultivated regions of the social sciences. In 1965, Roger Brown of Harvard, in the introduction to his well-known social psychology textbook, noted that he could list the subjects generally considered to belong to social psychology but could see no common denominator among them:

> I myself cannot find any single attribute or any combination of attributes that will clearly distinguish the topics of social psychology from topics that remain within general experimental psychology or sociology or anthropology or linguistics. Roughly speaking, of course, social psychology is concerned with the mental processes (or behavior) of persons insofar as these are determined by past or present interaction with other persons, but this *is* rough and it is not a definition that excludes very much.[2]

More than two decades later, in his second version of the book, Brown did not bother to say any of this but simply began, without a definition, *in medias res*. A good idea; let us do so, too. Here, as a first dip into the field, is a handful of famous examples of sociopsychological research:

An undergraduate volunteer—call him U.V.—arrives at a laboratory in the psychology building to take part in an experiment in "visual perception"; six other volunteers are there already. The researcher says the experiment has to do with the discrimination of the length of lines. At the front of the room is a card with a single vertical line several inches long (the standard), and to the right, on another card, three more lines, numbered 1, 2, and 3. The volunteers are to say which of the numbered lines is the same length as the standard. U.V. can easily see that 2 matches the standard and that 1 and 3 are both shorter. The other volunteers announce their choices, each speaking up for 2, as does U.V. in his turn. The experimenter changes the cards, and the procedure is repeated, with similar results.

But with the next card, the first volunteer says, "One," although to U.V.'s eye 1 is clearly longer than the standard. As each of the other volunteers, in turn, inexplicably says the same thing, U.V. becomes more disconcerted. By the time it is his turn, he is squirming, hesitant, nervous, and a little disoriented, and does not know what to say. When he, and others who are subjected to the same experience, do finally speak up, 37 percent of the time they go along with the majority and name as the matching line one they think is either shorter or longer than the standard.

In reality, only one person present at each session—in this case, U.V.—is an experimental subject; the other supposed volunteers are accomplices of Solomon Asch, the researcher, who has instructed them to name the wrong lines on certain trials. The aim of this classic experiment, conducted in the early 1950s, was to determine the conditions producing conformity—the tendency to yield to actual or imagined pressure to agree with the majority view of one's group. Research on conformity has continued ever since and many experiments have identified its various causes, among them the desire to be correct (if others all agree, maybe they're right) and the wish not to be considered a dissident or "oddball."[3]

Two student volunteers, after spending some time discussing and performing a routine clerical chore together, are asked by the experimenter to play a game called the Prisoner's Dilemma. Its premise:

Two suspects are taken into custody and separated. The district attorney is certain that together they committed a crime but he has insufficient evidence to convict them. He tells each one that if neither confesses, he can convict them on a lesser charge and each will get a year in prison. But if one confesses and the other does not, the confessing one will get special treatment (only half a year in prison) and the other the most severe treatment possible—almost surely a twenty-year sentence. Finally, if both confess, he will ask for lenient sentencing and each will get eight years.

Since Prisoner 1 cannot reach Prisoner 2 to agree on a plan, he thinks through the possibilities. If he confesses and 2 does not, he (1) will get only six months, the best possible result for himself, and 2 will get twenty years, the worst outcome for him. But 1 recognizes that it is risky to take that chance; if he and 2 both own up, each will get eight years. Perhaps he'd be better off not confessing. If he doesn't, and 2 also doesn't, each gets one year, not a bad outcome. But suppose he doesn't and 2 *does*— then 2 will get a mere six months and he a terrible twenty years.

Clearly, rational thinking cannot yield the best answer for either prisoner unless each trusts the other to do what is best for both. If one of them chooses on the basis of fear or of greed, both will lose. Yet it makes no sense to choose on the basis of what is best for both unless each is certain that the other will do likewise. And so the volunteers play, with any of a number of results, depending on the conditions and instructions laid down by the researcher. (Achieving what is best for both is only sometimes the outcome.)

The Prisoner's Dilemma has been used, in various forms, by many researchers for five decades to study trust, cooperation, and the conditions that create them and their opposites.[4]

A college student rings the doorbells of a number of homes in Palo Alto, California, introduces himself as a representative of Citizens for Safe Driving, and makes a preposterous request: permission to place on the front lawn a billboard bearing the message DRIVE CAREFULLY (preposterous because a photograph he produces shows a lovely house partly obscured by a huge, poorly lettered sign). Not surprisingly, most of the residents refuse. But some agree. Why do they? Because for them this was not the first request. Two weeks earlier, a different student, claiming to be a volunteer with the Community Committee for Traffic Safety, had asked them to display a neatly lettered three-inch-square sign reading BE A SAFE DRIVER, and they had agreed to this innocuous request. Of the residents who had not been softened up by the previous modest request, only 17 percent said yes to the billboard; of those who had previously agreed to display the three-inch sign, 55 percent did so.

The experiment, carried out in 1966, was the first of many to explore the foot-in-the-door technique, well known to fund raisers, of asking for a very small contribution and later returning to ask for a much larger one. The researchers, however, were not interested in raising funds or in safe driving but in the reasons that this method of persuasion works. They concluded that the people who agree to a first small request see themselves, in consequence, as helpful and civic-minded, and that this self-perception makes them more likely to help the next time, when the request is for something much larger. (The foot-in-the-door technique is still being used in experiments exploring the subtleties of motivation.)[5]

The staff of a large mental hospital says that Mr. X is schizophrenic. A well-dressed middle-aged man, he came in complaining of hearing voices; he told the admitting psychiatrist that they were unclear but that "as far as I can tell, they were saying 'empty,' 'hollow,' and 'thud.' " Since being admitted, he has said nothing more about the voices and has behaved normally, but the staff continues to consider him mentally ill. The nurses even make note in his chart of one frequent abnormal activity: "Patient engages in writing behavior." Several of his fellow inmates see him differently; as one of them says, "You're not crazy. You're a journalist or a professor. You're checking up on the hospital."

The patients are right, the staff wrong. In this 1973 study of how staffs of mental hospitals interact with their patients, a professor of psychology and seven research assistants got themselves admitted to twelve East Coast and West Coast hospitals by using the story about voices and, once they had been admitted, acting normally. As patients, they covertly observed staff attitudes and actions toward patients that they would never have had the chance to witness had they been identified as researchers. Among their disturbing findings:

— Once staff members had identified a patient as schizophrenic, they either failed to see, or misinterpreted, everyday evidence that he was sane. On the average, it took the pseudo-patients nineteen days of totally normal behavior to get themselves released.
— The staff, having come to think of the pseudo-patients as schizophrenic, spent as little time as possible in contact with them. Typically, they would react to a patient's direct question by ignoring it and moving on, eyes averted.
— Staff members often went about their work or talked to each other as if the patients were not present. As David Rosenhan, the senior author of the study, wrote: "Depersonalization reached such proportions that pseudo-patients had the sense that they were invisible or at least unworthy of account."[6]

In a campus psychological laboratory, six male sophomores sit in separate cubicles, each wearing a headset. Participant A, through his, hears the researcher say that at the countdown, participants A and D are to shout "RAH!" as loudly as possible, holding it for a few seconds. After the first round, A hears that now he alone is to shout at the countdown; next, that all six are to shout; and so on. Part of the time, these instructions are transmitted to all six students, but part of the time one or another is fed false instructions. Participant A, for instance, may be told that all six are to shout, although, in fact, all the others hear messages telling them not to. To conceal what is happening, all six hear recorded shouting over their headsets during each trial. (The experiment, like many others in social psychology, would not even have been conceived of before the development of modern communications equipment.)

All this bamboozlement has a serious purpose: it is part of a series of studies of "social loafing," the tendency to do less than one's best in group efforts unless one's output is identifiable and known to the others. The evidence in this case is the measured volume of each student's shouting (each student is separately miked). When a student believes he and one other are shouting together, he shouts, on average, only 82 percent as loudly as when he thinks he alone is shouting. And when he thinks all six are shouting, his average output drops to 74 percent of his solo performance. In their report the research team concludes, "A clear potential exists in human nature for social loafing. We suspect that the effects of social loafing have far-reaching and profound consequences . . . [It] can be regarded as a kind of social disease." A number of recent studies have explored ways to combat the disease by such means as instilling a sense of importance and responsibility in each person, making it clear that individual as well as group performance will be evaluated, and so on.[7]

No such sampling, however varied, can do justice to the range of subjects and research methods of social psychology, but perhaps these specimens give some idea of what the field is about—or at least what it is not about. It is not about what goes on strictly within one's head, as in Cartesian, Jamesian, or Freudian introspection, nor is it about large sociological phenomena, like stratification, social organization, and social institutions.

It *is* about everything in between—whatever an individual thinks or does as a result of what other individuals think or do, or what the first person *thinks* the others are thinking or doing. As Gordon Allport wrote many years ago, social psychology is "an attempt to understand and explain how the thought, feeling, and behavior of individuals are influenced by the actual, imagined, or implied presence of others."[8] That's less a definition than a thumbnail description, but having looked at some examples, we begin to see what he meant and to appreciate the difficulty of putting it into words.

A Case of Multiple Fatherhood

Social psychology is both a recent area of knowledge and an ancient one. It emerged in its modern form more than eighty years ago and did not catch on until the 1950s, but philosophers and protopsychologists had long been constructing theories about how our interactions with others affect our mental life and, conversely, how our mental processes and personality affect our social behavior. One could make the case, according to Allport, that Plato was the founder of social psychology, or if not he, then Aristotle, or if not he, then any of a number of later political philosophers such as Hobbes and Bentham, although what all these ancestors contributed was thoughtful musing, not science.[9] The claims of paternity grow more numerous but equally shaky in the nineteenth and early twentieth centuries: Auguste Comte, Herbert Spencer, Émile Durkheim, the American sociologists Charles Horton Cooley, William Sumner, and many others all wrote about social psychological issues, but their work was still largely armchair philosophizing, not empirical science.

In 1897, however, an American psychologist named Norman Triplett conducted the first empirical test of a commonsense sociopsychological hypothesis. He had read that bicycle racers reach higher top speeds when paced by others than when cycling alone, and it occurred to him that perhaps it is generally true that an individual's performance is affected by the presence of others. To test his hypothesis, he had children of ten and twelve wind fishing reels alone and in pairs (but did not tell them what he was looking for) and found that many of them did indeed wind faster when another child was present.[10]

Triplett did more than verify his hypothesis; he created a crude model of social psychological investigation. His method, an experiment that simulates a real-world situation, conceals from the volunteers what the researcher is looking for, and compares the effects of the presence and absence of a variable (in this case, observers), became the dominant mode of social psychological research. Moreover, his topic, "social facilitation" (the positive effect of observers on an individual's performance), remained the major problem—Allport even said the only one—studied by social psychologists for three decades.

(The basic problem—the "situational norm" induced by the presence of some variable in the environment—has continued to be of interest to the present. In studies reported in 2003, a research team found that participants who were told they would be visiting a library and then were asked to read words on a screen spoke softly; when told they would be visiting a railroad station, they spoke more loudly. When participants expected to be eating in a fancy restaurant, they ate more politely than usual, even biting a biscuit more neatly than other participants who did not expect to be going to the fancy restaurant.[11])

Social psychology gained a foothold in psychology in 1924 with the publication of Floyd Allport's *Social Psychology*, a book that became widely used in social psychology classes at American universities. Either because of that book or a spontaneous expansion of interest, social psychology research caught on. By the 1930s the new discipline was clearly distinguished from its sociological origins when *Experimental Social Psychology* by Gardner and Lois Barclay Murphy and *Handbook of Social Psychology* by Carl Murchison, both defined it as an experimental discipline separate from the more naturalistic observational techniques used in sociology.

Up to this point, social facilitation (Triplett's interest) had remained the central topic of social psychology research, but the field expanded significantly in the 1930s when Muzafer Sherif (1906–1988), a Turk who took graduate training in psychology at Harvard and Columbia, studied the influence of other people on one's judgment, not on one's performance. Sherif had his subjects, one at a time, sit in a dark room, stare at a tiny light, and tell him when it started to move and how far it moved. (They were unaware that the apparent movement is a common visual illusion.) Sherif found that each person, when tested alone, had a characteristic impression of how far the light moved, but when exposed to the opinions of others tended to be swayed by the group norm.[12] His experiments strikingly showed the vulnerability of individual judgment to social opinion and pointed the way for hundreds of conformity experiments in the following two decades. (Asch's famous length-of-lines conformity experiment, described above, came nearly twenty years later.)

An even more significant expansion of the domain of social psychology was a result of the rise of Nazism in Germany. A number of Jewish psychologists immigrated to America in the 1930s, among them some who had broader views of social psychology than those in the American tradition. Among the refugees was the man generally acknowledged to be the real father of the field, Kurt Lewin, of whom we heard earlier; he was the Gestaltist at the University of Berlin whose graduate student, Bluma Zeigarnik, conducted an experiment to test his hypothesis that uncompleted tasks are remembered better than completed ones. (He was right.) Although Lewin's name never became familiar to the public and is unknown today except to psychologists and psychology students, Edward Chase Tolman said of him after his death in 1947:

> Freud the clinician and Lewin the experimentalist—these are the two men whose names will stand out before all others in the history of our psychological era. For it is their contrasting but complementary insights which first made psychology a science applicable to real human beings and real human society.[13]

Lewin, heavily bespectacled and scholarly looking, was a rarity: a genius who was extremely sociable and friendly. He loved and encouraged impassioned, free-wheeling group discussions of psychological problems with colleagues or graduate students; at such times his mind was an intellectual flintstone that cast off showers of sparks—hypotheses that he freely handed to others and ideas for intriguing experiments that he often was happy to have them carry out and take credit for.

Lewin was born in 1890 in a village in Posen (then part of Prussia, today part of Poland), where his family ran a small general store.[14] He did poorly in school and showed no sign of intellectual gifts, perhaps because of the anti-Semitism of his schoolmates, but when he was fifteen his family moved to Berlin, and there he blossomed intellectually, became interested in psychology, and eventually earned a doctorate at the University of Berlin. Much of the course work in psychology, however, was in the Wundtian tradition. Lewin found the problems it dealt with petty, dull, and yielding no understanding of human nature, and he hungered for a more meaningful kind of psychology. Shortly after he returned to the university from military service in World War I, Köhler became head of the institute and Wertheimer a faculty member, and Lewin found what he was looking for in the form of Gestalt theory.

His early Gestalt studies dealt with motivation and aspiration, but he soon moved on to apply Gestalt theory to social issues. Lewin conceived of social behavior in terms of "field theory," a way of visualizing the total Gestalt of forces that affect a person's social behavior. Each person, in this view, is surrounded by a "life space" or dynamic field of forces within which his or her needs and purposes interact with the influences of the environment. Social behavior can be schematized in terms of the tension and interplay of these forces and of the individual's tendency to maintain equilibrium among them or to restore equilibrium when it has been disturbed.[15]

To portray these interactions, Lewin was forever drawing "Jordan curves"—ovals representing life spaces—on blackboards, scraps of paper, in the dust, or in the snow, and diagramming within them the push and pull of the forces in social situations. His students at Berlin called the ovals "Lewin's eggs"; later, his students at MIT called them "Lewin's bathtubs"; still later those at the University of Iowa called them "Lewin's potatoes." Whether eggs, bathtubs, or potatoes, they pictured the processes taking place within the small, face-to-face group, the segment of reality that Lewin saw as the territory of social psychology.

Although students at Berlin flocked to Lewin's lectures and research programs, like many another Jewish scholar he made little progress up the academic ladder. But his brilliant writing about field theory, particularly as applied to interpersonal conflicts and child development, brought him an invitation in 1929 to lecture at Yale and another in 1932 to spend six months as a visiting professor at Stanford. In 1933, shortly after Hitler became chancellor of Germany, Lewin resigned from the University of Berlin and with the help of American colleagues got an interim appointment at Cornell and later a permanent one at the University of Iowa.

In 1944, realizing a long-held ambition, he set up his own social psychology institute, the Research Center for Group Dynamics, at the Massachusetts Institute of Technology, and there assembled a first-rate staff and a group of top-notch students. It became the primary training center for mainstream American social psychology. In 1947, only three years later, Lewin, then fifty-seven, died of a heart attack; the Research Center for Group Dynamics soon moved to the University of Michigan, and there and elsewhere his former students continued to promulgate his ideas and methods.

Lewin's boldly imaginative experimental style, going far beyond that of earlier social psychologists, became the most salient characteristic of the field. A study inspired by his experience of Nazi dictatorship and passionate admiration of American democracy illustrates the point. To explore the effects of autocratic and democratic leadership on people, Lewin and two of his graduate students, Ronald Lippitt and Ralph White, created a number of clubs for eleven-year-old boys. They supplied each club with an adult leader to help with crafts, games, and other activities, and had each leader adopt one of three styles: autocratic, democratic, or laissez-faire. The boys in groups with autocratic leaders soon became either hostile or passive, those with democratic leaders became friendly and cooperative, and those with laissez-faire leaders became friendly but apathetic and disinclined to get things done. Lewin was

unabashedly proud of the results, which confirmed his belief in the dele-
terious effect of autocratic leadership and the salutary effect of democratic leadership on human behavior.[16]

It was topics and experiments like this that account for Lewin's powerful impact on social psychology. (Field theory enabled him to conceive
of such research, but it never became central to the discipline.) Leon
Festinger (1919–1989), Lewin's student, colleague, and intellectual
heir, has said that Lewin's major contribution was twofold. One part was
his gifted choice of interesting or important problems; it was largely
through him that social psychology began exploring group cohesive-
ness, group decision making, authoritarian versus democratic leadership, techniques of attitude change, and conflict resolution. The other
part was his "insistence on trying to create, in the laboratory, powerful
social situations that made big differences" and his extraordinary inven-
tiveness of ways to do so.[17]

Despite Lewin's catalytic influence, for some years social psychology
gained a foothold only in a handful of large metropolitan universities.
Elsewhere, behaviorism was still king, and its adherents found social
psychology too concerned with mental processes to be acceptable. But
during World War II the needs of the military gave rise to several important social-psychological studies of soldier morale and behavior, and in
the postwar years a number of social influences and problems brought
about a surge of interest in the young discipline. Among them: the
increasing mobility of the American population and the many social
and interpersonal problems that it created; the search in the expanding
business world for new and more persuasive sales techniques; the effort
by social scientists to comprehend Nazi genocide and, more broadly,
the sources and control of aggression; the gradual return of cognitivism
to psychology; the rise of Senator McCarthy, which stimulated interest
in the phenomenon of conformity; and incessant international negotiations, which turned social psychologists' attention to group dynamics
and bargaining theory.

During the 1950s, social psychology expanded explosively and soon
was offered by virtually every university psychology department in the
United States. The rebelliousness of American youth in the 1960s, the
disruptions caused by the Vietnam War, the activism of blacks, women,
and gays, and other social problems made it an increasingly pertinent
field of study. All too often, however, when businessmen and legislators

turned to social psychologists for answers, they were exasperated at hearing that social psychologists were only beginning their work and had no ready answers. Yet it was not long before the data the researchers were gathering did have profound effects on American society, as a single example attests. The United States Supreme Court, in its 1954 *Brown* v. *Board of Education* decision, said that the evidence of "modern authority" showed that Negro children were harmed by segregated education, and cited numerous social-psychological studies demonstrating that segregated schooling, even if equal, left Negro children with a sense of inferiority, low self-esteem, and hostility toward themselves. Lewin, had he been alive, would surely have been proud of his offspring.

Closed Cases

Many social psychologists feel that their field is unusually subject to fads; many "hot topics" have come and gone in its fifty-odd years as a leading discipline, and certain subjects that once seemed the very essence of social psychology have been relegated to storage.

The main reason, however, is not faddism so much as the nature of social psychology. In most other sciences knowledge about a particular group of phenomena accumulates and deepens, but social psychology deals with a range of problems that have little in common and do not add up. In consequence, many a phenomenon has captured the attention of social psychologists, been intensively studied, and essentially explained. When only details remain to be filled in, for all intents and purposes the file is marked "Solved" and the case closed.[18]

Herewith four famous closed cases.

Cognitive Dissonance

This was without question the most influential theory in social psychology and the dominating subject in the field's journals from the late 1950s to the early 1970s. Thereafter it slowly lost its position as the center of attention and today is an accepted body of knowledge but no longer an area of active research, although a number of recent studies apply the theory to special problems.

Cognitive dissonance theory says that the human being feels tension and discomfort when holding inconsistent ideas (for instance, "So-and-so is a windbag and a bore" but "I need So-and-so as a friend and ally"), and will seek ways to decrease that dissonance ("So-and-so isn't so bad, once you get to know him," or "I don't really need him; I can get along fine without him").

In the 1930s, Lewin had come close to the subject when he explored how a person's attitudes are changed by his or her being a member of a group that reaches a decision, and how such a person will tend to hold fast to that decision, ignoring later information that conflicts with it. Lewin's student Leon Festinger carried this line of inquiry further and developed the theory of cognitive dissonance.[19]

As a young graduate student, Festinger had gone to the University of Iowa in 1939 expressly to study under Lewin—not social psychology, in which he had no interest, but Lewin's early work on motivation and aspiration. Under Lewin's spell, however, he was drawn into social psychology and in 1945 became an assistant professor at Lewin's new Research Center for Group Dynamics at MIT.

For some years after Lewin's death, Festinger, who moved to the University of Minnesota, wore Lewin's mantle, thanks to his fine intellect, the excitement he brought to teaching, and the daring with which he undertook research that overstepped the boundaries of propriety to obtain otherwise unavailable data. In part he was emulating Lewin's boldness, but in part expressing his own personality. A peppery fellow of moderate size and a lover of cribbage and chess, both of which he played with fierce competitiveness, Festinger had the tough, brash, aggressive spirit so often found in men who grew up between the world wars on the tempestuous Lower East Side of New York.

A prime instance of Festinger's boldness and unconventionality was a research project in which he and two young colleagues, Henry W. Riecken and Stanley Schachter (who had been his student at MIT), acted as undercover agents for seven weeks. They had read a newspaper story, in September 1954, about a Mrs. Marian Keech (not her real name), a housewife in a town not far from Minneapolis, who claimed that for nearly a year she had been receiving messages from superior beings she identified as the Guardians on the planet Clarion. (The messages came in the form of automatic writing that she produced while in a trance.) She revealed to the press that on December 21, according to the Guardians, a great flood would cover the northern hemisphere, and all who lived there, except a chosen few, would perish.

Festinger, who was already working out his theory, and his junior colleagues saw a golden opportunity to study cognitive dissonance at first hand. As they stated their hypothesis in *When Prophecy Fails*, the report they published in 1956:

> Suppose an individual believes something with his whole heart; suppose further that he has a commitment to this belief, that he has taken irrevocable actions because of it; finally, suppose that he is presented with evidence, unequivocal and undeniable evidence, that his belief is wrong: what will happen? The individual will frequently emerge, not only unshaken, but even more convinced of the truth of his beliefs than ever before.[20]

The three social psychologists felt that Mrs. Keech's public statements and the ensuing events would be an invaluable real-life demonstration of the development of a paradoxical response to contradictory evidence. They called on Mrs. Keech, introducing themselves as a businessman and two friends who were impressed by her story and wanted to know more. Riecken gave his real name, but Schachter, who had an irrepressible sense of humor, introduced himself as Leon Festinger, leaving a stunned Festinger no option but to say he was Stanley Schachter and maintain that identity in all his contacts with Mrs. Keech and her followers.[21]

Mrs. Keech, they learned, had already gathered a small coterie that met regularly, was making plans for the future, and was awaiting final directions from the planet Clarion. The team drew up a research plan calling for the three of them, plus five student assistants, to be "covert participant observers." In the guise of true believers, they visited cult members and took part in their meetings sixty times over a seven-week period. Some visits lasted only an hour or two, but others involved nonstop séance-like sessions running twelve to fourteen hours. The research was physically and emotionally exhausting, partly because of the strain of concealing their reactions to the absurd goings-on at the meetings, and partly because of the difficulty of making a record of the words of a Guardian as voiced by Mrs. Keech and others in their trances. As Festinger later recalled:

> At intervals infrequent enough not to arouse comment, each of us would go to the toilet to make notes in private—that was the only place in that house where there was any privacy. Periodically, one or two of us together would announce we were taking a short walk to get some

fresh air. We would then dash madly to the hotel room to dictate from our notes . . . By the time the study was terminated we all literally collapsed from fatigue.[22]

At last Mrs. Keech received the long-awaited message. Spaceships would come to a certain place at a specific time to rescue the believers and take them to safety. But the spaceships failed to arrive either then or at several later promised times, and December 21 came and went without any flood.

At that point, Mrs. Keech received word that, thanks to the goodness and light created by the believers, God had decided to call off the disaster and spare the world. Some of the members, particularly those who had been doubtful or unsure, could not reconcile the failure of the prophecies with their beliefs and dropped out, but the members who had been most deeply committed—some had even quit their jobs and sold their possessions—behaved just as the researchers had hypothesized. They came away more strongly convinced than ever of the truth of Mrs. Keech's revelations, thereby eliminating the conflict between what they believed and the disappointing reality.

Festinger went on to develop and publish his theory of cognitive dissonance in 1957. It immediately became the central problem of social psychology and remained the principal topic of experimental research for over fifteen years. In 1959 he and a colleague, J. Merrill Carlsmith, conducted what is usually cited as the classic cognitive dissonance experiment. They artfully deceived their volunteer subjects about the purpose of the study, since the subjects, had they known the researchers wanted to see whether they would change their minds about some issue to minimize cognitive dissonance, might well have felt embarrassed to do so.

Festinger and Carlsmith had their undergraduate male subjects perform an extremely tedious task: they had to put a dozen spools into a tray, remove them, put them back, and repeat the process for half an hour. Then they had to turn each of forty-eight pegs in a board a quarter turn clockwise, then another quarter turn, and so on, again for half an hour. After each subject had finished, one of the researchers told him that the purpose of the experiment was to find out whether people's expectation of how interesting a task is would affect how well they performed it, and that he had been in the "no-expectation group" but others would be told that the task was enjoyable. Unfortunately, the researcher went on, the assistant who was supposed to tell that to the next subject had just called in to say he couldn't make it. The researcher said he needed someone to take the assistant's place and asked the subject to help out. Some subjects were offered $1 to do so, others $20.

Nearly all of them agreed to tell what was obviously a lie to the next subject (who, in reality, was a confederate). After they had done so, the subjects were asked how enjoyable they themselves had found the task. Since it had unquestionably been boring, lying about it to someone else created a condition of cognitive dissonance ("I lied to someone else. But I'm not that kind of person"). The crucial question was whether the size of the payment they had received led them to reduce dissonance by deciding that the task had really been enjoyable.

Intuitively, one might expect that those who got $20—a substantial sum in 1959—would be more likely to change their opinion of the task than those who got a dollar. But Festinger and Carlsmith predicted the opposite. The subjects who got $20 would have a solid reward to justify their lying, but those who got a dollar would have so little justification for lying that they would still feel dissonance, and would relieve it by convincing themselves that the task had been interesting and they had not really lied. Which is exactly what the results showed.*[23]

Festinger and Carlsmith were exhilarated; social psychologists find it particularly exciting to discover something that is not obvious or that contradicts usual impressions. As Schachter has often told his students, it's a waste of time to study *bubbe* psychology; that's the kind that when you tell your grandmother—*bubbe*, in Yiddish—what you found, she says, "So what else is new? They pay you for this?"[24]

Cognitive dissonance theory stirred up a good deal of hostile criticism, which Festinger scathingly dismissed as "garbage," and attributed to the fact that the theory presented a "not very idealistic" image of humankind.[25] Whatever the motives of the critics, a flood of experiments showed cognitive dissonance to be a robust (consistent) finding. And, moreover, a fertile theory. Reminiscing, the eminent social psychologist Elliot Aronson said, "All we had to do was sit around and we could generate ten good hypotheses in an evening . . . the kinds of hypotheses that no one would even have dreamed of a few years earlier."[26] The theory also explained a number of kinds of social behavior

---

*All the students, after the true purpose of the experiment was revealed, were asked to return the money. Only one student—who had received $1—objected (Aron and Aron, 1989:115).

that could not be accounted for within behaviorist theory. Here are a few examples, all verified by experiments:[27]

— The harder it is to gain membership in a group (as, for instance, when there is grueling screening or hazing), the more highly the group is valued by a person who is accepted. We convince ourselves we love what has caused us pain in order to feel that the pain was worthwhile.

— When people behave in ways they are likely to see as either stupid or immoral, they change their attitudes so as to believe that their behavior is sensible and justified. Smokers, for instance, say that the evidence about smoking and cancer is inconclusive; students who cheat say that everyone else cheats and therefore they have to in order not to be at a disadvantage.

— People who hold opposing views are apt to interpret the same news reports or factual material about the disputed subject quite differently; each sees and remembers what supports his views but glosses over and forgets what would create dissonance.

— When people who think of themselves as reasonably humane are in a situation where they hurt innocent others, as soldiers often harm civilians in the course of combat, they reduce the resulting dissonance by derogating their victims ("Those SOBs are helping the enemy. They'd knife you in the back if they could"). When people benefit from social inequities that cause others to suffer, they often tell themselves that the sufferers aren't capable of anything better, are content with their way of life, and are dirty, lazy, and immoral.

Finally, one case of a "natural experiment" that illustrates the human tendency to reduce cognitive dissonance by rationalization:

— After a 1983 California earthquake the city of Santa Cruz, in compliance with a new California law, commissioned Dave Steeves, a well-regarded engineer, to assess how local buildings would fare in a major earthquake. Steeves identified 175 buildings that would suffer severe damage, many of them in the prime downtown shopping area. The city council, aghast at the report and what it implied about the work that would have to be done, dismissed his findings and voted unanimously to wait for clarification of the state law. Steeves was called an alarmist and his report a threat to the well-being of the town, and no further action was taken. On October 17, 1989, an earthquake of magnitude 7.1 hit just outside Santa Cruz. Three hundred homes were destroyed and five thousand seriously damaged in Santa Cruz County; the downtown area was reduced to ruins; five people were killed and two thousand injured.

Because of its explanatory power, cognitive dissonance theory easily survived all attacks. Twenty-five years after Festinger first advanced it and sixteen years after he left social psychology to study archaeology, a survey of social psychologists found that 79 percent considered him the person who had contributed most to their field.[28] Today, a generation later, Festinger's name and fame have dimmed, but cognitive dissonance remains a bedrock principle of social psychological theory. But one criticism of cognitive dissonance research has been difficult to rebut. The researchers almost always gulled the volunteers into doing things they would not ordinarily do (such as lying for money), subjected them without their consent to strenuous or embarrassing experiences, or revealed to them aspects of themselves that damaged their self-esteem. The investigators "debriefed" subjects after the experiment, explaining the real purpose, the reason deception had been necessary, and the benefit to science of their participation. This was intended to restore to them their sense of well-being, but critics have insisted that it is unethical to subject other people to such experiences without their knowledge and consent.[29]

The Psychology of Imprisonment

These ethical problems were not peculiar to dissonance studies; they existed in more severe form in other kinds of sociopsychological research. A famous case in point is an experiment conducted in 1971 by Professor Philip G. Zimbardo, a social psychologist at Stanford University, and three colleagues.[30] To study the social psychology of imprisonment, they enlisted undergraduate men as volunteers in a simulation of prison life, in which each would play the part of a guard or a prisoner. All volunteers were interviewed and given personality tests; twenty-one middle-class whites were selected after being rated emotionally stable, mature, and law-abiding. By the flip of a coin, ten were designated as prisoners, eleven as guards, for the duration of a two-week experiment.

The "prisoners" were "arrested" by police one quiet Sunday morning, handcuffed, booked at the police station, taken to the "prison" (a set of cells built in the basement of the Stanford psychology building), and there stripped, searched, deloused, and issued uniforms. The guards were supplied with billy clubs, handcuffs, whistles, and keys to the cells; they were told that their job was to maintain "law and order" in the prison and that they could devise their own methods of prisoner control. The warden (a colleague of Zimbardo's) and guards drew up a list of sixteen rules the prisoners had to obey: they were to be silent at meals, rest periods, and after lights out; they were to eat at mealtimes but no other time; they were to address one another by their ID number and any guard as Mr. Correctional Officer, and so on. Violation of any rule could result in punishment.

The relations between guards and prisoners quickly assumed a classic pattern: the guards began to think of the prisoners as inferior and dangerous, the prisoners to view the guards as bullies and sadists. As one guard reported:

> I was surprised at myself . . . I made them call each other names and clean out the toilets with their bare hands. I practically considered the prisoners cattle, and I kept thinking I have to watch out for them in case they try something.

In a few days the prisoners organized a rebellion. They tore off their ID numbers and barricaded themselves inside their cells by shoving beds against the doors. The guards sprayed them with a fire extinguisher to drive them back from the doors, burst into their cells, stripped them, took away their beds, and in general thoroughly intimidated them.

The guards, from that point on, kept making up additional rules, waking the prisoners frequently at night for head counts, forcing them to perform tedious and useless tasks, and punishing them for "infractions." The prisoners, humiliated, became obsessed by the unfairness of their treatment. Some grew disturbed, one so much so that by the fifth day the experimenters began to consider releasing him before the end of the experiment.

The rapid development of sadism in the guards was exemplified by the comments of one of them who, before the experiment, said that he was a pacifist, was nonaggressive, and could not imagine himself maltreating another person. By the fifth day he noted in his diary:

> I have singled him [one prisoner] out for special abuse both because he begs for it and because I simply don't like him . . . The new pris-

oner (416) refuses to eat his sausage . . . I decided to force feed him, but he wouldn't eat. I let the food slide down his face. I didn't believe it was me doing it. I hated myself for making him eat but I hated him more for not eating.

Zimbardo and his colleagues had not expected so rapid a transformation in either group of volunteers and later wrote in a report:

What was most surprising about the outcome of this simulated prison experience was the ease with which sadistic behavior could be elicited from quite normal young men, and the contagious spread of emotional pathology among those carefully selected precisely for their emotional stability.

On the sixth day the researchers abruptly terminated the experiment for the good of all concerned. They felt, however, that it had been valuable; it had shown how easily "normal, healthy, educated young men could be so radically transformed under the institutional pressures of a 'prison environment.' "

That finding may have been important, but in the eyes of many ethicists the experiment was grossly unethical. It had imposed on its volunteers physical and emotional stresses that they had not anticipated or agreed to undergo. In so doing, it had violated the principle, affirmed by the Supreme Court in 1914, that "every human being of adult years and sound mind has a right to determine what shall be done with his own body."[31] Because of the ethical problems, the prison experiment has not been replicated; it is a closed case.*

Even this was bland in comparison with another experiment, also of major value, and also now a closed case. Let us open the file and see what was learned, and by what extraordinary means.

Obedience

In the aftermath of the Holocaust, many behavioral scientists sought to understand how so many normal, civilized Germans could have behaved toward other human beings with such incomprehensible savagery. A massive study published in 1950, carried out by an interdiscipli-

---

*At least, in social psychology, but not, alas, elsewhere; the horrendous behavior of American prison guards at Abu Ghraib was Zimbardo's experiment writ large.

nary team with a psychoanalytic orientation, ascribed prejudice and ethnic hatred to the "authoritarian personality," an outgrowth of particular
kinds of parenting and childhood experience.[32] But social psychologists
found this too general an explanation; they thought the answer more
likely to involve a special social situation that caused ordinary people to
commit out-of-character atrocities.

It was to explore this possibility that an advertisement in a New Haven
newspaper in the early 1960s called for volunteers for a study of memory
and learning at Yale University.[33] Any adult male not in high school or
college would be eligible, and participants would be paid $4 (roughly
the equivalent of $25 today) an hour plus carfare.

Forty men ranging from twenty to fifty years old were selected and
given separate appointments. Each was met at an impressive laboratory
by a small, trim young man in a gray lab coat. Arriving at the same time
was another "volunteer," a pleasant middle-aged man of Irish-American
appearance. The man in the lab coat, the ostensible researcher, was
actually a thirty-one-year-old high school biology teacher, and the middle-aged man was an accountant by profession. Both were accomplices
of the social psychologist conducting the experiment, Stanley Milgram
of Yale, and would act the parts he had scripted.

The researcher explained to the two men, the real and false volunteers, that he was studying the effect of punishment on learning. One of
them would be the "teacher" and the other the "learner" in an experiment in which the teacher would give the learner an electric shock
whenever he made an error. The two volunteers then drew slips of paper
to see who would be which. The one selected by the "naïve" volunteer
read "Teacher." (To ensure this result, both slips read "Teacher," but the
accomplice discarded his without showing it.)

The researcher then led the two subjects into a small room, where the
learner was seated at a table, his arms strapped down, and electrodes
attached to his wrists. He said he hoped the shocks wouldn't be too
severe; he had a heart condition. The teacher was then taken into an
adjoining room from which he could speak to and hear the learner but
not see him. On a table was a large shiny metal box said to be a shock
generator. On the front was a row of thirty switches, each marked with
the voltage it delivered (ranging from 15 to 450) plus descriptive labels:
"Slight Shock," "Moderate Shock," and so on, up to "Danger: Severe
Shock" at 435, and finally two switches marked simply "XXX."

The teacher's role, the researcher explained, was to read a list of word
pairs (such as *blue, sky* and *dog, cat*) to the learner, then test his memory

by reading the first word of one pair and four possible second words, one of which was correct. The learner would indicate his choice by pushing a button lighting one of four bulbs in front of the teacher. Whenever he gave a wrong answer, the teacher was to depress a switch giving him a shock, starting at the lowest level. Each time the learner made an error, the teacher was to give him the next stronger shock.

At first the experiment proceeded easily and uneventfully; the learner would give some right answers and some wrong ones, the teacher would administer a mild shock after each wrong answer, and continue. But as the learner made more mistakes and the shocks became greater in intensity—the apparatus was fake, of course, and no shocks were delivered—the situation grew unpleasant. At 75 volts the learner grunted audibly; at 120 he called out that the shocks were becoming painful; at 150 volts he shouted, "Get me out of here. I refuse to go on!" Whenever the teacher wavered, the researcher, standing beside him, said, "Please continue." At 180 volts the learner called, "I can't stand the pain!" and at 270 he howled. When the teacher hesitated or balked, the researcher said, "The experiment requires that you continue." Later, when the learner was banging on the wall, or still later, when he was screaming, the researcher said sternly, "It is absolutely essential that you continue." Beyond 330, when there was only silence from the next room—to be interpreted as equivalent to an incorrect answer—the experimenter said, "You have no other choice; you must go on."

Astonishingly—Milgram himself was amazed—63 percent of the teachers did go on, all the way. But not because they were sadists who enjoyed the agony they thought they were inflicting (standard personality tests showed no difference between the fully obedient subjects and those who at some point refused to continue); on the contrary, many of them suffered acutely while obeying the researcher's orders. As Milgram reported:

In a large number of cases the degree of tension reached extremes that are rarely seen in sociopsychological laboratory studies. Subjects were observed to sweat, tremble, stutter, bite their lips, groan, and dig their fingernails into their flesh . . . A mature and initially poised businessman enter[ed] the laboratory smiling and confident. Within 20 minutes he was reduced to a twitching, stuttering wreck who was rapidly approaching a point of nervous collapse . . . yet he continued to respond to every word of the experimenter, and obeyed to the end.[34]

Milgram did not, alas, report any symptoms he himself may have had while watching his teachers suffer. A spirited, feisty little man, he gave no indication in his otherwise vivid account that he was ever distressed by his subjects' misery.

His interpretation of the results was that the situation, playing on cultural expectations, produced the phenomenon of obedience to authority. The volunteers entered the experiment in the role of cooperative and willing subjects, and the researcher played the part of the authority. In our society and many others, children are taught to obey authority and not to judge what the person in authority tells them to do. In the experiment, the teachers felt obliged to carry out orders; they could inflict pain and harm on an innocent human being because they felt that the researcher, not they themselves, was responsible for their actions.

In Milgram's opinion, his series of experiments went far to explain how so many otherwise normal Germans, Austrians, and Poles could have operated death camps or, at least, accepted the mass murder of the Jews, Gypsies, and other despised groups. (Adolf Eichmann said, when he was on trial in Israel, that he found his role in liquidating millions of Jews distasteful but that he had to carry out the orders of authority.)

Milgram validated his interpretation of the results by varying the script in a number of ways. In one variation, a phone call would summon the researcher away before he said anything to the teacher about the importance of continuing to ever higher shock levels; his place would be taken by a volunteer (another confederate) who seemed to hit on the idea of increasing the shocks as far as needed and kept telling the teacher to continue. But he was a substitute, not the real authority; in this version of the experiment only 20 percent of the teachers went all the way. Milgram also varied the composition of the team. Instead of an affable, pudgy, middle-aged learner and a trim, stern, young researcher, he reversed the personality types. In that condition, the proportion of teachers going all the way decreased but only to 50 percent. Apparently, the roles of authority and victim, not the personalities of the persons who played the parts, were the crucial factor.

A disturbing adjunct to Milgram's results was his investigation of how people *thought* they would behave in the situation. He described the experimental set-up in detail to groups of college students, behavioral scientists, psychiatrists, and laymen, and asked them at what level of shock people like themselves would refuse to go on. Despite the differences in their backgrounds, all groups said people like themselves would defy the experimenter and break off at about 150 volts when the victim asked to be released. Milgram also asked a group of undergraduates at what level one *should* disobey; again the average answer was at about 150 volts. Thus, neither people's expectations of how they would behave nor their moral views of how they should behave had anything to do with how they actually behaved in an authority-dominated situation.

Milgram's obedience study attracted immense attention and won the 1964 award of the American Association for the Advancement of Science for sociopsychological research. (In 1984, when Milgram died of a heart attack at fifty-one, Roger Brown called him "perhaps the most gifted experimentalist in the social psychology of our time.") Within a decade or so, 130 similar studies had been undertaken, including a number in other countries. Most of them confirmed and enlarged Milgram's findings, and for some years his procedure, or variations of it, was the principal one used in studies of obedience.[35] But for more than two decades no researcher has used such methods, or would dare to, as a result of historical developments we'll look at shortly.

The Bystander Effect

In March 1964, a murder in Kew Gardens, in New York City's borough of Queens, made the front page of the *New York Times* and shocked the nation, although there was nothing memorable about the victim, murderer, or method. Kitty Genovese, a young bar manager on her way home at 3 A.M., was stabbed to death by Winston Moseley, a business-machine operator who did not know her, and who had previously killed two other women. What made the crime big news was that the attack lasted half an hour (Moseley stabbed Genovese, left, came back a few minutes later and stabbed her again, left again, and returned to attack her once more), during which time she repeatedly screamed and called for help, and was heard and seen by thirty-eight people looking out the windows of their apartments. Not one tried to defend her, came to help when she lay bleeding, or even telephoned the police. (One finally did call—after she was dead.)

News commentators and other pundits interpreted the inaction of the thirty-eight witnesses as evidence of the alienation and inhumanity of modern city dwellers, especially New Yorkers. But two young social psychologists living in the city, neither one a native New Yorker, were troubled by these glib condemnations.[36] John Darley, an assistant professor at New York University, and Bibb Latané, an instructor at Columbia University who had been a student of Stanley Schachter's, met at a party soon after the murder and found that they had something in common. Though unlike in many ways—Darley was a dark-haired, urbane, Ivy League type; Latané a lanky, thatch-haired fellow with a Southern country-boy accent and manner—they both felt, as social psychologists, that there had to be a better explanation of the witnesses' inactivity.

They talked about it for hours that night and had a joint flash of inspiration. As Latané recalls:

> The newspapers, TV, everybody, was carrying on about the fact that thirty-eight people witnessed the crime and nobody did anything, as if that were far harder to understand than if one or two had witnessed it and done nothing. And we suddenly had an insight: maybe it was the very fact that there *were* thirty-eight that accounted for their inactivity. It's an old trick in social psychology to turn a phenomenon around and see if what you thought was the effect was actually the cause. Maybe each of the thirty-eight knew that a lot of other people were watching—and *that* was why they did nothing.[37]

Late though it was, the two immediately began designing an experiment to test their hypothesis. Many weeks later, after much planning and preparation, they launched an extended investigation of the responses of bystanders, under varied circumstances, to an emergency.

In the study, seventy-two NYU students in introductory psychology courses took part in an unspecified experiment in order to fulfill a class requirement. Each arriving participant was told by Darley, Latané, or a research assistant that the experiment involved a discussion of the personal problems of urban university students. The session was to be conducted in two-person, three-person, or six-person groups. To minimize embarrassment when revealing personal matters, they would be in separate cubicles and would communicate over an intercom system, taking turns and talking in an arranged sequence.

Whether the naïve participant was supposedly talking to only one other person or to two or five others—supposedly, because in fact everything he heard others say was a tape-recorded script—the first voice was always that of a male student who told of difficulty adjusting to life in New York and to his studies, and confided that under stress he was prone to epileptic seizures. The voice was that of Richard Nisbett, then a graduate student at Columbia University and today a professor at the University of Michigan, who in tryouts had proved the best actor. The second time it was his turn to talk, he started to sound disordered and incoherent; he stammered and panted, said that he had "one of these things coming on," started choking and pleading for help, gasped, "I'm gonna die—er-er—help—er-er—seizure-er," and, after more choking sounds, fell silent.

Of the participants who thought that they and the epileptic were the only ones talking to each other, 85 percent popped out of their cubicles to report the attack even before the victim fell silent; of those who thought four other people were also hearing the attack, only 31 percent did so. Later, when the students were asked whether the presence of others had influenced their response, they said no; they had been genuinely unaware of its powerful effect on them.

Darley and Latané now had a convincing sociopsychological explanation of the Kew Gardens phenomenon, which they called "the social inhibition of bystander intervention in emergencies," or, more simply, "the bystander effect." As they had hypothesized, it was the presence of other witnesses to an emergency that made for passivity in a bystander. The explanation of the bystander effect, they said, "may lie more in the bystander's response to other observers than in presumed personality deficiencies of 'apathetic' individuals."[38]

They suggested later that three processes underlie the bystander effect: hesitancy to act in front of others until one knows whether helping or other action is appropriate; the feeling that the inactive others understand the situation and that nothing need be done; and, most important, "diffusion of responsibility"—the feeling that, since others know of the emergency, one's own obligation to act is lessened.[39] A number of later experiments by Latané and Darley, and by other researchers, confirmed that, depending on whether bystanders can see other bystanders, are seen by them, or merely know that there are others, one or another of these three processes is at work.

The Darley and Latané experiment aroused widespread interest and generated a crop of offspring. Over the next dozen years, fifty-six studies conducted in thirty laboratories presented apparent emergencies to a total of nearly six thousand naïve subjects who were alone or in the presence of one, several, or many others. (Conclusion: The more bystanders, the greater the bystander effect.) The staged emergencies were of many kinds: a crash in the next room followed by the sound of a female moaning; a decently dressed young man with a cane (or, alternatively, a dirty young man smelling of whiskey) collapsing in a subway car and struggling unsuccessfully to rise; a staged theft of books; the experimenter himself fainting; and many others. In forty-eight of the fifty-six studies, the bystander effect was clearly demonstrated; overall, about half the people who were alone when an emergency occurred offered help, as opposed to 22 percent of those who saw or heard emergencies in the presence of others.[40] Since there is less than one chance in fifty-one million that this aggregate result is accidental, the bystander effect is one of the best-established hypotheses of social psychology. And having been so thoroughly established and the effects of so many conditions having been separately measured, it has ceased in recent years to be the subject of much research and become, in effect, another closed case.

However, research on helping behavior in general—the social and psychological factors that either favor or inhibit nonemergency altruistic acts—continued to grow in volume until the 1980s and has only lately leveled off. Helping behavior is part of prosocial behavior, which, during the idealistic 1960s, began to replace social psychology's postwar obsession with aggressive behavior, and it remains an important area of research in the discipline.

A Note on Deceptive Research: One factor common to most of the closed cases dealt with above—and to a great many other research projects in social psychology—is the use of elaborately contrived deceptive scenarios. There is almost nothing of the sort in experimental research on personality, development, or most other fields of present-day psychology, but for many years deceptive experimentation was the essence of social psychological research.

In the years following the Nuremberg Trials, criticism of experimentation with human subjects without their knowledge and consent was on the rise, and deceptive experimentation by biomedical researchers and social psychologists came under heavy attack. The Milgram obedience experiment drew particularly intense fire, not only because it inflicted suffering on people without forewarning them and obtaining their consent, but because it might have done them lasting psychological harm by showing them a detestable side of themselves. Milgram, professing to be "totally astonished" by the criticism, asked a sample of his former subjects how they felt about the experience, and reported that 84 percent said they were glad they had taken part in the experiment, 15 percent were neutral, and only 1 percent regretted having participated.[41]

But in the era of expanding civil rights, the objections on ethical grounds to research of this sort triumphed. In 1971 the Department of Health, Education, and Welfare adopted regulations governing eligibility for research grants that sharply curtailed the freedom of social psychologists and biomedical researchers to conduct experiments with naïve subjects. In 1974 it tightened the rules still further; the right of persons to have nothing done to them without their informed consent was so strictly construed as to put an end not only to Milgram-type procedures but to many relatively painless and benign experiments relying on deception, and social psychologists abandoned a number of interesting topics that seemed no longer researchable.

Protests by the scientific community mounted all through the 1970s, and in 1981 the Department of Health and Human Services (successor to DHEW) eased the restrictions somewhat, allowing minor deception or withholding of information in experiments with human beings provided there was "minimum risk to the subject," the research "could not practicably be carried out" otherwise, and the benefit to humanity would outweigh the risk to the subjects.[42] "Risk-benefit" calculations, made by review boards before a research proposal is considered eligible for a grant, have permitted deceptive research—though not of the Milgram obedience sort—to continue to the present. Deception is still used in about half of all social psychology experiments but in relatively harmless forms and contexts.[43]

Still, many ethicists regard even innocuous deception as an unjustifiable invasion of human rights; they also claim it is unnecessary, since research can use nonexperimental methods, such as questionnaires, survey research, observation of natural situations, interviews, and so on. But while these methods are practical in many areas of psychology, they are less so, and sometimes are quite impractical, in social psychology.

For one thing, the evidence produced by such methods is largely correlational, and a correlation between factor X and factor Y means only that they are related in some way; it does not prove that one is the cause of the other. This is particularly true of sociopsychological phenomena, which involve a multiplicity of simultaneous factors, any of which may seem to be a cause of the effect under study but may actually be only a concurrent effect of some other cause. The experimental method, however, isolates a single factor, the "independent variable," and modifies it (for instance, by changing the number of bystanders present during an emergency). If this produces a change in the "dependent variable," the behavior being studied, one has rigorous proof of cause and effect. Such experimentation is comparable to a chemical experiment in which a single reagent is added to a solution and produces a measurable effect. As Elliot Aronson and two co-authors said in their classic *Handbook of Social Psychology*, "The experiment is unexcelled in its ability to provide unambiguous evidence about causation, to permit control over extraneous variables, and to allow for analytic exploration of the dimensions and parameters of a complex phenomenon."[44]

For another thing, no matter how rigorously the experimenter controls and manipulates the experimental variables, he or she cannot control the multiple variables inside the human head unless the subjects are deceived. If the subjects know that the investigator wants to see how they react to the sound of someone falling off a ladder in an adjoining room, they are almost sure to behave more admirably than they otherwise might. If they know that the investigator's interest is not in increasing memory through punishment but in seeing at what point they refuse to inflict pain on another person, they are very likely to behave more nobly than they would if ignorant of the real purpose. And so, for many kinds of sociopsychological research, deceptive experimentation is a necessity.

Many social psychologists formerly prized it not just for this valid reason but for a less valid one. Carefully crafted deceptive experimentation was a challenge; the clever and intricate scenario was highly regarded, prestigious, and exciting. Deceptive research was in part a game, a magic show, a theatrical performance; Aronson has likened the thrill felt by the experimenter to that felt by a playwright who successfully re-creates a piece of ordinary life.[45] (Aronson and a colleague once even designed an experiment in which the naïve subject was led to believe that she was the confederate playing a part in a cover story. In fact, her role as confederate was the actual cover story and the purportedly naïve subject was the actual confederate.[46]) In the 1960s and 1970s, by which time most undergraduates had heard about deceptive research, it was an achievement to be able still to mislead one's subjects and later debrief them.

During the 1980s and 1990s, however, the vogue for artful, ingenious, and daring deceptive experiments waned, although deceptive research remains a major device in the social psychologists' toolbox. Today most social psychologists are more prudent and cautious than were Festinger, Zimbardo, Milgram, Darley, and Latané, and yet the special quality of deceptive experimentation appeals to a certain kind of researcher. When one meets and talks to practitioners of such research, one gets the impression that they are a competitive, nosy, waggish, daring, stunt-loving, and exuberant lot, quite unlike such sobersides as Wundt, Pavlov, Binet, and Piaget.

Ongoing Inquiries

Of the wide variety of topics in the vast, amorphous field of social psychology, some, as we have seen, are closed cases; others have been actively and continuously investigated for many decades; and many others have come to the fore more recently. The currently ongoing inquiries, though they cover a wide range of subjects, have one characteristic in common: relevance to human welfare. Nearly all are issues not only of scientific interest but of profound potential for the improvement of the human condition. We will look closely at two examples and briefly at a handful of others.

Conflict Resolution

Over half a century ago social psychologists became interested in determining which factors promote cooperation rather than competition and whether people function more effectively in one kind of milieu than another. After a while, they redefined their subject as "conflict resolution" and their concern as the outcome when people compete, or when they cooperate, to achieve their goals.

Morton Deutsch, now a professor emeritus at Teachers College, Columbia University, was long the doyen of conflict-resolution research. He suspects that his interest in the subject may have its roots in his childhood.[47] The fourth and youngest son of Polish-Jewish immigrants, he was always the underdog at home, an experience he transmuted into the lifelong study of social justice and methods for the peaceful resolution of conflict.

It took him a while to discover that this was his real interest. He became fascinated by psychology as a high school student when he read Freud and responded strongly to descriptions of emotional processes he had felt going on in himself, and in college he planned to become a clinical psychologist. But the social ferment of the 1930s and the upheavals of World War II gave him an even stronger interest in the study of social problems. After the war he sought out Kurt Lewin, whose magnetic personality and exciting ideas, particularly about social issues, convinced Deutsch to become a social psychologist. For his doctoral dissertation he studied conflict resolution, and continued to work in that area throughout his long career. The subject was congenial to his personality: unlike many other social psychologists, he is soft-spoken, kindly, and peace-loving, and as an experimenter relied largely on the use of games that involved neither deception nor discomfort for the participants.

A particular focus of his research was the behavior of people in "mixed-motive situations," such as labor-management disputes or disarmament negotiations, where each side seeks to benefit at the other's cost yet has interests in common with, and does not want to destroy, the other. In the 1950s he studied such situations intensively in the laboratory by means of his own modification of the Prisoner's Dilemma game.[48] In Deutsch's version, each player seeks to win imaginary sums by making one of two choices—with results that depend on which of two choices the other player makes at the same time. Specifically, Player 1 can choose either X or Y, and Player 2 simultaneously can choose either A or B. Neither, in deciding what to do, knows what the other is going to do, but both know that every combination of their choices— XA, XB, YA, and YB—has different consequences. Player 1, for instance, thinks: "If I do X and he does A, we each win $9—but if he does B, I lose $10 and he wins $10. What if I do Y? If I do, and he does A, I win $10 and he loses $10—but if he does B, we each lose $9." Player 2 is confronted by similar dilemmas.

Since neither knows what the other is doing, each has to decide for himself what move might be best. But as in the original Prisoner's Dilemma, logical reasoning doesn't help; only if both players trust each other to do what is best for both will they choose X and A respectively, and each win $9. If either mistrusts the other or tries to do the best for himself without regard to the other's welfare, he may win $10 while the other loses that much—but is equally likely to lose $10 while the other wins that much, or, along with the other player, lose $9.

Deutsch varied the conditions under which his student volunteers played so as to simulate and test the effects of a number of real-life circumstances. To induce cooperative motivation, he told some volunteers, "You should consider yourself to be partners. You're interested in your partner's welfare as well as your own." To induce individualistic motivation, he told others, "Your only motivation should be to win as much as you can for yourself. You are to have no interest whatever in whether the other person wins or loses. This is not a competitive game."

Finally, to induce a competitive mind-set, he told still others, "Your motivation should be to win as much money as you can for yourself and also to do better than the other person. You want to make rather than lose money, but you also want to come out ahead of the other person." ·

Usually, players made their choices simultaneously without knowing each other's choice, but sometimes Deutsch had the first player choose and then transmit his choice to the second player, who would then make his choice. At other times, one or both players were allowed to change their choice when they heard what the other had chosen. And sometimes both were allowed to pass each other notes stating their intentions, such as, "I will cooperate, and I would like you to cooperate. That way we can both win."[49]

As Deutsch had hypothesized, when the players were oriented to think of each other's welfare, they behaved in a trusting fashion (they chose X and A)—and did the best, collectively, even though either one would have been the big loser if the other had double-crossed him. But when they were told to try to win the most and to best the other, each usually assumed that the other was also out to win at his expense and made choices that were good for only one and bad for the other, or bad for both.

An encouraging result, Deutsch has said, is that "mutual trust can occur even under circumstances in which the people involved are clearly unconcerned with each other's welfare, provided that the characteristics of the situation are such that they lead one to expect one's trust to be fulfilled."[50] That is the case when, for instance, one player is able to propose to the other a system of cooperation, with rules and penalties for infractions; or when one knows, before committing himself to a choice, what the other was going to do; or when one can influence the outcome for the other, with the result that it is not in the other's interest to violate an agreement.

Deutsch's use of the modified Prisoner's Dilemma game was a seminal event in social psychology. It led to hundreds of similar studies by others who modified and varied the conditions of play in order to explore a range of other factors that encouraged either cooperative or competitive styles of conflict resolution.

Deutsch himself soon moved on to another game that he and a research assistant, Robert M. Krauss, constructed to investigate how threats affect conflict resolution. Many people, during conflicts, believe they can induce the other side to cooperate by making threats. Embattled spouses hint at separation or divorce in an effort to change each other's behavior; management warns strikers that unless they come to terms it will close down the company; nations in conflict mass troops on the border or conduct weapons tests in the attempt to wrest concessions from the other side.

In Deutsch and Krauss's Acme-Bolt Trucking Game there are two players, both "truck drivers," one with the Acme Company, the other with the Bolt Company. This map represents the world in which they interact.

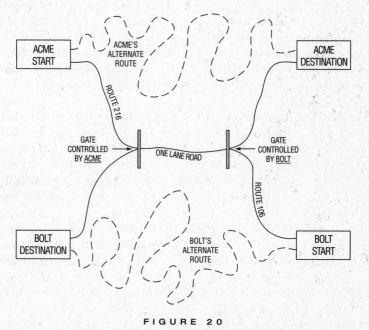

FIGURE 20

Which works better—toughing it out or cooperating?

Time is of the essence for each player. Quick trips mean profit; slow ones, loss. Each begins moving his truck at the same time and at the same speed (the positions appear on control panels), and each can choose to go by the circuitous route or the short one. The latter, although obviously preferable, involves a stretch of one-lane road that accommodates only one truck at a time. If both players choose that route at the same time, they reach a bumper-to-bumper deadlock and one or both have to back out, losing money. Obviously, the best course is for them to agree to take turns on the one-lane road, thus allowing both to make maximum and nearly equal profits.[51]

To simulate threat making, Deutsch and Krauss gave each player control of a gate at his end of the one-lane strip. Each player, when bargaining, could threaten to close his gate to the other's truck unless the other agreed to his terms. The experiment consisted of twenty rounds of play in each of three conditions: bilateral threat (both players controlled gates), unilateral threat (only Acme controlled a gate), and no threat (neither player controlled a gate). Another important variable was communication. In the first experiment, the players communicated their intentions only by the moves they made; in a second one, they could talk to each other; in a third, they *had* to talk to each other at every trial. Since the goal of both players was to make as much money as possible, the total amount of money they made in twenty rounds of play was a direct measure of their success in resolving the conflict. The major findings:

— The players made the greatest profit (collectively) when neither could make a threat; fared less well in the unilateral threat condition; and, contrary to common belief, did worst when each could threaten the other. (Could our former belief in "mutual deterrence" as the way to avoid nuclear war have been an unthinkably expensive misjudgment from which, through luck, we did not suffer?)

— Freedom to communicate helped little toward reaching an agreement, particularly if each could threaten the other. Nor did the obligation to communicate if both could threaten, although it did if only one could.

— If the players were coached about communicating and told to try to offer fair proposals to each other, they reached agreement more swiftly than when not tutored.

— When both players could make threats, verbal communication following a deadlock led to a useful agreement more quickly than if they were allowed to communicate only before the deadlock. Apparently, becoming deadlocked was a motivating experience.

— The higher the stakes, the more difficulty they had reaching agreement.

— Finally, when the experiment was run by an attractive female research assistant instead of a male, the players—male undergraduates—acted in a more macho fashion, used their gates more frequently, and had significantly more trouble reaching cooperative agreements.[52]

The Acme-Bolt Trucking Game instantly became a classic, was widely cited, and won the prestigious AAAS award for social science research.* Like many another ground-breaking study, it was the target of criticism, much of which questioned whether the variables it was based on are found in real life. But with time that question has been fairly well settled. The notion that a conflict can be thought of as a problem, and approached by thinking "What is the best way for us to solve it?" has been borne out by many other studies and has been turned into a number of programs of practical training. In 1986 Deutsch founded the International Center for Cooperation and Conflict Resolution at Teachers College, and this institute, the Program on Negotiation at Harvard Law School, the Conflict Resolution Consortium at the University of Colorado, and other similar centers have had considerable success in teaching constructive methods of settling disputes to negotiators for management and labor, divorce and corporate lawyers, government officials and legislators, teachers and students, tenants and landlords, family members, and others in conflict situations. If unresolved conflict is all too rife in our world, it's because all too few embattled individuals and peoples know about—or care about—peaceful resolutions of their disputes.

Research on the topic continues. Heidi Burgess, co-director with Guy Burgess of the Colorado Consortium, says that currently the areas of special interest are "the way people frame conflicts" and how this affects "the way the conflict process is conducted and/or resolved" (thus carrying on Deutsch's original work), and, branching out to other aspects of the field, "the impact of humiliation, anger, fear, and other strong emotions on conflicts and their resolution, the social-psychological effects of trauma, and approaches to trauma healing."[53]

Attribution

In the 1970s, cognitive dissonance was displaced as the leading topic of social psychology by a new subject, attribution. The term refers to the

---

*One of many awards to Morton Deutsch. The latest is the 2006–2007 James McKeen Cattell Award of the Association for Psychological Science—its highest award in applied psychological science.

process by which we make inferences about the causes of events in our lives and the behavior of others.

Our attributions, whether correct or incorrect, are more responsible than objective reality for how we think, what we feel, and how we behave. Studies have shown, for example, that we commonly attribute greater warmth, sexiness, and other desirable traits to good-looking people than to homely people, and behave toward them accordingly. Again, those who ascribe women's lower employment status and pay scales to their fear of success and lack of assertiveness treat them differently from those who believe the causes are male prejudice, male dominance in the workplace, and traditional attitudes about woman's proper role. All these are examples of what social psychologists call the "fundamental attribution error"—namely, "the strong tendency to interpret other people's behavior as due to internal (dispositional) causes rather than external (situational) ones."[54]

The phenomenon of attribution is captured in an old joke. Two men, one a Protestant and the other a Catholic, see a priest entering a brothel. The Protestant smiles sourly at the evidence of the hypocrisy of Catholics, the Catholic smiles proudly at the evidence that a priest will go anywhere, even into a brothel, to save the soul of a dying Catholic.

For those who prefer a more serious example, attribution is illustrated by an early experiment conducted by two former students of Lewin's, John Thibaut and Henry Riecken. They assigned naïve volunteers, one at a time, to work on a laboratory project, in the course of which each realized that he needed the help of two other people present, one a graduate student, the other a freshman. (Both were accomplices of the researchers.) Each volunteer sought their help and eventually got it. When the volunteers were later asked why they thought the others had helped them, most said the graduate student had helped because he wanted to, the freshman because he felt obliged to. These attributions were based not on anything they had experienced but on the volunteers' preconceptions about social status and power.[55]

Much other research has examined an extremely serious form of attribution error—the reasons given by people as to why other people tolerated or committed acts of hatred against groups and even accepted genocide of the hated people. A 2003 study asked Jewish and German visitors to Anne Frank's home in Amsterdam, now a museum, whether the behavior of Germans during the Holocaust was due to their aggressive nature (an internal cause) or to the historical context in which the events occurred (external factors). By a considerable margin, the Jewish respondents attributed the German behavior to German aggressiveness, the German respondents to external factors (thus more or less absolving themselves of inner evil).[56]

Fritz Heider, an Austrian psychologist, had suggested the concept of attribution as early as 1927, but little notice was taken of it for many years. In 1958, Heider, who had long since immigrated to the United States, broadened the concept, proposing in his *Psychology of Interpersonal Relations* that our perceptions of causality affect our social behavior, and that we respond not to actual stimuli but to what we think caused them. An example: If a wife is trying to annoy her husband by not talking to him, he may think either that she is worried or that he has done something to offend her, and his actions will depend not on the real reason for her behavior but on what he attributes it to.[57] Heider also made a valuable distinction between those attributions which point toward external causes and those which point toward internal ones. This preceded by eight years Julian Rotter's important work on the attribution of internal versus external locus of control as a key personality trait.

Psychologists found Heider's ideas exciting, since knowledge of the factors that lead people to make attributions would greatly increase the predictability of human behavior. Interest in attribution grew throughout the 1960s, and by the 1970s it had become one of the hot topics in social psychology.

But more a topic than a theory; indeed, it was a mass of small theories, each a reworking in attributional terms of some previous explanation of a sociopsychological phenomenon.[58] Cognitive dissonance was reinterpreted as the self-attributing of one's behavior to what one supposed one's beliefs and feelings must be. (If circumstances compel me to behave badly toward someone, I tell myself that he deserves it and attribute my behavior to my perception of his "real" nature.) The foot-in-the-door phenomenon was similarly explained anew: if I give a little to a fund raiser the first time, and therefore give more a second time, it is because I attribute the first donation to my being a good and kindly person. And so on. Large areas of the territory of social psychology were invaded and laid claim to by the attributionists.[59]

More important than the reinterpretation of previous findings was the multitude of new discoveries resulting from attribution research. A few notable examples:[60]

— Lee Ross and two colleagues asked pairs of student volunteers to play a "quiz show game." One was appointed questioner, the other contestant. Questioners were asked to make up ten fairly difficult questions to which they knew the answers, then pose them to the contestants. (Contestants averaged about six correct answers.) Afterward, all participants were asked to rate one another's "general knowledge." Nearly all the contestants said they considered questioners more knowledgeable than themselves; so did impartial observers of the experiment. Even though they knew that questioners had asked questions they knew the answers to, they attributed superior general knowledge to them because of the role they had played.

— Investigators discovered that we commonly attribute the behavior of highly noticeable, different-looking, or strikingly dressed people to inherent qualities, and the behavior of forgettable or ordinary-looking people to external (situational) forces.

— People's reactions to the poor, alcoholics, accident victims, rape victims, and other unfortunates were explained in terms of the "just world hypothesis"—the need to believe that the world is orderly and just, and that it rewards us according to our deserts. This leads to the attribution of victims' misfortunes to their own carelessness, sloth, risk taking, seductiveness, and the like. Some studies have found that the worse the plight of the victim, the more he or she is seen as responsible for it.

— Male college students were asked by the psychologist Stuart Valins to look at slides of nude women and rate their attractiveness. While looking at them, each man, through earphones, heard what was supposedly his own heartbeat but was in reality recorded sound controlled by Valins. The *lub-dub, lub-dub* the volunteers heard was speeded up when they looked at certain slides but not others. When they later rated the appeal of the women, they named as particularly attractive those who seemed to have caused their heartbeat to speed up.

— Volunteers given false reports of how well they had done on tests tended to attribute supposed success to their own efforts or abilities, supposed failure to external causes such as the unfairness of the test, distracting noises, and so on.

— Researchers asked a group of nursery school children who had previously enjoyed drawing with multicolored felt-tip pens to play with them in order to receive Good Player awards. They asked a control group to play with the pens but said nothing about an award. Some time later, both groups were given access to the pens during free-play periods. The children who had received awards were much less interested in using them than the no-award group. The attributional interpretation: children who had expected a reward implicitly thought, "If I do it for the reward, I must not find drawing with it very interesting."

Since the 1980s attribution theory has been largely absorbed into the broader field of "social cognition," or the study of how people think about social issues, an expansive domain that includes such intriguing topics as self-fulfilling prophecies, how attitudes affect behavior, persuasion and attitude change, stereotyping and prejudice, and much more. Within that framework attribution remains a central concept in contemporary social psychology. It has added substantially to psychology's patchwork explanation of human behavior.

It has also yielded a number of practical applications in education (students are led to attribute their failures to lack of effort rather than inability), the treatment of depression (depressed persons are induced to minimize their sense of personal responsibility for negative events in their lives), the improvement of performance and motivation of fearful and defeatist persons (they are led to attribute feared failures to lack of practice and skill rather than to character defects), and so on.[61]

Many other topics of both scientific interest and potential practical value have been explored by social psychologists in recent years and continue to be actively researched. Here are some of them, along with a few sample findings of each:

Interpersonal relations: Communication between spouses, friends, co-workers, and others, often ambiguous and misinterpreted, is usually much improved by experience in T-groups (T for training), therapy groups, and marital counseling. Participants are alerted to their own communication flaws and made more sensitive to what others are saying . . . Rules for clear and fair argument, taught to spouses in conflict, can considerably improve their communication and relationship . . . Only a fraction (possibly less than a tenth) of the information in emotional communications is conveyed by the words, the rest by body language, eye contact or avoidance, distance maintained between persons, and the like; nonverbal communication skills, too, can be taught . . . Guilt has social benefits; it protects and strengthens interpersonal relationships by, among other things, keeping people from acting in ways that would harm their relationships . . . Jealousy has adaptive functions, serving to keep mates together (signals of jealousy by one partner may inhibit the other from straying).[62]

Mass communication and persuasion: Political, sales, and other presentations that do not indicate in advance that they will attempt to persuade are more successful than those which honestly announce what they're about to do . . . Two-sided presentations, offering and refuting the opposition's view, then offering and supporting one's own view, are far more persuasive than powerful presentations of a single view . . . Forthright arguments on any controversial topic are listened to chiefly by the already convinced and shunned by those who hold an opposite view; indirect, emotionally appealing, deceptive, and unfair methods are, regrettably, more effective in changing attitudes than straight talk about issues . . . People can be persuaded via the *central route* (rational thinking about a rational argument) or the *peripheral route* (being distracted by, say, a sexy celebrity while the message is being delivered—obviously the favored and more effective choice of many advertisers).[63]

Attraction: An unromantic reality: Physical proximity and membership in groups are major determinants of romantic preferences and of friendships . . . Within the parameters of nearness and group membership, physical beauty is by far the strongest factor in the initial attraction toward dating partners, yet persons with low or moderate self-esteem avoid approaching the most desirable partners out of fear of rejection . . . In both friendships and mate choices, similarity of personality and background have far more power to attract than the legendary appeal of opposite traits.[64]

Attitude change (or persuasion): Persons low in self-esteem are more readily made to change their attitudes than persons with high self-esteem . . . People are more influenced by the statement of an authority than by an equally or even better documented statement of a nonauthority . . . They are also more easily persuaded by overheard information than by information directed at them, and by actions they have been induced to perform (as in Festinger's cognitive dissonance experiment) than by logical reasoning . . . Simply being repeatedly exposed to something—a name, a product, a slogan—often changes one's attitude toward it, generally in a favorable way (again, obviously, a psychological reality well-known to advertisers and politicos).[65]

Prejudice: When people are assigned to or belong to a group, generally they come to think of it as better than other groups in order to maintain their self-esteem and positive self-image . . . People assume that others who share one of their tastes, beliefs, or attitudes are like them in other ways, and that those who differ with them on some issue are unlike them in other ways . . . The mutual antipathy of people in rival or hostile groups dissipates if the groups have to cooperate to achieve some goal valuable to both of them . . . Stereotyping can lead to prejudice, which may be conscious and intentional, conscious and unintentional, and, perhaps most serious, unconscious and unintentional.[66]

Group decision making: Groups make either riskier or more conservative decisions than individuals, largely because group discussion and the airing of opinions frees many of the members to take a more extreme position than they would have on their own . . . Groups perform better than individuals on tasks where everyone's effort adds to the result but not on tasks where there is only one correct solution and where, if one member discovers it but is not supported by at least one other, the group may ignore the correct solution . . . In groups organized to solve a particular problem, two people assume particular importance: the task specialist, who speaks most, has the most ideas, and is seen as the leader; and the socioemotional specialist, who does the most to promote harmony and morale.[67]

Altruism: The bystander effect, discussed above, can be counteracted by knowing about it. In an experiment, students who had heard a lecture on the bystander effect were helpful to a hurt stranger in a situation where normally they would have been passive . . . Self-interest is the major motivation of many altruistic acts (one helps a person in distress to relieve one's own discomfort or guilt at seeing that person's pain), but some altruistic acts are motivated solely by a perception of the other person's needs and by empathy that social experience has transformed into true compassion . . . Altruism, or at least empathy, can be successfully taught in the classroom by role playing in little psychodramas, projective completion of stories, group discussions, and other methods.[68]

Social neuroscience: Many social psychological processes are now being investigated by means of brain scans to see if observable differences in neural activity and blood flow occur when certain interpersonal events take place. In one study, for instance, photos of whites,

blacks, females, and males were shown for one second each to participants almost all of whom were white. Recordings of several kinds of
brain potentials showed that photographs of black persons elicited more
attention than those of white persons, and females more than males —
and that the differences were manifested within one hundred milliseconds of seeing each photo, an indication that we very swiftly assign
people we see to categories.[69]

This is only a sample of the active fields and topics in social psychology.
Others range from excuse-making and self-handicapping (arranging
things so that one is likely to fail and has an excuse for failure) to the
effects of TV violence on behavior; from changing patterns of love and
marriage to the decision-making processes of juries; and from territoriality and crowding to race relations and social justice. No wonder it is all
but impossible to draw the boundaries of social psychology; like the former British Empire, it sprawls across a vast world of human thought,
feeling, and behavior.

The Value of Social Psychology

Like that empire and many another, social psychology has undergone
attacks from without and rebellions from within. Its hodgepodge of topics,
overextended battle lines, bold and sometimes offensive experimental
methods, and lack of integrating theory have all made it an inviting target.

The most intense attack came from within. For half a dozen or more
years beginning in the early 1970s, during the so-called Crisis of Social
Psychology, social psychologists were engaged in an orgy of self-
criticism. Among the sundry charges they lashed themselves with were
that their field paid too little attention to practical applications (but conversely that it paid too little attention to theory); that it devoted far too
much effort to studies of trivial details (but conversely that it hopped
from one big issue to another without completing studies of the details);
and that it made unjustifiable generalizations about human nature on
the basis of mini-experiments with American college undergraduates.

This last criticism was the most troubling. In 1974, when self-criticism
was at its peak, college students were the experimental subjects in 87 percent of the studies reported in one leading journal and 74 percent of
those in another.[70] Such laboratory research, critics said, might be inter-

nally valid (it showed what it said it showed), but might not be and probably was not externally valid (what it showed did not necessarily apply to the outside world). A laboratory situation as highly artificial and special as the Milgram obedience experiment, and the behavior it elicited, could hardly be compared, they said, with a Nazi death camp and the confident, unfaltering barbarity of the officers and guards who daily herded crowds of naked Jews into the "showers" and turned on the poison gas.

The most disturbing assault, expanding the charge that the findings of sociopsychological research lack external validity, was made by Kenneth Gergen of Swarthmore College in 1973. In a journal article that torched his own profession, he asserted that social psychology is not a science but a branch of history. It claims to discover principles of behavior that hold true for all humankind but that really account only for phenomena pertaining to a given sample of people in a specific cultural setting at a particular time in history.[71]

As examples, Gergen said the Milgram obedience experiment was dependent on contemporary attitudes toward authority but that these were not universal; cognitive dissonance claims that human beings find inconsistency unpleasant, but early existentialists welcomed it; and conformity research reports that people are swayed more by the views of friends than of others, a conclusion that may hold good in America but not in societies where friendship plays a different role. Gergen's drastic conclusion:

> It is a mistake to consider the processes in social psychology as basic in the natural science sense. Rather, they may be largely considered the psychological counterpart of cultural norms . . . Social psychological research is primarily the systematic study of contemporary history.

For some years following the publication of Gergen's scathing critique, social psychologists held many soul-searching symposia devoted to his thesis. Edward Jones said that since Gergen's pessimistic conclusions were not especially novel, "one can wonder why contemporary social psychologists paid such lavish attention to them," and suggested that "a widespread need for self-flagellation, perhaps unique to social psychologists, may account for some of the mileage of the Gergen message."[72] Whence that special need? Jones does not say, but perhaps it was penance for the brashness, egotism, and *chutzpa* characteristic of the profession up to that point.

Eventually, the debate did yield sound answers to the barbed questions hurled by Gergen and others, and restored the image of social psychology as a science.

To the charge that what is true of college undergraduates may not be true of the rest of humankind, methodologists replied that for purposes of testing a hypothesis, the population being studied is not a critical issue. If variable X leads to variable Y, and in the absence of X there is no Y, the causal connection between X and Y is proven for that group; to the extent that it is also found true of other groups, it is likely to be a general truth. (The recent emphasis on cross-cultural psychology has proven that to be the case with many a finding, including the Milgram obedience phenomenon and Latané's social-loafing principle, each of which has been demonstrated in varied groups of experimental subjects in this country and in other countries.)

In a thoroughgoing rebuttal of Gergen's charges, Barry Schlenker of the University of Florida pointed out that the physical sciences, too, began with limited and contradictory observations and gradually developed general theories that harmonized their seeming inconsistencies. In the same way, the social sciences have identified, in limited contexts, what seem to be human universals, and brought together wider-ranging proof. Anthropologists and sociologists, for instance, first supposed and later demonstrated that all societies have incest taboos, some form of the family, and some system for maintaining order. Social psychology, said Schlenker, was following the same route, and the principles of social learning, conformity, and status dominance were among the findings that have already been shown to have multicultural validity.[73]

By the end of the 1970s the crisis was abating, and a few years later Edward Jones could view it and the future of the field with optimism:

> The crisis of social psychology has begun to take its place as a minor perturbation in the long history of the social sciences. The intellectual momentum of the field has not been radically affected . . . The future of social psychology is assured not only by the vital importance of its subject matter but also by its unique conceptual and methodological strengths that permit the identification of underlying processes in everyday life.[74]

Nonetheless, from that time to this, again and again some wannabe proclaims, usually in an obscure, offbeat journal, that social psychology is wrongly oriented and points out which way it should go, not that anyone pays such preachments any attention. It remains true that social psychol-

ogy has no unifying theory, but many of its middle-range theories have
been widely validated, and their jumbled mass of findings impressively
adds to humankind's understanding of its own nature and behavior.

But from Triplett's day to the present, the value of social psychology
has been as much a matter of practical application to real-life concerns
as of deeper understanding of fundamental principles. The beneficial
uses of social psychology are remarkable: among them are ways to get
better compliance by medical patients; the use of cooperative rather
than competitive classroom methods; social support groups and networks for the widowed and divorced, substance abusers, and others in
crisis; training in interpersonal communication in T-groups; the improving of the mood and mental functioning of nursing home patients by
giving them greater control and decision-making power; new ways of
treating depression, loneliness, and shyness; classroom training in
empathy and prosocial behavior; control of family conflict by means of
small-group and family therapy.[76]

Some years ago, after the Crisis in Social Psychology had passed and
the discipline was back in good health, Elliot Aronson voiced what he
and many other social psychologists felt about their field:

[It] is my belief that social psychology is extremely important—that
social psychologists can play a vital role in making the world a better
place . . . [and can have] a profound and beneficial impact on our lives
by providing an increased understanding of such important phenomena as conformity, persuasion, prejudice, love, and aggression.[76]

Today, nearly two decades later, social psychologists retain that passionate affirmative belief in the value of their discipline. As the authors
of a leading textbook proclaimed in 2006:

*Virtually everything we do, feel, or think is related in some way to the
social side of life.* In fact, our relations with other people are so central
to our lives and happiness that it is hard to imagine existing without
them . . . Survivors of shipwrecks or plane crashes who spend long
periods of time alone often state that not having relationships with
other people was the hardest part of their ordeal—more difficult to
bear than lack of food or shelter. In short, the social side of life is, in
many ways, the core of our existence. It is this basic fact that makes
social psychology—the branch of psychology that studies all aspects of
social behavior and social thought—so fascinating and essential.[77]

That view of the discipline may be why, despite the compelling attractions of the glamorous newer fields of cognitive science, evolutionary psychology, and cognitive neuroscience, the membership of the Society for Personality and Social Psychology has grown by 50 percent in just the past dozen years and now has 4,500 members.

What matter, then, if social psychology has no proper boundaries, no agreed-upon definition, and no unifying theory?

FOURTEEN

The Perception
Psychologists

Interesting Questions

Aminnow, with almost no brain to speak of, can see (more or less); so can an ant, whose entire nervous system consists of only a few hundred neurons; and so can many another creature that has nothing remotely akin to a mind. It might seem, therefore, that visual perception is a physiological function and, though it influences many psychological processes, is not itself one of them.*

Throughout the centuries, however, most philosophers and psychologists have considered perception, at least in human beings, a fundamentally psychological function; it is the mind's link to external reality, of which we know only what our senses tell us. The derivation of knowledge from perceptions raises a host of interesting questions (interesting not in the lay sense of "absorbing" but in the scientific sense of "important" or "potentially illuminating"). But although philosophers have thought about perception for twenty-five hundred years and physiologists and psychologists have researched it for nearly four hundred, some of these questions remain moot and some have been answered in ways that raise new and equally puzzling questions. With the advent of cognitive neuroscience, however, a number of the most interesting questions have recently been, or are currently being, definitively answered.†

---

*Since most of the psychological research on perception has concerned vision, we will bypass the other senses.
†In this chapter we will touch only lightly on cognitive neuroscience but come to grips with it in a later chapter.

Consider one that the Greek philosophers were the first to ask: How do images of the outside world reach the intellect within?

Plato speculated that the eye actively seeks information by sending forth emanations of some kind that encompass objects—palpating them visually, so to speak. Democritus disagreed, arguing that perception works in the other direction: each object constantly imprints its likeness on the atoms of air, and these replicas, traveling to the viewer, interact with the atoms of the eye and re-create the likeness there, whence it passes to the mind. It was a better guess than Plato's but wrong in all its details.

In 1604 the German astronomer Johannes Kepler made a leap forward in the understanding of vision. Recent developments in optics and optical instruments enabled him to recognize that the clear body in the front of the eye is a lens that bends rays of light coming from any object, casting an image of the object on the eye's screenlike retina, from which the resulting nerve impulses are transmitted to the brain.

Ever since, the notion has prevailed that the eye is a kind of camera; the metaphor fits the facts of nearsightedness, farsightedness, and astigmatism, and their correction by eyeglasses. But while it is valid in some respects, it is seriously misleading in many others. Ralph N. Haber, long a leading figure in perception research, has called it "one of the most potent though misguided metaphors in psychology" and the source of much "mischief."[1]

What sort of mischief? For one thing, in a camera the image projected by the lens is upside down, and in 1625 Christoph Scheiner, an astronomer, showed that this is also true of the eye. He carefully peeled away the outer coating of the back of an ox's eye and through the semitransparent retina saw an upside-down version of whatever he aimed the eye at. But if we see the image that is formed on the retina, why do we not see the world upside down? The question was to plague psychologists for three centuries.[2]

Another difficulty created by the eye-as-camera metaphor became evident with the advent of photography. To form a sharp image, a camera must be held still during the exposure or, in the case of a movie camera, open and close its shutter many times a second; our eyes, however, constantly jiggle back and forth, even when we look steadily at some point, yet do not produce blurred images. Although we are not aware of and do not normally experience these movements, we can see them by means of a simple procedure. Look steadily at the black dot in the cen-

ter of the diagram below for about twenty seconds, then quickly shift to
the white dot and gaze at it fixedly. You will see an illusory pattern of
black lines wavering slightly to and fro. The black lines are an afterimage, due to temporary fatigue of the retinal receptors on which the white
lines fell for twenty seconds; the wavering is the never-ending movement in question.

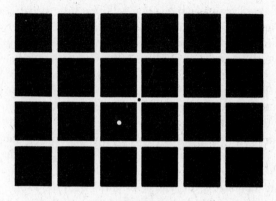

FIGURE 21

Test pattern for perceiving constant eye movement

The meaning of the demonstration is that the eye may be somewhat like
a camera, but seeing is nothing like taking pictures.

A second interesting question: Is what we see actually out there? A corollary question: Does it look like what we see? Folk wisdom has always
held that we see what exists and what we see is a faithful account of what
exists. We see a closed door before us, reach out to the doorknob, and it
is where we expected it to be and does what we expected it to do; we
lower ourselves onto a chair and it is real and solid, as it appeared to be;
we raise a forkful of fettuccini Bolognese to our mouth and it is rich,
meaty, and chewy, just as we anticipated. Common sense and philosophy agree that perception is contact with reality. Only a few rare birds,
like Bishop Berkeley, have ever doubted that there is a world outside
ourselves that corresponds to our perceptions.

But though nearly all of us reasonably assume our perceptions to be
truthful, physicists now assure us that the colors we see do not exist as
colors outside our heads. The red of a ripe apple, for instance, does not

exist as red in the apple; what does is a surface that absorbs all visible light except in the region of 650 nanometers wavelength, which it reflects. When that specific radiation reaches the human eye, the brain perceives it as what we call red. It may be disconcerting to think that the whole splendid colorful world we see on a spring day doesn't really look like that outside of our own minds. But perhaps we should set aside this philosophic/metaphysical issue and consider a much more approachable problem of vision, namely, that we often have visual experiences we know are misleading or erroneous but cannot will ourselves to correct. The moon, on the horizon, looks huge; we are aware that it does not change size but cannot make ourselves see it as no larger than it is when overhead. We stare at a bright light and, looking away, see an afterimage—a perception, but not of anything outside ourselves. We have dreams in which we see persons, places, and actions that are not before us, as they seem to be, or may not even exist.

There are, furthermore, the many illusions that psychologists have studied in the past and the present century. In the following diagram the gray tones of the inner areas look quite different from each other, but actually are identical, as you can determine by cutting a small hole in a piece of paper and centering it over first one and then the other. The mind, or at least the brain's visual cortex, judges lightness in terms of contrast, not absolute intensity. What you see is not what exists.

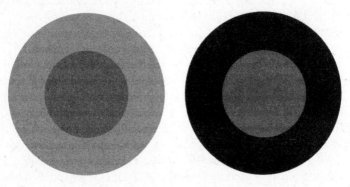

FIGURE 22
Which central area is darker? Wrong!

Here are several other classical illusions, each named for its discoverer: (1) the Zöllner, (2), the Poggendorf, (3) the Jastrow, and (4) the Hering:

Contrary to what your eyes tell you (and as you can verify with a ruler), the straight lines in (1) are parallel to one another, the angled lines in (2) are aligned, not offset from each other, the figures in (3) are the same size, and the heavy lines in (4) are perfectly straight.

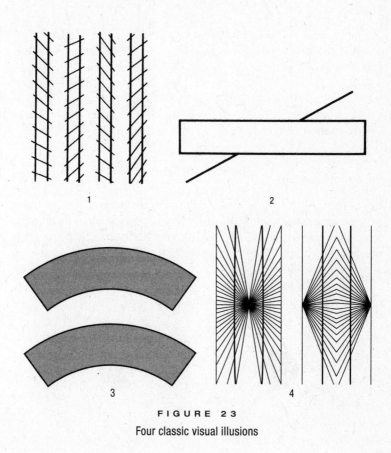

FIGURE 23
Four classic visual illusions

Another category of illusion consists of ambiguous figures that we can will ourselves to see as either one or the other of two different things. Two examples:

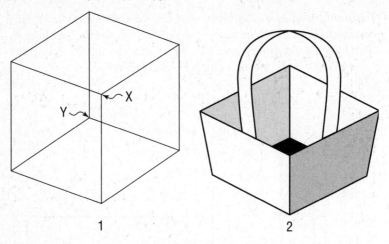

FIGURE 24
Two reversible figures

In (1) you can will yourself to see the familiar Necker cube as if you were looking down on it, with corner X closest to you, or as if you were looking up at it, with corner Y closest to you. In (2) you can see the handles attached inside the two white sides of the basket—or, if you choose, attached inside the gray sides.

Finally, in the following diagram there appears to be a triangle that is distinctly whiter than the surrounding area,

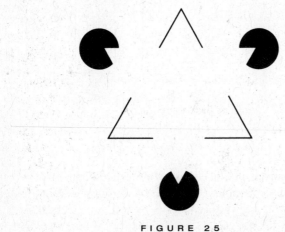

FIGURE 25
The triangle that does not exist

but it was you who created both the triangle and its brightness; no such figure is there, nor is the paper any whiter where the triangle seems to be than in the adjacent background.

As we proceed, we will learn the explanations for some of these illusions; for now, the point is that perception in human beings is not simply a physiological process that transmits representations of outside stimuli to the central nervous system; it often involves higher mental processes that make sense (and sometimes nonsense) of the impulses arriving via the optic nerves.

A third interesting question—Edwin Boring, in his monumental *History of Experimental Psychology*, calls it "the first mystery of vision"[3]—is that we have two eyes yet do not see everything doubled. Galen long ago rightly hypothesized that this is because the nerve fibers from both eyes lead to the same part of the brain. But that is only a partial answer. The two retinas receive somewhat different images of all but distant objects, as is easily confirmed by alternately opening and closing each eye while looking at a nearby object. (Each eye sees more of one side of the object than the other, and sees the object in a different relationship to things in the background.) But if these somewhat different images overlap in the brain, why is the result not blurred?

Perception researchers now answer that "fusion" of the dissimilar images takes place in the visual cortex, resulting in a single three-dimensional image. By tracing the axons of the two optic nerves—which are made up of a million ganglion cells—and by using modern brain scan techniques to see what brain areas are activated by vision, perception researchers have been able to identify the intricate routing and processing of the incoming neural impulses. Omitting the bewildering details, suffice it to say that the impulses are split up and separated into thirty different pathways to areas of the visual cortex for *pattern recognition* (how things look), *place recognition* (where things are), color, and other characteristics. Then these and other arriving data are coordinated through a host of other pathways of the brain's visual system to yield a final perception of a unified visual scene.[4]

Another interesting question, one of the most baffling, is how the image on the retina is viewed in the brain. Nerve impulses from the retina travel to the brain's visual cortex, but what then? No screen exists in the brain on which they can be projected, so how is the incoming flow of data seen? And if it is displayed in some way there or elsewhere in the brain, who or what sees it? The question revives the ancient (and now thoroughly discredited) supposition that there is a homunculus or little man—the "I" of the mind—who perceives what arrives at the cortex. But if the homunculus is seeing that image, with what is it doing so? Eyes of some sort? Then who or what is looking at what arrives at the homunculus's visual center? And so on, ad infinitum.

Allied to this puzzle is the question of visual memory. Every adult has an immense repertoire of images stored in his or her brain—familiar faces, houses, trees, leaves, cloud formations, beds slept in. They have been recorded, in some fashion, after even a single quick viewing. Though we cannot call all of them clearly to mind, it is by means of them that we recognize something we see a second time. In 1973 a Canadian psychologist, Lionel Standing, a man of great patience, showed ten thousand snapshots of miscellaneous subjects to volunteers at the rate of two thousand a day for five days. Later, when he showed them some of these pictures mixed in with new ones, they correctly identified two thirds of the old ones as pictures they had already seen.[5] Where had they stored all the briefly seen images and in what form? When they saw a picture the second time, how did they locate and view the image in memory to compare it with the incoming one? Not by projecting the stored one on a cerebral screen, since none exists. And however they displayed it, what inside them looked at both the stored and incoming images—ah! there's that troublesome little man again.

(Forget the little man and the screen he's looking at. Research done in the past two decades has come up with a more realistic but more complicated answer, based in considerable part on studies of people with specific kinds of brain damage due, usually, to strokes. One woman, for instance, when asked to describe a banana, could say that it was a fruit and grows in southern climates but could not name its color. Another patient, asked to describe an elephant, said correctly that it had long legs but incorrectly that it had a neck that could reach the ground to pick things up.

(From many such studies, plus the results of brain scans showing what areas are activated by the effort to visualize something, it has become fairly clear that mental images are not located like filed pictures in any one or several places, but that the *components* of each image—its shape, its color, its texture, and so on—are filed away separately and that sum-moning up a mental image uses many of the same processes that per-ception itself does, calling up and coordinating these several elements into one final, more or less complete image. But not a pictorial image; just as the letters of this sentence symbolize things they don't physically resemble, the patterns of firing of brain neurons represent objects and events in the outside world.[6] Why did evolution devise this scheme? Let the evolutionary psychologists figure out that one.)

These are but a few of the mysteries of visual perception; perhaps no area of psychology has produced as much research data and as relatively few definitive answers. Some years ago, James J. Gibson, a controversial but noted perception theorist, flatly asserted that most of what percep-tion researchers had learned in the past hundred years was "irrelevant and incidental to the practical business of perception."[7] A trifle more moderately, the perception psychologists Stephen M. Kosslyn and James R. Pomerantz said in 1977 that, despite all the accumulated data, perception is still poorly understood.[8] Still, they added, "we do know some things about it." And, they could add today, they now know a good deal more about it. Indeed, enough to begin to understand it, to answer at least some of the interesting questions, and to discard others in favor of more cogent ones.

Styles of Looking at Looking

For centuries, philosophers debated about whether we are born with mental equipment that makes sense of what we see (the Kantian or nativist view), or must learn from experience to interpret what we see (the Lockean or empiricist view). When psychology became experimen-tal, the findings of perception research not only failed to answer the question but added to the evidence for each side. Although today the terms have been redefined and the hypotheses have become more sophisticated, the debate continues.

Locke, Berkeley, and other philosophers and psychologists sometimes fantasized a test case that would definitively resolve the issue: a person blind from birth who, through an operation or some other intervention, suddenly gains sight. Would he know, without touching what he was looking at, that the object was a cube rather than a sphere, a dog rather than a cat? Or would his perceptions be meaningless until he learned what they meant? Such a person's experiences might hold the key.

In recent centuries a handful of such cases have, in fact, turned up. The most carefully reported was that of an Englishman with opaque corneas who, in the early 1960s, at the age of fifty-two was able to see for the first time.[9] S.B., as he is called by Richard L. Gregory, a British psychologist and perception expert who studied him closely, was an active and intelligent man who had made a good adaptation to his blindness: He was skilled at reading Braille, made objects with tools, often chose to walk without the customary white cane even though he sometimes bumped into things, and would go bicycling with a friend holding his shoulder to guide him.

In S.B.'s middle years, corneal transplants became possible, and he underwent an operation. According to Gregory's report, when the bandages were removed from his eyes, he heard the surgeon's voice and turned toward what he knew must be a face. He saw only a blur.

Experience, however, rapidly clarified his perceptions: Within days he could see faces, walk along a hospital corridor without touching the walls, and recognize that the moving objects he saw through the window were cars and trucks. Spatial perception, however, came to him more slowly. For a while, he judged the distance to the ground below his hospital window to be such that he could touch it with his toes if he hung by his hands from the windowsill, although it was ten times that distance.

S.B. was soon able to identify at first sight articles he had known by touch, such as toys, but many objects that he had never touched were mysteries to him until he was told or discovered what they were. Gregory and a colleague took him to London, where he recognized most of the animals at the zoo because he had petted cats and dogs and knew how other animals differed from them. But in a science museum S.B. saw a lathe—a tool he had always wanted to use—and could make nothing of it until, with his eyes closed, he ran his hands over it. Then, opening his eyes and looking at it, he said, "Now that I've felt it, I can see."

Interestingly, when Gregory showed S.B. some illusions, he failed to be misled by them; he did not, for instance, perceive the straight lines of the Hering illusion as curved or the parallel ones of the Zöllner as divergent. Such illusions evidently depend on one's having learned cues that denote perspective, and those cues, given by the other lines in the illusions, meant nothing to S.B.

The conclusions one can draw from his case are thus disappointingly mixed; some of the evidence favors innateness, some, experience. Besides, the evidence is contaminated: S.B. had had a lifetime of sensory experiences and learning with which to interpret his first visual perceptions, and his story does not reveal the extent to which the mind, before experience, is prepared to understand visual perceptions. Nor is the question answered by developmental research with infants, since it is unclear how much the development of an infant's perceptual abilities at any juncture is due to maturation and how much to experience. Only impermissible experiments that would deprive an infant of perceptual and other sensory experience could tease the two apart and measure their relative influence.

Making a still worse muddle of the matter is the question of whether perception is primarily a physiological function or a mental one.

The founders of scientific psychology in the nineteenth century and the early decades of the present one tried to evade this issue by asserting that mind was unobservable and perhaps illusory, and by limiting themselves to the study of physical realities. Those who were interested in perception investigated the physiology of the sensory systems, especially the visual one, and over the course of more than a century, a number of them in Europe and America assembled a mass of data on the mechanics of that system. By the early years of the twentieth century they had determined that the retina of each eye, a thin sheet of specialized neural tissue, contains about 132 million photoreceptor cells of two types, rods and cones, both of which convert light into nerve impulses; that the rods, more common in the periphery of the retina, are more sensitive and respond only to very low levels of illumination; that the cones, more common in the center, respond at higher levels of illumination; and that there are three species of cone, one containing primarily chemicals that absorb light of short wavelengths (and thus react to blue and green), another, of middle wavelengths (green), and a third, of longer wavelengths (yellow, orange, and red).[10]

They had also traced out much of the complex wiring scheme by which the rods and cones send their impulses to the brain. From the retinas, the bundles of optic nerve fibers make their way to the visual cortex, an area at the lower part of the back of the brain. En route, the fibers carrying messages from the left half and from the right half of each eye's field of vision are sorted out and redirected; the messages from each eye's right-hand field of vision end up at the left visual cortex, the left-hand field of vision at the right visual cortex. (To this day, no one has the least idea why evolution arranged this crisscross.)

Many psychologists were long reluctant to accept the evidence that visual functions are centered in the visual cortex; such localization smacked of phrenology. Late in the nineteenth century, however, brain localization—not of the phrenological type, and only of certain functions—gained new credibility after Wernicke and Broca discovered that speech functions are carried out in two small areas in the left half of the brain. This inspired researchers to look for an area where visual messages are received and understood, and through autopsies of brain-damaged human beings and operations on monkeys they identified it, in general terms, as the rear of the brain.

More precise pinpointing of the visual cortex was a byproduct of weaponry used in the Russo-Japanese War of 1904–1905.[11] In that conflict the Russians introduced a new rifle, the Mosin-Nagant Model 91, which fired bullets of smaller diameter and higher velocity than the rifles of earlier wars. The bullets often penetrated the skull without shattering it, and in some cases destroyed, partly or totally, the victim's vision without killing him. Tatsuji Inouye, a young Japanese army doctor who worked with wounded soldiers, plotted the extent to which each patient's visual field had been lost by each eye, determined from the site of the bullet's entry and exit which parts of the brain had been damaged, and, putting these data together, identified the precise location and extent of the visual cortex.

Among his findings was that the areas of the visual cortex that receive the retinal messages are grossly disproportionate to the areas of the retinal image. A very large part receives impulses coming from the fovea, the small central area of the retina where vision is sharpest, and only a small part from the larger peripheral area. (Later research showed the disparity in proportions to be about 35 to 1.[12]) That settled one great issue: what arrives at the brain is in no way an image corresponding in layout to the image on the retina.

The inescapable implication of Inouye's and others' findings, gradually accepted over the next several decades, was that the retinal cells are "transducers" that change light signals into a different form of energy— bursts of nerve impulse—and that these "coded" impulses or signals, when received in the brain, are not turned back into images in the visual cortex, even though "seen" there or elsewhere in the brain.[13] How they are seen remained a mystery, but perception physiologists did not trouble themselves with this question; their style of looking at looking dealt with the flow of neural impulses and stopped short at the borders of mind.

Another style of so-called perception research—it was only peripheral to perception—was in the Wundtian tradition. Its practitioners studied sensations (the immediate simple responses to sounds, lights, and touches), which they considered reflexive, elemental, and scientifically investigable, and the perception of those simple sensations. But they ignored all the complex interpretive aspects of perception, which they correctly deemed the result of the mind's processing of sensations and incorrectly believed to be beyond objective scrutiny. This approach, popular in the early part of the twentieth century, yielded a huge store of data about sensations but added almost nothing to the understanding of the psychology of perception.

Yet another style of perception research is psychophysics, which also stops short of looking at mental processes. Fechner and his followers, as we saw, measured sensory thresholds (the weakest sound, light, or other stimulus a subject could perceive) and "just noticeable differences" between pairs of stimuli. While such inquiries touched on conscious mental processes, the psychophysicists asked no questions about *how* the subject noticed a stimulus or judged differences but stuck to objective data—the magnitude of the stimuli and the subject's statements that he did or did not perceive a stimulus or a difference between two stimuli. Psychophysics was therefore acceptable during the dominance of behaviorism, when perception was otherwise largely ignored because it assumes that a representation of the world exists in the mind, a concept the behaviorists rejected.[14]

But psychophysics was plagued by a chronic problem: subjects were inconsistent in their responses. If given the same threshold stimulus a number of times, sometimes they would see or hear it, sometimes not. If a light at an intensity below a subject's threshold was gradually increased, he might begin to see it at a given level, but if it was presented above that threshold and gradually decreased, he might cease to see it at a somewhat different level.[15]

To solve this problem, in 1961 the psychologist J. A. Swets proposed applying to psychophysics the engineering concepts of signal detectability and information theory, which psychologists had come into contact with during World War II. Swets and his collaborators even gave their approach a name betokening the impersonality and objectivity of engineering—the Theory of Signal Detection. It held, first, that there would always be some random variation in the number of neurons excited by any signal and in the amount of "noise" (extraneous or accidental excitations) entering the neural system, and it corrected for these variations by statistical theory. It held, second, that a subject's response on any trial is partly determined by his expectations and his effort to maximize his rewards and minimize his costs; these variables could be accounted for by decision-making theory.

Although "decision making" sounds mental, the Theory of Signal Detection remains outside the mind; it predicts the likelihood of correct and incorrect responses according to purely mathematical parameters. Signal detection theory was a major advance in psychophysics and is a part of the standard repertoire of experimental methods today, but it concerns only certain objective results of perception and casts no light on how perception takes place.[16]

All along, however, a small number of psychologists had been exploring the internal or cognitive aspects of perception. They were mentalists, but not in the metaphysical sense; rather, in the tradition of James, Freud, and Binet, they believed that higher mental processes are the heart of psychology and can be experimentally investigated.

In 1897, even as Thorndike and others were beginning to turn toward animal experimentation and what would become behaviorist psychology, an American psychologist named George Stratton undertook a perception experiment of a human and distinctly cognitive kind. For a week, allowing himself no respite, he wore lenses that turned his view of the world upside down. At first he had so much difficulty getting about and reaching for objects that he would often close his eyes and rely on touch and memory. But by the fifth day he was automatically making the right movements and by the end of the week felt that things were where he saw them and even, at times, that they "seemed upright rather than inverted." When at last he removed the lenses, everything was bewildering. For several hours he found that he was reaching for objects in the wrong direction; then he relearned where things were when seen normally. The experiment dramatically showed that spatial perception, at least in human beings, is in some part learned and can be relearned.[17]

Striking as these findings were, the outlook of most psychologists in the early decades of the century was so antimentalist that there was little follow up of Stratton's work and almost no cognitively oriented perception research until half a century later. But by the 1940s several unrelated strains of cognitively oriented psychology—Freudian, Gestalt, personality research, and the nascent discipline of social psychology—were gaining strength, and psychologists who found any of them congenial took a wholly different approach to perception research from that of psychophysiologists and psychophysicists.

Some, in America and elsewhere, rediscovered Stratton's work and conducted new optical-distortion experiments. In 1951, Ivo Kohler, an Austrian psychologist, persuaded volunteers to spend fifty days seeing the world through prism goggles that displaced part of their visual field 10 degrees to the right and made straight vertical lines slightly curved. For days his subjects found the world unstable and had difficulty walking and performing even simple tasks, but after a week to ten days most things looked normal to them, and after a few weeks one volunteer was even able to ski. Like Stratton, they felt disoriented when they finally removed the prisms but soon adapted to normal vision.[18]

Other psychologists revived the long-neglected study of illusions, and by the 1950s it was again a topic of active research. The remarkable subjective triangle shown in Figure 25, created in 1950 by Gaetano Kanizsa, an Italian psychologist, was only one of many new illusions used to investigate mental processes of vision. A special kind of illusion was used to explore the mind's interpretation of ambiguous figures. The following classic example, created in 1930 by Boring, can be seen at will either as an old hag turned partly toward the viewer or as a young woman turned partly away.

FIGURE 26

What kind of woman is this?

That depends on what you choose to see.

The capacity to see either of two different images in ambiguous figures like this one or in figure-ground reversal patterns like the Rubin vase (Figure 12) cannot be explained by any known physiological mechanism, the British psychologist Stuart Anstis has said, but is the result of higher perceptual processes.*[19] The same is true of the mind's acceptance of, or bewilderment by, the "impossible objects" created by perception researchers in the 1940s and 1950s, of which these are classic examples:

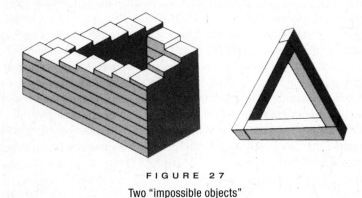

FIGURE 27

Two "impossible objects"

It is the mind, not the retina, optic nerves, or specialized cells of the neural cortex, that interprets the cues in such a figure as a picture of an object and simultaneously realizes that no such object could exist in the real world.

Another cognitive approach to perception was that of a number of American psychologists who, beginning in the 1940s, sought to discover how needs, motivations, and mental sets affect perception. Jerome Bruner and Leo Postman of Harvard, two leaders in this endeavor, showed toys and plain blocks, all three inches in height, to young children, and asked them to judge the objects' size; the children thought the toys were taller. In an extension of the experiment, they told the children they would get to keep the toys, but temporarily broke their promise. When the toys seemed unavailable, the children judged them as

---

*Some perception researchers attribute the reversal effect to neural satiation (the retinal neurons become fatigued with one image and the other replaces it). But this does not explain why we can switch images at will.

even larger than they had previously. Other researchers asked hungry and not-hungry subjects to estimate the size of food items; the hungry ones saw them as bigger than did the others. These and similar experiments demonstrated that need, desire, and frustration influence perception.[20]

So do certain traits of personality, according to other studies of that era. By means of a written test and an interview, Else Frenkel-Brunswik, a psychologist who was trained in Vienna and had immigrated to America, rated a group of children on ethnic prejudice, a trait she associated with the rigid "authoritarian personality pattern." She then showed the children a picture of a dog, followed by a series of transitional pictures in which the image gradually became that of a cat. Those who had scored high on prejudice tended to see the image as a dog longer than the unprejudiced, who were more flexible. Much the same was true when she asked children to identify the color of a series of cards that changed from one hue to another.[21]

Other cognitive studies of perception in the 1940s and 1950s explored "perceptual defenses"—forms of mental resistance to seeing something disturbing. Researchers used tachistoscopes to flash words on a screen very briefly (for a hundredth of a second or so), and found that subjects were less likely to recognize taboo words than neutral ones. The effect was strongest when the subjects were females and the experimenter male. One team used a tachistoscope to display achievement-related words like "compete" and "mastery," and neutral words like "window" and "article"; subjects who had a strong need for achievement, as measured by Henry Murray's TAT, could read the achievement-related words more quickly and easily than the neutral ones.[22]

Mental set, or the expectation of what one might see, was another topic of this kind of research. Bruner and Postman used the tachistoscope to show subjects very brief views of playing cards, most of which were standard but some of which were not, like a red four of spades. Habit and expectation caused twenty-seven of their twenty-eight subjects to see the abnormal cards as normal, but once the subjects knew about the cards, their mental set was changed and they made far fewer incorrect identifications.[23]

By 1949 such studies had become so numerous that psychologists, borrowing a term then current in women's fashions, spoke of the New Look in perception research. For about a decade, the New Look flourished, amassing data on the extent to which needs, motives, memory, and mental sets affect perception. Then, lacking detailed theory with which to explain the processes through which this took place, the movement lost steam. Much later, perception researchers came up with a cognitive description (rather than a theory) of visual recognition processing, lumpily called "bottom-up, top-down," that made sense of the accumulated data. In bottom-up processing the mind assembles the various bits of data coming in, achieving higher levels of recognition and meaning as it sees them fit together. But top-down processing, drawing on stored memory, context, and the like, may influence the lower levels of perception, either by making ambiguous information clear or by inducing a conception—or misconception—of what is being reported at the lower level. An often-cited example is the middle letter in each of these words:

TAE CAT

FIGURE 28

Bottom-up processing alone would leave us unsure what we were seeing; context—top-down processing—leads us to see the first one as an H, the second one as an A, although they are identical. Similarly, in the ambiguous images we saw above in Figure 24, it is whatever top-down influence we choose to exert that yields what we finally see.)

After the New Look petered out, perception research revived with the advent of a new and powerful theory, information processing, which in the 1960s and 1970s was beginning to transform cognitive psychology with its vision of an orderly series of processes by which sensations are transformed into thought, and thought to action. This theory postulates (and provides experimental evidence of) the metamorphosis of sensory input in a sequence of steps, including very brief storage in the sense organ, encoding into nerve impulses, short term memory storage in the mind, rehearsal or linkage with known material, long-term memory storage, retrieval, and so on. The theory made it possible for psychologists to be specific about how the mind handles incoming sensory material, and it revived interest in the cognitive approach to perception. By the 1970s research in the field of cognition was proliferating, as we will see in a later chapter.

But by then many significant discoveries had been made about the physiology of perception. Ever since, the two styles of looking at looking, the physiological and the cognitive, have existed side by side, seemingly opposed to each other but in reality focused on different aspects of the same phenomena, as discussed from here on.

Seeing Form

How do we see the shapes of things? The question may seem absurd — how could we *not* see them? But the perception of form is neither automatic nor foolproof. We see a shadowy figure in the park at night and cannot tell whether it is a bush or a lurking person; we read a carelessly scrawled signature and do not know whether it starts with C, G, or O; we arrive home exhausted after a long flight, spot our car in the vast airport parking lot, and trudge toward it, only to find as we draw near that it is a lookalike of another make; we enjoy a jigsaw puzzle precisely because we find it challenging and rewarding to locate the piece that will fit into the edge we have just created.

Research on form perception seeks to identify the mechanisms, both neural and cognitive, that enable us to recognize shapes — and that sometimes fail us. Much of that research in the past half century has taken the cognitive approach. The Gestaltists and their followers explored the mind's tendency to group related elements into coherent forms, fill in gaps in what we see, distinguish figures from background, and so on. They and others also said it was inborn higher mental processes that account for the "constancy phenomenon" — our seeing things as unchanged despite distortions of the retinal image, as when we perceive a book lying at an angle to us as having square corners although on the retina, as in a photograph, the book is a rhomboid with two acute and two obtuse angles.

But such perceptions are results, not processes. By what steps does the mind achieve them? It is one thing to say that we fill in gaps in familiar but incomplete forms that we see; it is quite another to determine by what specific means we achieve this. Many studies exploring cognitive processing of visual information in fine detail have identified some of them. A few examples of the findings:

—Research on the subjective-contour phenomenon (as in the illu-sory triangle in Figure 25 above) indicates that we create the imagined contours partly through association (the three angles remind us of previously seen triangles) and partly through clues that experience has taught us signify interposition (an object's obstructing our view of another one). As the perception researcher Stanley Coren pointed out, the gaps in the circles and in the existing triangle suggest that something else—the illusory tri-angle—is in the way, partially obscuring them. Because of the apparent interposition, the mind "sees" the imaginary tri-angle.[24]

—Some experiments have explored how we recognize a shape we are searching for, particularly when it is lost in a jumble of other shapes. One important process is "feature detection"—conscious searching for known and recognizable elements of a particular fig-ure so as to distinguish it from similar shapes. In each of the follow-ing columns there is a single X. If you time your own search for it with a sweep-second hand, you will find that you locate it far faster in the first list than in the second:[25]

ORDQCG	WEFIMZ
CRUDOQ	EVLMZW
QUORDC	VIMWZE
CUORCD	ZIVFEW
DROCUD	VIZELM
DOCURD	MFWIVZ
DRGCOD	ZVXIEW
ORCDUQ	WVLZIE
ODQRUC	EWMZFI
DRXOQU	MEZFIV
DUGQOR	IWEMVZ
RGODUC	WEZMFV
GCUDOC	EFLMIV
DGOCDR	WZIEFV

The task of matching the pattern of the X retrieved from memory to what we are looking at is far easier and quicker when the hidden X is among rounded letters than among letters made up of straight lines and angles, like the X itself, in which case we must pay close attention to minor features. Or, as another explanation has it, we often identify visual images by "preattentive" processes—automatic ones concerned with overall image—but when that does not suffice, we shift to "focused attention" and consciously search for minor distinguishing features of the sought object.[26]

— In 1954 Fred Attneave, of the University of Oregon, asked subjects to represent certain figures by a series of ten dots; they tended to place the dots on those points where the direction of the outline changed most sharply. Attneave's conclusion was that one way we recognize patterns is by means of analysis of its "points of change."[27] He also created some figures, greatly simplified from reality, by drawing straight lines from one point of change to another. Although this reduces curves to straight lines, the figures are still immediately recognizable, as in this example:

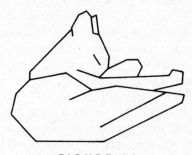

FIGURE 29

No curve exists, yet one sees a curved object.

— Skilled readers see words as wholes, without identifying them letter by letter, as beginning readers do. But even in rapid reading, a great deal of high-speed feature detection goes on, as shown by experiments conducted by Eleanor J. Gibson (the wife of James Gibson, mentioned above) and colleagues at Cornell in the 1960s. They made up a batch of nonsense monosyllables, some of which obey English rules of spelling and therefore are pronounceable ("glurck," "clerft") and then switched the consonant groups around to make others, with the same letters, that violate the rules and are not pronounceable ("rckugl," "ftercl"). When skilled readers saw the words in tachistoscopic flashes, they could read the legal combinations far more easily than the illegal ones, even though none of the letter groups was a known word. One possible explanation was that they pronounced the words to themselves and were better able to hold pronounceable ones in short-term memory than unpronounceable ones. But Gibson repeated the experiment at Gallaudet College with deaf students who had never heard words pronounced, and she got the same results. This could only mean that in perceiving each pseudo-word, readers distinguished all the letters and instantly recognized which groups of them obeyed the rules of legitimate patterns of spelling in English and which did not.[28]

— Researchers working with visual illusions found that if subjects were instructed to look long at an illusion, and in some cases to let their eyes wander back and forth over it, the force of the illusion would wane. Even though the cues in the illusion mislead the mind, attentive looking enables the mind to extract much of the reality from the cues.[29]

— In the late 1950s and early 1960s, Irvin Rock, a young psychologist who would become a leading figure in perception research, showed subjects a square tilted at 45 degrees and asked them what it looked like; they said a diamond. He then tilted *them* by 45 degrees, causing the figure to be projected as a square on their retinas. But they saw it in a room with respect to which it was tilted and could feel themselves tilted with respect to that room; these two sources of information, processed by the mind, caused them still to see the square as a diamond. This simple experiment profoundly influenced Rock's thinking about perception and led him to conclude that until perceptual phenomena have been analyzed from a psychological viewpoint, it is premature to do so on a neurophysiological level.[30]

These findings, and many more from studies made in the succeeding decades, made it clear that form is the most important cue for object recognition. Early in life toddlers learn to identify objects by their shape; they quickly gain the ability to distinguish between a dog and a cat, and having learned what an apple is, they recognize green ones, yellow ones and red ones as apples. Not long ago the psychologist Barbara Landau showed three-year-olds a meaningless shape and told them it was a "dax"; then she showed them other objects with the same shape but made of different materials, sizes, and colors, but the children identified each of them as a "dax."[31]

And yet to this day, say Michael Gazzaniga and Todd Heatherton, "how we are able to extract an object's form from the image on our retina is still somewhat mysterious."[32] They cite such commonplace mysteries as our ability to recognize objects from different perspectives and in unusual orientations, and to tell where one object ends and another begins, as in the case of a horse and rider. Hypotheses about how we do it are plentiful; proven theories are nonexistent.

From the 1940s on, neurophysiologists were making discoveries about visual perception that were as significant as those of the cognitivists. As early as the 1930s, they were able to record the electrical activity of small groups of nerve cells, and by the 1940s laboratory researchers had perfected glass probes containing electrodes so fine—the hairlike tip might be a thousandth of a centimer in diameter—that they could be inserted into a single cell of the retina, geniculate body, or visual cortex of a cat or a monkey that had been given local anesthetic. With this kind of apparatus, researchers could observe the individual cell's electrical discharges when the animal was shown a light or some other display.[33]

This technique produced a historic discovery about form perception. In the late 1950s, David Hubel and Torsten Wiesel, two brilliant neurophysiologists at Harvard Medical School, were testing the responses of visual cortical cells in cats. They would implant a microelectrode in a cell of a cat's visual cortex; although they could not pick a particular cell, by inserting the probe at about the right spot and right angle they knew what area they were reaching. Wiesel once likened the process to spearing cherries from a bowl with a toothpick; you may not be able to see which cherry you're spearing, but you're sure to hit something. The cat would be restrained in a harness while the researchers shone spots or bars of light and other figures on a screen. By securely fixing the position of the cat's head, the researchers could know which part of the retina the image fell on and link this with the cortical area being probed. Through an amplifier and loudspeaker, they could hear the cell fire; at rest, it might produce a few "pops" per second, but chatter away at fifty or a hundred pops per second when stimulated.[34]

Since both the retina and the cortex are complicated structures, it took great patience to discover which cells, at what location and in which layer of the cortex, respond to messages from different areas of the retina.[35] One day in 1958, this excruciatingly fine-detailed work yielded an astonishing and half-accidental finding. Hubel and Wiesel had positioned an electrode tip in a cell but for hours couldn't induce rapid firing. As Hubel recalled, a few years ago:

We tried everything short of standing on our heads to get it to fire. (It did fire spontaneously from time to time, as most cortical cells do, but we had a hard time convincing ourselves that our stimuli had caused any of that activity.) To stimulate, we were using mostly white circular spots and black spots. After about five hours of struggle, we suddenly had the impression that the glass with the [black] dot was occasionally producing a response, but the response seemed to have little to do with the dot. Eventually we caught on: it was the sharp but faint shadow cast by the edge of the glass [slide] as we slid it into the slot that was doing the trick. We soon convinced ourselves that the edge worked only when its shadow was swept across one small part of the retina and that the sweeping had to be done with the edge in one particular orientation.[36]

In short, the cell responded strongly to a horizontal line or edge but only weakly or not at all to a dot, a tilted line, or a vertical line.

Hubel and Wiesel (and other researchers) went on to show that some other cells are specifically responsive to lines at an angle or to vertical lines or to right angles or to distinct edges (where there is a contrast between an object and what surrounds it). It became clear that the cells of the visual cortex are so specialized that they respond only to particular details of images on the retina. Hubel and Wiesel won a Nobel Prize in 1981 for this and related brain research.

One bizarre offshoot of the Hubel and Wiesel work was the notion of the "grandmother cell"—a parody, by J. Y. Lettvin, at the time of Hubel and Wiesel's work, of what he considered the simplistic notion that single neurons in the brain might detect and represent every object, including one's grandmother. The parody had enough appeal to be seriously considered by some perception specialists but actually became shorthand for all the overwhelming practical arguments against a one-to-one object coding scheme.[37]

In any case, Hubel and Wiesel's line-detector cells are a proven reality. Interestingly, this response is partly acquired, even though it is neurological. In a 1970 experiment kittens were reared in a vertical cylinder lined with vertical stripes and never saw horizontal lines. When they were tested for vision, at five months, they were blind to horizontal lines or objects. The neural explanation is that the cortical cells that respond to horizontal lines had failed to develop during the early stages of the kittens' lives.[38] Similarly, people reared in cities have more exposure to vertical and horizontal lines during early childhood than to lines oriented otherwise, and develop a greater sensitivity to the former. A research team tested a group of city-reared college students and a group of Cree Indians who grew up in traditional tents and lodges with few verticals and horizontals. The city-reared students exhibited the oblique effect; the Crees did not.[39]

You can also experience the specificity of the vertical, horizontal, and oblique detector cells of your retina by staring fixedly at the center of this pattern:

FIGURE 30

A pattern that confuses the retina's line-detector cells

The whirling and vibrating you see are probably due to the fact that when you look at the center, where rays of varied angles are close together, the eye's continual movements cause the image on the retina to shift from one kind of angled line to another, sending a jumble of signals that confuses the cortical receptors of specialized directional sensitivity.

The line detection ability of specific neurons is also exemplified by the following two displays, in each of which one object "pops out" because its lines have a unique stimulus property for those neurons:

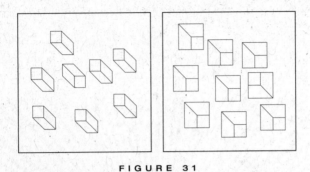

FIGURE 31

Line Detection: The one inconsistent figure in each set "pops out."

The microelectrode technique enabled neurophysiologists to decipher the architecture of the visual cortex—the neurons are arranged vertically, about a hundred in a column, and in layers that run through the columns—and to measure the responses of neurons in every part of the visual cortex to a broad variety of stimuli. The result was a detailed picture of how different cells in different parts of the visual cortex distinguish among all sorts of shapes, contrasts in brightness, colors, movements, and depth cues. A neuron-to-neuron and column-to-column synaptic hook-up of immense complexity links the responses of all these cells, presenting the brain with a composite message of the coded information of what had been a retinal image.[40]

Where and how that assembled message is "seen" by the mind was not apparent, although it was clear, from much of the cognitive perception research, that the specialized responses of the visual cortical cells are not the final product, at least not in human beings. In simple animals the neuronal responses may be enough to produce appropriate action (either flight or attack). In human beings, the neural messages are often meaningless until they are interpreted by cognitive processes. In the case of the illusory triangle, the viewer's mind, not cortical cells, supplies the missing parts of the figure. The same is true of many other incomplete or degraded images, where the viewer, consciously invoking higher mental processes, fills in the missing parts and sees what is not there. A case in point:

FIGURE 32

A degraded image. What is it?

At first, most people see this figure (by Irvin Rock) as a meaningless array of dark fragments. How the reversal to the white regions and to perception of the hidden word comes about is not known, but once it has been seen, the mind is almost unable to see the figure again as meaningless fragments.

Seeing Movement

The metaphor of the eye as camera implies that we see the world in snapshots, but our visual experience is one of unbroken movement. Indeed, the perception of our movement through the environment and the movement of things in the environment is one of the most important aspects of seeing. Vision without perception of movement would be almost valueless, perhaps even worse than no vision, to judge from a rare case reported in the journal *Brain* in 1983.

The patient was a woman who was admitted to a hospital after experiencing severe headaches, vertigo, nausea, and, worst of all, a disabling loss of the perception of movement. A brain scan and other tests showed that she had suffered damage to a part of the cerebral cortex outside the primary visual receiving area that is known to be crucial to movement perception.[41] From the report:

> [She had] a loss of movement vision in all three dimensions. She had difficulty, for example, in pouring tea or coffee into a cup because the fluid appeared to be frozen, like a glacier. In addition, she could not stop pouring at the right time since she was unable to perceive the movement in the cup (or a pot) when the fluid rose . . . In a room where more than two other people were walking she felt very insecure and unwell, and usually left the room immediately, because "people were suddenly here or there but I have not seen them moving" . . . She

could not cross the street because of her inability to judge the speed of a car, but she could identify the car itself without difficulty. "When I'm looking at the car first, it seems far away. But then, when I want to cross the road, suddenly the car is very near."[42]

Even without such evidence, we can tell that movement perception is of paramount importance. Perception of our own movement guides us in making our way through our environment; perception of objects coming toward us enables us to escape harm; perception of the movement of our hands provides data vital to control when we are reaching for an object or doing fine manual work; perception of our minute bodily movements when standing keeps us from weaving or losing balance. (If you stand with your feet close together and shut your eyes, you will find it difficult to remain perfectly steady.)

Much research on movement perception for the past half-century has dealt with external variables: how the size, speed, location, and other characteristics of moving objects affect the way they appear to us. Such research is akin to psychophysics: it gathers objective data but says nothing of the internal processes responsible for the experiences. Still, it has provided important clues to those processes, both of the innate neural and the acquired cognitive kinds.

A typical finding about an innate low-level process: Researchers projected a shadow or boxlike figure on a screen in front of infants, then made the shadow or figure rapidly expand. When it did, the infants reared back as if to avoid being hit. The reaction is not a result of experience; a newborn who has never been hit by an approaching object will react in this fashion, as will many young and inexperienced animals. The avoidance response to a "looming" figure is evidently a protective reflex built into us by evolution; the visual impression of an object coming at us triggers escape behavior without involving higher mental processes.[43]

A typical finding about an acquired high-level process: In 1974 the psychologists David Lee and Eric Aronson built a floorless little room that could be slid one way or another across an unmoving floor. When they placed in it a toddler of anywhere from thirteen to sixteen months and slid the room in the direction he or she was facing—that is, away from the child's face—the child would lean forward or fall; if they slid it in the other direction, the child would lean backward or fall. The explanation is that when the walls moved away, the child felt as if he or she were falling backward and automatically tried to compensate by leaning forward, and vice versa. This seems to be acquired behavior. The child learns to use "optic flow" information when beginning to walk. (Optic flow is the movement of everything within our visual field when we move. As we walk toward some point, for instance, everything around it expands outward toward the limits of our vision.)[44]

These and other fruitful studies of movement perception revealed additional defects of the long-held notion that the eye is a kind of camera. One such defect is that although the eye has no shutter, moving objects do not cause a blur, nor do we see a blur when we move our eyes as we do on a photograph if the camera is moved during exposure. Accordingly, much research on motion perception has sought to discover why there is no blurring. One hypothesis that gained favor was based on the finding by Ulric Neisser and various others that when we view an image flashed on a screen by a tachistoscope for even a tiny fraction of a second, we can briefly see it afterward in the mind's eye. In 1967 Neisser used the term "icon" for this very brief visual memory, measured its duration as about half a second (later research reported as little as a quarter of a second) to two seconds, and found that it is erased if a new pattern is presented before it has faded.[45] Other vision researchers then suggested that since the eye sweeps across the field of vision or follows moving objects in a series of jumps known as "saccades," it sees nothing while moving but at every momentary stop sends an iconic snapshot to the brain. The snapshots are assembled there into a perception of motion, somewhat as if one were watching a movie.[46]

This hypothesis was widely accepted in the 1970s and the early 1980s. But some leading investigators began to doubt that the icon, observed only under unnatural laboratory conditions, exists in normal perception; if it does not, the saccadic-iconic hypothesis of movement perception collapses. As Ralph Haber saw it:

> Such presentations have no counterpart in nature, unless you are trying to read during a lightning storm. There are no natural occasions in which the retina is statically stimulated for less than about a quarter of a second, preceded and followed by blankness . . . There is never a fixed snapshot-like retinal image, frozen in time, but rather a continuously changing one . . . The icon was born in the laboratory, and it has life only there and nowhere else.[47]

The screen of the eye is not a photographic emulsion, and moving images on it are not captured, unblurred, in the form of stills. Rather, the retina is a tissue made up of millions of receptors, each of which, when stimulated, fires many times per second. As an image moves across the retina, a continuous flow of impulses from a series of receptors proceeds to the visual cortex. There is no blur, because the system generates not a series of stills but an unbroken stream of changing information.

And indeed, a dramatic discovery about movement perception, made four decades ago, was that some neurons in the retina and in the visual cortex fire in response to movement but that many others do not; the detection of movement begins at the single-cell level. This ancient evolutionary development helps prey avoid being eaten, and also helps predators locate and seize their prey. A frog will efficiently snap at any small moving object but starve to death if presented only with dead flies or worms, which it does not perceive as food;[48] many other simple predators show similar behavior. The frog's retina and brain apparently have neurons that respond to movement (and size), a capacity that has more survival value than other aspects of vision.

In the 1960s and 1970s, Hubel and Wiesel, among others, demonstrated the existence of movement detectors. They showed, when recording the activity of single cells in cats and monkeys by the microelectrode technique, that in both the retina and the visual cortex certain cells, and only these, respond strongly to movement. Some, in fact, fire in response only to movement in a particular direction, others only to movement in the opposite direction.[49]

Other investigators confirmed this by entirely different methods. In 1963 Robert Sekuler and a colleague projected an image of a grate moving upward, established the threshold (minimum speed) at which each human subject could see it moving, and then had each one look steadily at the moving image. After several minutes, subjects could no longer see the movement when the grate was crawling at the original threshold speed, although they could still do so when the speed was doubled, and could see downward motion at the slower speed. The results indicated that there were upward-motion detectors, which had become fatigued, and downward-motion detectors, which had not. Comparable results were obtained in reverse when the subjects watched a downward-moving grating for several minutes.[50]

Most of us have experienced movement-detector fatigue without knowing its neural basis. If we look steadily for some time at a waterfall (or another continuously moving stream, like an assembly line) and then look away, we see illusory movement in the opposite direction. "This is called the *waterfall effect*," note Gazanniga and Heatherton, "because if you stare at a waterfall and then turn away, the rocks and trees will seem to move upward for a moment."[51] The cells in the visual cortex that fire at a high rate in response to movement in one direction become temporarily fatigued and cease firing, while those that fire in response to movement in the opposite direction continue to do so at their normal low level, temporarily producing a sense of movement in their preferred direction.

None of this, however, explains two other mysteries of motion perception. If we move our eyes or head to follow a flying bird or other moving object, we perceive movement even though the image remains at the center of the retina. Conversely, if we move our eyes, images sweep across the retina but we see the world as still.

There must, then, be some other source of information that confirms or corrects the information coming from the retina. Two possibilities have long been put forward: Either the brain's commands to the eyes and head to move, in order to keep the image of a moving object on the center of the retina, or the eye and head movements themselves are relayed to the visual cortex and there interpreted as the object's movement. Similarly, when we scan a still background, either the brain's commands or the eye and head movements send signals to the visual cortex that enable it to recognize the moving retinal image as that of an unmoving scene.[52]

The matter has not been resolved; laboratory experiments with animals provide some evidence for each theory. By one means or another, eye and head movements provide part of the information essential to movement perception. Studies of afterimages prove the point. If subjects stare at a bright light for a little while, then look away toward a relatively dark area, they see an afterimage of the light. If they move their eyes, the afterimage moves in the same direction, although the source of the afterimage, the fatigued area of the retina, does not move. This means that the visual cortex, receiving messages that the eyes are moving but that the image is not moving across the retina, interprets them to mean that the eyes are tracking a moving image.[53]

Another possible explanation is the *frame of reference effect*. If you are looking at some background, such as the tennis court across the net, your opponent starts to move cross-court, and you turn your head to keep your eyes on him, the result is an array of images across your retinas. But you know that the other player moved, not the tennis court, which had been established in your brain as the frame of reference.[54]

Much recent neuroscientific research has investigated the neural pathways involved in various forms of disorders of motion perception. Thus far, it has neither confirmed nor amended the above hypotheses, but may well be on the brink of doing so.

Seeing Depth

In nature, unlike the laboratory, neither form nor movement exists apart from three-dimensionality; to understand form and motion perception in everyday life, it is essential to understand depth perception.[55] Psychologists have always considered this a central puzzle about perception; a bibliography of all their writings on depth perception would fill more than a volume.[56]

The basic question has always been both obvious and simple: How do we see the world as three-dimensional when our source of information, the image on the retina, is essentially two-dimensional? Why do we not see the world as flat, like a color photograph in which distance and the three-dimensional qualities of every object are merely suggested by size, perspective, shading, and other cues?

Such cues are, in fact, the answer offered by a group of theories. These take many forms but all hold that depth perception is not automatic and innate. Some say that it comes about as a result of experiences that lead us to associate depth with the cues; others that it is the product of learned mental processes by means of which we infer depth from the cues.

The argument that depth perception is the product of our associating cues with our experiences of depth began with Locke and Berkeley. From their time to the present, psychologists in the associationist-behaviorist tradition have maintained that unconsciously or consciously we link the cues in the two-dimensional retinal image with our experiences of how far away the objects are that produce those cues.

The alternative notion, that we perceive depth as a result of a kind of logical reasoning about what we see, was first voiced in 1843 by J. S. Mill, who said of perception that what we observe is one-tenth observation and nine-tenths inference. Later in the century, Helmholtz argued, in more detail, that we unconsciously infer three-dimensional reality from the two-dimensional retinal data. From then until now, a number of cognitively oriented psychologists have held that perception, including that of depth, is partially or even largely a product of higher mental functions—"thoughtlike processes," Irvin Rock terms them—of which inference from cues is only one.[57]

Whichever view one prefers, the cues to depth are familiar enough in everyday life, and their role in perception has been demonstrated in many hundreds of experiments. Here are the principal cues and a few representative experiments:[58]

— Apparent size: The farther away any object is, the smaller it seems, but if we already know how big it is—a person, for instance—we judge how far away it is from its apparent size even if it is on a featureless plain that gives no cue. In a 1951 experiment, one researcher made up playing cards ranging from half the normal size to twice the normal size and showed them to subjects under laboratory conditions in which there were no cues to distance. The subjects thought the double-size cards were close to them and the half-size cards far from them. All were at the same distance.[59] Everyone, moreover, has experienced the moon illusion—the full moon looks remarkably larger when it is on the horizon than when overhead. Of the explanations currently offered, the most persuasive is that when the moon is close to objects on the horizon, they affect our judgment of its size; when it is overhead, away from all such clues, we judge it differently.

— Perspective: Parallel lines running away from the viewer, such as railroad tracks or the edges of walls, converge with distance. How powerfully we are influenced—or, one should say, informed—by this cue was shown earlier in Figure 13 on page 331: The perspective gradient enables us to perceive the farther figure as roughly the same size as the nearer one, although in fact, as shown, the image of the former is only a third the size of the latter.

— Interposition: When an object is partly concealed by another we realize that the concealed one is farther from us than the concealing one. In looking out over a cityscape, we easily sense the distance of a remote tall building from the fact that closer ones obscure its lower floors; at sea, on the other hand, the distance of a floating object is much harder to judge.

— The texture of a surface—a grassy field, a cement sidewalk—is constant, but the increasingly finer grain of the texture at greater distances makes it an important cue to the distance of anything on that surface.

— Faraway buildings or hills are pale and hazy compared with nearby ones, owing to the greater amount of atmosphere between them and us.

— Motion parallax — the changing relationship of things to each other as we move — is an important source of depth information, particularly when nearby objects are seen in relation to distant ones.

— Convergence and accommodation: When we look at something very close to us, our eyes angle inward and the muscles around each lens strive to keep it in focus. When we look at something far away, our eyes are parallel and the lenses relaxed. The concomitant visceral sensations are important cues to the distance of objects ten feet or less from us.

— Binocular disparity: When we look at something relatively close to us, its image falls on the fovea — center of the retina — of each eye, and the images of other objects equally far away fall on corresponding parts of both retinas. The images of objects either nearer or farther away, however, fall on different parts of the two retinas, as this diagram indicates:

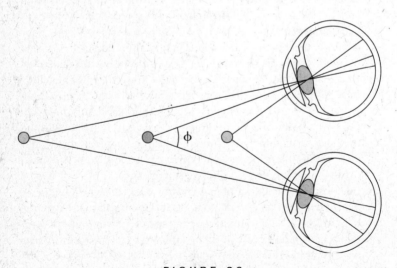

FIGURE 33
How binocular disparity conveys depth

The disparity between the retinal images is interpreted by the brain to indicate which object is farther from us. Binocular disparity is most effective from close up to somewhere between eight hundred to nineteen hundred feet.[60] Some perception theorists regard it as the most important of all cues to depth.

All the foregoing redundant cues to depth can be explained in terms of innate mechanisms or of learned behavior. But the innate aspect of depth perception is supported by other and more convincing evidence.

A historic series of experiments indicating that depth perception is instinctive was performed at Cornell in the late 1950s and early 1960s by Eleanor Gibson, whose work on high-speed reading of pronounceable and unpronounceable words we saw earlier, and a colleague, Richard Walk. Gibson, who had a lifelong aversion to cliffs, and Walk, who during World War II had trained paratroopers to jump off a high platform, jointly conceived of and created a "visual cliff" to determine whether rats learn depth perception or are born with it. The visual cliff was a thick sheet of glass with tile-patterned wallpaper on the underside of half of it and the same paper under the other half but several feet below. The question was whether creatures that had had no experience of depth—that had never tumbled off a high place of any sort—would automatically shun what looked like a drop-off.

The researchers reared chicks, rats, and other animals in the dark, depriving them of any experience of depth, then placed them on a board that crossed the glass between the shallow side and the seemingly deep one. The results were dramatic. The animals, though they had never experienced depth, almost always avoided the deep side and stepped off the board onto the shallow side.

Gibson and Walk then tried human infants. As Gibson recalled later:

We couldn't very well rear the infants in the dark, and we had to wait until they could locomote on their own to use avoidance of the edge as our indicator of depth discrimination, but infants of crawling age did avoid the "deep" side. They may have learned something in the months before they could crawl; but whatever it was, it could not have been externally reinforced, since the parents never reported that the babies had fallen from a height.[61]

The mother of each infant would stand at one side or the other of the apparatus and beckon to her child. In nearly all instances, the infant crawled readily toward her when she was on the shallow side, but only three out of twenty-seven ventured onto the deep side when their mothers were there.[62]

Later laboratory work by others, however, weakens the Gibson-Walk conclusion somewhat, suggesting that the fear of heights in human infants is learned through locomotor experience in general.[63] But impressive evidence that depth perception is built into the nervous system came in 1960 from an unlikely source, AT&T's Bell Laboratories, and an unlikely researcher, a young electrical engineer who was a specialist in TV signal transmission. Bela Julesz, born and educated in Hungary, came to the United States after the abortive revolution of 1956, and was hired by Bell Labs in Murray Hill, New Jersey, to develop ways to narrow the band widths used by TV signals. But Julesz was drawn to more interesting questions and from 1959, with Bell Labs' acquiescence, devoted himself to research on human vision. Though he never acquired a degree in psychology, he became a widely known, award-winning perception psychologist, the head of visual perception research at Bell Labs, a MacArthur Fellow, and, in 1989, director of the Laboratory of Vision Research at Rutgers University.[64]

Julesz had barely begun vision research when he came up with the idea that made him instantly famous in psychological circles. He had been surprised to find, in reading about stereoscopic depth perception, general acceptance of stereopsis as the result of the brain's matching cues to form and depth in each eye's image. This was thought to lead to fusion of the images and depth perception. Julesz, who had had some experience in Hungary as a radar engineer, felt sure that this was wrong.

> After all, in order to break camouflage in aerial reconnaissance, one would view aerial images (taken from two somewhat different positions) through a stereoscope, and the camouflaged target would jump out in vivid depth. Of course, in real life, there is no ideal camouflage, and after a stereoscopic viewing one can detect with a single eye a few faint cues that might discriminate a target from its surroundings. So I used one of the first big computers, an IBM704 that had just arrived at Bell Labs, to create *ideally camouflaged* stereoscopic images.[65]

These consisted of randomly created patterns of black and white dots, as in this pair:

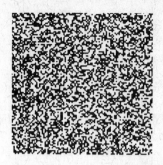

FIGURE 34

When these patterns are stereoscopically merged,
the center floats upward.

There are no cues to depth in these two patterns when each is looked at alone. But although they are largely identical, a small square area in the center has been slightly shifted to one side by the computer so that when each image is seen by one eye and the patterns merged, that area produces a binocular disparity—and seems to float above the rest of the background. (To see this remarkable effect, hold a 4″ × 6″ card or a sheet of paper vertically in front of and perpendicular to the page so that each eye sees only one image. Focus on one corner of the pattern, and in a little while the two images will migrate toward each other and fuse. At that point the center square will appear to hover an inch or so above the page.)

The random-dot stereogram is far more than an amusing trick. It proves that stereoscopic vision does not depend on cues in each retinal image to create the experience of three-dimensionality, and that, on the contrary, the brain fuses the meaningless images and thereby reveals the hidden cues to three-dimensionality. This is not a cognitive process, not a matter of learning to interpret cues to depth, but an innate neurological process taking place in a particular layer of the visual cortex. That is where a highly organized mass of interacting cells performs a correlation of the dots in the patterns, yielding fusion and the perception of the three-dimensional effect.[66] (Stereopsis is not the only way we achieve depth perception. Julesz's work does not rule out others, including those which involve learning.)

Julesz is proud that his discovery led Hubel and Wiesel and others to turn their attention from form perception to the investigation of binocular vision, but modestly adds:

I never regarded my role of introducing random-dot stereograms into psychology as a great intellectual achievement, despite its many conse-

quences for brain research. It was just a lucky coincidence, a clash
between two cultures, an association between two foreign languages
(that of the psychologist and the engineer) in the head of a bilingual.[67]

Yet another theory about depth perception was proposed several
decades ago—one that was neither specifically neural nor specifically
cognitive. Not that its proponent tactfully combined the two; on the
contrary, he virtually ignored the neural theory and dismissed the cognitive theories as unnecessary and based on wrong assumptions.

Only a thoroughgoing maverick would reject a century's worth of
depth-perception research and claim to have found a totally different
and correct approach. Only a true nonconformist would assert that we
perceive depth neither by neural detection nor inference from cues but
"directly" and automatically. Only a brash individualist would present a
radical epistemology in which the physics of light is said to give us an
accurate, literal experience of depth and that we need not interpret what
we see because we see what is as it is.

Such a one was the late James J. Gibson (1904–1979), whose admirers considered him "the most important student of visual perception of
the twentieth century" and "the most original theoretician in the world
in the psychology of perception," but whose theory is considered by the
majority of perception specialists "extremely implausible" (one reviewer
even called it too "silly" to merit discussion) and has few advocates.[68]

Born in a river town in Ohio and reared in various parts of the Mid-
west, Gibson was the son of a railroad surveyor.[69] He went to Princeton
University but felt out of place in a social world that revolved around
clubs, and preferred to associate with what he called "the eccentrics."
For a while he vacillated between philosophy and acting (he was wavy-
haired, square-jawed, and good-looking enough for leading roles), but in
his senior year he took a course in psychology and at once heard the call.
In 1928, he received a faculty appointment at Smith, where for some
years, he was interested in relatively traditional perception research.
Then, during World War II, he was asked by the Army Air Corps's Aviation Psychology Program to develop depth-perception tests for determining who had the visual aptitudes needed for flying, particularly for
making successful take-offs and landings.

He considered the classical cues to depth perception, including shadows and perspective, of little worth. In his opinion they were based on
paintings and parlor stereoscopes rather than on three-dimensional reality, and on static images rather than on movement. What seemed to him

much more useful and realistic were two other kinds of cues: texture gradient, like the uniformly changing roughness of the runway as seen by a pilot during the final leg of an approach; and motion perspective, or the flow of changing relationships among objects as one moves through the environment, including all that a pilot sees during take-offs and landings.[70] These cues soon became, and are today, accepted components of the cue-based theory of depth perception.

Gibson's Air Corps work held the germ of his later view. The crucial mechanism in depth perception (in all perception, according to Gibson) is not the retinal image, with all its cues, but the changing flow of relationships among objects and their surfaces in the environment that the perceiver moves through. During the 1950s and 1960s, he did a considerable amount of research at Cornell that tested his belief in texture gradients. In some experiments he placed diffusing milk-glass between an observer and textured surfaces; in others he dilated the observer's eyes to prevent sharp focus on texture; in still others he cut Ping-Pong balls in half and made goggles of them so that what his subjects saw was foglike, without surfaces or volume.[71] From these and other experiments, plus a careful consideration of his research on air-crew testing and training, Gibson came to reject texture gradients and to stress movement by the observer through the environment as the key to depth perception. However large or small the movement, it results in changes in the optic array—the structured pattern of light reaching the eye from the environment—such as is suggested in this drawing:

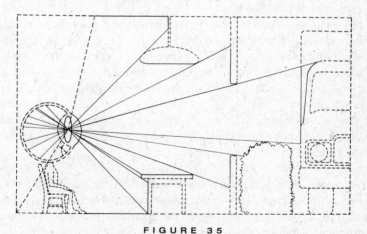

FIGURE 35
How optic array conveys depth

The optic array, rich in information as seen from any point, becomes infinitely richer with movement by the observer. Even minor movements of the head change the array, transforming what is seen of an object and the relationships among objects, and yielding optic flow of one kind or another. Gibson came to believe that optic array and flow convey depth and distance directly, without the need of mental calculation or inference from cues.[72]

This is how Gibson explained depth perception in his sweeping "ecological" theory of "direct perception." The pity is that he felt obliged to throw out the baby with the bathwater. For it is possible to acknowledge both the neural and cognitive views of depth perception as correctly explaining different aspects of the phenomenon and the Gibsonian view as supplementary to them. But it wasn't possible for James J. Gibson.

His name and theory have faded from view, but the cues he was so enamored of have remained accepted components of contemporary accounts of depth perception.

Two Ways of Looking at Vision

"Visual perception," Bela Julesz said fifteen years ago, "is in the same state as physics was prior to Galileo or biochemistry was prior to the discovery of the double helix by Watson and Crick."[73] Since then, a good deal more has been learned, and yet it remains true that each of the two major approaches—the neural and the cognitive—explains only some of the phenomena; there is not yet a comprehensive and unifying theory of visual perception. Perhaps some great organizing concept remains undiscovered, or perhaps visual perception is so complex that no one theory can embrace all of its concepts and that the two different approaches deal with events occurring at radically different levels of complexity.

We have seen something of each of these approaches. Here, to round out the picture, are brief sketches of how each explains visual perception in general.

The neural approach answers questions that preoccupied nineteenth-century physiologists: How can sensory nerves, though alike in structure, transmit different sensations to the brain? And how does the brain turn those incoming impulses into vision?

The answer, worked out in great detail over recent years,[74] is that the nerve impulses themselves do not differ; rather, receptors that respond to specific stimuli send their messages separately to the striate or primary area of the visual cortex. The process begins on the retina, where rods are sensitive to low levels of illumination, cones to more intense levels; cones are of three types, each responsive to different wavelengths of visible light, and some, as we have already heard, sensitive to special shapes and motions.

From the rods and cones, the same kinds of nerve impulses travel along parallel pathways but end up in different areas of the brain—more than 90 percent of them in particular parts of the primary visual cortex and 10 percent in other subcortical structures. Thus the messages delivered to the brain have been analytically separated into color, shape, movement, and depth, and delivered to specialized receptive areas. By means of staining techniques that trace the neuron pathways in laboratory monkeys from retina to visual cortex, researchers have been able to identify more than thirty such distinct cortical visual areas.

What happens then? The brain puts it all together: Using single-cell recordings and two kinds of brain scans (PET, positron emission tomography, and fMRI, functional magnetic resonance imaging), perception researchers have puzzled out the extremely intricate architecture of the primary visual cortex and its wiring scheme (far too complex to take up here), which integrates the individual impulses and blends the information from the two eyes. The result is that the image cast on the retina winds up as the excitation of groups of complex neurons, but the pattern of these excitations in no way resembles the image on the retina or the scene outside the eye. Rather, as already mentioned, it is analogous to writing about a scene, which conveys what it consists of but does not in the least look like it.

It is not an image but a coded *representation* of the image, somewhat as the patterns of magnetism on a tape recording are not sounds but a coded representation of sounds. The representation, however, is not yet a perception; the primary visual cortex is in no sense the end of the visual path. It is just one stage in the processing of the information it handles.

From the striate region the partly assembled and integrated information is sent to other areas of the visual cortex and to higher areas of brain cortex beyond it. There, the information is finally seen by the mind and recognized as something familiar or something not seen before. How that takes place is still moot, according to most neuroscientists. A few, however, boldly guess that somewhere at the higher brain levels are cells that contain "traces" of previously seen objects in the form of synaptic connections or molecular deposits, and these cells respond when an incoming message matches the trace. The response to a match is an awareness ("I know that face"); a nonmatch produces no response, which is also an awareness ("I don't know that face").[75]

The neural approach tells us much about the workings of visual perception at the micro level but little at the macro level, much about the machinery of vision but little about its owner and operator, much about neuronal responses but little about the *experience* of perception. As one cognitive theorist put it, "Trying to understand perception by studying only neurons is like trying to understand bird flight by studying only feathers."[76]

The cognitive approach deals with the mental processes at work in such perceptual phenomena as shape constancy, feature identification, form recognition, cue-derived depth perception, recognition of figures when much of the information is missing, and so on.

The mental processes that yield these results are made up of billions of neuronal events, but cognitive theorists say that it takes macrotheories, not microtheories, to explain these processes. A physicist studying how and when a wave changes form and breaks as it nears the shore cannot derive the laws of wave mechanics from the interactions of trillions of water molecules, not even with a number-crunching mainframe computer. Those laws express mass effects that exist at a wholly different level of organization. The sounds made by a person talking to us are made up of vibrations of the molecules of atmospheric gases, but the meaning of the words cannot be explained in those terms.

So too with the mental processes of visual perception; they are organized mass effects of neural phenomena expressed by mental, not neurophysiological, laws. We have already seen evidence of this, but there is one particularly intriguing and historic example worth discussing. What happens, and at what level, when we call up an image from memory and see it in the mind's eye? Experiments by cognitive theorists show that this can be explained only in high-level cognitive terms. The most elegant and impressive of such experiments are those of Roger Shepard (now emeritus) of Stanford University on "mental rotation." Shepard asked subjects to say whether the objects in each of these three pairs are identical:

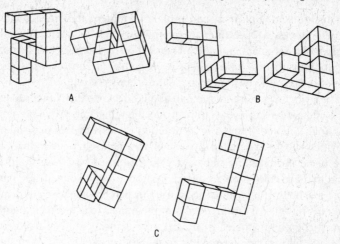

A

B

C

FIGURE 36

Mental rotation: Which pairs are identical?

Most people recognize, after studying them for a little while, that the objects in A are identical as are those in B. Those in C are not. When asked how they reached their conclusions, they say that they rotated the objects in their minds much as if they were rotating real objects in the real world. Shepard demonstrated how closely this procedure mirrors real rotation by another experiment, in which viewers saw a given shape in degrees of angular difference. This set, for example, shows a single shape in a series of positions:

FIGURE 37

Mental rotation: The greater the distance, the longer it takes.

When subjects were shown pairs of these figures, the time it took them to identify them as the same was proportional to the angular difference in the positions of the figures; that is, the more one figure had to be rotated to match the other, the longer it took for identification.[77]

This is only one of many perceptual phenomena that involve higher mental processes operating on internalized symbols of the external world. For some years a number of perception researchers have been trying to formulate a comprehensive cognitive theory of what those processes are and how they produce those perceptions.

There are two schools of thought about how to do this. One uses concepts and procedures drawn from artificial intelligence (AI), a branch of computer science. The basic assumption of AI is that human mental activities can be simulated by step-by-step computer programs—and take place in that same step-by-step programmed way.[78] Partly in the effort to make computers recognize what they are looking at, and partly to gain a better understanding of human perception, AI experts have written a number of form-recognition programs. To achieve elementary form recognition—to recognize triangles, squares, and other regular polygons, for instance—a program might follow a series of if-then steps. If there is a straight line, then follow it and measure it to its end; if another line continues from there, then call that point a corner and measure the angle by which it changes direction; if that other line is straight, follow it until . . . and so on, until the number of sides and angles has been counted and matched against a list of polygons and their characteristics.

The chief argument in favor of the AI approach to visual perception is that there is no projector or screen in the brain and no homunculus looking at pictures; hence the mind must be dealing not with images but coded data that it processes step by step, as a computer program does.

Fifteen years ago the chief argument against the AI idea was that no existing program of machine vision had more than a minuscule capacity, compared with that of human beings, to recognize flat shapes, let alone three-dimensional ones, or to know where they are within the environment, or to recognize the probable physical qualities of the rocks, chairs, water, bread, or people it was seeing. But since then there have been extraordinary developments in machine vision. Formerly limited to two-dimensional representation, it is now capable of 3-D, and methods of identifying shapes and distances have greatly improved. Robots guided by machine vision now run operations in a great many factories; AI systems using machine vision have guided driverless automobiles across the desert, avoiding obstacles and ravines; security systems can now match a seen face to a photograph of that face, and so on.

Having said all that, it remains true that machine vision has only a very limited capacity, compared with that of human beings, to recognize all sorts of objects *for what they are*; it doesn't *understand*, it doesn't *know*, it doesn't *feel*. Basically, that's because it isn't hooked up to the immense information base of the human mind: its vast store of mental and emotional responses built in by evolution, its immense accumulation of learned meanings of perceptions, its huge compilation of interconnected information about the world. As remarkable as the achievements of the designers of machine vision are, their work has led to a greater understanding of how to make machine vision work but not to a deeper understanding of how human vision works.

The other school of thought about how cognitive perceptual processes work has long relied and continues to rely on laboratory studies of human thinking rather than machine simulations of thinking. This view, going far beyond the Helmholtz tradition that perception is the result of unconscious inference from incomplete information, includes conscious thought processes of other kinds. Its leading exponent in recent years was Irvin Rock (1922–1995) of the University of California at Berkeley. His book, *The Logic of Perception*, was described in the *Annual Review of Psychology* as "the most inclusive and empirically plausible explanation of perceptual effects that seem to require intelligent activity on the part of the perceiver."[79]

Rock, though an outstanding perception psychologist, was far from outstanding in his early undergraduate years; in fact, in an intellectual family he was the black sheep. But during World War II his unit was dive-bombed by enemy planes, he felt sure he would be killed, and "I vowed to myself," he said, "that if I survived I would try to do more with my life than I had until then."[80] After the war he became a top-notch student. He began graduate school in physics but switched to psychology when he realized that there was greater opportunity in that young field for a significant contribution to knowledge.

At the New School for Social Research Rock fell under the spell of the Gestaltists who were there and became an ardent one himself. Certain basic Gestalt laws of organization and relational thinking are still part of his theory. But those laws describe essentially automatic processes, and Rock came to believe that many perceptual phenomena could be accounted for only by mental processes of a thoughtlike character.[81]

This idea first occurred to him when he conducted the 1957 experiment, described above, in which he tilted a square so that it looked like a diamond, then tilted the perceiver. Since the perceiver still saw the square as a diamond, Rock reasoned that he must have used visual and visceral cues to interpret what he saw. Rock spent many years devising and conducting other experiments to test the hypothesis that, more often than not, perception requires higher-level processes than those taking place in the visual cortex. These studies led him, finally, to the thesis that "perception is intelligent in that it is based on operations similar to those that characterize thought."[82]

And indeed, Rock has said, perception may have led to thought; it may be the evolutionary link between low-level sensory processes in primitive organisms and high-level cognitive processes in more complex forms of life. If what the eye sees, he argues, is an ambiguous and distortion-prone representation of reality, some mechanism had to evolve to yield reliable and faithful knowledge of that reality. In his words, "Intelligent operations may have evolved in the service of perception."[83]

This is not to say that all perception is thoughtlike; Rock specifically cited the waterfall illusion as explicable in low-level neural terms. But most facts about motion perception and other kinds of perception seemed to him to require high-level processes. Unconscious inference, as in our use of texture gradient cues to sense distance, is only one of them.[84] Description that results in interpretation is another. In the ambiguous old hag–young woman figure by Boring, what one sees is not the result of simply recognizing an image but of describing to oneself what a particular curve is like: like a nose or like a cheek. Many perceived forms or objects are not instantly recognizable; recognizing what they are comes about through such a process.[85]

Perception also often calls for problem solving of one sort or another. One hardly thinks of perception as the solving of problems, but Rock marshaled a considerable amount of evidence—much from earlier studies by others, some from his own original experiments—to show that in many cases we seek a hypothesis to account for what we see, weigh that hypothesis against other possibilities, and choose the one that seems to solve the problem of making sense of what we see. All of this usually takes place in a fraction of a second.

One example: In a laboratory phenomenon known since the time of Helmholtz, if a wavelike curved line is passed horizontally behind a slit,

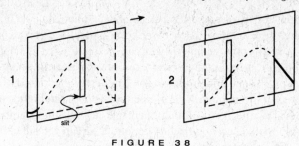

FIGURE 38

Anorthoscopic perception: The dot moves up and down
but the mind figures out what is happening.

as in the above figure, most observers first see it as a small element moving
up and down, but after a while some of them will suddenly see the sinu-
ous line moving at right angles to and behind the aperture. What produces their altered and correct perception? Rock found that one clue they
use is the changing slope of the line as it passes the slit; another is the end
of the curved line, if it comes into view. Such clues suggest to the mind an
alternative hypothesis — that a curve is moving past the slit horizontally,
rather than that a small element is moving up and down. This hypothesis
is so much better that the mind accepts it and sees the line as it really is.[86]

Rock summed up his theory as follows:

> On a theoretical level, at least according to the theory presented here,
> both perception and thought entail reasoning. In some cases, general-
> izations or rules are arrived at in perception by induction. These rules
> are then used deductively as premises from which inferences are drawn.
> Perception in some cases can be characterized as the result of creative
> problem solving, in the sense of searching for the grounds (or internal
> solution) from which a specific interpretation follows. Perception entails
> decisions, just as does thought. Operations that culminate in perceptual
> experience are of the same kind that characterize thinking.[87]

Where does all this leave us?

We have seen two richly detailed bodies of information deriving from
two basic ways of explaining visual perception: the cognitive, thoughtlike approach and the neurological, stimulus-based approach (and perhaps, but to a lesser extent, a third one, Gibson's "ecological" or "direct

perception" theory). But these accounts of perception are not contradictory but complementary; each describes a part of the full reality. To employ a well-worn metaphor, you can describe what is happening when you type at your computer in terms of the program you are using (Word, WordPerfect, and so on); or you can describe it in terms of what takes place in the microprocessor, circuits, monitor, and other parts of the hardware. So it is with human perception: Both the cognitive and the neurophysiological approaches are sound; we can consult either one or both, depending on what we want to understand.

With so long and rich a history of studies of the cognitive aspects of perception, plus the dramatic and abundant recent findings of cognitive neuroscience, it is not surprising that the emphasis of today's perception researchers is less on grand theory or even midrange theory than on special and rather fine-tuned topics. Any recent copy of APA's *Journal of Experimental Psychology: Human Perception and Performance* makes that obvious; here, for instance, are a few titles from the April 2006 issue of that journal:

"On the Surprising Salience of Curvature in Grouping by Proximity."
"Memory for Where, But Not What, Is Used During Visual Search."
"Sequence Learning and Selection Difficulty."
"Speeded Old-New Recognition of Multidimensional Perceptual Stimuli: Modeling Performance at the Individual-Participant and Individual-Item Levels."
"Eye Movements and Lexical Ambiguity Resolution: Investigating the Subordinate-Bias Effect."
"The Beneficial Effects of Additional Task Load, Positive Affect, and Instruction on the Attentional Blink."

But we need not concern ourselves further with this level of research. We have seen enough to know that perception, despite its remaining puzzlements, is now a relatively developed area of psychological knowledge. We know a great deal more about perception than has been known up to now—but also know that far more remains to be known. For as Michael Gazanniga and Todd Heatherton sum up the situation, "the big puzzle that occupies the minds of modern psychological scientists is unraveling the nature of the connection between electrochemical activity within the neural circuits and the complex information processing that culminates in our perception of the world."[88]

Or to put it simplistically: How do our neural processes become *us*?

FIFTEEN

The Emotion
and Motivation Psychologists

Fundamental Question

If you were to stand on the bank of some quiet estuary of a Long Island bay on a spring day, you might be lucky enough to see a female muskrat swimming desperately and uttering anguished yelps as a male muskrat paddles furiously after her. (He invariably catches her, or perhaps she invariably allows him to.) If you were to sit on a deserted Long Island beach in spring, you might see a male sea gull furiously chase away a female gull who was sidling up in hope of a bite of the crab he is pecking at, but a week later you'd see him allow her to snatch a piece, and a week or so after that actually put a morsel into her beak. (A day or two later he will mount her, with her acquiescence.)

As far as one can tell, these creatures never wonder why the other acts as he or she does or why they themselves act as they do. It is only human beings who ask, "Why do we do what we do?"—perhaps the most important question we ever ask ourselves, and the fundamental question of psychology.

Primitive peoples had a variety of answers: Human behavior is governed by spirits, magical spells, the eating of particular parts of certain animals, and so on. The semiprimitive Homeric Greeks were only a little more sophisticated; they thought the gods put ideas and impulses directly into their minds. But the Greek philosophers of the sixth and fifth centuries B.C. made a historic leap: they attributed human behavior to internal forces—bodily feelings and thoughts.

They regarded those two sources, however, as opposed. Plato, for one, held that we are ruled by our appetites except to the extent that reason shows us the better way and that the will achieves a balance between the two forces. The idea that the passions—desires and emotions by which we are passively driven—are evil and that reason is good was to dominate Western ideas about behavior throughout the centuries, influencing thinkers as dissimilar as Paul, the great apostle of Christianity, and Spinoza, the supreme rationalist. Here is Paul lamenting the power of the passions:

> For the good that I would I do not; but the evil that I would not, that I do.
> Now if I do that I would not, it is no more I that do it, but sin that dwelleth in me.
> I find then a law, that, when I would do good, evil is present within me.
> For I delight in the law of God after the inward man:
> But I see another law in my members, warring against the law of my mind, and bringing me into captivity to the law of sin which is in my members.
>
> —Romans 7:19–23

And here, seventeen centuries later, is Spinoza introducing his analysis of "human bondage" (the fourth part of his *Ethic*):

> The impotence of man to govern or restrain the passions I call bondage, for a man who is under their control is not his own master, but is mastered by fortune, in whose power he is, so that he is often forced to follow the worse, although he sees the better before him.

Although Paul and Spinoza advocated different ways of controlling the passions—Paul through salvation by means of faith in God's grace, Spinoza through the use of reason and knowledge—both saw them, if uncontrolled, as causing humans to behave badly.

Aside from the conflict between reason and the passions, philosophers were never much interested in the influence of the passions on behavior; they were far more concerned with the workings of the intellect and the sources of knowledge. When they did discuss human behavior, it was generally in the context of moral philosophy—how we ought to behave—rather than the causes of our behavior. The psychology of the passions received only perfunctory notice before the modern era;

Descartes, as we saw, did little more than name six primary emotions and interpret a number of others as combinations of them.[1] And although Spinoza dealt with the passions in some detail, he did so in austere, logical terms that convey no sense of their power or of emotional experience. Love, for instance, he defined as "nothing but joy accompanied with the idea of an external cause" and hatred as "nothing but sorrow with the accompanying idea of an external cause."[2]

The first person to scientifically explore the influence of the emotions on behavior was not a psychologist but the great naturalist Charles Darwin. In 1872, more than a dozen years after the appearance of his historic *Origin of Species*, Darwin published an intriguing minor work, *The Expression of the Emotions in Man and Animals*, in which he argued that emotions evolved because they lead to useful actions and increase a creature's chances of survival. Fear, anger, and sexual excitement produce, respectively, escape behavior, counterattacks on any enemy, and the propagation of the species. Human emotions, Darwin maintained, are derived from their animal precursors and have similar values and expressions. The baring of fangs by the wolf becomes the sneer of the human being; the bristling of an animal's body hair in anger or fear to make itself look larger becomes the angry human's hair standing on end, outthrust chest, and aggressive stance.[3]

But despite Darwin's eminence, most early scientific psychologists avoided the topic of the emotions. (William James and, of course, Freud and other psychoanalysts were notable exceptions.) Nowadays, because of the broad acceptance of psychotherapy, many people think of the emotions and the behavior they beget as the major concern of psychologists, but during the first half of the twentieth century, says Ernest Hilgard in his history of psychology in America, there was a "peculiar lack of interest among academic psychologists in the great emotional themes of literature and drama."[4]

This was the result of their naïve efforts, in those decades, to be as rigorously objective as physicists, with the result that they considered reports of subjective states, including feelings or emotions, to be outside the bounds of science. From the time of Thorndike's experiments with cats in puzzle boxes until midcentury, researchers sought to link behavior to observable physiological states, such as hunger, thirst, or pain, not to subjective states, such as the emotions.

Between the discomfort of such physiological states and the resulting behavior, however, there must be some directing mechanism or force. If not, why should hunger lead to prowling and seeking, or sexual desire to courting behavior, rather than to random agitated movement?

In the early years of the last century, psychologists were content to say that the behavior prompted by a physiological need or state is specified by instinct. This simplistic answer said nothing about how an instinct operates at the psychological level and offered no psychological condition that could be experimentally investigated. But in 1908 the psychologist William McDougall suggested an explanation and developed it more fully in 1923. A creature aroused by a physical need is in pursuit of a known goal, and its behavior is therefore *purposive* or *motivated;* the psychological impetus that results in the behavior, *motivation,* is a condition that can be experimentally manipulated, measured, and studied. A new field of psychology was launched.

Although human activities ranging from buttoning one's shirt to writing a sonnet are motivated, psychologists of the behaviorist era limited themselves chiefly to studying motivation in the laboratory rat. In that relatively simple animal, they could create basic physical needs like hunger that were quantifiable in terms of the hours or days of deprivation, and could easily and objectively measure the behavior produced, primarily prowling and maze running.

With the advent of the new cognitivism in the 1950s and 1960s, mental processes again became a legitimate field of study, and some researchers began investigating motivation and emotion in human beings. But for some years, most of the attention of cognitive psychologists was on "cold cognition" (information processing, reasoning, and the like). Only within the past twenty-five years or so has it turned more toward "hot cognition" and how it is related to motivation. Not until 1988 could Ross Buck of the University of Connecticut, a leading figure in motivation and emotion research, proclaim, "Psychology has rediscovered emotion," and it was only in the 1990s that emotions actually resumed a place on center stage of psychological enquiry.[5]

(Unfortunately, emotions and motivations are somewhat like a scrambled egg—yolk and white are both present but impossible to separate. Emotions or the physiological states that arouse them are often what power motivation (for instance, infatuation motivates the infatuated one to actively pursue the desired one), while motivation often generates emotions (one driven by ambition to rise in the political world may develop envy or even hatred of his or her competitors). The two phenomena are frequently discussed and researched as if they were separa-

ble, although the separation is arbitrary and unrealistic. But the problem is not ours to solve; our concern is the story of psychology, so let us
see what happened when emotion and motivation became a subdiscipline of that emerging science.)

Either because this was so recent a development or because the subject
is so heterogeneous, emotion researchers and theorists found it difficult
to agree on a definition of what they were studying. Ordinary people
have no such difficulty; even a child of three knows what he means
when he says he is happy, sad, or afraid—it's how he feels. But research
psychologists were looking much deeper; their definitions of emotion
included causes, physiological concomitants, and consequences, and
may strike the layman as ponderous and abstruse. An example:

> Emotions are changes in action readiness which have control prece-
> dence (which interrupt or compete with alternative mental and behav-
> ioral activities), changes caused by appraising events as relevant to
> concerns (hence giving rise to positive or negative feelings).[6]

But neither this nor any of the dozens of then-extant professional definitions of emotions was generally accepted by psychologists. As the
authors of one journal article commented in 1984, "Everyone knows
what an emotion is, until asked to give a definition." Even in 2004, long
after emotion had re-emerged as a key topic in psychology, the editor of
a book of research articles on the subject said, in his introduction,
"There is, at present, no consensus about what the emotions are . . . [or]
any good single definition of emotion."[7]

And although most psychologists said that there is a handful of basic
emotions and that the many others are derived from or related to these,
there was no agreement as to what the basic emotions are. Some experts
included "desire," others did not; some included "surprise," others
specifically excluded "startle," which most people would consider a
form of surprise; most psychotherapists used "affect" to mean either conscious or unconscious emotional states, but some academic psychologists said that sensory likes and dislikes are affects, emotions are not.

Seeking to filter out the essentials, in 1984 Robert Plutchik, a noted
emotion researcher at the Albert Einstein College of Medicine in New
York, asked volunteers to rate a long list of pairs of emotion-related
words in terms of their similarity. Factor-analysis of their ratings showed

which emotions had the greatest degree of overlap with others and thus were the most central. Plutchik concluded that there are eight basic emotions: joy, acceptance, fear, surprise, sadness, disgust, anger, and anticipation. Other common emotions, he found, are milder or stronger versions of these; for example, grief is sadness at an extreme, and pensiveness is sadness at a low level.[8] It's as good a list as exists, yet though it has often been cited, it did not become the standard among emotion researchers—nor did any other such list.

And there was not yet—nor is there today—a generally accepted theory of the emotions. Some theorists stress the causes of emotions, others their behavioral consequences; some say emotions consist of visceral states, others of higher mental processes, and still others of autonomic and central nervous system phenomena. The proliferation of theoretical ideas is typical of a science in its early, exploratory years; by 1985 one report said that there were roughly a hundred distinguishable theories of the emotions and that even when similar ones were grouped, there were still eighteen groups or types of theory.[9]

But one can group all those theories into three categories: those that focus on the physical changes accompanying an emotion, such as increased heart rate, skin temperature, palmar sweating, and activation of areas of the brain; those that center on how an emotion feels—the subjective experience that we seek when we ask someone, "How are you feeling?"; and those that are concerned with what people believe or understand about why they feel as they do.[10] The studies of the emotions throughout the twentieth century to the present essentially followed this very track: The early inquiries centered on somatic theory, the next group on ANS (autonomic nervous system) and CNS (central nervous system) aspects of emotions and motivation, and the third on the cognitive or thought processes involved.

All this may make emotion research sound remote from real life, and it is true that psychologists are interested in lofty questions about the emotions: what functions they serve, whether they are innate or acquired, whether they are universal or culturally variable, and how they are related to changes in the body and to mental processes. But psychologists are also interested in an eminently practical question: How are emotions related to behavior? Most of them agree that an emotion is not just a signal to the creature that some object or event is relevant to its needs; it is the means through which motivation becomes purposive action.[11]

Thus the ancient question—Why do we do what we do?—has

become central to modern psychology, and the emotions are now seen as a crucial part of the answer. The study of emotion and motivation began with philosophic speculations, in the scientific era turned first to the investigation of physical needs, then to that of nervous system functions, later to that of cognitive processes, and finally to that of brain activation. It is a paradigm of the evolution of psychology itself.

Somatic Theory

What sort of person would starve a captive rat for two days, then put it in a box with a food pellet at the far end, which the rat cannot reach without scurrying across an electrically charged grid that shocks its feet? What sort of person would put a mother rat at one end of that box and her babies at the other?

A sadist, you might think. But Carl J. Warden was a very decent young man and not in the least sadistic; he was simply a typical experimental psychologist of the behaviorist era. The time was 1931, the place Columbia University, the apparatus his invention, the Columbia Obstruction Box, by means of which he was seeking to measure, as objectively as possible, the strength of two sources of motivation, the hunger drive and the maternal drive.

His data, he hoped, would validate the simple hypothesis that the greater the rat's need, the greater its drive or motivation to allay that need. The measure of the need for food was simply how long the rat had been without any; the measure of the resulting drive was how frequently the rat would cross the electric grid for another morsel of food. The experiment proved Warden's hypothesis correct up to the third day of deprivation; after that the rat became weakened and less driven to cross the grid. Motivation research could hardly have been more objective. (The trials with the mother and her babies yielded less satisfying results; the absence of the pups did not create as clear-cut a need as hunger.)[12]

In Warden's report, as in other behaviorist writing, there was no talk of instinct. Behaviorists believed that almost everything a higher-order creature (like a mammal) does is the result of learning, and they viewed instinct theory as reactionary. By the 1920s they were calling the goal-directed energy of motivated behavior "drive" rather than instinct. Robert S. Woodworth, who proposed the concept of drive in 1918, said that although organisms possess innate mechanisms for such activities as seeking and devouring food, these lie idle until activated by a drive that directs the creature toward goals it has learned will allay the need. Behaviorists found drive a comfortable concept. Moreover, unlike instinct, it was one they could experimentally generate, measure, and modify by conditioning in the effort to determine the laws of motivation.

One of those hypotheses—a rather obvious one—was that the stronger a physiological need and the greater the drive to satisfy it, the more activity the creature will manifest. To test this hypothesis, in 1922 a Johns Hopkins University psychologist named Curt Richter mounted cages on springs and automatically recorded the movements of rats. Gratifyingly, the traces showed that hungry ones prowled around more than fed ones. In 1925 at the University of North Carolina, J. F. Dashiell used a checkerboard maze for the same purpose. He counted the number of squares rats entered and found that hungry ones explored more squares than fed ones. In 1931 Warden's Columbia Obstruction Box was a still better method of measuring the same drive.

Throughout the 1920s and 1930s a good deal of such experimentation explored other primary drives, including those originating in the needs for fluids, oxygen, sex, a comfortable temperature, and the avoidance of pain. In 1943 these physiological aspects of motivation were merged in an elegantly simple theory by Clark Hull, the mathematical behaviorist, who asserted that all drives seek the same fundamental satisfaction—relief from the unpleasant tension created by a biological need—and that the ideal state sought by all creatures is the tranquillity that comes from the satisfaction of all drives.[13] Nearly half a century later, ethological research would indeed show that many animals are torpid for a while when they have filled their bodily needs; a lion, after a big meal, may lie in the same spot for twelve hours at a stretch.[14]

But many forms of behavior do not fit within the borders of Hull's theory. A dog will obey commands not to allay a biological need but to please its master; a hamster will run inside an exercise wheel for no apparent reason; a rat will learn to press a bar for a drop of saccharine-flavored water that has no nutritive value. To account for such behavior in accord with drive-reduction theory, behaviorists decided there were such things as "acquired" or "secondary" drives and motives. These arise from nonphysiological needs but gain their motive power by association with primary drives.[15] The dog, for instance, learns to obey its master because at first it is rewarded by food and approval; eventually it develops a drive for approval, and approval becomes the reward.

Yet this jerry-built repair of drive theory could not account for some other kinds of behavior. It could not explain the hamster's running or the rat's working to get saccharine water. And unless "secondary drive" was defined so broadly as to include behavior not linked by conditioning to a physiological need, it could not explain why monkeys in one experiment pushed open a window again and again (it remained open only for thirty seconds) in order to watch a toy electric train running, or why monkeys in another experiment repeatedly unlatched a battery of hooks and latches even after they learned that doing so opened no doors and yielded no reward.[16] Or why a music lover goes to a concert, a reformer labors to change the political system, a theologian strives to justify the ways of God to man, a penitent lashes his back with chains, a mountain climber scales the Matterhorn, or a psychologist investigates the phenomenon of motivation.

Hull's idea that drive reduction is the goal of all motivated behavior was further challenged by a much-publicized experiment in sensory deprivation conducted at McGill University in 1957. Volunteers, wearing padded mitts and translucent goggles that admitted light but no images, spent several days lying on a soft foam-rubber pad in a small chamber where the monotonous hum of an air conditioner masked all other sounds. (They were allowed out briefly from time to time to eat, relieve themselves, and be tested.) Most of them had looked forward to a long, pleasant rest but soon found the absence of almost all sensory stimulation disagreeable and disorienting. They had difficulty thinking coherently, their moods fluctuated between hilarity and irritability, their performance on standard tests of mental ability deteriorated markedly, a few of them experienced hallucinations, and nearly all asked to be released from the experiment after a few days.[17]

Clearly, many kinds of behavior are motivated by complex needs generated by the autonomic and central nervous systems and the mind; this was what emotion and motivation researchers had been ignoring.

Over the years, however, as researchers explored the complexities of conflicting motivations that could not all be accounted for by internal drives or needs, they recognized that some behavior is motivated by "incentives"—external stimuli or rewards not directly related to biological needs. Many people will stay up late watching a movie although they need, and know they need, to go to sleep; many will keep nibbling canapés at a party to be social, even though they feel overfull. Eventually, in 1989 and 2001, the British psychologist Michael Apter advanced a "reversal theory" of "metamotivation": We can switch from one motivational state to its equally rewarding opposite, but can never be in a state where both pertain. For instance, we are in an achievement-oriented motivational state when working on some important project, but may at some point reverse to an enjoyment-motivated state to take a break and have a snack; both states gratify needs but in opposite ways. Apter's team asked parachute jumpers about their feelings just before and after jumping: In both conditions the reward was one of great arousal, but before jumping the arousal was due to great anxiety, afterward to great pleasure.[18]

But now we must get back to our story.

Although behaviorists could observe and measure the external activities associated with motivation, they could neither observe nor measure physical indices of emotion. A rat could not tell them what it was feeling, and though a human being could, they regarded such information as unverifiable and scientifically valueless.

Not all psychologists, however, felt bound by the behaviorist prescription for acceptable evidence; some were willing to accept a human being's identification of what he or she was feeling. But even they, during the early decades of the century, were interested chiefly in the physiological changes accompanying the emotions the subjects said they felt and which, the researchers believed, were the source of those emotions.

This theory, as we saw earlier, had been advanced by William James in 1884 and almost simultaneously by Carl Lange, a Danish physiologist. The James-Lange theory held that—contrary to our impression that some fact excites an emotion in us and this gives rise to bodily changes—an exciting fact brings about bodily changes, and our perception of those changes is the emotion. (As James put it, we meet a bear and tremble, and because we tremble feel afraid.)

The James-Lange theory was generally accepted for many years, and by the 1920s, as new techniques of physiological measurement were developed, researchers were able to measure objectively the bodily states James had been able to describe only subjectively. Their aim was to see how specific changes in blood pressure, pulse, and respiration correlated with the emotions the subjects said they experienced.

In the free-wheeling spirit of the time, some of the researchers imposed stresses on their subjects that would be considered outrageous today. A psychologist named Blatz, for instance, told his volunteers that the experiment they were taking part in was a study of heart-rate changes over a fifteen-minute period. Each volunteer was tied in a chair, blindfolded, wired to equipment that monitored pulse, breathing, and skin conductance, and left alone for a quarter of an hour. After three such sessions during which nothing happened—some subjects actually fell asleep—at some point in the fourth session Blatz threw a switch causing the chair, hinged in front and standing on a trap door, to drop backward. It was smoothly stopped by a door check after falling through a 60-degree arc. The volunteers exhibited a burst of rapid and irregular heartbeat, the abrupt cessation of breathing followed by gasping, and a surge of skin conductance. All reported feeling fear (and, later, either anger or amusement). Presumably, the fall was so sudden and unexpected that there was no anticipatory emotion; as in the James-Lange theory, the fear was the experience of the bodily changes produced by the fall.[19]

Carney Landis, a psychologist interested in the physiological sources of severe emotional upsets, must have been a remarkable salesman. In the early 1920s, he was able to persuade three volunteers to fast for forty-eight hours, go without sleep for the last thirty-six of them, be hooked up to blood-pressure and chest-expansion monitors, swallow a small balloon attached to a rubber tube to allow gastric contractions to be measured, have a similar device inserted into their rectums, and breathe into an apparatus that measured their carbon dioxide output as an index of metabolic rate—and at that point receive an electric shock as strong as they could bear without struggling until they signaled that they could stand it no longer.

The shock caused the blood pressure to shoot up, the pulse to race and become irregular, and the rectal contractions to cease. (The data on stomach contractions were not consistent.) But despite the volunteers' commendable suffering for science, the results of the procedure were unclear. Although all three said they felt anger, they had little or no awareness of any specific physiological changes associated with and possibly causing the emotion. The only physical response Landis could find that regularly corresponded to a subjective state was that of surprise. An eye blink and a complex facial-bodily reaction immediately preceded awareness of the emotion and that, at least, was in accord with the James-Lange theory.[20]

But by 1927 other physiological experiments were yielding powerful evidence that contradicted the theory. They were the work of Walter Cannon (1871–1945), a distinguished investigator and theorist. Cannon was, like John B. Watson and James Gibson, one of those impecunious small-town youths who, though lacking important connections, was able in that era to scale the scientific heights through hard work and genius. He published research papers that attracted wide attention even before receiving his M.D. at Harvard, and, without any close links such as William James had had to the powers at that university, was appointed its George Higginson Professor of Physiology at the age of only thirty-five.

Although Cannon's discipline was physiology, he had studied under James and was a friend of Robert Yerkes. It may have been these influences that led him, after years of exploring the control of digestion by the ANS, to turn to the physiology of the emotions. After much investigation, he came to regard the James-Lange theory as thoroughly wrong, and in 1927 he published a historic paper that seemingly demolished it.[21] In the paper he offered five kinds of evidence based on his own and others' research. Of the five, the following three were particularly convincing:

— Visceral changes usually occur one to two seconds after a stimulus, but emotional reactions generally take less time; they therefore precede the physical changes. (Although this was based on laboratory evidence, it is a common experience that immediately after a near-accident we feel fear—after which our heart pounds, we feel weak, we have a strange taste in our mouth, and more.)

— There are some differences among the visceral responses associated with various emotions, but they are not so differentiated or sensitive as to provide distinctive cues for the range of emotions that human beings experience.

— Cannon surgically severed the viscera of cats from the sympathetic nervous system, as C. S. Sherrington, a British physiologist, had previously done with dogs. In both cases all messages from the heart, lungs, stomach, bowels, and other viscera in which, according to James, emotions originate, were cut off from the brain. Nonetheless, wrote Cannon:

> These extensively disturbing operations had little if any effect on the emotional responses of the animals. In one of Sherrington's dogs having a "markedly emotional temperament," the surgical reduction of the sensory field caused no obvious change in her emotional behavior; "her anger, her joy, her disgust, and when provocation arose, her fear, remained as evident as ever." And in the sympathectomized cats all superficial signs of rage were manifested in the presence of a barking dog—hissing, growling, retraction of the ears, showing of the teeth, lifting of the paw to strike . . .[22]

Yet studies in succeeding decades, down to the present, continued to find evidence that in limited ways the James-Lange theory is correct. Three examples:

— A medical team at the Washington University School of Medicine found in 1969 that injections of lactate (a byproduct of energy metabolism in the cells) produce the physiological symptoms associated with anxiety plus the subjective sensation of anxiety, the latter most strongly in those who are anxiety-prone.[23]

— In 1966 George Hohmann, a psychologist who was a paraplegic because of a spinal injury, interviewed twenty-five war veterans, all of whom had suffered severed spinal cords two years or more earlier. Hohmann asked them to describe episodes of fear, anger, sexual excitement, and grief experienced both before and since their injuries. They said that, except for grief, their emotions were different since the severing of the spine; there was a decline in quality, a muting or coldness to their feelings. Strikingly, the higher the lesion—and therefore the greater the number of body systems disconnected from the brain—the greater the change. As one man with a cervical (high) lesion said:

> I sit around and build things up in my mind, and I worry a lot, but it's not much but the power of thought. I was at home in bed one day and dropped a cigarette where I couldn't reach it. I finally managed to scrounge around and put it out. I could have burned up right there, but the funny thing is, I didn't get all shook up about it. I just didn't feel afraid at all, like you would suppose.[24]

— Psychologists have long debated whether emotions are universal or relative; that is, whether people in different cultures feel the same feelings. For more than two decades, Paul Ekman of the University of California, San Francisco, Medical School, and his colleagues have studied the matter. They asked people in different cultures to express six basic emotions (anger, disgust, happiness, sadness, fear, and surprise), and found that their facial expressions were basically similar, though somewhat modified by cultural rules. Both Ekman and his colleagues, and Carroll Izard of the University of Delaware, have shown to people in a number of very different cultures photographs of actors expressing a number of emotions. Almost always, the viewers identified them correctly.

While there are major differences in the cultural situations evoking particular emotions, the evidence strongly suggests that the basic emotions are universal and are accompanied by the same movements of facial muscles.[25]

This does not prove that physical sensations precede the perception of emotion, as James and Lange posited. But more than a dozen experiments by Ekman and by others have shown that when volunteers deliberately assume the facial expression of a particular emotion, the muscular efforts involved create small but measurable changes in pulse rate, respiration rate, and skin conductance, along with equally small but measurable changes in their feelings.[26] Ekman considers these results a feedback effect: the deliberately assumed expression brings about bodily changes, which then create the emotional feeling the person has simulated.

The same principle sometimes enables psychotherapists to alter the emotions of patients. By changing facial expression, posture, and body movements, the patient can to some extent replace a despondent or defeated mood with a more positive and cheerful one.[27] Again, this supports the James-Lange theory: What we sense in the body determines our feelings. (Make the experiment yourself. Wreathe your features in a great, sunny grin, hold it for some seconds, and see if you don't feel at least a modicum of the feeling that should go with it.)

For such reasons, the James-Lange theory survives — or at least is part of the contemporary understanding of the emotions. In recent decades, research by cognitive psychologists and by cognitive neuroscientists has yielded a complex, multifaceted explanation of the interaction between the physical symptoms of emotions and the neural processing of those symptoms and of the stimuli responsible. Which comes first, which produces the other? Each one, at times, depending on all sorts of conditions, and often both in a species of feedback. We will spare ourselves the intricacies for now; the net results suggest that both sides in the debate are right and that the neural systems of emotion and cognition are both independent and interdependent.[28]

In sum, the somatic theory is a valid but imperfect and limited part of the contemporary answer to the question about the sources of the emotions. Now let us go back to look at other theories explored during the last century that have contributed importantly to today's view of the matter.

ANS and CNS Theory

Walter Cannon, whose experimental work called into question the James-Lange theory, offered his own theories of emotion and motivation; each was influential for many years.

His motivation theory—sometimes irreverently referred to as the spit-and-rumble theory—held that peripheral clues are what motivate a creature: a dry mouth will prompt drinking, a rumbling stomach will lead to eating. These clues, sending messages to the ancient part of the brain, there give rise to the drive to seek water or food.[29] Ironically, Cannon was thus saying about motivation much the same thing he attacked in James's theory of the emotions.

But Cannon's theory of emotions was quite different. He held that peripheral or visceral conditions were not the cause of the emotions but concomitant effects of other causes. In gathering his evidence against the James-Lange theory, he decorticated some animals (removed their cortex), after which it took very little stimulus to elicit a rage reaction from them.

This led Cannon and a Harvard colleague, Philip Bard, to suggest that rage and other emotions originate in the thalamus, a primitive structure in the core of the brain that receives information from sense organs (except the nose) and relays appropriate messages to the cortex and the ANS. The cortex, according to the Cannon-Bard theory, usually controls and inhibits the thalamus, but when the thalamus sends it certain kinds of information—the sight of an enemy, for instance—the cortex relaxes its control. The thalamus then is able to send its emotional messages in two directions: to the nervous system, which produces the visceral responses of emotion and the appropriate behavior, and simultaneously back to the cortex, where the feeling of emotion is produced. Thus, the experience of emotion and its visceral symptoms are parallel effects of the thalamic messages.[30]

Of Cannon's two theories, the spit-and-rumble account of drive, though dominant for some time, was eventually demolished by other experimental evidence. In 1939 two research studies used "sham drinking" to test it. A fistula surgically made in a dog's esophagus drained off water as the dog drank, so that none reached the stomach. Although its mouth was wet, the dog continued drinking copiously without allaying its thirst. Evidently, nothing as simple as dry mouth caused the thirst drive; it came from other and deeper visceral signals, turned into action by the nervous system.

The Cannon-Bard emotion theory, however, was strongly supported, although modified, by later research showing that the ANS, thalamus, and other primitive areas of the nervous system could generate emotions without any input participation by the viscera. In the late 1920s and the 1930s Walter Hess, a Swiss physiologist, inserted electrodes in the rear area of the hypothalamus (a part of the core of the brain located below the thalamus) of a laboratory animal and delivered a weak electrical stimulus; the animal acted enraged. When Hess sent the same current into the forward area of the hypothalamus, the animal became calm and sleepy. Much later, José Delgado, a Spanish neuroscientist, demonstrated this hypothalamic control of rage with Iberian flair. He implanted an electrode in the forward area of a bull's hypothalamus and then entered a bullring holding a control box that would send an electrical impulse through the electrode. The bull was released into the ring, saw Delgado, grew enraged, and charged. Delgado, unflinching, pushed the button, and the bull halted and turned away.[31]

At Yale in the 1950s, Delgado and several colleagues did equally impressive, if less theatrical, research with electrode implantations in rats and cats. By sending a weak current into a cat's or rat's amygdala—a part of the "limbic system" or ancient mammalian brain, a series of structures located between the thalamus and the cortex—they produced fear behavior. Later, Delgado and others did so with human patients during brain surgery. When one patient was receiving the current, he said he felt as if he had just been missed by a car, another as if "something horrible was about to happen" to her. The feelings ceased as soon as the current was turned off.[32]

A completely different kind of evidence supporting the limbic-system theory of the emotions was produced in the 1970s by J. E. Steiner, a developmental psychologist. He took pictures of newborn infants to whom, before their first feeding by breast or bottle, he gave water flavored sweet, sour, or bitter. The sweet water caused the babies to lick their lips, the sour water to purse them and wrinkle their noses, and the bitter water to open their mouths and spit or retch. Steiner then did the same with anencephalic newborns (anencephaly is a tragic anomaly in which the fetus develops no brain tissue above the brain stem; the newborn soon dies); they exhibited exactly the same facial expressions and reactions. Simple emotions and their facial expressions thus appear to be generated by the brain stem, although the responses are modified later, in normal children, by higher nervous centers as the children learn what is acceptable emotional behavior in their society.[33]

In the 1950s Magda Arnold, a Czech-born psychologist at Loyola University in Chicago (one of the few women to attain eminence in psychology before midcentury), and others proposed "arousal theory," an integrated explanation of both motivation and emotion that held their origin to be the "reticular formation" (a network of neurons connecting the brain stem to the thalamus) and the limbic system.

Arousal theory, supported by research using electrode stimulation of the brain, holds that incoming stimuli "activate" parts of the reticular formation and limbic system, which alert the cortex and ready the creature for action.[34] Sounds or smells, for instance, will awaken a sleeping animal; a baby's whimper will bring its sleeping mother wide awake and on her feet in an instant. Such stimuli as deprivation of water, food, or air, or an increase in sex hormone levels, were also shown by electroencephalograms (EEGs)—brain recordings—to activate the reticular formation and, through it, to increase heart rate and overall activity.[35] In sum, the theory envisioned the reticular formation as a regulatory device that, on receiving signals by the senses, turns on both physiological activity and emotional responses.

But as Phil Evans, senior lecturer in psychology at North East London Polytechnic, has ruefully said of arousal theory, "Few concepts in psychology have proven so bothersome and yet so superficially attractive."[36] For although it provides a neural explanation of both motivation and emotion, and makes sense of a wide array of data, it is too general. It presents only one dimension of emotion—the degree of arousal—which leaves unexplained the diversity of the emotions. Also, physiological measures of arousal like heart rate and skin conductance often fail to agree with EEG data and observed levels of activity. Finally, studies of sleep have shown that during periods of rapid eye movement (REM), an animal or human is deeply asleep yet has brain waves indicating high arousal of the reticular formation.[37]

The arousal theory has not been abandoned, but theorists now say that arousal is not the source of the emotions but a concomitant of them. Nor is it a unidimensional condition; there are different types of arousal—behavioral, ANS, and cortical—each with its own characteristics.[38]

The higher-level cortical influences on motivation and emotion, in fact, have been in the forefront of research for nearly half a century. A single recent case history will document the broad-ranging role of the frontal cortex—the center of cognitive processes—on emotions. "Elliot," a man in his early thirties, developed severe and incapacitating headaches, due to a large benign tumor behind his eyes. Surgeons removed it but could not help removing some of the surrounding frontal lobe tissue. Elliot recovered physically but lost the capacity to make decisions and, most curiously, had no emotional reactions to the many mistakes he began making in his career and personal life. The eminent neurologist Antonio Damasio examined him and reported, "I never saw a tinge of emotion in my many hours of conversation with him: no sadness, no impatience, no frustration with my incessant and repetitious questioning." When Elliot was shown disturbing pictures such as severely injured bodies, he said he knew the pictures were disturbing and that before the surgery he would have felt disturbed—but now felt nothing.[39]

Philosophic and religious traditions have held that our emotions and drives originate in our animal or physical side, but modern cognitive psychology, drawing on data of cases like that of Elliot and many other sources of more specific information, finds that many of our emotions and motivations are influenced by, or even originate in, the mind. Let us see the evidence.

Cognitive Theory

Psychologists, in stressing first the somatic and then the thalamic-limbic sources of motivation, were ignoring an everyday truth taken for granted by the average person: human beings and higher-level animals often exhibit emotions and motivations stemming from mental needs, not physiological ones.

Dog owners are well aware of this. They have seen their pet, turned loose in a new or unfamiliar house, immediately explore and sniff around the territory, driven not by hunger or any other somatic need but by a need to know.

Parents are aware of it. They have seen their small child happily push the buttons and pull the levers of a toy cash register or similar toy by the hour, driven by a need to find out how things work.

Everyone knows that after being housebound for a day or two by a storm or a minor illness, one feels a need to get out, look around, and see other places and faces, and after long hours of routine work, a need to do something refreshing to the spirit.

Hull, on a behaviorist basis, and Freud, on a psychodynamic one, held the basic motivation of creatures to be drive reduction, but in the 1960s, as cognition was again becoming the central concern of psychology, a number of researchers began to consider drive reduction theories seriously incomplete and to conduct experiments showing that more advanced creatures are often motivated by cognitive needs and processes.

We learned earlier of two such experiments. The monkeys that opened a window to watch a toy train and those that undid latches without any reward for doing so were motivated not by a physiological need or arousal of the primitive brain but by a cognitive need, namely, for mental stimulation.

Other experiments conducted in the 1950s and after showed that, contrary to behaviorist theory, rats will learn to behave in ways that are unrewarded—at least not by food, water, or other physical gratifications. In several studies, rats chose a path that led them not to food but into a maze, preferred to take a new path rather than a known one leading to food, learned to take a particular fork of a Y maze or to discriminate white from black for the reward of exploring a checkerboard maze, and learned to press a bar to turn on a light when their cage was dark or to turn it off when their cage was bright.[40]

Not only were the animals aroused by novelty; they actively sought novel situations in order to arouse themselves. Human beings are especially likely to try to arouse their own minds and feelings. We seek to frighten ourselves by going to horror movies, to stir ourselves up sexually by reading erotic material, to challenge ourselves by playing games against opponents as good as or better than ourselves, and to make our minds work by solving puzzles. One psychologist, Fred Sheffield, persuasively made the case that it is not drive reduction that reinforces human behavior so much as drive *induction*; we seek not so much the completion of the movie, book, or game as the excitement of watching, reading, or playing.[41]

Such behavior makes sense in terms of evolutionary theory. As the motivation theorist Robert White suggested in 1959, highly developed animals, in order to survive, must learn to deal effectively with their environment. To be curious about novel situations and to be self-arousing is to increase the chance of learning to deal effectively with the environment, and consequently of surviving and reproducing.[42]

But we do not like or seek as much arousal as possible; we prefer moderate stimulation and dislike what is unduly stressful, extremely frightening, or chaotic.[43] This, too, has survival value: we and other creatures function best at intermediate levels of arousal.[44] In one of many experiments attesting to this, volunteers were given up to a hundred seconds to solve each of twenty difficult anagrams for a small cash reward. Their level of motivation was measured by having them rate how attractive they found the goal; those who were moderately motivated solved the most anagrams.[45] The principle is familiar to everyone. All those who drive cars, play games requiring physical or mental skill, or work for others know that they do not do their best when bored or sleepy—or when under extreme pressure to do well.

Some of the best evidence that the motivation behind self-arousal and exploratory behavior is the desire to achieve competence and control of the immediate environment comes from Piaget's and others' studies of children's cognitive development through play and schooling. We heard about some of Piaget's relevant observations earlier, but one more example is apropos here. One day Piaget gave his son Laurent, aged ten months, a piece of bread; Laurent dropped the bread, picked it up, broke off pieces, and let them drop again and again, watching each fall with great interest. The next day, Piaget writes,

he grasps in succession a celluloid swan, a box, and several other small objects, in each case stretching his arm and letting them fall. Sometimes he stretches out his arm vertically, sometimes he holds it obliquely in front of or behind his eyes. When the object falls in a new position (for example on his pillow) he lets it fall two or three times on the same place, as though to study the spatial relation; then he modifies the situation.[46]

The obvious satisfaction such activities yield comes from finding out how the world works and achieving some degree of control over it. In Robert White's words:

The child appears to be occupied with the agreeable task of . . . discovering the effects he can have on the environment and the effects the environment will have on him. To the extent that these results are preserved by learning, they build up an increased competence in dealing with the environment. The child's play can thus be viewed as serious business, though to him it is merely something that is interesting and fun to do.[47]

This is true not only during childhood; in adulthood, though to a lesser extent, we are impelled to expand our knowledge of, and competence in dealing with, the world we live in.[48]

But this does not explain the intense motivation of some human beings to seek answers to questions that have no utilitarian value: the age and size of the universe, for instance, or the means by which bees tell each other where to find honey, or the extent to which human personality is genetically determined. As Daniel Berlyne, a gifted motivation theorist, wrote about the motivating force of curiosity:

> Few phenomena have been the subject of more protracted discussion than human knowledge. Yet this discussion has usually paid little attention to the motivation underlying the quest for knowledge . . . Strangely enough, many of the queries that inspire the most persistent searches for answers and the greatest distress when answers are not forthcoming are of no manifest practical value or urgency. One has only to consider some of the ontological inquiries of metaphysicians or the frenzy of crossword enthusiasts to be convinced of this.[49]

The desire to learn and understand, said Berlyne, could be accounted for in part by psychoanalytic theory, Gestalt psychology, and reinforcement theory, but a fuller explanation lies in the motivation of curiosity. In Berlyne's view, there is a subtler need behind curiosity than the desire for practical knowledge. Strange or puzzling situations arouse conflict in us, and it is the drive to reduce the conflict that impels us to seek answers.[50] What motivated Einstein to develop his general theory of relativity was not its immense practical consequences but what he called a "passion for comprehension"—specifically, a need to understand why his special theory of relativity was at odds with certain principles of Newtonian physics.

In the 1950s and 1960s, psychologists turned up, along with their new findings about cognitive influences on motivation, a wealth of evidence that the mind, rather than the viscera, thalamus, or limbic system, is often the major source of emotional experiences and their physical symptoms. Some of that evidence:

— For half a century it had been known that when a person guilty of some crime is read a list of words or asked questions, some of which are neutral and others of which relate to the crime, the latter often cause a rise in the suspect's blood pressure and galvanic skin conductance. In the 1950s and 1960s further research found other tell-tale symptoms and improved the technology of lie detection equipment. The premise that the conscious mind influences the emotions—or at least guilty anxiety and its associated physical symptoms—was confirmed.[51]

—In 1953 Howard S. Becker, a sociologist, studied fifty people who had become marijuana users. He found, among other things, that new users have to be taught to notice and identify what they feel, label the state as "high," and identify it as pleasant. The physiological feelings of the high acquire their meaning in considerable part from cognitive and social factors.[52]

—In 1958, in a celebrated experiment, Joseph Brady subjected pairs of monkeys to regular stress in the form of electric shock. One monkey of each pair could postpone the shock for twenty seconds by pressing a lever; the other monkey's experiences were linked to the first one's. (He was either not shocked or shocked according to what the first one did or failed to do.) Surprisingly, the monkeys who could avoid the shock developed ulcers, the passive ones did not. Evidently the anticipation and burden placed on the first monkey by the ability to control the shock produced anxiety and its somatic symptoms. Those in the shock-controlling group were soon dubbed "executive monkeys," their situation being likened to that of human executives working under high pressure and constant anticipation of crisis.[53] It was not, however, only anticipation that caused ulcers; it was also the uncertainty about when they had to take action. When a researcher named Jay Weiss repeated Brady's experiment (with rats instead of monkeys), he added a warning tone that signaled the executive rats (but not the passive ones) to take action. Both groups developed ulcers, but the executive rats, thanks to the security of the warning tone, developed distinctly fewer than the passive rats.[54]

—In 1960, Eckhard Hess (whom we saw, a while back, imprinting mallard ducklings on a mechanical mother) photographed the eyes of volunteers while they looked at different pictures. The pupils of the men widened when they saw pictures of women, especially pin-ups; the pupils of the women did so when they saw pictures of babies, particularly of one with his mother. The mind, recognizing and evaluating the content of the pictures, sent signals to the limbic system, which then generated both peripheral and central responses, namely, the pupillary widening and a sense of sexual interest.[55]

By far the most impressive experiment on cognitive influences on the emotions was conducted in 1962 by Stanley Schachter (1922–1997) and Jerome Singer; it yielded a theory that dominated emotion research for twenty years. Schachter, whom we last saw enacting with gusto the role of a true believer in a cult expecting a worldwide flood, was a bluff, craggy-faced man with a zany sense of humor and, in the 1960s, a taste for daring and deceptive experimentation. Only such a person could have conceived of and coolly carried out the historic work in question.

Schachter, after reviewing the evidence for and against the James-Lange and Cannon-Bard theories, had concluded that "the variety of emotion, mood, and feeling states are by no means matched by an equal variety of visceral patterns," and, like a number of other psychologists, came to believe that cognitive factors might be the major determinants of emotional states. He and Singer hypothesized that human beings cannot identify an emotion from the physical symptoms they are experiencing but must rely on external clues. The mind, using those clues, labels what the body is feeling as anger, joy, fear, and so on.

To test their hypothesis, Schachter and Singer asked volunteers for permission to inject them with Suproxin, supposedly a vitamin preparation, to investigate its effects on vision. In reality, the material injected was adrenaline, which causes the heart to race, the face to flush, and the hands to tremble—as do certain strong emotions. Some subjects were told in advance that Suproxin had these side effects, others were not.

Just before each subject began to feel the effects of the adrenaline, he was ushered into a room where he and another student (a confederate), who supposedly had also just had the vitamin injection, had to fill out a five-page questionnaire. The confederate enacted one of two scripts that he had rehearsed. In the presence of some subjects he would act giddy, silly, and happy. He would doodle, pitch crumpled paper into a distant wastebasket in a "basketball game," make a paper airplane and sail it around the room, play with a hula hoop, and so on, meanwhile saying things like "This is one of my good days. I feel like a kid again." With other subjects he would grumble about the length of the questionnaire and become annoyed by the questions (which grew ever more personal and insulting, one of the last being, "With how many men has your mother had extramarital relations?"—to which the lowest multiple-choice answer was "4 and under"). Finally he would rip up the questionnaire, throw the pieces on the floor, and storm out of the room.

Through a one-way screen, the researchers observed and rated each volunteer's behavior and afterward had him fill out a mood scale indicating how irritated, angry, or annoyed, or conversely how good or happy, he felt. The results were arresting. Of the volunteers who had not been told about the injection's effects, those who had seen the confederate being euphoric had also behaved, and said they felt, euphoric, and those who had seen him being irritated and angry had also behaved, and said they felt, irritated and angry. But volunteers who had been told in advance about Suproxin's physiological side effects gave no such responses; they already had an adequate cognitive explanation for their feelings. Schachter and Singer's historic conclusion:

> Given a state of physiological arousal for which an individual has no immediate explanation, he will label this state and describe his feelings in terms of the cognitions available to him. To the extent that cognitive factors are potent determiners of emotional states, it should be anticipated that precisely the same state of physiological arousal could be labeled "joy" or "fury" or "jealousy" or any of a great diversity of emotional labels depending on the cognitive aspects of the situation.[56]

The cognitive theory of emotional arousal was a smashing success. It not only illustrated the importance of cognition, the new passion of psychologists, but made sense of a mass of previously bewildering findings. Over the next two decades a huge amount of related research was conducted by psychologists, some of which qualified or contradicted the Schachter-Singer theory but most of which confirmed and added to it. A few highlights of the findings:

— Schachter and his colleague Larry Gross enlisted volunteers, some obese and some normal, in what they were told was a study of how somatic reactions are related to psychological traits. The experimenters conned each volunteer into handing over his watch when electrode paste was applied to his wrists; the electrodes being attached to him served only to disguise the removal of the watch. The researchers also left a box of crackers in the room and told the volunteer—who was alone during the experiment—to help himself. In the room was a doctored clock, running either at half speed or at double speed. After a while some volunteers thought it was their dinnertime although it was still early, others that it was not yet their dinnertime although it was late. The obese volunteers ate more crackers when they thought it was beyond their regular dinner hour than when they thought it was not yet their dinner hour; normal volunteers ate the same number no matter what time they thought it was. The conclusion: Not the stomach but the mind of the obese volunteers determined their feelings of hunger.[57]

— Another research team had an attractive female confederate approach men students as they were crossing either a swaying suspension bridge over a deep canyon or a low, solid bridge. In each situation the confederate's cover story was that for a research project she wanted them to fill out a questionnaire and make up a brief story about a picture. She gave each man her name and telephone number so that he could call her if he wanted to know more about the project. The men she approached on the frightening suspension bridge wrote stories with more sexual imagery and were more likely to call her and ask for a date than the men she approached on the low, firm bridge. The experimenters concluded that the men approached on the frightening bridge interpreted their anxiety as the first stage of sexual attraction. As per Schachter-Singer theory, the men had taken an external clue—the presence of the attractive woman—as the explanation of their physical feelings.[58]

— In the late 1970s Paul Rozin and Deborah Schiller of the University of Pennsylvania undertook an inquiry into how and why human beings develop a liking for a painful stimulus, in this case chili pepper in food. Rozin and Schiller interviewed college students in Philadelphia and Mexicans in a highlands village near Oaxaca, and discovered that initially the response to chili pepper by children is almost always strongly negative; this ruled out the possibility that chili lovers are relatively insensitive to the irritant. They found that the initial dislike of the painful sensation changed because of the mother's training and the social situation (especially in Mexico). The recognition that the burning sensation is considered desirable led the children to develop a liking for it—again, evidence that the mind decides how a sensation is to be interpreted.[59]

— Sexual arousal and mating behavior are automatically triggered in insects by pheromones (attractant secretions); even in mammals, odors produced by a female in heat switch on sexual desire and activity in the male, as every dog owner knows. Moreover, in many mammals hormone levels in both male and female determine when they have the mating urge. But in human beings, phero-mones and hormone levels have only a limited relation to sexual interest. A vast amount of anthropological, historical, and psycho-logical research data attest that human sexual arousal is largely a matter of cognitive responses—reactions to clues specific to each culture.[60] Three scraps of evidence, out of thousands available:

1. In some cultures, the female breast, normally concealed, is power-fully exciting to men; in those where it is routinely exposed, it is not. Similarly, at the turn of the century, a woman's ankle was an erotic sight for Western men; by the 1980s, in magazines like Playboy and Penthouse photographs of completely nude women were considered marginally erotic and only those featuring a clear view of the pudenda, preferably tumescent and open, were thought of as highly arousing.

2. Alfred Kinsey's historic surveys of American sexual behavior, con-ducted during the 1940s and published in 1948 and 1953, found that women were much less often stimulated by erotic materials than men. But a national survey made nearly three decades later found that the sexual revolution and the women's movement had made women far more arousable by erotic material than for-merly. Again, in Kinsey's era women were much less likely than men to experience orgasm in intercourse; by the time of the later survey they had become considerably more orgasmic.[61]

3. Volunteers in an experiment were exposed to erotica while carry-ing out difficult arithmetical tasks; although they were aware of the erotic stimuli, they did not become aroused. Apparently, to become excited by erotic material, the viewer or reader must fantasize himself or herself as part of the action; the partici-pants in the experiment were too preoccupied by their work to do so.[62]

As early as the 1930s, but chiefly from the 1950s on, researchers in other areas of psychology were also turning up evidence that cognitive processes are a major source of human emotions and motivations. To do justice to the diverse research would require volumes; we will content ourselves with a few paragraphs about each of four examples:

I

In the mid-1930s, as we have seen, the Harvard personality researcher Henry Murray developed the Thematic Apperception Test (TAT) to measure aspects of personality, especially unconscious ones. Drawing on psychoanalytic theory, he framed these in the form of thirty-five needs: for orderliness, dominance, deference, aggression, abasement, nurturance, affiliation (belonging and friendship), and others. Each of the thirty-five was a motivating force, and many were investigated from that angle in the following years.

Perhaps the most intensively researched was the need for achievement, or, as it is referred to in psychological literature, nAch. In the 1950s and 1960s, David McClelland and his colleagues at Wesleyan University in Connecticut produced a number of valuable studies of the personality and behavior of people with high nAch and of its sources. Among their findings: Persons high in nAch prefer tasks that offer concrete feedback and hence tend to choose work in which it is possible to see growth and expansion . . . Boys high in nAch had mothers who expected them, from an early age, to be independent and self-reliant, and who put fewer restrictions on them than mothers of low-nAch boys . . . A survey of twenty-three modern societies found that the value a society places on achievement is reflected in its children's stories and is correlated to its increase in electrical production in recent years.[63]

All of which indicates that motivation to achieve is acquired from one's parents and society, and is thus cognitive in nature.

II

Freud held that the ego or largely conscious self develops as the child learns to control his or her impulse to obtain immediate gratification, and to postpone seeking satisfaction for the sake of greater reward or social acceptability. Thus, motivation in the older child and adult, though powered by the drive to obtain pleasure, is cognitively directed.

In the 1950s and beyond, experimental evidence gathered by developmental psychologists supported Freud's ego-development theory. Walter Mischel and his collaborators, for example, offered children the choice of an immediate small reward or a delayed larger one. At seven, most children chose the immediate reward; at nine, most of them chose the delayed larger one.[64]

Meanwhile, the writings of the psychoanalysts Anna Freud and Heinz Hartmann had been bringing about a change in the focus of psychodynamic psychology. The ego was found to be more powerful and influential, the id less so, than had been thought. To psychologists who were psychodynamically oriented, this meant that in large part the human adult is motivated by conscious wishes, ego defense mechanisms, and values. By the 1950s, therefore, psychotherapists and academic psychologists were actively exploring positive cognitive forces used by the ego to combat stress, in particular *hope* to counteract anxiety when facing uncertainties, and *coping mechanisms* to deal with problems rather than irrational reactions and self-defenses.[65]

III

Most twentieth-century psychologists across the spectrum from Freud to Skinner were determinists. As scientists, they believed that human behavior, like all events in the real world, is caused; every thought and act is the result of antecedent events and forces. This premise seemed to them essential to the status of psychology as a science. In this view, if individuals could behave as they chose—if some or much of their behavior were determined by their will, operating freely, rather than by past experiences and present forces—there could not be a body of rigorous laws concerning behavior. Accordingly, the term "will" had largely disappeared from psychology by midcentury and ever since has not even been mentioned in passing in most textbooks, although an excellent current one does list it in the index as "will, illusion of conscious."[66]

But the concept has refused to die; it lives on in altered form and under other names, and for good reason.

For one thing, the goal of psychotherapy is to liberate the patient from the control of unconscious forces. This can only mean that the patient becomes capable of consciously weighing and judging the alternatives and deciding how to behave. But what is a decision if not a volitional act?

For another, developmental psychologists had found that a crucial feature of children's mental development is the gradual appearance of "metacognition"—awareness of their own thought processes and ability to manage them. Children slowly discover that there are ways to remember things, to formulate problem-solving strategies, to categorize objects; they begin to exercise conscious and voluntary control of their own thought processes.[67]

For yet another, cognitive psychology had to devise a modern equivalent of will to account for the phenomenon of decision making, observed in innumerable studies of thinking and problem solving. Artificial intelligence experts refer to the "executive functions" of programs that simulate thinking; that is, the parts of such programs that weigh the results achieved at any point and determine what steps to take next. Some theorists say that the human mind, likewise, has executive machinery that makes decisions. But the decisions made by an AI program are fully predictable, while predictions of decisions of a human being are often wrong. Why? Is there, after all, some area of freedom within human choice, some kind of free will within voluntary control? We will look further into this enigma in the final chapter; for now, it is enough to note that whether one views decision making as a fully predictable executive process or as a voluntary act, its motivation is of cognitive origin.[68]

IV

Murray suggested in the 1930s that social factors are often a source of motivation, but the suggestion lay fallow; in the 1950s, with the growth of social psychology and humanistic psychology, psychologists became interested in "social motivation."[69] This was an important component of an integrated theory of motivation put forward in 1954 by Abraham Maslow, the leader of the humanistic psychology movement of the 1950s and 1960s.

Maslow (1908–1970) was a complex, enthusiastic, and thoughtful man whose life had well fitted him to the task of theorizing about human motivations. One of seven children of an immigrant family in Brooklyn, he was an unhappy, neurotic child, and a chronic outsider. This motivated him to school achievement of a high order, largely overcoming his unhappiness and isolation. Moving upward through the academic ranks at Teachers College, Brooklyn College, and Brandeis, he worked closely with a variety of colleagues—behaviorists, animal psychologists, a leading neurologist, Gestaltists, and psychoanalysts (he himself underwent analysis)—seeking to understand human motivations and to fit all that he learned into a comprehensive scheme. He died of a heart attack at sixty-two, but not before completing that task.

Maslow pictured human needs and the motivations arising from them as a hierarchy or pyramid. Its broad base, on which all else rests, consists of the physiological needs; the next higher layer, of the safety needs (for security, stability, freedom from fear, and so on); still higher, of the psychological needs, which are largely of a social nature (the needs for belonging, love, affiliation, and acceptance; the needs for esteem, approval, and recognition); and finally, at the pinnacle, of the "self-actualization needs" (the need to fulfill oneself, "to become everything that one is capable of becoming").[70]

Research by others on social motivation explored many of these topics and spelled out how social motivation is tied into personality traits. Insecure people, for instance, have a strong need for approval; as a result, they consistently strive to convey socially desirable traits. On personality tests they will lay claim to sentiments that are admirable but rarely true, such as "I have never intensely disliked anyone," and deny others that are socially undesirable but generally true, such as "I like to gossip at times." Most people seek a degree of social approval in this fashion, but those with a particularly strong need for approval do so to such an extreme that others see them as sanctimonious and unlikable.[71]

Many other aspects of social motivation were hot topics in the field from the 1960s to the 1980s—more, indeed, than can be included in this brief account. Social motivation is so broad a topic that our sampling has given us only a taste of it. But we cannot spend more time here; there have been so many developments and discoveries in the field of emotion and motivation in the past generation, especially the past fifteen years, that we must hasten on to wander through a veritable sideshow of recent psychological curiosa.

Patchwork Quilt

We have come a long way from half-starved rats scurrying across an electric grid for a morsel of food, and from Cannon's cats, hissing with rage at barking dogs although their viscera had been disconnected from their brains.

As we followed the story, it may have seemed that early theories were disproved by later research and discarded in favor of new ones, but the reality is far more complicated: Still later evidence has often revalidated old theories without invalidating the newer ones. Once more it appears that in psychology few theories are ever proven dead wrong; rather, they are shown to be limited and incomplete but to have value when pieced together with other theories in an inclusive, if untidy, patchwork quilt of theory.

The James-Lange theory is the prime example of an early one that still occupies a place in the quilt. It seemed to be outmoded by Cannon's work, which located the source of emotion in the thalamus, and by the Schachter-Singer experiment, which found it to be in the mind, but in 1980 Robert Zajonc, a distinguished researcher and scientific provocateur, revived it in new form on the basis of his own finding that feeling states occur prior to cognitive evaluation.

Zajonc (pronounced "zye-onts") was born in Poland, and in 1940, when he was seventeen, fled from the German invaders; his life disrupted, he did not complete his doctorate until he was thirty-five. But despite the late start, he performed a great deal of significant research, especially in social psychology, and won a number of honors. The possessor of a restless mind, he has always preferred to look into questions that he has said "irritate him," answer them in bold outline, and move on, leaving the details to others.

In the late 1970s Zajonc conducted a number of experiments on the "mere-exposure effect"; this is the human tendency to develop a preference for a stimulus with which we become familiar, even though it has no meaning or value for us. Zajonc showed volunteers a number of Japanese ideographs, some only once, others up to twenty-seven times. He then displayed the ideographs again, asking the volunteers which they recognized and which they liked best. They preferred those they had seen most often, even though the symbols meant nothing to them—and even though they did not recognize them.

Aside from the disturbing implications of the finding—that we can be swayed to like and prefer products or persons merely through the repeated exposure of their names or images—Zajonc saw in it something of scientific import. Affective reactions (feeling states) can occur without cognition, can precede cognitive evaluation, and are more responsible for what we do than cognition. In an article in *American Psychologist*, which he titled—provocatively, by his own admission—"Feeling and Thinking: Preferences Need No Inferences," he came out flatly for the primacy of the physical source of the emotions:

> Affect should not be treated as unalterably last and invariably postcognitive. The evolutionary origins of affective reactions that point to their survival value, their distinctive freedom from attentive control, their speed, the importance of affective discriminations for the individual,

the extreme forms of action that affect can recruit—all these suggest something special about affect. People do not get married or divorced, commit murder or suicide, or lay down their lives for freedom upon a detailed cognitive analysis of the pros and cons of their actions.[72]

The article exasperated many cognitive psychologists and created lively controversy. Richard Lazarus, of the University of California at Berkeley, became Zajonc's chief opponent and vigorously disputed Zajonc's thesis. In the same journal he offered an array of contrary evidence, the most salient being his own data on how the emotions aroused in volunteers by motion pictures could be altered by versions of the soundtrack that gave different information. Lazarus had used a film of Australian aborigines performing subincision, the ritual slitting of the underside of the penis of a male adolescent with a sharp stone. The film distressed viewers greatly when the soundtrack emphasized its pain and cruelty but far less when the soundtrack stressed how the adolescents looked forward to undergoing the ritual and thereby earning the status and benefits of adulthood. Lazarus's conclusion:

> Cognitive activity is a necessary precondition of emotion because to experience an emotion, people must comprehend—whether in the form of a primitive evaluative perception or a highly differentiated symbolic process—that their well-being is implicated in a transaction, for better or worse. A creature that is oblivious to the significance of what is happening for its well-being does not react with an emotion.[73]

In fact, he later came to take "the strongest position possible" on the role of cognition in emotion, namely, that it is both a necessary and sufficient condition. "*Sufficient* means that thoughts are capable of producing emotions; *necessary* means that emotions cannot occur without some kind of thought."[74]

Zajonc and Lazarus continued their debate for some time, but the work of others indicated that both were right and their findings not incompatible.

One such indication is the finding of the developmentalist Michael Lewis and his colleagues, discussed earlier, that six primary emotions (joy, fear, anger, sadness, disgust, and surprise) appear at or shortly after birth, but that six others (embarrassment, empathy, envy, pride, shame, and guilt) do not appear until the child develops cognitive capacity and self-awareness.[75] Lewis and his team did not discuss the Zajonc-Lazarus debate, but their observations make room for both noncognitive and cognitive interpretations of emotion. (Carroll Izard's infant photos document much the same development of emotions and their expression.)

Social psychologist Ross Buck said that the resolution of the controversy lay in the recognition that there is more than one sort of cognition: "knowledge by acquaintance," or direct sensory awareness, and "knowledge by description," the cognitive interpretation of sensory data, a distinction expounded some decades ago by the philosopher Bertrand Russell. Feelings may occur first, said Buck, but are transformed by the mind's knowledge into cognitive judgments about the information they convey—which then modify the feelings. The process is a continuing interaction. "Feeling, expression, physiological responding, cognition, and goal-related behavior are interrelated processes, playing integrated and interacting roles in motivation and emotion."[76]

Robert Plutchik identified the Zajonc and Lazarus views as only parts of a larger whole. He defined an emotion as a chain of events in a complex feedback-loop system. A stimulus starts the process, but from then on there is an interplay between cognitive evaluations, feelings, and physiological changes, impulses to action, and overt actions, the results altering their own causes in a continuing process.[77] Plutchik interpreted both the Zajonc and Lazarus data as products of research methods that look at single events rather than the whole process:

> One can put an electrode in the brain of a cat, or of a human being, and produce emotional reactions without a cognitive evaluation of an external event . . . It is obviously possible to focus attention on any of the elements of the chain. One can then produce theories that emphasize, for example, the primacy of arousal, or the primacy of expressive behavior.[78]

The ancient theory that emotions are a major source of motivation that often overpowers the better judgment of the mind seemed to be made obsolete by the Darwinian evidence that emotions are signals and cues calling forth behavior with survival value. Yet how could the Darwinian view be reconciled with the ample evidence that we are often governed by useless or harmful emotions—panic, depression, jealousy, self-loathing, persistent grieving for a lost love, phobias, and even more crippling and tormenting emotional disturbances?

The question is quicksand; tread upon it and you may never escape. Let us be cautious; let us only look at it from afar and for an instant.

Although there is nothing like general agreement, a number of leading figures in the field hold a generally neo-Darwinian view of the emotions. They regard them as a source of information that enables us to appraise situations and judge what actions to take to achieve valued goals.[79] But the classic antagonism of emotions and intellect has largely vanished; in the light of cognitive psychology, it has come to appear that emotions and cognition serve the same end, self-preservation. Robert Plutchik has argued that in simple animals, emotions are the cues to actions with survival value, and in more complex animals, including humankind, cognitive capacity performs the same function, correcting or amplifying the predictions of the emotions—though we still need their power to produce the behavior:

> The appropriateness of an emotional response can determine whether the individual lives or dies. The whole cognitive process evolved over millions of years in order to make the evaluation of stimulus events more correct and the predictions more precise so that the emotional behavior that finally resulted would be adaptively related to the stimulus events. *Emotional behavior, therefore, is the proximate basis for the ultimate outcome of increased inclusive fitness.*[80]

This still left unanswered the question of why we so often experience emotions that mislead us, are useless, or are damaging. Nico Frijda of the University of Amsterdam, a leading emotion researcher, offered several answers, among them that dysfunctional emotions sometimes result from a faulty evaluation of the situation, sometimes from contingencies that are more than one can cope with, and sometimes are emergency reactions in situations where slower and more thoughtful evaluation would serve us better.[81]

Psychosomatic research has shown, too, that when we cannot escape from or take action against a threatening or tense situation, our emotions are no guide to action but a source of pain and illness.[82] The hostage held by fanatics, the front-line soldier, the terminal cancer patient, cannot benefit from most of their emotions but only be damaged by them. Finally, when we have opposing or incompatible desires, or desires that are in conflict with social constraints, we experience emotions that are pathological.

In recent years many researchers have been mining narrow lodes, not making large illuminating discoveries but adding bits and pieces of all sorts to an emerging multicausal—or, to put it more candidly, patch-work—theory of emotion and motivation. Their work ranges widely from the somatic to the neural, the cognitive, and elsewhere. What follows is a hodgepodge of latter-day examples; feel free to sample as much or as little as you like.

- Some researchers have explored how specific neurotransmitters influence emotion and motivation. The molecules of cholecystokinins, for instance, plug up certain neural receptors in the GI tract and the CNS, and thereby affect appetite; obese men, given doses of the chemical, eat less.[83]
- Others have sought to link specific emotions to particular parts of the body. In one such study, 172 volunteers named the parts in which they felt different emotions: shame mostly in the face, fear in many areas but especially the anal region, disgust in the stomach and throat, and so on. But the researchers did not feel that this meant the emotions were based primarily on bodily experience; rather, they saw the somatic information as part of a composite in which awareness, cognitive appraisal, and body feeling all interacted.[84]
- In seeking the sources of empathy, researchers have observed children over time to see when precursor emotions appear and develop. They have found that an infant will cry when it hears another infant cry, apparently out of a primitive form of empathy (the same infant will not cry if it hears a tape recording of its own crying). And as we saw earlier, a child nearing one year will react with distress to the sight and sound of another person in pain, but at two or three will try to comfort or even help the other person. The reasonable conclusion: Compassion is a product of personality development and socialization, building on the empathetic emotional foundation.[85]
- Antonio Damasio has distinguished between *emotional states* (bodily symptoms of an emotion) and *emotional feelings* (cognitive awareness of the symptoms). This far, he sounds like William James, but he goes beyond James by saying that emotional states and emotional feelings can be unconscious and that the physiological experience of a strong emotion, once learned, becomes a *somatic marker*—an automatic guide to swift action in emergencies and to swift decision-making. To prove the existence of somatic markers, Damasio tested patients who had ventromedial

frontal lobe damage and compared them with control subjects:
Both reacted to an innately alarming stimulus (a sudden loud
sound) with increased skin conductance, but when they were
shown pictures of disaster scenes or mutilations (stimuli which
should produce a learned emotional response), the control subjects showed a sharp spike in skin conductance; the patients with
ventromedial cortical damage showed none. What the patients had
learned was no longer connected to their somatic systems.[86]

— Other research, related to Damasio's, compared the startle responses of patients with damage to the amygdala (as mentioned
earlier, a small area of the medial temporal lobe involved in emotional processing) with those of normal people. People in both
groups were startled by a sudden loud noise, but when the noise
occurred in the context of a dark, empty street, the control subjects
showed a much stronger startle response and the amygdala-
damaged patients did not. Yet, most curiously, the patients were
able to say that the dark street stimulus was the far more arousing
one; they knew it was arousing—but were unaroused.[87]

— A number of researchers have been interested in the effects of emotions on perception and memory. In one very recent study, participants saw a key word flashed for $\frac{1}{10}$ of a second, and then two words,
one of which was the same one they had so briefly seen. If that key
word was related to either a positive or negative emotion, they were
more likely to identify it correctly than if it was emotionally neutral; evidently, we see more clearly if what we see has some emotional impact. As for memory, various studies found that
participants could more easily recall events or information when
they happened to be in the same mood as when they first had the
experience or learned the information. In a good mood, one can
recall more pleasant or positive events in one's life than when in a
bad mood.[88]

— For the past dozen years the subject of "emotional intelligence"
(EI) has been the focus of a good deal of research and theorizing.
What EI is depends on who's talking about it. From one point of
view, it is the ability to understand and regulate our emotions; from
another point of view, it is the reliance on emotions to aid us in
making judgments as to how to behave. Psychologist Daniel Goleman in his book *Emotional Intelligence* says that people can be
smart in a way that has nothing to do with IQ scores but with self-
awareness, impulse control, zeal and motivation, empathy and

social deftness; our emotions, in short, are often very smart—but, he admits, can also be very stupid. As for the research evidence: In a study employing personality tests and a special scale that rates EI, students who scored high in EI were more likely to report positive relationships with others, including greater perceived support from their parents and fewer negative interactions with their close friends, than those who scored low. In a study of people with careers in insurance, employees with higher EI scores were rated by their supervisors as more tolerant of stress, more sociable, and having greater potential for leadership than employees with lower EI scores. Higher scores were also related to higher salary and more promotions.[89]

These few examples illustrate the extent to which the old field of emotion and motivation is showing new vigor. Can the resulting mass of findings of the past eighty-odd years be pieced together into a unifying coherent theory?

A few psychologists believe they can, although no single overall scheme seems dominant. But the general view, to judge from a sampling of top textbooks, is that the three major theories—the James-Lange, the Cannon-Bard, and the cognitive appraisal (Schachter, Lazarus, and others)—all have grains of truth. But so do a number of the variants and developments of them that we have seen.[90] Not a simple answer, to be sure.

To hark back to the question asked at the beginning of this chapter— Why do we do what we do?—at this time there is no one integrated theory, no overall design, to what has become a theoretical patchwork quilt. Those who must have a simple, easily understood answer will not find it in psychology. At least, not yet.

SIXTEEN

The
Cognitivists

Revolution

In 1960, George A. Miller, though youthful and somewhat pixieish in appearance at forty, was a professor of psychology at Harvard and assured of his prestigious post and comfortable style of living for the rest of his career. Yet that year he felt compelled, despite deep misgivings, to reveal his true colors even if it meant giving up his place at Harvard.

His revelation would not be about radical politics or radical sex, both on the rise at that time, but about his interest in the mind.

The *mind*? What could be subversive or disreputable about that? Wasn't it the core concern of psychology?

No, not then, nor had it been since the beginning of the behaviorist dominion over American psychology four decades earlier. To behaviorists, the mind, invisible, nonmaterial, and conjectural, was an obsolete metaphysical concept that no experimental psychologist concerned about his career and reputation would talk about, much less devote himself to.

But Miller had become a covert mentalist over the years. Born and raised in Charleston, West Virginia, as a freshman in college he had been uninterested in and even a trifle hostile toward psychology; in a memoir he says, tongue in cheek (a frequent mode of his), that he saw drawings of the brain and other organs in a psychology textbook and, "raised by Christian Scientists, I had been trained to avoid *materia medica*, and I could recognize the devil when I saw him."[1]

Either education or infatuation changed his outlook. In his junior year at the University of Alabama, Miller, smitten with a girl (whom he later married), went to the informal seminars in psychology she was attending, given by Professor Donald Ramsdell at his home. Miller made such an impression on Ramsdell that a couple of years later, when he completed a master's in speech and communication, Ramsdell offered him a job teaching psychology to undergraduates, although Miller had never had a formal course in the subject. By then married and a father, Miller needed the job and took it; a year of teaching psychology made a convert of him.

He went to Harvard for graduate studies, received a solid grounding in behaviorist psychology, and so distinguished himself that after earning his doctorate he was made an instructor. For the next fourteen years, first at Harvard and then at the Massachusetts Institute of Technology, he conducted experimental studies in speech and communication. Despite his behaviorist training, this work, unlike rat-based research, forced him willy-nilly to think about human memory and other higher mental processes. He drifted still closer to mentalism after attending a summer seminar at Stanford, where he worked closely with the psycholinguist Noam Chomsky, and a sabbatical year at the Center for Advanced Study in the Behavioral Sciences at Palo Alto, where he was exposed to new ways of doing research on thinking, especially the simulation of thought processes by computer programs.

In the fall of 1960 Miller returned to Harvard a changed man. As he tells it in his memoir:

> I realized I was acutely unhappy with the narrow conception of psychology that defined the Harvard department. I had just spent a year romping wildly in the sunshine. The prospect of going back to a world bounded at one end by psychophysics and at the other by operant conditioning was simply intolerable. I decided that either Harvard would have to let me create something resembling the interactive excitement of the Stanford Center or else I was going to leave.

Miller confided in his friend and colleague, the social psychologist Jerome Bruner, about his discontent and the dream of a new center devoted to the study of mental processes. Bruner shared both his feelings and his vision. Together they approached McGeorge Bundy, provost of the university, won his approval, and with funding from the Carnegie Corporation established the Harvard Center for Cognitive Studies. Naming it that made Miller feel like a declared apostate:

To me, even as late as 1960, using "cognitive" was an act of defiance. It was less outrageous for Jerry [Bruner], of course; social psychologists were never swept away by behaviorism the way experimental psychologists had been. But for someone raised to respect reductionistic science, "cognitive psychology" made a definite statement. It meant that I was interested in the mind—I came out of the closet.

And became a leader of the movement that radically changed the focus and methods of psychology and has guided it ever since.

George Miller's coming-out typifies what was happening to experimental psychologists in the 1960s. At first a few, then many, and soon a majority abandoned rats, mazes, electric grids, and food-dispensing levers in favor of research on the higher mental processes of human beings. Within the decade, the movement had assumed such proportions as to earn the name "the cognitive revolution."

Many forces had been building toward it. During the two previous decades, Gestaltists, personality researchers, developmentalists, and social psychologists were all, in their different ways, exploring mental processes. Coincidentally, a series of developments in several other scientific fields (some of which we have already heard about, some of which we will hear about shortly) were producing knowledge of other kinds about how the mind works. Specifically:

— Neuroscientists, using microelectrode probes and other new techniques, were observing the neural events and cellular interconnections involved in mental processes.
— Logicians and mathematicians were developing information theory and using it to account for both the capabilities and limitations of human communication.
— Anthropologists, analyzing the thought patterns of people in other cultures, were discovering which mental processes vary among cultures, and which are universal and therefore possibly innate.
— Psycholinguists, studying language acquisition and use, were learning how the mind acquires and manipulates the intricate symbol system we call language.
— Computer scientists, a new hybrid (part mathematician, part logician, part engineer), were contributing a brand-new theoretical model of thinking, and designing machinery that seemed to think.

By the late 1970s, cognitive psychology and these related fields came to be known as the cognitive sciences; a number of enthusiasts called them collectively, "cognitive science" and regarded it as a new and distinctive field.[2] In the 1980s and early 1990s they expected it to replace the field of psychology; instead, standard psychology morphed, absorbing the new ideas of cognitive science. Today, most departments of psychology include many cognitive science topics, and the relatively few separate departments of cognitive science that exist include many or most classical psychology topics.[3] The bottom line: The cognitive revolution was more than a remarkable broadening and deepening of psychology; it was the extraordinary—indeed, wholly improbable—simultaneous development in six sciences of new knowledge bearing on mental processes.

Computer science had by far the greatest impact on psychology. This new field was the product of intense research during World War II, when Allied forces urgently needed calculating machines that could rapidly handle large sets of numbers to direct antiaircraft guns, operate navigation equipment, and the like. But even very high-speed calculating machines needed to be told by a human operator, after each calculation, what to do next, which severely limited their speed and introduced inaccuracies. By the late 1940s, mathematicians and engineers were starting to provide the machines with sets of instructions (programs) stored in their electronic memories. Now the machines could swiftly and accurately guide their own operations, carry out lengthy sequences of operations, and make decisions about what needed to be done next. The calculating machines had become computers.

At first, computers dealt only with numerical problems. But as the mathematicians John von Neumann and Claude Shannon and other computer experts soon pointed out, any symbol can represent another kind of symbol. A number can stand for a letter and a series of numbers for a word, and mathematical computations can represent relationships expressed by language. For instance, $=$ can stand for "is the same as," $\neq$ for "is not the same as," $>$ for "more than" or "too much." Given a set of rules by which to turn words into numbers and algebraic relationships and then back into words, a computer can perform operations analogous to some kinds of human reasoning.[4]

In 1948 the idea that the computer might in some ways function like a mind—at the time this seemed more like science fiction than science—was first broached by von Neumann and the neurophysiologist Warren McCulloch at a California Institute of Technology conference, "Cerebral Mechanisms in Behavior."

That notion captivated Herbert Simon, then a young professor of political science at the Carnegie Institute (now Carnegie-Mellon University).[5] "Professor of political science" hardly describes him, however. Simon, the son of an electrical engineer, was so bright that he was skipped in school and was considerably younger than his friends and classmates. Add to that his being unathletic and growing up in Wisconsin keenly aware of his Jewishness, and it is not surprising that he solaced himself by becoming an exceptional student. In college he liked to think of himself as an intellectual, but in fact his interests were freakishly wide-ranging; although he became a political scientist, he was interested and self-taught in mathematics, economics (for which he was awarded a Nobel Prize in 1978), administration, logic, psychology, and computer science.

In 1954, Simon and a brilliant young graduate student of his, Allen Newell, discovered that they shared passionate interests in computers and thinking (both men later earned degrees in psychology), and in creating a computer program that would think. For a first attempt, they chose a very limited kind of thinking, namely, proving theorems in formal logic, an entirely symbolic and almost algebraic process. Simon's task was to work out proofs of theorems while "dissecting as minutely as possible, not only the proof steps, but the cues that led me to each one." Then the two men together tried to incorporate this information in a flow diagram that they could turn into a computer program.

After a year and a half of work, Simon and Newell electrified the audience at a 1956 symposium on information theory at MIT with a description of their intellectual offspring, Logic Theorist. Running on JOHNNIAC, a gigantic, primitive, vacuum-tube computer, it was able to prove a number of theorems in formal logic in anywhere from under a minute to fifteen minutes per proof.[6] (On a modern computer it would do the same thing in virtually the blink of an eye.) Logic Theorist, the first artificial intelligence program, wasn't very intelligent; it could prove only logic theorems—at about the same speed as an average college student—and only if they were presented in algebra-like symbols. Still, as the first computer program that did something like thinking, it was a breathtaking achievement. (George Miller was at the presentation; he regards that day as the birthday of cognitive science, even though it took him another four years to declare his apostasy from behaviorism.[7])

By the end of the following year, 1957, Newell, Simon, and a colleague, Clifford Shaw, had created a much cleverer program, General Problem Solver (GPS), which incorporated a number of broad principles common to many intellectual tasks, including proving theorems in geometry, solving cryptarithmetic problems, and playing chess. GPS would make a first move or probe to begin determining the "problem space" (the area containing all possible moves between its initial state and the desired goal), look at the result to see whether the move had brought it closer to the goal, concoct possible next moves and test them to see which one would advance it toward the goal, back up to the last decision point if the train of reasoning veered off course, and start again in another direction. A simple problem that GPS solved easily early in its career went as follows (the problem was presented not in these words, which GPS could not understand, but in mathematical symbols):

A heavy father and two young sons have to cross a swift river in a deep wood. They find an abandoned boat that can be rowed across, but will sink if overloaded. Each young son weighs 100 pounds. Two sons weigh as much as the father, and more than 200 pounds is too much for the boat. How do the father and the sons cross the river?[8]

The solution, though simple, requires a seeming retreat in order to advance. The two sons get in and row across; one debarks and the other rows back and lands; the father rows across and gets out; the son on that side rows back, picks up his brother, and returns to the far shore. GPS, in devising and testing this solution, was doing something akin to human problem solving. By means of the same heuristic—a broad stratagem of exploration and evaluation—it was able to solve similar but far more difficult problems.

Two basic features of GPS and later artificial intelligence (AI) programs brought about a metamorphosis in cognitive psychology by giving psychologists a more detailed and workable conception of mental processes than any they had previously had, plus a practical way to investigate them.[9]

The first of those features is *representation*: the use of symbols to stand for other symbols or events. In GPS, numbers stand for words or relationships, and in the hardware (the actual computer) operated by GPS, groups of transistors, acting as binary switches that are either on or off, stand for those numbers. By analogy, cognitive psychologists could conceive of the images, words, and other symbols stored in the mind as representations of external events, and of the brain's neural responses as representations of those images, symbols, and thoughts. A representation, in other words, corresponds to the thing it represents without being at all similar to it. But this was actually an old discovery in new form; Descartes and Fermat discovered long ago that algebraic equations can be represented by lines drawn on a graph.

The second feature is *information processing*: the transforming and manipulating of data by the program in order to achieve a goal. In the case of GPS, incoming information—the feedback of each step—was evaluated as to where it had led, used to determine the next step, stored in memory, retrieved if needed again, and so on. By analogy, cognitive psychologists could conceive of the mind as an information-processing program that transforms perceptions and other incoming data into mental representations and, step by step, evaluates them, uses them to determine what to do next in the attempt to reach its goal, adds them to memory, and retrieves them for use again as needed.

The information-processing (IP) or "computational" model of thinking has been the guiding metaphor of cognitive psychology ever since the 1960s, and has enabled researchers and theorists to explore the inner universe of the mind as never before.

One specimen of such an exploration will exemplify how the IP model enables cognitive psychologists to ascertain what takes place in the mind. In a 1967 experiment, a research team headed by Michael Posner asked its subjects to say aloud, as fast as possible, whether two letters projected on a screen had the same or different names. When the subjects saw this

AA

they almost instantly said "Same," and when they saw this

Aa

they again almost instantly said "Same." But the researchers, using a highly accurate timer, measured a minuscule difference. On average, subjects replied to AA in 549 milliseconds and to Aa in 623 milliseconds. A tiny difference, to be sure—but a statistically significant one.[10] What could account for it?

The IP model envisions any simple cognitive process as a series of step-by-step actions performed on the data. The following simple flow diagram, typical of many drawn by cognitive psychologists, symbolizes what goes on when we see and recognize something:

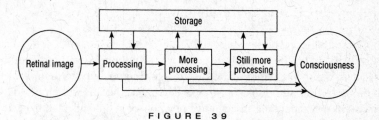

FIGURE 39

A typical information-processing diagram

That accounts for the reaction-time difference in the experiment. If an image proceeds directly from the first "processing" box to "consciousness," it does so in less time than when it must pass through two or three boxes. In order to identify the letters in AA as having the same name, subjects had to perform only visual pattern recognition on the visual image; to identify those in Aa as having the same name, they had to locate the name of each letter in memory and then see whether they were the same—additional processing that took 74 milliseconds more, a tiny but consequential difference, and strong evidence of how the mind performed this little task. In a follow-up experiment subjects had to say whether AU were both vowels, and in another whether SC were both consonants; the AU response took somewhat longer than AA or Aa had, and SC much longer (nearly a second). Again, these longer reaction times indicated that more steps of mental processing were required.[11] Thus even trifling experiments based on the IP model can reveal something of what goes on in the mind.

To be sure, the finding is an inference from results, not a direct observation of the process. But contrary to behaviorist dogma, inference of an unseen process from results is considered legitimate in the "hard" sciences. Geologists infer the events of the past from sediment layers, cosmologists the formation and development of the universe from the ancient light of distant galaxies, physicists the characteristics of short-lived atomic particles from tracks they leave in a cloud chamber or emulsion, and biologists the evolutionary path that led to *Homo sapiens* from fossils. So, too, with the interior universe of the mind: psychologists cannot voyage into it, but they can deduce how it works from the track, so to speak, made by an invisible thought process.

Revolution No. 2

What, another revolution so soon?

Well, not on the heels of the cognitive revolution, but not far behind it. This one, though long gathering force, would not burst forth until the 1980s, but we must look ahead to its emergence because much of what we will see happening in cognitive psychology will be affected by it. It was the cognitive neuroscience revolution.

That's a relatively new name for an old school of thought about the mind, the biological approach to mental processes that sought to explain them in terms of neuronal processes and events. We saw a notable example of it in Hubel and Wiesel's discoveries of retinal cells that respond only to specific shapes or directions of motion. That was recent, but the neuroscientific approach has antecedents going back at least to Descartes. Although he believed in the immateriality of mind, he conjectured, as we saw, that reflexes were caused by the flow of "animal spirits" through the nervous system, much as the movements of automata in the royal gardens were caused by the flow of water in pipes, and that memory was the result of the widening of the particular "pores of the brain" through which animal spirits had passed during learning.[12] Similarly, a century ago the young Freud confidently asserted that all psychological processes could be understood as "quantitatively determined states" of the neurons, though he soon admitted with chagrin that the time was not ripe for such understanding.

The same hope, though, had continued to inspire many researchers. And during the past sixty years, and especially the past twenty-five, extraordinary advances in cognitive neuroscience have led some enthusiasts to assert that it will soon replace the psychological approach to the mind and that concepts such as needs, emotions, and thoughts will be replaced by physiological data. When such data are available, Paul Churchland, a philosopher of neuroscience, asserted in 1984,

we will set about reconceiving our internal states and activities, within a truly adequate framework at last. Our explanations of one another's behavior will appeal to such things as our neuropharmacological states, the neural activity in specialized anatomical areas, and whatever other states are deemed relevant by the new theory.[13]

Most research in behavioral neuroscience in the decades immediately preceding its 1980s breakout as cognitive neuroscience was focused not on thought processes but on the physical events taking place (as thought occurs) in the "wetware"—the hundred billion or more neurons that make up the human brain. Cognitive neuroscientists—some were neurobiologists who had studied psychology, others were psychologists who had studied neurobiology—were interested in such phenomena as the flow of sodium and other ions into and out of the axon (main stem) of a neuron as electrical impulses pass along it; the molecular structure of the neurotransmitters (the chemicals produced in the synapses, the junctions at which the impulses are passed to other neurons); the bursts of neurotransmitter molecules that leap across the microscopic synaptic gaps from neuron to neuron carrying messages of excitation or inhibition; and the neuronal routes and networks activated by different kinds of stimuli and mental activities.

Behavioral neuroscientists (as they were then known), often white-coated, spent much of their time in operating rooms and laboratories, where, among other things, they surgically destroyed specific portions of animals' brains to learn what aspects of behavior those parts control; they interviewed and tested people who had suffered brain damage; they measured and recorded the spikes of activity of single neurons and the overall patterns of brain excitation ("brain waves") during various mental activities; they administered drugs that increase or decrease the production of particular neurotransmitters to determine what functions these perform; and they did chemical analyses of the brain tissue of laboratory animals and human cadavers to see what neurotransmitters were in either short supply or excess in individuals whose behavior is abnormal in some respect.

A good deal of their work, as we have already seen, involved testing patients with cerebral damage (most often strokes), pinpointing the affected brain area and identifying it as the cause of the patient's diminished or lost perceptual and mental abilities. But much other neuroscientific research, though arguably valuable, had its comical overtones. One investigator implanted sixteen microelectrodes into the muscles of a male grasshopper in order to record the electrical impulses of its neurons during courtship. Others inserted microelectrodes into the left front leg of a cockroach and the foot of a snail to measure the neural impulses that produce movement toward some goal; the investigators regarded this as research on "motivated behavior."[14]

Of all cognitive processes, especially in more advanced species, memory is the most basic, and for decades cognitive neuroscientists sought to identify how and where memory exists at the cellular level. A few examples of the ways in which they did so:

—As long ago as 1949, Donald Hebb, a Canadian psychologist, hypothesized that memories are stored by the modification of the synapses connecting neurons (an idea not unlike Descartes's). The repeated activation of a synapse in a learning experience, he said, somehow strengthens the synapse and links the two neurons into a circuit or "memory trace."[15] Hebb's hypothesis was more or less confirmed in 1973 when a British neurophysiologist, Timothy Bliss, and a colleague, Terje Lømo, measured the voltage in one neural pathway in the brain of a rabbit, then sent repeated bursts of electricity down the path, and afterward found that the pathway carried a higher voltage than before. The synapses had been strengthened by the electrical impulses. The implication was that that is what happens in learning.[16] (Later research, as we will see, has added many details and complexities to the explanation.)

—Also in the early 1970s, an American psychologist, William Greenough, raised rats in two environments, one containing toys, mazes, and other stimulating devices, the other without any. The rats in the stimulating environment developed heavier areas of cerebral cortex; the neurons in those areas had grown more dendrites and thus more synapses than those of rats in the dull environment. Later, by means of electron microscopy, Greenough and a colleague actually counted 20 to 25 percent more synapses in the affected cortical areas of the enriched-environment rats than those of the deprived ones. Learning had generated the extra connections; memory traces must somehow be recorded in them.[17]

—In the late 1980s Daniel L. Alkon and his colleagues at the National Institute of Neurological and Communicative Disorders and Stroke trained a sea snail, *Hermissenda crassicornis*, to respond to light in a way it does not normally do. *Hermissenda* instinctively swims toward light; also, when the water is turbulent it instinctively clenches its foot muscle in order to cling to a surface. Alkon combined these reactions. By flashing a light and simultaneously whirling the chamber in which he housed the snail, he conditioned it—taught it—to clench its foot muscle whenever it saw a flash of light. He then found that in certain of the snail's photoreceptor neurons, molecules of PKC, a calcium-sensitive enzyme, had moved from the interior of the neuron toward its membrane, where they reduced potassium-ion flow—a partial explanation of memory in molecular terms.[18]

— Over several decades, James L. McGaugh and other researchers did a number of studies in which they injected epinephrine (a hormone produced by the adrenal gland) and other catecholamine neurotransmitters into rats after training them to run a maze. Epinephrine, in particular, causes the rats to remember longer what they learned than rats not so dosed. The explanation, deduced from other studies, seems to be that a byproduct of the epinephrine combats opioids, a group of neurotransmitters that serve useful purposes but plug up receptors on the receiving side of synapses. The result: more receptors remain open, the synapses function more efficiently, and memory is strengthened.[19]

These and many other research studies made cognitive neuroscientists feel sure that they were on the right track to explaining the many mysteries of psychology. Their approach promised to end, once and for all, the ancient debate about body and mind by explaining all mental processes in terms of material substances and events. All high-level mental processes such as memory, language, and reasoning were only ions and molecules flowing hither and thither in the labyrinthine and infinitesimal plumbing of the brain.

But the great majority of cognitive psychologists, proud of their new dominance and excited by the amazing capacity of computers to mimic—and perhaps explain—human reasoning, were dismissive of cognitive neuroscience. In the 1950s, after Newell and Simon's dramatic presentation of Logic Theorist, whatever connection had existed between cognitive psychology and neuroscience fell apart; Simon, in fact, authoritatively declared that to "understand cognition, one needn't pay much if any attention to the underlying biology."[20]

For the next twenty-five or so years, most cognitive psychologists agreed with him, insisting that neural events do not provide an adequate or useful explanation of cognitive phenomena. Few were dualists in the sense of believing in immaterial mind, but they asserted that psychological processes, though constructed of neural events, were properties of the organization or metastructure of those components, not of the components themselves, even as shelter is not a property of bricks, beams, and shingles but of a house built of them.

Nobel Laureate Roger Sperry, though himself a brain scientist, offered another analogy: a higher-order mental process is like a wheel rolling downhill—the rolling is determined by the "overall system properties" of the wheel, not by the atoms and molecules of which it is made.

The developmentalist Jerome Kagan used a different analogy: the elegant laws of planetary motion illustrate phenomena that are not expressible in terms of the atoms of which the planets are made.

Another analogy, this from the cognitive scientist Earl Hunt: "We can tell from physical measures that the left temporal region of the brain is active when we read, but we cannot discriminate the activity induced by reading Shakespeare from that induced by reading Agatha Christie."

And a word from the cognitive psychologist George Mandler: "The mind has functions that are different from those of the central nervous system, just as societies function in ways that cannot be reduced to the function of individual minds."[21]

Most cognitive psychologists thus believed that a word retrieved from memory could not be equated with the firing of millions of neurons and the resultant millions or billions of synaptic transmissions, but was the product of the pattern or structure of those firings and transmissions. The neurobiological study of memory, valuable as it was, did not tell us how we learn anything, recognize things we have earlier experienced, or retrieve items from memory as needed—the words we use in speech, to give one example. Such phenomena, they insisted, were governed not by the laws of cognitive neuroscience but by those of cognitive psychology.

Martha Farah, a distinguished neuroscientist and director of the Center for Cognitive Neuroscience at the University of Pennsylvania, recalls that in 1980, when she was a graduate student of psychology at Harvard, "I asked to take a course in neuroanatomy—and got lectured. I was 'supposed to be studying how the mind worked, and looking at how the brain works was simply not relevant.' That was the received wisdom in those days. The '70s and '80s were the last hurrah of brain-free psychology."[22]

What ended the reign of brain-free psychology? Many things, including:

— the growing mass of data on neuronal transmission, on the functions of brain substructures, and on the molecular and other factors that strengthen synaptic connections in learning;

— the shortcomings of the computer model of cognition (it was becoming apparent that although computers could simulate some aspects of cognition, the mind processes information in vastly more complex ways than the linear step-by-step fashion of computer programs);

— the weakening resistance of some leading cognitive psychologists to valuable neuroscientific findings about brain processes; and

— the growing sense among neuroscientists by the late 1970s that they were doing far more than exploring brain biology and that their domain should be called "cognitive neuroscience."

But as has been the case in various other sciences, it was a new tool (actually a set of tools) that transformed the domain of neuroscience and produced a second revolution in the cognitive sciences. The tools were an array of brain scan devices—machines that could produce various kinds of images of the working brain and, most importantly, of the physical changes or events taking place in it when mental processes were in progress.

Prior to the 1980s, physiologists had been able to use EEG (electroencephalography) to show the form of brain waves; this was useful in studying the differences in brain wave activity during various wakeful and sleep states and the distortions of the waves during epileptic seizures. The method, however, was poor at localizing the brain activity of specific cognitive processes because it reflected overall electrical activity, not that of specific regions or structures of the brain.[23]

But in the 1980s several dramatic advances were made. One was the development of PET (positive emission tomography) scanning after many years of experiments in measuring blood flow in the brain. In a PET scan the subject lies supine on a narrow table which rolls into a large tubular machine. A nearby cyclotron generates a weakly radioactive isotope with a half-life of only two minutes which is then injected into the patient. The scanner, sensitive to the isotope, records blood flow in a "slice" (narrow cross-section) of the brain, the isotope showing where the brain is active. From a number of slices, a computer assembles three-dimensional images of the brain. The PET scan can be used clinically to study physical damage to, and abnormalities in, the brain, but cognitive psychologists and neuroscientists soon began using PET scans to see what areas of the brain had increased blood flow during—and thus were involved in—various kinds of mental activity.[24]

In 1983 another important tool was introduced—CT (computed tomography) scanning, also known as CAT scanning (computerized axial tomography). It proved to be a valuable medical tool for assessing many kinds of physiological problems, but also for studying brain structure and identifying brain lesions. In the CT scan, the subject is, as in a PET scan, supine, and eased into the scanner, which has an X-ray source and a set of radiation detectors. The scanner sends radiation through the target part of the subject from various angles. The density of biological materials varies; accordingly, the data gathered by the detectors reveal the hidden structure, and are assembled by a computer program to yield X-ray pictures of the entire scanned target. CT scans were and are used primarily for clinical medical analyses, but the method also had some value for cognitive research on brain structure, although the results are not very distinct and lack fine resolution.[25]

By far the most important and latest new tool is the MRI (magnetic resonance imaging) scan. Again the subject is supine inside a scanning machine, which is about the size of a small SUV, and which, while making a horrendous racket, generates a powerful magnetic field that permeates the subject's head. The magnetism, unlike the radiation of the CT scan, is harmless—and capable of revealing brain structure and activity far better than the CT scan.

It can do so because the protons of hydrogen, a major component of the water and fat in the brain, behave like tiny magnets and line up under the influence of the magnetic field (normally, their orientation, unaffected by earth's weak magnetism, is randomly distributed). Then, radio waves, passed through the subject's head, change the protons' orientation, but the instant the radio waves stop, the protons bounce back to the orientation created by the magnetic field and, in so doing, emit energy signals. These, picked up by detectors, yield scans much clearer, and with far finer resolution (a spatial resolution of one millimeter and a temporal resolution of about one second) than any other scanning method.

Best of all, from the cognitive researcher's viewpoint, if the subject performs some prescribed mental task while being scanned, the resulting fMRI (functional MRI) scan gives an intimate look at exactly which brain areas and substructures are active, and how active, during that kind of mental activity. Accordingly, the fMRI quickly became the workhorse of cognitive neuroscience. A dozen years ago, a mere handful of studies based on fMRI scans appeared in a year's worth of research literature; today, the annual output is several thousand.[26]

What has all this done to psychology, the science of the human mind? That depends on who is assessing the situation.

Most psychologists, focused on mental processes rather than wetware, continue to use research methods that were available before the advent of scanning, but many of them also rely on the help of scanning. They no longer see cognitive psychology and cognitive neuroscience as distinct and unrelated fields. As Robert J. Sternberg, a notable cognitive psychologist, says, "Biology and behavior work together. They are not in any way mutually exclusive."[27] Some use stronger terms to appraise the impact of cognitive neuroscience: Psychologists Stephen Kosslyn and Robin Rosenberg write, "It is fair to say that neuroimaging techniques have transformed psychology, allowing researchers to answer questions that were hopelessly out of reach before the mid-1980s."[28]

Does that suggest that cognitive neuroscience will become the psychology of the future? Not according to cognitivist Michael Posner, who has worked in both camps and whose work has been admired by researchers in both: "An impressive aspect of the anatomical methods such as PET and fMRI is how much they have supported the view that cognitive measures can be used to suggest separate neural structures," and he stresses the importance of the contributions of both fields to understanding brain function.[29]

But some cognitive neuroscientists think it possible, even likely, that their field will come to dominate mental science. Martha Farah, when asked if cognitive neuroscience would eventually become the overarching theory of psychology, said, "Yes, because it's a broader and more heterogeneous approach to studying the mind which encompasses cognitive psychology. It's a molecular-cellular-systems explanation of how the brain acts during all the classical processes of cognitive psychology—how we learn, think, behave, why we differ from each other, the sources of personality. All these things are in principle explainable by various levels of brain activity at various levels of description."[30]

We seem to be at the top of the ninth, score tied, and will have to see how the game plays out.

Now let us return to the story of cognitive psychology and look more closely at several of its major themes of recent decades.

Memory

In the 1960s, the cognitive revolution rapidly won the allegiance, at least in academia, of some senior psychologists, most junior ones, and most graduate students of psychology. At first, they concentrated on perception, the first step of cognition, but fairly soon they shifted their attention to the uses the mind makes of perceptions—its higher-level mental processes. By 1980, John Anderson, a theorist of those processes, defined cognitive psychology as the attempt "to understand the nature of human intelligence and how people think."[31]

In information-processing theory, the essential first step is the storing of incoming data in memory, whether for part of a second or for a lifetime. As James McGaugh said in a 1987 lecture:

> Memory is essential for our behavior. There is nothing of significance that is not based fundamentally on memory. Our consciousness and our actions are shaped by our experiences. And, our experiences shape us only because of their lingering consequences.[32]

How crucial memory is to thought is painfully apparent to anyone who has known a person suffering from advanced Alzheimer's disease. He may frequently forget what he wants to say partway through a sentence, get lost walking down the driveway to his mailbox, fail to recognize his children, and become upset by the unfamiliarity of his own living room.

In 1955—before the start of the cognitive revolution—George Miller had given an address at a meeting of the Eastern Psychological Association that has been called a landmark for cognitive theorists working on memory. In his typically breezy manner, Miller called the talk "The Magical Number Seven, Plus or Minus Two," and began by saying, "My problem is that I have been persecuted by an integer." The integer was 7, and what seemed to Miller both magical and persecutory about it was, as many experiments had shown, that it is the number of digits that one can usually hold in immediate memory.[33] (It is easy to remember briefly, after a moment's study, a number like 9237314 but not one like 5741179263.)

It is both noteworthy and mysterious that immediate memory, the limiting factor in what we can pay attention to, is so tiny. The limitation serves a vital purpose: it drastically prunes the incoming data to what the mind, at any moment, urgently needs to attend to and make decisions about, a function that undoubtedly helped our primitive ancestors survive life in the jungle or the desert.[34] But it raises perplexing questions. How can so small a field of attention handle the flood of perceptions we must attend to when driving a car or skiing? Or the welter of sounds and meanings when someone is talking to us—or when we are trying to say something to them?

One answer, Miller said, making good use of an idea that had lain fallow in psychology for a century, is that immediate memory is not limited to seven digits but to seven—more or less—*items*: seven words or names, for instance, or "chunks" such as FBI, IBM, NATO, telephone area codes, or familiar sayings, all of which contain far more information than single digits but are as easily remembered.

But even with chunking, the capacity of immediate memory is insignificant compared with the enormous amount of material—everyday experiences, language, and general information of all sorts—that we learn and store away in long-lasting memory and call up again as needed.

To explain this disparity and determine how memory works, cognitive psychologists conducted a great many experiments during the 1960s, 1970s, and 1980s; the findings, pieced together, gave shape to an information-processing picture of human memory. In it, memory consists of three forms of storage, ranging from a fraction of a second to a lifetime. Experiences or items of information needed only for an instant fade away as soon as used, but those needed longer are transformed and held for longer, or even worked into the semipermanent or permanent register of long-term memory. Researchers and theorists portrayed the three types and the transfer of information among them in flow charts something like the one on p. 608.

The briefest form of memory consists of sensory "buffers" in which incoming sensations are first received and held. By means of the tachistoscope, researchers verified that buffers exist and also measured how long memories endure in them before disappearing. In a classic experiment in 1960, the psychologist George Sperling flashed on a screen, before attentively watching volunteers, patterns of letters like this:

R B L A
T Y Q N
G K R X

The letters appeared for a twentieth of a second, too brief a time for the volunteers to have seen all of them, although immediately afterward

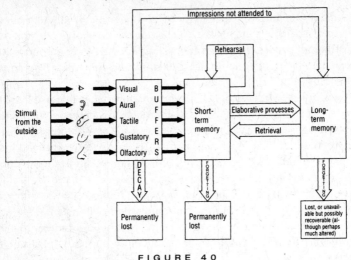

FIGURE 40

An information-processing model of human memory

they could write down the letters of any one line. (A tone, right after the flash, told them which line to record.) They could still "see" all three lines when they heard the tone, but by the time they had written down one line, they could no longer remember the others; the memory had vanished in less than a second. (Experiments by others yielded comparable results with sounds.) Evidently, incoming perceptions are stored in buffers, from which they vanish almost at once—fortunately, for if they lasted longer, we would see the world as a continuous blur.[35]

Since, however, we need to retain somewhat longer the things we are currently concerned with, there must be another and longer-lasting form of temporary storage. When we pay attention to material in a sensory buffer, we process it in any of several ways. A digit becomes not just a perceived shape but a symbol—a 4 gets a name (four) and a meaning (the quantity it stands for); similarly, words we read or hear get meanings. This processing transfers whatever we are attending to from the buffers to the immediate or short-term memory that Miller was talking about.

In lay usage, short-term memory refers to the retention of events of recent hours or days, but in technical usage it denotes whatever is part of current mental activity but is not retained after use. This form of memory is brief. We have all looked up a phone number, dialed it, gotten a busy signal, and had to look up the number again to redial it. Yet we can retain it for many seconds or even minutes by continuously repeating it to ourselves—psychologists call this activity "rehearsal"—until we have used it.

To measure the normal duration of short-term memory, therefore, researchers had to prevent rehearsal. A team at Indiana University did so by telling their subjects that they were to try to remember a set of three consonants, a very easy task, but that as soon as they had seen them, they were to count backward by threes in time with a metronome; this preempted their attention and made rehearsal impossible. The researchers cut the volunteers' backward counting short at different times to see how long they would retain the three consonants; none did so longer than eighteen seconds. Many later experiments confirmed that the decay rate of short-term memory is between fifteen and thirty seconds.[36]

Later, other studies distinguished between two kinds of short-term memory (not shown in the above diagram). One is verbal: the immediate memory for numbers, words, and so on that we have been discussing. The second is conceptual: the memory of an idea or meaning conveyed in a sentence or other expression of several parts (an algebraic equation, for instance). In a 1982 experiment, subjects were shown sentences, a word at a time, at a tenth of a second per word; they could easily remember plausible (though not necessarily true) sentences like this:

Tardy students annoy inexperienced teachers.

But they fared badly with nonsensical sentences of the same length, like:

Purple concrete trained imaginative alleys.[37]

A number of studies showed that we easily retain the message of a sentence in short-term memory but swiftly forget its exact words. Similarly, we retain in long-term memory for months, years, or a lifetime the content or meaning of some conversations we have had and books we have read, the gist of courses we have taken, and innumerable facts we have learned, but none, or at most a few, of the exact words in which any of these were couched. The mass of material stored away in this fashion is far larger than most of us can imagine: John Griffith, a mathematician, calculated that the lifetime capacity of the average human memory is up to 10^{11} (one hundred trillion) bits,* or five hundred times as much information as is contained in the *Encyclopaedia Britannica*.[38]

*A bit, in information theory, is the smallest unit of information: it is equal to a simple yes or no. A digit or a letter of the alphabet is equal to several bits.

New information in short-term memory is forgotten after we use it, unless we make it part of long-term memory by subjecting it to further processing. One form of processing is rote memorizing, as schoolchildren memorize multiplication tables. Another is the linking of new information to some easily remembered structure or mnemonic device, like a singsong jingle (the preschool alphabet song) or a rhyming rule ("When the letter C you spy, / Put the E before the I").

But a far more important kind, as became clear in the research performed in the 1960s and 1970s, is "elaborative processing," in which the new information is connected to parts of our existing organized mass of long-term memories. We splice it into our semantic network, so to speak. If the new item is a mango and we have never seen one before, we link the word and concept to the appropriate part of long-term memory (not a physical location—ideas and images are now thought to be scattered throughout the brain—but a conceptual one: the category "fruit"), along with the mango's visual image, feel, taste, and smell (each of which we also link to the categories of images, tactile qualities, and so on), plus what we learn about where it grows, what it costs, how to serve it, and more. In the future, when we try to think of a mango, we retrieve the memory in any one of many ways: by recalling its name, or thinking about fruit, or about fruit with a green skin, or about yellow sweet slices, or any other category or trait with which it is linked.

Much of what was learned about how all these kinds of information are organized was the product of reaction-time experiments such as asking subjects to name, in a brief period of time, as many things as they can that are red, or that are fruit, or that start with a given letter. Using that technique, Elizabeth Loftus found that in one minute volunteers could, on average, name twelve instances of "bird" but only nine of "yellow." Her conclusion was that we cannot readily look directly in memory for examples of a property but instead locate categories of objects (birds, fruit, vegetables), and scan each for that property.[39]

Similarly, as Loftus and a colleague, Allan Collins, found, it takes people longer to answer "true" or "false" to the statement "An ostrich is a bird" than to the statement "A canary is a bird." The implication: A canary is a more typical bird than an ostrich, is closer to the center of the category, so it requires less time to identify. Collins and Loftus, on the basis of such data, symbolically portrayed long-term semantic memory as an intricate network that is hierarchical (a general category is surrounded by specific instances) and associative (each instance is linked to a number of traits). They envisioned it as shown on p. 611.[40]

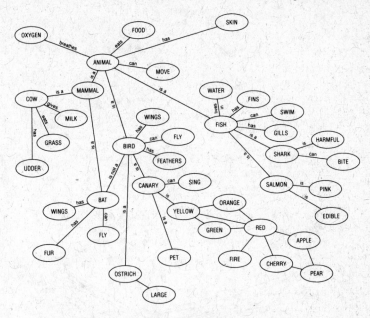

FIGURE 41

One portrayal of the long-term semantic memory network

This is only a minuscule sample of the semantic memory network. Every node shown here is connected to many other chains of nodes not shown: "Swim" might be linked to "cetaceans," "human swimmers," "sports," "healthful exercises," and each of those to other instances, characteristics, traits, and so on, and on.

A much later and much more detailed representation of the memory network relating to birds is bewilderingly complex; it is on page 612, as Figure 42, for those who care to puzzle it out.

Memory research has been so far-ranging and multifaceted over the last several decades that we must limit ourselves now to a handful of brief reports of major research findings and theories, and then move on.

Memory systems: The memory system portrayed in Figure 40, on p. 608, is now seen as too simple. According to the results of many studies, there are a number of interacting memory systems that encode and store different kinds of information in different ways. The memories stored about how to swim, drive a car, or sail a boat are very different from those concerning the names and identities of people you know, how to

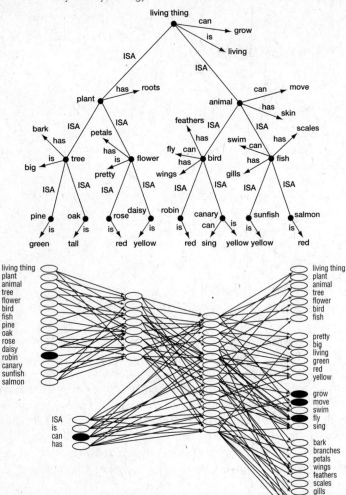

FIGURE 42

Network and connectionist representations of
concepts relating to birds

perform arithmetical procedures, or what a collie looks like. Each of these kinds of memory, and many others, require their own forms of processing and storage, and differ in the amount and kinds of effort required to enter and retain it in long term memory.

Moreover, memory researchers distinguish among types of memory in other ways: Explicit memory refers to information or knowledge that we can bring to mind and to personal experiences, and implicit memory to information that is available without conscious effort, including motor skills and automatic responses (such as avoiding bumping into others on the sidewalk), built-in attitudes and reactions to people, objects, and situations—all of these requiring different memory systems.[41]

Other studies have investigated the differing process of recognition and recall—a distinction familiar enough in everyday experience (we all recognize a great many words that we cannot easily or at all summon up voluntarily). In a socially valuable application of the difference, a series of studies tested whether witnesses to a crime (a staged one before groups of students who were not told what was going on until later) would be more likely to identify the actual culprit in a lineup or by seeing a number of suspects one at a time. The latter method proved so much the better that many police departments are now changing their standard lineup procedures.[42]

Cognitive neuroscientists have lately done brain scans during different kinds of memory activity and come up with an answer to an old question: Where are memories stored? The answer, in the past, has vacillated between "locally" and "widely distributed." Brain scans now show that "widely distributed" is the answer—and that different kinds of memories are differently distributed.[43]

Categorization: Much research indicates that the human mind has a tendency to spontaneously group similar objects in memory and, from their similarities, develop general concepts or categories. Even infants only a few months old seem to do simple categorizing. One research team showed four-month-old babies patches of varied blues, greens, yellows, and reds. After seeing a number of patches of one color group, the babies showed a preference for a patch of any other color. The conclusion: Hue categorization is either innate or develops soon after birth.[44]

Many other studies have documented how, as children acquire language, they gradually develop such categories as "animal" after experiences of dogs, cats, squirrels, and others. Parents, to be sure, teach these concepts to their children, but in part the tendency seems to be built in. It is so general among all people as to be presumed an innate human trait. The anthropologist Brent Berlin found that people in a dozen different primitive societies group plants and animals in remarkably similar fashion, namely, hierarchically, starting with subgroups similar to biological species, combining these in larger headings similar to biological genera, and lumping these together in categories similar to biological plant and animal kingdoms.[45]

The ability to categorize was probably selected by evolution. It has survival value, since from such groupings we can make valid inferences about things that are new to us. Rochel Gelman and a colleague showed subjects pictures of a flamingo, a bat, and a blackbird. The blackbird was portrayed so that it looked much like the bat. Subjects were told about the flamingo, "This bird's heart has a right aortic arch only," and about the bat, "This bat's heart has a left aortic arch only." Then they were asked about the blackbird, "What does this bird's heart have?" Almost 90 percent answered "right aortic arch only," correctly basing their answer not on the visual similarity of bat and blackbird but the common membership in the bird category of flamingo and blackbird. Even four-year-old children, when given a similar but simpler test, based their answers almost 70 percent of the time on category membership.[46]

Representation: Researchers were long at odds about the form in which the material is stored in long-term memory. Some believed it is represented both in images and words and that there is communication between the two data banks. Others, drawing on information theory and the computer model, argued that information is recorded in memory only in the form of "propositions." A proposition is a simple "idea unit" or bit of knowledge embodied in a conceptual relationship like that between bat and wings (a bat has them) or bat and mammal (a bat is one).

In the first view, a bat would be recorded in memory as an image, along with verbal statements about it; in the second view it would be recorded in the form of relationships (as in the bits of semantic networks in the figures above) which, though not verbal, are equivalent to "bat has wings," "salmon is red," and so forth. Another example of the propositional view is seen in these sentences:

The princess kissed the frog,

and its passive version,

The frog was kissed by the princess,

which mean the same thing; they are verbal expressions, differently focused, of the same proposition or unit of relationship knowledge.[47]

The proponents of each view have good evidence to back them up. The "mental rotation" experiments of Roger Shepard that we saw earlier indicate that we see objects "in the mind's eye" and deal with those images as if they were three-dimensional objects. Later studies by others confirmed and extended this finding. Several years ago, Stephen Kosslyn, who has long explored mental imagery, took a different tack: He had subjects memorize a map of a small roughly pear-shaped island with various things located here and there, among them a hut at one end, a lake nearby, a cliff somewhat farther off, a large rocklike object at the farthest end, and so on. Later, his subjects were asked to close their eyes, summon up the remembered image, focus on one location such as the site of the hut, and then find another named site and push a button as soon as they found it. The times of each mental search were recorded; most remarkably, the farther the second location was from the first, the longer it took them to find it. Obviously, they were scanning across the mental image.[48]

But the advocates of propositional representation have equally good grounds for their view. They contend that images cannot convey such relationships as "has," "causes," and "rhymes with," or represent categories and abstract concepts. Herbert Simon and William Chase found that chess masters could reproduce an entire board position after viewing it for just a few seconds—but only if it was a true board position in an actual game. If it was a random arrangement of the pieces, they could not. The implication: The masters' memory was not visual but was based on the geometrical relations—the attack and defense move potentials—of the pieces. Finally, information in computer programs is stored in propositional form, and if computability is a good model of cognition, it stands to reason that the mind stores information similarly.[49]

Quite reasonably, a third position has been taken for some time by many theorists: There are several types of representation—propositions, mental models, and images, each encoding information at a different level of abstraction. Finally, a fourth position is that different types of mental imagery use different brain networks: imagery involving spatial relations (as in imaginary rotation of an object) relies on a network in the parietal lobes, while imagery involving high-resolution shapes relies on a network in the occipital lobes.[50] (Even if true, that position doesn't help us understand how the masses of neuronal impulses arriving by either network get to be "seen" by us as mental images.)

Schemas: In 1932 the English psychologist Frederic Bartlett told subjects folk tales from non-Western sources and then asked them to recall the tales. They remembered the stories inaccurately, inadvertently fill-ing in gaps, modifying events so as to provide reasons for what hap-pened, and omitting details that made no sense to Western minds. Bartlett concluded that "remembering is not the re-excitation of innu-merable fixed, lifeless, and fragmentary traces" but "an imaginative reconstruction, or construction" based on our own organized mass of experiences. He called that organized mass "schemata"; others prefer the anglicized version "schemas."[51]

Bartlett's idea has been revived and elaborated in recent years. Schemas—also known as "frames" and "scripts"—are now thought of as packages of integrated information on various topics, retained in memory, on which we rely to interpret the allusive and fragmentary information that ordinary conversation—and even most narrative writ-ing—consists of. In 1978, David Rumelhart, then of the University of California in San Diego, reported on experiments in which he read stories, sentence by sentence, to his subjects to see how and when they formed a clear idea of what the stories were about. When, for instance, they heard this: "I was brought into a large white room, and my eyes began to blink because the bright light hurt them," some 80 percent at once assumed they were hearing either a hospital or interrogation scene, and supplied a wealth of information to the few words they had heard. If the next sentence or two contradicted this supposition, they changed it and filled out the story anew from a dif-ferent schema.[52]

Much other recent work on schemas and a related type of informa-tion package known as a "script" has firmly established that it is by draw-ing on our expectations and organized knowledge structures that we understand and interpret—or often misinterpret—what we hear, read, and experience. Memory, in sum, is not only an information register to be consulted as needed but a program that directs our thinking.[53]

Forgetting: Many studies have explored why we forget some things and not others, and what can be done to improve memory, particularly in the elderly, most of whom undergo some degree of nonpathological memory impairment. (Normal age-related memory problems can often be ameliorated by mnemonic and other training. There is also the possi-bility that not far down the road a pharmacological treatment, rebalanc-ing altered neurotransmitter output, will be found.)[54]

Much interesting research has concerned not the total loss of particular memories but the forgetting of important details and their replacement by new material. Our legal system relies heavily on the assumption that if we remember an event at all, we remember it as it was. The courts and many psychotherapists also believe that forgotten material retrieved through hypnosis is a true record of what happened. But psychotherapists have also long had evidence that we alter memories to make them more acceptable to the ego, and for many years Elizabeth Loftus has been amassing experimental evidence showing that the memory of a startling or traumatic event can be distorted by the trauma itself, that the memory of an event can be slanted by a skillful attorney's loaded questions, that we graft new information on to the memory of an event as time goes by and have no way of retrieving the original version, and that hypnosis sometimes retrieves deeply buried memories—and sometimes manufactured ones.[55] (In 2005, Loftus won a $200,000 Gravemeyer Award for her research on false recollections.)

Nearly all of us, however, feel sure that certain events are indelibly and accurately burned into our memories. Recollections of such experiences as first hearing about the assassination of President Kennedy or the explosion of the Challenger space shuttle are known to psychologists as "flashbulb memories," because they are vivid tableaus that seem utterly unforgettable. Ulric Neisser and an associate, Nicole Harsch, seized an extraordinary opportunity to study the phenomenon. The day after the Challenger disaster (which occurred on January 28, 1986), they asked a large sample of undergraduates to record, in detail, how they had heard the news of the explosion. Two and a half years later, those respondents who could still be reached were asked to answer a questionnaire about the event and six months later were interviewed.

Over a third of the students' recollections about time, place, who told them, and so on were dead wrong, as judged by their 1986 reports, and nearly another quarter were partly wrong. When the subjects were shown their original statements, Harsch and Neisser reported, "Many were quite upset by the discrepancies with their present memories . . . Interestingly, many continued to prefer their current 1989 recall to the version in the original 1986 record." Where did the errors come from? Harsch and Neisser call them "narrative reconstructions" of the type described by Bartlett in 1932.[56]

Sometimes, even in the fast-developing cognitive revolution, *plus ça change* . . .

Language

Scientists infer natural laws from specimens, events, natural phenomena, and experimental findings of one sort or another. The comparable raw materials for cognitive scientists are thoughts, but the neural discharges, or brainwaves, that indicate thought, though they can be seen by EEG (electroencephalography), reveal nothing of the content. Gestures, facial expressions, mathematical or artistic symbols, and demonstrations (as in sports training) convey thoughts, but within a very narrow range. The principal form in which thinking can be observed is language, which has accordingly been called "the window to the mind."

Or, one might also say, the spoor of thought, since language not only conveys thoughts but in its structure bears traces of how our minds work. The study of thought processes as revealed by these traces is the province of psycholinguistics. (Linguistics, an older discipline, deals with the characteristics of language itself.)

An example of such a trace: Small children tend to treat irregular verbs and nouns as if they were regular ("Doggy runned away," "Dat baby has two toofs"). But they have not heard adults make such mistakes, and therefore are not imitating them. The errors, psycholinguists say, show that children recognize such regularities in adult speech as adding "ed" to make a simple past tense, "s" or "es" to make a plural noun, and take these to be applicable to all verbs and nouns (the tendency is called "overregularization")—evidence that the human mind spontaneously generalizes from examples, then applies the generalization to new cases. Cognitive psychologists long had two different hypotheses about how this takes place: one, that regular past tense forms are generated by a rule and irregular ones retrieved from memory; and two, that both forms are generated by a single system and differ only in their reliance on sound and semantics. An fMRI-based study has just settled the issue: Brain area activation is the same for both regular and irregular verbs, thus confirming the single-system hypothesis.[57]

The acquisition of verb tenses is only one of a number of marks left by the thinking process that psycholinguists have found in language. They are not peculiar to English; analogous phenomena can be found in every language and seem to be characteristic of human thought. Human languages appear to be governed by the same universal principles and constraints.

The universality does not, of course, involve grammar and vocabulary; in those respects English, Swahili, and Basque, for instance, have nothing in common. Yet children who grow up hearing each of those languages recognize, without being taught, the difference between singular and plural forms of a noun, the verb forms that denote present and past, and so on, and construct for themselves the rules governing their language. Similarly, they intuit the basic rules governing word order and are able to construct simple declarative sentences made up of words in the proper sequence. No child of English-speaking parents ever says, "Milk more some want I," nor does a child of parents who speak any other language get its basic word order wrong.

Psychology had little relationship to linguistics before midcentury, but in the dawn of the cognitive revolution some cognitive psychologists and linguists dimly saw that new developments in each of their disciplines called for explanations by the other one. For instance, certain new theories of the linguists about how grammar works implied that the mind, when dealing with concepts, performs complex manipulations that are not accounted for by behaviorist psychology. In 1953, a number of psychologists and linguists held a conference at Cornell University, discussed their areas of common interest, and adopted the term "psycholinguistics" to designate the study of the psychology of language.

Psycholinguistics was still a little-known discipline when, four years later, a twenty-nine-year-old member of the Harvard Society of Fellows published a monograph that thrust the subject into the limelight. The theory proposed in that monograph has been called one of the two most important developments in psychology in that era (the other being artificial intelligence).[58] Its author was Noam Chomsky, some of whose ideas we heard about earlier.

Chomsky, a shaggy-haired, bespectacled, rumpled genius—the Central Casting stereotype of an intellectual—very nearly did not become a psycholinguist.[59] He grew up during the Depression years in the radical Jewish community of New York; his father, however, was a distinguished Hebrew scholar, and even as a youth Chomsky picked up some knowledge of the structure of the Semitic languages and some idea of what linguistics was about. These two themes, radical politics and language, have dominated his life ever since. His work in linguistics, the basis of his renown in cognitive psychology, came about when he met Zellig Harris, a professor of linguistics at the University of Pennsylvania.

Harris, who got him excited about linguistics, was trying to develop a system based on behaviorist principles—a system that could account for language patterns without reference to meaning. But his scheme was flawed, and for some years Chomsky labored diligently in the effort to make it work. When he could not, he abandoned Harris's theory and within two years had developed his own. It is ironic that Chomsky is a leftist; the central thesis of his theory, advanced in his monograph *Syntactic Structures*, is that certain aspects of linguistic knowledge and ability are innate, not learned, a doctrine that leftists, liberals, and behaviorist-trained psychologists considered mentalistic and reactionary.

The child, Chomsky maintained, makes sense of heard speech and acquires language not by means of the grammar of the language ("surface grammar," in his terminology) but by an inherent ability to recognize deep-lying syntactical relationships among the component phrases of the heard sentence—what he calls the "deep structure" of the underlying connections. As evidence he points to the ease with which children understand what is meant when one form of sentence is transformed into another—when, for example, a declarative statement is reworded as a question—and make such transformations themselves. If surface grammar were what children relied on, they would extract incorrect rules for transforming sentences. From instances like these:

The man is tall.
Is the man tall?

they would derive the rule: Start at the beginning, move on to the first appearance of "is" or another verb, and shift that verb to the front. But the rule is too simple; it fails as soon as one confronts a sentence like:

The man who is tall is in the room—

where the rule would lead them to say

Is the man who tall is in the room?

But children never make that mistake. They make trivial ones like "toofs" but not substantive ones; they sense the relationships among the elements of the thought—its syntactic constituents or "phrase structures." It is by means of this knowledge of "universal grammar" that children make sense of what they hear and effortlessly construct correct sentences they have never heard.

When and how do they come by a knowledge of universal grammar and deep structure? Chomsky's answer perfectly expresses the revolution against the behaviorist doctrine that the newborn's mind is a *tabula rasa.* Somewhere in the brain, he maintains, is a specialized neural structure—he calls it the Language Acquisition Device, or L.A.D.—that is genetically wired to recognize the ways in which the things and actions represented by noun phrases and verb phrases are related to one another as agent, action, and object.

Chomsky and the many psycholinguists who adopted his view or developed their own versions of it set out in new form the ancient question, banned during the behaviorist era, of whether knowledge exists in the mind before experience. Their answer: While language itself is learned, the brain is so constructed that children spontaneously extract the rules of speech from what they hear without being taught those rules and, making only minor errors, use them when constructing sentences.

Though usually serious and intense, Chomsky is certainly capable of wit. To illustrate the deep relationships among the components of a sentence, he concocted a completely absurd one that has become famous: "Colorless green ideas sleep furiously." Although totally nonsensical, it feels very different to the reader from an equally nonsensical rearrangement of the words: "Ideas furiously green colorless sleep." Anyone familiar with English finds the first version somehow comfortable—it almost seems to mean something—while the second is uncomfortable gibberish. The reason is that the first version obeys the rules of both surface grammar and deep structure; the second does not.

Chomsky's theory touched off fierce controversy, largely because of its innatism, although he did not posit inborn ideas but only the inborn capacity to experience language in useful ways. Some critics, rejecting the hypothesis of an L.A.D., agreed that the ability to acquire language is innate but said that it is a byproduct of general intellectual abilities. Others to whom the theory of an innate L.A.D. is unacceptable keep finding grounds on which to reject it. One such ground, for instance, is that genetically transmitted organs are subject to variations. If so, some children should have abnormal L.A.D.'s and be deficient in some areas of language comprehension, but there seems to be no evidence of that.[60]

Aside from the controversy, for half a century psycholinguists and cognitive psychologists have been gathering evidence that shows how language relates to thought and reveals thought processes. Some patiently observe the errors and self-corrections children make in learning language, some analyze language games, some study developmental language disorders like dyslexia and acquired language disorders produced by brain injuries, and some conduct reaction-time experiments. An instance of the last: Herbert Clark and others have found that when subjects are shown a simple pattern, such as a star above a plus sign, and alongside it either a true affirmation ("Star is above plus") or a true denial ("Star is not below plus"), it takes them two tenths of a second longer to say the denial is true than to say the affirmation is true. We seem to be programmed to think more easily about what is than about what is not, and we have to turn negative sentences into positive ones in order to deal with them.[61]

Today, many psycholinguists, as a result of their research, give more credit to environmental influences in language acquisition than Chomsky does. They stress, for instance, the informal language training provided by "motherese," the special way mothers (and some fathers) talk to small children. Nevertheless, while many psycholinguists question details of Chomsky's L.A.D. theory (which he himself has much qualified and modified over the years), most agree that human beings have a genetically determined ability to understand and acquire any language.

Psycholinguists have also explored other important questions about the relation of language to thought. Do we always or only sometimes think in words? Is thought possible without words? Do the words of our native language shape or limit our thinking? The issues have been much debated and much studied. A few highlights:

— The linguist Benjamin Whorf theorized in 1957 that thought is molded by the syntax and vocabulary of one's native language, and offered cross-cultural evidence to prove his point. One of his examples was that the Hopi Indian language does not distinguish, at least not as we do, between past, present, and future (a rare exception to a nearly universal rule). Instead, a Hopi speaker indicates through inflections whether he or she is talking about an event that actually happened, one that is expected to happen, or about such events in general. Whorf and his followers accordingly maintained that the language we use shapes or influences what we see and think.[62]

— On the other hand, anthropologists have found that in many other cultures people have fewer color terms than English-speaking people but experience the world no differently. The Dani of New Guinea have only two color terms: *mili* (dark) and *mola* (light), but tests of speakers of Dani and other languages that lack many explicit color names have shown that their memory for colors and their ability to judge differences between color samples are much the same as our own. At least when it comes to color, they can think without words.[63]

—The studies of children's thinking, carried out by Piaget and other developmental psychologists, show strong interactions between language and thought. Hierarchical categorization, for one thing, is a powerful cognitive mechanism that enables us to organize and make use of our knowledge; if we are told that an unfamiliar item in an ethnic grocery store is a fruit, says Philip Lieberman, we know at once that it is a plant, edible, and is probably sweet.[64] This inferential capacity is built into the structure of language and acquired in the normal course of development. Studies show that children begin verbal categorization at about eighteen months, and that one of the results is the "naming explosion," a phenomenon every parent has observed. Thus, says Lieberman, "particular languages do not inherently constrain human thought, because both capacities [language and thought] appear to involve closely related brain mechanisms."[65]

The physical locations of some of those brain mechanisms were pinpointed through the study of aphasia, a speech disorder caused by an injury to or lesion in a specific part of the brain. A lesion in Wernicke's Area, as we saw earlier, results in speech that is relatively fluent and syntactical but often nonsensical; victims either mangle or cannot find the nouns, verbs, and adjectives they want. Howard Gardner, a Harvard cognitive psychologist who has explored aphasia, has given this example, taken from a conversation he had with a patient:

"What kind of work have you done, Mr. Johnson?" I asked.
"We, the kids, all of us, and I, we were working for a long time in the . . . you know . . . it's the kind of space, I mean place rear to the spedwan . . ."
At this point I interjected, "Excuse me, but I wanted to know what work you have been doing."
"If you had said that, we had said that, poomer, near the fortunate, forpunate, tamppoo, all around the fourth of martz. Oh, I get all confused," he replied, looking somewhat puzzled that the stream of language did not appear to satisfy me.[66]

In contrast, a person with damage to Broca's area, though able to understand language, has great difficulty producing any; the speech is fragmented, lacking in grammatical structure, and deficient in modifiers of nouns and verbs.

This much is known at the macro level. Nothing, however, is known about how the neuronal networks within Wernicke's and Broca's areas carry out language functions in normal persons; those areas are still "black boxes" to psychologists—mechanisms whose input and output are known but whose internal machinery is a mystery.

But neuroscientists have found a few clues. Analyses of brain function in speech-impaired persons by means of electrode probes during surgery, PET and fMRI scanning, and other methods have shown that linguistic knowledge is located not only in Wernicke's and Broca's Areas but in many parts of the brain and is assembled when needed. Dr. Antonio Damasio of the University of Iowa College of Medicine is one of many researchers who have concluded that information about any object is widely distributed. If the object is, say, a polystyrene cup (Damasio's example), its shape will be stored in one place, crushability in another, texture in another, and so on. These connect, by neural networks, to a "convergence zone" and thence to a verbal area where the noun "cup" is stored.[67] This is strikingly similar to the abstract portraits of the semantic memory network we saw earlier in this chapter.

In the past several years, PET and fMRI scans of normal people have identified areas in the brain that are active when specific linguistic processes are going on. But despite a wealth of such information, the data do not tell us how the firing of myriad neurons in those locations becomes a word, a thought, a sentence, or a concept in the mind of the individual. The data provide a more detailed model than was formerly available of where language processes take place in the brain, but cognitive neuroscience has not yet yielded a theory as to how the neural events become language. As Michael Gazanniga and his co-authors say in *Cognitive Neuroscience*, "The human language system is complex, and much remains to be learned about how the biology of the brain enables the rich speech and language comprehension that characterize our daily lives."[68]*

"Much remains"? A memorable understatement.

Reasoning

Some years ago I asked Gordon Bower, a prominent memory researcher, a question about thinking and was taken aback by his testy

---

*The comment, made in 2002, still holds true.

reply: "I don't work on 'thinking' at all. I don't know what 'thinking' is."
How could the head of Stanford University's psychology department not
work on thinking at all—and not even know what it is? Then, rather
grudgingly, Bower added, "I presume it's the study of reasoning."

Thinking was traditionally a central theme in psychology, but by the
1970s the proliferation of knowledge in cognitive psychology had made
the term unhandy, since it included processes as disparate as momentary short-term memory and protracted problem solving. Psychologists
preferred to speak of thought processes in more specific terms:
"chunking," "reasoning," "retrieval," "categorization," "formal operations," "problem solving," and scores of others. "Thinking" came to
have a narrower and more precise meaning than before: the manipulation of knowledge to achieve a goal. To avoid any misunderstand-
ing, however, many psychologists preferred, like Bower, to use the
term "reasoning."

Although human beings have always viewed reasoning ability as the
essence of their humanity, research on it was long a psychological back-
water.[69] From the 1930s to the 1950s little work was done on reasoning
except for the problem-solving experiments of Karl Duncker and other
Gestaltists and the studies by Piaget and his followers of the kinds of
thought processes characteristic of children at different stages of intellectual development.

But with the advent of the cognitive revolution, research on reasoning
became an active field. The IP (information processing) model enabled
psychologists to formulate hypotheses that portrayed, in flow-chart fashion, what went on in various kinds of reasoning, and the computer was a
piece of apparatus—the first ever—with which such hypotheses could
be tested.

IP theory and the computer were synergistic. A hypothesis about any
form of reasoning could be described, in IP terms, as a sequence of specific steps of information processing; the computer could then be programmed to perform an analogous sequence of steps. If the hypothesis
was correct, the machine would reach the same conclusion as the reasoning human mind. By the same token, if a reasoning program written
for the computer produced the same answer as a human being to a
given problem, one could suppose that the program was operating in
the same way as, or at least in a similar fashion to, that of the human
mind.

How does a computer do such reasoning? Its program contains a routine, or set of instructions, plus a series of subroutines, each of which is

used or not used, depending on the results of the previous operations and the information in the program's memory. A common form of routine is a series of if-then steps: "If the input meets condition 1, then take action 1; if not, take action 2. Compare the result with condition 2 and if the result is [larger, smaller, or whatever], take action 3. Otherwise take action 4 . . . Store resulting conditions 2, 3 . . . and, depending on further results, use these stored items in such-and-such ways."[70]

But when computers carry out such programs, whether in mathematical computing or problem solving, are they actually reasoning? Are they not acting as automata that unthinkingly execute prescribed actions? The question is one for the philosopher. If a computer can, like a knowledgeable human being, prove a theorem, navigate a spacecraft, or determine whether a poem was written by Shakespeare, who is to say that it is a mindless automaton—or that a human being is not one?

In 1950, when only a few primitive computers existed but the theory of computation was being much discussed by mathematicians, information theorists, and others, Alan Turing, a gifted English mathematician, proposed a test, more philosophic than scientific, to determine whether a computer could or could not think. In the test, a computer programmed to solve a certain kind of problem is stationed in one room, a person skilled in that kind of problem is in another room, and in a third room is a judge in telegraphic communication with each. If the judge cannot tell from the dialogue which is the computer and which the person, the computer will pass the test: it thinks.[71] No computer program has yet won hands down, in publicly conducted contests, although some have fooled some of the judges. The validity of the Turing test has been debated, but at the very least it must mean that if a computer seems to think, what it does is as good as thinking.

By the 1960s, most cognitive psychologists, whether or not they agreed that computers really think, regarded computation theory as a conceptual breakthrough; it enabled them for the first time to describe any aspect of cognition, and of reasoning in particular, in detailed and precise IP terms. Moreover, having hypothesized the steps of any such program, they could translate them from words into computer language and try the result on a computer. If it ran successfully, it meant that the mind did indeed reason by means of something like that program. No wonder Herbert Simon said the computer was as important for psychology as the microscope had been for biology; no wonder other enthusiasts said the human mind and the computer were two species of the genus "information-processing system."[72]

The ability to solve problems is one of the most important applications of human reasoning. Most animals solve such problems as finding food, escaping enemies, and making a nest or lair largely by means of innate or partly innate patterns of behavior; human beings solve or attempt to solve most of their problems by means of either learned or original reasoning.

In the mid-1950s, when Simon and Newell undertook to create Logic Theorist, the first program that simulated thinking, they posed a problem to themselves: How do human beings solve problems? Logic Theorist took them a year and a half, but the question occupied them for more than fifteen. The resulting theory, published in 1972, has been the foundation of work in that field ever since.

Their chief method of working on it, according to Simon's autobiography, was two-man brainstorming. This involved deductive and inductive reasoning, analogical and metaphoric thinking, and flights of fancy—in short, any kind of reasoning, orderly or disorderly:

> From 1955 to the early 1960s, when we met almost daily . . . [we] worked mostly by conversations together, with the explicit rule that one could talk nonsensically and vaguely, but without criticism unless you intended to talk accurately and sensibly. We could try out ideas that were half-baked or quarter-baked or not baked at all, and just talk and listen and try them again.[73]

They also did a good deal of laboratory work. Singly and together they recorded and analyzed the steps by which they and others solved puzzles and then wrote out the steps as programs. A favorite puzzle, of which they made extensive use for some years, is a child's toy known as the Tower of Hanoi. In its simplest form, it consists of three disks of different sizes (with holes in their centers) piled on one of three vertical rods mounted on flat bases. At the outset, the largest disk is on the bottom, the middle-sized one in the middle, the smallest one on top. The problem is to move them one at a time in the fewest possible moves, never putting any disk on top of one smaller than itself, until they are piled in the same order on another rod.

The perfect solution takes seven steps, although with errors leading to dead ends and backtracking to correct them, it can take several times that many. In more advanced versions, the solution requires complex strategies and many moves. A perfect five-disk game takes thirty-one moves, a perfect seven-disk game 127 moves, and so on.* Simon has said, quite seriously, that "the Tower of Hanoi was to cognitive science what fruit flies were to modern genetics—an invaluable standard research setting."[74] (Sometimes, however, he ascribes this honor to chess.)

Another laboratory tool used by the team was cryptarithmetic, a type of puzzle in which a simple addition problem is presented in letters instead of numbers. The goal is to figure out what digits the letters stand for. This is one of Simon and Newell's simpler examples:

$$
\begin{array}{r}
S \ E \ N \ D \\
M \ O \ R \ E \\
\hline
M \ O \ N \ E \ Y
\end{array}
$$

The obvious first step: M must be 1, since no two digits—S + M in this case—can add up to more than 19, even with a carry.† Simon and Newell had volunteers talk out loud as they worked on such a puzzle, recorded everything they said, and afterward diagrammed the steps of their thought process in the form of a search track of moves, decisions at forks with more than one option, wrong choices pursued to dead ends, reversals to try another route from the last fork, and so on.

Simon and Newell made particular use of chess, a vastly more complex problem than either the Tower or cryptarithmetic. In a typical chess game of sixty moves, at each step there are on average thirty possible moves; to "look ahead" only three moves would mean visualizing twenty-seven thousand possibilities. A key question for Simon and Newell was how chess players deal with such impossibly large sets of

---

*Lacking the toy, you can play the game with three or more coins of different sizes. Draw three squares on a sheet of paper, pile the coins in one of them, decide which square the pile is to end up in, and start. The three-coin game is easy, the four-coin game not so easy, and the five-coin game quite hard.

†The solution continues as follows:

S must be either 8 or 9, depending on whether or not there is a carry. Substituting 1 for M, where S + 1 = O, we see that O can be only 0 or 1. But M is 1, so O must be 0; therefore S must be 9 and there is no carry.

In the second column from the left, E + 0 would be E unless there is a carry; hence there must be a carry. So E + 1 = N.

If E is odd, N is even, and vice versa. If E is odd, it can only be 3, 5, or 7 (1 and 9 are already assigned). Try 3. And so on.

contingencies. The answer: A skilled chess player does not consider all the possible moves he might make next and all the moves his opponent might make in response but only those few moves that make good sense and that follow elementary guidelines like "Guard the King" and "Don't give away a piece for one of lesser value." In short, the chess player makes a heuristic search—one guided by broad strategic principles of good sense—rather than a thorough but uninformed one.

The Newell and Simon theory of problem solving—for alphabetical reasons Newell's name is first on their joint publications—on which they worked for another fifteen years is that problem solving is a search for a route from an *initial state* to a *goal*. To get there, the problem solver has to find a *path* through a *problem space* made up of all possible states he might arrive at by making all the moves that obey the *path constraints* (rules or conditions of the domain).

In most such searches, the possibilities multiply geometrically, since each decision point offers two or more possibilities, each of which leads to another decision point offering another set of possibilities. In the sixty moves of an average chess game, each move, as already mentioned, has an average of thirty alternatives; the total number of paths in a game is 30^{60}—30 million trillion trillion trillion trillion trillion trillion—a number totally beyond human comprehension. Accordingly, as Simon and Newell's research demonstrated, problem solvers, in finding their way through such problem spaces, make no effort to look at every possibility.

In the massive tome they published in 1972 and straightforwardly called *Human Problem Solving*, Newell and Simon presented what they considered its general characteristics. Among them:[75]

— Because of the limits of short-term memory, we work our way through a problem space in serial fashion, taking one thing at a time.
— But we do not perform a serial search of every possibility, one after another. We use that method only when there are very few possibilities. (If, for instance, you don't know which one of a small bunch of keys opens a friend's front door, you try them one at a time.)
— In many problem situations trial and error is not practicable; if so, we search heuristically. Knowledge makes this very effective. As simple a problem as solving an eight-letter anagram like SPLOMBER would take fifty-six working hours if you wrote out all 40,320 permutations at a rate of one every five seconds, but most people can solve it in seconds or minutes by ignoring invalid beginnings (PB

or PM, for instance) and considering only valid ones (SL, PR, etc.).*

— One important heuristic commonly used to simplify the task is what Newell and Simon call "best-first search." At any fork in the search path, or "decision tree," we first try the move that appears to carry us closest to the goal. It is efficient to move toward the goal with every step (although sometimes we have to move away from it to circumvent an obstacle).

— A complementary and even more important heuristic is "means-end analysis," which Simon has called "the workhorse of GPS [General Problem Solver]." Means-end analysis is a mixture of forward and backward search. Unlike chess, which uses forward searching, in many cases the problem solver sees that he cannot proceed directly toward the goal but must first reach a subgoal from which the goal is attainable, or perhaps has to get first to an even earlier subgoal or one still earlier than that.

In a relatively recent review of problem-solving theory, Keith Holyoak offers a homely example of means-end analysis: Your goal is to have your living room freshly painted. The subgoal nearest that goal is the condition in which you can paint it, but that requires you to have paint and a brush, so you must first reach the earlier subgoal of buying them. To do so requires reaching the even earlier subgoal of being at a hardware store. So it goes, backward chaining until you have a complete strategy by which to move from your present state to the state of having a painted living room.[76]

As major an achievement as Newell and Simon's theory of problem solving was, it dealt only with deductive reasoning. Moreover, it considered only "knowledge-poor" problem solving—the kind applicable to puzzles, games, and abstract problems. To what extent the method described problem solving in knowledge-rich domains—the sciences, business, or law, for instance—was unclear.

For the past several decades, therefore, a number of researchers have been expanding the investigation of reasoning. Some have studied the psychological tendencies on which deductive and inductive reasoning are based; some whether either form, or some other, is what we use in everyday reasoning; some the differences in the kinds of reasoning used by experts and by novices in knowledge-rich situations. These investiga-

*The answer: PROBLEMS

tions have produced a wealth of insights into the formerly invisible workings of the reasoning human mind. Here are a few of the highlights:

Deductive reasoning: The traditional idea, going back to Aristotle, is that there are two kinds of reasoning, deduction and induction. Deduction extracts a further belief from one that is given; that is, if the premise or premises are true, so is the conclusion, since it is necessarily included in them. From the premises of Aristotle's classic syllogism

All men are mortal.
Socrates is a man.

it follows that

Socrates is mortal.

This kind of reasoning is tight, strong, easy to follow, and fully convincing. It is exemplified by proofs of logic and geometry theorems.

Yet many other syllogisms that have only two premises and contain only three terms are not so transparent; some are so difficult that most people cannot draw a valid conclusion from them. Philip Johnson-Laird, who has done research on the psychology of deduction, gives an example that he has used in the laboratory. Imagine that in a room there are some archaeologists, biologists, and chess players, and that these two statements are true:

None of the archaeologists is a biologist.
All the biologists are chess players.

What, if anything, follows from those premises? Johnson-Laird has found that few people can give the right answer.[77]* Why not? He believes that the ease of drawing the valid conclusion in the Socrates syllogism and the difficulty of doing so in the archaeologist syllogism are due to the way the arguments are represented in the mind—the "mental models" we create of them, a theory he has been developing and testing ever since.[78]

People with formal training in logic usually visualize such arguments in the form of geometrical diagrams, the two premises being repre-

*The only correct deduction is that some of the chess players are not archaeologists.

sented by circles, one inside the other, or overlapping it, or separate. But Johnson-Laird's theory, based on his research and validated by a computer simulation, is that people without such training use a more homespun model. In the Socrates syllogism, they unconsciously imagine a number of people, all mortal, imagine Socrates as related to that group, and then cast about for any other possibility (anyone outside the set—possibly Socrates). There being no such possibility, they correctly conclude that Socrates is mortal.

In the archaeologist syllogism, however, they imagine and try out first one, then another, and finally a third model, of increasing difficulty (we will spare ourselves the details). Some people rely on the first, unable to see that the second invalidates it, and others the second, not seeing that it, too, is discredited by the third and most difficult—which leads to the only valid conclusion.[79]

Mental modeling is not the only source of erroneous deductions. Experiments have shown that even where the form of a syllogism is simple and its mental model easy to create, people are apt to be misled by their beliefs and information. One research team asked a group of subjects whether these two syllogisms were logically correct:

All things that have a motor need oil.
Automobiles need oil.
Therefore, automobiles have motors.

All things that have a motor need oil.
Opprobines need oil.
Therefore, opprobines have motors.

More people thought the first one logically correct than did the second, although the two are identical in structure, differing only in the substitution of the nonsense word "opprobines" for "automobiles." They were misled by their knowledge of automobiles; knowing the conclusion of the first syllogism to be true, they thought the argument logically correct. But it is not, as they could see in the case of opprobines, about which they knew nothing and where they could recognize that there is no necessary overlap between opprobines and things with a motor.[80]

Inductive reasoning: By contrast, inductive reasoning is loose and inexact. It moves from specific beliefs to broader ones, that is, from limited cases to generalizations. From "Socrates is mortal," "Aristotle is mortal," and other instances, one infers, with a degree of confidence based on the number of cases, that "all men are mortal," although even a single case to the contrary would invalidate that conclusion.

A good deal of important human reasoning is of this type. Categorization and concept formation, crucial to thinking, are the products of induction, as seen in studies of how children arrive at categories and concepts. All the higher knowledge humankind possesses about the world—everything from the inevitability of death to the laws of planetary motion and galactic formation—is the product of the derivation of generalizations from a mass of particulars.

Induction is also the reasoning used where pattern recognition is the key to solving a problem. A simple example:

What number comes next?

2   3   5   6   9   10   14   15   ___

A ten-year-old can answer correctly after a while; an adult can see the pattern and the answer (20) in a minute or less. It is the very reasoning process employed by economists, public health officials, telephone system planners, and many others whose recognition of patterns is critically important to the survival of modern society.

(Disconcertingly, researchers have found that many people frequently fail to reason inductively from incoming information. All too often, we notice and add to our memory store only what supports a strongly held belief, ignoring any that does not. Psychologists call this "confirmation bias." Dan Russell and Warren Jones gave subjects materials to read, some confirming and some disproving the existence of ESP. Afterward, believers in ESP remembered the confirming materials 100 percent of the time but the negative materials only 39 percent of the time, while skeptics remembered both kinds about 90 percent of the time.[81])

Much of our reasoning combines deduction and induction, each of which serves its own purposes. How we came by both kinds of reasoning ability has been explained, at least hypothetically, by evolutionary psychology: Both methods are assets in the struggle to survive and were the products of natural selection.[82] The hypothesis seems validated by a recent study using PET scans: When subjects were asked to solve problems requiring deduction, two small areas on the right side of the brain showed increased activity; when the problems required inductive thinking, two brain structures on the left side showed it.[83] Natural selection, in short, developed brain structures capable of both kinds of reasoning.

Probabilistic reasoning: The human mind's abilities are the product of evolutionary selection, but we have lived in advanced civilized societies too short a time to have developed an inherited ability for sound reasoning about statistical likelihoods, though it is often called for in modern life.

Daniel Kahneman and Amos Tversky, who did much of the basic work in this area, asked a group of subjects which they would prefer: a sure gain of $80, or an 85 percent chance of winning $100 along with a 15 percent chance of winning nothing. Most people preferred the sure gain of $80, although statistically the average yield of the risky choice is $85. Kahneman and Tversky concluded that people are "risk-averse": They prefer a sure thing even when a risky thing is the better bet.

Turning to the obverse situation, Kahneman and Tversky asked another group of subjects whether they would prefer a sure loss of $80 or an 85 percent chance of losing $100 along with a 15 percent chance of losing nothing. This time a large majority preferred the gamble to the sure thing even though, on average, the gamble is costlier. Kahneman and Tversky's conclusion: When choosing between gains, people are risk-averse; when choosing between losses, they are risk-seeking—and in both cases are likely to make poor judgments.[84]

An even more disquieting finding came from a later experiment in which they posed two versions of a public-health problem to groups of college students. The versions are mathematically identical but different in wording. The first version:

Imagine that the U.S. is preparing for the outbreak of a rare Asian disease, which is expected to kill 600 people. Two alternative programs to combat the disease have been proposed. Assume that the exact scientific estimates of the consequences of the programs are as follows:

If Program A is adopted, 200 people will be saved.
If Program B is adopted, there is a ⅓ probability that 600 people will be saved, and a ⅔ probability that no people will be saved.
Which of the two programs would you favor?

The second version gave the same story but worded the alternatives as follows:

If Program C is adopted, 400 people will die.

If Program D is adopted, there is a ⅓ probability that nobody will die, and a ⅔ probability that 600 people will die.

Subjects responded quite differently to the two versions: 72 percent chose Program A over Program B, but 78 percent (of a different group) chose Program D over Program C. Kahneman and Tversky's explanation: In the first version, the outcomes are portrayed in terms of gains (lives saved), in the second version in terms of losses (lives lost). The same biases as shown by the experiments where money was at stake distorted subjects' judgment in this case, where lives were at stake.[85] (In 2002, Kahneman won the Nobel prize in economics for his work on probabilistic reasoning; Tversky, who would have shared it, unfortunately was dead by then.)

We reason poorly in these cases because the factors involved are "nonintuitive"; our minds do not readily grasp the reality involved in probabilities. This shortcoming affects us both individually and as a society; the electorate and its leaders often make costly decisions because of poor probabilistic reasoning. As Richard Nisbett and Lee Ross point out in their book *Human Inference*, many governmental practices and policies adopted during crises are deemed beneficial because of what happens afterward, even though the programs are often useless or worse. The misjudgment is caused by the human tendency to attribute a result to the action meant to produce it, although often the result stems from the normal tendency of events to revert from the unusual to the usual.[86]

It is reassuring, therefore, that a number of studies have found that unconscious mental processing often yields good evaluations and decisions—sometimes better than the results of conscious deliberation. In a series of studies reported in 2004, a Dutch psychologist asked subjects to make choices about complex real-world matters that had many positive and negative features such as choosing an apartment. One group was told to make an immediate (no thought) choice, another group to think for three minutes and then choose (conscious thought), and a third group to work for three minutes on a difficult distracting task and then choose (unconscious thought). In all three studies, the subjects in the unconscious thought condition made the best choices.[87]

Analogical reasoning: By the 1970s, cognitive psychologists had begun to recognize that much of what logicians regard as faulty reasoning is, in fact, "natural" or "plausible" reasoning—inexact, loose, intuitive, and technically invalid, but often competent and effective.

One such form of thinking is the analogical. Whenever we recognize that a problem is analogous to a different problem, one we are familiar with and know the answer to, we make a leap of thought to a solution. Many people, for instance, when they have to assemble a piece of knocked-down furniture or machinery, ignore the instruction manual and work by "feel"—looking for relationships among the parts that are analogous to the relationships among the parts of different kinds of furniture or machinery they assembled earlier.

Analogical reasoning is acquired in the later stages of childhood mental development. Dedre Gentner, a cognitive psychologist, asked five-year-olds and adults in what way a cloud is like a sponge. The children replied in terms of similar attributes ("They're both round and fluffy"), adults in terms of relational similarities ("They both store water and give it back to you").[88]

Gentner interprets analogical reasoning as a "mapping" of high-level relations from one domain to another; she and two colleagues even wrote a computer program, the "Structure-Mapping Engine," that simulates the process. When it was run on a computer and provided with limited data about both the atom and the solar system, the program, like the great physicist Lord Rutherford, recognized that they are analogous and drew appropriate conclusions.[89]

With difficult or unfamiliar problems, people generally do not use analogical reasoning because they only rarely spot a distant analogy, even when it would provide the solution to their problem. But if they consciously make the effort to look for an analogy, they are far more apt to see one that is not at all obvious. M. L. Gick and Keith Holyoak used Duncker's classic problem, of which we read earlier, about how one can use X-rays to destroy a stomach tumor without harming the surrounding healthy tissue. Most of their subjects did not spontaneously discover the solution; Gick and Holyoak then provided them with a story that, they hinted, might prove helpful. It told of an army unable to capture a fortress by a single frontal attack but successful when its general divided it into separate bands that attacked from all sides. Having read this and consciously sought an analogy to the X-ray problem, most subjects saw that many sources of weak X-rays placed all around the body and converging on the tumor would solve the problem.[90]

Expert reasoning: Many cognitive psychologists, intrigued by Newell and Simon's work, assumed that their theory would apply to problem solving by experts in fields of special knowledge, but found, to their surprise, that it did not. In a knowledge-rich domain, experts do more forward searching than backward searching or means-end analysis, and their thinking often proceeds not step by step but in leaps. Rather than starting with details, they perceive overall relationships; they know which category or principle is involved and work top-down. Novices, in contrast, lack perspective and work bottom-up, starting with details and trying to gather enough data to gain an overview.[91]

Since the 1980s, a number of cognitive psychologists have been exploring the characteristics of expert reasoning in different fields. They have asked experts in cardiology, commodity trading, law, and many other areas to solve problems; again and again they have found that experts, rather than pursuing a logical, step-by-step search (as a newly trained novice or an artificial intelligence program would do), often leap from a few facts to a correct assessment of the nature of the problem and the probable solution. A cardiologist, for instance, might from only two or three fragments of information correctly diagnose a specific heart disorder, while a newly graduated doctor, presented with the same case, would ask a great many questions and slowly narrow down the range of possibilities. The explanation: Unlike novices, experts have their knowledge organized and arranged in schemas that are full of special shortcuts based on experience.[92]

Is the Mind a Computer? Is a Computer a Mind?

Even in the first flush of enthusiasm for IP theory and computer simulations of reasoning, some psychologists, of a more humanistic than computer-technical bent, had reservations about the comparability of mind and machine. There are, indeed, major dissimilarities. For one, the computer searches for and retrieves items as needed—at blinding speed, nowadays—but human beings retrieve many items of information without any search: our own name, for instance, and most of the words we utter. For another, as the cognitive scientist Donald Norman has pointed out, if you are asked "What's Charles Dickens's telephone number?" you know right away that it's a silly question, but a computer would not, and would go looking for the number.[93]

For a third, the mind knows the meaning of words and other symbols, but the computer does not; to it they're only labels. Nor does anything about the computer resemble the unconscious or all that goes on in it.

These are only a few of the differences that have been obvious since the first experiments in computer reasoning. Yet, no less an authority than Herbert Simon categorically asserted that mind and machine were kin. In 1969, in a series of lectures published as *The Sciences of the Artificial*, he argued that the computer and the human mind are both "symbol systems"—physical entities that process, transform, elaborate, and generally manipulate symbols of various kinds.

Throughout the 1970s, small cadres of dedicated psychologists and computer scientists at MIT, Carnegie-Mellon, Stanford, and a handful of other universities, possessed of a zealotlike belief that they were on the verge of a great breakthrough, developed programs that were both theories of how the mind works and machine versions of human thinking. By the 1980s the work had spread to scores of universities and to the laboratories of a number of major companies. The programs carried out such varied activities as playing chess, parsing sentences, deducing the laws of planetary motion from a mass of raw data, translating elementary sentences from one language to another, and inferring the structure of molecules from mass spectrographic data.[94]

The enthusiasts saw no limit to the ability of IP theory to explain how the mind works and of AI to verify those explanations by carrying out the same processes—and eventually doing so far better than human beings. In 1981 Robert Jastrow, director of the Goddard Institute for Space Studies, predicted that "around 1995, according to current trends, we will see the silicon brain as an emergent form of life, competitive with man."[95]

But some psychologists felt that the computer was only a mechanical simulation of certain aspects of the mind and that the computational model of mental processing was a poor fit. The eminent cognitivist Ulric Neisser had become "disillusioned" with information-processing models by 1976, when he published *Cognition and Reality*. Here, much influenced by James Gibson and his "ecological" psychology, Neisser made the case that IP models were narrow and far removed from real-life perception, cognition, and purposeful activity, and fail to take into account the richness of experience and information we continually receive from the world around us.[96]

A number of other psychologists, though not saying they were disillusioned, sought to broaden the IP view to include the mind's use of

schemas, shortcuts, and intuitions, and its ability to function simultaneously on both the conscious and unconscious levels to conduct simultaneous processes in parallel (a critical issue we shall hear more of in a
moment).

Still others challenged the notion that computers programmed to
think like humans actually think. AI, they maintained, isn't anything
like human intelligence, and though it may vastly outperform the
human mind at calculations, it would never do easily, or at all, many
things the human mind does routinely and effortlessly.

The most important difference is the computer's inability to understand what it is thinking about. John Searle and Hubert Dreyfus, both
philosophy professors at Berkeley, the computer scientist Joseph
Weizenbaum at MIT, and others argued that computers, even when
programmed to reason, merely manipulate symbols without having any
idea what they mean and imply. General Problem Solver, for instance,
may have figured out how the father and two sons could get across the
river, but only in terms of algebraic symbols; it did not know what a
father, son, or boat were, what "sink" meant, what would happen if they
sank, or anything else about the real world.

But many programs written in the 1970s and 1980s did seem to deal
with real-world phenomena. This was especially true of "expert systems," computer programs written to simulate the reasoning, and make
use of the special knowledge, of experts in fields ranging from oncology
to investment and from locating veins of ore to potato farming.

Typically, such programs, designed to aid problem solving, ask the
person operating them questions in English, use the answers and their
own stored knowledge to move through a decision-tree pattern of reasoning, close off dead ends, narrow down the search, and finally reach a
conclusion to which they assign a certainty ratio ("Diagnosis: systemic
lupus erythematosus, certainty .8"). By the mid-1980s, scores of such
programs were in routine use in scientific laboratories, government, and
industry, and before the end of the decade many hundreds were.[97]

Probably the oldest and best-known expert system is MYCIN, created in
1976 and improved in 1984, which can be used to detect and identify
(and potentially even treat) about a hundred different kinds of bacterial
infections, and announce what degree of certainty it puts on its findings.
In tests against human experts, "MYCIN's performance compared favorably with that of faculty members in the Stanford School of Medicine . . . [and] outperformed medical students and residents in the same
school," notes the distinguished cognitivist Robert J. Sternberg in *Cogni-*

tive Psychology (2006), "[and] . . . had been shown to be quite effective in prescribing medication for meningitis." INTERNIST, another expert system, diagnoses a broader range of diseases, although in doing so, it loses some precision, resulting in diagnostic powers less than that of an experienced internist.

But although these and other expert systems are intelligent in a way that banking computers, airline reservation computers, and others are not, in reality they do not know the meaning of the real-world information they deal with, not in the sense that we know. CADUCEUS, an internal medicine consultation system, can diagnose five hundred diseases nearly as well as highly qualified clinicians, but an authoritative textbook, *Building Expert Systems,* long ago pointed out that it "has no understanding of the basic pathophysiological processes involved" and cannot think about medical problems outside or at the periphery of its area of expertise, even when plain common sense is all that is needed.[98] One medical diagnostic program failed to object when a human user asked whether amniocentesis might be useful; the patient was male and the system simply wasn't "aware" that the question was absurd. As John Anderson has said, "The major difficulty which human experts handle well is that of understanding the context in which knowledge is to be used. A logical engine will only yield appropriate results if that context has been carefully defined."[99] But to define contexts as broadly and richly as the human mind does would require an unimaginable amount of data and programming.

The most impressive demonstrations of computer reasoning have been the chess matches in which AI programs have defeated human chess champions. In 1997 a program called Deep Blue defeated the world's best chess player, Garry Kasparov. In large part, it did so by brute force—searching about 200 million possible moves each second (a human being does well to manage one move per second). Since then, other programs, using far less hardware and running far more slowly, but using more strategy—particularly the kinds of creative and original strategies that chess masters can make—have defeated most of their top-level human opponents. Some of the newer programs make some counterintuitive, even ridiculous-looking, moves that can prove to be highly creative.[100]

Among other arguments against the assertion that AI programs think, made by many psychologists and other scientists, are these:[101]

—AI programs of the expert system type or with broader reasoning abilities lack intuition, a crucial characteristic of human intelligence. Although computers can be excellent manipulators of symbols and can carry out complex prepackaged algorithms, they cannot act on the kinds of hunches that genuine experts can but people with only book knowledge cannot.

— AI programs have no sense of self or of their place in the world around them. This severely limits their ability to do much real-world thinking.

— They are not *conscious.* Even though consciousness is still proving extremely difficult to define, we experience it and they do not. They cannot, therefore, examine their own thoughts and change their minds as a result. They make choices, but these are determined by their built-in data and their programming. Computers thus have nothing that resembles free will (or, if you prefer, free choice).

— They cannot—at least not yet—think creatively except within the purely abstract realm of chess. Some programs do generate new solutions to technical problems, but these are recombinations of existing data. Others have written poetry and music and created paintings, but their products have made little dent in artistic worlds; as in Doctor Johnson's classic remark, they are "like a dog's walking on his hinder legs. It is not done well; but you are surprised to find it done at all."

— Finally, they have no emotions or bodily sensations, although in human beings these profoundly influence, guide, and not infrequently misguide, thinking and deciding.

Nonetheless, both the IP metaphor and the computer have been of immense value in the investigation of human reasoning. The IP model has spawned a profusion of experiments, discoveries, and insights about those cognitive processes which take place in serial fashion. And the computer, on which IP theories can be modeled and either validated or invalidated, has been an invaluable laboratory tool.

But the shortcomings of the IP model and the limitations of AI simulations led, by the 1980s, to a second stage of the cognitive revolution: the emergence of a radically revised IP paradigm. Its central concept is that while the serial model of information processing fits some aspects of cognition, most—especially the more complex mental processes—are the result of a very different model, parallel processing.

By astonishing coincidence—or perhaps through a cross-fertilization of ideas—this accorded with then-new findings of brain research showing that in mental activities, nerve impulses do not travel a single route from one neuron to another; they proceed by the simultaneous activation of multitudes of intercommunicating circuits. The brain is not a serial processor but a massively parallel processor.

Matching these developments, computer scientists got busy devising a new kind of computer architecture in which interlocking and intercommunicating processors work in parallel, affecting one another's operations in immensely complex ways that are more nearly analogous to those of the brain and mind than are serial computers.[102] The new computer architecture is not patterned on the neuron networks of the brain, most of which are still unmapped and too complex by an astronomical degree to be copied, but it does, in its own way, perform parallel processing.

The technical details of these three developments lie beyond the scope of this book. But their meaning and significance do not; let us see what we can make of them.

New Model

In 1908, Henri Poincaré, a French mathematician, labored for fifteen days to develop a theory of Fuchsian functions but without success. He then left to go on a geological expedition. Just as he boarded a bus, talking to a fellow traveler, the solution popped into his mind so clearly and unequivocally that he did not even interrupt his conversation to check it out. When he did so later, it proved correct.

The annals of creativity are full of such stories; they suggest that two (or possibly more) thoughts can be pursued simultaneously by the mind, one consciously, the other or others unconsciously. Anecdotes are not scientific evidence, but in the early years of the cognitive revolution several experiments on attention did suggest that the mind is not a single serial computer.

In one of the best known, conducted in 1973, subjects put on headphones after being told by the experimenters, James Lackner and Merrill Garrett, to pay attention only to what they heard with the left ear and to ignore what they heard with the right one. With the left ear they heard ambiguous sentences, such as "The officer put out the lantern to signal the attack"; simultaneously, with the right ear some heard a sentence that would clarify the ambiguous one if they were paying attention to it ("He extinguished the lantern"), while others heard an irrelevant sentence ("The Red Sox are playing a doubleheader tonight").

Neither group could say, afterward, what they had heard with the right ear. But when asked the meaning of the ambiguous sentence, those who had heard the irrelevant sentence with the right ear were divided as to whether the ambiguous one had meant that the officer *snuffed out* or *set out* the lantern, but nearly all of those who had heard the clarifying sentence chose the *snuffed out* interpretation. Apparently, the clarifying sentence had been processed simultaneously and unconsciously along with the ambiguous one.[103]

This was one of several reasons why, during the 1970s, a number of psychologists began to hypothesize that thinking does not proceed serially. Another reason was that serial processing could not account for most of human cognitive processes; the neuron is too slow. It operates in milliseconds, so human cognitive processes that take place in a second or less would have to comprise no more than a hundred serial steps. Very few processes are that simple, and many, including perception, recall, speech production, sentence comprehension, and "matching" (pattern or face recognition), require vastly greater numbers.

By 1980 or so, a number of psychologists, information theorists, physicists, and others began developing detailed theories of how a parallel-processing system might work. The theories are extremely technical and involve high-level mathematics, symbolic logic, computer science, schema theory, and other arcana. But David Rumelhart, one of the leaders of the movement, summed up in simple language the thinking that inspired him and fifteen colleagues to develop their version, "Parallel Distributed Processing" (PDP):

Although the brain has *slow* components, it has *very many* of them. The human brain contains billions of such processing elements. Rather than organize computation with many, many serial steps, as we do with systems whose steps are very fast, the brain must deploy many, many processing elements cooperatively and in parallel to carry out its activities. These design characteristics, among others, lead, I believe, to a general organization of computing that is fundamentally different from what we are used to.[104]

PDP also departed radically from the computer metaphor used until then in its explanation of how information is stored. In a computer, information is retained by the *states* of its transistors. Each is either switched on or off (representing a 0 or a 1), and strings of 0's and 1's stand for numbers symbolizing information of all sorts. When the computer is running, electric current maintains these states and the information; when you turn it off, everything is lost. (Permanent storage on a disk is another matter altogether; the disk is outside the operating system, much as a written memo is outside the mind.) This cannot be the mind's way of storing information. For one thing, a neuron is not either on or off; it adds up inputs from thousands of other neurons and, reaching a certain level of excitation, transmits an impulse to still other neurons. But it does not remain in an active state for more than a fraction of a second, so only very short-term memory is stored in the mind by neuronal states. And since memories are not lost when the brain is turned off in sleep or in the unconsciousness caused by anesthesia, it must be that longer-term storage in the brain is achieved in some other fashion.

The new view, inspired by brain research, is that knowledge is stored not in an "on or off" state of the neurons but in the *connections* among them formed by experience.* In the case of a machine, the connections exist among the "units" of a parallel distributed processor. As Rumelhart said,

> Almost all knowledge is *implicit* in the structure of the device that carries out the task ... It is built into the processor itself and directly determines the course of processing. It is acquired through the tuning of connections as these are used in processing, rather than formulated and stored as declarative facts.[105]

The new theory, accordingly, came to be known as "connectionism," and has remained the number one buzz word of current cognitive theory.[106] In an interesting reversal, cognitive psychologists no longer think of mental processes as taking place in computer-like serial fashion and

---

*Storage of information in the brain has long been thought to be the result of some kind of unexplained strengthening of the synapses involved in any learning experience. Recent neurophysiological research, too arcane to be fully spelled out here, has established that in any form of learning, a series of at least 15 steps involving 100 or more different molecules takes place, switching on certain genes. These make the post-synaptic neuron more easily activated by the presynaptic neuron's release of various neurotransmitters (Marcus, 2004:100). In addition, the process induces the growth of additional synaptic connections on the presynaptic side (Kandel, 2006, chaps. 14, 17, 19). These changes, in effect, record information, although any elementary item in memory—a shape, say, or a sound—may require that a vast number of strengthened synapses, linked in a network, fire together.

their connectionist model of mental processes—based on neurological evidence—has become the guiding standard for computer design.

Rumelhart and his collaborators were not the only psychologists to imagine how connectionism in the human mind might work; a number of other connectionist models have been drawn up in recent years. But the basic concept underlies them all, namely, that the brain functions by means of exceedingly intricate and complex networks of multiple interconnections among its neurons, enabling the mind, among other things, to work both consciously and unconsciously at the same time, make decisions involving multiple variables, recognize meanings of spoken or written words, and on and on.

For our purposes, the Rumelhart et al. model can serve to exemplify the whole genre. A diagram that Rumelhart and two of his collaborators drew up for their book on PDP will make the PDP idea clear if you are willing to take a minute or two to trace it through. It is a portrait not of a bit of brain tissue but of a bit of a theoretical connectionist network:

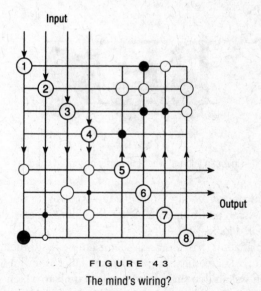

FIGURE 43

The mind's wiring?

A hypothetical example of a connectionist network

Units 1 to 4 receive inputs from the outside world (or some other part of the network), plus feedback from the output units, 5 to 8. The connections among the units are indicated symbolically by the unnumbered disks: The bigger an open disk, the stronger the connection, the bigger a filled disk, the stronger the inhibition or interference with transmission. Thus, unit 1 does not influence unit 8, but does influence 5, 6, and 7 to varying degrees. Units 2, 3, and 4 all influence 8 in widely varying degrees, and 8 in turn feeds back to the input units, affecting 1 almost not at all, 3 and 4 rather little, and 2 strongly. All this goes on at the same time and results in an array of outputs, in contrast to the single process and single output of serial design.

Although Rumelhart and his collaborators said that "the appeal of PDP models is definitely enhanced by their physiological plausibility and neural inspiration," the units in the diagram are not neurons and the connections are not synapses.[107] The diagram represents not a physical entity but what *happens*; the brain's synapses and the model's connections operate in different ways to inhibit some connections and strengthen others. In both cases, the connections are what the system knows and how it will respond to any input.[108]

A simple demonstration: What word is partly obscured by inkblots in this diagram?

FIGURE 44

How can you tell what the partly obscured word is?

You probably recognized instantly that the word is PEN. But how did you know that? Each partly obscured letter could have been other than the one you took it to be.

The explanation (based on a similar example by Rumelhart and Jay McClelland): The vertical line in the first letter is an input into your recognition system that strongly connects to units in which P, R, and B are stored; the curved line connects to all three. On the other hand, the sight of the straight line does not connect—or, one can say, is strongly inhibited from connecting—to any unit representing rounded letters like C or O. Simultaneously, what you can see of the second letter is strongly connected to units registering F and E, but crossfeed from the first letter connects strongly to E not F, because experience has established PE, RE, and BE but not PF, RF, or BF as the beginning of an English word. And so on. Many connections, all operating at the same time and in parallel, enable you to see the word instantly as PEN and not as anything else.[109]

On a larger scale, the connectionist model of information processing is in striking accord with other seminal findings of cognitive psychological research. Consider, for instance, what is now known about the semantic memory network in Figure 41. Each node in that network— "bird," "canary," and "sing," for instance—corresponds to a connectionist module something like the entire array in the last diagram but perhaps consisting of thousands of units rather than eight.[110] Imagine, if you can, enough such multithousand-unit modules to register all the knowledge stored in your mind, each with millions of connections to related modules, and . . . But the task is too great for imagination. The connectionist architecture of the mind is no more possible to visualize in its entirety than the structure of the universe; only theory and mathematical symbols can encompass it.

The connectionist model is strongly analogous to actual brain structure and function. The late Francis Crick, who shared a Nobel Prize for discovering the structure of DNA and then did neuroscience research at the Salk Institute, said that the concept of the brain as a complex hierarchy of largely parallel processors "is almost certainly along the right lines."[111] Paul Churchland and Patricia Churchland—each a philosopher of cognitive science—have said that the brain is indeed a parallel machine "in the sense that signals are processed in millions of different pathways simultaneously." Each aggregation of neurons sends millions of signals to other aggregations and receives return signals from them that modify its output in one way or another. It is these recurrent patterns of connection that "make the brain a genuine dynamical system whose continuing behavior is both highly complex and to some degree independent of its peripheral stimuli."[112] Thus could Descartes, lying abed all morning, think about his own thoughts, as has many a psychologist since.

Possibly the most remarkable development of all is, as noted above, the change in the relationship between computer and mind. A generation ago, it seemed that the computer was the model by which the reasoning mind could be understood. Now the order has been reversed: The reasoning mind is the model by which a more intelligent computer can be built. Artificial intelligence researchers have been writing programs that simulate the parallel processing of small neural networks, their aim being to create AI programs that are more nearly intelligent than those based on serial processing, and to create programs that simulate hypothesized mental processes so that they can be tested on a computer.

A wonderful irony: The brain that makes mind possible turns out to be the best model for the machine that had been thought vastly superior to it, a model so complex and intricate that it is all the computer can do, for now, to replicate a few of its multitude of functions and make only symbolic simulations of a handful of others.

As David, the greatest of psalmists, sang twenty-five centuries before the cognitive revolution and the computer age, "I will praise thee; for I am fearfully and wonderfully made."

And the Winner Is—

We have followed the revolutionary development of cognitive psychology and the later but equally revolutionary development of cognitive neuroscience, which currently coexist, overlapping and infiltrating each other. But will they continue to do so or is one likely to dominate and absorb the other, becoming the psychology of the future? The answer would seem to depend on which discipline offers the better scientific explanation of mental processes and behavior.

Cognitive psychology, as we have seen, has compiled a remarkable record over the past six decades. Escaping from the severe limitations of behaviorist theory, it rediscovered the mind and found innumerable ways to investigate the unseen processes, among them perception, learning, memory, emotion, personality development, and social behavior, that take place in it. Cognitive psychologists were free to ask, once again, the great questions the Greek philosophers asked so long ago, summed up in the megaquestions "How do we know what we know, and why do we behave as we do?"

As is the case with other sciences, the proliferation of hypotheses and collecting of empirical evidence by cognitive psychologists has often produced corrections and drastic revisions of theories, minitheories, and data, but seen in perspective, cognitive psychology has been a cumulative, self-correcting, self-transforming science.

Its one great shortcoming has always been its lack of an adequate explanation of how the activity of billions of neurons in the brain can result in thoughts, emotions, and voluntary actions. As the neuropsychologist V. S. Ramachandran and science writer Sandra Blakeslee wrote a few years ago, "Many people find it disturbing that all the richness of our mental life—all our thoughts, feelings, emotions, even what we regard as our intimate selves—arise entirely from the activity of little wisps of protoplasm in the brain. How is this possible? How could something as deeply mysterious as consciousness emerge from a chunk of meat inside the skull?"[113]

In an effort to answer this question, ever since the early days of the cognitive revolution many psychologists have reached beyond the classic boundaries of their field to explain what they were studying in terms of hormonal, genetic, and other physiological factors. And for the past two and a half decades, as we have seen throughout this chapter, many psychologists have turned to the methods of cognitive neuroscience, especially brain scanning, to help validate their psychological hypotheses. But valuable as all this is, it still does not tell us how a blizzard of neural impulses becomes thought or other mental processes.

Cognitive neuroscience, especially since the advent of brain scans, has been compiling a record of advances in knowledge as impressive as that of cognitive psychology. The neuroscientists have traced neuronal pathways from sense receptors to various loci in the brain, located the areas where emotions are generated, shown that memories are stored in distributed network fashion, and in general extended their research deep into the territory of cognitive psychology, amassing a great deal of information about what areas of the brain are active in mental imagery, attention, speech, learning, voluntary and involuntary action, and other areas of classic psychological interest.

All of which is impressive and almost certainly will be the foundation on which some day a fuller explanation of how the brain becomes mind may be forthcoming. But not yet. The authors of one impressive tome of neuroscience write, "In this book, we explore how the brain actually does enable mind"[114]—but by "enable" they seem to mean something less than explain how the synaptic events become mental events. I asked Martha Farah, director of the Center for Cognitive Neuroscience at the University of Pennsylvania, if the problem were not akin to that of trying to account for the movement of a wave in terms of the movements of individual molecules of water; she laughed and said, "Fluid mechanics is independent of molecular physics. But cognition may not be describable without some details of neuronal function being in the picture."

Thus, a mental process as simple as a word retrieved from memory

cannot be equated with the firing of millions of neurons and the resultant billions of synaptic transmissions but is the product of the pattern or
structure of those firings and transmissions. Mental phenomena such as
speech, memory retrieval, and reasoning are governed not by the laws of
neural activity but by those of cognitive psychology. The former logo of
the journal *Cognition* is a striking example of this distinction:

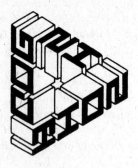

FIGURE 45

Levels of reality: molecules, letters, words, impossible objects

The design is made up of molecules of ink on paper, a reality that has
nothing to do with its meaning. At a higher level of organization, the
molecules make up letters, which individually are symbols without
meaning but as here organized make up the word "cognition." But we
are not done. The design, though it looks real and three-dimensional, is
an object that cannot exist in the real world; the paradoxical illusion is a
mental epiphenomenon. Explain that, if you can, in terms of molecules
of ink, letters, or bursts of energy in the neurons of the visual cortex.

Whether or not there is ever a full and satisfying explanation of mental events in neural terms, the revolutions of cognitive psychology and
cognitive neuroscience have been successful side by side, overlapping,
and in concert with each other.

As for the title of this section, "And the Winner Is—," we now seem to
be at the top of the tenth (or eleventh? or twelfth?)—and still tied.

SEVENTEEN

The
Psychotherapists

Growth Industry

Let us indulge in a bit of fantasy. Wilhelm Wundt, invisible except to us, returns from Somewhere to see what has become of the science he launched more than a century ago.

Stern and formal in his black lecture gown, the shade of the Herr Professor stares uncomprehendingly as some of his intellectual descendants, at a cognitive science conference, discuss the molecular basis of memory in the giant sea snail, while others speak of a computer program that simulates parallel distributing processing. Elsewhere, however, he permits himself an uncharacteristic beaming smile when he hears that six decades ago there were only about 4,000 psychologists in America but today there are some 180,000, (about half at the doctorate level, half at the master's level), a nearly forty-five-fold growth.[1]

When, however, the vaporous Dr. Wundt drifts into the offices of the American Psychological Association, his smile turns to a dark scowl. For here he learns that during the past several decades most new Ph.D.'s in psychology have become not researchers but industrial, educational, and—by far the largest number—clinical and counseling psychologists.[2] Wundt had adamantly opposed educational psychology and similar practical applications of the science, but *this*—listening and talking to people about their personal problems—is the worst, a detestable degradation of psychology. And he is horrified when he hears that most Americans, these days, think of a psychologist as someone who treats patients with mental health problems.[3] *Schrecklich!*

Of all the ways in which psychology influenced Americans during the past three quarters of a century, none has been more pervasive than the change it brought about in how they think of and deal with emotional and mental disorders. Many miseries, failures, disabilities, dissatisfactions, and misbehaviors that their forefathers attributed to weakness of character, wickedness, or Fate came to be seen by most Americans as psychological disorders that could be treated by mental health practitioners.

Acting on this conviction, in recent years some 10 million Americans made 86 million visits to psychotherapists annually, and in-patients in mental hospitals and psychiatric wards of general hospitals accounted for another several million sessions. Cumulatively, nearly one out of three persons—80 or 90 million—have had some experience with psychotherapy.[4]

About a third of these "consumers" of psychotherapy were treated by psychologists, about a third by physicians (but probably more of the total visits were made to psychologists than to physicians, since many users visited a physician only once to receive medication rather than talk therapy). The rest of the visits were made to clinical social workers, clinical mental health counselors, lay (nonmedical) analysts, and pastoral counselors. (Dr. Abe Wolf, current president of Division 29—psychotherapy—of the American Psychological Association, ruefully says in a recent online message from his division, "Psychologists struggle to maintain a distinct identity, competing with other professionals who all practice psychotherapy.") Most of the above professionals (except for the physicians dispensing medication), despite their dissimilar backgrounds and allegiance, practice therapies that are psychological, as distinguished from such other approaches to mental illness as the physiological, social, and religious.[5]

The rise in the use of medication, however, has been notable; the nonmedical therapists now often refer their clients to a physician for medication (to be taken along with talk therapy), and many emotionally or mentally ailing people ask their own family physicians for mood-influencing medications. Some psychotherapists believe that medication has somewhat reduced the practice of psychotherapy, though they have no hard data on the issue. But Dr. Mark Olfson, an associate professor of clinical psychiatry at Columbia University and the lead author of the latest survey of psychotherapy usage, recently told Erica Goode of the *New York Times*, "With all the attention given to antidepressants and other medications, the role of psychotherapy can be easily overshad-owed . . . but [it is] clear that psychotherapy continues to play an impor-tant role in the mental health care of many Americans."[6]

Psychology was not originally an applied science, and its training cen-ters produced not "health care providers" but researchers and theorists. The discipline grew rapidly after World War II, as did all the sciences, with the number of science Ph.D.'s granted yearly increasing more than tenfold between 1945 and 1970. But then the baby boom of undergrad-uates ebbed, new degree holders had difficulty finding teaching posi-tions, and doctorate production declined steeply in all the sciences—except psychology, which kept growing.

By the 1970s, however, psychology was growing not as a pure science but as several forms of applied science, of which health care was far and away the largest. The total output of Ph.D.s in psychology grew steadily from 1966 to 2000, with only a slight drop off to 2004, but the percent-age of research psychologists fell off sharply after the mid-1970s while the output of health care providers (clinical, counseling, and school psy-chologists) continued to increase. Although the absolute number of research psychologists has grown since 1970, it has steadily shrunk as a percentage of the discipline and now comprises a small minority of all doctoral and master's level psychologists. Clinical and counseling psy-chologists, most of whom practice psychotherapy (the rest do primarily testing and assessment), now make up about half.[7]

Despite the growing numbers of clinical psychologists, about two thirds of the demand for psychotherapy is, as already mentioned, met by others: two thirds of the nation's 45,000 psychiatrists who spend much of their time in private practice; 96,000 clinical social workers, most of whom practice some psychotherapy in agency and hospital settings but some of whom do so in private practice; 80,000 certified clinical mental health counselors; 3,000 pastoral counselors; and an unknown number of other people who call themselves psychotherapists—the use of the term is not controlled by law in most states—and who have anywhere from a fair amount of training to none at all.[8]

Psychotherapists in all these disciplines now treat a far broader spec-trum of patients than ever. ("Patients" is the term used by psychiatrists and psychologists; many other therapists call them "clients" to avoid the medical connotations of the word "patient." The terms in this context are synonymous.)

Formerly, psychotherapy was used chiefly with people whose contact with reality was unimpaired but who suffered from anxiety, phobias,

obsessions and compulsions, hysteria, hypochondriasis, physical problems of psychological origin—in short, all those said to have neuroses.*
Today, many people seek psychotherapeutic help for marital conflict,
parent-child problems, job-related troubles, loneliness, shyness, failure
to succeed, and indeed anything that comes under the general heading
of "problems of living."

In addition, psychotics, who used to be treated by prolonged soaking
in tepid water, insulin or electroconvulsive shocks, and even lobotomy
but rarely by psychotherapy—which often couldn't reach them—are
now brought back to reality or lifted out of the depths of depression by
psychoactive drugs and thereby enabled to benefit from psychotherapy.
In the 1950s, well over half a million people were locked away in the
nation's state mental hospitals; since the introduction of chlorpro-
mazine and other psychoactive drugs in the middle of that decade, the
number has declined radically, to fewer than 44,000.[9] A majority of the
kinds of patients who formerly were confined now live in the community, and their mental disorders are treated in community mental health
centers by means of medication and psychotherapy.

Although psychotherapy has thus grown vastly in influence and acceptability, it has long been assailed both by those who regard psychology as
a spurious science and those who regard psychotherapy as a spurious
healing art.

One line of attack has stressed that clinical psychologists and other
psychotherapists themselves admit that what they do is more intuitive
than rational, more an art than a science. Many academic and research
psychologists have therefore long held that psychotherapy is unworthy
to be called a part of their science. In 1956, a psychologist, David Bakan,
wrote in *American Psychologist*, a publication of the American Psychological Association:

> There is a prevailing sense of the scientific untenability of clinical psy-
> chology [i.e., psychotherapy] among many psychologists. Frequently,
> clinical psychology is envisaged as an art; or if the critic is inclined to

DSM-III, the 1980 edition of the American Psychiatric Association's bible of diagnosis,
and *DSM-III-R*, the 1987 revision, omit "neuroses" as a diagnostic category and identify
the disturbances formerly grouped under that label as separate categories of mental disorder. "Neurosis" and "neurotic" are, however, still informally used by both practitioners
and the laity, and will be so used here.

be more critical, it may be conceived of as an attempt to obtain knowledge mystically and effect changes magically.[10]

A few years later the psychologists Marvin Kahn and Sebastian Santoste-
fano wrote, again in *American Psychologist*, that clinical psychology was
"in a state of anxiety, great ambivalence, insecurity, and self-doubt.
Clinical psychology states that it is a science, and then says that it is an
art."[11] In 1972 and again in 1986, E. Fuller Torrey, himself a psychiatrist, devoted an entire book to the thesis that psychotherapists were akin
to witch doctors and medicine men, and achieved changes in their
patients by comparable nonscientific means.[12]

Attacking psychotherapy as nonscience has continued ever since, the
attackers ignoring or belittling the many hundreds of controlled studies
and meta-analyses of those studies validating aspects of the discipline
that have been performed over the decades (we'll hear about them
later). Typical of such attacks is one of the latest, an op-ed piece in the
New York Times in 2006 by Adam Phillips, a British child psychoanalyst:

> Psychoanalysis is having yet another identity crisis. It . . . [is] trying to
> make therapy into more of a "hard science" by putting a new emphasis
> on measurable factors . . . It would clearly be naïve for psychothera-
> pists to turn a blind eye to science, or to be "against" scientific method-
> ology. But the attempt to present psychotherapy as a hard science is
> merely an attempt to make it a convincing competitor in the market-
> place. It is a sign, in other words, of a misguided wish to make psy-
> chotherapy both respectable and servile to the very consumerism it is
> supposed to help people deal with.[13]

Thomas Szasz, a perennial gadfly to his fellow psychiatrists and other
psychotherapists, made a different and radical attack on clinical psychology. Mental illness, he charged, is a "myth" fabricated by clinicians
who, acting as lackeys of the establishment, diagnose forms of socially
disapproved deviant or individualistic behavior as mental disorders.[14]

Still others have charged that psychotherapists falsely claim therapy
to be useful against a wide variety of disorders although, these critics
assert, it is helpful against only a limited number. In 1983 Bernie Zilbergeld, an Oakland psychologist and psychotherapist, said in his
Shrinking of America that psychotherapy is effective for a few problems
but that for most others it is of little or no value and is inferior to drugs or
simply talking to a friend.[15]

Another favorite criticism in recent years has been that a number of conditions psychotherapists say they can treat are actually of physiological origin and are poorly remediable by psychotherapy but far better dealt with by medications.

Clinical (severe) depression, for one, has been shown to be of biological origin in many cases. Particularly in elderly people, it is often associated with an age-related imbalance in certain neurotransmitters. Research studies of recent years have shown, according to current information from SAMHSA (Substance Abuse and Mental Health Services Administration), that antidepressant drugs "chemically restore the balance and relieve the depression . . . [and] are effective across the full range of severity of major depressive episodes in major depressive disorder and bipolar disorder. [The named drugs are the tricyclic and heterocyclic antidepressants, MAOIs (monoamine oxidase inhibitors), and SSRIs (selective serotonin reuptake inhibitors.)] . . . The mode of action of antidepressants is complex and only partly understood. Put simply, most antidepressants are designed to heighten the level of a target neurotransmitter at the neuronal synapse."[16]

Tourette syndrome—uncontrollable tics, grunts, barks, often the compulsive repetition of foul language—was long attributed by psychotherapists to profound psychological disturbances and interpreted as having hostile and anal meanings, but psychotherapy consistently failed to help. What *has* helped is the administration of dopamine blocking agents, which suggests that the disorder is due to a dopaminergic excess of organic origin.[17]

Compulsive gambling and other forms of sensation seeking have been seen by psychotherapists as disorders for which psychotherapy is appropriate, but by 1989 studies based on urinalysis and spinal taps showed that compulsive gamblers and sensation seekers have a chronic deficit of the neurotransmitter norepinephrine. That deficit, it was hypothesized, leads to a low level of alertness and a feeling of boredom, which victims try to alleviate by seeking danger—a condition in which the brain produces extra norepinephrine and which, though it makes most people extremely uncomfortable, makes these people feel good.[18]

Obsessive-compulsive disorder, in which certain obsessive ideas cause such persistent senseless actions as washing the hands dozens of times a day, has also been found by means of PET scans to be associated with abnormally high rates of glucose metabolism in the basal ganglia, a region of the brain between the limbic system and the cerebral cortex. By the late 1980s, clomipramine, an antidepressant, was found to sharply reduce the symptoms over a period of weeks, but it had unpleasant side effects, including sleepiness, difficulty starting urination, dry mouth, and a drop in blood pressure when rising from a seated position. Currently, therefore, the medication of choice is usually one of the SSRIs—fluvoxamine (Luvox), fluoxetine (Prozac), sertraline (Zoloft), paroxetine (Paxil), or citalopram (Celexa). If an SSRI does not work, clomipramine is the fall-back treatment.[19] (Another SSRI now coming into favor is escitalopram oxalate [Lexipro]).

Given the long-standing derogation of psychotherapy and the many assertions that it is not science but, at best, a form of magical belief and, at worst, fraud, how can we account for its vast growth and wide acceptance? Some people offer sweeping social explanations: We live in a disconnected and alienated age; we seek sources of comfort and reassurance and turn to those who offer them for pay; in a secular age, psychotherapy takes the place of religious belief and is a secular sanctuary. And so on.

But if we meet some of the practitioners, eavesdrop on their clinical sessions, and look at the accumulated evidence of outcomes, we may arrive at a more empirical and less ideological explanation of the success of the psychotherapists and of psychotherapy.

Freud's Offspring: The Dynamic Psychotherapists

One of the few generalizations that can be made about psychotherapy today is that few generalizations can be made about it. By now it is practiced in accord with half a dozen or more major methods, of which there are hundreds of variants. At one extreme is the patient lying on the couch—now very rare—and pouring out random thoughts while the psychoanalyst murmurs *mmm* from time to time; at the other, an alcoholic, after taking a dose of Antabuse (disulfiram) or Temposil (citrated calcium carbimide), is served a generous whiskey-and-soda in a treatment room and soon after drinking it gasps, breaks into a sweat, complains of rapid and irregular heartbeat, dizziness, nausea, difficulty breathing, and headache, and vomits violently into a handy basin.

Nonetheless, one legitimate generalization about modern psychotherapy is that a majority of all psychotherapists use forms of dynamic therapy (also called "psychoanalytically oriented psychotherapy") at least part of the time.* These are based on dynamic psychology, which conceives of psychological problems as resulting from intrapsychic conflicts, unconscious motivations, and the interplay of external demands with components of the personality structure.

This conception, though psychological, had its origin, as we saw, not in psychology itself but in the chance discovery of a neurologist—Freud—that he had more success treating hysterics with "the talking cure" than with physiotherapy or hypnosis. Psychology was slow to adopt his discovery and theories; during the early decades of the twentieth century, while psychoanalysis was gaining ground among physicians and psychologists in Europe, clinical psychologists in America were still chiefly performing psychological testing and measurement. Some universities did open psychological clinics before World War I, but these were limited to the testing and training of children with learning problems. Psychotherapy remained an exotic and alien treatment that was practiced largely in Europe.

American medicine was equally slow to adopt psychoanalytic methods. Early in the century, American psychiatrists mainly treated hospitalized psychotics and almost entirely by physical methods: constraint, tub soaks, exercise, and physical work. But World War I produced a bumper crop of veterans with traumatic neuroses, and in consequence a number of psychiatrists, aware that psychoanalytic therapy was said to have considerable success with severe neurotics, began to take an interest in it.[20]

A few went to Europe for training, and when several psychoanalytic institutes opened in American cities, a trickle of psychiatrists and others began analytic training. Some better mental hospitals, such as the Institute of Pennsylvania Hospital in Philadelphia, invited European psychoanalysts to come train their staffs. Eventually, organized psychiatry made psychoanalysis one of its specialties and, through its psychoanalytic societies, limited training to physicians, although only a minority of psychiatrists ever took training in it and practiced it. Psychologists and others who were not physicians but wanted training had to get it in

---

*Overall data are hard to come by, because psychotherapy is not a regulated profession and many kinds of professionals practice it. Paul Crits-Christoph, director of the Center for Psychotherapy Research at the University of Pennsylvania, said in an interview for this book that a 1990 survey of 423 psychotherapists found that over two thirds identified themselves as eclectic in orientation, but that the majority of these eclectic therapists said that they most often used a psychodynamic orientation, and an additional 17 percent identified themselves as purely psychodynamic. (But as we will see, later estimates indicate that somewhat lower figures now prevail.)

Europe. Later a few institutes were founded in the United States for "lay analysts" (nonmedical analysts).

During the 1920s psychoanalysis became a favorite topic among the avant-garde, and psychodynamic concepts were taken up by the psychological establishment. As we saw, they were a major influence on Henry Murray, creator of the Thematic Apperception Test, and his research group at Harvard. By the 1930s, when a number of European psychoanalysts fleeing Nazism arrived here and the number of training institutes grew, psychoanalysis attained the status of a movement.

Like the earlier movement in Europe, however, it underwent frequent fissions. In the 1930s, some psychoanalysts in America altered and significantly added to Freudian doctrine, often distancing themselves from the main psychoanalytic body. Most notable were various "neo-Freudians" who worked out systems of their own and set up institutes to teach them. Although they did not reject Freudian dynamics, they gave social and cultural factors equal or even greater importance in character development and mental disorders. The gentle philosophic Erik Erikson, whose developmental theory we have already seen, was one of them; the fiercely independent protofeminist Karen Horney, another; and the poetic social-reformist refugee from Nazism, Erich Fromm, a third.

Another neo-Freudian of note was the psychiatrist Harry Stack Sullivan. He was an only child and the only Catholic child in his upstate New York farming community. Perhaps because of his loneliness, he became interested in the relationship between the growing child and the caretaking adult and how it affected character and behavior. The dynamic treatment he devised, "interpersonal therapy," was based in part on Freud, but rather than relying on free association, it called for the therapist and patient to engage in face-to-face discussion, with the former behaving as a real person, not as a shadowy figure on whom the patient projects transference images.

Since, in the 1930s, the usual regimen of therapy by Freudians and neo-Freudians consisted of four or five sessions per week—Freud preferred six—for at least several years, the number of patients in treatment remained limited to the few who were both well-to-do and able to spare the time. But World War II produced far more psychologically damaged veterans than had World War I—in 1946, Veterans Administration hospitals alone had forty-four thousand of them as in-patients[21]—and an urgent need for a larger corps of psychotherapists and for briefer forms of treatment. The result was a sharp growth in the numbers of psychiatrists and clinical psychologists, who were increasingly beginning to use psychodynamic concepts and methods.

At the same time, psychoanalytic notions about the human psyche, popularized by such writers as André Breton, Thomas Mann, and Arthur Koestler, and by surrealist painters, became a fad among the intelligentsia; undergoing analysis was almost a rite of passage for the avant-garde. Psychoanalytic ideas were also reaching millions of ordinary folk; Dr. Benjamin Spock's *Book of Baby and Child Care*, which advocated child-rearing practices based on Freudian views of human development, sold over twenty-four million copies between the late 1940s and 1970s and was the most important single vehicle by which Freudian psychology influenced American society.[22] Unfortunately, psychoanalytic ideas were often distorted by enthusiasts who used them as license to blame their failures on their parents. As Erik Erikson ruefully said, "Even as we were trying to devise a therapy for the few, we were led to promote an ethical disease for the many."

The impact of psychoanalysis was extraordinary, considering how few analysts and analysands there were. At the height of its popularity in the mid-1950s, there were only 619 medical analysts and about 500 lay analysts in the country and perhaps a thousand in training in some twenty institutes for physician analysts and a dozen for lay analysts.[23] While no census exists of analysands, if most analysts worked eight hours a day and saw each patient four or five times a week, the total number in treatment at any time could have been only about nine or ten thousand, an insignificant fraction of all those with mental disorders. Nor could the relatively few psychoanalysts who specialized in treating children handle more than the select few with rich parents. A case report in *The Psychoanalytic Study of the Child* in 1949 concerned a five-year-old boy who was afraid to be in school without his mother and who was cured by a psychoanalysis that lasted three years. (The analyst never considered, and perhaps did not know of, any briefer way to treat the boy's phobia.)[24]

The cost, time required, and disruption of daily life caused by regular appointments were bound to prevent the therapy from becoming widely used. But there were other obstacles. The cognoscenti soon learned, and made sport of the fact, that it often seemed a swindle, with the patient spending money, time, and effort while the psychoanalyst did and said almost nothing. Classically trained Freudians, who still consti- tuted the great majority of psychoanalysts, had become more distant and unapproachable than Freud had ever been. (Freud once said, "I am not a Freudian."[25]) Many spoke very little but simply listened to their patients, fending off questions about what they thought of the patient's narrations or symptoms with evasions like "Why does that seem impor- tant to you?" and "Why do you think I would feel that way?"

The rationale was (and still is) that the analyst's expressions of thought and feeling would make him or her a real person instead of a vague fig- ure and thereby interfere with the patient's transference—projection onto the therapist of an important figure from the patient's childhood. Such transference was, as it remains for many analytic practitioners, an essential mechanism in the curative process. But even the most rigid analyst had to communicate now and then. Psychoanalytic training stressed that changes were produced by making the unconscious con- scious through free association and through three processes requiring the analyst to speak (though not about his or her personal feelings): the interpretations of dreams, of transference, and of resistance.[26]

But though analysts did talk from time to time, many patients were aware chiefly of their silences and refusals to answer questions, and were infuriated—but unable to break away. One analyst wrote of treating an attractive young woman "who bawls me out unmercifully almost every hour, calling me immature, a quack, cold, a sex maniac, and so on, yet at the end of the hour she gives me a deep, longing look and says softly, 'See you next time.' "[27] In *The International Journal of Psycho-Analysis* another reported the following diatribe (here somewhat abridged) of a patient on one of her bad days:

> I'm fed up. A whole year I've been at this—a mixed-up, miserable, wasted year. And for what? Nothing. Not a goddam thing. One of these days I'm going to find the guts to walk out on you and not come back. Why should I come back? You do nothing for me, nothing. Year after year, you just listen. How many years do you want? Who the hell do you think you are? How can you do it?—changing no one, curing no one, raking in the money and spending your weekends in Bermuda, too gutless to admit that you're selling false merchandise. There's more humanity in my garbageman than in you.[28]

Occasionally an analyst might even let a patient who was unable to voice his or her thoughts lie silent on the couch for the whole hour, or even a number of hours, without trying to help the patient break through—yet would charge for the time spent. Humorists and satirists made this seem a common occurrence, although it was actually very rare. Apart from a sense of obligation to help the patient, most analysts would have found such hours of silence unendurable.

What were they like, these formidable authorities who could exert such power over their patients while remaining aloof and seemingly uncaring? Some, outside their clinical hours, played a role that they gradually came to believe was their real self: wise, philosophic, penetrating of gaze, given to ruminative silences, formal, witty, fiercely competitive, and easily wounded—in short, as much like Freud as possible.[29] But in truth they were no more all of a piece than are physicists, violinists, or plumbers. Psychoanalysts came (and still come) in all models, ranging from the glacial to the warm, from the austere to the amiable, from the strong to the weak. Nonetheless, some qualified observers were able to make a few generalizations about them. Arthur Burton, a lay analyst who edited a volume of short autobiographies by analysts, said that many of them feel special and lonely, are wise rabbinical teachers (even the non-Jews among them), possess certain so-called feminine qualities ("mothering," intuition, sensitivity, emotionality), and tend to be both agnostic and liberal.[30]

A very different picture was painted by the author and educator Martin Gross in a vitriolic assault in *The Psychological Society* (1978). He portrayed psychoanalysts as aloof, money-grubbing, arrogant, addicted to oneupmanship, brainwashers of their patients, exaggerators of their results, and either self-deluded believers or self-aware charlatans. There might have been a modicum of truth in his charges, but by and large nonpartisan surveys and studies of psychoanalysts portrayed them far more positively.[31] By the 1950s, moreover, many of them were shifting toward ego analysis, adopting some of the neo-Freudian emphasis on realistic interaction with their patients, and dealing actively not only with the patient's unconscious and the past but also with his or her conscious processes and present problems.

Still, the many disadvantages of psychoanalysis, even in modified form, and the development of briefer, less costly treatments, brought about a decline in its prestige and popularity during the 1960s. There were also larger reasons for its loss of status. As Glen O. Gabbard, then at the Menninger Foundation, wrote in 1990, "The post–World War II enthusiasm for psychoanalysis as a panacea for social problems led to a bitter disenchantment in the 1960s"[32]—unjustly, since psychoanalysis had never been presented as a remedy for social ills but only for individual problems. Scores of articles in professional journals and popular magazines spoke of the "crisis in psychoanalysis," of its "status decline," and of the lack of evidence that it was an effective treatment. Summing up, Dr. Judd Marmor, an eminent psychoanalyst, wrote that "the handwriting is on the wall for all to see. Psychoanalysis is in serious danger."

That was in the 1960s, and psychoanalysis has not yet disappeared. But for many years it dwindled steadily in prestige and use. By the late 1980s Helen Fischer, administrative director of the American Psychoanalytic Association, ruefully admitted that "almost no one"—she was speaking of medical psychoanalysts—"is now in the full-time practice of psychoanalysis." As for psychologists, by 1990 the American Psychological Association reported that only 2.5 percent of its clinical members considered themselves primarily psychoanalysts. Some psychotherapists, both medical and nonmedical, were still using analysis with certain patients—those who could afford it—for whom major character change, reaching deep into the unconscious, was the goal, but psychoanalysis was no longer the model and ideal of therapy, nor was it at the frontier of therapeutic knowledge and research.[33]

But as noted in the earlier discussion of Freud's life and work, the ranks of psychoanalysts, though still very small, have swelled somewhat in the past half dozen years, and psychoanalysis, gleefully pronounced dead many times in recent decades by its enemies, has regained some of its éclat, particularly because most of its practitioners have greatly modified their procedures.

True, a few hard-liners such as Glen Gabbard, who is now professor of psychiatry and director of the Baylor Psychiatry Clinic at the Baylor College of Medicine, still define psychoanalysis as "an intense treatment, four to five times per week for 45–50 minutes, generally lasting between three to eight years, [in which] the patient generally lies on the couch and free associates—that is, says whatever comes to mind—facing the ceiling, and not the therapist."[34] But even Dr. Gabbard says that Freud wouldn't recognize psychoanalysis today: "Freud believed that just recalling repressed memories would be curative, but now we understand that recollection alone is not sufficient. Also, Freud conceived of the unconscious as a sort of reservoir of sexual and aggressive impulses.

Now, thanks in part to modern neuroscience, we think of unconscious mental processes as, at least in part, procedural memory, also known as habit memory or muscle memory. The way we relate to people in early life gets internalized and repeated, in much the same, automatic way our fingers 'remember' how to play the piano. The analyst will point out these patterns of behavior—an approach quite different from Freud's notion that repressed memories will simply pop over the repression barrier."[35]

Most present-day medical psychoanalysts and the small percentage of psychologists who do psychoanalysis operate very differently from the way their predecessors in the profession did. Their practice, though the core psychoanalytic conception of the human personality and of neurotic disorders lives on in it, takes other forms that are less expensive, easier, and briefer. In one important group of variations, known as psychoanalytic, psychoanalytically oriented, or dynamic psychotherapy, typically the therapist sees the patient only once or twice a week (and sometimes less often); the patient sits and faces the therapist (Freud, you recall, could not tolerate that); and the therapist becomes a real person to the patient, discussing, querying, advising, sharing experience and knowledge, and in general being as much an educator as an elicitor and interpreter of unconscious material.

(In addition, many M.D. psychoanalysts now supplement therapy with medication and many non-M.D. psychoanalysts refer their patients to an M.D. for medication. In fact, a number of psychiatrists now practice psychopharmacology, all but laying aside psychotherapy except for enough patient-physician talk to establish diagnosis.)

The bottom line of all this is that for many of the psychologists who practice various forms of nonanalytic psychotherapy, it remains the case that psychodynamic concepts prevail and are the heart of the treatment process. Transference, for instance, can exist and be used even in weekly face-to-face therapy, though differently from the way it is in classical analysis, as in this description by the clinical mental health counselor Bernice Hunt of her relationship to a young woman she treated several years ago (the case, though relatively recent, is typical of what has been taking place in dynamic therapies for a number of decades):

She had no mothering beyond infancy—in fact, she became a caretaker before she was three, when her mother was permanently paralyzed as the result of an accident. In the therapeutic relationship I soon became the good mother hers hadn't been able to be. I sympathized, I supported, I consoled, I "gave her permission" to play as well as work, and to express her anger to others and to me. She underwent what Franz Alexander [of the Chicago Psychoanalytic Institute] called a "corrective emotional experience" and more or less relived her childhood in different form. When, as in normal development, she began to internalize our relationship, she became able, like any healthy adult, to individuate—to be mother to herself.[36]

By the 1970s and 1980s a handful of psychiatrists and psychologists were developing the techniques of "short-term dynamic therapy" based on psychoanalytic principles. The distinguished science writer Dava Sobel reported in 1982 that although short-term dynamic psychotherapy had existed in various stages of research and refinement for about twenty years, it was now "burgeoning into a recognizable force, drawing converts and controversy."[37] Focusing on a single current problem troubling the patient, these methods do not use free association, probe the unconscious, strive for insight, or overhaul the personality; they rely chiefly on the patient's transference.[38] Unlike the psychoanalyst, the therapist actively confronts the patient with the evidence that he or she is behaving toward the therapist in an unrealistic way carried over from other relationships. The therapist sometimes does this even in the first session, as described (in abridged form here) by Peter E. Sifneos, a Boston psychiatrist:

PATIENT: I put on an act. I wear a mask. I give the impression that I'm different from what I really am. Before my girlfriend broke off our relationship, she said that she didn't like going out with someone who is "a phony." Mary, my previous girlfriend, had said the same thing, using different words, and so did Bob, my best friend. I know what they are all talking about. At times, even here, I have this great urge to show off and make you admire me.

THERAPIST: And where does this urge come from?

P: From very long ago. I used to put on an act to impress my mother. I remember one time when I made up a whole story about school. I told her that the teacher had said I was the best student she ever had. My mother was impressed, but you know, doctor, it wasn't true. The teacher had complimented me, but I exaggerated it. I blew it out of proportion.

T: So you were trying to impress your mother, you are trying to impress your girlfriends, and Bob, and even here—

p: What do you mean by "even here"?

t: A minute ago you said that even here you had such a tendency.

p: Did I say that?

t: Yes, you did. Furthermore, why does it surprise you? If you put on an act with everyone else, why wouldn't you put on an act with me?

p: It did occur to me that it was possible, but this is precisely what I don't want to do. I'm here to understand why I do it so I can stop pretending. I want you to help me.[39]

In classical psychoanalysis, that point might not have been reached for months.

Going still further with this approach, in 1990 Moshe Talmon, a clinical psychologist at the Kaiser Permanente Medical Center in Hayward, California, wrote a book called *Single-Session Therapy*, in which he discussed how much could be achieved with some patients in the first session—often, especially in clinics, the only session—not by the offer of advice but by dynamic interactions.

In general, however, short-term psychodynamic therapy takes between six and twenty weekly sessions to achieve its limited goal, and has been reported effective for stress and bereavement disorders, late-life depression, and for certain emotional and personality disorders.[40] For many psychotherapists, dynamic therapies, especially the shorter and more interactive forms, are now the treatment of choice for most neurotic disorders and problems of living. There is good evidence, in fact, that much benefit takes place within a relatively few hours of therapy. A typical study shows that half of all weekly patients are significantly relieved of their acute symptoms of distress by the eighth session, although chronic and more fundamental problems take much longer.[41]

In recent years, partly due to the tight-purse policies of managed care administrators, short-term psychotherapy has established a firm place in the therapy world. A number of studies have dealt with doubts about its effectiveness; in 2001 a careful review of such studies by Bernard L. Bloom, a psychologist at the University of Colorado, found "brief psychotherapy consistently helpful, particularly for mild to moderate levels of depression . . . The frequent severity and chronicity of these conditions suggests, however, that several brief episodes of care may be necessary to achieve optimal effect."[42]

In 1990, about a third of all psychotherapists in the APA were basically psychodynamic in orientation,[43] but ever since the 1960s a number of other therapeutic approaches, very different from the psychodynamic, have been attracting sizable followings. Some of these methods seemed, when new, to be the ultimate challenge to dynamic therapy, but none has ousted it; all methods, the old and the new, continue to be practiced. Some therapists use only or mainly one; many others classify themselves as eclectic and use any of several different methods of treatment, according to need. In recent years there has been an interest in "psychotherapy integration"—the harmonizing of the several major theories of psychotherapy and the use of any and all of the major methods, depending on the nature of the problem and the needs of the patient.[44]

Let us look at these newer therapies and try to find out why, despite their profound differences, they are all, most improbably, credited with similar rates of success.

The Patient as Laboratory Animal:
Behavior Therapy

In 1951 Howard Liddell, a benign, gentle, gray-haired professor of psychobiology at Cornell, was doing research that any outsider would have considered sadistic. He was systematically creating neuroses—or symptoms analogous to those of neurotic human beings—in sheep, goats, and a large pig named Tiny. On a farm outside Ithaca, Liddell or one of his several helpers would attach a wire to one leg of a sheep in a small chamber; then he would flash a light in the chamber, and ten seconds later give the sheep a jolt of current.

At first the sheep would merely jump, but after scores of shocks it learned the meaning of the signal, and when the light flashed, it would race about the chamber as if to avoid the shock—to no avail. After about a thousand such cycles, as soon as the sheep was led into the test chamber it would begin twitching and jerking, and at the first signal would grind its teeth, pant, roll its eyes, and become rigid, staring at the floor. At this stage, even when it was turned out to pasture, it behaved abnormally; it stayed as far from its fellows as possible. It had developed the animal equivalent of a full-blown stress neurosis.[45]

Liddell also sought to reverse the process. A badly traumatized sheep would be wired up in the test chamber and would see the light flash but not experience any subsequent shock. Since a sheep is not a particularly intelligent animal, a great many innocuous flashings were necessary before it began unlearning its fear responses to the signal; eventually it would be thoroughly deconditioned.

Pigs, in contrast, are smart. Tiny had become phobic about her laboratory feed box after getting shocked a few times when she lifted the lid, so she would not go near it even when she saw food being put into it. To dispel her phobia, a graduate student fed her outside the pen, where she felt safe, until she came to trust him; then he took her into the laboratory, put a juicy piece of apple in her feed box, and talked to her soothingly while scratching her back. "What's the matter, Tiny?" he said. "Why don't you eat your apple? Go ahead, try it." He pointed to it and continued to talk softly and to pat her. Tiny grunted, tentatively tried the box, and got the apple without being shocked. After only a few such sessions she would open the box and eat from it as long as the student was near; later, if anyone was near; and finally when no one was near. She had been cured.

The induction of neurosis in animals was standard Pavlovian psychology—Pavlov himself had done something like it, and so had other experimenters in the United States—but Liddell was going further by studying deconditioning to cure the neurosis. ("Rest cures"—time spent away from the laboratory—were ineffective; the animal would improve, but on re-entering the laboratory would immediately relapse.) Liddell pursued his work and published his findings for over two decades without suggesting to any clinical therapist that the method might be applicable to human beings. When I queried him in 1952, he was reluctant to speculate but admitted that he hoped it would prove to be useful.*

It did so far sooner than he expected it to. In Johannesburg, South Africa, a general practitioner named Joseph Wolpe read the Pavlovian literature while studying psychiatry at the University of Witwatersrand in 1947 and 1948, and was greatly impressed. He conducted experiments of his own similar to Liddell's but using cats, which he made neurotic by shocking them while feeding them in a cage in the experiment room; after a while they would not eat in the cage even when half-starved. Wolpe then sought to reverse the conditioning by offering them food pellets in a room that looked quite different. Their anxiety was low

*Apparently, he was not aware that in 1924 a psychologist named Mary Cover Jones had used classical conditioning techniques to cure a three-year-old boy of a phobia of furry things by pairing the appearance of a rabbit, first far off and then closer, with his enjoyment of favorite foods.

there because of the surroundings, and they soon learned to eat in a cage in that room. Wolpe then fed them in a cage in a room somewhat like the experiment room, then in a third still more like it, and finally in the experiment room itself.[46]

He called this method "reciprocal inhibition" or "desensitization"; his theory was that if a pleasurable response (such as feeding) that inhibits anxiety occurs in the presence of anxiety-producing stimuli, it will weaken the power of those stimuli.[47] In the case of his cats, the pleasurable response to food became associated with the cage and eventually with the cage in the experiment room, overcoming the anxiety that had been created there.

Wolpe began seeking a comparable technique that might be used with his human patients. (The feeding response would rarely be strong enough in humans, and in any case would not be practical in office visits.) Retraining human beings by desensitization seemed to him an obviously more scientific way to treat neurosis than by dynamic psychotherapy. It may also have appealed to Wolpe, a small, chilly, authoritarian man, for other reasons. Many years later, a study of the personalities of therapists would find that behavior therapists—those whose methods are based on behaviorist principles—tend to be unemotional and to prefer objectivity and distance, while dynamic therapists tend to be emotional and to prefer subjectivity and interpersonal involvement.[48] Wolpe's dislike of and contempt for psychodynamic psychotherapy was absolute; as he later wrote, "There is no scientific evidence for the Freudian conception of neurosis . . . A neurosis is just a habit—a persistent habit of unadaptive behavior, acquired by learning."[49]

After some years of experimenting and reading, Wolpe found a method he thought would work; it became the basis of most of his practice from then on. He would induce a pleasant trancelike state in the patient, link its agreeable feelings by associative training with the fear-inducing stimulus, and thereby overcome the fear. (This pertains only to a neurotic fear; the procedure would be useless against fear aroused by a real and continuing danger, like living in a city under enemy bombardment.)

Wolpe would begin such treatment by spending a few hours taking a new patient's history and indoctrinating him or her with the theory that the neurosis was only one or more habits induced by experience and easily replaceable by new habits, without any need to dig into the unconscious or childhood traumas.

He would then teach the patient deep muscle relaxation, which involves the "letting go" of muscle groups first in the forehead, then the face, and so on down to the toes, until a fully relaxed, half-trancelike state is achieved. While the patient was becoming adept at achieving this, he or she and Wolpe would construct a "hierarchy," or graded list of stimuli, according to their power to arouse anxiety. Wolpe would have the patient envision the feeblest of them while in the relaxed state. Once it no longer caused any discomfort, they would tackle the next one. The patient would become progressively deconditioned, until the last and worst stimulus was associated with the relaxed state and rendered innocuous.

In a typical case report, Wolpe told of Mrs. C.W., a fifty-two-year-old Johannesburg housewife, who came to him because of overpowering fears of rejection, illness, and death, along with fears of the symptoms created by these feelings. He and she assembled a hierarchy for each of her fears. That for physical symptoms comprised nine items, the mildest of which was fear of pain in the left hand (caused by an old injury); the most severe, fear of irregular heartbeats. By her eighteenth desensitization session, he had deconditioned her to all but the three most severe items on the list, and at that session worked on her third worst fear, that of pain in her left shoulder. First, he got her deeply relaxed and had her concentrate on her pleasant feelings. Then he proceeded as follows:

> If by chance any scene should disturb you, you will indicate it by raising your left hand. First, we are going to have something already familiar to you at these sessions—a pain in your left shoulder. [In previous sessions she had said she was disturbed at imagining this.] You will imagine this pain very clearly and you will not be at all disturbed . . . Stop imagining this pain and again concentrate on your relaxing . . . Now again imagine that you have this pain in your left shoulder . . . Stop imagining this pain and again relax . . . [A third cycle followed.] If you felt in the least disturbed by the third presentation of this scene, I want you now to indicate it by raising your left hand. *(The hand does not rise.)* [The patient later reported that the first presentation of the imagined pain had slightly disturbed her, but by the third presentation it had not done so at all.][50]

By this method, Wolpe claimed, he had been able to cure not only phobias but neuroses of many sorts—usually in about one-twentieth the number of therapeutic sessions required by psychoanalytic therapy. Many of his cases were more dramatic than that of Mrs. C.W.; they ranged from an extreme fear of driving to an equally extreme fear of urine (by a youth who had been a bedwetter). Even when the presenting symptoms sounded like the kind of neurosis that would require dynamic therapy, Wolpe found explanations based on simple phobias. A twenty-seven-year-old woman came to him complaining of frigidity (Wolpe's word) and serious problems in her marriage, notably an inability to assert herself. Wolpe, rather than searching for deep psychological fears of domination, as Freudians might have, concluded after questioning that her anxiety was triggered by situations involving the sight or touch of a penis, which she found revolting.

He and she then worked up a hierarchy in which the least fearful situation, for her, was seeing a nude male statue in a park thirty feet away. After she overcame anxiety at imagining this scene, he brought her closer and closer, until she could imagine herself handling the stone penis. He then switched to a series of scenes in which she imagined herself at one end of the bedroom, seeing her husband's penis from a distance of fifteen feet. Through desensitization, she was brought closer and closer until she could imagine herself briefly touching the penis, and then doing so for longer periods of time. By about the twentieth session she reported that she was enjoying sexual relations with her husband and having orgasm about half the time.[51]

Such systematic desensitization, according to Wolpe, proved to be the method of choice for about 70 percent of his patients; for the other 30 percent he worked out other techniques. During the early 1950s, he began making his work known through journal articles, and in 1958 presented a full-scale treatment of it in the book *Psychotherapy by Reciprocal Inhibition*.

By then, a handful of other therapists had followed suit and begun practicing desensitization and developing other forms of behavior therapy. The most influential were Arnold Lazarus, another South African, who had come to the United States and was the first person to use the term "behavior therapy,"[52] and H. J. Eysenck in England. For a while, behavior therapy of neurotic conditions remained a novelty and rarity. Few clinicians practiced it, because it was diametrically opposed to the dominant dynamic tradition, and, in any case, there was no place in the United States to get training in it. But in 1966, Wolpe, by then at Temple University School of Medicine in Philadelphia, launched a program of research and training in behavior therapy. The same year, a nonprofit clinic and training center called the Behavior Therapy Institute opened in Sausalito, California; a new book, *Behavior Therapy Techniques*, by Wolpe and Lazarus (by then his colleague at Temple), appeared; and the following year Wolpe and behavior therapy were introduced to the nation's intelligentsia by an article in the *New York Times Magazine*.[53]

From that point on, research on behavior therapy and publication of articles about it increased rapidly; by the 1970s it had become a leading method of therapy and has remained so, though it has never supplanted dynamic therapy, as Joseph Wolpe felt it should. Some psychotherapists practice it exclusively; many more use it in combination with cognitive therapy (which we will look at shortly and which they call cognitive behavioral therapy); and a number of others, including some whose primary allegiance is to dynamic therapy, use behavior therapy now and then for the treatment of specific phobias such as fear of driving, flying, cats, or crowded places, which often can be cured without concomitant dynamic treatment.

A particularly interesting use of the desensitization technique is in treating sexual dysfunctions, especially impotence and female lack of orgasm. In the late 1960s, William Masters and Virginia Johnson, both sex researchers but neither one a psychologist, developed what has ever since been one of the key treatments of such difficulties when they result from anxiety, not from an organic condition. The method pioneered by Masters and Johnson involved instruction in, and the practice of, step-by-step desensitization—the procedures were carried out by the couple at home over a period of days or weeks—starting with the partners touching each other's bodies, gradually coming to fondle each other's genitals (intercourse is barred, to prevent performance anxiety), eventually inserting the penis in the vagina but without coital movement, and finally, when that condition is anxiety-free, proceeding to full coition. Unlike treatment of the simpler phobias, however, sex therapy generally required discussion of and education in the couple's relationship.[54]

The Masters and Johnson form of sex therapy was rapidly adopted and used by a wide variety of therapists. The results, however, were often less than hoped for, and over a number of years sex therapists modified the basic desensitization therapy into more of a cognitive-behavioral process, often including bibliotherapy. In one form or another, it continued to be one of the techniques used by some psychotherapists, especially those who specialize in treating sexual dysfunctions.[55]

Desensitization remains the most frequently used technique of behavior therapy, but for certain conditions different techniques developed by Wolpe and others work better. They are:

Aversive conditioning: The goal of this technique is to eliminate undesired behavior, such as alcoholism, drug use, or deviant sexuality. According to behaviorist theory, when a response to a stimulus is linked with pain or punishment, the response becomes weakened or inhibited. As a treatment, it calls for causing the patient discomfort when he or she does, or thinks of doing, whatever act is to be eliminated.

In an early form of aversive conditioning used with hospitalized alcoholics, mentioned earlier in this chapter, the patient would take a nausea-producing drug along with an alcoholic drink; the drink was followed by nausea and vomiting. After a number of such experiences, the patient might find the sight or even the thought of a drink repellent.

Later, electric shock became the preferred method for treating motivated alcoholics, heavy smokers, overeaters, persons plagued by obsessive-compulsive routines, and sexual deviants. An example: A thirty-three-year-old man sought treatment for his lifelong interest in women's undergarments and his impotence with women. He would buy panties or steal them from clotheslines, put them on, and masturbate. In treatment, he would look at a pair of panties or a picture of them or would think of them; as he did so, the therapist would give him a brief but painful shock. After forty-one sessions and 492 shocks over a fourteen-week period, the patient said that panties no longer aroused him; with this obstacle cleared away, he and his therapist were able to treat his impotence by other methods.[56]

Some therapists used aversive conditioning to treat male homosexuals, delivering a shock to them when they looked at pictures of nude males but not when they looked at pictures of nude females.[57] There were reports of modest success with this method, but when homosexuality came to be redefined during the 1970s as a sexual preference rather than a mental disorder, this use of aversive therapy was abandoned.

A mild form of aversive conditioning is called covert sensitization. Patients are trained to punish themselves by thinking some loathsome thought when they are about to do whatever it is they want to stop doing. A drinker, for instance, may be taught that as soon as he walks into a bar to buy a drink, he should visualize himself becoming nauseated, vomiting all over his hands, shirt, and suit, and on the bar and the bartender, but, as soon as he turns away and heads out, feeling better. Evidence of this method's usefulness has been scanty.

By and large, the stronger aversive methods have fallen into disfavor and now are rarely used. Not only did they involve risks to health, but aroused ethical concerns, patient resistance, and negative public perception of procedures that customarily (and intentionally) cause extremely uncomfortable consequences. These effects often lead to poor compliance with treatment, high dropout rates, potentially hostile and aggressive patients, and public relations problems. Social critics and members of the general public alike often consider this type of treatment punitive and morally objectionable.[58] The benefits, moreover, have not proven long-lasting unless alternative ways of behaving replace the inhibited one. For such reasons, most psychotherapists consider aversive therapy a last resort.

Assertiveness training: This is not a single technique but several; all aim to help patients overcome social anxieties and inhibitions and act more assertively in situations in which they have been timid and passive. Treatment begins with education: The therapist and patient discuss threatening situations and identify appropriate responses. The patient is then encouraged to try out those behaviors in mildly threatening situations, and, as he begins to feel some control, extend them to more severe ones.

An important part of assertion training is "behavior rehearsal." The patient enacts his or her role in a threatening situation, with the therapist playing the part of the threatening person (employer, spouse, neighbor). The patient has the opportunity to practice saying and doing whatever he or she needs to do in real life, with feedback and direction coming from the therapist, until the patient is skilled in the role and comfortable with the new behavior, and begins to see himself or herself in different terms.[59]

Modeling: Albert Bandura of Stanford University developed this technique based on his theory that most human behavior is learned by identifying with and imitating others of personal importance. The heart of the treatment consists of the patient's watching the therapist behave in a particular way, learning by imitation, and modifying his or her behavior accordingly. As Bandura has pointed out, this is the process by which millions of people, watching and imitating others at Toastmasters Clubs, have overcome their fear of public speaking.[60]

Modeling, first used to change the behavior of children, was soon found useful in combating phobias in adults. Typically, treatment consists of having the patient watch the model in contact with the feared object in a relatively unthreatening situation, then in a series of increasingly threatening ones. In dealing with snake phobia, for instance, the model first touches the snake, then holds it, and finally allows it to crawl over his body. The therapist encourages the patient to go through the same series of activities, even guiding the patient's hand and praising him for his efforts. Gradually, the therapist reduces the degree of demonstration, protection, and guidance until the patient, alone and without help, is able to confront the feared experience.[61]

Operant conditioning: After the success of the experiment in the 1960s and 1970s in which the behavior of hospitalized psychotics was modified by the use of rewards, many mental hospitals instituted programs based on such operant conditioning. Nurses and psychiatric technicians were trained to give tokens (poker chips, cards, or imitation coins) to patients for such desirable acts as grooming themselves, keeping their rooms neat and clean, behaving normally toward other patients, and taking on job responsibilities. The tokens were exchangeable for such privileges as a movie, a special food, a private room, or a weekend pass. Positive results were widely achieved, particularly with patients who had been withdrawn and apathetic for years. "Token economy" programs, as they are called, have also been used successfully with retarded persons, delinquents, and disturbed schoolchildren.[62]

All in the Mind: Cognitive Therapy

Nearly two thousand years ago, the Stoic philosopher Epictetus composed an apothegm that anticipated the theory behind a major form of current psychotherapy: "People are disturbed not by things but by the view which they take of them."[63]

Some may find this shallow, others too pat, but its validity is shown by the effectiveness of cognitive psychotherapy. Albert Ellis, one of the originators of this form of therapy, has summed up its basic principle in what could almost be a rewording of Epictetus's apothegm: "You largely feel the way you think, and you can change your thinking and thereby change your feeling."[64]

Cognitive psychotherapy is often called "cognitive-behavior therapy," since it incorporates elements of behavior therapy. But though the two forms overlap, they have a somewhat different focus. Behavior therapy often treats the patient like the sheep or pig whose behavior and reactions can be shaped by desensitization and other forms of conditioning; cognitive therapy seeks to modify the patient's feelings and behavior by modifying his or her conscious thoughts.

The cognitive approach to mental disorders emerged in the early years of the cognitive revolution in psychology. In the 1940s and early 1950s, several psychologists theorized that flawed cognitive processes, rather than unconscious conflicts, were responsible for many neurotic conditions. One of the therapists was Julian Rotter (whose work on internal and external locus of control we looked at earlier); both an academic and a therapist, he devised "social learning" therapy, a method of getting the patient to rethink his or her faulty expectations and values.[65]

Albert Ellis, a cognitive therapist well known to the public, has said that he was "spurred on" by Rotter's and others' writings but that he began practicing and promoting his own rational-emotive therapy (RET), a form of cognitive therapy, in 1955, and was therefore "the first major cognitive-behavioral therapist" and "the father of RET and the grandfather of cognitive-behavioral therapy."*[66]

Not exactly a modest statement, but Ellis was not a modest man. He has unblushingly written that he was "one of the most distinguished alumni of Teachers College" and "one of the best-known clinical psychologists, as well as one of the most famous sexologists, in the United States and in the world." "My 'old age,' during the 1980s," he wrote in 1991, when he was eighty-eight, "has seen my professional and public popularity, as well as that of rational-emotive therapy and cognitive-behavior therapy, steadily progress."[67] He said that "when not absorbed in something big, ongoing, and creative, [I am] easily bored," and admitted to being a workaholic — but a healthy one — whose typical workday was seventeen hours long, running from 8:30 A.M. to 1:15 A.M.[68] Not surprisingly, at ninety-three he was lean, even skinny; his long face was often saturnine but could break into a demonic grin, and except for the lack of a pointed black beard, he looked something like the operatic conception of Mephistopheles.

Even if one discounts the hyperbole, Ellis's achievements and energy were extraordinary, considering the poor start he had.[69] He has described his father as a spendthrift and runaround who gave him no fathering and his mother as given over to bridge, mah-jongg, and other

*Since 1993 it is also sometimes called "rational emotive behavior therapy," or REBT.

diversions. Young Ellis, who grew up in the Bronx, was hospitalized eight times for nephritis between the ages of five and eight, and was forbidden to play active sports, developed into "something of a sissy" where such activities were concerned, and was shy, introverted, and phobic about speaking in public. All this, he has said, helped him become a "stubborn and pronounced problem solver":

> If life, I said to myself, is going to be so damned rough and hassle-filled, what the devil can I do to live successfully and happily nevertheless? I soon found the answer: use my head! So I figured out how to become my nutty mother's favorite child, how to get along with both my brother and sister [despite] their continual warring with each other, and how to live fairly happily without giving up my shyness.[70]

In his teens and twenties, Ellis's ambition was to become a writer; he produced many unsuccessful manuscripts, but, being practical, took a degree in accounting and another in business and, despite the Depression, was able to get decent jobs. Among his unpublished manuscripts was a vast tome on sexuality, and friends often asked him for sexual advice. He liked counseling them so much that he decided to become a clinical psychologist, and, while holding down a job managing a gift-and-novelty firm, went to graduate school at Teachers College, Columbia University, and received his doctorate in 1947, at thirty-four.

For any normal man, so late an entry into the field would have meant a minor career, but not for Ellis. While working in the New Jersey mental health system for some years, he took four years of psychoanalytic training, began seeing patients of his own in 1948, and by 1952 had a full-time practice in Manhattan. He also began the abundant production of both professional and popular books on sexuality and allied matters; his radical views and frequent penchant for vulgar language made him something of a scalawag in psychotherapy, a role he seems to have delighted in all his life.

Between 1953 and 1955, Ellis began to rebel against psychoanalysis; he found it too slow, too passive (on the part of the analyst), and not suited to his personality. As he explained to Claire Warga, a psychologist who wrote about him in *Psychology Today* a few years ago:

> Patients temporarily *felt* better from all the talk and attention but didn't seem to *get* better . . . I began to wonder why I had to wait passively for weeks or months until a client showed through his or her own interpre-

tive initiative that he or she was "ready" to accept my interpretation. Why, if clients were silent most of the hour, couldn't I help them with some pointed questions or remarks? So I began to become a much more eclectic, exhortative-persuasive, active-directive kind of therapist.[71]

After experimenting for two years with techniques more to his taste, he worked out rational-emotive therapy, and in 1955 began practicing it and writing about it. Its essence, he wrote in an early paper, is that the emotions associated with neurosis are "the result of illogical, unrealistic, irrational, inflexible, and childish thinking," and that the cure lies in the therapist's "unmasking" the client's illogical and self-defeating thinking and teaching him how to think "in a more logical, self-helping way."[72] The overall tone of the therapist's—or at least Ellis's—approach is indicated by certain key words. The therapist should "make a forthright, unequivocal *attack* on the client's general and specific irrational ideas," "try to induce him to adopt more rational ones in their place," and "keep pounding away, time and again, at the illogical ideas which underlie the client's fears."

It is not easy to convey on the printed page the essence of RET, as practiced by Ellis; his provocative and challenging manner has to be imagined. The following sample (abridged here) does however capture something of the flavor and process of his method. It is part of an early session with a twenty-six-year-old commercial artist who has a steady girlfriend and has sex with her regularly but is afraid of becoming a homosexual.

THERAPIST: What's the main thing that's bothering you?

CLIENT: I have a fear of turning homosexual—a *real* fear of it!

T: Because "*if* I became a homosexual—" what?

C: I don't know. It really gets me down. It gets me to a point where I'm doubting every day. I do doubt everything, anyway.

T: Yes. But let's get back to—answer the question: "If I were a homosexual, what would that make me?"

C: [*Pause*] I don't know.

T: Yes, you do! Now, I can give *you* the answer to the question. But let's see if you can get it.

C: [*Pause*] Less than a person?

T: Yes. Quite obviously, you're saying, "I'm bad *enough*. But if I were homosexual, that would make me a *total* shit!" ... Why would you be?

c: [*Pause*]
T: Not, why would you *think* you were? But why would you actually *be* a shit if you were the one out of a hundred who couldn't make it with girls and the other ninety-nine could?*
c: [*Long pause*]
T: You haven't proved it to me yet! *Why* would you be no good? Worthless?
c: [*Long pause*] Because I'm not.
T: You're not what?
c: I'm not part of the ninety-nine.
T: "I'm not part and I should—"
c: I should be.
T: Why? If you really are homosexual, you are a homosexual. Now, why should you be *non*homosexual if you're really a homosexual? That doesn't make sense.
c: [*Long pause*]
T: See what a bind you're in?
c: Yeah.
T: You're taking the sane statement "It would be *desirable* to be heterosexual if I were gay," and translating it into "Therefore, I *should* be." Isn't that what you're doing?
c: Yeah.
T: But does that make sense? It doesn't![73]

And a brief passage from a session with another client:

T: The same crap! It's always the same crap. Now if you would look at the crap—instead of "Oh, how stupid I am! He hates me! I think I'll kill myself"—then you'd get better right away.
c: You've been listening! (laughs)
T: Listening to what?
c: (laughs) Those wild statements in my mind, like that, that I make.
T: That's right! And according to my theory, people couldn't get upset unless they made those nutty statements to themselves . . . If I thought you were the worst shit who ever existed, well that's my opinion. And I'm entitled to it. But does it make you a turd?

*Ellis was using the patient's own figures for the sake of argument (the number of homosexuals per hundred males is, of course, rather larger). He also has said (in a personal communication) that he was not agreeing with the patient that being a homosexual is bad but merely showing him that thinking it would be bad would not actually make him a bad person.

 c: No.

 t: What makes you a turd?

 c: Thinking that you are.

 t: That's right! Your belief that you are. That's the only thing that could ever do it. And you never have to believe that. See? You control your thinking. I control my thinking—my belief about you. But you don't have to be affected by that. You always control what you think.[74]

Some of this may seem hard on the patient, but Ellis has always said that confrontational RET works better than nonconfrontational RET. Warmth, on the other hand, can be harmful, in Ellis's opinion. When still in his psychoanalytic phase, he tried being warm over a ten-month period and found that it pleased his clients and made them feel good but made them sicker—more dependent and needy—than they had been, and he gave it up.[75]

Ellis formalized his ideas as "the ABC theory of RET." Activating Events (A's) in people's lives are intermingled with their Beliefs (B's) about those A's, and largely because of the B's the result is Consequences (C's)—emotional and behavioral disturbances. Later on, he spelled out in detail the multiple interactions and feedbacks among the A's, B's, and C's. For instance, a bad C—emotional reaction—feeds back into the belief system and strengthens the B (belief about an experience, and that in turn influences how the sensory system actually evaluates an experience (A).[76] The goal of RET is to get the client to make a "profound Basic Philosophic change . . . to see, to surrender, and to stop reconstructing their core musts that are at the bottom of their dysfunctional Basic Philosophic Assumptions." In sum: Rational thinking is the source of mental and emotional health.

This sounds simplistic, but it has proven to have considerable appeal. After a slow start, and despite opposition by dynamically oriented therapists, it began to catch on during the 1960s through Ellis's own ceaseless promoting, the growth of cognitive therapies in general, and the incorporation of RET in textbooks of cognitive and behavioral therapy. Ellis's practice grew ever busier. In 1959 he had founded an Institute for Rational-Emotive Therapy, bought a building on East Sixty-fifth Street in Manhattan to house it, and from then on kept the building filled from morning to late evening with clients, students, and staff.

By the 1970s, although Ellis, his students, and his methods were often attacked in professional journals, RET institutes were being founded in other cities and in Europe. In 1982, a survey of eight hundred clinical and counseling psychologists published in the APA's *American Psychologist* showed that Ellis was regarded as currently the second most influential psychotherapist (the first was Carl Rogers, of whom more shortly), and a review of references in three counseling journals found Ellis the most cited author in the early 1980s.[77] In 1985 the American Psychological Association gave Ellis its Award for Distinguished Professional Contributions, saying, in part:

> Dr. Albert Ellis' theoretical contributions have had a profound effect on the professional practice of psychology. His theories on the primacy of cognition in psychopathology are at the forefront of practice and research in Clinical Psychology. Dr. Ellis' theories have importantly encouraged an active-directive approach to psychological treatment, combined with a deep humanistic respect for the uniqueness of the individual.[78]

But the field of psychotherapy has always been one of many new developments and shifts of popularity. Over the past two decades, Ellis's key idea has been borrowed, adapted, and practiced within a host of differently named methodologies (generally in a less aggressive manner) by many others. By 2002, the APA annual convention included a roundtable titled "Will the Real Behavior Therapy Stand Up?" Dr. Ellis said on that occasion that his version was the first, and, in his view, still the most effective, but that "the entire field of psychotherapy is more eclectic since the 1980s," that "behavior therapy has become more multimodal," and that the future would be one in which "everyone is stealing from everyone . . . Within ten years I predict that all behavior therapies will be equally efficacious."[79]

To conclude this narrative on a rather dismal note, a few years after the APA roundtable, Ellis and the board of directors of his institute fell into a nasty dispute over administrative issues, and in 2005 the board forced him out. He continued, embittered but undaunted, to practice REBT elsewhere in New York City until his death two years later. Despite his ouster, he was still the winner, because his basic method, the rational treatment of mental and emotional ills, has become one of the arrows in the quiver of most psychotherapists, whatever their major orientation.

The therapist, who has done the most to advance and develop cognitive therapy did not originally owe anything to Ellis but later incorporated his fundamental premise—and often acknowledged his indebtedness to him. He is Aaron "Tim" Beck, whose name conjures respect and admiration throughout the world of contemporary psychotherapy.

At about the same time that Ellis was publishing his first papers on RET, Beck, a psychiatrist on the faculty of the department of psychiatry at the University of Pennsylvania, was taking his first step along a similar route. At that time a youthful man of modest height with a dense thatch of straight hair and a disarming smile, Beck practiced psychoanalysis, but in his own life he had earlier used behavioral and rational techniques on himself to conquer two severe phobias. As a child, he had had a series of operations, and from then on the sight of blood would make him feel faint. By the time he reached his teens he decided to defeat the phobia. "One of the reasons I went into medicine was to confront my fear," he has said, and in his first year in medical school he made himself watch operations from the amphitheater and in his second year elected to be a surgical assistant. By making himself experience blood as a normal phenomenon, he dispelled his fear. Later in life he similarly tackled a fear of tunnels, manifested as involuntary shallow breathing and faintness (he attributes the phobia to a childhood fear of suffocation caused by a bad bout of whooping cough). He got rid of the fear by pointing out to himself repeatedly that the symptoms would show up even before he entered a tunnel. Proving to himself that they were unrealistic, he gradually reasoned the fear away.[80]

Beck, until his late thirties, believed in and used psychoanalytic therapy with his patients. He was particularly interested in depression, which, according to psychodynamic theory—as he interpreted it—is the result of hostility choked back and turned on oneself, where it takes the form of a "need to suffer." The depressed person satisfies this need by behaving in ways that provoke others to reject or disapprove of him or her.

It troubled Beck that the theory was not well accepted by many psychiatrists and psychologists, and he set out to gather data from his own clinical experience to validate it. At first the evidence seemed to support the theory, but after a while he noticed contradictions and anomalies in his data. In particular, the depressed patients he was studying seemed not to be trying to be rejected by others but to win acceptance and approval. Beck underwent a loss of faith. "This marked discrepancy between laboratory findings and clinical theory," he has written in retrospect, "led to an 'agonizing reappraisal' of my own belief system."[81]

Beck, looking for a new faith, caught a glimpse of one when he resumed the study of the dreams of one depressed patient. In those dreams the patient was always a failure, unable to achieve some goal, losing an object of value, or appearing diseased, defective, or ugly. Beck had formerly interpreted the dreams as expressions of a wish to suffer; now he had an epiphany:

> As I focused more on the patient's descriptions of himself and his experiences, I noted that he consistently embraced a negative construction of himself and his life experiences. These constructions—similar to the imagery in his dreams—seemed to be distortions of reality.[82]

By means of a series of tests, Beck found that the patient "had a global negative view of himself, the outside world, and the future, which apparently was expressed in the wide range of negative cognitive distortions."

That being so, he reasoned, it should be possible "to correct his distortions through the application of logic and rules of evidence and to adjust his information processing to reality." Perhaps not just this patient but most patients could be healed by such therapy. As Beck has said, quoting the humanistic psychologist Abraham Maslow, "The neurotic is not only emotionally sick—he is cognitively wrong."[83]

This concept is the basis of the cognitive therapy of depression that Beck developed and wrote about in journal articles in 1963 and 1964, and in a 1967 book, *Depression: Clinical, Experimental, and Theoretical Aspects.* Later, through years of weekly conferences and case discussions with colleagues in the department of psychiatry, he extended the use of cognitive therapy to other neurotic conditions, and still later adapted it to the treatment of problems in couples' relationships.

For some years Beck's ideas were ignored and he was considered something of a pariah in the profession. But by the 1970s, as cognitivism pervaded psychology and, to some extent, psychiatry, his ideas were absorbed into the major theories of personality and behavior. A growing number of clinicians began relying on his methods, especially with depressed patients, and over the years some of them have modified or added to Beck's formulations and worked out their own versions. Beck, not a self-promoting person, is still not widely known among the psychologically attuned laity, but within psychology and psychiatry he is generally acknowledged as the creator of cognitive therapy. In his version and others it is now one of the leading treatments used in the United States. About a third of all psychotherapists are primarily cognitive or cognitive-behavioral; many others use cognitive-behavior therapy part of the time.[84]

Cognitive therapy did not spring full-grown from Beck's brain. He himself says that it owes something to the cognitive revolution in psychology and to the behavior therapy movement, which, to the extent that its therapy requires the patient to think about the mental steps needed to achieve change, is partly cognitive. Beck did not know of Ellis's RET when he first conceived of cognitive therapy, but he has said that Ellis's work played a major part in the development of cognitive-behavior therapies.[85]

Although Beck's system has some resemblances to Ellis's, Beck has been more decorous, gentle, and supportive than Ellis in his personal style. Beck also differs from Ellis in that he offers a more detailed cognitive theory of the neurotic disorders. In discussing depression, for instance, he has identified and labeled three causative factors:

— "the cognitive triad": the depressive's distorted view of himself or herself, his world, and his future ("I'm no good," "My life is disappointing," "Things will never improve");
— "silent assumptions": unexpressed beliefs that negatively affect the individual's emotional and cognitive responses ("If someone's angry, it's probably my fault," "If I am not loved by everyone, I'm unworthy");
— "logical errors": overgeneralization (taking one instance to represent a pattern), selective attention (focusing on some details and ignoring others), arbitrary inference (drawing conclusions unwarranted by logic or the available evidence), and others.[86]

He has made similar analyses of the cognitive distortions responsible for a number of other neurotic and even psychotic disorders.

Beck's cognitive therapy involves much more than merely pointing out to the patient his or her cognitive distortions. A crucial part in getting the patient to recognize the distortions is the therapist-patient relationship; Beck makes much of the need for the therapist to be warm, empathetic, and sincere. He has employed a variety of cognitive and behavioral techniques, among them role playing, assertion training, and behavior rehearsal.* He has also used "cognitive rehearsal." He would ask a depressed patient who cannot carry out even an old, familiar, well-learned task to imagine and discuss with him each step in the process; this counteracts the tendency of the patient's mind to wander and offsets the sense of incapacity. Patients often report that they feel better as a result of completing a task in imagination.

Beck also assigned "homework." The patient, between sessions, had to monitor his or her thoughts and behavior, make deliberate efforts to alter them, and carry out specific tasks. This not only overcame the patient's inertia and lack of motivation but also yielded actual accomplishments that tended to correct the patient's incorrect belief that he or she was unable to achieve anything. Toward the same ends, Beck also often asked the patient to write a weekly report of his or her activities and tell the degree to which each was gratifying.

The crucial work of the therapy, however, was examining, in the office sessions, the patient's ideas and correcting his or her cognitive distortions. Beck's manner of doing so was very different from Ellis's. One severely depressed woman told Beck, "My family doesn't appreciate me," "Nobody appreciates me, they take me for granted," and "I am worthless." Her evidence was that her adolescent children no longer wanted to do things with her. Here is how Beck led her to test the reality of her view of her children's feelings:

PATIENT: My son doesn't like to go to the theater or to the movies with me anymore.
THERAPIST: How do you know he doesn't want to go with you?
P: Teenagers don't actually like to do things with their parents.
T: Have you actually asked him to go out with you?
P: No. As a matter of fact, he did ask me a few times if I wanted him to take me . . . but I didn't think he really wanted to go.
T: How about testing it out by asking him to give you a straight answer?
P: I guess so.
T: The important thing is not whether or not he goes with you, but whether you are deciding for him what he thinks instead of letting him tell you.

*Past tense, because these days Beck limits himself to research and training. The Beck Institute for Cognitive Therapy and Research that he founded in 1994 is now headed by Dr. Judith Beck, his daughter; there, she and others provide therapy and training.

P: I guess you are right but he does seem to be inconsiderate. For example, he is always late for dinner.

T: How often has that happened?

P: Oh, once or twice . . . I guess that's really not all that often.

T: Is his coming home late for dinner due to his being inconsiderate?

P: Well, come to think of it, he did say that he had been working late those two nights. Also, he has been considerate in a lot of other ways.[87]

The patient later found out that her son was, in fact, willing to go to the movies with her.

As this example illustrates, the crucial aspect of Beck's style of cognitive therapy is Socratic questioning to get the patient to produce information contradicting his or her assumptions or conclusions, thereby correcting these cognitive distortions. The technique is even more apparent in this excerpt from a therapy session with a twenty-five-year-old woman who wanted to commit suicide because her husband was unfaithful and she regarded her life as "finished":

T: Why do you want to end your life?

P: Without Raymond I am nothing . . . I can't be happy without Raymond. But I can't save our marriage.

T: What has your marriage been like?

P: It has been miserable from the very beginning. Raymond has always been unfaithful. I have hardly seen him for the past five years.

T: You say that you can't be happy without Raymond. Have you found yourself happy when you are with Raymond?

P: No, we fight all the time and I feel worse.

T: Then why do you feel that Raymond is essential for your living?

P: I guess it's because without Raymond I am nothing.

T: Before you met Raymond, did you feel you were "nothing"?

P: No, I felt I was somebody.

T: If you were somebody before you knew Raymond, why do you need him to be somebody now?

P: (puzzled) Hmmm . . .

T: Have any men shown an interest in you since you have been married?

P: A lot of men have made passes at me but I ignore them.

T: Do you think there are other men as good as Raymond around?

P: I guess there are men who are better than Raymond because Raymond doesn't love me.

T: Is there any chance of your getting back together with him?

P: No . . . he has another woman. He doesn't want me.

T: Then what have you actually lost if you break up the marriage?

P: I don't know (crying). I guess the thing to do is just make a clean break.

T: Do you think that if you make a clean break, you will be able to get attached to another man?

P: I've been able to fall in love with other men before.[88]

Following this session the patient no longer felt suicidal; she began questioning her assumption "Unless I am loved, I am nothing," and after thinking over the questions Beck had asked her, she decided to seek a legal separation. Eventually she got a divorce and went on to lead a normal life.

Although by the 1970s many therapists had tinkered with Beck's detailed prescriptions, cognitive therapy technique had become fairly standardized. It generally required anywhere from six sessions (Beck prefers to call them "interviews") to many months. At each one, the therapist and patient review the latter's reactions to the previous session and its results, plan the coming steps in therapy, agree on the next tasks and homework, and apply logic, investigation, and reality testing to the patient's current perceptions and thoughts about what is happening to him or her.

By the 1980s, cognitive psychotherapy had become part of the mainstream, and in addition to the one third of all psychotherapists who were primarily cognitive-behavioral, about another third were eclectic, most of them using cognitive-behavior therapy at times.[89] It had become widely considered the treatment of choice for certain problems, particularly depression and low self-esteem. Beck, by then white-haired and benign, had become a doyen of psychotherapy. In 1989 the American Psychological Association gave him its Distinguished Scientific Award for Applications of Psychology, citing him thus:

For advancing our understanding and treatment of psychopathology. His pioneering work on depression has profoundly altered the way this disorder is conceptualized. His influential book, *Cognitive Therapy of Depression*, is a widely cited, definitive text on the subject. The systematic extension of his approach to conditions as diverse as anxiety and phobias, personality disorders, and marital discord demonstrates that his model is as comprehensive as it is rigorously empirical.[90]

That's not all. In 2004 the Grawemeyer Foundation of the University of Louisville gave him its annual $200,000 prize for outstanding ideas in the field of psychology—and in 2006 he was the recipient of the prestigious Lasker Award for Clinical Medical Research, which consisted of $100,000 and acknowledgment of the "major advance" he had made in psychotherapy.

By the time of Beck's APA award in 1989, cognitive therapy and cognitive-behavior therapy were on the rise, and since then their use has caught on almost throughout the field among professionals of many orientations. For several decades, but especially the past one, Beck, his colleagues, and other cognitive therapists have been modifying and expanding cognitive therapy to enable them to apply it to a wide variety of disorders. His original focus was on the use of cognitive therapy (CT) to treat depression, but by now special variants of it have been developed to treat such disparate problems as suicidal tendencies, anxiety disorders and phobias, panic disorder, personality disorders, substance abuse, and the psychical miseries engendered by a variety of physical ailments.

Among these variant forms of cognitive therapy are, for instance, teaching emotional regulation skills to highly reactive patients, having phobic or anxious patients expose themselves to feared situations, restructuring the meaning of early trauma through imagery, and working through a fear hierarchy with a panic disorder patient (getting the patient to tolerate a minimal fear object, then a slightly worse one, and so on step by step).[91]

A mass of research has validated the use of CT, CBT (cognitive behavior therapy), and their variants. There are now some four hundred research reports of outcome studies of CT and nearly as many of CBT.[92] Summing up the results, a number of meta-analyses—sophisticated statistical poolings of the results of these research studies—have reported various levels of positive effects, most of them relatively large. A few of the findings: large effect sizes for unipolar depression, generalized anxiety disorder, panic disorder, and a few other disorders; moderate effect sizes for CBT of marital distress, anger, and chronic pain; and small effect sizes for sexual offenders.[93]

There is no available statistic concerning the total number of people currently receiving CT and CBT, but it is undoubtedly large—and would be considerably larger except for the recent trend toward the medication of mood disorders. "Where have all the 'easy cases' gone?"

Aaron Beck recently mused. "Our hunch is that most patients respond reasonably well to their first-line treatment—by primary care doctors or psychopharmacologists. The relative nonresponders eventually may be referred to cognitive therapy—which now represents a secondary or even a tertiary—level of care."[94]

But in his introduction to a book by Judith Beck about treating these more difficult cases, he points out that she regards them as a challenge rather than a burden. Such is the admirable ethos of the cognitive therapist.[95]

A Miscellany of Therapies

The three families of therapy we have looked at—dynamic, behavior, and cognitive—are presently the major forms of psychotherapy, but a great many other kinds are available, nearly all said by their developers to be more effective, cheaper, quicker, or better in various ways than any of the big three. Before 1950, there were only about a dozen or so versions of psychotherapy, but by the early 1970s Morris Parloff, then director of psychotherapy research at the National Institute of Mental Health, counted 130; by 1988 Alan Kazdin, of the University of Pittsburgh School of Medicine, searched the key resource material and offered "a conservative estimate" of over 230 alternative treatments; and currently Paul Crits-Christoph, who, you will recall, is the director of the Center for Psychotherapy Research at the University of Pennsylvania, says that recent estimates have put the number at around 600.[96]

Bewildering as this may seem, the therapies actually fit into a relatively small number of categories: the three we have already seen, a few others that have had some significant impact on psychotherapeutic thinking and practice, and a host of others that have been flashy and newsworthy but account for very little in the real world of psychological treatment.

First, then, some of the few that are serious entrants in the historical record:

Humanistic therapies: In the 1950s humanistic psychology, the core of the "human potential movement"—whose leading spokesman was Maslow—emerged as a "Third Force" or alternative to Freudian psychoanalysis on the one hand and behaviorist psychology on the other.

The humanists, more philosophic than scientific, objected to the psychoanalytic doctrine that the individual's personality and behavior are totally determined by his or her life experiences, especially those of childhood, and also to the behaviorist view that the individual's behavior is only a set of conditioned responses to stimuli. Humanistic psychology stressed the individual's power to choose how to behave and the right to fulfill oneself in one's own way; it held that behavior should be judged not in terms of supposedly objective scientific standards but in terms of the individual's own frame of reference. If a person considered an easy-going, noncompetitive, "laid-back" life ideal, that was a valid goal for him or her, not a symptom of a character flaw; so, too, with singleness rather than marriage, sexual freedom rather than monogamy, and other departures from social norms. Humanist psychology therefore had great appeal, especially for the young, during the individualistic, rebellious 1960s.

Out of this psychology emerged a crop of variant related therapies. Though widely disparate, they are all based on the doctrine that everyone possesses inner resources for growth and self-healing and that the goal of therapy is not to change the client but to remove obstacles, such as poor self-image or the denial of feelings, to the client's use of these inner resources. The therapist does not guide clients toward a scientific ideal of mental health but helps them grow toward their own best selves. In the late 1980s about 6 percent of clinical psychologists and probably a like percentage of other psychotherapists considered themselves primarily humanistic.[97] Today the figure is undoubtedly smaller because of the dominance of the big three and the availability of psychotropic medications.

Client-centered therapy: This, the most important of the humanistic therapies, was the creation of Carl Rogers, who, born and raised on a midwestern farm, started out to become a minister. He switched to psychology and was trained in psychoanalysis but after some years concluded that it was unproductive, and made another major switch to a very different form of therapy of his own devising. A chronically optimistic man, Rogers felt that therapy should focus on present problems, not past causative factors. He also believed that people are naturally good and can solve their own problems once they accept that they are in charge of their fate, and he translated these views into a technique in which the therapist echoes or reflects what the client—Rogers rejected the term "patient"—says. This is supposed to convey a sense of respect of the client and "faith or belief in the capacity of the individual to deal with his psychological situation and with himself."[98] Here is a sample of the process from a session (abridged here) with a depressed twenty-year-old woman:

> CLIENT: It's an effort for me to walk down the street sometimes. It's a crazy thing, really.
>
> THERAPIST: Even just little things—just ordinary things, give you a lot of trouble.
>
> C: M-hm, that's right. And I don't seem to be able to conquer it. I mean it just—every day seems to be over and over again the same little things that shouldn't matter.
>
> T: So, instead of making progress, [you find that] things don't really get any better at all.
>
> C: I sort of persecute myself in a sort of way—sort of self-condemnation all the way through.
>
> T: So that you—condemn yourself and don't think much of yourself and that's gradually getting worse.
>
> C: That's right. I don't even like to attempt things. I feel like I am going to fail.
>
> T: You feel that you're whipped before you start in.[99]

This may sound like a parody of therapy, but Rogers deeply believed that by his method he created "a facilitative climate in which [the client] can explore her feelings in the way that she desires and move toward the goals that she wishes to achieve."[100] Most dynamically oriented therapists were unimpressed with Rogers's method, but in the 1950s and 1960s client-centered therapy was widely adopted and practiced by those psychologists and other psychotherapists who had not had training in dealing with unconscious processes.[101] Thereafter its influence waned; today it is the preferred technique of only a few clinical psychologists and other psychotherapists, although its humane philosophy is said to affect the way many therapists treat their clients.[102]

Gestalt therapy: Quite unlike Rogers's method, though sharing its philosophy of human health and self-direction, this is the technique developed by Frederick (Fritz) Perls, a psychiatrist. He called it Gestalt therapy, although, as noted earlier, it has little in common with Gestalt psychology. Perls's aim was to make patients aware of feelings, desires, and impulses they had "disowned" but that were actually part of them, and to get them to recognize those they think are a genuine part of themselves but were actually borrowed or adopted from others.[103]

Perls's technique for achieving this was vigorously confrontational and often harsh, and included a variety of "experiments," "games," and "gimmicks" designed to provoke, challenge, and force the patient to acknowledge the truth about his or her feelings. In filmed episodes of therapy, Perls seems at times almost sadistic, but with some patients he was very effective. Gestalt therapy was popular and deemed important in humanistic circles during the 1960s and 1970s; today it plays only a very minor part in the world of psychotherapy.

Transactional analysis: TA was in vogue in the 1960s and is the only recognized psychotherapy to have been the subject of two books on the national best-seller list for over a year (Eric Berne's *Games People Play* and Thomas A. Harris's *I'm Okay—You're Okay*). TA is based on dynamic principles, is concerned with interpersonal behavior, and deals with neurotic problems on a "rational" basis—not, however, through reasoning, like RET and cognitive therapy. It works through the therapist's interpretations of which of three ego states are responsible for a particular behavior by the patient.

These ego states or selves are the ways in which the patient acts in his or her "transactions." In any given transaction—the basic unit of social interaction—each person behaves toward another either as Child (the child self, largely emotional, that remains embedded within each of us), Parent (the set of precepts and beliefs—the "shoulds" and "should nots"—we internalized from our childhood perceptions of our parents), or Adult (the cognitive self, the mature and rational ego).

Although the three ego states are based on unconscious feelings, in TA the therapist deals with them on a conscious level, pointing out the ways in which the patient and the people he or she is dealing with are either communicating successfully or engaging in "crossed transactions." The therapist also spells out the many "games"—fraudulent or ulterior transactions that conceal the real meaning of the interaction—they play in their inappropriate roles. Patients learn to recognize which self they are being in their transactions with others (and with the therapist), and which the others are being with them. Under the therapist's guidance, they learn to utilize their Child for fun but have their Adult in charge of their serious behavior.[104] Today, TA is one of many special techniques used occasionally by some therapists.

Interpersonal psychotherapy: This short-term insight-oriented (psycho-dynamic) therapy has proven particularly useful in treating depression. It focuses on the client's current relationships with peers and family members and aims to discover how what happens in them is connected to the client's mood; its goal is to improve the way those relationships work on the assumption that this will improve the client's emotional state. The therapist helps the client think about the consequences of how he or she behaves in those relationships, alter those actions, improve communication and openness with the others, and thus modify the relationships in a beneficial fashion, all toward the end of relieving the client's symptoms.[105]

Group, couples, and family therapy: These are not specific therapeutic techniques but "modalities"; a modality is a type of therapy classified by the unit of treatment (individual, couple, family, group).

Group therapy: At least a hundred varieties exist or have existed; new ones appear every year, but many soon die out.

In the 1960s and 1970s, in keeping with the spirit of the times and the idealization of communes, "encounter groups" flourished and the group milieu was seen in humanistic circles as more therapeutic than one-on-one therapy. Later, the general view came to be that group therapy is useful primarily for interpersonal and social problems, although it does also address internal ones; members of a group provide one another with support and empathy as well as with feedback on how the social self each presents is perceived and which aspects of it are welcomed and which not.[106]

Group activities can range from discussion of one another's problems and self-revelation to role playing, and from group support of a grieving or troubled member to group attack of a member whose behavior is objectionable. In most groups the therapist steers interactions to some extent and actively intervenes to prevent the group from attacking a member destructively.

Groups range in size, although most therapists consider eight an ideal number. They usually meet once a week, cost only a fraction of what individual therapy costs, and last anywhere from eight weeks to years, depending on their goals and the therapists' orientations. Group psychotherapy used to be an American specialty but now is practiced in many countries; there are still, however, more group therapists in this country than any other. The American Group Psychotherapy Association has close to three thousand members; probably ten times that many therapists not in the association conduct groups at least part of the time.[107]

Couples therapy: Couples therapy was originally known as marriage counseling but today often proceeds at a deeper level than old-time counseling and is offered not only to married couples but to premarital, extramarital, and homosexual couples, all of whom have somewhat similar relationship problems.

The therapist's role in couples therapy is a tightrope act: If he or she is perceived by either member of the couple as siding with the other member, the therapy may be abruptly broken off. The therapist therefore seeks to avoid transferences that would generate strong feelings by either client; acts as interpreter, adviser, and teacher; and stresses that the troubled relationship, not either individual, is the client.

The therapist solicits information and makes interpretations; teaches communications skills and problem solving; plays back to the couple how they sound and look in their interaction ("Are you aware that you sat as far apart as possible?"); brings up sensitive issues that they avoid discussing with each other but can safely fight about in the relative safety of the therapist's office; and assigns homework to teach them new and more satisfying patterns of behavior. Couples therapy is usually conducted on a weekly basis, and most problems can be resolved in a year or less. In some cases, the partners in couples therapy recognize that what one or both really want is the end of the relationship. In that case, the therapist sometimes is able to help them separate cooperatively rather than combatively and minimize the damage to themselves and to the children, if there are any.[108]

Family therapy: Family therapy was developed almost simultaneously in several different places in the United States in the 1950s, most notably in Palo Alto and New York. Its basic assumption is that psychological symptoms and difficulties of all sorts stem from faulty relationships within the family rather than from individual intrapsychic mechanisms (although these are not ruled out).

Even though the family may come in with an "identified patient"—a scapegoat or supposedly sick member on whom the family blames its troubles—the therapist regards the family as the patient, or, to be more precise, the family's interactions, rules, roles, relationships, and organization. All these make up the "family system"; family therapy draws heavily on systems theory, which was borrowed and adapted from biology. In systems theory terms, the family members may be either overly or insufficiently involved with one another; cut off from outside influences by rigid family boundaries; conversely, lacking in a sense of familial belonging because of vague family boundaries; and so on.[109]

The therapist diagnoses the family's problems in systems theory terms by means of genograms (diagrams of family patterns over three generations), by determining what the alliances are within the family, and by using other methods special to family therapy. There are several schools of family therapy, each of which has developed its own intervention techniques. Family therapy is offered not only privately but in clinics and community mental health centers.

The American Association for Marriage and Family Therapy now has more than 23,000 members, who come from various disciplines and have met the association's requirement of training and supervised postgraduate experience as marriage and family therapists. Many other thousands of psychotherapists, who may or may not have had extensive training in marital and family therapy, call themselves marital and family therapists—the term is not controlled by law in most states—to indicate that they deal with couples and family problems as well as individual ones.[110]

Odds and ends: In addition to all the above, a large selection of other brands of therapy is available, at least in America's major cities and particularly in California. Some are strange but based on sound psychology; others are even stranger and based on pseudo-scientific or mystical ideas. All told, they are essentially trifling in their contribution to mental health treatment. A random sample:

Primal theory requires the client to engage in prolonged screaming in order to release infantile rage. The client is taught to do this at home when necessary.

Morita therapy, developed in Japan, is based on Zen principles and begins with four to seven days of total bed rest, isolation, and sensory deprivation. Thereafter, the patient is taught to accept his feelings and symptoms and to live actively in the present, directing his thinking away from himself and toward the world around him.

696   The Story of Psychology

Ordeal therapy assigns the patient to a task or situation worse than the presenting problem, such as getting up in the middle of the night, every night, to exercise.

Paradoxical prescription, employed to break down powerful resistances, consists of telling the patient to keep on with his problem behavior or even to step it up. The permission to do the impermissible is supposed to defuse it, rob it of its perverse value, and lead to a breakthrough.

Positive psychology, discussed in an earlier chapter, is an umbrella term for a therapeutic regimen that, while not ignoring what is known about human suffering and disorders, stresses positive emotions, positive character traits, peak experiences, and an understanding of happiness. It has been widely publicized by its originator, Martin Seligman, but accounts for only a minuscule percentage of psychotherapy patients.

Hypnosis or, more precisely, post-hypnotic suggestion, sometimes helps people control their smoking or overeating, overcome stage fright, and deal temporarily with other undesirable traits.

EMDR (Eye Movement Desensitization and Reprocessing): After several initial stages of preparation, the client focuses on the image of the cause of the disorder and moves his/her eyes back and forth following the therapist's fingers as they move across his/her field of vision for twenty to thirty seconds or more. This is repeated a number of times during the session. It is supposed to eliminate the influence of the source of the image.

est (Erhard Seminars Training), popular in the 1970s, consisted of two weekends spent in a ballroom (at a cost of $250). Bathroom privileges were denied except at official breaks, and the audience was subjected to a day-long barrage of abuse by the leaders ("You are all assholes . . . You're nothing but a goddamn machine"). When the clients were sufficiently exhausted and humiliated, the secret of life was revealed: You *are* a machine, cannot be anything but, and can be happy only by being what you are. Werner Erhard stopped holding sessions in 1991, but a firm called Landmark Forum continues to run est-type meetings.

Special-purpose workshops last half a day or all day, and sometimes for a whole weekend, with time out only for food, toilet use, and sleep. Lectures, group therapy, sensitivity training, and other activities are all used to deal with feelings and emotional symptoms stemming from a problem the attenders share: child abuse, incest, spousal abuse, fear of revealing oneself, and many others.

And all those others: What shall we call them? Well, let's not call them anything but merely mention a few in passing: orgone therapy (in which the patient sits in a special box that supposedly collects a curative energy pervading the universe), dance therapy, past lives therapy, miracles therapy, healing through visionary experience, aromatherapy, mindfulness, therapeutic touch . . . but it is time to call a halt. We have gone beyond the bounds of science, even though many people think of these fringe activities as psychotherapies based on psychology.

But Does It Really Work?

In his autobiography, the late H. J. Eysenck proudly termed himself "rebel with a cause." Indeed, many causes. After leaving Germany for England in his youth, he enthusiastically laid about him in sundry educational, political, and scientific battles, even while making solid contributions in several areas of psychology. Long a professor and researcher at the Institute of Psychiatry, University of London, and with an impressive list of published and widely cited contributions on intelligence, testing, and personality, he, like Ellis (but on a serious plane), was always a resolutely cheerful bad boy of psychology.

None of his imbroglios was more heated than the one brought about by his historic assault on psychotherapy in 1952. Eysenck had always been contemptuous of psychotherapy, which he felt was unsupported by any scientific evidence. To prove the point he reviewed the data of nineteen studies reporting the results of psychotherapy and came to some shocking conclusions. The different studies claimed "improvement" in as few as 39 percent and as many as 77 percent of the cases, a range so broad as to justify suspicion, he said, that something was amiss. Far worse, Eysenck added up the findings and calculated that, on average, 66 percent of the patients had improved—and then cited other studies reporting that of neurotic patients who had custodial care but no psychotherapy, 66 to 72 percent had improved. His conclusion: There was no evidence that psychotherapy was responsible for its supposed effects. His radical corollary to that conclusion: All training in psychotherapy should be abandoned forthwith.[111]

"The sky fell in," he later commented. "I immediately made enemies of Freudians, of psychotherapists, and of the great majority of clinical psychologists and their students."[112] As was to be expected, many of his newly made enemies—including prestigious names in British and American psychology—wrote angry replies. Anger aside, they had good grounds for discrediting his findings, and published rebuttals in a number of leading British and American psychology journals. Their most telling criticisms were that Eysenck had lumped together data derived from different forms of therapy, different kinds of patients, and different definitions of improvement; moreover, the untreated group was not truly comparable to the treated groups.[113] Still, he had thrown down the gauntlet; it was now up to those who believed in psychotherapy to prove that it was effective, a task they had never seriously undertaken.

Ever since, there has been a steady flow of psychotherapy outcome studies—many hundreds, in fact—differing greatly in scientific quality, in the size of the samples studied, in the criteria of improvement, and in the use or lack of use of control groups. Their findings, accordingly, have shown great variation.

But meta-analyses that rate the studies by scientific quality, adjust for differences in method, and only then sum up the results, have repeatedly found that the weight of evidence is clearly in favor of psychotherapy. In 1975, a painstaking meta-analysis of nearly a hundred controlled studies, by Lester Luborsky of the University of Pennsylvania, concluded that most of them found a high proportion of patients benefiting from psychotherapy. And, contrary to Eysenck's claim, two thirds of the studies showed that significantly more treated than untreated patients improved.[114] (If studies involving minimal treatment had been excluded from the Luborsky review, the superiority of therapy over no therapy would have appeared still greater.)

A comprehensive review of outcome studies made in 1978 by a team at the National Institute of Mental Health came to a similar conclusion.[115] In 1980 a still more comprehensive meta-analysis by another team of psychologists reviewed and evaluated the findings of 475 studies, using a wide range of outcome measures to compare the experience of patients who received psychotherapy with untreated members of control groups. Its conclusions were unequivocal: Therapy yields benefits in most, though not all, cases.

Psychotherapy benefits people of all ages as reliably as schooling educates them, medicine cures them, or business turns a profit . . . The average person who receives therapy is better off at the end of it than 80% of the persons who do not. This does not, however, mean that everyone who receives psychotherapy improves. The evidence suggests that some people do not improve, and a small number get worse.[116]

But one aspect of the findings of these meta-analyses seemed baffling: All forms of therapy appeared to benefit about two thirds of the patients. Yet if each kind of therapy works for particular reasons—as spelled out by the theory it is based on—how could all work equally well? Luborsky's team wondered whether it was really true that, as in the dodo bird race in *Alice in Wonderland*, "everyone has won and all must have prizes," and concluded that it did seem to be true. Their explanation was that there are common components among the psychotherapies, most notably the helping relationship between therapist and patient. Other researchers pointed to other common factors, especially the chance to test reality in a protected environment, and the hope of relief, generated by therapy, that motivates the patient to change.

Yet the dodo bird hypothesis is exceedingly counterintuitive; common sense and lifetime experience tell us it is most unlikely that despite the great differences in therapeutic methods, they all work equally well for all conditions. The meta-analyses assure us that psychotherapy does work, but the overall figures they give do not link particular techniques to the outcomes of particular disorders. Moreover, they average out the results achieved by different therapists in each study.

Luborsky and colleagues, seeking to demystify their own findings, did a later study of therapists who used three different approaches in treating drug-dependent patients and found that the choice of therapy was less important than the personality of the therapist.[117] More important has been the development, in recent years, of a genre of outcome studies that test the results of specific techniques in the treatment of specific disorders. Such research has furnished ample evidence that certain forms of therapy are anywhere from somewhat to much more effective than others in the treatment of particular conditions.

We have already heard of some of these results; among others, a technique known as "cognitive-behavioral treatment with response prevention" is markedly superior to other methods of treating OCD (obsessive-compulsive disorder); CT with exposure to a feared object or situation yields better results with anxiety disorders than other methods; psychodynamic therapy is effective in the treatment of depression if the therapist is a warm and supportive person (but, overall, CT and interpersonal therapy do as well); both CT and CBT are more effective than medication in the treatment of anxiety symptoms; CBT is more effective than medication for treating insomnia; and similar findings show other techniques to be especially effective with other disorders.[118] Some of these results have been further substantiated by cognitive neuroscience: Brain scans have shown, for instance, that CBT produces changes in the brain of a depressed patient quite different from those of medication. Both methods relieve symptoms, but medication produces a bottom-up change while psychotherapy produces a top-down and hence more lasting change.[119]

The new outcome studies are, moreover, part of a movement within medicine and psychotherapy known as "evidence-based treatment." In recent years the American Psychological Association, the American Psychiatric Association, the U.S. Agency for Health Care Policy and Research, and several managed care companies all have proposed psychotherapy practice guidelines based on treatments of mental disorders that have been empirically proven effective. Paul Crits-Christoph calls this movement "the biggest change in therapy of the last ten years."

That's a change? Haven't psychotherapists always been guided by the evidence of outcomes of various forms of treatment? Yes, by the outcomes of their own practices. But no, not by empirical research studies. The editors of A Guide to Treatments That Work, a massive 2002 review of empirical studies of psychotherapies and psychotropic medications, acerbically note the "lamentably low value psychotherapists and other mental health professionals more generally continue to attach to psychotherapy research . . . The clinical activities of most psychotherapists remain largely untouched by findings from empirical research. Many clinicians continue to utilize methods and procedures that lack empirical support."[120]

One reason for this is the well-documented phenomenon known as the "expectancy effect." Therapists (like physicians and scientists) tend to see the results, in their own work, that they expect to see. The results reported by any therapist based on his or her own practice fall far short of the guidelines of scientific rigor. To be genuinely empirical, evidence must be produced by impartial researchers, and by comparing the outcome in a treated group with that in a control group (a strictly similar but untreated group), which enables the researchers to subtract the expectancy effect, the placebo effect, and other distortions from the apparent effect of treatment.

When the APA's Division of Psychotherapy raised the issue of evidence-based therapy a decade ago, there was a fierce backlash from therapists who feared they would be controlled by managed care officers who would refuse to reimburse them if empirical evidence did not back up the therapy they preferred to use. A heated debate—a "major controversy," according to an APA Web page offering a course in evidence-based psychotherapy—has continued ever since.

Yet the concept of empirical evidence as a guide to treatment is not new; in medicine it goes back a century or more, and it has been part of the world of psychotherapy for decades. "What's different today," says Crits-Christoph, "is that the label 'evidence-based therapy' now has political clout. From the early sixties through the nineties there was no process for turning research into practice. No one was pressuring anyone to sign on the dotted line that you would translate empirical research findings into practice." In England, under socialized medicine, evidence-based therapy is enforced; here, it is beginning to be enforced by managed care providers—and by moral suasion.

For despite the resistance to the evidence-based movement, says Crits-Christoph, "It has raised consciousness of the importance of empirical evidence. The concept of evidence-based therapy has become a fundamental guiding principle. It's getting very hard to disagree with the idea that empirical evidence should shape practice."[121]

Very hard to disagree with the idea—and with the evidence assembled in *A Guide to Treatments That Work* (and other more recent compilations). The *Guide* presents the results, primarily of rigorous studies plus some less than rigorous, of dozens of pharmacological and psychotherapeutic treatments of over two dozen major disorders. We heard above of some of the treatments that work; here are a few others:

— bipolar disorders: lithium and several other medications are effective; psychosocial treatments, including CBT, increase medication adherence.
— bulimia: antidepressant drugs produce significant short-term reduction in binge eating and purging; CBT ends binge eating and purging in roughly half the patients.
— major depressive disorder: behavior therapy, CBT, and interpersonal therapy all yield substantial reductions in depression.
— OCD: SSRIs reduce or eliminate both obsessions and compulsions; CBT involving exposure and ritual prevention methods is also a first-line treatment.

— panic disorders: CBT, in vivo exposure, and coping skills acquisition have proved effective.
— social phobia: exposure-based procedures and multicomponent CBT effectively reduce or eliminate the symptoms.
— specific phobias: exposure-based procedures, especially in vivo exposure, eliminate most or all components of specific phobia disorders.

All of which is as convincing an answer to the question "But does it really work?" as anyone could ask for.

The new forms of outcome research and the moral (and financial) pressure of the evidence-based ethos are making psychotherapy, in alliance with psychopharmacology, increasingly scientific and increasingly effective. Perhaps even the specter of Wundt, were he presented with the data, might relax his dark scowl and grudgingly nod approval.

EIGHTEEN

Users and Misusers
of Psychology

Knowledge Is Power

Whatever the phantom of Wilhelm Wundt might think of present-day clinical psychology, the flesh-and-blood Wundt was incensed at the sight of his science put to other disgracefully practical uses — and by some of his favorite students.

One of them, Ernst Meumann, committed what Wundt saw as apostasy, abandoning pure research in order to apply psychological principles to education. Even worse, two others hawked their knowledge to business and the public. In 1903 Walter Dill Scott, a professor at Northwestern University, published a book on the psychology of salesmanship and advertising, and in 1908 a prize pupil of Wundt's, Hugo Münsterberg, whom William James brought over to be director of the psychology laboratory at Harvard, published a book on the psychology of courtroom testimony and in 1915 another on applications of psychology to everyday problems.

Münsterberg, although an archetypal German professor, reactionary in his social views (he vehemently maintained that woman's place was in the home) and of formidable appearance (austere mien, pince-nez, jutting chin, a pointed guardsman's mustache), had become a leading figure in American psychology. As such, he seems to have been ambivalent about his identity. Although he energetically promoted applied psychology in books, articles in popular magazines, and lectures before large audiences, he sought to preserve his status as a scientist by producing a number of ponderous tomes of abstruse psychological theory. He could have spared himself the effort: His applied psychology had major impact; his theoretical work, none.

Many psychologists were affronted by Münsterberg's advocacy of applied psychology, but the public liked it. Of greater consequence, a few adventurous businessmen asked Münsterberg and his students to use their psychological knowledge to improve workers' efficiency, make advertising more persuasive, and help select the job applicants best able to perform specific tasks.

On behalf of a telephone company, for instance, Münsterberg developed a test to identify women with the aptitudes needed for competent switchboard operation. To check up on him, the company secretly included several skilled operators among the thirty job applicants it sent him; happily for Münsterberg, the skilled operators scored at the top of the list.

Less happily, at the outset of World War I Münsterberg made a number of pro-German public statements that destroyed his prestige; when he died in 1916 the American Psychological Association, of which he had once been president, published not one word of eulogy.[1]

Münsterberg's efforts to be both an applied and pure psychologist symbolizes an age-old debate about the value of knowledge. Most intellectuals have held that it is worth pursuing for its own sake, without any thought of possible utility; many if not most scientists have prided themselves on conducting research without thought of its potential business applications, and considered applied research less prestigious, more commercial, and soiled by the goals of sales and profit. But most leaders of society and most ordinary people have felt that scientific research — including psychological research — is worthwhile only if it has some practical use. This view has been particularly dominant in the pragmatic, industrial-technological society of America, with whose values it is in harmony.

Not surprisingly, therefore, as basic psychology blossomed during the past century, applied psychology soon caught on and flourished. Today it is manifest in a myriad of university departments, a number of applied psychology journals, textbooks, and several societies and annual conferences.

Moreover, the long-dominant view that research moved in one direction — from basic to applied — has recently been challenged in various ways. In 1997 Donald Stokes, a political scientist, made a convincing case in *Pasteur's Quadrant* that, rather than a single straight line of development from basic to applied research, the two are different dimensions between which there is an area of multidirectional interaction; Pasteur's great work, he pointed out, was applied, practical, and basic all at the same time.

Not long afterward, Rodney Nichols, president of the New York Academy of Sciences, proclaimed, "Revolutionary advances also come out of mission-oriented research. It is possible—indeed, often natural—to fulfill a social goal *and* create even richer scientific results than pure curiosity engenders."[2] A current textbook of applied cognitive psychology says, "When a product or service is especially compelling, researchers seek to derive the basic principles that made the product or service useful in the first place."[3] Significantly, a number of recent government research grants have backed the concept that applied research can lead to new basic knowledge.[4]

And some basic researchers who have switched to applied research find it intellectually (as well as economically) rewarding. Donald Norman, for years a leading figure in cognitive science, left academia for applied research in 1993 (but now holds positions in both camps); what intrigues him about applied cognitive psychology, he says, is that "technology expands the human mind, its perceptions, its interactions with the world. Consider the screwdriver: It extends your perceptual system. That's a metaphor for all sorts of technological advances. My book, *Things That Make Us Smart*, is about things that are not just tools but extensions of our minds."[5]

That pertains to product design, but applied psychology takes many other forms and exerts many other influences on society and everyday life. We have already seen a number of early applications of basic psychological research and theory to practical ends, among them:

— intelligence testing by the Army in the two world wars to screen out unfit draftees;
— intelligence and ability testing by many schools throughout the nation in order to group children in classes according to their ability to learn;
— the use of perception principles in the testing of candidates for pilot training by the Army Air Corps in World War II;
— the citing by the Supreme Court of psychological research findings in its momentous *Brown* v. *Board of Education* decision, and the resulting integration of public schools;

— the education of parents, through the popular media and other means, in the normal stages of child development and the kinds of parent behavior that most benefit the child at each stage;
— and, of course, all the forms of psychotherapy and their huge impact on the mental health and behavior of Americans. And on their physical health: A number of studies have shown that people who make heavy use of medical services reduce that use by as much as a third after mental health treatment.[6]

These are only a few of the ways in which psychological knowledge has been applied over the past century. In recent decades the field has burgeoned. Clinical and other applied psychologists now make up well over half the total membership of the American Psychological Association and probably at least that proportion of nonmember psychologists, and American society is profoundly influenced by their work in the following (and many other) ways:

— Each year, the plans of 1.5 million high school seniors are determined in large part by their scores on SATs (formerly known as Scholastic Aptitude Tests) and over 1 million by their scores on ACTs (American College Testing), both designed by educational psychologists; many schools do not even consider for admission those who score below some cutoff point.
— The hiring of millions of people for positions ranging from assembly-line jobs to managerial posts is governed in considerable part by their scores on tests of intelligence, aptitude, honesty, and personality traits.
— As a people, we spend billions of dollars each year to improve our performance at work, in sports, and in personal relationships through various forms of training, many based on psychological findings.
— A multibillion-dollar flood of TV and radio commercials and print-media advertisements significantly influences our tastes, purchases, everyday behavior, and voting preferences. Much of that communication uses techniques of persuasion recommended by psychological consultants (or, to call them by the disquieting term now used by some textbooks of applied psychology, "compliance professionals").
— Countless products, appliances, gadgets, medications, food supplements, books and magazines, insurance programs—and so on and

on—that we buy and use have been partly or wholly designed in accordance with psychological research about our preferences (or in many cases susceptibilities) or the preferences of particular age groups, racial groups, gender, and other criteria.

All of which raises the question: Does applied psychology use scientific knowledge to better the human condition, or misuse it for selfish goals and at considerable cost to its targets?

It does both, of course. All scientific knowledge can serve good ends or bad ones, often both at the same time. The norms and structure of each society determine which choice or mixture of choices prevails. For example, American society, by richly rewarding the healing of the ill and the postponement of death, has fostered the development of such measures as respirators and devices to maintain nutrition and hydration, but by failing to modify its traditions and laws, obliges doctors to prolong life in the terminally ill, the permanently unconscious, and the hopelessly agonized.

So, too, with psychology. Of its many applications, some improve individual and collective life while others benefit their practitioners but harm those they are used on. Knowledge, once gained, cannot be expunged from our collective consciousness, nor would we want it to be, but as a society we have not yet learned to encourage the uses of psychology and at the same time recognize and limit or even prevent its misuses.

What follows is not an overview of the broad range of applied psychology (which would require a book as thick as this one) but a series of brief sketches of a few of its beneficial and harmful influences on our lives today.

Improving the Human Use of the Human Equipment

A number of applications of psychology enable human beings to make more efficient or more salutary use of their capabilities and responses. Among them:

Health psychology: Some of these applications ameliorate or cure mental and physical illnesses linked to psychological factors. Psychotherapy, of course, is the major example. Others include diagnostic procedures and situational or social interventions. A few instances:

— The Type A Behavior Pattern (TABP), that of people who are unusually ambitious and aggressive, tense, given to rapid speech and quick action, and easily irritated and provoked to hostility, was suspected for many years to be a cause of coronary heart disease. By 1981, a number of studies offered enough evidence for the National Heart, Lung, and Blood Institute to conclude that TABP was associated with increased risk of CHD. Since then, however, further research has modified this conclusion; recent studies have found that it is the "Anger/Hostility" dimension—only a part of TAPB—that is most predictive of CHD. While TABP and its anger-hostility component seem to be an innate personality tendency, stress reduction training can mitigate it greatly. Also, the situational factors that provoke it can be minimized or avoided. Informed parents, for instance, can consciously play down their emphasis on a child's need to achieve; they can also select schools that minimize competition. Adults with TABP can change to a less competitive work environment or even, if necessary, a less competitive career.[7]

— Social psychologists and epidemiologists have found a statistical connection between the disruption of social ties and networks by events like migration, divorce, or death and a number of physical and psychological illnesses. For instance, depression and a concomitant weakening of immune response are markedly more common among divorced and widowed people than married ones. The antidote recommended by psychologists is social support, which, much recent research has shown, moderates the vulnerability to stress. Accordingly, support groups of many kinds have proliferated throughout the country. There are groups for the elderly, impaired, families of substance abusers, and cancer patients (particularly women who have undergone mastectomy), and hospice programs that tend to the needs of the terminally ill and their family members.[8]

— The normal decline of memory in the aging is often a cause of severe distress, lowered self-esteem, depression, and withdrawal from social situations. Lately, clinics in a number of universities and other centers have been offering training in mnemonic and other associative techniques that compensate. One leading clinic has reported that after a two-week course, middle-aged and older trainees could recall the names that went with faces as well as or better than they could when young.[9] Research-based methods of memory improvement are now also available in books, on the Web, and on CD-ROMs.

— Many health maintenance organizations and medical clinics use methods derived from the psychology of motivation to get patients to take their prescribed drugs and carry out recommended activities. Among the techniques: presenting patients with indisputable evidence of benefit; providing proof that recognized authorities back the procedures; and rewarding patients, particularly those on weight-loss diets, with encouragement, approval, and chart displays of their progress.

Educational psychology: By the 1960s, psychologists and educators had amassed evidence that disadvantaged children are cognitively and culturally ill-prepared for school, and that this is why they fall farther behind other children year by year. Head Start, begun in the 1960s as part of President Johnson's War on Poverty, was a large-scale experiment intended to offset the learning difficulties of poor children by giving them special education to supply the skills and background they need to succeed in school.

But for political reasons Head Start was launched hurriedly, without plans for properly assessing its effects. Only after the program had been running for some years did Congress ask to have it evaluated. Researchers then compared a number of first-, second-, and third-grade children who had taken part in Head Start with similar children who had not, and found, distressingly, that the Head Start students were doing no better in school than the others. The finding touched off a raging controversy. Defenders of the program said that the two groups were not really equivalent—that Head Start had attracted those who needed it most and would have done even worse without it. Attackers said the program had proven that compensatory special education had no lasting effect and that the children's poor environment prevailed.[10]

The debate continued year after year, with some studies reporting success and others reporting failure, and with other programs designed by researchers rather than social activists yielding more hopeful data. By 1982, the pooled findings of eleven well-designed studies of early enrichment programs showed that children in the programs had done better than the control groups of comparable children and had scored higher on IQ tests for several years.[11] Unfortunately, the gains were not permanent, and for a fundamental reason: after three decades of experience, a careful summary of the evidence yielded a mixed finding and an explanation:

> The empirical literature . . . delivers good news and bad news. The bad news is that neither Head Start nor any preschool program can inoculate children against the ravages of poverty. Early intervention simply cannot overpower the effects of poor living conditions, inadequate nutrition and health care, negative role models, and substandard schools. But good programs can prepare children for school and possibly help them develop better coping and adaptation skills that will enable better life outcomes, albeit not perfect ones.[12]

In many other ways and on a far larger scale, psychology has been applied in education for several decades. We have already seen most of them and can pass by with a summary note of how things stand today: Throughout the nation some 25,000 school psychologists test and assess students and provide short-term therapy, and several thousand educational psychologists use learning theory and research data to design effective teaching methods and teach them to students in teachers' colleges.

Human engineering: Early in the century, engineers who designed machinery, automobiles, appliances, and other mechanical devices occasionally gave thought to making the controls and gauges of the equipment fit natural human perceptual and motor capabilities. Even in early automobiles, for instance, the steering wheel was linked to the front wheels in such a way that to turn left, the driver turned the wheel to the left. This may seem an obvious design, but the very first automobiles were steered by a tiller, which the driver had to push to the right to make the car turn to the left, and vice versa. Similarly, some designers tried, on an intuitive basis, to make the dials and controls of radios, power tools, and factory machinery operate in what felt like a natural way.

But as long as this was left to engineers—as was largely the case until World War II—a great deal of equipment had dials and controls that were hard to interpret or hard to fine-tune. Some required unnatural or needlessly complicated human movements that swelled the likelihood of mistakes and accidents. An example was the British Mosquito, a

World War II fighter-bomber designed before psychologists appeared on the scene. The throttles were on the pilot's left and the landing-gear control on the right. Consequently, at take-off the pilot had to let go the throttles in order to hold the wheel with his left hand so that he could reach over with his right to raise the landing-gear lever, although the throttles, when he let them go, tended to jiggle back, reducing power just when maximum power was essential.

During the war, when many kinds of new and more complicated military equipment were being developed, the military services and their contractors began hiring psychologists to help make the products compatible with human perceptions and responses; this was the start of what became known as human engineering or engineering psychology. Psychologists redesigned equipment to increase the legibility of instrument dials, the ease with which an operator could make fine adjustments of controls, the naturalness of the movements required, and the like.[13]

Jack Dunlap, a naval officer in charge of a unit doing research on gunnery training, had been a professor of psychology at Fordham. His firsthand experiences of gunnery equipment and his understanding of the psychological difficulties in using it led him, after the war, to form the first human-engineering firm, Dunlap & Associates. A short, rotund, ebullient man, Dunlap had both the expertise and exactly the right outlook for applied psychology. "Balls of fire!" he genially roared at one visitor in 1951. "I can't stand all this academic horseshit about pure science. Science isn't worth a damn unless it makes life better for people."[14]

The firm's growth was phenomenal. Dunlap started it in 1948 with a capital investment of $21,000 and within three years was grossing over $700,000 from work for the Department of Defense, an airplane manufacturer, an office machine company, a maker of heavy electrical equipment, and a flashlight manufacturer, among others.

A typical bit of Dunlap & Associates human engineering solved a pharmaceutical company's problem of incorrect pill counting (overcounts meant lost income, undercounts violated federal law, and both were far too frequent). A workman counting pills would not actually count them but would slide an aluminum board with, say, a hundred little indentations into a bin of pills. When he slid it back out, pills rested in nearly every hole, and at a glance he could see that he merely had to add four or five by hand to what the board had picked up, then dump the lot into a hopper for automatic bottling. At least, that's how it should have worked, but the pill counters kept making errors. A Dunlap staffer, after studying the process, realized that the color of the boards did not contrast sharply with the color of many pills. He added a dab of orange paint to the bottom of each indentation with the result that any hole not filled by a pill showed up like a warning light. Accuracy shot up instantly; problem solved.

Since the 1950s human engineering has been a recognized branch of applied psychology; its practitioners work on everything from jumbo jets and subway control centers to cell phones and home computers. Psychologists in human engineering have researched scores of such questions as whether a rotating calibrated dial that moves past a fixed marker is easier to read than a pointer that rotates around a fixed calibrated dial (the rotating dial is easier), and how to make the handles of controls easier to recognize (one way: by color coding them; another: by giving them shapes that signify their use even without one's looking at them — for instance, giving a landing-gear handle a round, wheel-like end, a flap handle a flaplike wedge shape).[15]

Until recently, the most potentially disastrous equipment in America, its nuclear power plants, was designed largely without the benefit of human engineering. After the 1979 accident at the Three Mile Island nuclear power plant, the Nuclear Regulatory Commission belatedly realized that there had been a dearth of human engineering psychologists on the staffs of firms that designed and built America's nuclear plants. That may have been why the operator-machine system at Three Mile Island had serious flaws. The indicator that should have warned operators of a stuck valve in the automatic shutdown system was not designed to call attention to itself; almost 30 percent of the system displays were too high to be read by operators; colors that signified normal conditions on some control panels signified a problem on others. As a result of these findings, the NRC hired about thirty psychologists and, heeding their recommendations, issued new regulations and guidelines for the nation's nuclear plants.[16]

A few other typical findings by specialists in human engineering:

— Equipment users can read data faster and with far fewer errors from analog displays such as the hands of a watch or an aircraft altimeter than from digital displays with numbers appearing in a control panel window.
— They comprehend bar graphs, pie charts, and other visual displays more readily than alphanumeric displays.
— They can grasp at a glance the information and relationships of sev-

eral kinds of data that must be read simultaneously if the data are presented on a monitor as a single symbolic shape, like a polygon with sides of varying length.

— Finally, a surprising recent finding: Attractive things are easier to use—and work better—than ugly things. In a study by two Japanese researchers and another by an Israeli, people found ATMs with attractive layouts easier to use than ATMs with unattractive layouts, even though the screens, the number of buttons, and how they operated were identical.[17] "These and related findings," says Donald Norman, "suggest the role of aesthetics in product design: Attractive things make people feel good, which in turn makes them think more creatively. How does that make something easier to use? Simple, by making it easier for people to find solutions to the problems they encounter."[18]

Environmental psychology: This latter-day specialty deals with the ways in which human beings use and are influenced by their physical environment. Three examples:

Territoriality: Like most animals, human beings have a strong impulse to control the space around them. When a group of people feel that a certain area belongs to them collectively, they tend to act together and on one another's behalf rather than as isolated individuals. In 1972 Oscar Newman, a noted urban planner, analyzed patterns of crime in public housing projects and identified the placement of buildings—what views they opened onto, what spaces they half-enclosed or commanded, and so on—that instilled in their inhabitants feelings of community and responsibility, and were thereby associated with lower crime rates.[19] Since then, a number of environmental psychologists and architects have amplified the study of what kinds of neighborhood layouts foster collective territoriality and mutuality.[20]

Privacy: In different societies and different parts of our own society, people have dissimilar needs for privacy, but in general some degree of privacy is important to nearly everyone. The environmental psychologist tries to meet this need architecturally. In large offices, for instance, the use of partitions or walls providing freedom from direct visibility by supervisors, rather than open-plan design, has been found to yield greater job satisfaction and better, not worse, performance.[21]

Crowding: Living and working where the density of human beings is constantly high is stressful. When density cannot be lowered, environmental psychologists offset its effects by architectural and visual manipulation. One team of environmental psychologists tested three minor architectural variations within a college dormitory to see how much they differed in creating the feeling of crowding. One was a long corridor with rooms housing forty students; the second, two short corridors, each with rooms housing twenty students; the third, a long corridor housing forty students but with a lounge in the middle, where students could meet, set off from each half of the corridor by doors. Although the last arrangement had as high a density as the other two, students perceived it as less confining and crowded, more congenial and social.[22]

Performance psychology: This specialty is concerned with expanding the mental abilities and motor skills used in learning and in many skilled activities, including sports.

In the past two decades, some reputable psychologists (and some who are less than reputable) have made extraordinary claims for the effectiveness of certain performance-increasing methods of training, many of them New Age techniques outside the mainstream of scientific psychology. These include sleep learning, accelerated learning, neurolinguistic programming, biofeedback, the mental rehearsal of athletic skills, extrasensory perception, psychokinesis (moving or altering physical objects by mental effort alone), and others.

Because extensions of human capabilities would be valuable in combat, in 1984 the Army Research Institute asked the National Academy of Sciences to evaluate a number of these unorthodox techniques. The NAS's National Research Council created a fourteen-member Committee on Techniques for the Enhancement of Human Performance; it consisted largely of psychologists (reputable) and was headed by Robert A. Bjork of the University of California at Los Angeles. The committee and its subcommittees visited ten laboratories to observe techniques, listened to presentations by advocates of the new methods as well as independent consultants, and reviewed a huge literature. The conclusions, some predictable and others surprising, were published in two reports, the first in 1988 and the second in 1991.[23] Here are a few of the salient findings about somewhat unorthodox methods of expanding human capabilities. (Later we will hear the conclusions about the more unorthodox ones.)

Training regimes: Many physical trainers and coaches stress the value of "massed practice"—intensive, prolonged practice of a skill. An example is the training offered in tennis "camps," where students work at their tennis many hours a day for a week or two. Such regimens, the committee reported, do boost performance to high levels in a short time, but the gain is evanescent:

> In general, massing of practice on some component of the to-be-learned task produces better performance in the short term (e.g., during training) but much poorer performance in the long term than does spacing of practice. In some cases massed practice yields long-term recall performance less than one-half the level that results from spaced practice, and two massed practices are often not appreciably better than a single study trial.[24]

The spacing effect holds true not just for motor skills but for verbal ones, particularly language learning. Although this has been known to psychologists for many decades, the short-term gain in skill during massed practice continues to impress coaches and instructors, and to beguile their students. The committee's findings and the advice of sports psychologists will probably not counteract the sales pitches of the promoters of massed-practice training programs.

Mental practice of motor skills: For some time, sports psychologists have been counseling athletes, musicians, and other practitioners of motor skills to rehearse mentally what they mean to do physically, claiming that this will improve actual performance. A number of athletes and others have testified to the effectiveness of the method. Jack Nicklaus, for one, has said that he never takes a golf shot without first visualizing the precise trajectory of his swing and the flight of the ball. A Chinese pianist, imprisoned for seven years during the Cultural Revolution, played as well as ever soon after his release, and explained that he could do so because during his captivity he had practiced every day in his mind.

Anecdotes, of course, do not prove a hypothesis. The committee therefore examined a mass of research data and found that in controlled studies of motor skills, people who mentally rehearsed did perform distinctly better than people who did not. But physical practice alone yielded better results than mental practice alone, and a combination of the two yielded still better results in those skills where physical practice is difficult or costly and in those requiring planning and decision making rather than automatic responses. The committee concluded that the claims of sports psychologists as to the benefits of mental practice are exaggerated.[25]

While some sports psychologists continue to use these methods, the current emphasis seems to be more in the therapeutic mode: helping athletes think of themselves as winners, maintain focus during competition, heighten their own motivation, and cope with their intense feelings. Bob Rotella, well-known sports psychologist and author, is an exemplar, according to Gazzaniga and Heatherton: "He helps athletes train their minds to focus on their goals and teaches them to deal with their doubts, worries, and frustrations . . . For Rotella, this means that how athletes view themselves, their beliefs, and their performance expectations shape how they actually perform."[26]

Improving the Fit Between Humans and Their Jobs

We have already seen two ways in which psychologists have improved the compatibility of humans and machines: through testing individuals for specific machine-handling aptitudes, and through designing equipment to suit human perceptions, responses, and movements. Two other approaches to heightening workers' effectiveness consist of adapting their movements and modifying the work environment.

Early in the century, "efficiency experts" armed with stopwatches and tape measures analyzed and modified the actions needed for each task. They studied an employee's movements to determine whether, say, he could pack books into a shipping carton faster while seated or standing, using one hand or two, with the books piled to the right, left, or in front of the carton.[27] But such modifications, aimed solely at increasing output, often made industrial jobs more stressful and fatiguing, created worker hostility, and caused higher rates of errors and defects in the product.

During and after World War II, the increasing complexity of technology led to a new and larger concept, the "operator-machine system." This went beyond applying the elements of human engineering; it called for adapting the environment of the workplace to human psychological capacities and needs by modifying lighting, noise, rest periods, communications, and other working conditions in ways that would lessen fatigue, improve job satisfaction and employee commitment, and lower absenteeism and turnover.

From the factory, industrial psychologists gradually moved into the office, testing managerial job applicants for leadership qualities, recommending changes in job requirements to prevent burnout, and suggesting modifications of the chain of command and internal communication to improve team functioning and team problem solving. What had been industrial psychology became, in the post–World War II era, industrial/organizational (I/O) psychology, the specialty of 7 percent of all today's psychologists.[28] Some of them, trying to look like pure scientists, spend much of their time on research and theory, but most are concerned with understanding those aspects of people's behavior in the world of work that will enable them to solve employment problems and improve efficiency;[29] they act as if they were a hybrid of scientist and manager. A statement made several years ago by an I/O psychologist with United Brands Company is illuminating:

> As a "practitioner," I have focused on day-to-day organizational problems and opportunities: starting-up new plants, reorganizations, increasing teamwork, selecting and developing managers, improving morale, etc. . . . My interests have shifted from knowledge for its own sake to knowledge for action, from correct methodology to activity that is results-oriented, from what isn't being done perfectly to what can be done better. I am much more likely to read *Harvard Business Review* than *Journal of Applied Psychology*.[30]

Many of the functions of I/O psychologists, it is apparent, are primarily managerial; accordingly, we pass these by. But other functions, though serving management's ends, are primarily psychological. A look at two of them will give some notion of how I/O psychologists apply their science to improving the fit between human beings and their jobs.

Fitting the job to the person: This consists in part of human engineering, but includes much more.

The human engineering aspects include a number of physical features of the workplace and job that I/O psychologists pay attention to. Among them:[31]

— the "work-space envelope," including such factors as privacy and crowding, lighting, the spatial relationships of desks and chairs in relation to shelves, files, and doors, the best height for work surfaces, and many similar matters;

—noise in the workplace, which can generate stress and interfere with cognitive processes;

—specialization of the job, which makes for efficiency and high output, but workers who do the same thing all day (welding one corner of a car door, skinning chicken breasts, entering deposits and withdrawals on a computer) find their work monotonous, fatiguing, and lacking in meaning.

Psychologists can make useful suggestions about these workplace characteristics, but all of them cost money, although the argument has been made that more comfortable and less bored workers actually do more and better work and that employee turnover is reduced.

But human engineering is only one facet of the much larger subject of job satisfaction, a major concern of I/O psychologists. This is a broad and complex subject; we will content ourselves here with merely noting, first, the major *organizational causes* of job satisfaction, as summarized by psychologist Robert Baron of Rensselaer Polytechnic Institute and two co-authors.[32]

—a comfortable, pleasant work setting (the result of good solutions to the three engineering problems just mentioned),

—a fair reward system,

—high respect for the boss,

—participation in decision making, and

—appropriate workload.

In addition, there are four *personal causes* of job satisfaction:

—the individual's status,

—seniority,

—a good match between the employee's interests and work, and

—genetic factors. *Genetic factors?* Yes. Studies of identical twins separated at birth and raised apart have found that despite their different life upbringing and life experience, they have very similar levels of job satisfaction, which strongly suggests that innate personality traits play a considerable part in it.[33]

Fitting the person to the job: In large part this consists of assessing the ability of potential employees to perform a particular job. But in the case of managers, it also calls for appraising them after some years on the job in order to determine who has been moving up and looks like high-level material, and who seems stuck and unlikely ever to contribute much. Companies have good reason to want to know which prospective employees to bet on. One insurance company reckoned in 1974 that it cost $31,600 to replace a salesperson and $185,000 to replace a sales manager; the figures would be roughly four times as large today.[34]

Employee testing began, as we saw, before World War I. It has grown steadily ever since; nowadays a majority of large organizations and some smaller ones use tests in personnel selection. The evidence is that it pays off. A typical study, made for an artificial ice plant, found that of applicants for maintenance positions whose test scores ranged from 103 to 120, 94 percent were later rated as superior on the job; of those whose scores ranged from 60 to 86, only 25 percent were rated that highly.[35]

Tests for blue-collar jobs range from paper-and-pencil quizzes measuring knowledge of the job to "work sample tests" in which the applicant performs tasks similar to those of the actual job. White-collar job tests similarly range from written ones measuring verbal fluency, numerical ability, reasoning ability, and other cognitive skills, to those in which the applicant does filing, gives directions based on maps, handles emergency phone calls, and the like.

At many companies, applicants for managerial positions undergo a rigorous evaluation procedure known as assessment. Henry Murray, of TAT fame, and others developed assessment during World War II as a means of selecting intelligence agents for the OSS (Office of Strategic Services, the predecessor of the CIA). OSS assessment, as we saw in an earlier chapter, relies on personality tests and observations of the candidates in several artfully contrived situations. After the war, some of the psychologists who had worked in the OSS assessment project adapted the method to other purposes at the Institute for Personality Assessment and Research in Berkeley. Abandoning the qualifications of spies for more mundane concerns, they developed assessment protocols for dozens of specialties ranging from law school student to Mount Everest climber and from M.B.A. candidate to mathematician.[36]

But it was Douglas Bray, a psychologist at AT&T, who worked out the method of personnel assessment that became the model for American business and industry. Bray, born in Massachusetts, had made his way as far as graduate school at Clark University, where he earned a master's in psychology before being drafted in 1941. He was assigned to the Air Corps's aviation psychology program, where he helped create paper-and-pencil tests, psychomotor skills tests, and simulations to screen candidates for training as pilots, navigators, bombardiers, and aerial gun-ners.[37]

The work gave Bray an abiding interest in assessment. After the war he earned a doctorate in social psychology at Yale and taught for some years, but in 1955 he had the lucky break that started him on the real work of his life. A former professor recommended him to AT&T, which needed a psychologist to conduct a long-term study on selecting people who could become highly effective managers. At the time, AT&T was hiring as many as six thousand college graduates a year and promoting thousands more from vocational jobs to management jobs; knowing how to pick winners would be of immense value.

In Bray, it had picked a winner before having a method for doing so. Within a year he had assembled a staff, devised an assessment protocol, and begun using it in an "assessment center" in the headquarters of Michigan Bell in St. Clair. (Michigan Bell was the first company in the AT&T system to participate in the managerial-career study.) At the assessment center, twelve management candidates at a time would spend three days undergoing interviews, completing a battery of cogni-tive tests, personality inventories, attitude scales, and projective tests, and taking part in three major behavioral simulations—leaderless group discussion, a business game, and "In-Basket," an individual exercise in which each participant was handed a sheaf of •memos, letters, and requests, and had to make decisions, write replies, and take other appro-priate actions. Eight assessors, chiefly psychologists, spent a week observing and evaluating the participants in each group.[38]

As in all longitudinal research, the hardest part for Bray was waiting to gather evidence that the assessment method was valid. Eight years and again twenty years after each participant's assessment Bray conducted reassessments. The results strongly validated his method. After twenty years, 43 percent of the college graduates who had been rated the most promising had reached the fourth (of six) level or higher of manage-ment, as against only 20 percent of those judged less promising. Of non-college men, 58 percent of those highly rated by the assessment had made it to the third level or higher, but only 22 percent of those not highly rated had risen that far.[39]

Bray's assessment center and method did not catch on for some years, but in the expansive economic atmosphere of the 1970's it mushroomed; by 1980 there were about a thousand assessment centers, and by 1990 some two thousand.[40] Since then, the number has decreased somewhat because costs proved too high to be practical for most positions, but Assessment Centers continue to be widely used in the U.S. and almost every industrialized country for identifying or selecting senior-level talent.[41] Today, assessment in a center can take as little as one day, and evaluation has been much speeded up by replacing paper-and-pencil tests with computerized Q-and-A programs, and group exercises with computerized and video-aided simulations.

Many of the Bray techniques, in simplified and speeded-up form, are being used by the multitude of assessment organizations now operating on the Web.[42] Bray has won six awards for his work as an applied psychologist, including one from the American Psychological Association, which presented him in 1991 with the Gold Medal for Life Achievement in the Application of Psychology.

The Use and Misuse of Testing

The testing of job applicants by employers is only a small part of what is now one of psychology's most extensive influences on American life. Each year scores of millions of Americans take standardized multiple-choice tests published by over a hundred companies, some of which are *multi*-multi-million-dollar enterprises. Thanks to the federal No Child Left Behind Law, in 2006 every student from the third to eighth grade and one high school grade had to take state tests—about 45 million in all. (It was estimated by the Government Accounting Office that states would spend anywhere from $1.9 billion to $5.3 billion from 2002 to 2008 to implement No Child Left Behind–mandated tests.[43]) Add to that all the IQ tests given in schools throughout the nation, the standardized tests required for certification in the professions, the tests administered to many would-be employees by companies, the SAT, ACT, and other tests that play a role in college admissions, the personality and other tests given to patients by psychotherapists, and many others, and it is evident that testing is one of psychology's most successful applications to daily life. It has become a major means by which our society makes decisions about people's lives in education, employment, physical and mental health treatment, the civil service, and the military. And even love and mating: A number of dating services now use personality and other tests to generate "matches" between people.[44]

Binet's aim in developing intelligence tests, early in the century, was to benefit both the children and society by determining which children needed special education. Similarly, psychological and employment tests have always been basically diagnostic, meant to benefit the people being tested and those who deal with them. The extraordinary expansion of testing in the past several decades is evidence that it does serve these purposes. Testing is, in fact, essential to the functioning of modern society; schools, universities, large industries, government, and the military would be crippled and all but inoperable if they were suddenly deprived of the information they gain from it.

Yet testing can lend itself to misuse, the most serious example being the favoring of certain racial and economic groups and the handicapping of others. The obvious case in point is the effect of testing on the educational and employment opportunities of whites as compared with blacks, Hispanics, and other disadvantaged groups.

To people with an unqualified hereditarian view of human abilities, the use of intelligence and achievement tests poses no ethical problem. They believe that middle- and upper-class people do better on such tests, on the average, than lower-class people simply because they are better intellectually endowed by nature. As we saw, the followers of Galton were convinced that heredity accounts for the differences between the average scores on IQ and other mental tests of people of different classes and races. It was on this basis that schools throughout the country began testing students fairly early in the century and placing the higher-scoring in academic programs and the lower-scoring in "vocational" programs, thus preparing students for what were taken to be their manifest stations in life.

If that reasoning were correct, such testing and placement would be not only fair but in the best interests of the individuals and of society. But what if the test scores reflect the influence of environment? What if poverty and social disadvantage prevent children and adults from developing their latent abilities, causing them to score lower than those from favored backgrounds? If that is the case, the use of test scores to measure supposedly innate ability and to determine each individual's educational and employment opportunities is a grave injustice and a major source of social inequity.

Time and again, for more than sixty years, controversy has raged over the extent to which the scores of IQ and other cognitive ability tests measure innate abilities and the extent to which they reflect life experience. But it became clear in recent decades that the data used by both hereditarian and environmentalist psychologists, chiefly derived from cross-sectional samples (samples of people of different ages), did not adequately explain the processes observed by Piaget and other developmental psychologists. Longitudinal studies tracing the course of development in individuals revealed that nature and nurture are not static, fixed components but are interactive and highly variable over time. At any point in life, an individual's intellectual and emotional development is the product of the continuing interaction of his or her experiences and innate capabilities.

Then, too, most developmentalists have come to believe that different genotypes are affected to different degrees by environment; each has its own "reaction range." As Irving Gottesman, emeritus professor at the University of Minnesota Medical School, has explained, an individual with mongolism may, in an enriched environment, attain a level of intellectual development only modestly higher than he would in a restricted poor environment; an individual with the hereditary equipment of a genius may, in an excellent environment, reach a level of development very much higher than he would in a poor environment.[45] Thus, at low levels of innate ability the influence of environment is far less than it is at high levels.

Such generalizations, however, tell us only about categories, not about the relative influences of nature and nurture on any one person; there are too many idiosyncratic and incalculable factors in each person's history to permit analysis of the relative roles of heredity and environment on the individual's development. It is therefore impossible, at least at present, to precisely determine innate intellectual ability from an individual's test scores.

That being so, how can testing be used to determine schooling and job placement without unfairly benefiting privileged middle-class persons and unfairly penalizing the disadvantaged? The answer, so far, has been to control testing by political and legal means. The Civil Rights Act of 1964 and its amendments gave minority and other disadvantaged groups a legal toehold from which to attack testing as discriminatory and to demand remedial action. They challenged educational and employment tests in court, sometimes successfully, on the grounds that some of the materials are familiar to whites but not to most minority groups and, more broadly, that minority groups, particularly blacks and Hispanics, grow up under such social disadvantages that any test, even one based on symbols rather than words and ostensibly "culture fair," is unfair.

The radical remedy demanded by some activist groups at the height of the civil rights ferment in the 1960s was the abandonment of testing, and, as mentioned earlier, in New York, Washington, D.C., and Los Angeles city administrations actually banned intelligence testing in the elementary schools.[46] But the opponents of testing had majority power only in a few large cities, and in any case placing slow learners and the handicapped in the same classrooms as normal and gifted children so slowed down the education of the latter group that the efforts to eliminate testing soon failed.

Similar attacks on the use of college qualifying tests were made by some civil rights activists and groups. Ralph Nader, for one, charged in 1980 that the SATs discriminate against minority students, most of whom come from culturally impoverished backgrounds. Complaints and pressure against the SATs continued. Spokespersons for minorities have lately kept up a drumfire of charges against the SAT, claiming among other things that analogies used in the test are culture-bound and unfair to students with nonwhite, non-middle-class backgrounds, as are certain items using special, class-related words like "regatta," and that the readers who grade a new writing section in the SAT are likely to emphasize stylistically and grammatically Standard English, marking students down whose style employs idioms, phrases, or word patterns more common to communities of color. The College Board vigorously denies all of these charges, asserting that there is no research indicating that analogy questions are culturally biased, that data about the use of "regatta" show that minority students found the question using it no more difficult than did white students, and that the English teachers who read the essays "are trained to ignore errors in grammar, spelling, or punctuation until those errors are so bad as to get in the way of making sense of the student's argument."[47] The jury is still out.

In the realm of employment testing, activists scored a major success, at least temporarily. The General Aptitude Test Battery (GATB), which measures a number of cognitive abilities and some aspects of manual dexterity, was developed in the 1940s by the U.S. Employment Service and was long used by that bureau and many of its state and local offices as the basis of referrals to employers. But the average GATB scores of minority groups were well below those of the majority groups, so if test scores resulted in, say, 20 percent of whites being referred for a particular job, only 3 percent of blacks and 9 percent of Hispanics might be referred for the same job.

The amended Civil Rights Act made it illegal to use the scores in this way, not because the tests failed to measure abilities wanted by employers but because national policy required giving the disadvantaged compensatory advantages.[48] Rulings by the Equal Employment Opportunity Commission and a number of court decisions led to a solution known as "within-group norming" or "race norming." Under this policy, test takers were referred for jobs not on the basis of their raw scores but according to where they ranked within their own racial or ethnic group. A black who scored in the eighty-fifth percentile of black test takers would be put on an equal footing with a white who scored in the eighty-fifth percentile of the whites, even though the black's score was lower than the white's. A black with the same score as a white would be rated higher than the white.[49] In the 1980s the employment services of thirty-eight states used race norming, some more than others. Employers, by and large, went along with the method, mainly because it helped them meet government affirmative action requirements.

Some psychologists attacked race norming as a travesty of testing and a distortion of the test's measure of job fitness,[50] and political conservatives attacked it as an illegal "quota" system, unfair to whites. A 1989 study by a committee of the National Research Council backed race norming but recommended that the Employment Service base job referrals not only on the GATB but on the applicant's experience, skills, and education. The committee saw the merit of both sides in the dispute:

> The question of the fair use of the GATB is not one that can be settled by psychometric considerations alone — but neither can referral policy be decided on the basis of equity concerns alone. If there is a strong federal commitment to helping blacks, women, and certain other minority groups moving into the economic mainstream, there is also a compelling interest in improving productivity and strengthening the competitive position of the country in the world market.[51]

The race-norming question was a hot potato in the congressional debate over the Civil Rights Act of 1991. In the struggle to pass an act that President George H. W. Bush would not veto, congressmen who favored race norming had to yield to those who opposed it. The act as finally passed prohibited "test score adjustment" on the basis of race, and the practice has since been banned at all eighteen hundred state and local offices of the Employment Service.

How one views this matter—whether one considers referring job applicants on the basis of race norming a proper use or a misuse of testing—depends on one's political philosophy.

We will spare ourselves a thorough review of the many other ways in which testing of one kind or another is, or can be, misused by opportunistic, misguided, inept, or extremist individuals. But three particularly suspect uses are worth noting:

Dumbing down: In the 1980s, when minority groups were militantly fighting against testing, one "solution" to the alleged unfairness of pre-employment tests was to revise them or modify their scoring so as to upgrade the scores of minority test takers. An example: In 1984 the Golden Rule Insurance Company of Indianapolis agreed not to use any tests in which the average scores of blacks were more than 10 percent lower than those of whites. In 1985 the state of Alabama reached a settlement under which it would not use teacher certification tests that produced differences greater than 5 to 10 percent between whites and blacks. In other cases, the solution has been to make the tests so easy that everyone can pass: In the early 1990s Texas gave a teacher examination that nearly 97 percent of candidates passed.[52]

For years, many states have deliberately made the tests schoolchildren take easy in order to create a fraudulent appearance of progress. This was so before the No Child Left Behind Act was passed, and although that law sought to achieve quality schooling in exchange for federal dollars, the dumbing-down tradition has continued. A recent study conducted by Policy Analysis for California Education, a research institute run by Stanford University and the University of California, found that many states were continuing to make their students look better than they were in reality. The study, as cited in a *New York Times* editorial, showed that "students who performed brilliantly on state tests scored dismally on the federal National Assessment of Education Progress, the strongest, most well-respected test in the country."[53] The *New York Times* reported in July 25, 2006, that Secretary of Education Margaret Spellings had rejected as inadequate the testing systems of Maine and Nebraska; federal money will be withheld from both. Other states may be in jeopardy.

Honesty testing: "Integrity tests" have been marketed for several decades and their use by employers has recently grown substantially, and for two good reasons. One is that employee theft has been rising, year by year; various recent estimates range from $30 billion to $60 billion.[54] The other is that in 1988 Congress passed the Employment Polygraph Protection Act, which prohibited the use of lie-detection equipment in most employment settings; as a result, the use of paper-and-pencil and computerized integrity tests soared. Some integrity tests probe attitudes toward dishonest behavior by means of direct questions such as "Do you think it is stealing to take small items home from work?" or by inquiries about the applicant's views on tardiness and absenteeism. Others use an indirect approach, measuring personality traits from which psychologists infer the applicant's attitude toward honesty. Such tests ask questions like "How often do you blush?", "How often are you embarrassed?", and "Do you make your bed?"[55]

Not surprisingly, there has been considerable opposition to integrity tests by labor groups on several grounds: that they are neither valid nor reliable and therefore falsely rate some honest people as dishonest, damaging their reputations and opportunities; that they are an invasion of privacy; and that they have an "adverse impact" on minority groups, eliminating higher percentages of them than of whites from job opportunities. Nonetheless, the integrity testing business has grown and thrived in recent years.

In 1991 a task force of the American Psychological Association, after making an exhaustive two-year study of honesty tests, concluded that the publishers of many tests offer no substantiation of their validity and utility. The association therefore strongly urged employers not to use such tests. But for the few tests for which information was available, the task force found:

> The preponderance of the evidence is supportive of their predictive validity . . . To the extent that evidence is available, it is consistent with the idea that these tests reflect aspects of personal integrity and dependability, or trustworthiness.[56]

Later studies by the APA and other sources again found that some integrity tests have respectable levels of validity and that others do not. The would-be employee who is asked to take an integrity test is at risk of being incorrectly rated dishonest.

Emotional stability testing: In November 1989 a man named Sibi Soroka, who had applied for the job of security officer at a Target Store in California and been required to take two tests, the Minnesota Multiphasic Personality Inventory and the California Psychological Inventory, filed suit against Target's owner, the Dayton Hudson Corporation, charging invasion of privacy. The tests (discussed in an earlier chapter), have many purposes, among them to screen out emotionally unstable applicants for "safety sensitive" positions such as police officer, airline pilot, and nuclear plant operator. They include hundreds of items, some touching on religion ("My soul sometimes leaves my body," "I feel sure there is only one true religion") and some on sex ("I wish I were not bothered by thoughts about sex," "I am very strongly attracted by members of my own sex").

Soroka complained that he had been upset by the tests, which had invaded his privacy. He asked for a preliminary injunction preventing Target from using the results or continuing such testing. His lawsuit made headlines; there had been many privacy-invasion suits over drug testing in employment settings, but the claim that standard personality tests used in employment screening were an invasion of privacy broke new ground. The court denied Soroka's request for a preliminary injunction but an appeals court granted it. That court did not rule out all such testing but only whatever contained unjustifiably invasive items, like those pertaining to sex and religion. In 1993 Target Stores reached a $1.3 million settlement with Soroka and other plaintiffs in a class-action lawsuit filed in Alameda Superior Court, though Target admitted no legal wrongdoing.[57]

Soroka's case established a beachhead in the attack against personnel testing. Other recent suits have attacked it on the grounds of defamation and the inflicting of emotional distress. The borderline between the justifiable use of testing and its misuse is being redrawn; where it will finally lie, one cannot now be sure.

Covert Persuasion: Advertising and Propaganda

"Nothing in life is more pervasive than persuasion," wrote psychologist Eleanor Siegel in the APS *Observer* some years ago, adding:

> Nearly every social interaction between humans—and between members of many nonhuman primate species—has a strong element of persuasion. Knowledge about the psychological processes that affect people's decision making therefore carries tremendous positive potential.[58]

And tremendous negative potential. Until the modern era, human beings who sought to persuade others to believe in their gods, make love, or sell them goods for less than the announced price did so by generally known and customary means, of which the others were presumably aware. The Roman senators listening to Cicero deliver his attacks on Catiline, the near-mutinous crewmen hearing Columbus's firm assurances, the Puritan worshippers dutifully attending to the Reverend Cotton Mather's fulminations against sin and portrayals of damnation, surely recognized that their minds and hearts were being played upon in culturally prescribed fashion, and made their judgments within that context.

But with the advent of scientific psychology, it became possible for informed people to use certain findings of the new science to influence the minds and feelings of others by methods not generally recognized as persuasive techniques.

This can be well-intended. The sophisticated techniques used by teachers in motivating children to learn and by psychotherapists to inspire patients to change are examples of the many ways in which covert psychological persuasion is employed for the benefit of others.

But the techniques can also be used to induce behavior that is harmful to the subjects, not merely in terms of concrete costs but at the price of freedom of choice. Those who are persuaded may be deprived of their rationality and become little better than Skinner's Ping-Pong-playing pigeons, mindless creatures blindly obeying the will of others, heedless of their own best interests.

The use or abuse of psychology to persuade had become so pervasive by the early 1990s that social psychologists Anthony Pratkanis and Elliot Aronson called their 1992 study of the subject *The Age of Propaganda*. They meant not just political or religious propaganda but any "communication of a point of view with the ultimate goal of having the recipient of the appeal come to 'voluntarily' accept this position as if it were his or her own."[59]

Since we are interested in the misuse of covert persuasion, we will bypass overt forms of persuasion, like honest advertising; techniques of propaganda that rely not on covert use of psychological principles but on "disinformation" (the [George W.] Bush administration's fraudulent assertions that Iraq had weapons of mass destruction); deceptive labeling (the administration's switch, when no WMD were found, to the claim that the U.S. invaded Iraq to liberate the Iraqis from oppression); unconcealed appeals to easily aroused emotions (a picture of an adorable baby sitting in a Michelin tire, or of the Marines raising the flag at Iwo Jima); and, finally, certain military uses of psychology, including nontorture POW interrogation techniques and brainwashing, which are hardly covert and, in any case, are considered ethically justifiable during warfare.

But the use of psychological knowledge to persuade covertly is very common in advertising. Much advertising, to be sure, forthrightly portrays the product in an attractive light, praises its virtues, and states its price. However, a considerable part of the $400 billion spent each year in America on advertising of all types pays for messages conveyed by covertly persuasive techniques derived from psychological principles. As the journalist Vance Packard revealed long ago in *The Hidden Persuaders*, a muckraking 1957 exposé of these methods, psychoanalytic principles were then being used on a large scale—and, he later said in 1980, still were—to "channel our unthinking habits, our purchasing decisions, and our thought processes . . . Many of us are being influenced and manipulated, far more than we realize, in the patterns of our everyday lives."[60]

The early applications of psychological principles to advertising by Walter Dill Scott, John B. Watson, and others were relatively aboveboard, but in the late 1940s devious, cunning, and more potent applications were introduced by several people acquainted with Freudian theory. The best-known of them was the late Ernest Dichter. Born in Vienna, he earned a doctorate in psychology at the University of Vienna and briefly practiced psychoanalysis but, being Jewish, fled the Nazis in 1938 and came to the United States. Unlike most other refugee psychoanalysts, who resumed the practice of their profession in their new surroundings, he recognized that American advertisers were bigger game than neurotics, and began peddling his services as an expert who could identify unconscious desires in consumers by which they could be motivated to buy the client's products.

Dichter was not the only one with this idea; others aware of the psychology of the unconscious were beginning to do similar work. But he was the key figure in what was known as "motivational research." He used psychoanalytic theory to formulate hypotheses that he then tested by means of interviews, questionnaires, and sample ads on several hundred families in Croton-on-Hudson, New York, where he had his headquarters. Ebullient and dynamic, Dichter unabashedly proclaimed that a successful advertising agency "manipulates human motivations and desires and develops a need for goods with which the public has at one time been unfamiliar—perhaps even undesirous of purchasing."[61]

A good example of his work is the first study in which he used motivational research. His client was Compton, the agency that had the Ivory Soap account. As Dichter recalled years later, he told agency executives, "Bathing is a psychologically liberating ritual. You cleanse yourself not only of dirt but of guilt." The evidence he produced by means of interviews and questionnaires convinced them; with his help they adopted as their ad copy "Be smart and get a fresh start with Ivory Soap . . . and wash all your troubles away."[62]

He also radically changed the thrust of cigarette advertising. In the early 1950s, cigarette ads either stressed enjoyment or reassured readers about the effects of smoking on health. Dichter considered both approaches feeble. The typical American, in his analysis, was basically puritanical and tended to feel guilty when using any self-indulgent product. Accordingly, Dichter told agency people handling a cigarette account, "Every time you sell a self-indulgent product, you have to assuage guilt feelings and offer absolution." To identify such guilt-reducing rationalizations for smoking, he made an in-depth study of 350 smokers and discovered a dozen "functional" reasons why one should smoke: to relieve tension, to be sociable, to convey a sense of virility, and more. As a result, his client's ads, and soon many others', showed people smoking under pressure, in company, and out on the range.[63]

For some years, motivational research was the hot idea in advertising and still is used to some extent. But by the 1970s advertisers had become less enamored of psychoanalytic trickery—it had not paid off as dramatically as they expected—and began turning to later psychological research for techniques of covert persuasion.

One useful finding, first made in the late 1960s and reaffirmed repeatedly in more recent years, was Robert Zajonc's discovery of the "mere exposure" effect. As we saw earlier, Zajonc found that repeated exposure to even a meaningless symbol creates in the viewer a sense of familiarity and a favorable response. Psychological consultants to advertising agencies advised their clients that frequent brief repetition of the brand name and logo, even without reasoned and time-consuming argument, would sway the viewer. Many advertising agencies tested the method and found that it worked. The endless reiteration of a product name during a long football game or tennis match (along with, of course, macho or sexy imagery, scenes of fun in the sun, and the like) has its effect. When fans shop for beer or tennis shoes and come on the name they have seen so often, they have an automatic and unthinking favorable response.[64]

Over the past several decades, the method has also become endemic in TV commercials for political candidates, to the detriment of the democratic process. In place of reasoned argument about issues, the prevalent practice is to subject viewers to a barrage of thirty-second or even shorter commercials hammering home the candidate's name and simplistic "sound bites" that change many people's preferences through sheer repetition. One could call this propaganda, but there is little difference between such propaganda and covert advertising; in both cases something is being sold to the viewer by devious means. Similarly, in many small towns and city neighborhoods the current campaign tactic of sticking little signs along roadsides or on front lawns bearing only the candidate's name—no message and not even a party affiliation—is intended to make the name so familiar that it will incline the wavering voter to choose it without knowing quite why.

Some other laboratory findings that have recently been put to use in product advertising and propaganda:

—In an experiment based on classical conditioning theory, subjects saw pens of one color while hearing pleasant background music, and pens of another color while hearing unpleasant background music. Later, when offered a choice of pens, they tended to pick the color that had been paired with pleasant music. The principle, widely used in TV commercials, sounds innocuous, but it induces people to make a choice without an awareness of why they choose as they do.[65]

—In contrast to this short-term conditioning effect, a long-term "sleeper effect" has been experimentally demonstrated. Over a period of time, the emotional response created by an ad is dissociated from the product name, even though the emotion causes the name to be remembered. Thus, an ad that commands attention by creating unpleasant emotions—a recent TV commercial for a laxative shows a man grimacing while a deep male voice groans in discomfort—can be productive rather than counterproductive.[66] Viewers may think it stupid of the advertiser to use an irritating or annoying commercial, but in the long run they remember the product, not the disagreeable reaction.

—More generally, if the message is presented in ways that arouse fear, it is more likely to work than would factual or rational argument. The method is often used in public service messages that portray the dire consequences of certain kinds of behavior, and in commercials for fire or flood insurance, pest control, air bags, and the like.[67]

— Various characteristics of the person delivering the message can have a significant covert persuasive influence. Fast speakers are generally more persuasive than slow speakers.[68] Handsome, beautiful, sexy presenters, and celebrities in general, are believed by advertisers to exert important covert influence. Clothing can have a similar effect; for years, though less often now, advice about medications or diet was usually delivered by an actor wearing a white lab coat.

— A particularly subtle technique, in selling political positions, is for the speaker to present both sides of the argument, particularly when likely to be heard by people opposed to his or her own view. A presenter who does not seem to be obviously trying to persuade listeners to change their attitude is often, paradoxically, more effective than one clearly seeking to do so.[69]

— An experiment conducted by Leon Festinger and Elaine Walster many years ago showed that overheard discussions are more likely to change a hearer's mind than those in which the hearer knows the speakers are aware of his or her presence. Unconsciously, we are more swayed by a communication not intended to persuade us than by one intended to do so. A commercial for a well-known brokerage firm used to show all the people in a room falling silent and straining to overhear a person privately giving his companion a piece of that firm's advice. The same principle underlies the many "candid camera" commercials in which a person, unaware of being filmed, testifies to the virtues of some product.[70]

— A team of social psychologists conducted an experiment to find out the effect of distraction on the person listening to a persuasive message. They discovered that listeners who were distracted during a reasoned argument were more convinced by it than those who were not distracted; the effect was strongest when the argument was weak. The researchers' explanation: Distraction interferes with the viewer's or listener's ability to evaluate or mentally argue against the message. Pratkanis and Aronson say that TV advertisers have made use of that finding:

> Advertisers can, for example, "compress" a thirty-six-second commercial into a thirty-second time by running the ad at 120 percent of its normal speed. Psychologically, time-compressed ads are harder to argue against. Metaphorically, the advertiser is persuad-

ing at 100 miles an hour while you maintain the speed limit and try to defend yourself at 55 miles an hour. You are bound to lose.[71]

TV viewers may wonder why so many recent commercials are a pell-mell series of brief flashes of images plus a rat-a-tat-tat of words; that's why.

—A particularly immoral method of covert persuasion is the use of symbols based on repressed hatreds or fears. A notorious example is the series of commercials conceived of by the late Lee Atwater, architect of George H. W. Bush's 1988 presidential campaign, charging that Michael Dukakis was responsible for the weekend furlough of the convicted murderer Willie Horton, who, while out of prison, tortured a man and raped his fiancée. But the real intent of the commercial was the impact created by the picture of Horton, an ugly, fierce-looking, dark-skinned black man.

—In a brand-new ploy, demonstrated in two experiments at Simon Fraser University, participants who had to solve an anagram (GANECY) before seeing the name of a brand of product were more likely to say they had seen the brand before than participants who were not asked to solve the anagram, and when shown a list of brand names in the same category, preferred the one they thought they had seen before. Why did they? The researcher, Antonia Kronlund, says the "Aha!" experience of solving the puzzle (AGENCY) generates a good feeling that is then misattributed to the first brand name seen. Says Ms. Kronlund, "Such techniques can be used by marketers in magazine layouts, in store displays—the possibilities are endless."[72]

—Finally, the ethos of covert persuasive techniques is candidly, almost proudly, displayed in the online ad of John Wiley publishers for its 2006 book *Covert Persuasion: Psychological Tactics and Tricks to Win the Game* by Kevin Hogan and James Speakman:

A guide to all the tricks salespeople need to turn "no" into "yes"!

Covert Persuasion synthesizes the latest research in the field of influence with the extensive experience of psychologist and public speaker Kevin Hogan to produce an unbeatable guide to the psychological tricks that win sales battles. Based on cutting-edge science, Hogan and James Speakman reveal dozens of previously

unknown verbal and nonverbal tricks and tactics that will have
customers saying "yes" before they even realize it. A salesperson
fully aware of all the nonverbal and verbal cues and hints that
lead a customer to a particular response will always have the
upper hand. *Covert Persuasion* reveals more than ten keys to sub-
tly elicit agreement from even the most stubborn customer.

This is but a sampling of the use of unconscious persuasive factors in
advertising and propaganda. We have seen others in our journey
through psychological history, among them the foot-in-the-door technique of fund raising (asking for a small favor, then returning for a larger
one), and Kahneman and Tversky's experiments in skewed decision
making (an alternative couched in terms of the chance of winning was
chosen by many more people than a statistically identical alternative
couched in terms of the chance of losing). Thousands of studies have
investigated all sorts of other factors affecting persuasion, and many of
the findings have been and are being used by advertisers, politicians,
religious leaders, activists of all sorts, and others in the persuasion business. To the extent that these findings are used to manipulate Americans
into making consequential decisions on the basis of unconscious motivations and fears, they are misuses of psychology—not as serious as the
misuse of physics in nuclear bombs or of biology in germ warfare, but
neither trifling nor innocuous.

But let us end this discussion on a happier note. One of the most alarming forms of covert persuasion turned out to be nothing to fear. In 1957
James Vicary, a market researcher, announced that he had had the messages DRINK COCA-COLA and HUNGRY? EAT POPCORN flashed on the screen
in a Fort Lee, New Jersey, movie theater for 1/3000 of a second every five
seconds during showings of the movie *Picnic.* No viewer, he said, had
been aware of the messages, but in the course of a six-week trial Coca-Cola
sales had gone up by 18.1 percent and popcorn sales by 57.7 percent.[73]

The story was a sensation. The public was horrified, social critics
issued alarms, subliminal advertising on radio and TV became big business during the 1970s, department stores played background music
tapes containing undetectable warnings against shoplifting, and the
Federal Communications Commission ruled that the use of subliminal
messages could result in the loss of a broadcast license.

All utter nonsense. In *The Age of Propaganda* Pratkanis and Aronson
reported on their examination of more than two hundred academic

papers on subliminal messages. Most found no evidence that such messages influence behavior, and those that did were "either fatally flawed on methodological grounds or cannot be reproduced."[74]

For good measure, Pratkanis and Aronson cited a droll experiment in which the Canadian Broadcasting Corporation subliminally flashed the message PHONE NOW 352 times during a popular Sunday night show, after telling viewers that a subliminal message would be sent and asking them to say what it was. The message had no effect on the volume of phone calls placed during the experiment, and not one of the nearly five hundred viewers who wrote in to say what they thought they perceived had the right answer. Many, however, apparently aware of the Vicary story, said they became hungry or thirsty during the show.[75]

But all who believed the Vicary story had been gulled. An article in *Advertising Age* in 1984 said that Vicary admitted his original experiment was a fake, intended to increase customers for his failing marketing business.[76]

Psychology in the Courtroom

The formidable Hugo Münsterberg was the first to recommend that psychology be applied to the justice system, the very foundation of the structure of governance. In his 1908 book *On the Witness Stand*, he summarized existing psychological knowledge of the factors influencing testimony and said that applied psychology would be helpful to judges, lawyers, and juries—all of whom he took to task for "thinking that their legal instinct and their common sense supply them with all that is needed, and somewhat more."[77] But the book had little effect; during the next half century psychologists rarely served as expert witnesses, they tested candidates for only a handful of big-city police departments, and the studies they conducted on the psychology of the justice system had no direct effect.

Since the 1960s, however, there has been an explosive growth of interest in and application of psychology within the justice system. Although legal professionals and psychologists continue to have a strained relationship, applied psychology now pervades the courts, judicial chambers, and probation hearing rooms. The 2005 edition of the *Handbook of Forensic Psychology*, edited by the psychologists Irving B. Weiner and Allen K. Hess, runs to 912 pages and contains chapters on over a score of areas of application, each involving many specific activities, in both civil and criminal actions. To name but a few of these, psychologists now:

- — act as consultants to the court in custody disputes where there is a question about parental competency, and render opinions based on clinical methods of assessment.
- — testify in compensation cases where an employee claims that a physical or psychological disability is the result of injuries in the workplace. Such claims, running to many billions of dollars per year, often involve malingering or fakery; the psychologist's job is to interview and test the plaintiff, and report his or her clinical impressions.
- — testify on the fairness of a lineup procedure that was used to identify a criminal suspect. The psychologist draws upon a body of research findings on fair and unfair lineups. An unfair lineup may make identification obvious by such means as using "foils"—stand-ins—very different from the suspect in appearance, or in the cases of photo lineups, by using a scowling or frowning photo of the suspect and neutral or smiling ones of the foils.
- — act as observer and adviser to a judge and attorneys when they interview a child to determine his or her competence as a witness.
- — obtain evidence in sexual abuse cases from children too young to testify in court. Using methods borrowed from child therapy, psychologists watch children play with dolls and look for the enactment of activities similar to those of the alleged crime.
- — interview and test a criminal suspect pleading the insanity defense. That defense is successfully used far less often than the public supposes. Surveys have found that the public thinks about 40 percent of criminals use the insanity plea and that a third of them succeed, but in 1991 a major eight-state study commissioned by the National Institute of Mental Health found that less than 1 percent of county court cases involved the insanity defense, and that of those, only around one in four was successful.[78]

Certain other applications of psychology to justice processes are of more doubtful value, since they are not well accepted by court professionals or have uncertain outcomes. Cases in point:

Predictions of dangerousness: Probation boards often ask psychologists to predict how likely it is that a prisoner convicted of a violent crime will commit additional violent crimes if released. Willie Horton gave a bad name to the psychological evaluation of future violence, as have other killers who, freed, have killed again.

A much-cited review of five studies of predictions of violence found that the clinicians were correct in their predictions only a third of the time.[79] (Many of their errors, however, were innocuous "false positives"—predictions of violence by an individual who, after being released, did *not* commit further acts of violence.) The U.S. Supreme Court reviewed the capital conviction of one Thomas Barefoot, whose lawyer claimed that testimony predicting Barefoot's future violence should not have been considered in deciding his sentence. In 1983 the Supreme Court disagreed, holding that such testimony is not necessarily unreliable.[80] But even the American Psychiatric Association argued in an *amicus curiae* brief that predictions of dangerousness are wrong too often to be used where a death penalty is involved, and throughout the 1980 and 1990s, most mental health professionals maintained that dangerous behavior could not be predicted. Some recent studies, however, suggest that if certain basic rules were followed, clinicians could indeed predict dangerousness in certain situations—a not thoroughly reassuring conclusion.[81]

Lie detector tests: The usefulness and validity of lie detector tests have been debated for many years by psychologists, legislators, lawyers, judges, and the press. As we have seen, anxiety about lying, particularly when the subject is asked questions containing key words or phrases related to the crime, will produce accelerated heart rate, accelerated breathing, and increased skin conductance, all of which the polygraph clearly shows. But the large research literature on the subject provides a great deal of evidence against, as well as for, the theory. An analysis of ten careful studies of the use of lie detection equipment showed that polygraphs do 64 percent better than pure chance—a lot better, but still far too inaccurate to warrant their use as evidence.[82] That 1985 conclusion has been reaffirmed repeatedly. In 2002 an expert panel convened by the National Academy of Sciences found no scientific evidence to warrant the use of polygraphs on a regular basis, pointing out that while thousands of employees of the FBI, CIA, and other governmental agencies have been given lie-detector tests, not one has ever been found to be a spy—not even Aldrich Ames, who passed the test but was later convicted of selling secrets to the Russians.[83]

Leonard Saxe, formerly at Boston University and now at Brandeis, has offered a convincing explanation of the weakness of polygraph evidence. The polygraph, he says, is not a lie detector but a fear detector. If people are afraid the machine will expose their lying, they develop a fear reaction that the machine reports—but if they do not believe the machine can do so, they lie without being afraid, and the machine reports that they have told the truth.[84]

Because of the unreliability and doubtful validity of polygraph testing, most courts do not usually admit the results as evidence and psychologists rarely do polygraph testing. (It is generally done by technicians who call themselves "polygraphers.") But polygraph results are not entirely barred from the courtroom; the Supreme Court has left it to the courts of each jurisdiction to determine how and when to allow them, or to exclude them altogether (*United States* v. *Scheffer*, 523 U.S. 303 [1998]). A number of jurisdictions that otherwise exclude polygraph evidence nonetheless allow the parties to stipulate to the admissibility of the evidence before the test is administered. These courts typically set requirements on matters such as the qualifications of the polygraph examiners and the conditions under which the tests are to be given.[85]

Plaintiffs and defendants sometimes take a polygraph test before the trial and, if the results favor them, release the news to the press. The results do not become evidence, but the public and, unfortunately, some jurors in the case may form an opinion on the basis of the so-called evidence.

Scientific jury selection: The courtroom application of psychology in jury selection is of very questionable social value. Its proponents claim that it makes jury trials fairer, but its aim is to select jurors predictably biased in favor of the psychologist's client.

Scientific jury selection, which has existed for over three decades, is a specialized service that can cost a plaintiff or defendant anywhere from fifty thousand to hundreds of thousands of dollars; accordingly, it is used chiefly in major damage suits and key civil rights cases, although some low-cost services have recently become available for smaller, low-budget cases.[86] The service is provided mostly by market research and management consultant firms that have on their staffs, or hire for the purpose, sociologists and psychologists whose research furnishes the client's lawyers with information about what kinds of jurors to avoid and what kinds to select.

Lawyers, of course, have a number of their own rules of thumb as to what kinds of jurors are desirable or undesirable in different cases, and they try in the *voir dire* (the questioning of potential jurors) to select those they think are not biased against—or, even better, are biased in favor of—their client. The system is reasonably fair only because both sides question each candidate in order to select or reject him or her. Scientific jury selection adds to this process covertly gathered significant information about the personality traits and background characteristics of potential jurors from which the expert predicts, with considerably greater accuracy than the lawyer, how they will react to the two sides in the case.

An early, but still archetypal, example of the genre is the scientific jury selection conducted in 1975 by the defense in the murder trial of Joan Little, a black prisoner who had allegedly been raped by a prison guard and then killed him with an icepick. A team of sociologists and psychologists working for the defense began with demographics. They ascertained that Beaufort County, North Carolina, where the crime occurred, was 30 percent black but that the jury pool was only 13.5 percent black, and so advised the defense lawyers. For that reason and others the judge granted the defense motion for a change of venue.

In the new venue the research team conducted a community survey of attitudes toward defendants in criminal trials. Using social-psychological methodology, they analyzed the data and produced profiles of "good" and "bad" jurors. Black women and young Democrats with at least a college education, for instance, would be likely to have social values predisposing them to be sympathetic toward Little.

The next phase was purely psychological. An expert on body language observed prospective jurors during the *voir dire*, judging their truthfulness and anxiety level from their posture, movements, eye contact, vocal intonation, and hesitancy in speech. (Some jury researchers also take such characteristics to indicate whether a juror makes decisions on an emotional or a rational basis.) The body-language expert passed his evaluations on to the lawyers, who used them, along with the attitude profiles from the community survey, as the basis for selecting or rejecting jurors. Despite the opposing efforts of the prosecution, the jury selected was thoroughly pro-Little and after a five-week trial found her not guilty on all counts.[87]

Some of the notable cases in which scientific jury selection has been used include the trial of Angela Davis, the Wounded Knee trials, the trials of the Vietnam Veterans Against the War, Vietnam veterans against the manufacturers of Agent Orange, Mark David Chapman (John Lennon's assassin), Attorney General John Mitchell, and the criminal trial of O. J. Simpson. Many of these and other front-page trials ended with verdicts favorable to the side employing jury selection experts.[88]

In many such trials, scientific jury selection has reduced the unknowns by adding to the selection process predictions based on particular jurors' feelings about giant corporations, leftists, widows, blacks, competitive marketing, the police, homosexuals, paraplegic accident victims, and so on and on.

The basic premise of scientific jury selection is thus in direct conflict with the principle that a defendant is to be judged by a fairly and representatively assembled group. As one jury researcher candidly put it, "Anybody who tells you that jury research is designed to pick a fair jury is out of his bird. Lawyers want to pick a jury that favors their side — they'd be foolish if they didn't — and jury research gives them a rational way of going about it."[89] In choosing jurors on the basis of their predictable behavior, scientific jury selection undermines the ethical foundation of jury trial.

Beyond the Fringe

As a drowning man will catch at a straw, so people in troubled times will seize on mystical beliefs in the hope of salvation. This may account for the vast popularity in recent decades of New Age (and post–New Age) mystical beliefs, practices, and nostrums said to endow their believers and users with mental health, spiritual power, peace, understanding, and joy. To name but a few: pyramid power, crystal power, aromatherapy, past lives therapy, memory recovery, messages from extraterrestrials, channeling, out-of-body experiences, rebirthing, reparenting, Scientology, thought field therapy, and repressed memory therapy.

We heard of a few such oddities in the chapter on psychotherapies and will pass them by now, noting only that almost all are lacking in any scientific validation; they offer anecdotal and case history evidence but have had no randomized controlled studies and no replication studies by double-blind impartial evaluators. A massive recent review by a team of thirty-seven respected academics considers almost all of them unproven, unevaluated, unscientific, and, in some cases, potentially harmful in a number of ways.[90]

But enough of that. Our attention now is focused on unorthodox theories and practices that are alleged to enlarge human psychic powers, a potent appeal that has enabled some of these systems, if one can call them that, to far outstrip the popularity of mainstream scientific psychology. The question we ask here is whether these offbeat forms of psychology are "outliers"—instances of real science at its outmost borders—or, like mesmerism and phrenology, forms of pseudoscience that delude the credulous and the uninformed.

An enormous literature has been generated by both believers and nonbelievers, but we can take a shortcut: You will recall from an earlier chapter that in 1988 and 1991 the National Research Council (of the National Academy of Sciences) appointed a Committee on Techniques for the Enhancement of Human Performance to advise the Army of any psychological techniques that could extend human capabilities.[91] Let us look at the committee's findings on five particularly popular techniques or theories, adding notes on any later studies that add anything significant to those findings.

Subliminal self-help: Annual sales of subliminal self-help tapes, available by mail order and on racks in supermarkets and bookstores, now exceed $50 million. Their producers claim that by using them one can reduce pain, break the smoking habit, control eating, build self-esteem, counter depression, overcome impotence, and achieve other worthy goals.

Unlike subliminal advertising, the messages in the tapes are presented not in microsecond doses but at normal spoken speed, although they are hidden by music, the susurrus of the surf, or other covering sounds. A tape said to build self-confidence may contain, imperceptible beneath such sounds, the repeated message "I believe in myself more and more each day." The claim is that hidden messages are subconsciously perceived and powerfully affect the user's feelings, thoughts, and behavior.

The most conclusive study reviewed by the committee was a double-blind experiment in which volunteers were tested for memory and self-esteem, then for five weeks used commercially produced subliminal self-help tapes either for memory improvement or self-esteem enhancement, and later were retested. What they did not know was that only half of them got the tapes they thought they were getting; of the other half, those who were told they got self-esteem tapes actually got memory-improvement tapes and vice versa.

The results achieved with all these groups showed that the tapes "had no appreciable effect, positive or negative, on any measure of either self-esteem or memory, but many of the subjects believed otherwise."

Another research team that did similar work said less discreetly that sub-liminal self-help audio tapes are "fraudulent" and "complete scams."[92]

Later studies of these and other kinds of subliminal self-help items, and legal actions against them, have been equally damning. Several companies have marketed gadgets that deliver flashing lights and sounds through modified eyeglasses and headphones; typically, the Relaxman Synchroenergizer was claimed to improve digestion and sexual function and control pain, habits, and addictions. Because such flashing lights can trigger epileptic seizures in susceptible individuals, including some with no prior history of seizures—and did so—in 1993 the FDA initiated a seizure of the manufacturer's entire supply, which a judge subsequently ordered destroyed.[93]

The FDA also stopped the marketing of the InnerQuest Brain Wave Synchronizer, which was said to provide diet control, stress relief, pain relief, and increased mental capacity; the FDA also ordered Zygon International, Inc., to make refunds to users of its Learning Machine (and to develop proof of claims for it) from which people were supposed to learn foreign languages overnight, quadruple their reading speed, expand their psychic powers, build self-esteem, and replace bad habits with good ones.[94]

But the latest news on this matter is depressing: A scan of the Web in late 2006 found only a handful of articles or book chapters repeating or amplifying the National Research Council committee's findings about subliminal self-help devices but over thirty thousand entries promoting and offering such devices for sale.

Learning during sleep: From 1916 to the 1970s a number of psychologists tried softly playing to people, while they were sleeping, material to be learned, on the theory that it would be heard at an unconscious level and effortlessly absorbed. The committee reported that the early research was inconclusive, since there was no hard evidence that the subjects were truly asleep. But later research, which included EEG recordings of alpha-wave brain activity to verify that the sleepers were soundly asleep, yielded only negative results; no learning took place.

Still, some evidence existed that learning might take place during the lighter stages of sleep. One researcher, some years ago, treated a group of nail biters by playing, three hundred times a night while they were asleep, for fifty-four nights, a recording of the message "My fingernails taste terribly bitter." Forty percent of the group stopped biting their nails. A possible explanation: Since most people's sleep ranges through different levels in the course of a night, learning had taken place during periods of lighter sleep. The NRC committee's conclusions:

> The committee finds no evidence to suggest that learning occurs during verified sleep (confirmed as such by electrical recordings of brain activity). However, waking perception and interpretation of verbal material could well be altered by presenting that material during the lighter stages of sleep. We conclude that the existence and degree of learning and recall of materials presented during sleep should be examined again.

As it has been, again and again, sometimes with positive and sometimes negative results. The reason for this inconsistency has been clarified in a major new work, *Memory: The Key to Consciousness*, by psychologists Richard F. Thompson and Stephen A. Madigan:

> An important qualification in many of these studies is that no measures were taken of whether the person was actually asleep or instead had been wakened to some degree by the taped message. One recent experiment on learning during sleep eliminated these problems by monitoring the electrical activity of the brain while word lists were read repeatedly to sleeping subjects, and making sure that the subjects remained in REM sleep. The results of the experiment were clear: There was no evidence for any kind of memory formation for events that occurred during sleep, in tests of either implicit or explicit memory.[95]

But, of course, as with all beyond-the-fringe psychological gimmickry, plenty of sleep-learning applications are for sale on the Net. To which one can only say: Let the sleeper beware.

Neurolinguistic programming: This system of procedures, originally developed by two reputable psychotherapists, Richard Bandler and John Grinder, is marketed by a large number of individuals and firms in many countries as training in a set of valuable skills. The trainers do a lively business teaching it for a fee at NLP workshops, seminars, and institutes.

The aim of NLP, as expressed by its proponents and teachers, is often as opaque as pea soup: It provides, they say, "a general philosophy and approach (together with tools and methodologies) that will assist a person seeking change to find a path through an unfamiliar landscape to a goal which he or she desires but lacks a means to reach."[96] In reality, its appeal is practical and, in some eyes, Machiavellian.

The use of NLP is said to increase one's influence and effectiveness in dealing with other people. Its core concept is that people, in their mental and physical activities, use particular sensory systems—visual, auditory, tactile, and so on—to represent to themselves the material they are dealing with. According to NLP theory, they are most strongly influenced by materials presented in whatever representational system they prefer or are using at the moment. The person trained in NLP relies on clues like eye movements, posture and respiration rate, and language. With this information he or she practices "mimesis" (mimicking the other person's posture, respiration rate, and choice of metaphors), and "anchoring" (a form of conditioning to elicit a specific response) and thereby enlarges his or her influence over the other person's thoughts, feelings, and opinions. The technique has great appeal, for obvious reasons, to executives, managers, and salespersons.

The committee, however, found no scientifically acceptable evaluations of the effectiveness of NLP, since, as it said, "the proprietors, purveyors, and practitioners of NLP are not experimentalists and are not interested in conducting such studies." The evidence of the few halfway credible studies that exist "is either neutral or negative . . . Overall, there is little or no empirical evidence to date to support either NLP assumptions or NLP effectiveness."

Quite possibly, the committee added, some aspects of NLP do have some merit; maintaining eye contact with another person and paying close attention to his or her choice of topics and metaphors may well make for better communication. But the committee found that these possibly effective aspects of NLP are neither peculiar to it nor related to NLP theory.

Since then, a vast mass of literature about NLP has piled up, almost none of which meets the minimal requirements for scientific validity and most of which is either hard sell or passionate sermonizing. This is not to say that NLP doesn't work. A good summation was recently offered by Dr. Robert T. Carroll, a philosopher at Sacramento City College:

While I do not doubt that many people benefit from NLP training sessions, there seem to be several false or questionable assumptions upon which NLP is based. Their beliefs about the unconscious mind, hypnosis, and the ability to influence people by appealing directly to the subconscious mind are unsubstantiated . . . NLP makes claims about thinking and perception which do not seem to be supported by neuroscience . . . NLP itself proclaims that it is pragmatic in its approach: what matters is whether it *works*. However, how do you measure the claim "NLP works"? . . . Anecdotes and testimonials seem to be the main measuring devices. Unfortunately, such a measurement may reveal only how well the trainers teach their clients to persuade others to enroll in more training sessions.[97]

Biofeedback: This is the use of electronic and other monitoring equipment to provide an individual with information about his or her biological functions, the goal being to train the person to exert voluntary control over processes that are normally involuntary. Among those activities are heart rate, blood pressure, body temperature (particularly of the extremities), and alpha-wave activity.

Typically, a trainee with hypertension will watch a continuous blood pressure readout and in some unspecified way come to associate certain unconscious processes with any observed drop in pressure. After a while, without knowing how he does it, the trainee can voluntarily lower his blood pressure. Similarly, subjects watching monitors of right-brain and left-brain activity learn to increase one and decrease the other, the result being an improvement of such cognitive abilities as mentally solving arithmetic problems. Trainees who learn to reduce tension in specific muscle groups have been able to improve their musical skills, sprinting performance, and hand-eye tracking.

Impressive as this sounds, the committee found that there were serious limitations to the gains achieved through biofeedback. Subjects could not decrease their heart rate under conditions of stress; only two of ten studies on muscle relaxation showed evidence of it and none showed much benefit in stressful situations; control of alpha-wave activity improved performance only on simple cognitive tasks; and body temperature control, potentially valuable in preventing frostbite, did not work except when the subject was in a resting state.

As with other fringe/alternative treatments, biofeedback has a huge literature, much of it unsubstantiated claims, some of it reasonably solid research. A credible up-to-date overall appraisal comes from the Blum Patient and Family Learning Center of the Massachusetts General Hospital:

Biofeedback training as a tool for relaxation and stress reduction enjoyed a brief surge of popularity following its inception in the late 1960s, but exaggerated claims based on poor-quality studies led to a reaction against it, and biofeedback largely slipped out of the public view during the 1970s and 1980s. In the 1990s, however, properly designed studies were performed, and biofeedback began to regain respect.

Currently, incomplete but encouraging evidence suggests that biofeedback may indeed offer at least modest benefits for a variety of medical conditions, including hypertension, anxiety, Raynaud's syndrome, low-back pain, insomnia, fecal incontinence in children, irritable bowel syndrome, and migraine and tension headaches. Biofeedback does not appear to be effective for asthma.[98]

Parapsychology: For many decades a number of committed parapsychologists—some are physicists, psychologists, and members of other scientific disciplines, many others laypersons—have been conducting experiments in such "psychic" phenomena as extrasensory perception (ESP), clairvoyance (seeing things that are out of sight), psychokinesis (the ability to move objects or influence machinery by mental power), telepathy, out-of-body experiences, near-death experiences, and channeling. The American Society for Psychical Research, founded in 1885, has a substantial endowment fund, publishes a newsletter and a journal, and regularly holds lectures, symposia, and meetings. A Gallup poll in 2005 found that four out of ten Americans believe in ESP, nearly a third in telepathy, and over a quarter in clairvoyance.[99]

Nearly all parapsychological phenomena, if real, would have practical value (and indeed police and others sometimes pay psychics to try to locate missing persons). The National Research Council committee therefore visited parapsychology laboratories to witness demonstrations and experiments, discussed parapsychological experiments with a number of parapsychologists, and reviewed studies by both believers and skeptics.[100] Of this mass of material, the two most positive findings were these:

—Of the vast number of reports of remote viewing achieved by telepathy, only nine were scientific studies, but eight of the nine had serious flaws (the "senders" had unintentionally provided the "receivers" with clues in between trials), and the ninth had a differ-

ent but equally serious flaw. A later and more rigorous study did produce some results, but below the level of statistical significance.
— Of 332 reports of psychokinetic influence over random number generators, 188 had some claim to scientific status; of these, 58 reported statistically significant results. The two most careful and extensive of these experiments used random number generators that turned out either 0's or 1's, averaging 50 percent of each over the long term. Subjects who tried to influence the machines by psychokinesis were able to produce 50.5 percent of 1's in one laboratory and 50.02 percent in the other, that is, one extra 1 per hundred trials in one laboratory, two extra 1's in every twenty-five hundred trials in the other laboratory. In view of the large number of trials, these results are statistically significant but they indicate "an extremely weak effect."

That being the most impressive evidence of parapsychological phenomena, the committee's conclusion was categorical:

The committee finds no scientific justification from research conducted over a period of 130 years for the existence of parapsychological phenomena.

In the committee's view, the best scientific evidence does not justify the conclusion that ESP—that is, gathering information about objects or thoughts without the intervention of known sensory mechanisms— exists.

Nor does scientific evidence offer support for the existence of psychokinesis—that is, the influence of thoughts upon objects without the intervention of known physical processes.[101]

The parapsychological community was, of course, unshaken in its beliefs by the committee's summary of the evidence. But that was to be expected; you will recall that Festinger, Riecken, and Schachter, in their study of a cult that expected the world to be destroyed by a flood, ruefully reported that when an individual with a commitment to a belief, who has acted upon that belief, is presented with evidence that it is wrong, he "will frequently emerge, not only unshaken, but even more convinced of the truth of his beliefs than ever before."[102] The human mind, that most wonderful and powerful apparatus for making sense of the world, seems equally apt at justifying its own nonsense.

If you will surf the Web for an hour or two for documents on parapsychology, you will see that in 2007, a time when our culture is perfused by scientific psychology, and particularly the twin revolutions of cognitive psychology and cognitive neuroscience, a very sizable part of our population believes fervently in many of the phenomena of parapsychology. For some of these the believers think they have evidence, although it never meets the reasonable criterion that "extraordinary claims require extraordinary evidence." A recent meta-analysis of 380 research studies of psychokinesis would indeed have been extraordinary evidence—had the results been positive; in fact, the net effect was so minuscule and meaningless that the authors suggest it was an artifact of publication bias (a result of papers with positive results getting published and those with none or negative results being rejected).[103]

But many believers are unconcerned about research evidence; they believe because they experience things best explained by parapsychology. They're right about one aspect of the matter: Their experience is real—it's an actual event in the brain. They're wrong only in thinking that the subject of their experience was real. If a person sees the face of Jesus in a wet, oil-slicked street, it's a reality—that is, the experience is; what's in the street is something else altogether.

As for the vast mass of papers, books, speeches, journal articles, and other forms of communication that purport to present evidence—

Enough! This book is a history of psychology, the science of the mind; parapsychology is not psychology and not science. We have strayed off course. Let us abandon the subject and return to our story, of which there is only one more chapter.

NINETEEN

Psychology Today

Portrait of a Psychologist

Although most thoughtful people consider the use of stereotypes small-minded and prejudiced, we all rely on generalizations about others to enable us to behave appropriately toward them. If we are seated at dinner next to a woman we have never met and learn that she is a Presbyterian minister, we speak to her somewhat differently from the way we would if we learn she is the author of scandal-mongering unauthorized celebrity biographies. Generalized expectations, though often oversimplified and inaccurate, are necessary hypotheses about people; without them we would function no better at the dinner or in other social situations than a Korowai tribesman just arrived from the wilds of Papua New Guinea.

So, what would come to your mind if you heard that the stranger seated next to you at a dinner is a psychologist?

To most people, it would mean that he or she has special insight into human nature and treats troubled people. But you, having read this far, are disabused of any such erroneous generalization. You know that "psychologist" denotes not one but a broad spectrum of occupations, many of which have nothing to do with insight into human nature, and that many psychologists are scientists, not healers. No generalization, no single image, can encompass the proficiencies and activities represented by the following handful of specimens of contemporary psychologists at work:

— In a laboratory, a young woman wearing headphones, her head inside a large scanning machine, hears a male voice uttering what she has been told are sentences; her task is to push any one of four buttons to indicate how "meaningful" each sentence is. Here are some samples of what she hears:

"the man on a vacation lost a bag and wallet"
"the freeway on a pie watched a house and window"
"on vacation lost then a and bag wallet man then a"
"a ball the a the spilled librarian in sign through fire"
"the solims on a sonting grilloted a yome and a sovier"
"rooned the sif into hlf the and the foig aurene to"

The so-called sentences, some of which sound like a bad simulation of Jabberwocky, range from the "semantically congruent" (they make sense) through the "semantically random" (the individual words make sense but the sentence does not) to the "pseudoword list" (nonwords in no syntactical order).

The young woman's choices of which buttons to push don't actually matter; what the four researchers are interested in is what the fMRI scans show about her brain activity as she hears the spoken words. And in fact what they show is exciting, although the researchers, in their report, couch their findings in the usual impassive academese: "Syntactic and semantic processes engaged during sentence comprehension occur in distinct but overlapping parts of the temporal and parietal lobes. These regions make use of syntactic and semantic information in different ways." The details, too recondite to repeat here, add up to an intriguing finding: The human brain has different specialized circuits for interpreting the semantics (meaning) and the syntax (sentence structure) of heard speech.[1]

— A white-coated man, scalpel in hand, bends over a laboratory table and, slowly laying open the body of a brown Australian marsupial mouse, searches for its tiny adrenal glands. The mouse, a male, had died after many hours of continuous copulation; all males of this species, *Antechinus stuartii*, expire after a nonstop bout of five to twelve hours of sexual activity, which they engage in only during a two-week period of the year. Examination of the adrenals of a number of such mice leads to an explanation: The length of daylight and average temperature during the reproductive season induce extreme hyperactivity of the male mouse's adrenals, which trigger the prolonged and stressful copulation that ends in death.[2] The study adds to a growing body of knowledge of seasonal influences on the behavior of mice . . . and men.

— In a room designed to look like a cocktail lounge, a small group of volunteers meet, are served drinks (some get vodka and tonic, some only tonic, though what they are told they're getting isn't necessarily the truth). After fifteen minutes of drinking and chatting, they are shepherded into a back room where they watch a twenty-five-second video of two basketball teams passing balls back and forth, and are asked to count the number of times the white-shirted team passes the ball. During the action, a woman dressed in a gorilla suit walks into the middle of the screen, beats her chest, and walks off. When the video is over, the researchers interview each participant; they find, remarkably, that of the forty-six who took part in a dozen small sessions, only 18 percent of those who had a real drink had noticed the gorilla—and even more remarkably, that fewer than 50 percent of those who got a placebo (nonvodka) drink had noticed it. The two significant implications: Even mild intoxication strongly affects the ability to notice anything other than what one is paying attention to (passing the basketball), and even sober people are not likely to notice an unexpected and unusual object if they are paying attention to something else—a finding that could be of crucial importance to eyewitness testimony in court cases.[3]

— In a psychology lab, two student volunteers stand at opposite sides of a narrow table; a central curtain hangs between them, screening them from each other, and they have been instructed not to speak. Each grasps a handle of a crank that runs under the table from one to the other. On the table is a large, flat, blue disk, with two small marks at its edge, one on each side. From above, a target area (a small white oblong) is projected onto each side of the disk. The participants can rotate the disk by means of the crank handles, and when told, they try to move the mark on the disk into the target area as quickly as possible, then wait for a new target to appear. Since each student has a handle of the crank and no instructions as to how to proceed, the participants are as likely to inadvertently combat each other as to collaborate. But in fact after only a few trials they begin to work together, one partner speeding the disk toward the target, the other slowing it down to avoid overshooting. They evidently communicate wordlessly by their handling of the crank—and do better as a team than volunteers who perform the task alone. The findings, a valuable addition to "motor control theory," illuminate how people manage to wordlessly coordinate many kinds of movements with each other—everything from moving furniture to waltzing.[4]

—On a winter day, at the edge of a pond where ducks are paddling about, two bundled-up researchers stand thirty yards apart; one throws a chunk of bread into the water every five seconds, the other every ten seconds. After a few days of this feeding, twice as many ducks cluster near the five-second thrower as the other. But some days later the researchers introduce a change: The ten-second thrower tosses in chunks twice as large as the five-second thrower. At first the ducks continue to assemble as they have been doing, two to one in favor of the faster thrower, but within five minutes they have redistributed themselves and are divided equally between the two—evidence, the researchers believe, of a sophisticated innate foraging strategy in which the ducks take into account not only the rate at which edible items appear but their average size.[5] The study adds to knowledge of how time and quantity are nonverbally represented in the brains of animals and humans.

—A team of researchers gingerly positions miniature microphones inside the ear canals of a volunteer seated in the center of a circular framework on which six loudspeakers are mounted at different heights. The researchers then send white noise (a broad-spectrum hiss) through one speaker after another, rotating the apparatus 15 degrees at a time, until they have sent sound from 144 locations. Each time the volunteer identifies the position of the speaker by giving its direction and elevation in degrees. Later, using recordings of what the microphones picked up, the researchers transmit sound to the volunteer through earphones instead of the loudspeakers; he identifies the apparent directions from which the noise is coming in virtually perfect agreement with where it had come from in the actual condition. The experiment adds to knowledge of how the mind determines the direction of a sound source from the difference in time at which the sound reaches the ears.[6]

To this hodgepodge of images we could add any of the scores of others that have already been described or alluded to—everything from a psychotherapist Socratically leading a patient to recognize his unrealistic beliefs to a developmental psychologist recording the eye movements of an infant watching images flashed on a screen, and from a behavioral neuroscientist injecting epinephrine into a rat that has learned a maze to see how the hormone affects its memory to a cognitive scientist painstakingly constructing the thousands of steps of a computer program that, presented with hundreds of sentences, will learn language more or less as an infant does.

Beyond all this are many psychologists whose special interests and activities we have not taken time to explore, although some are of considerable relevance to everyday life. A few instances:

— Some are investigating the psychology of love and mate selection. At one time this was a much-researched field; then, being deemed too "soft"—not rigorously testable—it was sidelined. In the past couple of decades, however, there has been something of a resurgence of love research based on sophisticated statistical analyses of survey data and interviews, brain scans, cross-cultural data, and neurotransmitter science. Researchers have been using all these methods to distinguish between kinds of love (passionate, romantic, intimate, companionate, and so on), how some of these interact with sexuality, and how love changes over time.[7] These sound like familiar and classic topics, but some of the methods of inquiring into them are strictly contemporary and cutting-edge. An example: Helen Fisher, a psychologically oriented anthropologist, says in her latest book, *Why We Love: The Nature and Chemistry of Romantic Love*, that the feeling of love is the result of elevated levels of either dopamine or norepinephrine or both, as well as decreased levels of serotonin. She argues that this hypothesis is supported by fMRI scans of the areas of the brain that light up when subjects who are passionately in love are shown pictures of their adored one. (Still, one might interpret this as an *effect* of feeling romantic love rather than its *cause*.)

— Teams of researchers have been conducting long-term longitudinal studies of individuals who suffer recurrent periods of depression. Typically, they track the events and changes of their subjects' lives, correlate these with their emotional states, and statistically disentangle the influence of each possible cause of depression. Findings have lent weight to such stressful influences as childhood abuse, family conflicts, spousal abuse, and other traumas, and the counteracting force of such compensatory factors as the support of friends and relatives.[8] The Stirling County Study, the longest-running of all such studies (it was started in 1948), has yielded a mass of published results. One recent example is the finding that women born after World War II are at greater risk for depressive illness than older women, possibly because many of the younger women entered the labor force and employment is a major stressor. Another finding is that men with long-term depression have far higher mortality and morbidity rates than long-term depressed women, perhaps because men are less willing to seek treatment.[9]

— The nature of intelligence has been explored intensively for many decades, but in recent years some current researchers have advanced the concept that intelligence is neither overall intellectual ability nor a collection of correlated abilities but a set of different processes and strategies that may operate at different levels in the same person. As mentioned earlier, Howard Gardner of Harvard, for one, argues that each individual has seven distinct intelligences: linguistic, logical-mathematical, spatial, bodily kinesthetic, musical, interpersonal, and intrapersonal. Robert J. Sternberg of Yale, for another, offers research data pointing to a "triarchic" structure of intelligence: the mind's knowledge of its own abilities, its use of its accumulated experience, and its appraisal of the existing situation.

— A good many researchers are probing deeper than ever into the sources of gender role behavior and sexual preference. Some focus on prenatal influences on brain development, some on genetic anomalies, others on familial influences, and still others on cultural factors. Each group portrays its factors as the most influential, but the emerging view is that all are involved and to varying degrees in each case; it is the specific kinds of interactions, in any individual's history, that determine the outcome.

— The nature of consciousness, possibly the most profound puzzle of psychology, was long set aside as either not investigable or not useful either theoretically or practically. However, since the cognitive revolution and the cognitive neuroscience revolution, it has again been seen by some investigators as a question of paramount importance, and one they believe can eventually be answered. A few years ago Francis Crick suggested that a continuous, semi-oscillatory firing of sets of neurons creates a temporary unity of neural activity in many parts of the brain; the self-activating nature of the pattern is the basis of consciousness. Philip Johnson-Laird has likened consciousness to a computer's "operating system," a set of instructions that direct and control the flow of information in whatever programs are running. Gerald Edelman has proposed two levels of consciousness. A low-level form arises from the interaction between the part of the brain governing internal physiological drives and the part processing information from the outside world. A high-level form arises from the interaction between the linguistic and concept-forming parts of the brain, with the ability to label things and fit them into categories, thereby freeing the mind from subservience to events in real time and enabling it to be aware of its own thoughts.

Finally, there is "spin-mediated consciousness" theory (which you need not try to decode into comprehensible language). It holds that quantum spin is the seat of consciousness: In the words of one theorist, "Consciousness is intrinsically connected to the spin process and emerges from the self-referential collapses of spin states . . . The nuclear spins inside neural membranes and proteins form various entangled quantum states some of which survive decoherence through quantum Zeno effects."[10] Whatever.

So much for the vain effort to stereotype the special interests and activities of psychologists. But can we not at least picture the typical psychologist as a person? We cannot. Psychologists come in both sexes and in all sizes, shapes, colors, ages, and levels of training and status.

Many people envision a psychologist as white, male, a "doctor," and, as mentioned, the possessor of special insight into human nature and a healer of the mentally ailing. The last two descriptors, having to do with insight and healing, do apply to about 60 percent of the more than 102,000 doctorate-level psychologists. But nearly a third of the 102,000 are academics and researchers who have nothing to do with healing, and smaller minorities perform various services in industry, government agencies, other service settings, and schools.[11] But the first descriptor, white, is reasonably correct: Nationally, fewer than 4 percent of all employed doctorate-level psychologists are black, 3.4 percent are Hispanic, and fewer than 3 percent are Asian.[12] (Within the APA, for unclear reasons, only 1.7 percent of members are black, 2.1 percent Hispanic, and 1.9 percent Asian.[13])

The second descriptor, male, once was accurate but has long since ceased to be. In 1910, only 10 percent of doctorate-level psychologists were women, but by 1938 the figure was 22 percent, and by 1990 40 percent, while today women make up 50 percent nationally (and within the APA, 53 percent).[14] This shift is largely due to the growth of clinical psychology, which has always been relatively open to women. Academic psychology has not; for many decades, male psychologists all but excluded women from academic posts with the rationalization that they would abandon their research for years or permanently when they had children. Accordingly, male psychologists produced most research papers and held nearly all high-level academic and research positions. Only in relatively recent years have women come close to sharing academic appointments, but they still lag far behind as to equality in tenure; and while women's names now appear on research papers as often as men's, as of 2000 (the most recent year for which a report is available) they held fewer of the important chairs in psychology departments than their numbers warrant.[15]

The title "doctor," meaning holder of a Ph.D. or other doctorate degree, is another inaccurate component of the stereotype. True, three quarters of the APA's 90,000 members and an even higher proportion of the 12,000 full members of the APS (Association for Psychological Science, formerly known as the American Psychological Society) do hold Ph.D.'s or, in a few cases, Psy.D.'s, or Ed.D.'s. But at a lower level of advanced training there are well over 50,000 psychologists, most of them outside APA and APS, who hold only master's degrees but who perform useful services, including testing, counseling, psychotherapy, and various routine psychological services in industry, nursing homes, schools, clinics, government agencies, and private practice.[16]*

All of which demonstrates that psychologists come in a variety of models, some as unlike others as if they had nothing in common except the generic name.

---

*The 50,000 figure is an estimate carefully calculated from many sources by APA's Online Research Office. The Bureau of Labor Statistics says ten thousand (see www.bls.gov/emp#data); apparently, BLS uses a rigorous criterion in its count.

Portrait of a Science

What is true of psychologists and their activities is equally true of their field of interest: Although called a science, it is too heterogeneous to be defined or described in any simple, clear-cut fashion.

The vignettes above and what we have seen throughout this history document psychology's sprawl and diversity. But to get a still better idea of how diversified and chaotic a field psychology has become, one has only to leaf through half a dozen volumes of *Annual Review of Psychology*. Each year's volume contains about a score of chapters reviewing recent work in such disparate major areas of psychology as perception, reasoning, and motor skill acquisition, others covering more recondite and remote subjects such as brain dopamine and reward, auditory physiology, social and community intervention, hemispheric asymmetry, music psychology, various applications of brain scanning, and the psychology of religion. In the course of half a dozen years the *Annual* covers roughly a hundred different fields, each with its own subtopics, any of which could consume a researcher's full time and effort.

An even clearer and more variegated picture emerges from the gargantuan programs of the APA's conventions. Consider, for instance, this random sampling of the titles of the plenary sessions at the August 2006 meeting:

— "Emerging Findings from Multicultural Psychiatric Epidemiology"
— "Fear and Anxiety: Breaking News from Neuroscience"
— "Uses and Abuses of Evolutionary Psychology"
— "The Anatomy of Human Destructiveness"
— "Failure of Visual Awareness"
— "How Do People Change?"

A similarly random sampling of the vast array of addresses, sessions, and workshops at that meeting would yield a taste not of a consommé but a mulligan stew of psychological science.

The contents page of APS's *Current Directions in Psychological Science*, though research oriented—APS allows clinical material in only through a crack in the door—is just as variegated and wide-ranging; here are a few titles of articles in recent issues:

— "Infants' Differential Processing of Female and Male Faces"
— "The Structure of Emotion: Evidence from Neuroimaging Studies"
— "Talking and Thinking with Our Hands"
— "Comparing Exemplar- and Rule-Based Theories of Categorization"
— "Brain Mechanisms for Interpreting the Actions of Others from Biological-Motion Cues"
— "Stress and Adaptation: Toward Ecologically Relevant Animal Models"

Can any discipline so untidy, multifarious, and disorganized be called a science? Are we justified in believing that its statements about human nature and the human mind are scientific truths?

A century ago William James, after brilliantly setting forth what psychology was at the time, ruefully said that it was not yet a science but only "the hope of a science." We have seen how he characterized it:

> A string of raw facts; a little gossip and wrangle about opinions; a little classification and generalization on the mere descriptive level; a strong prejudice that we have states of mind, and that our brain conditions them; but not a single law in the sense in which physics shows us laws, not a single proposition from which any consequence can causally be deduced.[17]

Compare that with what psychology has become: a massive accretion of facts, observations, and laboratory research findings, not raw but digested by sophisticated statistical analysis; much gossip and wrangle, but mostly about testable interpretations and theories, not mere opinions; a wealth of classifications and generalizations at the theoretical level; and a profusion of laws and propositions about our states of mind and their relation to brain events whose consequences can be, and regularly are, causally deduced and put to the proof. Psychology has long since grown beyond the hope of a science to become the reality of a science.

But one unlike most others in perplexing and troubling ways.

In the natural sciences, knowledge is cumulative and moves toward a deeper understanding of nature. Relativity theory did not disprove Newtonian physics but absorbed it and went beyond it to deal with phenomena Newton could not observe; modern evolutionary theory does not disprove Darwinism but adds details, exceptions, and complications that take into account evidence Darwin did not know of. Psychology, in contrast, has spawned many special theories that either were disproved or turned out to apply to so limited a range of phenomena as to provide no basis for a larger and more inclusive theory. Behaviorism is the prime example. It brilliantly explored and explained a variety of psychological processes—and completely ignored almost all of the phenomena of mind; psychology was able to progress only when it escaped from the behaviorist cage.

Psychology, furthermore, is rife with what Jerome Kagan has called "unstable ideas"—concepts and theoretical statements that do not refer to fixed and unchanging realities but are subjective and variable. Unlike the phenomena in physics, which are events in the physical world, many of those in psychology concern the *meanings* of certain events to human beings; two psychologists using the same term may be speaking of quite different things, especially at different periods of time and in different sociocultural settings.

Some years ago, Kagan, looking back at his earlier writings, said, "I realized, to my embarrassment, that I had assumed fixed meanings for ideas like maturation, memory, and continuity of mood and habit." But with the perspective of years, he could see that the meanings of those and many other ideas in psychology vary according to how a researcher gathers evidence. One defines and studies fear as a set of biological events, another as the inner experiences of his subjects when they are feeling afraid. But the two sets of data are not coterminous; often the biological signs are missing in a person feeling fear and the emotion is absent in a person exhibiting its biological signs. The truth of supposedly scientific statements about fear depends on what one means by the term.[18] The same is true of so central a subject in psychology as emotion: As we have seen, emotion has been defined and redefined, decade by decade, since the time of William James, and despite the accumulation of a plethora of data, the question of the nature of emotion is still being explored by probing analytical discourses.

Again unlike physics, psychology has many laws that hold good only within the culture where the observations were made. In recent years psychologists have become interested in the cross-cultural validity of the laws of their science and have identified a number that appear to be universal, including some of Piaget's observations on stage development, the sequence in which children acquire the components of language, the spontaneous human tendency toward categorization, the tendency toward social loafing, and others. But they have also found that many other laws of developmental phenomena hold good only where they were deduced or in culturally similar settings. Among these are the definitions and development of masculinity, femininity, love, and jealousy; the tendency to conform to the majority and to obey authorities; the use of logic in reasoning; and the development of feelings of kinship and belonging.[19]

None of this means that psychology is not a science. But it is not a coherent science with a coherent and comprehensive theory; it is an intellectual and scientific jumble sale.

Forty-odd years ago, when the cognitive revolution was breaking out of the confines of behaviorism, the profusion of possibilities was, at first sight, stimulating and exhilarating, but on closer inspection proved to be bewildering and troubling. One psychologist, David L. Krantz of Lake Forest College, has described how psychology appeared to him initially and later:

> When I first became aware of psychology, I was most excited by its enormous range and diversity . . . I was only vaguely aware, and largely unconcerned, that the chapters in the introductory textbook did not relate to each other. Actually, their non-overlap just heightened the freshness of discovery.
>
> Later in graduate school the excitement created by such variety was tempered by an increasing emphasis on specialization, a pressure to dwell on only one or two chapters in the text. I was also becoming aware that psychology's diversity was often negatively seen as an indicator of incoherence, or even worse, as a hallmark of "non-science."[20]

That's how it looked to him four decades ago, when he and many other psychologists were troubled by the diversity and discontinuity of their field. And they continued to be troubled for years. One commentator predicted only sixteen years ago in *American Psychologist* that within the next fifty years the major fields of psychology would split off, achieve separate identities, and establish their own departments in universities, and that psychology would be viewed in perspective as a temporary phase in the development of the multiple behavioral sciences.[21] Other theorists were both less and yet more optimistic, holding that no unifying theory was possible and that none was needed. Sigmund Koch, who spent many years looking at the larger issues of the field, concluded over two decades ago that "the noncohesiveness of psychology [should] finally be acknowledged by replacing it with some such locution as 'the psychological studies.' "[22]

But others have long argued that some new conception, theory, or metaphor will be, and must be, found to unite the semiautonomous specialties of psychology; they see a desperate need for "grand unifying principles" that will prevent disintegrative fractionation.[23] They feel sure that a new and unifying metaphor or conception is bound to appear. Yet how little consensus there currently is about what those principles might be we can gather from listening to big-theory suggestions by two of the most respected senior psychologists of our time.

First, the eminent cognitive psychologist Albert Bandura: He has long espoused and continues to develop a broad and pervasive "agentic theory" that encompasses virtually all of human behavior. Bandura holds that the emergence of the human ability to symbolize the world (in language and signs) gave us the power to become agents of our own lives, not just passive products of the forces and influences acting upon us. "Psychology is the one discipline that uniquely encompasses the complex interplay among biological, intrapersonal, interpersonal, and sociostructural determinants of human functioning . . . The exercise of individual and collective agency is contributing increasingly, in virtually every sphere of life, to human development, adaptation, and change."[24]

Second, the Nobel laureate neuroscientist Eric Kandel: He says, "Understanding the human mind in biological terms has emerged as the central challenge for science in the 21st century." Biology, with its vast new armamentarium of knowledge and methodology, has "turned its attention to its loftiest goal: understanding the biological nature of the human mind." Future historians, looking back, will see that "the most valuable insights into the human mind . . . did not come from the disciplines traditionally concerned with mind—philosophy, psychology, or psychoanalysis. Instead they came from a merger of these disciplines with the biology of the brain . . ."[25]

There could hardly be a greater difference of opinion as to what kind of psychological Theory of Everything is about to emerge. But while nothing we have seen in this history since the onset of the cognitive revolution indicates that such a theory is imminent, in practical terms much that we have seen points to the very opposite of fractionation and noncohesiveness. Admittedly, many psychologists are working on ever-smaller, more specialized subjects—but a great deal of current research is multidisciplinary, and researchers, in pursuing almost any topic worthy of inquiry, will now draw on the insights and enrichment of cultural psychology, evolutionary psychology, computation theory, the infrastructure findings of neuroscience, and so on. As Michael Gazzaniga, the eminent cognitive neuroscientist and 2006 president of the APA recently wrote,

> As we study the mind, complex mechanisms will be common . . . [and] frequently, what we see will not be what we think it is. In order to chase down the true mechanisms, we will need to know many things from many fields of study. If we divide ourselves up into sub-subspecialties, we will never figure things out.[26]

For forty years, and especially for the last twenty, what has been taking place has been a disorderly integration, a loose, untidy interweaving, a semifusion, of the many dissimilar sciences within the broad realm of psychology. It may well be that no Theory of Everything will appear that neatly explains both the actions of neurotransmitters and the mental processes of writing a poem, both the configurations of neural networks and the course of true love. A Theory of Everything was possible in psychology when we knew very little; it may never be so again. And maybe we don't really need one.

Schism

Even if the fear that psychology will break apart into shards of disconnected subdisciplines is belied by the developments of recent years, one important schism did take place almost two decades ago, the organizational split between academician-scientists and clinician-practitioners.

Schisms between academic and applied psychologists were nothing new in the APA, the professional organization that had long represented psychology in the United States. The association was founded in 1892 as a learned society whose members were primarily teachers and researchers. From the beginning, applied psychologists were looked down on and rarely elected to important offices; their values and goals were considered venal, commercial, unscientific, and, in a word, grubby. John B. Watson was cast out of academia because of sexual scandal, but the APA ignored him for decades not for that reason but because he sold his skills to the advertising world.

Clinicians in particular were considered by academicians a lesser breed. At the 1917 APA convention, a small group of aggrieved clinicians—there were only a handful in the APA at the time—feeling that their interests were being ignored, decided to found their own society, the American Association of Clinical Psychologists. It grew, and the APA took action. It created a clinical section of its own, announced that it would accept all members of the AACP as members of the APA, and revised its bylaws, stating that its purpose was to advance psychology as a science and as a profession. The ploy worked: The renegades came home and the AACP was dissolved.

Similar events recurred as the number of clinical psychologists and applied psychologists in the APA grew. Each time the discontented formed another organization of their own, the APA made further changes in its structure to keep them in or bring them back. But genuinely harmonizing the interests, outlooks, and values of academics and clinicians was all but impossible. In *American Psychologist* in 1984, a psychologist, borrowing a concept from C. P. Snow, wrote sorrowfully of "psychology's two cultures," mutually uncomprehending, hostile, and alien.

What brought the matter to critical mass was money. During the 1970s third-party payments for clinical services had been available through health insurance, but by the 1980s that source of payment began to shrink as a result of Reagan administration policies and the growth of health maintenance organizations. The clinicians in the APA—by this time nearing a majority—demanded that the organization step up lobbying and publicity on their behalf. This alarmed the academics. They feared that the APA, historically a scientific organization, was becoming a professional association with monetary and political goals, and would soon be dominated by the practitioners.

During the mid-1980s the board of directors of the APA sought to avert mass defections of the scientists by devising plans of reorganization to protect their interests, but all were rejected by the APA's council of representatives. With a crisis imminent, a patchwork reorganization plan, satisfactory to neither side, was approved by the council, submitted to the membership in 1988—and rejected by an almost two-to-one margin.

That was the decisive event. At the APA's 1988 convention in Atlanta, a group of former presidents of the association and eminent academics, among them Albert Bandura, Kenneth Clark, Jerome Kagan, George Miller, and Martin Seligman, caucused in a hotel room and, in a spirit of defiance and rebellion, announced the formation of a new organization, the American Psychological Society, for academic and science-oriented psychologists. In the ensuing weeks hundreds of scientists resigned from the APA to join the APS, and hundreds more joined but retained their APA memberships. Within a year, the APS had 6,500 members and now has nearly 12,000 full members and over 5,000 student members. It is and always will be far smaller than the APA, which currently has nearly eight times that many members, but it is thriving. To more sharply distinguish itself and its purpose from the APA, the APS, while preserving its acronym, recently changed its name from the American Psychological Society to the Association for Psychological Science.

Today, like divorced parents who have worked out a modus vivendi for the sake of the children, the APA and the APS no longer publicly attack each other. Representatives of the two groups have occasionally had discussions aimed at finding ways to cooperate when possible. The APA even offered, some years ago, to publish the new APS journal, *Psychological Science* (today the APS publishes four journals), and although the APS chose another publisher, it sent a letter of appreciation to the APA. The two organizations compete in trying to attract graduate students and new doctorate holders, but today many APS members think it wise to belong to both groups. Present indications are that the APS will continue to grow and to serve the scientific community. The APA, also growing every year, will have an ever-larger percentage of clinician-professionals but continue to have a sizable minority of academician-scientists, publish journals for them, and represent their interests in Washington and elsewhere.

If all this is confusing, how could it be otherwise? In psychology nothing is simple, nothing is clear; the field nicely mirrors the untidy, complex human mind that it studies.

Psychology and Politics

— Nearly one tenth of all doctoral scientists in the United States are psychologists.
— Psychological knowledge has become vital to the successful operation of our schools, industries, clinics and mental hospitals, and the military. All will function still better as research yields greater understanding of human nature.
— Basic research in psychology, unlike many other sciences, does not

yield salable products and hence is not self-supporting. It must be funded largely by the federal government for the public good.

What, then, would be a reasonable sum for the federal government to invest in psychological research?

Twenty billion dollars a year?

Ten?

Five?

The actual figure: for fiscal year 2005, $574.4 million, a little over half a billion.[27]

Basic research in psychology currently receives one seventh as much federal support as does research in the physical sciences, one twenty-seventh as much as the life sciences, and only 2 percent of all federal support of scientific research.

The APA and the APS regularly send representatives to Capitol Hill to plead for greater support, but there they encounter serious obstacles. Most of the federal funding of psychological research comes from various agencies within the National Institutes of Health, modest amounts from branches of the Department of Defense, less than $4 million from the National Science Foundation, and minor sums from other agencies.[28]* The associations' representatives must therefore make their case before a number of committees and subcommittees; that spreads the risk but means fighting on many fronts without any overall high-level support.

In earlier decades, when psychological research was as simple as Thorndike's building a few puzzle cages out of scrap wood and buying a few cats and dogs, funding was a minor problem. But modern surveys, magnetic resonance scanning equipment, mainframe computers, and longitudinal studies by teams of specialists cost substantial amounts of money. Even so, psychological research is nickel-and-dime stuff compared with research on new weapons or space travel. Yet we, a nation more enamored of psychology than any other and eager for its knowl-

*Much of the funding of basic psychological research has been coming from NIMH, but in 2005–2006 the director announced that in the future funding priority would be assigned to basic research aimed at understanding and treating mental illness, while basic research of a more fundamental kind would get lower priority, if any. The result may be a considerable shrinkage of federal funding of basic research in psychology (National Science Foundation: Survey of Federal Funds for Research and Development FY 2003, 2004, and 2005).

edge and the benefits it confers, invest in psychological research a little more than .2 percent (two tenths of 1 percent) of the 2005 federal budget.

Today we shake our heads about the Romans, who spent vast sums to build their great cities, roads, and aqueducts but made no effort to study and arrest the declining fertility and work productivity of the native Roman stock. One wonders whether future creatures, poring over the ruins of our world, will shake their heads in wonder at our having spent immense sums for so many things but so little for the research on human nature that might have been the key to our survival.

The government is not only niggardly in its support of psychological research; it interferes with or even forbids certain kinds of research, sometimes for admirable reasons, often for ignoble or partisan ones.

As we saw earlier, during the expansion of civil rights in the 1960s the Public Health Service adopted regulations governing biomedical research that protected human rights, and in 1971 the Department of Health, Education, and Welfare extended them to all research in human behavior; the regulations, though not laws, assumed the force of law by denying federal funds to those who did not conform. The crucial regulation required researchers to obtain the informed consent of patients and subjects to any experimental procedure. But this laudable extension of the rights of the individual, when rigidly applied, made deceptive psychological research or concealment of the experimenter's goal impermissible; even relatively innocuous experiments requiring deception were ruled out.

After years of anguished protests over the strangling of social psychological research, the regulations were eased somewhat in 1981, and deceptive research again became fundable. Still, the constraints have remained so tight that much potentially valuable research is neither attempted nor considered. As one eminent social psychologist put it after the easing of the requirements, "The regulations and IRBs [Institutional Review Boards] exert a profound influence on researchers' thinking. You don't even consider tackling a problem that would require deception of a kind that will create trouble with the IRB. Whole lines of research have been nipped in the bud."[29]

More deplorable forms of political interference with psychological research are the politically motivated attacks on specific projects and on behavioral research in general by officials of the administration and by members of Congress.

In a classic instance, Representative William Dannemeyer, a California Republican, raised a storm of conservative objections in 1991 to an approved teenage sex survey and managed to kill it off. Emboldened, he broadened his attack and introduced an amendment to a 1991 NIH reauthorization bill that would have prohibited HHS from conducting or supporting any national survey of human sexual behavior. Even in a time of intellectual conservatism this was too much for the House of Representatives, which voted 283 to 137 to defeat the amendment.[30] Still, 137 members of the House voted for it, an alarming show of extremism.

More recently, there have been a number of attempts by various members of Congress to cut back or altogether prohibit federal funding of specific areas of psychological and sociological research—or, more ambitiously, all of it. A few instances:

— In 2003, during consideration of the 2004 NIH budget (as part of the Labor, HHS, Education appropriations bill), Representative Pat Toomey (R-PA) introduced an amendment to defund five approved NIH grants because he felt that research on sexual behavior and health was not a proper area for NIH to fund studies in. The House defeated the Toomey amendment by a razor-thin margin of two votes.[31]

— In 2004 and 2005, Representative Randy Neugebauer (R-TX) ambitiously went the whole way, sponsoring amendments to the NIH appropriations bill to defund all mental health grants. Each time, the bills were approved by the House with the amendments included. What would have become of mental health research in our country is hard to say; fortunately, the amendments died in the House-Senate conference committee.[32]

— In 2005, during consideration of the fiscal year 2006 Science, State, Justice, and Commerce appropriations bill, which includes funding for the National Science Foundation, Representative Anthony Wiener (D-NY) tried to reduce NSF's Research and Related Activities account by $147 million in order to boost funding for the Community Oriented Police program. Wiener's amendment failed.[33]

— In 2005 and 2006, Senator Kay Bailey Hutchison (R-TX), chair of the Senate Science and Space Subcommittee, submitted an amendment to an act affecting the National Science Foundation that would have directed NSF not to fund grants in the social, behavioral, and economic sciences. An uproar from the scientific community and an opposing amendment offered by Senator Frank Lautenberg (D-NJ) resulted in a bipartisan compromise amendment that allowed NSF to continue funding all the sciences.[34]

What motivates these members of Congress to oppose social and behavioral research? It is possible that they really feel some of the targeted studies are "improper" or wasteful or potentially refutative of their political and social beliefs. But it is also possible that they are primarily playing to the audience of their constituents—those elements of American society that are fearful of science or hostile to scientific research that threatens their belief systems. Whatever the answer, it is clear that government funding of research in the social and behavioral sciences, relatively minor though it is, will probably continue to be attacked by congresspersons whenever it suits their purposes.

In addition to administration officials and legislators, many special-interest and advocacy groups outside the government have attacked particular kinds of research, sometimes succeeding in hampering work, sometimes actually aborting projects. Ironically, this has been happening during the several recent decades in which psychology has been making its most striking advances. More ironically, these efforts to block research have been made not only by conservative groups but by liberal, radical, antiestablishment, and politically middle-of-the-road groups.

One such essentially middle-ground force is the "animal rights" movement, whose followers have often resorted to violence, breaking into medical and psychology laboratories, destroying equipment and records, and sometimes making off with the animals. Leaders of the animal rights movement argue that animal and human lives are morally equivalent and that performing experiments on animals that would be unacceptable on human babies is "speciesism." Animal research, in their view, is immoral regardless of the benefits. Their ethical stance was epitomized some years ago by Chris DeRose, founder and director of Last Chance for Animals, who said, "If the death of one rat cured all diseases, it wouldn't make any difference to me."[35]

Many other areas of psychological research have been regularly, fiercely, and often successfully opposed by other special-interest and advocacy groups, some of the politically correct kind, others politically conservative, and yet others of a traditionalist middle ground. To evince interest or pursue research in any of the topics blacklisted by these groups can result in anything from hate mail, public demonstrations, threats of violence, and physical assaults to, in academe, failure to be promoted, ostracism by one's colleagues, lack of tenure, and rejection of research papers by journals—in sum, academic oblivion. Here are a few such areas of research:

— genetic differences in IQ (attacked by minorities, radicals, and some liberals for nearly forty years as being racist);
— genetic differences in mental abilities and emotional responses of males and females (attacked by feminists ever since the 1960s as sexist);
— biological bases for differences in male and female sex roles (again, long attacked by feminists as blatant sexism);
— biological influences on violence and crime (assailed by minority groups, liberals, and others as racist, since violence and crime rates are higher among blacks than whites);
— sex surveys of teenagers (fiercely opposed by conservative groups, who regard sex surveys as impermissibly violative of privacy and parental rights);
— many forms of memory research (attacked by lawyers and "repressed memory" experts because the findings are a threat to court cases of sexual abuse in childhood).

The record is far longer,[36] but this handful of items is enough to illustrate that many of psychology's findings are as unpopular, repellent, and detestable to various segments of our population as Galileo's argument that the earth circled the sun was to the Catholic Church in 1633.

But popularity is not the test of truth, the legitimacy of research is not determined by its social appeal, and academic freedom does not mean freedom to inquire only into subjects that are politically safe. Research considered offensive, dangerous, or politically incorrect may prove to be valueless or even harmful—or may increase our understanding of humankind and lead to an improvement of the human condition. We saw that in 1909, when Freud lectured at Clark University, Weir Mitchell, a distinguished physician and a pioneer in the application of psychology to medicine, called him a "dirty, filthy man," and a dean of one Canadian university said that Freud seemed to advocate "a relapse into savagery."[37] Those worthies were too close to his work to see its future value; we are too close to much of the work under recent or current attack to know exactly how much, if anything, it will add to knowledge and benefit society. But unless we seek new knowledge, we are certain not to gain it. That being so, efforts to block psychological and behavioral research for political, religious, or other nonscientific reasons are no better than the Catholic Church's forcing Galileo, on pain of imprisonment, to swear that the truth was other than he knew it to be and to abstain from teaching, writing, or discussing heretical heliocentric theory.

Status Report

How far into the terra incognita of the mind has our journey taken us?

An explorer making his way across an unmapped landmass knows, when he sees the ocean in the distance, that he has reached the far shore, the end of his trek. But for us there is no far shore; in science there is never a finite amount to be known about the nature of reality. We cannot know how far we have gone toward the end of the journey, since there is no end. As with all other sciences, psychology, in answering questions, also discovers the more detailed and profound ones it can ask.

We have, though, come far enough to answer many of the classic questions asked by Greek philosophers so long ago and by other thinkers ever since. The answers to their questions about the nature of the soul, the dual substances of mind and body, and the ways in which mind and body interact are implicit in what is now known about the real-world chemical and electrical events taking place at many levels and in organized forms that yield the complex thoughts and feelings that we call mind. Here is a paradigm of the levels of those events and forms of organization:

— at the lowest level, circa ten angstroms (one billionth of a meter): the neurotransmitter molecules, issuing in bursts from the synaptic vesicle of a firing neuron into the gap between it and the dendrite of another neuron;

— several orders of magnitude larger (an order of magnitude covers a range up to about tenfold in size): the synaptic gap, about one micron (one millionth of a meter) wide, across which the neuro-

transmitter molecules leap, carrying the impulse from the transmitting neuron to the receiving one;

— two orders of magnitude higher: the neurons, about one hundred
microns or one ten-thousandth of a meter long, down whose axons
the transmitted impulses travel, and from which they are sent on to
connecting neurons;

— another order higher: the simplest circuits, about a millimeter
long, of a few linked neurons that fire in sequence, producing such
elemental reactions as a response to a directionally oriented visual
stimulus;

— one to two orders higher: circuits of anywhere from one centimeter
to ten centimeters in length, composed of millions of linked neurons — the hardware (or, more accurately, wetware) in which the
programs run that we experience as mental maps, thoughts, and
language;

— finally, another order higher: the entire central nervous system,
roughly a meter or so in length, in which all the above take place at
their own levels of organization.[38]

Mind, in short, is the programmed flow of information made possible
by the organized patterns of billions of neural events.

Perception, emotion, memory, thought, personality, and self are the
mind's programs at work, drawing on and using the information and
experience stored in the brain's circuitry in the form of synaptic connections to respond to stimuli in one fashion or another.

This is the dominant view in contemporary psychology — dominant
but not accepted by everyone in the field. Apart from parapsychologists
and others beyond the fringe, a few philosophic psychologists still argue
for a kind of vitalism or "idealism," a contemporary version of classic
dualism in which mind or consciousness is something separate from
brain processes. They no longer call it "soul" — that term has disappeared altogether from psychology textbooks except in historical perspective — and their accounts of it are couched in up-to-date, if virtually
incomprehensible, physical/cosmological terminology. Here is how one
speaker at the 2006 Tucson Conference on Consciousness, Pim van
Lommel, explained how consciousness, separate from the brain, is constructed of quantum phenomena:

Based on the universal reported aspects of consciousness experienced
during cardiac arrest, we can conclude that the informational fields of

our consciousness, consisting of waves, are rooted in phase-space, in an invisible dimension without time and space, and are present around and through us, permeating our body. They become available as our waking consciousness only through our functioning brain in the shape of measurable and changing electromagnetic fields.[39]

The only thing wrong with this theory is that there's no credible, tested evidence for it. It's wholly imaginary, but it fills a need of some sort for Dr. van Lommel. So, too, other beliefs in consciousness or identity not rooted in the physical brain apparently meet a need for those who believe in them. Though there are provable and proven explanations of an ever-increasing number of real-world mental phenomena, for deep-seated emotional and social reasons they need to believe in something else, unprovable and undisprovable. The majority of scientists, however, feel more as did the mathematician and astronomer Pierre-Simon Laplace two centuries ago; when Napoleon asked him why God was not mentioned in his immense work of cosmology, *Traité de la Mécanique Céleste*, he replied, "Sire, I had no need of that hypothesis."

Another enduring question that contemporary psychology and its associated sciences have answered is that of nature versus nurture. Generally given a hereditarian answer early in the century, a behaviorist answer later on, in the past few decades it has been definitively answered in interactionist terms. The details, some of which we have already seen, need not be reviewed again, but here is the core of the matter: Many kinds of evidence show that innate propensities, the product of evolution, are developed and molded by experiences (in genetic terms, various genes are "turned on" by environmental influences), which then lead the person to interact differently with the environment. The developing human being is thus shaped by an unfolding and continually changing interaction between innate predispositions or potentialities and environment or experience.[40]

A similar answer applies to the old question about where our ideas come from: They are the product of experience and learning as filtered through and shaped by built-in neural propensities. Language acquisition is a case in point. The child's brain has specialized areas that are able, with little help, to perceive syntactical patterns, extract meaning from speech, and group related objects into abstract categories. When the built-in wiring is defective, learning is difficult or impossible. One who is innately low in verbal ability cannot deal with difficult abstractions, no matter how much experience he or she has.

We need not restate contemporary psychology's answers to certain other ancient questions: how perception works; how the mind solves problems; how we reason and why we often reason invalidly; how and when our actions are determined by emotions, conscious judgment, and the interplay of the two; and how selfish or altruistic, hostile or kindly patterns of behavior are constructed out of latent tendencies by familial and social experiences.

Certain other questions, however, have been called "luxury problems." Ignorance of them does not impede scientific progress or affect the daily routine of research; seeking to answer them therefore seems unnecessary, and most psychologists, accordingly, ignore them. The nature of consciousness is one such; its use or function in human psychology is unclear, and for many years most researchers, including cognitive psychologists, neglected it and paid attention to more manageable phenomena. But as we have seen, consciousness is now receiving attention in several quarters, and this suggests that as psychology probes ever deeper into cognitive processes, it will find that consciousness plays a major role in mental phenomena and that it can no longer be considered a luxury problem. As has often been pointed out, the most sophisticated computer is vastly inferior in important ways to any ordinary person precisely because it is not conscious of itself as an entity.

Even freedom and will, two concepts all but missing from psychology for some decades, have lately come back into view. Behaviorists had swept them aside as mentalist illusions, and even cognitive psychologists had avoided them because a freely willed act seems an uncaused act—a concept anathema to science. But cognitive psychologists have been unable to sidestep or ignore choice—a meaningless concept if one insists that past and present forces determine what the individual chooses, and yet an inescapable and observable phenomenon.

An answer now proposed by a number of psychologists is that the operating system of the mind can run in a self-reflective mode, examining its own thoughts and behavior, deliberately evaluating the outcomes of various actions and possible actions, deciding which is the best, and intentionally choosing to carry it out. When we do not pursue this process, we make choices for less conscious reasons—the condition Spinoza referred to as human bondage. When we choose on the basis of self-reflection and evaluations, we approximate human freedom. Albert Bandura has made much the same point time and again. In his therapeutic research on "self-efficacy," he has argued that freedom should not be conceived of negatively as the absence of external coercion but positively as the exercise of self-influence: "Through their capacity to manipulate symbols and to engage in reflective thought, people can generate novel ideas and innovative actions that transcend their past experiences . . . By the exercise of [self-regulation] they help to determine the nature of their situations and what they become."[41] This is the very core of his current agentic theory, mentioned above: "The evolutionary convergence of advanced symbolizing capacity enabled humans to transcend the dictates of their immediate environment and made them unique in their power to shape their life circumstances and the courses their lives take. In this conception, people are contributors to their life circumstances, not just products of them."[42]

Where do we go from here?

Every issue of *Annual Review of Psychology* is full of forecasts and predictions of the future of the field. Many of them suggest that on a number of fronts psychology is breaking through into previously unknown and unimagined realms of knowledge and that the broad, sweeping, crude formulations of the past are giving way to narrow, specific, testable theories. However, contrary to this view of a fragmenting science, much of what we have seen above shows that in recent decades the many psychological sciences have been overlapping and interacting despite the absence of an all-embracing megatheory.

But we have also seen that one candidate for a Theory of Everything is knocking on the door, if not yet admitted. Martha Farah, you will recall, said that cognitive neuroscience might become the overarching theory of psychology because it is a cellular-systems explanation of how the brain acts during all the classical processes of cognitive psychology: how we learn, think, behave; why we differ from each other; the sources of personality. In sum, "All these things are in principle explainable by various levels of brain activity at various levels of description." For good measure, she later added, "Neuroscience is showing that character, consciousness, and a sense of spirituality are all physical functions of the brain."

Maybe . . . but it is not clear to everyone how neuroscience can become the Theory of Everything, although it will surely be a major component of that theory. For even if all the mental processes that make up mind are the result of physical functions of the brain, the great—indeed, the greatest—of questions, currently unanswered, is: How do those physical functions become our own individual thoughts, memories, hopes, joys, sorrows? Or as asked earlier in this book: How do our neural processes become *us*?

Whatever the tomorrow of psychology is, it is almost certain that many of the discoveries of the future will, like those of the past, prove useful to humankind in ways ranging from the trivial to the highly consequential—from tips on child care and memory improvement, say, to the radical improvement of education and the reduction of racial and ethnic hatreds.

Finally, to a far greater extent than ever, psychology surely will satisfy that purest, noblest, and most truly human of desires, the wish to understand. Albert Einstein once said, "The most incomprehensible thing in the world is that the world is comprehensible," but psychology is proving the great man wrong. It is making our comprehension of the world comprehensible.

NOTES

PROLOGUE

1. Herodotus, *The Persian Wars*, bk. II, chaps. 2–3.

2. BBC News, April 29, 2004, citing report of findings in northern Israel as reported in *Science*.

3. George A. Barton, *The Royal Inscriptions of Sumer and Akkad* (New Haven: American Oriental Society, 1929), p. 61, cited in Jaynes, 1976:181.

4. Jaynes, 1976:69–70.

5. Ibid.:72–73.

6. Herodotus, *The Persian Wars*, bk. I, chap. 209.

7. Bruno Snell, in *The Discovery of the Mind* (Harvard University Press, 1953), says that this development was definitely post-Homeric.

8. *Carnegie Institution of Washington Yearbook*, 1923, 22:335–337, cited in Thackray and Merton, 1972:491–492.

CHAPTER 1

1. Bertrand Russell, 1945:3.

2. *De Anima*, chap. II.

3. Cited in Theophrastus, *On the Senses*, 50–58.

4. Democritus, frag. 9, in C. Bakewell, *Source Book in Ancient Philosophy* (New York, 1909).

5. Bertrand Russell, 1945:43.

6. *On the Sacred Disease* (epilepsy). This may have been written by one of Hippocrates' followers, but it is generally held to be faithful to his ideas.

7. Quoted in Diogenes Laertius, *Plato*, 27.

8. See the *Meno* dialogue.

9. See the *Phaedo* dialogue.

10. See the last book of the *Republic*.

11. *Republic*, bk. VII.

12. *Phaedo*.

...blic, bk. IX, 571.

...d., bk. IV.

...obert Watson, 1978:36.

Encyclopaedia Britannica: Macropaedia, "Aristotle."

...7. Robinson, 1989:ix–x.

18. *De Anima*, bk. II, chap. v; bk. III, chaps. vii–ix.

19. David Ross, *Aristotle* (1964), quoted in Robinson, 1989:25.

20. *De Generatione Animalium*, quoted in *Encyclopaedia Britannica: Macropaedia*, "Aristotle":1163.

21. *De Anima*, bk. III, chap. iv.

22. Ibid., bk. II, chap. ii.

23. Robert Watson, 1978:67.

24. Robinson, 1989:34–35.

25. *De Memoria*, 2, 45lb, 17.

26. David Murray, 1988:30.

27. Robert Watson, 1978:69.

CHAPTER 2

1. Theophrastus, *On the Senses*, 47.

2. Quoted in Bertrand Russell, 1945:243.

3. Diogenes Laertius, *Lives*, "Epicurus," 118.

4. Ibid.:23.

5. Bertrand Russell, 1945:233.

6. Zeller, 1870:503.

7. Bertrand Russell, 1945:255–256.

8. Diogenes Laertius, *Lives*, "Zeno," 58.

9. Bertrand Russell, 1945:266–267.

10. Ibid.:278.

11. *On the Nature of Things*, bk. III.

12. Tacitus, *Annals*, xv, 61; Suetonius, *Nero*, 35.

13. Epictetus, *Discourses*, frag. 1.

14. *Discourses*, I, 12, 21; frag. vi, 25.

15. Ibid., bk. IV, sec. 440A.

16. L. Thorndike, *A History of Magic and Experimental Science During the First Thirteen Centuries of our Era* (New York: Macmillan, 1923), I, cited in Robert Watson, 1978:83.

17. Plotinus, *Enneads*, IV, 8, 1.

18. Bertrand Russell, 1945:288–291.

19. Boorstin, 1983:100.

20. *De Spectaculis*, 30.

21. *Ad Uxorem*, I, 1–3.

22. *De Anima*, bk. IV.

23. Ibid., bk. V.

24. Ibid., bk. XII.

25. Ibid., bk. XVI.

26. Commentary in "John the Evangelist," xxix, 6, and "Sermon 43."

27. *On Christian Doctrine*, cited in Robert Watson, 1978:98.

28. In *The Nicene and Post-Nicene Fathers* (Christian Literature Company, 1886), vol. 1:227.

29. *On the Trinity*, bk. X, chap. xi.

30. *City of God*, bk. XIII, 19; bk. XIV:2–6.

31. *Confessions*, 1886 ed.:145ff.

32. *City of God*, bk. XI:26.

33. Alexander and Selesnick, 1966:53–54.

34. *Confessions*:145ff.

35. David Murray, 1988:53.

36. *City of God*, bk. XIV, chaps. 24 and 26.

37. *On the Unity of the Intellect Against the Averroists*, quoted in Durant, 1950:962.

38. David Murray, 1988:58, 62.

39. "Treatise on Man," Q.83, A.3, in *Summa Theologica*.

40. "Treatise on Man," Q.82, A.3, in *Summa Theologica*.

41. Bertrand Russell, 1945:454–455.

42. David Murray, 1988:64, citing Cardinal Mercier, *The Origins of Contemporary Psychology* (1918), and R. Brennan, *History of Psychology from the Standpoint of a Thomist* (1945).

43. David Murray, 1988:77.

44. F. Watson, 1915.

CHAPTER 3

1. Bacon, 1905 [1605]:167.

2. Robert Watson, 1978:146.

3. *Passions of the Soul*, excerpted in Flew, 1964:136.

4. *Discourse on Method*, part IV.

5. Ibid., part IV.

6. *Meditations*, "The Existence of Material Things."

7. *Treatise of Man*:21.

8. Hothersall, 1984:30.

9. Fancher, 1979:29–30.

10. Robert Watson, in Benjamin, 1988:46.

11. *Passions of the Soul*, article XXXI.

12. Ibid., article XLI.

13. Ibid., "What Sensation Is."

14. Ibid., article LXXIX.

15. Fancher, 1979:36–37.

16. Robert Watson, 1978:164–165.

17. *Ethics*, part V, preface.

18. Ibid., part I.

19. Ibid., part III, props. 6 and 7.

20. Alexander and Selesnick, 1966:100.

21. Robert Watson, 1978:166.

22. Boorstin, 1983:395.

23. *Leviathan*, part I, chaps. 2, 7.

24. Ibid., chap. 46.

25. Ibid., chap. 1.

26. Ibid., chap. 2.

27. Ibid., chap. 3.

28. Ibid., chap. 3.

29. Ibid., chap. 3.

30. Hobbes, 1658, quoted in David Murray, 1988:94–95.

31. *Essay*, "The Epistle to the Reader."

32. Ibid., introduction.

33. Robert Watson, 1978:191.

34. *Essay*, bk. 1, chap. 4, secs. 8–9.

35. Ibid., bk. II, chap. 1, para. 1.

36. Ibid., chap. 1, para. 2.

37. Ibid., chap. 23, para. 12.

38. Ibid., chap. 23, paras. 15, 29.

39. Ibid., bk. IV, chap. 3, para. 6.

40. Ibid., "The Epistle to the Reader."

41. *Principles of Human Knowledge*, no. 92, in *New Theory of Vision*:159.

42. Ibid., para. 18.

43. Hume, 1956 [1738], introduction, vol. I:5.

44. Ibid., part 4, sec. 6.

45. Ibid., part 1, sec. 4.

46. Ibid., part 3, sec. 6; vol. I, part 4, sec. 1.

47. Ibid., part 4, sec. 2.

48. Boring, 1950:194.

49. Ibid.:196.

50. Hilgard, 1987:5; Brooks, 1976.

51. Robert Watson, 1978:214.

52. Leibniz, 1696, XIV, 10.

53. Bertrand Russell, 1945:584.

54. From *Journal des Savants*, June, 1695, quoted in Flew, 1964:150.

55. *Critique of Pure Reason*, preface.

56. Ibid.

57. Ibid., excerpt no. 105 in Herrnstein and Boring, 1965.

58. Boring, 1950:249.

59. Leary, 1978; Leary, 1982.

CHAPTER 4

1. Biographical details from Fancher, 1979; Boring, 1950; and *Dictionary of Scientific Biography*, "Mesmer."

2. H. F. Ellenberger, in Benjamin, 1988:136–137.

3. Council et al., 1996; Kirsch & Council, 1992.

4. Blakeslee, 2005.

5. On Lavater: Asendorpf, 1986. Darwin's statement is quoted in J. Graham, "Lavater's Physiognomy in England," *Journal of the History of Ideas* 22:561–572.

6. Details on Gall and phrenology are from Fancher, 1979; Boring, 1950; and the *Dictionary of Scientific Biography*, "Gall."

7. Gall, *Sur les fonctions du cerveau, etc.*, excerpted in Herrnstein and Boring, 1966:211. Omissions not indicated.

8. Fancher, 1979:52.

9. Details on Flourens are from Fancher, 1979.

10. Details on "Tan": Broca, 1861.

11. Hunt, 1982b:220.

12. Boring, 1950:72.

13. Lowry, 1971; Boring, 1950; Robert Watson, 1978; and David Murray, 1988.

14. Quoted in Lowry, 1971:81.

15. Hearnshaw, 1987:124.

16. *Dictionary of Scientific Biography*, "Johannes Müller"; Fancher, 1979.

17. Müller, *Handbuch der Physiologie*, bk. V, excerpted in Rand, 1966 [1912]:538, 541–542. Omissions not indicated.

18. James, 1948 [1892]:12.

19. Müller, *Handbuch der Physiologie*, bk. V, law VII, excerpted in Rand, 1966 [1912]:542.

20. David Murray, 1988:170.

21. Müller, *Handbuch der Physiologie*, bk. V, law VIII, excerpted in Rand, 1966 [1912]:543.

22. Boring, 1950:101.

23. Weber, "Über den Raumsinn und die Empfindungskreise in der Haut und im Auge," excerpted and translated in Herrnstein and Boring, 1966:141.

24. Based on Weber, as quoted in Herrnstein and Boring, 1966:141ff.

25. David Murray, 1988; Hothersall, 1984; Boring, 1950.

26. Weber, *Der Tastsinn*, excerpted in Rand, 1966 [1912]:557, 559.

27. Hothersall, 1984:134.

28. Koenigsberger, 1965 [1906]; Fancher, 1979; *Dictionary of Scientific Biography*, "von Helmholtz"; Boring, 1950.

29. Boring, 1950:42.

30. David Murray, 1988:195–197; Brooks and Brooks; 1978.

31. Brooks and Brooks, 1978.

32. Helmholtz, *Treatise on Physiological Optics*, chap. 26, excerpted in Shipley, 1961:105, 108–109.

33. Ibid.: 101–103

34. Robert Watson, 1978:249–250; Balance and Bringmann, 1987.

35. Balance and Bringmann, 1987.

36. Quoted in Balance and Bringmann, 1987.

37. Fechner, *Elements of Psychophysics*, cited in Robert Watson, 1978:241.

38. Cited in David Murray, 1988:183.

39. James, 1948 [1892]:23.

40. Edwin G. Boring, in Benjamin, 1988:168.

41. James, *A Pluralistic Universe*, quoted by Edwin G. Boring in Benjamin, 1988:169.

42. Edwin G. Boring, in Benjamin, 1988:169; Robert Watson, 1978:248–249.

43. Boring, 1950:294–295.

CHAPTER 5

1. Wundt's diagram for such an experiment is in Woodward and Ash, 1982:186.

2. Wolfgang G. Bringmann et al., in Benjamin, 1988:190–191.

3. Lawrence Hall: Myers, 1986:486.

4. Bringmann, Balance, and Evans, 1975:293.

5. Quoted in Hilgard, 1987:44.
6. Wundt, 1862, excerpted in Shipley, 1961:70–73.
7. Quoted in Fancher, 1979:132–133.
8. Blumenthal, 1975.
9. On Wundt's life up to Leipzig, the principal source drawn on is Bringmann, Balance, and Evans, 1975; for his life in general, Boring, 1950; Fancher, 1979; Robert Watson, 1978; and David Murray, 1988.
10. Wolfgang G. Bringmann et al., in Benjamin, 1988:189–195.
11. Wundt, 1977, as excerpted in *History of Psychology* 21(2):53–55 (1989).
12. Quoted in Hothersall, 1984:97.
13. Quoted in Fancher, 1979:128.
14. Fancher, 1979:136.
15. Kagan and Havemann, 1972:15.
16. Wundt, *Outlines of Psychology*; 3rd ed. (1897), excerpted in Rand, 1966 [1912]:707–708.
17. Ibid.:710.
18. Wundt, *Outlines of Psychology* (1897), quoted in Mandler and Mandler, 1964:132–133.
19. Ibid., Blumenthal, 1975.
20. James, 1948 [1892]:125, 710.
21. Ibid.:126.
22. Boring, 1950:328.
23. Quoted in Boring, 1950:346.
24. Lowry, 1971:105; Blumenthal, 1975.
25. David Murray, 1988:206.
26. Blumenthal, 1975; Boring, 1950:332.
27. Boring, 1950:335–337.
28. Wundt, *Outlines of Psychology*, 3rd ed. (1907), excerpted in Rand, 1966 [1912]:697, 701.
29. Robert Watson, 1978:287.
30. Fancher, 1979:128.
31. M. D. Boring and E. G. Boring, 1948.
32. David Murray, 1988:212.
33. Garrett, 1951:103–104.
34. Slamecka, 1985; Anderson, 1985.
35. Robert Watson, 1978:308.
36. Ibid.:283.
37. Mandler and Mandler, 1964:133.
38. Boring, 1950:403–404; Mandler and Mandler, 1964, chap. 4.
39. David Murray, 1988:276–277; Mandler and Mandler, 1964, chap. 4.
40. Robert Watson, 1978:309–310.
41. Ludy T. Benjamin, in Benjamin, 1988:180–181.
42. Boring, 1950:343–345.

CHAPTER 6

1. Letter to Francis Child, 1878, quoted in Barzun, 1983:30.
2. Quoted in Hothersall, 1984:260.

3. James, 1948 [1892]:468. Omissions not indicated.

4. Ibid.:468.

5. Quoted in Barzun, 1983:265.

6. James, 1890, vol. I,:296.

7. Ibid.:421.

8. Ibid.:169.

9. Biographical details are largely from Gerald Myers, 1986, and Barzun, 1983, with some additions from Fancher, 1979, Hilgard, 1987, and Watson, 1978.

10. Quoted in Fancher, 1979:149.

11. James, 1902:150. Omissions not indicated.

12. Barzun, 1983:26.

13. James, 1920, vol. I:147–148. Omissions not indicated.

14. "Hate": quoted in Boring, 1950:511; "horror": quoted in Perry, 1935, vol. II:195.

15. James, 1890, vol. I: footnote to 666–667.

16. Ibid.:244.

17. Ibid.:185.

18. Ibid.:185.

19. Hilgard, 1987:50.

20. Introduction to James, 1948 [1892].

21. "I find myself": James, 1911:198, quoted in Myers, 1986:10; "Theoretically": quoted in Barzun, 1983:241.

22. *Journal of Philosophy, Psychology, and Scientific Methods* 7, no. 19 (1910):506, quoted in Myers, 1986:1. Omissions not indicated.

23. James, 1890, vol. I:138.

24. Ibid.:185.

25. Flanagan, 1984:40–41.

26. James, 1890, vol. I:216ff.

27. Ibid.:224–225. Omissions not indicated.

28. Ibid.:144.

29. Flanagan, 1984:35–36.

30. James, 1890, vol. I:141.

31. Ibid.:239.

32. Ibid.:332.

33. Ibid.:330.

34. Hilgard, 1987:53.

35. James, 1890, vol. I:330.

36. Ibid.:334–336.

37. Ibid.:344.

38. James, 1948 [1892]:203.

39. Gardner Murphy, for one, cited in Woodward, 1984:148.

40. James, 1890, vol. II:486.

41. Ibid.

42. Ibid.:501, 522ff.

43. Ibid.:524–525.

44. Ibid.:561–562.

45. Ibid.:572–576.

46. Myers, 1988:197.

47. James, 1890, vol. I:141–142, 144.

48. Ibid., vol. II:547.

49. Ibid.:496.

50. Ibid.:520.

51. Ibid., vol. I:201.

52. Ibid.:206.

53. Ibid.:206ff.

54. Ibid., vol. II:614–615.

55. Murray, 1988:252.

56. Quoted in Hearnshaw, 1987:147.

57. James, 1890, vol. II:449–450. He had advanced this idea years earlier; see James, 1884.

58. James, 1890, vol. II:450.

59. Hothersall, 1984:257–258.

60. Cannon-Bard Theory and Cognitive Appraisal Theory, summarized in Gerrig & Zimbardo, 2005:400–401.

61. Ekman, 1992.

62. Allport, 1966:146.

63. Allport, 1943.

64. Hilgard, 1987:65.

65. Fancher, 1979:168.

66. Quoted in Barzun, 1983:298.

CHAPTER 7

1. Major sources of biographical material: Gay, 1988; Ronald Clark, 1980; Ernest Jones, 1953–1957; Freud, 1954 [letters to Fliess]; and autobiographical writings in S.E.

2. Quoted in Roazen, 1976:537.

3. "An Autobiographical Study" (1925), S.E. XX:70.

4. Letter to Romain Rolland, May 13, 1926, in Ernest Freud, 1964:370.

5. "Jokes and Their Relation to the Unconscious" (1905), S.E. VIII:31.

6. Ibid.:61.

7. "The Question of Lay Analysis" (1926), S.E. XX:253.

8. Letter to Martha Bernays, January 16, 1884, in Ernst Freud, 1964:89.

9. Details of the case: Studies on Hysteria, part II, case 1, S.E. II:21ff; "Five Lectures on Psycho-Analysis" (1910), S.E. XI:9–16.

10. Letter of Freud to Stefan Zweig, June 2, 1932, quoted in Gay, 1988:67.

11. Ibid.

12. Karpe, 1961; Ellenberger, 1972.

13. Letter to Fliess, December 28, 1887, in Freud, 1954:53.

14. "On the Psychical Mechanism of Hysterical Phenomena: Preliminary Communication" (1893), S.E. II:3–17.

15. "Studies," S.E. II:101–102.

16. Ibid.:63.

17. Ibid., part II, case 5, S.E. II:135–181.

18. Ibid., part IV, S.E. II:270.

19. James Strachey, note on p. 110, S.E. II.

20. "Fragment of an Analysis of a Case of Hysteria" (1905), S.E. VII:118.

21. Ibid.:116–117.

22. *The Interpretation of Dreams* (1900), chap. VII, S.E. V:608.

23. Ibid., chap. II, S.E. IV:125.

24. Ibid.:118–119.

25. "Further Remarks on the Neuro-Psychoses of Defence" (1896), S.E. III:164; see also note on that page by James Strachey, editor of S.E.

26. S.E. III:191–221.

27. Letter to Fliess, quoted in Gay, 1988:93.

28. Letter to Fliess, September 21, 1897, in Freud, 1954:215–218.

29. Letter to Fliess, June 12, 1897, in Freud, 1954:211, and see editor's note, same p.; letter to Fliess, August 14, loc. cit.: 213.

30. Letter to Fliess, August 14, 1897, in Freud, 1954:213–214.

31. Letter to Fliess, October 27, 1897, in Freud, 1954:225–227.

32. Letter to Fliess, October 3, 1897, in Freud, 1954:218–221.

33. Ernest Jones, 1953:265–267.

34. "Project for a Scientific Psychology" [1895], S.E. I:295–343; Pyles, 1999; Gay, 1988:78–79, 123.

35. Ernest Jones, 1953:383.

36. Letter to Fliess, September 22, 1898, in Freud, 1954:264–265.

37. Bettelheim, 1983:69–78.

38. Jones, 1953:365–368; Gay, 1988:119, 222.

39. Major source: *The Interpretation of Dreams*, esp. chap. VII, S.E. V:509–621.

40. Ernest Jones, 1953:397.

41. "The Ego and the Id" (1923), S.E. XIX:50n.

42. Major source: *The Interpretation of Dreams*, chap. VII, S.E. V:599–611.

43. "Project," S.E. I; *The Interpretation of Dreams*, S.E. V:598ff.

44. Ernest Jones, 1953:400.

45. Strachey note in S.E. II:63; Bettelheim, 1983:89–90.

46. "Formulations on the Two Principles of Mental Functioning (1911): S.E. XII:223.

47. *The Interpretation of Dreams*, S.E. IV:260–266.

48. According to James Strachey (see S.E. IV:263n.), Freud's first use of the term is in "The Psychology of Love" (II): S.E. XI:171.

49. Major sources: *Studies on Hysteria*, S.E. II, passim, but esp. 268–269; *The Interpretation of Dreams*, passim, but esp. chap. VII, S.E. IV and V. The concept occurs throughout Freud's writings.

50. Major sources: "Project," S.E. I; *Studies on Hysteria*, part III, S.E.:197; *The Interpretation of Dreams*, chap. VII, S.E. V:565n.

51. *Studies on Hysteria*, part III, S.E.:197.

52. Ibid.:202.

53. "On Narcissism" (1914), S.E. XIV:85.

54. Preface to 3rd ed., *The Interpretation of Dreams*, quoted by Strachey in S.E. IV:xx.

55. Gay, 1988:154–156.

56. Quoted in Gay, 1988:59, 163.

57. Quoted in Karier, 1986:210.

58. Roazen, 1976:45–46, 56.

59. *Everyday Life*, S.E. VI:59.

60. Ernest Jones, 1955:286.

61. The data: Ernest Jones, 1955:286; Strachey, in S.E. VII:126.

62. Ernest Jones, 1955:57.

63. The anecdote, told by Franz Alexander, is quoted in Hilgard, 1987:641n.

64. "The Question of Lay Analysis," S.E. XX:252.

65. "An Outline of Psycho-Analysis" (1940), S.E. XXIII:157n.

66. Solms, 2004; Zaretsky, 2004:5 (italics are Zaretsky's).

67. January 24, 1925, quoted in Gay, 1988:454.

68. "An Autobiographical Study," S.E. XX:73.

69. Ibid.:72.

70. Roazen, 1976:133–134; Rieff, 1961:1, 11.

71. "Psycho-Analysis" (1934), S.E. XX:266–267.

72. "Introductory Lectures on Psycho-Analysis" (1916–1917), S.E. XV:26–27.

73. Major sources: *Three Essays on Sexuality* (1905), part II, S.E. VII; lecture XXXIII in "New Introductory Lectures on Psycho-Analysis" (1933), S.E. XXII.

74. "Five Lectures on Psycho-Analysis" (1910), S.E. XI:42.

75. Major sources: "On Narcissism" (1914), S:E. XIV; *The Ego and the Id* (1923), S.E. XIX.

76. Gay, 1988:515.

77. Major sources: *Beyond the Pleasure Principle* (1920), S.E. XVIII; "The Ego and the Id" (1923), S.E. XIX.

78. "Some Psychical Consequences of the Anatomical Distinction Between the Sexes" (1925), S.E. XIX:257–258.

79. Adapted from Kline, 1984:19.

80. Major sources: *Beyond the Pleasure Principle* (1920), S.E. XVIII; "The Ego and the Id" (1923), S.E. XIX.

81. Bettelheim, 1983:103–104.

82. Major sources: "Introductory Lectures on Psycho-Analysis" (1916–1917), S.E. XV, XVI; "Inhibitions, Symptoms and Anxiety" (1926), S.E. XX; "New Introductory Lectures on Psycho-Analysis" (1933), S.E. XXII.

83. "Inhibitions, Symptoms and Anxiety" (1926), S.E. XX:94–95.

84. "Analysis of a Phobia in a Five-Year-old Boy" (1909), S.E. X:5–149.

85. "New Introductory Lectures" (1933), S.E. XX:83–84.

86. "On the History of the Psycho-Analytic Movement" (1914), S.E. XIV:16; "Repression" (1915), S.E. XIV:146–158, and James Strachey's "Editor's Note" to same, 143–144.

87. "Introductory Lectures," S.E. XVI; "A Disturbance of Memory on the Acropolis" (1936), S.E. XXII:245; "Analysis, Terminable and Interminable" (1937), S.E. XXIII:235–236.

88. Grünbaum, 1984:277.

89. Ibid.:278.

90. Fisher and Greenberg, 1977:393, 395–396.

91. Kline, 1981:432, 437, 446.

92. Zaretsky, 2004:334–335; Solms, 2004.

93. Fisher & Greenberg, 1977:viii.

94. Quoted in Rudolf M. Lowenstein, *Freud: Man and Scientist* (New York: International Universities Press, 1951):17.

95. Hearnshaw, 1987:156–157.

96. Fancher, 1979:248.

97. Quoted in Adler, 2006.

98. Zaretsky, 2004:343–344.

99. Adler, 2006.

100. Solms, 2004.

101. Quoted in Solms, 2004.

CHAPTER 8

1. Forrest, 1974:181; Fancher, 1979:250–251.

2. Galton, 1907 [1883]:19–21.

3. Major biographical sources: Galton, 1908; Forrest, 1974.

4. Galton, 1908:287–289.

5. Quoted in Forrest, 1974:88.

6. *Hereditary Genius* (Galton, 1891 [1869]), quoted in Forrest, 1974:89.

7. Galton, 1891 [1869]:79.

8. Ibid.:1.

9. Galton, 1907 [1883]:17n.

10. Article in *Frazier's* magazine, quoted in Forrest, 1974:136.

11. Galton, 1970 [1874]:12.

12. Galton, 1907 [1883]:167.

13. Boring, 1950:485–486.

14. Galton, 1908:304; Forrest, 1974:192.

15. Correlation of .47: Forrest, 1974:199.

16. George Miller, 1962:145.

17. Fancher, 1979:293–294.

18. Boring, 1950:482.

19. Angell, 1907; Robert Watson, 1979:424.

20. Major source: Woodworth, 1944.

21. Watson, 1979:408.

22. Murray, 1988:379; Watson, 1979:409–410.

23. Solomon Diamond, in Benjamin, 1988:265.

24. Major biographical sources on Binet: Wolf, 1973; Hothersall, 1984; Robert Watson, 1978.

25. Stephen Jay Gould, 1981:146, quoting Binet, 1898:294–295.

26. Reprinted in Binet and Simon, 1980 [1916]:40.

27. Ibid.:45–68.

28. Ibid.:41.

29. Ibid.:276 (adapted); for the three-year-old test: 184–195.

30. Boring, 1950:574.

31. Binet and Simon, 1980 [1916]:42.

32. Ibid.:37.

33. Ibid.:16–17, 101, 104, 257; Binet, cited in Gould, 1981:154.

34. Goddard's introduction to Binet and Simon, 1980 [1916]:6.

35. Michael Sokal, in Benjamin, 1988:316.

36. Fancher, 1987.

37. Hothersall, 1984:308–309.

38. Terman, 1916:xi.

39. Goddard, 1914:571.

40. Goddard, 1912:65–66.

41. Goddard, 1914:561.

42. Gould, 1981:164–168, citing Goddard, 1917.

43. *Encyclopaedia Britannica* (1935 edition): "Migration," vol. 15:468.

44. Terman, 1916:19–20:

45. Terman biographical details from Hilgard, 1987:465–466, and Hothersall, 1984:267–268.

46. Terman, 1916:51, 127.

47. Ibid.:21.

48. Ibid.:6–7.

49. Gould, 1981:175, and 175n.

50. Hothersall, 1984:323–324; Gould, 1981:194.

51. Gould, 1981:194–195; Garrett, 1951:244.

52. Advertisement from Terman et al., 1923, reproduced in Gould, 1981:178; 7,000,000: Hothersall, 1984:324.

53. Gould, 1981:293; Lewontin, Rose, and Kamin, 1984:87.

54. Hothersall, 1984:323–324; Block and Dworkin, 1876:2–3.

55. Terman, 1916:91–92.

56. Lippmann, quoted in Block and Dworkin, 1976:19.

57. Gould, 1981:199–200.

58. Ibid.:196.

59. Hunt, 1999:94. See also Jensen, 1991:179; Snyderman and Rothman, 1998: 140–141, 250.

60. Benson, 2003.

61. Loehlin, 1985; Plomin and Daniels, 1987; Hilgard, 1987:484–489; Bouchard, 1986.

62. Grigorenko, 2000; Neisser et al., 1996; Plomin and Petrill, 1997.

63. Flynn, James, 1984, 1999.

64. Neisser, Ulric, et al., 1996.

65. Sternberg, 1985, 1999.

66. Gardner, 1983, 1999.

67. Benson, 2003.

68. Ibid.

69. Giles, Jim, 2006. "Scans suggest IQ scores reflect brain structure," *Nature* 440, March 30:588.

CHAPTER 9

1. Lloyd Morgan's work, mentioned in Hothersall, 1984:291.

2. Thorndike, 1898.

3. Pavlov's work described by Gregory A. Kimble in Koch and Leary, 1985:287–288.

4. Morgan, 1909 [1894]:53.

5. Loeb, 1900, chap. 15, excerpted in Herrnstein and Boring, 1966:468–472.

6. Major biographical sources: Thorndike, 1936; Joncich, 1968.

7. Thorndike, 1936:165.

8. Thorndike, 1911:64.

9. Ibid.:287.

10. Major biographical sources: Babkin, 1949; Asratyan, 1953.

11. Pavlov, 1927, lecture I, in Shipley, 1961:789.

12. R. Watson, 1978:441; Lashley, 1929.

13. Pavlov, 1927, lecture 1, in Shipley, 1961:789.

14. Pavlov, 1960 [1927]:291.

15. Yerkes and Morgulis, 1909.

16. J. Watson, *Encyclopaedia Britannica* article on behaviorism (ca. 1928), quoted in Skinner, 1981.

17. Coleman, 1988:104.

18. Garrett, 1951:17. Skinner, 1981, gives a more modest appraisal of Pavlov's influence.

19. Major biographical sources: John B. Watson, 1961; Hannush, 1987; David Cohen, 1979; Buckley, 1989.

20. Hannush, 1987.

21. J. Watson, 1961:276.

22. Ibid.

23. J. Watson, 1913.

24. Samelson, 1981.

25. J. Watson, 1916.

26. J. Watson, 1919:200–201.

27. Ibid.:214.

28. J. Watson and Rayner, 1920.

29. J. Watson, 1924:104.

30. Fancher, 1979:337.

31. J. Watson, 1930:18.

32. Bowers, 1973:316.

33. Bakan, 1966.

34. Gregory Kimble, in Koch and Leary, 1985:316.

35. Sigmund Koch, in Koch and Leary, 1985:931.

36. The examples are drawn from Bugelski 1975; Hintzman, 1978; and Levine, 1975, in all of which the original sources are cited.

37. J. Watson, 1919:14.

38. Quoted in Kitchener, 1977:19.

39. Ibid.:27.

40. Hull, 1967.

41. Boring, 1950:652. On details of Hull's system: Gregory Kimble, in Koch and Leary, 1985:300–301; Murray, 1988:326–327.

42. Hull, 1943:119.

43. Benjamin, 1988:434–435; Gregory Kimble, in Koch and Leary, 1985:318.

44. Gonnezano and Coleman, 1985.

45. Hothersall, 1984:394–395.

46. Major biographical sources: Skinner, 1967, 1976, 1979, 1983.

47. Skinner, 1979:117; Skinner, 1953:19–21; Cohen, 1977:279.

48. Skinner, 1967:410.

49. Quoted in Hothersall, 1984:395.

50. Skinner, 1972:7.

51. The first sentence: Skinner, 1972:12–13; the rest: Skinner, 1974:115.

52. Cohen, 1977:283.

53. Guttman, 1977.

54. Cohen, 1977:273.

55. Skinner, 1979:35.

56. Hilgard, 1987:194–199.

57. Fancher, 1979:364.

58. Skinner, 1953:92.

59. E. Hunt, 1982:59, citing Hintzman, 1978, and Levine, 1975.

60. As, for instance, according to Science Citation Index for the period May–August 1990.

61. Hintzman, 1978:194–196.

62. Ayllon and Azrin, 1968; Kazdin, 1978.

63. Bachrach et al., 1965.

64. Early years: Kinkade, 1972; status in 2006: Twin Oaks Web page, and e-mail communiqué from Twin Oaks.

65. Skinner, 1967:408.

66. Skinner, 1956.

67. Hintzman, 1978:180–181; Gregory Kimble, in Koch and Leary, 1985:315–316; Stephen Glickman, in Koch and Leary, 1985:766–768.

68. Braginsky and Braginsky, 1974:48.

69. Tolman, 1938.

70. Tolman and Honzick, 1930.

71. Tolman, 1948.

72. Tolman, 1938; Gregory Kimble, in Koch and Leary, 1985:303–305.

73. Guthrie, 1935:172.

74. Tolman, 1932:3; Tolman, 1938; "Neobehaviorism," in Benjamin, 1988:434–436.

75. Kuhn, 1970.

76. Gregory Kimble, in Koch and Leary, 1985:313–314.

77. Gerrig and Zimbardo, 2005:195.

78. Ibid.:196.

79. Kosslyn and Rosenberg, 2004:235.

80. Bandura, 1997:324–325, 333–337.

81. Shull and Grimes, 2006.

CHAPTER 10

1. Major sources of biographical details on Wertheimer: Luchins, 1987; Michael Wertheimer, 1980; Luchins and Luchins, 1986; Newman, 1944.

2. Major sources of biographical details on Köhler: Ash, 1985; Mandler and Mandler, 1968; Zuckerman and Wallach, 1987. On Koffka: Ash, 1985; Harrower, 1983; Grace Heider, 1979.

3. Wertheimer, 1961 [1912].

4. Ibid.

5. Mandler and Mandler, 1968:378.

6. "Gestalt Psychology," in Benjamin, 1988:517.

7. Wertheimer, 1959 [1945]: chap. 2.

8. Wertheimer, 1955b [1912].

9. Ash, 1985.

10. "More than half": Murray, 1988:284, referring to the period 1922–1928.

11. Wertheimer, 1955a [1923].

12. Helson, 1933.

13. Hothersall, 1984:171.

14. Zeigarnik, 1955 [1927].
15. Both studies: Koffka, 1963 [1935]:88–89.
16. Koffka, 1963 [1935]:161.
17. Adapted from Kohler, 1948 [1917], chap. 5.
18. Wertheimer, 1955c [1925] and Wertheimer 1959 [1945].
19. Kohler, 1988 [1967].
20. Hothersall, 1984:180.
21. Kohler, 1925a:190.
22. Kohler, 1925b:14.
23. Kohler, 1957 [1917]:150.
24. Kohler, 1925b:127.
25. Hothersall, 1984:180–181.
26. Ibid.:181.
27. Alpert, 1928.
28. Dunker, 1945 [1935]:69–70.
29. Ibid.
30. Ibid.:2–3.
31. Ibid.:86–88.
32. Kohler, 1955 [1918].
33. Asch 1969.
34. Boring, 1950:613.
35. Koffka; 1963 [1935]:355–356; R. Watson, 1978:481.
36. Koffka, 1963 [1935]:628–647.
37. Ibid.:52, 62–66; Hilgard, 1987:427.
38. Lashley, Chow, and Semmes, 1951; Sperry and Miner, 1955.
39. Koffka, 1963 [1935]:542.
40. Ibid.:557–558.
41. Boring, 1950:610.
42. Michael Sokal, in Benjamin, 1988:535–536.
43. Henle, 1986:121–123; Hilgard, 1987:139–145.
44. Feldin, Goldman-Meadow, and Gleitman, 1978.
45. Michael Sokal, in Benjamin, 1988:539.
46. Heidbreder, 1933.
47. Luchins and Luchins, 1978, vol. 2:505.
48. David Navon, cited in Rock and Palmer, 1990.
49. Ibid.
50. Gleitman, Fridlund, and Reisberg, 1999:319; Gerrig and Zimbardo, 2005:266.
51. Murray, 1988:295; R. Watson, 1978:604–605.
52. Koffka, 1963 [1935]:21.
53. Boring, 1950:600. Omissions not indicated.
54. Rock and Palmer, 1990. Omissions not indicated.

FISSION AND FUSION

1. Heidbreder, 1933.
2. Sanford, 1963:577.
3. Kessen and Cahan, 1986.
4. Gazzaniga, 2006.

CHAPTER 11

1. *Historia Animalium*, bk. I, viii, 891b.
2. McReynolds and Ludwig, 1984.
3. Pervin, 1985:85.
4. Cattell, 1974:65.
5. Woodworth, 1919; Loevinger, 1987:107.
6. Allport, 1965:424.
7. Ibid.:436; Loevinger, 1987:107.
8. Mischel and Peake, 1983:237.
9. Hartshorne and May, 1928:385.
10. Main source of biographical details: Allport, 1967.
11. Allport, 1968:383–384.
12. Allport, quoted in Evans, 1976:200–201.
13. Allport and Allport, 1928.
14. Allport, 1965:341–342, 347.
15. Ibid.:386–387.
16. Allport and Vernon, 1933.
17. Lawrence A. Pervin, cited in Buss and Cantor, 1989:33; Gleitman, Fridlund, and Reisberg, 1999, ch. 16.
18. Allport, 1965:353–355; the original source is Allport and Odbert, 1936.
19. Caspi and Roberts, 2001, cited in Harris, 2006.
20. Singer, 1984:148–150; Kline, 1983:26–27.
21. Kline, 1983:27.
22. Ibid.:28–29.
23. Singer, 1984:154–155.
24. *American Psychologist* 20:990 (1965), quoted in Singer, 1984:154.
25. Gough, 1988a; Singer, 1984:156; Aiken, 1979:256–257; Gough, 1988b. On versions in use ca. 1993: Gough, personal communication. On ranking today: various issues of *Mental Measurements Yearbook* from 1972 on, and Gough, personal communication.
26. Taken from Mischel, 1976:132.
27. Kline, 1983:35; Mischel, 1981:87.
28. Aiken, 1979:261.
29. "Leading topic": Hilgard, 1987:516. Pro-Rorschach: Singer, 1984:161. Anti-Rorschach: Aiken, 1976:263.
30. Murray, 1967.
31. Kazin, 1993; "Christiana Morgan" in *Gale Encyclopedia of Psychology*, 2nd ed., 2001.
32. Murray et al., 1938:144–145.
33. Ibid.:537–538.
34. Ibid.:531, 545.
35. McAdams and Valliant, 1982.
36. Aiken, 1979:260.
37. OSS, 1948:8.
38. Kline, 1983:37, 71.
39. Allport, 1958.
40. Eysenck, 1970 [1953]:19.
41. Eysenck and Rachman, 1965.

42. Most biographical details from Cattell, 1974.

43. Ibid.:64.

44. Cattell, 1969 [1946]:294–299.

45. Cattell and Stice, 1957, quoted in Singer, 1984:156.

46. Skinner, 1953:202–203, 285.

47. Dollard and Miller, 1950.

48. Rotter, 1954:102–103.

49. Rotter, personal communication.

50. Rotter, 1966.

51. Rotter, personal communication; Singer, 1984:247; Kosslyn and Rosenberg, 2004:466–467.

52. The examples are cited in Singer, 1984:247–248; Mischel, 1990:125; and Baron, Byrne, and Kantowitz, 1980:484–486.

53. Singer, 1984:248; Baron, Byrne, and Kantowitz, 1980:486. Heider quote: Edward E. Jones, 1990b:ix.

54. Kelly, 1955.

55. Jones and Berglas; 1978.

56. Seligman, 1991:19–21.

57. Overmier and Seligman, 1967.

58. Abramson, Seligman, and Teasdale, 1978.

59. Ibid.; Seligman, 1991:32–43, 66–67.

60. Cited in Krebs and Blackman, 1988:701–702.

61. Seligman, personal communication.

62. Sutterfield, 2001; Seligman et al., 2005.; www.ppc.sas.upenn.edu/.

63. Terman and Miles, 1936, quoted in Garrett, 1961:192–193.

64. Fearful: Maccoby and Jacklin, 1974, vol. 1:184–189. Nurturance: ibid.:220. Compassion: Staub, 1978a:254; Piliavin, Dovidio, et al., 1981:199–202.

65. Aggressiveness: Maccoby and Jacklin, 1974, vol. 1:241–247; Maccoby and Jacklin, 1980; Deaux, 1985. Verbal ability: Maccoby and Jacklin, 1974, vol. 1:2–3 and chap. 7. Nonverbal cues: Deaux, 1985. The recent review of brain studies: Hines, 2004:211. The thorough survey: Hines, 2004:11–13.

66. Deaux, 1985.

67. Kosslyn and Rosenberg, 2004:472–474; omissions not indicated; sources omitted.

68. Kretschmer, 1925.

69. Hilgard, 1987:495.

70. Sheldon and Stevens, 1942; Sheldon, Stevens, and Tucker, 1940.

71. Gardner Lindzey, in Lindzey and Hall, 1965:348.

72. Ibid.:348–349.

73. McConnell, 1974:652.

74. Berger, 1980:91–92, citing Thomas, Chess, and Birch, 1963.

75. Chess and Thomas, 1986, appendix B.

76. Mussen, Conger, et al., 1979:50.

77. Ibid.:51.

78. Powledge, 1983:26; Time, January 12, 1987:63.

79. Tellegen, Lykken, et al., 1988; Bouchard, Lykken, et al., 1990.

80. Loehlin, 1986.

81. Scarr, Webber, et al., 1981.

82. Bouchard and McGue, 2003.

83. Costa and McCrae, 1984.

84. The two studies: Rosenman, et al., 1975; Haynes, Feinleib, et al., 1980. Later studies: Carson, 1989.

85. Peterson, Seligman, and Vailliant, 1988; Seligman, 1991; Seligman et al., 2005; www.ppc.sas.upenn.edu/.

86. Eysenck, 1989.

87. Digman, 1990; McCrae, 1989; Costa et al., 1991.

88. Gerrig and Zimbardo, 2005:439–440.

89. Mischel, 1990:131.

90. Roberts et al., 2006.

CHAPTER 12

1. Sources of the following vignettes: Greenough, Black, and Wallace, 1987:549; Kisilievsky et al., 2003; Colombo and Richman, 2002; Hunt, 1982b:197, from personal observation; Piaget, 1948:13; Hunt, 1990:50, based on videotape seen at NIMH and on Zahn-Waxler, Radke-Yarrow, and King, 1979:321; Osherson and Markman, 1974–1975; Rest, 1986:22–23.

2. White, 1983.

3. Gelman, 1978:327.

4. *The Organisation of Thought*, quoted in Merton, 1968:1.

5. Skinner, 1953:59, 156.

6. In *British Journal of Psychology*, May 1982:1.

7. Kagan, 1989:91.

8. Ibid.

9. Major sources of biographical material: Piaget, 1952a; Evans, 1973; Ginsburg and Opper, 1969; Cohen, 1983.

10. Piaget, 1952b:42–43, 407–419.

11. Piaget, 1969.

12. The details: Flavell, 1963; Ginsburg and Opper, 1969; Mussen, Conger, et al., 1979; and Cohen, 1983. All give references to Piaget's own writings (which are relatively inaccessible due to his special terminology).

13. Piaget, 1952b:337–338.

14. Piaget, 1951, quoted in Berger, 1980:54.

15. Quoted in Mussen, Conger, et al., 1979:173.

16. Ginsburg and Opper, 1969:90.

17. Mussen, Conger, et al., 1979:176.

18. Piaget, 1958:70–71.

19. Piaget and Inhelder, 1969:132.

20. Kagan, 1989:193–194.

21. Papousek, 1959.

22. Sullivan, Rowe-Collier, and Tynes, 1979.

23. Kagan, 1989:189.

24. Sroufe, Cooper, and Marshall, 1988:351–352.

25. Eleanor Gibson, 1988.

26. Kagan, 1989:229–30.

27. Ginsburg and Opper, 1969:85, 171–172.

28. Bruner, 1964.

29. Kuenne, 1946.

30. Gagne and Smith, 1964.

31. Clark and E. Clark, 1977:266.

32. Moskowitz, 1978.

33. Bickerton, 1998.

34. Cohen, 1983:100–101.

35. Gelman, 1978.

36. On theory of mind: Somerville and Woodword, 2005; Gergely and Csiba, 2003; Baldwin and Baird, 2001. The fMRI-based study: R. Saxe and Powell, 2006.

37. Morton Hunt, 1982:180–182, citing work of Merry Bullock and Rochel Gelman.

38. Rogoff, 2003; Lourenço and Machado, 1996.

39. Fish, 2000.

40. Serpell, 2000; Rogoff, 1990.

41. Schlitz, 1997.

42. Various sources cited by Gerrig and Zimbardo, 2005:259–260, 305, 306, 329–330, 336, 460.

43. Farah et al. (in press).

44. Snibbe, 2003.

45. Buss, 2004:xix.

46. Kosslyn and Rosenberg, 2004:18.

47. Ibid.:19, citing Brown, 1991.

48. Buss, 2004:47.

49. Ibid.:59.

50. Ohman, Flykt, and Esteves, 2001.

51. Buss, 2004:93.

52. Ibid., xix, 373.

53. Pinker, 2002:135.

54. de Villiers and de Villiers, 1978:90.

55. McGraw, 1935

56. "Science and the Citizen: Growing Up," *Scientific American*, July 1987:30–32.

57. Dennis, 1935; Dennis, 1938.

58. Lorenz, 1937.

59. Hess, 1959.

60. Macfarlane, 1977; Kennell, Jerauld, et al., 1974.

61. Fantz, 1961.

62. Haaf, 1977; Aslin and Smith, 1988; Clarke-Stewart, Friedman, and Koch, 1985.

63. Nyengaard et al., 2001.

64. Siegler, 1989c:358–359; Gazzaniga and Heatherton, 2005:436–437.

65. Greenough et al., 1987

66. Bowlby, 1980, cited in Kagan, 1989:80; Bretherton, 1985:4; Peter Evans, 1977.

67. Gewirtz, 1965.

68. Bretherton, 1985:15; Ainsworth, Blehar, et al., 1978; Kagan, 1984:44; Sroufe and Cooper, 1988:221–223.

69. Sroufe, Cooper, and Marshall, 1988:222; Kagan, 1984:44–45.

70. Kagan, 1984:60–61.

71. Ibid.:61.

72. Lewis, Feiring, et al., 1984

73. Lewis, et al., 1989; Izard, Huebner, et al., 1980; Hyson and Izard, 1985.

74. Morton Hunt, 1990:49–50; Zahn-Waxler, Radke-Yarrow, and King, 1979. Brain scans: Decety and Jackson, 2006.

75. Sroufe, Cooper, and Marshall, 1988:302.

76. Lewis, et al., 1989b.

77. Staub, 1979; Martin Hoffman, 1971b.

78. Gray and Steinberg, 1999; Maccoby and Martin, 1983; Maccoby, 1980; Shaffer, 1985.

79. Mussen, Conger, et al., 1979:206–211; Hetherington and Morris, 1978; Bryan and Walbeck, 1970.

80. Mussen, Conger, et al., 1979:114–115; Parke, 1990.

81. Bowers, 1973; Mussen, Conger, et al., 1979:227–228.

82. Mueller and Lucas, 1975.

83. Sroufe, Cooper, and Marshall, 1988:385.

84. Berger, 1980:343–344.

85. Collins and Gunnar, 1990.

86. Darley and Shultz, 1990.

87. Lewis, et al., 1989a.

88. Sroufe, Cooper, and Marshall, 1988:385–387; Connolly and Doyle, 1984.

89. Broughton, 1978.

90. Sroufe, Cooper, and Marshall, 1988:467; Mussen, Conger, et al., 1979:305; Berndt, 1979.

91. Anne Peterson, 1988.

92. Kling et al., 1999.

93. Morton Hunt, 1990, passim.

94. Four-stage: Hoffman, 1982. Five-stage: Eisenberg, 1986:135–145. Six-stage: Krebs and Van Hesteren, 1994.

95. Piaget, 1948 [1932]; Ginsburg and Opper, 1969:99–109.

96. Main biographical sources: Who Was Who in America; "Memorial Minute," Harvard Gazette, December 15, 1989; Boston Herald, January 30, 1987; Boston Globe, April 8, 1987; and memorabilia contributed by Mrs. Lucille Kohlberg.

97. Kohlberg, 1984:640–641.

98. Ibid.:624–639; Kohlberg, 1969:379. The typical responses are adapted from Rest, 1968, in Kohlberg, 1984:49–55.

99. Kurtines and Gewirtz, 1984; David Cohen, 1983:125; Krebs, Denton, and Higgins, 1988.

100. Gilligan, 1977.

101. Gielen, 1996:313; Lind, 2003.

102. Denton and Krebs, 1990.

103. Krebs, in submission.

104. Main biographical sources: Snarey, 1987; Hilgard, 1987; Goleman, 1988a.

105. Adapted from Erikson, 1950:247–274.

106. Baltes, Reese, and Lipsitt, 1980.

107. Gazanniga and Heatherton, 2005, chap. 11; Kosslyn and Rosenberg, 2004, chap. 12.

108. Peterson, 1988.

109. Silbereisen and Noack, 1988.

110. Offer and Schonert-Reichl, 1992.

111. "Thrive or muddle through": sociologist Michael Farrell and social psychologist

Stanley Rosenberg, cited in Rosenfeld and Stark, 1987; "can adapt sufficiently": Baltes, Reese, and Lipsitt, 1980; Mussen, Conger, et al., 1979:419; "do cope": Rowe and Kahn, 1998.

112. The reanalysis: Havighurst et al., 1968; the Duke Longitudinal Study reports: Morton Hunt, 1985:70–71; Baltes et al., 1992; Freund and Baltes, 1998.

CHAPTER 13

1. The first definition: K. Shaver, 1987:2. The second one: Gerrig and Zimbardo, 2005:541.

2. Brown, 1965:xx.

3. Asch, 1951, 1955.

4. Luce and Raiffa, 1957:95; M. Deutsch, 1985:121–124.

5. Freedman and Fraser, 1966, Guadagno et al., 2001.

6. Rosenhan, 1973; Slater, 2004; Jaffe, 2006.

7. Latané, Williams, and Harkins, 1979; recent studies: Kosslyn and Rosenberg, 2004:711.

8. Quoted in Lindzey and Aronson, 1985, vol. I:3, unchanged from the 1954 edition.

9. Quoted in Lindzey and Aronson, 1968, vol. I:2–5.

10. Triplett, 1897.

11. Sherif, 1935, 1936.

12. Aarts and Dijksterhuis, 2003.

13. Marrow, 1969:ix.

14. Main sources of biographical details: Marrow, 1969; Allport, 1968, chap. 19; Hothersall, 1984.

15. M. Deutsch, 1968.

16. Lewin, Lippitt, and White, 1939.

17. Leon Festinger, in Festinger, 1980:238–239.

18. Edward Jones, in Lindzey and Aronson, 1985:57.

19. Biographical details: Leon Festinger, in Festinger, 1980; Aron and Aron, 1989; D. Cohen, 1977.

20. Festinger, Riecken, and Schachter, 1964 [1956]:3.

21. Leon Festinger, "A Personal Memory," in Grunberg, Nisbett, et al., 1987:5.

22. Ibid.:6.

23. Festinger and Carlsmith, 1959.

24. Aron and Aron, 1989:127.

25. Cohen, 1977:138.

26. Aron and Aron, 1989:117.

27. The examples are from Aronson, 1988a:153; Aronson, in Festinger, 1980:21; and Aronson, 1988a:122–124, 159. The Santa Cruz episode: Pratkanis and Aronson, 1992:35–36.

28. Lewicki, 1982.

28. Baumrind, 1977; M. Hunt, 1982a; Edward Jones, in Lindzey and Aronson, 1985:97.

30. Details are from Zimbardo, Haney, et al., 1974.

31. *Schloendorff* v. *The Society of the New York Hospital*, 1914. (The decision was written by Justice Benjamin Cardozo.)

32. Adorno, Frenkel-Brunswik, et al., 1950.

33. The details that follow are from Milgram, 1963, 1965, and 1974.

34. Milgram, 1963.

35. Brown, 1985:6.

36. The following account of their teaming up is from M. Hunt, 1985:132–134.

37. Personal communication, in M. Hunt, 1985:133.

38. Darley and Latané, 1968.

39. Latané, in Grunberg, Nisbett, et al., 1987:79.

40. Latané and Nida, 1981.

41. Aronson, 1988a:383.

42. "Code of Federal Regulations," *Federal Register* 46:16 (January 26, 1981):8389–8390.

43. Ortmann and Hertwig, 1998.

44. "The Laboratory Experiment," in Lindzey and Aronson, 1985, vol. I:443.

45. Quoted in Aron and Aron, 1989:93.

46. Aronson and Linder, 1965.

47. Biographical details: personal communication.

48. The work is summarized in Morton Deutsch, 1973.

49. M. Deutsch, 1973:183–185, 196.

50. Ibid.:214.

51. M. Deutsch, 1985:125.

52. Ibid.:128.

53. Heidi Burgess, personal communication.

54. Kosslyn and Rosenberg, 2004:693.

55. Thibaut and Riecken, 1955.

56. Doosje and Branscombe, 2003.

57. Heider interview in R. Evans, 1980:20–21.

58. Harvey and Weary, 1984:429.

59. Lindzey and Aronson, 1985, vol. I:90.

60. The examples are from, or cited in, Ross, Amabile, and Steinmetz, 1977; Kelley and Michela, 1980; Valins, 1966; Harvey and Weary, 1984:439–440; and Lepper, Greene, and Nisbett, 1973.

61. Kelley and Michela, 1980; Harvey and Weary, 1984:450–452.

62. Aron and Aron, 1989:57–58; Aronson, 1988a:328–330; Baumeister et al., 1994; Buss, 2000.

63. Aronson, 1988a:99, 103–111, 88–90; Petty et al., 2003.

64. Ellen Berscheid, in Lindzey and Aronson, 1985, vol. II, chap. 21; Kosslyn and Rosenberg, 2004:695–696.

65. Petty, Ostrom, and Brock, 1981:178; Lindzey and Aronson, 1985, vol. I:76, 236; and Festinger, 1957.

66. Stephan and Stephan, 1985:354–356; Tajfel, as reported in Brown, 1985:545–547; Sherif, Harvey, et al., 1961; Carter and Rice, 1997.

67. Stephan and Stephan, 1985:331–333; Aron and Aron, 1989:55; Stephan and Stephan, 1985:324–326; Zajonc, 2001.

68. M. Hunt, 1990:207–208, 180–181; 217–218.

69. Ito and Urland, 2003.

70. Hilgard, 1987:610.

71. Gergen, 1973.

72. Edward Jones, in Lindzey and Aronson, 1985, vol. I:99.

73. Schlencker, 1974.

74. Edward Jones, in Lindzey and Aronson, 1985, vol. I:100.

75. Judith Rodin, in Lindzey and Aronson, 1985, vol: II, passim.

76. Aronson, 1988a:xi.

77. Baron, Byrne, and Branscombe, 2006:5–6.

CHAPTER 14

1. Haber, 1978.

2. Boring, 1950:677.

3. Ibid.:675.

4. Pasternak et al., 2003; Rao et al., 1997; Gerrig and Zimbardo, 2005:106; Ramachandran, 2004:25.

5. Standing, 1973.

6. Farah, 1988; Kosslyn et al., 1993; Gazzaniga et al., 2002:238–239; Ramachandran, 2004:25.

7. Gibson, 1985:227.

8. Kosslyn and Pomerantz, 1977.

9. Gregory, 1970:194–200, citing R. L. Gregory and J. G. Wallace, 1963.

10. Livingstone, 1988.

11. Glickstein, 1988.

12. Hubel and Wiesel, 1979.

13. Boring 1950:675–676; Ralph N. Haber, in Koch and Leary, 1985:261–262; Schneider and Tarshis, 1980:153–155.

14. Attneave, 1962.

15. Forgus and Melamed, 1976:32–38.

16. Ibid.:38–45; Hilgard, 1987:113–114; Gerrig and Zimbardo, 2005:101–102. (The negative appraisal is mine. —M.H.)

17. Stratton, 1897.

18. Kohler, 1962.

19. Stuart Anstis, in Gazzaniga and Blakemore, 1975:316.

20. The experiments are cited in Forgus and Melamed, 1976:340, and Bruner and Krech, 1968 [1949]:3, 20.

21. Else Frenkel-Brunswik, in Bruner and Krech, 1968 [1949]:128–129.

22. Forgus and Melamed, 1976:342; David C. McClelland and Alvin M. Lieberman, in Bruner and Krech, 1968 [1949]:236–251.

23. Bruner and Postman, 1949.

24. Coren, 1972.

25. Idea borrowed from Coren, Porac, and Ward, 1984:436.

26. Goldstein, 1989:213–214, citing Neisser, 1967, and Treisman, 1986.

27. Attneave, 1954.

28. Gibson, Shurcliff, and Yonas, 1970.

29. Coren and Girgus, 1978:182–184.

30. Rock and Helmer, 1957; Rock and McDermott, 1964; and personal communication.

31. Landau, 1994.

32. Gazzaniga and Heatherton, 2006:188.

33. Goldstein, 1989:38.

34. Kanigel, 1984.
35. Hubel and Wiesel, 1959, 1962, 1968.
36. Hubel, 1988:69–70. Omissions not indicated.
37. Connor, 2005.
38. Blakemore and Cooper, 1970.
39. Annis and Frost, 1973.
40. Bloom, Lazerson, and Hofstadter, 1985:68–69.
41. Goldstein, 1989:281.
42. Zihl, von Cramon, and Mai, 1983.
43. Schiff, 1965.
44. Lee and Aronson, 1974.
45. Neisser, 1967, cited in Neisser, 1976:46–47.
46. Haber, 1978.
47. Ralph Haber, in Koch and Leary, 1985:276.
48. Marler and Hamilton, 1966:237.
49. Hubel and Wiesel, 1979.
50. Sekuler and Ganz, 1963.
51. Gazanniga and Heatherton, 2006:197.
52. Coren, Porac, and Ward, 1984:323–330; Gazanniga and Heatherton, 2006:197.
53. Ibid.:329.
54. Ibid.:198.
55. Ralph Haber, in Koch and Leary, 1985:265–266.
56. De Valois and De Valois; 1988:vii.
57. Mill, 1889 [1843]:420; Helmholtz, quoted in Cutting, 1986:232; Rock, 1984:1, 17.
58. Coren, Porac, and Ward, 1984:283–294.
59. Ittelson, 1951.
60. Coren, Porac, and Ward, 1984:293–300; Forgus and Melamed, 1976:288.
61. Eleanor Gibson, 1989:258–259.
62. Gibson and Walk, 1960; Walk and Gibson, 1961.
63. Bennet Bertenthal and Joseph Campos, in Rovee-Collier and Lipsitt, 1990:39–45.
64. Bernstein, 1984, and Julesz, personal communication.
65. Julesz, 1986:1602.
66. Julesz, 1991a:25.
67. Julesz, 1986:1602.
68. Admirers: Reed, 1987:90; Lombardo, 1987:xiii. Detractors: quoted in Reed, 1988:6.
69. Biographical details: J. Gibson, 1967, and Reed, 1988.
70. Reed, 1987:91.
71. Reed, 1988:160–162.
72. Gibson, 1950; Gibson, 1966; Gibson, 1968.
73. Julesz, 1991b:332.
74. Gazanniga et al., 2002:150–167.
75. Bloom, Lazerson, and Hofstadter, 1985:76.
76. Marr, 1982:27.
77. Shepard and Metzler, 1971; Cooper and Shepard, 1984.
78. Marr, 1982; Banks. and Krajicek, 1991.
79. Banks and Krajicek, 1991.
80. Unpublished autobiographical sketch.

81. Personal communication.
82. Rock, 1983:1.
83. Ibid.:1–2.
84. Ibid.:251.
85. Ibid., chap. 3.
86. Ibid.:108–110, 176–191.
87. Ibid.:339–341. Omissions not indicated.
88. Gazanniga and Heatherton, 2006:200.

CHAPTER 15

1. *The Passions of the Soul.*
2. *Ethic*, part III, prop. XIII, Scholium.
3. Darwin, 1872, cited in Plutchik, 1991b:37–38.
4. Hilgard, 1987:343.
5. Buck, 1988:vii; Evans, 2004:xi, in Evans and Cruse, 2004.
6. Shaver, Wu, and Schwartz, 1992.
7. Fehr and Russell, 1984; Evans, in Evans and Cruse, 2004:188.
8. Plutchik, 1984.
9. Joseph de Rivera, in Koch and Leary, 1985:364.
10. Gazanniga and Heatherton, 2006:393.
11. Buck, 1988:23–25; Frijda, 1986:475.
12. Warden, 1931.
13. Hull, 1943.
14. Angier, 1991.
15. Dálbir Bindra, in Koch and Leary, 1985:355.
16. The toy trains: Butler, 1953. The latches: Harlow, Harlow, and Meyer, 1950.
17. Heron, 1957.
18. Apter, 1989; Apter, 2001.
19. Blatz, 1925.
20. Landis, 1926.
21. Cannon, 1927.
22. Ibid.
23. Pitts, 1969.
24. Hohmann, 1966.
25. Ekman and Friesen, 1975; Ekman and Oster, 1979; Izard, Huebner, et al., 1980; Trotter, 1983.
26. Ekman and Oster, 1979; Ekman, Levenson, and Friesen, 1983; Laird, 1984; Leventhal and Tomarken, 1986.
27. Fensterheim and Baer, 1975.
28. Gazanniga et al., 2002:545.
29. Cannon, 1932.
30. Cannon, 1927; Bard, 1934.
31. Delgado, 1969.
32. Delgado, 1966; Schneider and Tarshis, 1980:378, 383.
33. Buck, 1988:97–99.
34. Evans, 1989:90.

35. Berlyne, 1978:155.

36. Evans, 1989:90.

37. Buck, 1988:101–102.

38. Evans, 1989:91.

39. Damasio, 1994:45.

40. Buck, 1988:356; Baron, Byrne, and Kantowitz, 1980:320.

41. Sheffield, 1966.

42. White, 1959.

43. Pittman and Heller, 1987.

44. Buck, 1988:76–77.

45. Ford, Wright, and Haythornthwaite, 1985.

46. Piaget, 1952b:269.

47. Robert White, 1959.

48. Buck, 1988:9–10.

49. Berlyne, 1954.

50. Ibid.

51. Thompson, 1988:127–130.

52. Becker, 1953.

53. Brady, Porter, et al., 1958.

54. Jay Weiss, 1971a, 1971b.

55. Hess and Polt, 1960; Hess, 1965.

56. Schachter and Singer, 1962.

57. Schachter and Gross, 1968.

58. Dutton and Aron, 1974.

59. Rozin and Schiller, 1980.

60. Ford and Beach, 1951; M. Hunt, 1959; M. Hunt, 1974.

61. Kinsey, Pomeroy, et al., 1949, 1953; M. Hunt, 1974.

62. Geer and Fuhr, 1976:

63. Summarized in Buck, 1988:382–385.

64. Mischel, 1958, 1976.

65. Hilgard, 1987:373–374, citing French, Mowrer, Lazarus, and others.

66. Gazzaniga and Heatherton, 2006.

67. Henry Gleitman, in Koch and Leary, 1985:429–434.

68. Hilgard, 1987:376–377; Damasio, 2003:275–276.

69. Geen, 1991.

70. Maslow, 1970, chap. 4 and passim.

71. Crown and Marlowe, 1964.

72. Zajonc, 1980.

73. Lazarus, Opton, et al., 1965.

74. The two quotations: Lazarus, 1984; Lazarus, 1991.

75. Lewis, Sullivan, et al., 1989.

76. Buck, 1988:11, 398–399.

77. Plutchik, 1985, 1990a, 1991b.

78. Plutchik, 1985.

79. Joseph de Rivera, in Koch and Leary, 1985:366–367; Frijda, 1986:475; Gazzanniga and Heatherton, 2006:393.

80. Plutchik, 1990a.

81. Frijda, 1986:475–476.

82. Seligman, 1991, chap. 4.

83. Woods and Stricker, 1999.

84. Nieuwenhuyse, Offenberg, and Frida, 1987.

85. Plutchik, 1990a; M. Hunt, 1990, chap. 4.

86. Damasio, 1994; Evans and Cruse, 2004:164–165.

87. Gazzaniga et al., 2002:560–561.

88. Flashed words: Zeelenberg et al., 2006. Mood-dependent memory: Eich and Macaulay, 2000.

89. Goleman, 1995; Salovey and Grewall, 2005.

90. E.g., Kosslyn and Rosenberg, 2004:394–395; Gerrig and Zimbardo, 2005:398–401. Gazzaniga and Heatherton, 2006, prefer to sum up present theory by listing fourteen main points about emotions (pp. 426–427) and nine main points about motivations (pp. 378–379).

CHAPTER 16

1. Biographical data: George Miller, 1989.

2. Gardner, 1985:36–37; Hilgard, 1987:257; Earl Hunt, 1989.

3. Donald Norman, personal communication; Cosmides, 2006.

4. Newell and Simon, 1972, chap. 2.

5. Biographical details from Simon, 1980, and Simon, 1991.

6. Newell, Shaw, and Simon, 1963.

7. Miller, quoted in Gazanniga et al., 2002:18

8. General Problem Solver is described in Newell and Simon, 1972:455–502. The river-crossing problem: adapted from Newell and Simon, 1972:853–854.

9. Mandler, 1985a:10–13; Gardner, 1985:38–41.

10. Posner and Mitchell, 1967.

11. Posner, 1986.

12. *The Passions of the Soul*, article 62.

13. Churchland, 1984, quoted in Flanagan, 1991:222.

14. Grasshopper: cited in Gazzaniga and Blakemore, 1975:16. Roach and snail studies cited in, and interpreted as motivation by: Gallistel, 1980.

15. Hebb, 1949, cited in Lieberman, 1991:30–31.

16. Bliss and Limo, 1973.

17. The work is reviewed in Greenough, Black, and Wallace, 1987.

18. Alkon, 1989.

19. McGaugh, 1990; Introini-Collison and McGaugh, 1991.

20. Quoted in Nadel and Piatelli-Palmarini, 2003.

21. Sperry, 1980; Kagan, 1989:194; Earl Hunt, 1989; Mandler, 1985:28–29.

22. Farah, personal communication.

23. Gazzaniga et al., 2002:129–131.

24. Gazzaniga et al., 2002:20–21; Kosslyn and Rosenberg, 2004:103.

25. Gazzaniga et al., 2002:114–115.

26. On fMRI characteristics: Farah and Wolfe, 2004; Gazzaniga and Heatherton, 2006:58. On the annual output of reports: Mitchell, 2005:28, and Farah, personal communication.

27. Sternberg, 2006:57.

28. Kosslyn and Rosenberg, 2004:102.

29. Quoted in Gazzaniga et al., 2006:144.

30. Farah, personal communication.

31. John Anderson, 1980:3.

32. McGaugh, 1987.

33. Miller, 1956.

34. Mandler, 1985:66.

35. Sperling, 1960.

36. The three-consonant experiment: Peterson and Peterson, 1959. Later replications: Gardner, 1985:122.

37. Potter, 1982, cited in Osherson and Smith, 1990:22–23.

38. Cited in Horn and Hinde, 1970.

39. Loftus, 1972.

40. Collins and Loftus, 1975.

41. Gazanniga and Heatherton, 2006:259–261.

42. Kolata and Peterson, 2001; Steblay et al., 2001.

43. Gazanniga and Heatherton, 2006:276–272.

44. Marc Bornstein, 1979:51.

45. Berlin, 1978.

46. Gelman and Markman, 1986.

47. Henry Gleitman, in Koch and Leary, 1985:422.

48. Denis and Kosslyn, 1999.

49. Pylyshyn, 1978; Chase and Simon, 1973; Johnson-Laird, 1988:51–52.

50. Gardner, 1985:368–369; Sternberg, 2006, chap. 8, esp.:296–297, 307–308. On the two networks, letter from Stephen Kosslyn in *Sci. Amer. MIND*, June/July 2006:4.

51. Bartlett, 1932, cited in Gardner, 1985:114–116.

52. Rumelhart, 1978.

53. Gazanniga and Heatherton, 2006:263–264, 301–302.

54. On training: Yesavage, 1985; Yesavage and Sheik, 1988. On pharmacological treatment: Crook, 1989, and personal communication.

55. Loftus, 1980, passim, esp.:56–57.

56. Harsch and Neisser, 1989.

57. de Villiers and de Villiers, 1978:206 ; Desai et al., 2006.

58. Frederick J. Crosson, in Koch and Leary, 1985:438.

59. Biographical details: Cohen, 1977.

60. Lieberman, 1991:130–131.

61. Clark and Clark, 1977:102, 105–110.

62. Whorf, 1956.

63. Heider [Eleanor. Rosch], 1972; Heider and Olivier, 1972.

64. Lieberman, 1991:144.

65. Ibid.:148.

66. Gardner, 1978.

67. Damasio, 1989, 1990.

68. Gazzaniga et al., 2002:399n.

69. Rips, 1990.

70. Adapted from Neisser, 1967:8.

71. Turing, 1950.

72. Simon: quoted by Frederick J. Crosson, in Koch and Leary, 1985:440; "other enthusiasts": Allen Newell, in Koch and Leary, 1985:444.

73. Simon, 1991:200–201.

74. Ibid., caption to photo opposite p. 195.

75. Newell and Simon, 1972, passim.

76. Keith J. Holyoak, in Osherson and Smith, 1991:122.

77. Johnson-Laird, 1988:228–229.

78. Ibid.:231–233; Johnson-Laird, 2001.

79. Ibid., 1988:229–230; Johnson-Laird, 2001.

80. Experiments cited in Rips, 1990.

81. Russell and Jones, 1980.

82. Cosmides, 1989; Kosslyn and Rosenberg, 2004.

83. Parsons and Osherson, 2001.

84. Kahneman and Tversky, 1981.

85. Ibid.

86. Nisbett and Ross, 1980.

87. Dijksterhuis, 2004.

88. Gentner, 1988.

89. Falkenhainer, Forbus, and Gentner, 1989.

90. Gick and Holyoak, 1983.

91. Earl Hunt, 1989; Gardner, 1985:97.

92. Sternberg, 2006:424.

93. Richard Evans, 1976:98.

94. M. Hunt, 1982b:330–332.

95. Jastrow, 1981.

96. Neisser, 1976, introduction, and personal communication.

97. Linden, 1988.

98. Hayes-Roth, Waterman, et al., 1983:40–41, 54.

99. John Anderson, in Linda Murray and John Richardson, 1989:93.

100. Kosslyn and Rosenberg, 2004:334–335.

101. Sternberg, 2006:524–526; Neisser, 1988, 1991; Pratt, 1987, chapter 14; Johnson-Laird, 1988:353–392; Alvin Goldman, in Osherson, Kosslyn, and Hollerbach, 1990; Steven Harnad, quoted in Raley, 2006:81.

102. Igor Aleksander, in Linda Murray and John Richardson, 1989:48.

103. Lackner and Garrett, 1973.

104. Rumelhart, 1989.

105. Ibid.:135–136.

106. Thagard, 2005, chap. 7.

107. McClelland, Rumelhart, and Hinton, in Rumelhart, McClelland, and the PDP Research Group, 1986, vol. 1:11.

108. Rumelhart, Hinton, and McClelland, in Rumelhart, McClelland, and the PDP Research Group, 1986, vol. 1:49.

109. James McClelland and David Rumelhart, 1981.

110. Mary C. Potter, in Osherson and Smith, 1990:14.

111. Crick and Koch, 1990b.

112. Churchland and Churchland, 1990.

113. Ramachandran and Blakeslee, 1998.

114. Gazzaniga et al., 2002:21.

CHAPTER 17

1. Bureau of Labor Statistics, U.S. Dept. of Labor, *Occupational Outlook Handbook*, 2006–2007 ed.

2. Ibid.

3. National Institute of Mental Health, 1990:253.

4. Olfson, et al., 2002. For in-patient episodes, National Institute of Mental Health, 1990:3. For one out of three total: ibid.

5. Olfson, et al., 2002; National Institute of Mental Health, 1990:200; Goode, 2002.

6. Olfson et al., 2002; Goode, 2002.

7. National Science Foundation, Institute of Mental Health, 1990:206; National Science Foundation, Division of Science Resources, Science and Engineering Doctorate Awards, 2004, table 2; and data provided directly by National Association of Social Workers, American Mental Health Counselors Association, and American Association of Pastoral Counselors.

8. Data provided by Amer. Psychiatric Assn.; Natl. Assoc. of Social Workers; American Mental Health Counselors Assoc., and American Association for Pastoral Counselors.

9. Natl. Assoc. of State Mental Health Program Directors Research Inst., 2002, online.

10. Quoted in Gilgen, 1982:167–168.

11. Ibid.:168.

12. Torrey, 1986; Trotter, 1991.

13. *New York Times*, op-ed page, February 26, 2006.

14. Szasz, 1961.

15. Zilbergeld, 1986.

16. SAMHSA, [2006], online: http://www.mentalhealth.samhsa.gov/features/surgeon-generalreport/chapter4/sec3_2.asp.

17. Schachter, 1980.

18. Goleman, 1989.

19. Rapaport, 1989; 2006 data: Medline Plus, online: "Medical Encyclopedia: Obsessive-Compulsive Disorder."

20. Alexander and Selesnik, 1966:217.

21. Hilgard, 1987:633.

22. Gilgen, 1982:66–67.

23. "Psychoanalysis," *Encyclopaedia Britannica*, 1960 edition; M. Hunt, 1957.

24. B. Bornstein, 1949.

25. Quoted in Reuben Fine, "Search for Love," in Burton, 1972.

26. Freud, "Five Lectures on Psycho-Analysis" (1910), S.E., XI; Bibring, 1954; Hinsie and Campbell, 1970:608; Wallerstein, 1989.

27. Reuben Fine, "Search for Love," in Burton, 1972.

28. Quoted in Hunt, 1957.

29. Personal impressions formed over four decades. —M.H.

30. Burton, 1972:3–22, 312–316.

31. See, for instance, Henry, Sims, and Spray, 1973.

32. Gabbard, 1990.

33. Fischer: quoted in M. Hunt, 1987. APA data: APA Directory Survey, 1990.

34. Quoted in May 21, 2002, program of Lichtenstein Creative Media (online at LCM@LCMedia.com).

35. Ibid.

36. Personal communication; Ms. Hunt, an eclectic in methodology, is the wife of the author of this book.

37. Sobel, 1982.

38. Hirschfeld and Shea, 1989.

39. Sifneos, 1987:79–80.

40. "Therapy FAQ by Toronto psychotherapist Beth Mares," 2006 (online); slightly higher figures were given by Jarrett and Rush, 1986:29; and by Goldfried, Greenberg, and Mannar, 1990.

41. Kenneth I. Howard, Northwestern University, cited in Goleman, 1988b.

42. Bloom, 2001.

43. On psychologists: 1990 APA Directory Survey. On clinical social workers: National Association of Social Workers, personal communication. On psychiatrists: Parloff, 1984. On eclectics: Norcross, Prochaska, and Gallagher, 1989.

44. The Society for the Exploration of Psychotherapy Integration now has seven hundred members and publishes the *Journal of Psychotherapy Integration*.

45. M. Hunt; 1952b.

46. M. Hunt, 1967.

47. Wolpe, 1958:71.

48. Coan, 1979:98, 101.

49. Quoted in M. Hunt, 1967.

50. Abridged from Wolpe, 1958:146–147.

51. Wolpe, 1969:86.

52. Morse and Watson, 1977:273.

53. M. Hunt, 1967.

54. Masters and Johnson, 1970.

55. J. van Lankfeld et al., 2001; AASECT, personal communication.

56. Kushner, 1970.

57. Feldman and MacCulloch, cited in Korchin, 1975:345.

58. *Gale Encyclopedia of Mental Disorders*, 2002, "Aversive Therapy."

59. Ibid., "Assertiveness Training"; Burke, 1989:136–139.

60. Bandura, 1971; Bandura, 1997:93, 398.

61. Bandura, Blanchard, and Ritter, 1969.

62. Joseph D. Matarazzo, in Kimble and Schlesinger, 1985:244–245; S. Jordan et al., 2003; *Gale Encyclopedia*, "Token Economy System."

63. *Enchiridion*.

64. A. Ellis, 1991b:14.

65. Burke, 1989:336–351.

66. A. Ellis, 1989:8.

67. A. Ellis, 1991d.

68. A. Ellis, 1983.

69. Biographical details from A. Ellis, 1991d, and Warga, 1988.

70. A. Ellis, 1991d.

71. Warga, 1988.

72. A. Ellis, 1975.

73. Ibid.

74. A. Ellis, 1982.

75. A. Ellis, 1991b:24–26.

76. A. Ellis, 1991c.

77. D. Smith, 1982; Heesacker, Heppner, and Rogers, 1982.

78. *American Psychologist*, April 1986, v. 41:380.

79. APA Convention 2002: www.fenichel.com/behavior.shtml.

80. Diffily, 1991.

81. Beck, Rush, et at., 1979, preface (unpaged).

82. Ibid.

83. Beck, 1976:76.

84. Crits-Christoph, 2006.

85. Beck, 1979:10.

86. Beck, 1967, 1976.

87. Beck 1979:155–156.

88. Ibid.:217–219.

89. D. Smith, 1982.

90. *American Psychologist*, April 1990:458.

91. J. Beck, 2005:15–16; J. Beck, personal communication.

92. On CT: J. Beck, personal communication; J. Beck and P. Bieling, 2006. On CBT: J. Arehart-Treichel, 2006.

93. A. Beck, 2005:953.

94. A. Beck, introduction to J. Beck, 2005:viii.

95. Ibid.

96. Parloff, personal communication; Kazdin, 1988, cited in Kazdin, 1990; Crits-Christoph, personal communication.

97. Norcross, Prochaska, and Gallagher, 1989.

98. Rogers, 1951:23.

99. Rogers, 1947.

100. Quoted in Bozarth, 1990.

101. Gilgen, 1982:181; Burke, 1989:73.

102. Gerrig and Zimbardo, 2005:528.

103. Perls, Hefferline, and Goodman, 1951.

104. Berne, 1964; T. Harris, 1969.

105. International Society for Interpersonal Psychotherapy Web page.

106. Gilgen, 1982:189.

107. Amer. Group Psychotherapy Assoc., personal communication.

108. Napier, 2000; Johnson, 2003.

109. Fishman and Fishman, 2003.

110. Amer. Assoc. for Marriage and Family Therapy Web page.

111. Eysenck 1952.

112. Eysenck, 1980:165.

113. Summarized in Reisman, 1976:352.

114. Luborsky, Singer, and Luborsky, 1975.

115. Parloff et al., 1978.

116. M. L. Smith, Glass, and Miller, 1980:87.

117. Luborsky, McLellan, et al., 1985.

118. Gerrig and Zimbardo, 2005:537; A. Beck, 2005:956; Crits-Christoph, personal communication; *JAMA*, June 28, 2006.

119. Goldapple, 2004; Judith Beck, personal communication.

120. P. Nathan and J. Gorman, 2002:643, 651.

121. Crits-Christoph, personal communication.

CHAPTER 18

1. Hilgard, 1987:705–706.
2. Nichols, 1997.
3. Herrmann et al., 2006:203.
4. Childress, 1999.
5. Donald Norman, personal communication.
6. APA Practice Directorate, 1991a.
7. Niaura et al., 2002; Rodin and Salovey, 1989.
8. Holahan et al., 1997; Kuijer et al., 2000; D. Russell and Cutrona, 1991.
9. Yesavage and Sheikh, 1988; Herrmann et al., 2006:69; Davis et al., 2005.
10. L. Saxe and M. Fine, 1981:14.
11. Lazar and Darlington, 1982.
12. Zigler and Styfco, 1994:129.
13. Hilgard, 1987:719–721.
14. M. Hunt, 1952a.
15. W. Gregory and W. Burroughs, 1989:56–61.
16. Jewell and Siegall, 1990:238–239.
17. Tractinsky, 1997; Tractinsky et al., 2000.
18. Norman, 2004:19.
19. O. Newman, 1972.
20. Giovannini, 2000; Sundstrom, Burt, and Kamp, 1980.
21. Gladwell, 2000.
22. Baum and Davis, 1980.
23. Druckman and Swets, 1988; Druckman and Bjork, 1991.
24. Druckman and Bjork, 1991:30.
25. Druckman and Swets, 1988:70; Druckman and Bjork, 1991:204–210.
26. Gazzaniga and Heatherton, 2006:29.
27. Jewell and Siegall, 1990:239.
28. Dave Nershi, executive director, Society for Industrial and Organizational Psychology.
29. Baron et al., 2006:538.
30. Jean B. Lapointe, quoted in K. Murphy and Saal, 1990:7.
31. Jewell and Siegall, 1990:251, 259–260; Smither, 1988:323, 325.
32. Baron et al., 2006:541–542
33. Arvey et al., 1989, cited in Baron et al., 2006:541–542.
34. Gregory and Burroughs, 1989:98, adjusted to 2006 dollar values.
35. Ibid.
36. Harrison Gough, personal communication (in 1992) about the Institute of Personality Assessment and Research, Berkeley, CA.
37. Dixon, 1988.
38. Bray, 1982; Bray and Byham, 1991.
39. Bray, 1982.
40. Hollenbeck, 1990; Byham, 1986; Bray and Byham, 1991.
41. *Advantage Hiring Newsletter*, January 2002 (www.advantagehiring.com/newsletter/0102/AssessmentCenters.htm); APA online, 2006.
42. See any of hundreds of commercial Web pages in Google (2007) under "employee testing" and "assessment centers."

43. Miner, 2004–2005.

44. Carter, 2005.

45. Gottesman, 1981; Turkheimer and Gottesman, 1991.

46. M. Hunt, 1971.

47. For charges against the SAT, see Wise, 2002, and others. The rebuttal: personal communication from Caren Scoropanos, Public Affairs, of the College Board.

48. Wigdor, 1990; see also National Research Council, 1989.

49. Wigdor, 1990.

50. E.g., Gottfredson, 1991, 1994.

51. National Research Council, 1989:261.

52. M. Hunt, 1999:95.

53. *New York Times*, op-ed page, July 2, 2006.

54. See, for instance, University of Wisconsin news release on www.uwsp.edu/news/pr/scEmployeeTheft.htm.

55. U.S. Congress, Office of Technology Assessment, 1990:1–2.

56. APA Science Directorate, 1991.

57. Arnold, 1991; *Reid Bulletin* (Reid Psychological Systems, Chi., IL), Fall/Winter, 1991. On the settlement: Coyne, 2002.

58. *APS Observer*, May 1991:8.

59. Pratkanis and Aronson, 1992:9.

60. Packard, 1981 [1957]:1.

61. Quoted in Packard, 1981 [1957]:25.

62. Clark, 1988:73.

63. Packard, 1981 [1957]:55–56.

64. Engel, Blackwell, and Kollat, 1978:430–431; John T. Cacioppo and Richard E. Petty, in Alwitt and Mitchell, 1985; Zajonc, 1980, 2001.

65. Gorn, 1982; Hawkins, Best, and Coney, 1983.

66. D. Moore and J. Wesley Hutchinson, in Alwitt and Mitchell, 1985.

67. Leventhal et al., 1965.

68. N. Miller et al., 1976.

69. Kosslyn and Rosenberg, 2004:681.

70. Pratkanis and Aronson, 1992:98–99.

71. Ibid.:142.

72. Kronlund and Bernstein, 2006.

73. Trenholm, 1989:46; Pratkanis and Aronson, 1992:199.

74. Pratkanis and Aronson, 1992:201.

75. Ibid.:201–202

76. "Another Look at Subliminal 'Facts'," *Advertising Age*, October 15, 1984:46.

77. Münsterberg, 1908:11.

78. "The public thinks": Gregory and Burroughs, 1989:340. The eight-state study: *Bulletin of the American Academy of Psychiatry*, 19 (4), 1991.

79. Monahan, 1984.

80. 463 U.S. 880; 103 S.CT. 3383 (1983).

81. Quinsey, 1995; Serin & Amos, 1995.

82. L. Saxe et al., 1985.

83. Gazzaniga and Heatherton, 2006:403.

84. L. Saxe, 1991; L. Saxe et al., 1985.

85. Faigman et al., n.d., post-2003.

86. Cleary, n.d., post-2002.

87. Ibid.; McConahay, Mullin, and Frederick, 1977.

88. Cleary, n.d., post-2002.

89. Roger Seasonwein, quoted in M. Hunt, 1982c.

90. Lilienfeld, et al., 2003, esp. chapter by Tavris.

91. Druckman and Swets, 1988; Druckman and Bjork, 1991; Bjork, 1991a, 1991b.

92. Druckman and Swets, 1988; Druckman and Bjork, 1991; Bjork, 1991a, 1991b; Philip Merikle and Timothy Moore, quoted in "Subliminal Advertising, Messages, and Conspiracy," *APS Observer*, September 1991.

93. Stehlin, I., 1995. "Unapproved devices seized," *FDA Consumer* 29(7):32–33.

94. *FDA Consumer* 28(2):41–43, 1994; *NAAG Consumer Protection Report*, March/April 1996:10–11.

95. Thompson and Madigan, 2005.

96. Quoted in *Wikipedia*.

97. Carroll, 2003, "NLP."

98. Underhill, 2006.

99. Gallup Poll News Service, June 16, 2005.

100. Druckman and Swets, 1988:167–208.

101. Ibid.:22, 167–168.

102. Festinger, Riecken, and Schachter, 1964 [1956]:3.

103. Bösch et al., 2006.

CHAPTER 19

1. Humphries et al., 2006.

2. Cited in Nelson, 1990:93–94.

3. Clifasefi et al., 2006.

4. Reed, 2006.

5. Cited in Gallistel, 1990a:2.

6. Cited in Middlebrooks and Green, 1991:154–155.

7. Baron et al., 2006:309–321.

8. Stressful influences: Coyne and Downey, 1991.

9. The Stirling County Study: Molloy, 2002.

10. Biophysicist Huping Hu, his collaborator Maoxin Wu, and others, quoted in the online encyclopedia *Wikipedia*.

11. Kosslyn and Rosenberg, 2004:25.

12. National Science Foundation, *Characteristics of Doctoral Scientists and Engineers in the United States, 2003*.

13. APA Online Research Office.

14. See notes 12 and 13.

15. APA Online, "Women in Academe: Two Steps Forward, One Step Back"; APA *Monitor on Psychology* 31, 10 (Nov. 2000), "In Search of Equality."

16. See notes 12 and 13; for non-Ph.D.'s, estimate provided by APA Online Research Office.

17. James, 1948 [1892]:468.

18. Kagan, 1989:3–4.

19. Shirav and Levy, 2006, passim: Buss, 2004, passim.

20. Krantz, 1987.

21. T. Scott, 1991.

22. Sigmund Koch, in Koch and Leary, 1985:93–94.

23. Fowler, 1990.

24. Bandura, 2006.

25. Kandel, 2006.

26. Gazzaniga, 2006.

27. National Science Foundation, *Federal Funds for Research and Development*, *FY 2003–2005*, table 23.

28. Ibid.

29. Edward Jones of Princeton, personal communication, circa 1992.

30. APA *Psychological Science Agenda*, September/October 1991:7.

31. COSSA (Consortium of Social Science Organizations) *UPDATE*, July 14, 2003.

32. COSSA (see note 31) *UPDATE*, Sept. 13, 2004.

33. Ibid., June 27, 2005.

34. Howard J. Silver, executive director, COSSA (see note 31), personal communication and undated COSSA press release.

35. Animal Research Data Base, 1994.

36. For a detailed report on these and other proscribed areas of research, see Hunt, 1999.

37. Ernest Jones, 1955:57.

38. Churchland and Churchland, 1990.

39. johnsparker.tripod.com/index.blog (a report of the April 14, 2006, session of the Tucson Conference, "Toward a State of Consciousness").

40. Kosslyn and Rosenberg, 2004:110–111.

41. Bandura, 1989.

42. Bandura, 2006.

REFERENCES

Abramson, L., et al., 1978. "Learned Helplessness in Humans: Critique and Reformulation." *J. Abnormal Psychol.* 87:49–74.

Adorno, T., et al., 1950. *The Authoritarian Personality.* New York: Harper and Brothers.

Aiken, L., 1979. *Psychological Testing and Assessment.* Boston: Allyn and Bacon.

Ainsworth, M., et al., 1978. *Patterns of Attachment.* Hillsdale, NJ: Erlbaum.

Alexander, F., and Selesnick, S., 1966. *The History of Psychiatry.* New York: Harper and Row.

Alkon, D., 1989. "Memory Storage and Neural Systems." *Scientific American,* July:42–50.

Allport, G., 1943. "The Productive Paradoxes of William James." *Psychol. Rev.* 50:95–120.

——, 1958. "What Units Shall We Employ?" In Lindzey, G., ed., *The Assessment of Human Motives* (New York: Rinehart).

——, 1965. *Pattern and Growth in Personality.* New York: Holt, Rinehart and Winston.

——, 1966. "William James and the Behavioral Sciences." *J. Hist. Behav. Sciences* 2:145–147.

——, 1967. "Gordon Allport," in Boring and Lindzey, 1967.

——, 1968. *The Person in Psychology.* Boston: Beacon Press.

——, and Allport, F., 1928. "A Test for Ascendance-Submission." *J. Abnormal and Soc. Psychol.* 23:118–136.

——, and Odbert; H., 1936. *Trait-names: A Psycho-lexical Study. Psychol. Monographs,* no. 211,

——, and Vernon, P., 1933. *Studies in Expressive Movement.* New York: Macmillan.

Alpert, A., 1928. "The Solving of Problems by Pre-school Children: An Analysis." *Teachers Coll. Contrib. to Educ.,* no. 323.

Alwitt, L., and Mitchell, A., eds., 1985. *Psychological Processes and Advertising Effects: Theory, Research, and Applications.* Hillsdale, NJ: Erlbaum.

American Association of University Women, 1991. *Shortchanging Girls, Shortchanging America.* Washington, DC: American Association of University Women.

American Psychiatric Association, 1980. *Diagnostic and Statistical Manual of Mental Disorders,* 3rd ed. Washington, DC: American Psychiatric Association.

——, 1987. *Diagnostic and Statistical Manual of Mental Disorders,* 3rd ed., revised. Washington, DC: American Psychiatric Association.

American Psychological Association: See also APA entries.

American Psychological Association, 1990. *1990 APA Directory*, Washington, DC: American Psychological Association.

American Psychological Society, 1991. Unpublished reply to International Union of Psychological Societies Survey Questionnaire.

Anderson, J., 1980. *Cognitive Psychology and Its Implications*. San Francisco: Freeman.

———, 1985. "Ebbinghaus's Century." *J. Experimental Psychol.: Learning, Memory, and Cognition* 11(3):436–438.

Angell, J., 1907. "The Province of Functional Psychology." *Psychol. Rev.* 14:61–91.

Angier, N., 1991. "Busy as a Bee? Then Who's Doing the Work?" *New York Times*, July 30, C1.

Annis, R., and Frost, B., 1973. "Human Visual Ecology and Orientation Anisotropies in Acuity." *Science* 182:729–731.

Anstis, S., 1975. "What Does Visual Perception Tell Us About Visual Coding?" In Gazzaniga and Blakemore, 1975.

Aoki, C., and Siekevitz, P., 1988. "Plasticity in Brain Development." *Scientific American*, December:56–64.

APA Education Directorate, 1991. *1991 Doctorate Employment Survey*. Washington, DC: American Psychological Association.

APA Online 2006: "Psychology Matters: Assessment Centers Help Companies Identify Future Managers."

APA Practice Directorate, 1991a. "Medical Cost Offset." Washington, DC: American Psychological Association.

———, 1991b. "Prevalence of Depression and the Effectiveness of Psychotherapy in Ameliorating Depressive Symptoms." Washington, DC: APA Practice Directorate, April 22.

APA Science Directorate, 1991. "Questions Used in the Prediction of Trustworthiness in Pre-Employment Selection Decisions: An APA Task Force Report." Washington, DC: American Psychological Association.

Aquinas, Thomas. *The Soul: A Translation of St. Thomas Aquinas' De Anima*. St. Louis: B. Herder, 1951.

———, *Summa Theologica*, trans. by Fathers of the English Dominican Province. New York: Benziger Brothers, 1948.

Arehart-Treichel, J., 2006. "Increasing Use of CBT Suggests Promising Future." *Psychi. News*, February 5.

Aries, P., 1962. *Centuries of Childhood*. New York: Knopf.

Aristotle. *De Anima*. In Aristotle's *Psychology*, trans. by W. A. Hammond. London: Swan, Sonnenschein, 1902.

———, *De Memoria. Historia Animalium*. In *The Works of Aristotle*, J. A. Smith and W. D. Ross, eds. 12 vols. Oxford: Clarendon Press, 1910–1952.

Arnold, D., 1991. "Invasion of Privacy: A Rising Concern for Personnel Psychologists." *The Industrial-Organizational Psychologist* 28(2):37–39.

Aron, A., and Aron, E., 1989. *The Heart of Social Psychology: A Backstage View of a Passionate Science*, 2nd ed. Lexington, MA: Lexington Books.

Aronson, E., 1988. *The Social Animal*, 5th ed. New York: W. H. Freeman.

———, and Linder, D., 1965. "Gain and Loss of Esteem as Determinants of Interpersonal Attractiveness." *J. Experim. and Soc. Psychol.* 1:156–171.

Arvey, R., et al., 1989. "Job Satisfaction: Genetic and Environmental Components." *J. of Applied Psychol.* 74:187–192.

Asch, S., 1951. "Effects of Group Pressure Upon the Modification and Distortion of Judgment." In Guetzkow, M. H., ed., *Groups, Leadership and Men*. Pittsburgh: Carnegie.

———, 1955. "Opinions and Social Pressure." *Scientific American*, May:31–35.

——, 1956. "Studies of Independence and Conformity: A Minority of One Against a Unanimous Majority." *Psychol. Monogr.* 70, no. 9 (whole no. 416).

——, 1969. "A Reformulation of the Problem of Associations." *Amer. Psychologist* 24(2):92–102.

Ash, M., 1985. "Gestalt Psychology: Origins in Germany and Reception in the United States." In Buxton, C., ed., *Points of View in the Modern History of Psychology*. New York: Academic Press.

——, and Woodward, W., eds., 1987. *Psychology in Twentieth-Century Thought and Society*. New York: Cambridge University Press.

Aslin, R., and Smith, L., 1988. "Perceptual Development." *Ann. Rev. Psychol.* 39:435–473.

Asratyan, E., 1953. *I. P. Pavlov: His Life and Work*. Moscow: Foreign Languages House.

Attneave, F., 1954. "Some Informational Aspects of Visual Perception." *Psychol. Rev.* 61:183–193.

Augustine. *Confessions. Letters*. In *The Nicene and Post-Nicene Fathers*, vol. 1. Buffalo: Christian Literature Co., 1886.

——, *City of God. Treatises on Marriage*. In Fathers of the Church series. New York: Fathers of the Church, 1947.

Ayllon, T., and Azrin, N., 1968. *The Token Economy: A Motivational System for Therapy*. New York: Appleton-Century-Crofts.

Babkin, B., 1949. *Pavlov: A Biography*. Chicago: University of Chicago Press.

Bachrach, A., et al., 1965. "The Control of Behavior in an Anorexic by Operant Conditioning Techniques." In Ullman, L. P., and Krasner, L., eds., *Case Studies in Behavior Modification*. New York: Holt, Rinehart and Winston.

Bacon, F., *Advancement of Learning. Novum Organum*. In *Philosophical Works*, J. M. Robertson, ed. (London, 1905).

Bahrick, H., 1985. "Associationism and the Ebbinghaus Legacy." *J. Experimental Psychol.: Learning, Memory and Cognition* 11:439–443.

Bakan, D., 1966. "Behaviorism and American Urbanization." *J. Hist. Behav. Sciences* 2:5–28.

Balance, W., and Bringmann, W., 1987. "Fechner's Mysterious Malady." *Hist. Psychol.* 19(I/2):36–47.

Baltes, P., et al., 1980. "Life-Span Developmental Psychology." *Ann. Rev. Psychol.*, 31:65–110.

Bandura, A., 1971. "Psychotherapy Based on Modeling Principles." In Bergin, A., and Garfield, S., eds., *Handbook of Psychotherapy and Behavior Change: An Empirical Analysis*. New York: Wiley.

——, 1989. "Perceived Self-Efficacy in the Exercise of Personal Agency." *The Psychologist: Bull. of the British Psychol. Soc.* 10:411–424.

——, 1997. *Self-Efficacy: The Exercise of Control*. New York: W. H. Freeman.

——, 2006. "Toward a Psychology of Human Agency." *Perspectives on Psychol. Sci.* 1 (2):164–180.

——, et al., 1969. "The Relative Efficacy of Desensitization and Modeling Approaches for Inducing Behavioral, Affective, and Attitudinal Changes." *J. Personality and Soc. Psychol.*, 13:173–199.

Banks, W., and Krajicek, D., 1991. "Perception." *Ann. Rev. Psychol*, 42:305–331.

Bard, P., 1934. "Central Nervous System Mechanisms for Emotional Behavior Patterns in Animals." *Res. Publications, Assoc. for Res. into Nervous and Mental Disorders* 19:190–218.

Baron, R. et al., 1980. *Psychology: Understanding Behavior*. New York: Holt, Rinehart and Winston.

——, et al., 2006. *Social Psychology*, 4th ed. Boston: Pearson.

Bartlett, F., 1932. *Remembering*. Cambridge: Cambridge University Press.

Barzun, J., 1983. *A Stroll with William James*. New York: Harper and Row.

Bassuk, E., and Gerson, S., 1978. "Deinstitutionalization and Mental Health Services." *Scientific American*, February:46–53.

Batson, C., et al., 1986. "Where Is the Altruism in the Altruistic Personality?" *J. Personality and Soc. Psychol.* 50 (1):212–220.

Baum, A., and Davis, G., 1980. "Reducing the Stress of High-Density Living: An Architectural Intervention." *J. Personality and Soc. Psychol.* 38:471–481.

Baumrind, D., 1972. "Socialization and Instrumental Competence in Young Children." In Hartup, W., ed., *The Young Child: Reviews of Research* 2.

———, 1977. "Snooping and Duping: The Application of the Principle of Informed Consent to Field Research." Paper presented at the San Diego meeting of the Society for Applied Anthropology.

Beck, A., 1967. *Depression: Clinical, Experimental, and Theoretical Aspects*. New York: Hoeber.

———, 1976. *Cognitive Therapy and Emotional Disorders*. New York: International Universities Press.

———, 2005. "The Current State of Cognitive Therapy: A 40-Year Retrospective." *Arch. Gen. Psychiatry* 62:953–959.

———, et al., 1979 [1967]. *Cognitive Therapy of Depression*. New York: Guilford Press.

Beck, J., 2005. *Cognitive Therapy for Challenging Problems*. New York: Guilford Press.

———, and Bieling, P., 2006. "Cognitive Therapy: An Introduction to Theory and Practice." In Dewan, M., Greenberg, R., and Steenbarger, B., eds., *The Art and Science of Brief Psychotherapies: A Practitioner's Guide*. Washington, DC: American Psychiatric Press.

Beck, R., et al., 1988. "False Physiological Feedback and Emotion: Experimental Demand and Salience Effects." *Motivation and Emotion* 12 (3):217–236.

Becker, H., 1953. "Becoming a Marihuana User." *Amer. J. Sociol.* 59:235–242.

Benjamin, L., 1985. "Ebbinghaus and Fechner: A Memento." *Hist. Psychol.* 17(2):42–50.

———, 1988. *A History of Psychology: Original Sources and Contemporary Research*. New York: McGraw-Hill.

Benson, E., 2003. "Intelligent Intelligence Testing." *APA OnLine: Monitor on Psychology* 34 (2), February.

Berger, K., 1980. *The Developing Person*. New York: Worth.

Berkeley, G., n.d. *A New Theory of Vision, and Other Writings*. London: J. M. Dent.

———, 1709. *Essay Towards a New Theory of Vision*. In *Berkeley: A New Theory of Vision, and Other Writings*. London: J. M. Dent, 1954.

———, 1710. *Treatise Concerning the Principles of Human Knowledge*. In *Berkeley: A New Theory of Vision, and Other Writings*. London: J. M. Dent, 1954.

Berlin, B., 1978. "Ethnobiological Classification." In Bosch, E., and Lloyd, B., eds., *Cognition and Categorization*. Hillsdale, NJ: Erlbaum.

Berlyne, D., 1954. "A Theory of Human Curiosity." *Brit. J. Psychol.* 45:180–191.

———, 1978. "Curiosity and Learning." *Motivation and Emotion* 2 (2):97–175.

Berndt, T., 1979. "Developmental Changes in Conformity to Peers and Parents." *Developmental Psychol.* 15:608–616.

Berne, E., 1964. *Games People Play*. New York: Grove Press.

Bettelheim, B., 1983. *Freud and Man's Soul*. New York: Knopf.

Bibring, E., 1954. "Psychoanalysis and the Dynamic Psychotherapies." *J. Amer. Psychoanalytic Assoc.* 2:745–770.

Binet, A., 1898. "Histoire des recherches sur les rapports de l'intelligence avec la grandeur et la forme de la tête." *L'Année psychologique* 5:245–298.

———, and Simon, T., 1980 [1916]. *The Development of Intelligence in Children.*

Nashville, TN: Williams Printing Company. (Facsimile of the 1916 edition published by Williams and Wilkins, Baltimore.)

Bishop, S., et al. (in press). "COMT Genotype Influences Prefrontal Response to Emotional Distraction." *Cognitive, Affective and Behavioral Neuroscience.*

Bjork, R., 1991a. "How Do You Improve Human Performance?" *APS Observer,* November.

———, 1991b. "On Giving Psychology Away." *APS Observer,* November.

Blakemore, C., 1975. "Central Visual Processing." In Gazzaniga and Blakemore, 1975.

———, and Cooper, G., 1970. "Development of the Brain Depends on the Visual Environment." *Nature* 228:447–478.

Blakeslee, S., 2005. "3, 2, 1: This Is Your Brain Under Hypnosis." *New York Times,* November 22, F1.

Blatz, W., 1925. "The Cardiac, Respiratory, and Electrical Phenomena Involved in the Emotion of Fear." *J. Experimental Psychol.* 8:109–132.

Bliss, T., and Lømo, T., 1973. "Long-lasting Potentiation of Synaptic Transmission in the Dentate Area of the Unanesthetized Rabbit Following Stimulation of the Perforant Path," *J. Physiol.* (London) 232:357–374.

Block, N., ed., 1981. *Readings in Philosophy of Psychology.* Language and Thought series, vol. 2. Cambridge, MA: Harvard University Press.

———, and Dworkin, G., eds., 1976. *The IQ Controversy.* New York: Random House.

Bloom, B., 2001. "Planned Short-Term Therapy for Depression: Recent Controlled Outcome Studies." *Brief Treatment and Crisis Intervention* 1:169–189.

Bloom, F., et al., 1985. *Brain, Mind, and Behavior.* New York: W. H. Freeman.

Blumenthal, A., 1975. "A Reappraisal of Wilhelm Wundt." *Amer. Psychologist* 30:1081–1088.

Backus, F., 1980. *Couple Therapy.* New York: Jason Aronson.

Bolles, R., 1975. *Theory of Motivation,* 2nd ed. New York: Harper and Row.

Boorstin, D., 1983. *The Discoverers.* New York: Random House.

Boring, E., 1950. *A History of Experimental Psychology,* 2nd ed. New York: Appleton-Century-Crofts.

———, et al., 1968. *A History of Psychology in Autobiography.* New York: Russell and Russell.

———, and Lindzey, G., eds., 1967. *A History of Psychology in Autobiography.* New York: Appleton-Century-Crofts.

Bornstein, B., 1949. "The Analysis of a Phobic Child." *Psychoanal. Study of the Child* 3–4:181–226.

Bornstein, M, 1979. "Perceptual Development: Stability and Change in Feature Perception." In Bornstein, M., and Kessen, W., eds., *Psychological Development from Infancy.* Hillsdale, NJ: Erlbaum.

Bösch, H., et al., 2006. "Examining Psychokinesis: The Interaction of Human Intention with Random Number Generators—a Meta-Analysis." *Psychol. Bull.* 132 (4):497–523.

Bouchard, T., 1986. "Diversity, Development and Determinism: A Report on Identical Twins Reared Apart." In Amelang, Manfred, ed., *Bericht über den 35. Kongress der Deutschen Gesellschaft für Psychologie.* Gottingen: Verlag für Psychologie, 417–435.

———, and M. McGue, 2003. "Genetic and Environmental Influences on Human Psychological Differences." Online: www.interscience.wiley.com.

———, Lykken, D.,et al., 1990. "Sources of Human Differences: The Minnesota Study of Twins Reared Apart." *Science* 250:223–228.

———, Segal, N., et al.,1990. "Genetic and Environmental Influences on Special Mental Abilities in a Sample of Twins Reared Apart." *Acta Genet. Med. Gemellol* 39:193–206.

Bower, T., 1964. "Discrimination of Depth in Premotor Infants." *Psychonomic Science* 1:368.

Bowers, K., 1973. "Situationism in Psychology: An Analysis and a Critique." *Psychol. Rev.,* 80 (5):307–336.

Bowlby, J., 1952. *Maternal Care and Mental Health.* Geneva: World Health Organization.

———, 1971, 1973, 1980. *Attachment and Loss.* 3 vols. New York: Basic Books.

Bozarth, J., 1990. "The Evolution of Carl Rogers as a Therapist." *Person-Centered Rev.* 5 (4):387–393.

Brady, J., et al., 1958. "Avoidance Behavior and the Development of Gastroduodenal Ulcers." *J. Experimental Anal. Behavior* 1:69–73.

Braginsky, B., and Braginsky, D., 1974. *Mainstream Psychology: A Critique.* New York: Holt, Rinehart and Winston.

Bray, D., 1982. "The Assessment Center and the Study of Lives." *Amer. Psychologist* 7 (2):180–189.

———, and Byham, W., 1991. "Assessment Centers and Their Derivatives." *J. Continuing Higher Educ.* Winter:8–11.

Brehm, J., and Self, E., 1989. "The Intensity of Motivation." *Ann. Rev. Psychol.,* 40:109–131.

Bretherton, I., 1985. "Attachment Theory: Retrospect and Prospect." In Bretherton, Inge, and Waters, Everett, eds., *Growing Points of Attachment Theory.* Child Development Monographs, no. 209. Chicago: University of Chicago Press.

Bringmann, W., et al., 1975. "Wilhelm Wundt 1832–1920: A Brief Biographical Sketch." *J. Hist. Behav. Sciences* 11:287–297.

Bronowski, J., 1973. *The Ascent of Man.* Boston: Little, Brown and Company.

———, and Mazlish, B., 1960. *The Western Intellectual Tradition: From Leonardo to Hegel.* New York: Harper and Brothers.

Brooks, G. P., 1976. "The Faculty Psychology of Thomas Reid." *J. Hist. Behav. Sciences* 12:65–77.

———, and Johnson, R., 1980. "Contributions to the History of Psychology: XXIV. Johann Caspar Lavater's Essays on Physiognomy." *Psychol. Reports* 46:3–20.

Broughton, J., 1978. "Development of Concepts of Self, Mind, Reality, and Knowledge." *New Directions for Child Development* I:75–100.

Brown, R., 1965. *Social Psychology.* New York: The Free Press.

———, 1985. *Social Psychology,* 2nd ed. New York: The Free Press.

Brožek, J., 1988. "A Contribution by J. E. Purkinje (1787–1869) to the History of Psychology." *Hist. Psychol.* 20 (1/2):33–36.

Bruner, J., 1964. "The Course of Cognitive Growth." *Amer. Psychologist* 19:1–15.

———, and Goodman, C., 1947. "Value and Need as Organizing Factors in Perception." *J. Abnorm. Soc. Psychol.* 42:33–44.

———, and Krech, D., eds., 1968. *Perception and Personality: A Symposium.* New York: Greenwood Press.

———, and Postman, L., 1949. "On Perception of Incongruity: A Paradigm." *J. Personality* 18:206–223.

Bryan, J., and Walbeck, N., 1970. "The Impact of Words and Deeds Concerning Altruism on Children." *Child Development* 41:747–757.

Buck, R., 1985. "Prime Theory: An Integrated View of Motivation and Emotion." *Psychol. Rev.* 92 (3):389–413.

———, 1988. *Human Motivation and Emotion.* 2nd ed. New York: Wiley.

Buckley, K., 1989. *Mechanical Man: John Broadus Watson.* New York: Guilford Press.

Bugelski, B., 1975. *Empirical Studies in the Psychology of Learning.* Indianapolis: Hackett.

Bureau of Labor Statistics, U.S. Dept. of Labor, *Occupational Outlook Handbook,* 2006–2007 ed.

Burke, J., 1989. *Contemporary Approaches to Psychotherapy and Counseling: The Self-Regulation and Maturity Model.* Pacific Grove, CA: Brooks/Cole Company.

Burton, A., ed., 1972. *Twelve Therapists: How They Live and Actualize Themselves.* San Francisco: Jossey-Bass.

Burtt, E., ed., 1939. *The English Philosophers from Bacon to Mill.* New York: Modern Library.

Buss, D., 2004. *Evolutionary Psychology: The New Science of the Mind.* Boston: Pearson.

——, and Cantor, N., eds., 1989. *Personality Psychology: Recent Trends and Emerging Directions.* New York: Springer-Verlag.

Butler, R., 1953. "Discrimination Learning by Rhesus Monkeys to Visual-Exploration Motivation." *J. Comparative and Physiol. Psychol* 46:95–98.

Byham, W., 1986. *The Assessment Center Method and Methodology: New Applications and Technologies.* Pittsburgh: Development Dimensions International.

——, 1989. *The Assessment Center Method in Perspective*, videocassette. Pittsburgh: Development Dimensions International.

Cabeza, R., et al., 2001. "Can Medical Temporal Lobe Regions Distinguish True from False? An Event-Related fMRI Study of Veridical and Illusory Recognition Memory." *Proc. Nat. Acad. Sci. USA.*

Cannon, W., 1927. "The James-Lange Theory of Emotions: A Critical Examination and an Alternative Theory." *Amer. J. Psychol.* 39:106–124.

——, 1932. *The Wisdom of the Body.* New York: W. W. Norton.

Carey, B., 2006. "Living on Impulse," *New York Times*, April 4, F1.

Carroll, R., 2003. *The Skeptic's Dictionary.* Hoboken, NJ: John Wiley.

Carson, R., 1989. "Personality." *Ann. Rev. Psychol.* 40:227–248.

Carter, S., 2005. "For Modern-Day Cupids, Data Replaces Dating." *APA Observer* 18 (2) February.

Case, R., 1986. "The New Stage Theories in Intellectual Development: Why We Need Them; What They Assert." In vol. 19 of *Minnesota Symposia on Child Psychology.* Hillsdale, NJ: Erlbaum.

Caspi, A., and Roberts, B., 2001. "Personality Development Across the Life Course." *Psychol. Inquiry* 12. 49–66.

Cattell, R., 1957. *Personality and Motivation Structure and Measurement.* Yonkers, NY: World Book Company.

——, 1963. "The Nature and Measurement of Anxiety." *Scientific American*, March: 96–104.

——, 1969 [1946]. *Description and Measurement of Personality.* Yonkers, NY: World Book Company.

——, 1973. "Personality Pinned Down." *Psychology Today* July:40–46.

——, 1974. "Raymond B. Cattell." In Lindzey, G., ed., *A History of Psychology in Autobiography.* vol. 7. New York: Appleton-Century-Crofts.

——, and Stice, G., 1957. *Handbook for the Sixteen Personality Factor Questionnaire.* Champaign, IL: Institute for Personality and Ability Testing.

Cautela, J. R., 1966. "Treatment of Compulsive Behavior by Covert Sensitization." *Psychol. Record* 16:33–41.

——, 1967. "Covert Sensitization." *Psychol. Reports*, 20:549–568.

Chase, W., and Simon, H., 1973. "Perception in Chess." *Cognitive Psychol.*, 4:55–81.

Chess, S., and Thomas, A., 1986. *Temperament in Clinical Practice.* New York: Guilford Press.

Chomsky, N., 1957. *Syntactic Structures.* The Hague: Mouton.

——, 1975. *Reflections on Language.* New York: Pantheon.

Churchland, Paul, 1984. *Matter and Consciousness.* Cambridge, MA: MIT Press.

——, and Churchland, Patricia, 1990. "Could a Machine 'Think?' " *Scientific American* January:32–37.

Clark, E., 1988. *The Want Makers*. London: Hodder and Stoughton.

Clark, H., and Clark, E., 1977. *Psychology and Language*. New York: Harcourt Brace Jovanovich.

Clark, M., and Reis, H., 1988. "Interpersonal Processes in Close Relationships." *Ann. Rev. Psychol.* 39:609–672.

Clark, R., 1980. *Freud: The Man and the Cause*. New York: Random House.

Clarke-Stewart, A., et al., 1985. *Child Development: A Topical Approach*. New York: Wiley.

——, et al., 1988. *Lifelong Human Development*. New York: Wiley.

Cleary, A., n.d. [post-2002]. "Scientific Jury Selection: History, Practice, and Controversy." www.publications.villanova.edu.

Clifasefi, S., et al., 2006. "Blind Drunk: The Effects of Alcohol on Inattentional Blindness." *Applied Cog. Psychol.* 20:697–704.

Coan, R., 1979. *Psychologists: Personal and Theoretical Pathways*. New York: Irvington.

Cohen, D., 1977. *Psychologists on Psychology: Modern Innovators Talk about Their Work*. New York: Taplinger.

——, 1979. *J. B. Watson: The Founder of Behaviorism*. London: Routledge and Kegan Paul.

——, 1983. *Piaget: Critique and Reassessment*. New York: St. Martin's Press.

Cohen, J., and Chakravarti, D., 1990. "Consumer Psychology." *Ann. Rev. Psychol.* 41:243–288.

Coleman, S., 1982. "B. F. Skinner: Systematic Iconoclast." *The Gamut* 6:53–75.

——, 1988. "Assessing Pavlov's Impact on the American Conditioning Enterprise." *Pavlovian J. Biol. Science* 23:102–106.

Collins, A., and Loftus, E., 1975. "A Spreading Activation Theory of Semantic Processing." *Psychol. Rev.* 82:407–428.

Collins, W., ed., 1982. *The Concept of Development*. Vol. 15 of *Minnesota Symposia on Child Psychology*. Hillsdale, NJ: Erlbaum.

——, and Gunnar, M., 1990. "Social and Personality Development." *Ann. Rev. Psychol.* 41:387–416.

Commins, S, and Linscott, R., eds., 1947. *Man and the Universe: The Philosophers of Science*. New York: Random House.

Connolly, J., and Doyle, A., 1984. "Relations of Social Fantasy Play to Social Competence." *Developmental Psychol.* 20:797–806.

Cooper, L., and Shepard, R., 1984. "Turning Something Over in the Mind." *Scientific American*, December.106–112.

Coopersmith, S., 1967. *The Antecedents of Self-Esteem*. San Francisco: W. H. Freeman.

Coren, S., 1972. "Subjective Contours and Apparent Depth." *Psychol. Rev.* 79:359–367.

——, and Girgus, J., 1978. *Seeing Is Deceiving: The Psychology of Visual Illusions*. Hillsdale, NJ: Erlbaum.

——, et al., 1984. *Sensation and Perception*. 2nd ed. New York: Academic Press.

Cosmides, L., 1989. "The Logic of Social Exchange: Has Natural Selection Shaped How Humans Reason?" *Cognition* 31:185–276.

Costa, P., and McCrae, R., 1984. "Personality as a Lifelong Determinant of Wellbeing." In Malatesta, C., and Izard, C., eds., *Emotion in Adult Development*. Beverly Hills: Sage.

——, 1986. "Personality Stability and Its Implications for Clinical Psychology." *Clin. Psychol. Rev.* 6:407–423.

——, et al., 1983. "Recent Longitudinal Research on Personality and Aging." In Schaie, K. W., ed., *Longitudinal Studies of Adult Psychological Development*. New York: Guilford.

——, et al., 1987. "Environmental and Dispositional Influences on Well-Being: Longitudinal Follow-Up of an American National Sample." *Brit. J. Pychol.* 78:299–306.

——, et al., 1991. "Facet Scales for Agreeableness and Conscientiousness." *Personality and Individual Differences* 81:887–898.

Costanzo, P., 1970. "Conformity Development as a Function of Self-Blame." *J. Personality and Soc. Psychol.* 14:366–374.

Council, J., et al., 1996. "Imagination, Expectancy and Hypnotic Responding." In R. G. Kunzendorf, et al., eds., *Hypnosis and Imagination*. Amityville, NY: Baywood.

Coyne, I., "Assessing the Effectiveness of Integrity Tests: A Review." *Internat. J. of Testing* 2 (1):15–34.

Coyne, J., and Downey, G., 1991. "Social Factors and Psychopathology." *Ann. Rev. Psychol.* 42:401–425.

Cravens, H., 1987. "Recent Controversy in Human Development: A Historical View." *Human Development* 30:325–335.

Crawford, T., and Ellis, A., 1989. "A Dictionary of Rational-Emotive Feelings and Behaviors." *J. Rational-Emotive and Cognitive-Behavior Therapy* 7 (1):3–28.

Crews, F., 1993. "The Unknown Freud." *The New York Review of Books*, November 18:55–66.

——, 1997 [1993, 1994]. "The Memory Wars: Freud's Legacy in Dispute." *The New York Review of Books*.

——, 1998. *Unauthorized Freud: Doubters Confront a Legend*. New York: Viking.

Crick, F., and Koch, C., 1990. "Towards a Neurobiological Theory of Consciousness." *Seminars in the Neurosciences* 2:263–275.

Crits-Christoph, P., 2006. (See footnote to p. 658). Personal communication.

Crook, T., 1989. "Diagnosis and Treatment of Normal and Pathological Memory Impairment in Later Life." *Seminars in Neurol.* 9 (1):20–30.

Crown, D., and Marlowe, D., 1964. *The Approval Motive: Studies in Evaluative Dependence*. New York: Wiley.

Cutting, J., 1986. *Perception with an Eye for Motion*. Cambridge, MA: MIT Press.

Damasio, A., 1989. "The Brain Binds Entities and Events by Multiregional Activation from Convergence Zones." *Neural Computation* 1:123–132.

——, 1990: "Synchronous Activation in Multiple Cortical Regions: A Mechanism for Recall." *Neurosciences* 2:287–296.

Darley, J., and Latané, B., 1968. "Bystander Intervention in Emergencies: Diffusion of Responsibility." *J. Personality and Soc. Psychol.* 8 (4):377–383.

——, and Shultz, T., 1990. "Moral Rules: Their Content and Acquisition." *Ann. Rev. Psychol.* 41:525–556.

Darwin, C., 1965 [1872]. *The Expression of the Emotions in Man and Animals*. Chicago: University of Chicago Press.

Davis, M., et al., 2005. "The Efficacy of Mnemonic Components of the Cognitive Interview." *Applied Cognitive Psychol.* 19:75–94.

Deaux, K., 1985. "Sex and Gender." *Ann. Rev. Psychol.* 36:49–81.

Decety, J., and Jackson, P., 2006. "A Social-Neuroscience Perspective on Empathy." *Current Directions in Psychological Science* 15 (2):54–58.

Delgado, J., 1969. *The Physical Control of the Mind: Toward a Civilized Society*. New York: Harper and Row.

Dennett, D., 1991. *Consciousness Explained*. Boston: Little, Brown and Company.

Dennis, W., 1935. "The Effect of Restricted Practice Upon the Reaching, Sitting, and Standing of Two Infants." *J. Genet. Psychol.* 47:17–32.

——, 1938. "Infant Development Under Conditions of Restricted Practice and of Minimum Social Stimulation: A Preliminary Report." *J. Genet. Psychol.* 53:149–157.

——, 1973. *Children of the Crèche*. New York: Appleton-Century-Crofts.

Denton, K., and Krebs, D., 1990. "From the Scene to the Crime: The Effect of Alcohol and Social Context, on Moral Judgment." *J. Personality and Soc. Psychol.* 59 (2):242–248.

Desai, R., et al., 2006. "fMRI of Past Tense Processing." *J. of Cognitive Neurosci.* 18 (2):278–297.

Descartes, R., 1637a. *Discourse on Method.* In Commins and Linscott, 1947.

——, 1637b. *Treatise of Man,* trans. Thomas Steele Hall. Cambridge, MA: Harvard University Press, 1972.

——, 1642. *Meditations.* In *Philosophical Works,* trans. E. S. Haldane and G. R. T. Ross. Cambridge: Cambridge University Press, 1911.

——, 1649. *The Passions of the Soul.* In *Philosophical Works,* trans. E. S. Haldane and G. R. T. Ross. Cambridge: Cambridge University Press, 1911.

Deutsch, M., 1968. "Field Theory." In *Internat. Encyclopedia of the Soc. Sciences.* New York: Macmillan Company and The Free Press.

——, 1973. *The Resolution of Conflict: Constructive and Destructive Processes.* New Haven: Yale University Press.

——, 1982. "Conflict Resolution: Theory and Practice." Copy of inaugural lecture as Edward Lee Thorndike Professor, Teachers College, Columbia University, April 22, 1982.

——, 1985. *Distributive Justice: A Social-Psychological Perspective.* New Haven: Yale University Press.

De Valois, R., and De Valois, K., 1980. "Spatial Vision." *Ann. Rev. Psychol.* 31:309–341.

——, 1988. *Spatial Vision.* New York: Oxford University Press.

de Villuis, J., and de Villiers, P., 1978. *Language Acquisition.* Cambridge, MA: Harvard University Press.

Dictionary of Scientific Biography, 1970–1980. New York: Charles Scribner's Sons.

Diffily, A., 1991. "Father and Child: Tim Beck and His Uncommon Common Sense." *Brown Alumni Monthly,* Winter.

Digman, J., 1990. "Personality Structure: Emergence of the Five-Factor Model." *Ann. Rev. Psychol.* 41:417–440.

Dijsterhuis, A., 2004. "Think Different: The Merits of Unconscious Thought in Preference Development and Decision Making." *J. of Personality and Soc. Psychol.* 87:586–598.

Diogenes Laertius, *Lives of Eminent Philosophers,* trans. by R. D. Hicks. Loeb Classical Library. Cambridge, MA: Harvard University Press, 1966.

Dixon, G., 1988. *What Works at Work: Lessons from the Masters.* Minneapolis: Lakewood Books.

Dollard, J., and Miller, N., 1950. *Personality and Psychotherapy.* New York: McGraw-Hill.

Donchin, E., 1985. "Can the Mind Be Read in Brain Waves?" Presentation at a Science and Public Policy Seminar, Federation of Behavioral, Psychological, and Cognitive Science, Washington, DC.

Druckman, D., and Bjork, R., eds., 1991. *In the Mind's Eye: Enhancing Human Performance.* Washington, DC: National Academy Press.

Druckman, D., and Swets, J., eds., 1988. *Enhancing Human Performance: Issues, Theories, and Techniques.* Washington, DC: National Academy Press.

DSM-III and *DSM-III-R:* See American Psychiatric Association, 1980 and 1987.

Duncker, K., 1945 [1935]. "On Problem-Solving." *Psychol. Monogr.* 58 (5), whole no. 270.

Durant, W., 1939. *The Story of Civilization: The Life of Greece.* New York: Simon and Schuster.

——, 1944. *The Story of Civilization: Caesar and Christ.* New York: Simon and Schuster.

——, 1950. *The Story of Civilization: The Age of Faith.* New York: Simon and Schuster.

——, 1953 [1926]. *The Story of Philosophy: The Lives and Opinions of the Greater Philosophers.* New York: Pocket Books.

——, 1954 [1935]. *The Story of Civilization.* Vol. 1, *Our Oriental Heritage.* New York: Simon and Schuster.

——, 1963. *The Story of Civilization: The Age of Louis XIV.* New York: Simon and Schuster.

Dutton, D. and Aron, A., 1974. "Some Evidence for Heightened Sexual Attraction under Conditions of High Anxiety." *J. Personality and Soc. Psychol.* 30:510–517.

Edelman, G., 1989. *The Remembered Present: A Biological Theory of Consciousness.* New York: Basic Books.

EEOC: *See* Equal Employment Opportunity Commission.

Egeland, J., et al., 1987. "Bipolar Affective Disorders Linked to DNA Markers on Chromosome 11." *Nature* 325:783–787.

Ehrenberg, O., and Ehrenberg, M., 1986. *The Psychotherapy Maze: A Consumer's Guide to Getting In and Out of Therapy.* New York: Simon and Schuster.

Eisenberg, N., 1986: *Altruistic Emotion, Cognition, and Behavior.* Hillsdale, NJ: Erlbaum.

——, ed., 1982. *The Development of Prosocial Behavior.* New York: Academic Press.

——, and Strayer, J., eds., 1987. *Empathy and Its Development.* New York: Cambridge University Press.

Ekman, P., 1992. "Facial Expressions of Emotion: New Findings, New Questions." *Psychol. Science* 3:34–38.

——, and Friesen, W., 1975. *Unmasking the Face.* Englewood Cliffs, NJ: Prentice Hall.

——, et al., 1983. "Autonomic Nervous System Activity Distinguishes Among Emotions." *Science,* 221:1208–1210.

——, and Oster, H., 1979. "Facial Expressions of Emotion." *Ann. Rev. Psychol.* 30:527–554.

Elkin, I., et al., 1985. "NIMH Treatment of Depression Collaborative Research Program." *Arch. Gen. Psychi.* 42:305–316.

Ellenberger, H., 1970. *The Discovery of the Unconscious: The History and Evolution of Dynamic Psychiatry.* New York: Basic Books.

——, 1972. "The Story of 'Anna O.': A Critical Review with New Data." *J. Hist. Behav. Sciences* 8:267–279.

Ellis, A., 1958. "Rational Psychotherapy." *J. Gen. Psychol.* 59:35–49.

——, 1975. *Growth Through Reason.* North Hollywood, CA: Wilshire Book Company.

——, 1982. "Self-Direction in Sport and Life." *Rational Living* 17:27–33.

——, 1983. "My Philosophy of Work and Love." *Psychotherapy in Private Practice* 1 (1):43–49.

——, 1989. "The History of Cognition in Psychotherapy." In Freeman, A., Simon, K., et al., eds., *Comprehensive Handbook of Cognitive Therapy.* New York: Plenum.

——, 1991a. "Rational-Emotive Family Therapy." In Home, A. M., and Passmore, J. L., eds., *Family Counseling and Therapy,* 2nd ed. Ithaca, NY: F. E. Peacock.

——, 1991b. "Using RET Effectively." In M. E. Bernard, ed., *Using Rational-Emotive Therapy Effectively.* New York: Plenum.

——, 1991c. "The Revised ABC's of Rational-Emotive Therapy (RET)." *J. Rational-Emotive and Cognitive-Behavior Therapy* 9 (3):139–172.

——, 1991d. "My Life in Clinical Psychology." In Walker, C. E., ed., *The History of Clinical Psychology in Autobiography,* vol. 1. Pacific Grove, CA: Brooks/Cole.

——, et al., 1987. "Cognitive Therapy and Rational-Emotive Therapy: A Dialogue" *J. Cognitive Psychotherapy* 1 (4):205–255.

Ellis, W., ed., 1955 [1938]. *A Source Book of Gestalt Psychology.* London: Routledge and Kegan Paul.

Encyclopaedia Britannica, 1980. Chicago: Encyclopaedia Britannica, Inc.

Engel, J., et al., 1978. *Consumer Behavior,* 3rd ed. Hinsdale, IL: Dryden Press.

Epictetus, *Works.* London: Loeb Library.

——, *Discourses.* In *Works.* London: Loeb Library.

Equal Employment Opportunity Commission, 1978. "Adoption by Four Agencies of the 'Uniform Guidelines on Employee Selection Procedures.'" *Federal Register* 43:38290–38315.

Erikson, E., 1950. *Childhood and Society*. New York: W. W. Norton.

Evans, Peter, 1977. "A Visit to John Bowlby." *Amer. Psychol. Association Monitor*, May.

Evans, Phil, 1989. *Motivation and Emotion*. London and New York: Routledge.

Evans, R., 1973. *Jean Piaget: The Man and His Ideas*. New York: E. P. Dutton.

———, 1976. *The Making of Psychology: Discussions with Creative Contributors*. New York: Knopf.

———, 1980: *The Making of Social Psychology: Discussions with Creative Contributors*. New York: Gardner Press.

Eysenck, H., 1952. "The Effects of Psychotherapy: An Evaluation." *J. Consulting Psychol.* 16:319–324.

———, 1970 [1953]. *The Structure of Human Personality*. London: Methuen and Company.

———, 1980. "Hans Jurgen Eysenck." In Lindzey, 1980.

———, 1989. "Health's Character." *Psychology Today*, December:28–35.

———, 1990. "Maverick Psychologist." In Eysenck, H. J., *Rebel with a Cause*. London: W. H. Allen.

———, and Rachman, S., 1965. *The Causes and Cure of Neurosis*. San Diego: Knapp.

———, and Wilson, G., 1973. *The Experimental Study of Freudian Theories*. London: Methuen and Company.

Faigman, D., et al., undated [post-2003]. "The Limits of the Polygraph." National Academy of Sciences: *Issues on Line: Flaws in Forensic Science*. www.issues.org/20.1/faigman.html.

Falkenhainer, B., et al., 1989. "The Structure-Mapping Engine: Algorithm and Examples." *Artificial Intelligence* 41:1–63.

Fancher, R., 1979. *Pioneers of Psychology*. New York: W W. Norton.

———, 1989. "Terman and His Works." *Science* 244, June:1596–1597.

———, 1987. "Henry Goddard and the Kallikak Family Photographs." *Amer. Psychologist* 42 (6):585–590.

Fantz, R., 1961. "The Origin of Form Perception." *Scientific American*, May:66–72.

Farah, M., 2004. "Neuroethics." http://www.amaassn.org/ama/pub/category/12727.html.

———, 2004a. *Visual Agnosia*. Cambridge, MA: The MIT Press.

———, 2006. "Neuroethics: The Practical and the Philosophical." *Cognitive Science* 9 (1):35–40.

———, and Feinberg, T., eds., 2006. *Patient-Based Approaches to Cognitive Neuroscience*. Cambridge, MA: The MIT Press.

———, and Wolfe, P., 2004. "Monitoring and Manipulating Brain Function: New Neuroscience Technologies and Their Ethical Implications." *Hastings Center Report*, May/June:35–45.

Fehr, B., and Russell, J., 1984. "Concept of Emotion Viewed from a Prototype Perspective." *J. Experimental Psychol.: General*, 113:464–486.

Feldman, H., et al., 1978. "Beyond Herodotus: The Creation of Language by Linguistically Deprived Children." In Lock, A., ed., *Action, Gesture, and Symbol: The Emergence of Language*. New York: Academic Press.

Fellows, L., and Farah, M., 2003. "Ventromedial Frontal Cortex Mediates Affective Shifting in Humans." *Brain* 1126:1830–1837.

Fensterheim, H., and Baer, J., 1975. *Don't Say Yes When You Want to Say No*. New York: David McKay.

Festinger, L., 1957. *A Theory of Cognitive Dissonance*. Stanford: Stanford University Press.

———, ed., 1980. *Retrospections on Social Psychology*. New York: Oxford University Press.

———, and Carlsmith, J., 1959. "Cognitive Consequences of Forced Compliance." *J. Abnormal and Soc. Psychol.* 58:203–210.

Festinger, L., et al., 1964 [1956]. *When Prophecy Fails*. New York: Harper Torchbooks.

Fish, J., 2000. "What Anthropology Can Do for Psychology." *Amer. Anthropologist* 102 (3):552–563.

Fisher, S., and Greenberg, R., 1977. *The Scientific Credibility of Freud's Theories and Therapy.* New York: Basic Books.

Fishman, H., and Fishman, T., 2003. "Structural Family Therapy." In Sholevar, G., and Schwoeri, L., eds., *Textbook of Family and Couples Therapy: Clinical Applications.* Washington, DC: American Psychiatric Publishing.

Flanagan, O., 1984, 1991 (2nd ed.). *The Science of the Mind.* Cambridge, MA: MIT Press.

Flavell, J., 1963. *The Developmental Psychology of Jean Piaget.* Princeton: D. Van Nostrand.

Flew, A., ed., 1964. *Body, Mind, and Death.* New York: Collier Books.

Flynn, J., 1984. "The Mean IQ of Americans." *Psychol. Bulletin* 95:29–51.

———, 1999. "Massive IQ Gains in 14 Nations." *Psychol. Bulletin* 101:171–191.

Ford, C., et al., 1985. "Task Performance and Magnitude of Goal Valence" *J. Res. on Personality* 19:253–260.

Ford, C., and Beach, F., 1951. *Patterns of Sexual Behavior.* New York: Harper and Hoeber.

Forgus, R., and Melamed, L., 1976. *Perception: A Cognitive-Stage Approach*, 2nd ed. New York: McGraw-Hill

Forrest, D., 1974. *Francis Galton: The Life and Work of a Victorian Genius.* London: Paul Elek.

Fowler, R., 1979. "Use of the Computerized MMPI in Correctional Decisions." In Butcher, J., ed., *New Developments in the Use of the MMPI.* Minneapolis: University of Minnesota Press.

———, 1985. "Landmarks in Computer-Assisted. Psychological Assessment." *J. Consulting and Clin. Psychol* 53 (6):748–759.

———, 1990. "Psychology: The Core Discipline" *Amer. Psychologist* 45 (1):1–6.

———, 1992. "APA: 1985 to 1992." In Evans, R. B., Sexton, V. S., and Cadvallader, T. C., eds., *The American Psychological Association: A Historical Perspective.* Washington, DC: American Psychological Association.

Freedman, J., and Fraser, S., 1966. "Compliance Without Pressure: The Foot-in-the-Door Technique." *J. Personality and Soc. Psychol.* 4 (2):195–203.

Freud, M., 1958. *Sigmund Freud: Man and Father.* New York: Vanguard Press.

Freud, S., 1953–1966. *The Standard Edition of the Complete Psychological Works of Sigmund Freud.* James Strachey, ed. 23 vols. London: Hogarth Press.

———, 1954. The *Origins of Psycho Analysis: Letters to Wilhelm Fliess, Drafts and Notes: 1887–1902.* Marie Bonaparte, Anna Freud, and Ernst Kris, eds. New York: Basic Books.

———, 1964. *The Letters of Sigmund Freud.* Ernst L. Freud, ed. New York: McGraw-Hill.

Frijda, N., 1986. *The Emotions.* Cambridge: Cambridge University Press.

Fromkin, V., 1985. "Implications of Hemispheric Differences for Linguistics." In Benson, D., and Zaidel, E., eds., *The Dual Brain.* New York: Guilford Press.

———, 1988. "The State of Brain/Language Research." In Plum, F., ed., *Language, Communication, and the Brain.* New York: Raven Press.

Fulker, D., et al., 1988. "Genetic Influence on General Mental Ability Increases Between Infancy and Middle Childhood." *Nature* 336:767–769.

Furumoto, L., 1988. "The New History of Psychology." Paper presented at the meeting of the American Psychological Association, Atlanta.

———, and Scarborough, E., 1986. "Placing Women in the History of Psychology: The First American Women Psychologists." *Amer. Psychologist* 41:35–42.

Gabbard, G., 1990. "Basic Principles of Dynamic Psychiatry." *Menninger Perspective* 21 (3):16–23.

Gagné, R., and Smith, E., 1964. "A Study of the Effects of Verbalization on Problem-Solving." *J. Experimental Psychol.* 63:12–18.

Gale Encyclopedia of Mental Disorders, 2002. Farmington Hills, MI: Thomson Gale

Gallistel, C., 1980. "From Muscles to Motivation." *Amer. Scientist* 68:398–409.

———, 1989. "Animal Cognition: The Representation of Space, Time, and Number." *Ann. Rev. Psychol.* 40:155–189.

———, 1990a. *The Organization of Learning.* Cambridge, MA: MIT Press.

———, 1990b. "Representations in Animal Cognition: An Introduction." *Cognition* 37:1–22.

Galton, F., 1892 [1869]. *Hereditary Genius: An Enquiry into Its Laws and Consequences.* Cleveland: World Publishing [1962 reprint of 1892 edition].

———, 1907 [1883]. *Inquiries into Human Faculty and Its Development.* London: Everyman's Library.

———, 1908. *Memories of My Life.* London: Methuen and Company.

———, 1970 [1874]. *English Men of Science.* London: Frank Cass.

Gardner, H., 1978. "The Loss of Language." *Human Nature,* March.

———, 1983. *Frames of Mind: The Theory of Multiple Intelligences.* New York: Basic Books.

———, 1985. *The Mind's New Science: A History of the Cognitive Revolution.* New York: Basic Books.

———, 1999. *Intelligence Reframed: Multiple Intelligences for the 21st Century.* New York: Basic Books.

Garrett, H., 1951. *Great Experiments in Psychology,* 3rd ed. New York: Appleton-Century-Crofts.

Gay, P., 1988. *Freud: A Life for Our Time.* New York: W. W. Norton.

Gazzaniga, M., 2006. "Divided We Lose." *APS Observer* 19 (2).

———, and Blakemore, C., 1975. *Handbook of Psychobiology.* New York: Academic Press.

———, et al., 2002. *Cognitive Neuroscience: The Biology of the Mind.* New York: W. W. Norton.

Geen, R., 1991. "Social Motivation." *Ann. Rev. Psychol.* 42:377–399.

Geer, J., and Fuhr, R., 1976. "Cognitive Factors in Sexual Arousal: The Role of Distraction." *J. Consulting and Clin. Psychol* 44:238–243.

Gelman, R., 1978. "Cognitive Development." *Ann. Rev. Psychol.* 29:297–332.

———, and Markman, E., 1986. "Categories and Induction in Young Children." *Cognition* 23:183–209.

Gentner, D., 1988. "Metaphor as Structure Mapping: The Relational Shift." *Child Development* 59:47–59.

———, and Toupin, C., 1986. "Systematicity and Surface Similarity in the Development of Analogy." *Cognitive Sci.* 10:277–300.

Gergen, K., 1973. "Social Psychology as History." *J. Personality and Soc. Psychol.* 26:309–320.

Gerrig, R., and Zimbardo, P., 2005. *Psychology and Life.* Boston: Pearson.

Gerstein, D., et al., eds., 1988. *The Behavioral and Social Sciences: Achievements and Opportunities.* Washington, DC: National Academy Press.

Gewirtz, J., 1965. "The Cause of Infant Smiling in Four Child-Rearing Environments in Israel." In Foss, B., ed., *Determinants of Infant Behavior,* vol. 3. London: Methuen and Company.

Gibson, E., 1988. "Exploratory Behavior." *Ann. Rev. Psychol.* 39:1–41.

———, 1989. "Eleanor J. Gibson." In Lindzey, 1989.

———, et al., 1970. "Utilization of Spelling Patterns by Deaf and Hearing Subjects." In Levin, H., and Williams, J., eds., *Basic Studies on Reading.* New York: Basic Books.

Gibson, E., and Walk, R., 1960. "The 'Visual Cliff.' " *Scientific American,* April:64–71.

Gibson, J., 1950. *The Perception of the Visual World.* Boston: Houghton Mifflin.

———, 1966. *The Senses Considered as Perceptual Systems.* Boston: Houghton Mifflin.

———, 1967. "James J. Gibson." In Boring and Lindzey, 1967.

———, 1968. "Depth Perception." In *International Encyclopedia of the Social Sciences.* New York: Macmillan.

——, 1979. *The Ecological Approach to Visual Perception*. Boston: Houghton Mifflin.

——, 1985. "Conclusions from a Century of Research on Sense Perception." In Koch and Leary, 1985.

Gick, M., and Holyoak, K., 1983. "Schema Induction and Analogical Transfer." *Cog. Psychol.* 15:1–38.

Gielen, U., 1996. "Moral Reasoning in Cross-Cultural Perspective: A Review of Kohlbergian Research." *World Psychology* 2:313–333.

Gilgen, A., 1982. *American Psychology Since World War II: A Profile of the Discipline*. Westport, CT: Greenwood Press.

Gilligan, C., 1977. "In a Different Voice: Women's Conceptions of the Self and of Morality." *Harvard Educ. Rev.* 47:481–517.

Gillihan, S., and Farah, M., 2005. "Is Self Special? A Critical Review of Evidence from Experimental Psychology and Cognitive Neuroscience." *Psychol. Bull.* 131 (1):76–97.

Ginsburg, H., and Opper, S., 1969. *Piaget's Theory of Intellectual Development*. Englewood Cliffs, NJ: Prentice Hall.

Giovannini, J., 2000. "Lost in Space." *New York Magazine*, November 27.

Gladwell, M., "Designs for Working." *The New Yorker*, December 11.

——, 2005. *Blink*. New York: Little Brown.

Glass, G., 1983. "Effectiveness of Different Psychotherapies." *J. Consulting and Clin. Psychol.* 31:28–41.

Gleitman, H., et al., 1999. *Psychology*. New York: W. W. Norton.

Glickstein, M., 1988. "The Discovery of the Visual Cortex." *Scientific American*, September:118–127.

Goddard, H., 1912. *The Kallikak Family: A Study in the Heredity of Feeble-Mindedness*. New York: Macmillan.

——, 1914. *Feeble-mindedness: Its Causes and Consequences*. New York: Macmillan.

——, 1917. "Mental Tests and the Immigrant." *J. Delinquency* 2:243–277.

Goldapple, K., et al., 2004. "Modulation of Cortical-Limbic Pathways in Major Depression." *Arch. of Gen. Psychiatry* 61 (1):34–41.

Goldfried, M., et al., 1990. "Individual Psychotherapy: Process and Outcome." *Ann. Rev. Psychol.* 41:659–688.

Goldstein, E., 1989. *Sensation and Perception*, 3rd ed. Belmont, CA: Wadsworth.

Goleman, D., 1988a. "Erikson, in His Own Old Age, Expands His View of Life." *New York Times*, June 14, C1.

——, 1988b. "When to Challenge the Therapist—and Why." *New York Times Magazine*, October 9.

——, 1989. "Biology of Brain May Hold Key for Gamblers." *New York Times*, October 3, C1.

Goode, E., 2002. "Psychotherapy Shows a Rise Over Decade." *New York Times:* November 20, 2002.

Goodheart, C., et al., 2006. *Evidence-Based Psychotherapy: Where Practice and Research Meet*. Washington, DC: APA Books

Gopher, D., and Kimchi, R., 1989. "Engineering Psychology." *Ann. Rev. Psychol.* 40:431–455.

Gormezano, I., and Coleman, S., 1985. "An Essay Review of *Mechanisms of Adaptive Behavior: Clark L. Hull's Theoretical Papers, with Commentary*," Amsel, A., and Rashotte, M., eds. *Behaviorism* 13 (2):171–182.

Gorn, G., 1982. "The Effects of Music in Advertising on Choice Behavior: A Classical Conditioning Approach." *Jour. Marketing* 46:94–101.

Gottesman, I., 1981. "Developmental Genetics and Life-span Orthogenetic Psychology." In Medwick, S. A., and Baert, A. E., eds., *Prospective Longitudinal Research*. Oxford: Oxford University Press.

Gottfredson, L., 1986. "Societal Consequences of the g Factor in Employment," *Jour. Vocational Behav.* 29:379–410.

———, 1988. "Reconsidering Fairness: A Matter of Social and Ethical Priorities." *Jour. Vocational Behav.* 33:293–319.

———, 1991. "When Job-Testing 'Fairness' is Nothing But a Quota." *Industrial-Organizational Psychologist* 28 (3):65–67.

———, 1994. "The Science and Politics of Race Norming." *Amer. Psychologist* 49 (11):955–963.

Gough, H., 1988a. "Along the Way: Recollections of Some Major Contributors to Personality Assessment." *J. Personality Assessment* 52 (1):5–29.

———, 1988b. "California Psychological Inventory Revised." *California Psychologist*, July 1988.

Gould, J., and Marler, P., 1987. "Learning by Instinct." *Scientific American*, January:74–85.

Gould, S., 1981. *The Mismeasure of Man.* New York: W. W. Norton.

Gray, J. A., 1979. *Ivan Pavlov.* New York: Viking.

Greene, N., 1985. "The Therapist Who Analyzes Therapy." *Pennsylvania Gazette*, December.

Greenough, W., 1991. "The Animal Rights Assertions: A Researcher's Perspective." APA *Psychological Science Agenda*, May–June.

———, et al., 1987. "Experience and Brain Development." *Child Development* 58:539–559.

Gregory, R. L., 1966. *Eye and Brain: The Psychology of Seeing.* London: Weidenfeld and Nicolson.

———, 1970. *The Intelligent Eye.* New York: McGraw-Hill.

———, and Wallace, J., 1963. "Recovery from Early Blindness: A Case Study." *Experimental Psychol. Soc. Monographs*, no. 2.

Gregory, W., and Burroughs, W., eds., 1989. *Introduction to Applied Psychology.* Glenview, IL: Scott, Foresman.

Grigorenko, E., 2000. "Heritablility and Intelligence." In Sternberg, R. J., ed., *Handbook of Intelligence.* Cambridge, UK: Cambridge University Press.

Grobstein, C., 1979. "External Human Fertilization," *Scientific American*, June:57–68.

Gross, M., 1978. *The Psychological Society.* New York: Random House.

Grünbaum, A., 1984. *The Foundation of Psychoanalysis: A Philosophical Critique.* Berkeley: University of California Press.

Grunberg, N., et al., eds., 1987. *A Distinctive Approach to Psychological Research: The Influence of Stanley Schachter.* Hillsdale, NJ: Erlbaum.

Guthrie, E. R., 1935. *The Psychology of Learning.* New York: Harper and Brothers.

Guttman, N., 1977. "On Skinner and Hull: A Reminiscence and Projection." *Amer. Psychologist* 32:321–328.

Haaf, R. A., 1977. "Visual Response to Complex Facelike Patterns by 15- and 20-week-old Infants." *Developmental Psychol.* 73:77–78.

Haber, R., 1978. "Visual Perception." *Ann. Rev. Psychol.* 29:31–59.

———, 1985. "Sensory Processes and Perception." In Koch and Leary, 1985.

Hall, G., 1904. *Adolescence.* New York: Appleton.

Hannush, M., 1987. "John B. Watson Remembered: An Interview with James B. Watson." *J. Hist. Behav. Sciences* 23:137–151.

Harlow, H., and Harlow, M., 1966. "Learning to Love." *Amer. Scientist* 54 (3):244–272.

Harlow, H., et al., 1950. "Learning Motivated by a Manipulation Drive," *J. Experimental Psychol.* 40:228–234.

Harris, J., 2006. *No Two Alike: Human Nature and Human Individuality.* New York: W. W. Norton.

Harris, M., 1972. "The Effects of Performing One Altruistic Act on the Likelihood of Performing Another." *J. Soc. Psychol* 88 (1):65–73.

———, and Samerotte, G., 1975. "The Effects of Aggressive and Altruistic Modeling on Subsequent Behavior." *J. Soc. Psychol.* 95:173–182.

Harris, T., 1969. *I'm Okay—You're Okay.* New York: Harper and Row.

Harrower, M., 1983. *Kurt Koffka: An Unwitting Self-Portrait.* Gainseville, FL: University Presses of Florida.

Harsch, N., and Neisser, U., 1989. "Substantial and Irreversible Errors in Flashbulb Memories of the Challenger Explosion." Paper presented at poster session, Psychonomic Society meeting, November.

Hartigan, J., and Wigdor, A., eds., 1989. *Fairness in Employment Testing.* Washington, DC: National Academy Press.

Hartshorne, H., and May, M., 1928. *Studies in Deceit.* New York: Macmillan.

Harvey, J., and Weary, G., 1984. "Current Issues in Attribution Theory and Research." *Ann. Rev. Psychol.* 35:427–459.

Hauert, C-A., ed., 1990. *Developmental Psychology/Cognitive, Perceptuo Motor and Neuropsychological Perspectives.* Vol. 64 of *Advances in Psychology.* North-Holland: Elsevier Science.

Havighurst, R., et al., 1968. "Disengagement and Patterns of Aging." In Neugarten, B., ed., *Middle Age and Aging.* Chicago: University of Chicago Press.

Hawkins, D., et al., 1986. *Consumer Behavior.* Plano, TX: Business Publications.

Hayes-Roth, F., et al., 1983. *Building Expert Systems.* Reading, MA: Addison-Wesley.

Haynes, S., et al., 1980. "The Relationship of Psycho-social Factors to Coronary Heart Disease in the Framingham Study. III." *Amer. J. Epidemiol.* 111:37–58.

Hazen, C., and Shaver, P., 1987. "Romantic Love Conceptualized as an Attachment Process." *J. Personality and Soc. Psychol.* 52:511–524.

Hearnshaw, L., 1987. *The Shaping of Modern Psychology.* London: Routledge and Kegan Paul.

Hebb, D., 1949. *The Organization of Behavior: A Neuropsychological Theory.* New York: Wiley.

Heesacker, M., et al., 1982. "Classics and Emerging Classics in Psychology." *J. Counseling Psychol.* 29:400–405.

Heidbreder, E., 1933. *Seven Psychologies.* New York: Century Company.

Heider, E., 1972. "Universals in Color Naming and Memory." *J. Experimental Psychol.* 93:10–12.

———, and Olivier, D., 1972. "The Structure of Color Space in Naming and Memory for Two Languages." *Cog. Psychol.* 3:337–354.

Heider, G., 1979. "Kurt Koffka." In Sills, 1979.

Helson, H., 1933. "The Fundamental Propositions of Gestalt Psychology." *Psychol. Rev.* 40:13–32.

Hendrick, C., 1977. "Social Psychology as an Experimental Science." In Hendrick, C., ed., *Perspectives on Soc. Psychol.* Hillsdale, NJ: Erlbaum.

Henle, M., 1978a. "Gestalt Psychology and Gestalt Therapy." *J. Hist. Behav. Sciences* 14:23–32.

———, 1978b. "One Man Against the Nazis—Wolfgang Köhler." *Amer. Psychologist* 33:939–944.

———, 1986. *1879 and All That: Essays in the Theory and History of Psychology.* New York: Columbia University Press.

Henry, W., et al., 1973. *Public and Private Lives of Psychotherapists.* San Francisco: Jossey-Bass.

Herodotus. *The Persian Wars.* New York: Modern Library.

Heron, W., 1957. "The Pathology of Boredom." *Scientific American,* January:52–56.

Herrnstein, R., and Boring, E., eds., 1966. A *Source Book in the History of Psychology.* Cambridge, MA: Harvard University Press.

Hershenson, M., ed., 1989. *The Moon Illusion.* Hillsdale, NJ: Erlbaum.

Hess, E., 1959. "Imprinting." *Science* 130:133–141.

——, 1965. "Attitude and Pupil Size." *Scientific American*, April:46–54.

——, and Polt, J., 1960. "Pupil Size as Related to the Interest Value of Visual Stimuli." *Science* 132:349–350.

Hetherington, E., and Morris, W., 1978. "The Family and Primary Groups." In Holtzman, W. H., ed., *Introductory Psychology in Depth: Developmental Topics.* New York: Harpers College Press.

Hilgard, E., 1987. *Psychology in America: A Historical Survey.* New York: Harcourt Brace Jovanovich.

Hines, M., 2004. *Brain Gender.* New York: Oxford University Press.

Hinsie, L. E., and Campbell, R. J., eds., 1970. *Psychiatric Dictionary.* New York: Oxford University Press.

Hintzman, D., 1978. *The Psychology of Learning and Memory.* San Francisco: W. H. Freeman.

Hippocrates. *Hippocrates*, W. H. S. Jones, ed. Cambridge, MA: Harvard University Press, 1923.

Hirschfeld, R., and Shea, M., 1985. "Affective Disorders: Psycho-social Treatments." In Kaplan, H. I., and Sadock, B., eds., *Comprehensive Text-book of Psychiatry*, 4th ed. Baltimore: Williams and Wilkins.

——, 1989. "Affective Disorders: Psycho-social Treatments." In Kaplan, H. and Sadock, B., eds., *Comprehensive Textbook of Psychiatry*, 5th ed. Baltimore: Williams and Wilkins.

Hobbes, T., 1650. *Human Nature.* In *The English Works of Thomas Hobbes*, W. Molesworth, ed. London: John Bohn, 1839, 1840.

——, 1651. *Leviathan.* In Burtt, 1939.

Hoffman, M., 1971a. "Father Absence and Conscience Development." *Developmental Psychol.* 4 (3):400–406.

——, 1971b. "Identification and Conscience Development." *Child Development* 42:1071–1082.

——, 1981. "Is Altruism Part of Human Nature?" *J. Personality and Soc. Psychol.* 40 (1):121–137.

——, 1982. "Development of Prosocial Motivation: Empathy and Guilt." In Eisenberg-Berg, N., ed., *Development of Prosocial Behavior.* Hillsdale, NJ: Erlbaum.

Hohmann, G., 1966. "Some Effects of Spinal Cord Lesions on Experienced Emotional Feelings." *Psychophysiol.* 3:143–156.

Holahan, C., et al., 1997. "Social Support, Coping, and Psychological Adjustment: A Resource Model." In Pierce, G. R., et al., eds., *Sourcebook of Social Support and Personality.* New York: Plenum.

Holden, C., 1988. "Research Psychologists Break with APA." *Science* 241:1036.

Hollenbeck, G., 1990. "The Past, Present, and Future of Assessment Centers." *Industrial-Organizational Psychologist* 28 (2):13–17.

Holroyd, K., et al., 1984. "Change Mechanisms in EMG Biofeedback Training: Cognitive Changes Underlying Improvements in Tension Headache." *J. Consulting and Clin. Psychol.* 52:1039–1053.

Holst, von, E., 1954. "Relations Between the Central Nervous System and the Peripheral Organs." *Brit. J. Animal Behav.* 2:89–94.

Honzik, M., 1984. "Life-Span Development." *Ann. Rev. Psychol.* 35:309–331.

Horn, J., and Hinde, R., eds., 1970. *Short-Term Changes in Neural Activity and Behaviour.* New York: Cambridge University Press.

Hothersall, D., 1984. *History of Psychology.* Philadelphia: Temple University Press.

Howard, A., 1990. *The Multiple Facets of Industrial-Organizational Psychology: Membership Survey Results.* Lexington, IL: Society for Industrial and Organizational Psychol.

Howard, A., et al., 1986. "The Changing Face of American Psychology." *Amer. Psychologist* 41 (12):1311–1327.

Hubel, D., 1988. *Eye, Brain, and Vision.* New York: Scientific American Library.

Hubel, D., and Wiesel, T., 1959. "Receptive Fields of Single Neurons in the Cat's Striate Cortex." *J. Physiol.* 148:574–591.

———, 1962. "Receptive Fields, Binocular Interaction, and Functional Architecture in the Cat's Visual Cortex." *J. Physiol.* 160:106–154.

———, 1968. "Receptive Fields and Functional Architecture of Monkey Striate Cortex." *J. Physiol.* 195:215–243.

———, 1979. "Brain Mechanisms of Vision." *Scientific American*, September:130–144.

Hull, C., 1943. *Principles of Behavior: An Introduction to Behavior Theory.* New York: Appleton-Century-Crofts.

———, 1967. "Clark L. Hull." In Boring and Lindzey, 1967.

Hume, D., 1956 [1738]. *A Treatise of Human Nature.* London: Everyman's Library (J. M. Dent).

Humphries, C., et al., 2006. "Syntactic and Semantic Modulation of Neural Activity during Auditory Sentence Comprehension." *J. Cognitive Neuroscience* 18:665–679.

Hunt, E., 1989. "Cognitive Science: Definition, Status, and Questions." *Ann. Rev. Psychol.* 40:603–629.

Hunt, M., 1952a. "Doctor for Push Buttons." *Nation's Business*, April.

———, 1952b. "Neurosis Factory." *Esquire*, July.

———, 1955. "The Art of Intelligent Drinking." *True*, May.

———, 1957. "How the Analyst Stands the Pace." *New York Times Magazine*, November 24.

———, 1959. *The Natural History of Love.* New York: Knopf.

———, 1967. "A Neurosis Is 'Just' a Bad Habit." *New York Times Magazine*, June 4.

———, 1969. "Crisis in Psychoanalysis." *Playboy*, October.

———, 1971. "The Intelligent Man's Guide to Intelligence." *Playboy*, February.

———, 1974. *Sexual Behavior in the 1970s.* Chicago: Playboy Press.

———, 1982a. "Research Through Deception." *New York Times Magazine*, September 12.

———, 1982b. *The Universe Within: A New Science Explores the Human Mind.* New York: Simon and Schuster.

———, 1982c. "Putting Juries on the Couch." *New York Times Magazine*, November 28.

———, 1985. *Profiles of Social Research: The Scientific Study of Human Interactions.* New York: Russell Sage Foundation.

———, 1986. "Beat Your Bad Moods for Good." *Reader's Digest*, June.

———, 1990. *The Compassionate Beast: What Science Is Discovering About the Humane Side of Humankind.* New York: William Morrow.

———, 1999. *The New Know-Nothings: The Political Foes of the Scientific Study of Human Nature.* New Brunswick, NJ: Transaction.

Huxley, J., et al., 1956. "Centenary of Psychology: 1856–1956." *Amer. Psychologist* 11 (10):558–562.

Hyson, M., and Izard, C., 1985. "Continuities and Change in Emotion Expressions During Brief Separation at 13 and 18 Months." *Developmental Psychol.* 21 (6):1165–1170.

Introini-Collison, I., and McGaugh, J. L., 1991. "Interaction of Hormones and Neurotransmitter Systems in the Modulation of Memory Storage." In Frederickson, R., McGaugh, J., and Felten, D., eds., *Peripheral Signaling of the Brain.* Toronto: Hogrefe and Huber.

Ittelson, W. H., 1951. "Size as a Cue to Distance. Static Localization." *Amer. J. Psychol.* 64:54–67.

Ivie, S., 1988. "A Romantic in Our Time" [Carl Rogers]. *Person-Centered Rev.* 3 (1):19–29.

Izard, C., 1986. "Why Feelings Are First: The Biological and Social Functions of Emotions." Distinguished Faculty Lecture. Newark, DE: University of Delaware.

——, et al., 1991. "Emotional Determinants of Infant-Mother Attachment." *Child Development* 62:905–917.

——, et al., 1980. "The Young Infant's Ability to Produce Discrete Emotion Expressions." *Developmental Pychol.* 16 (2):132–140.

James, W., 1884. "What Is an Emotion?" *Mind* 9:188–205.

——, 1890. *Principles of Psychology.* New York: Henry Holt.

——, 1902. *The Varieties of Religious Experience.* Undated reprint. New York: Dolphin Books, Doubleday and Company.

——, 1911. *Memories and Studies.* London: Longmans, Green.

——, 1920. *The Letters of William James,* H. James, ed. Boston: Atlantic Monthly Press.

——, 1948 [1892]. *Psychology.* Cleveland: World.

Janov, A., 1970. *The Primal Scream.* New York: Putnam.

Jarrett, R., and Rush, A., 1986. "Psychotherapeutic Approaches for Depression." In Cavenar, J., ed., *Psychiatry,* vol. 1. Philadelphia: J. B. Lippincott.

Jastrow, R., 1981. "The Post-Human World." *Science Digest,* January–February.

Jaynes, J., 1976. *The Origin of Consciousness in the Breakdown of the Bicameral Mind.* Boston: Houghton Mifflin Company.

Jensen, A., 1991. "Spearman's g and the Problem of Educational Equality." *Oxford Rev. of Educ.* 17 (2):169–187.

Jewell, L., and Siegall, M., 1990. *Contemporary Industrial/Organizational Psychology,* 2nd ed. St. Paul: West Company.

Johnson, G., 1988. "Artificial Brain Again Seen as a Guide to the Mind." *New York Times,* August 16, C1.

Johnson, S., 2003. "The Revolution in Couple Therapy: A Practitioner-Scientist Perspective." *J. of Marriage and Family Therapy* 29:365–384.

Johnson-Laird, P., 1988. *The Computer and the Mind: An Introduction to Cognitive Science.* Cambridge, MA: Harvard University Press.

——, 2001. "Mental Models and Deduction." *Trends in Cognitive Science* 51:434–443.

Joncich, G., 1968. *The Sane Positivist: A Biography of Edward Lee Thorndike.* Middletown, CT: Wesleyan University Press.

Jones, Edward, 1985. "Major Developments in Social Psychology since 1930." In Lindzey, G., and Aronson, E., 1985.

——, 1990a. *Interpersonal Perception.* New York: W. H. Freeman.

——, 1990b. Foreword to Higgins, R., et al., *Self-Handicapping: The Paradox That Isn't.* New York: Plenum Press.

——, and Berglas, S., 1978. "Control of Attributions about the Self Through Self-Handicapping Strategies." *Personality and Soc. Psychol. Bull.* 4:200–206.

Jones, Ernest, 1953, 1955, 1957. *The Life and Work of Sigmund Freud.* 3 vols. New York: Basic Books.

Julesz, B., 1986. "Stereoscopic Vision." *Vision Res.* 26 (9):1601–1612.

——, 1991a. "Early Vision and Focal Attention." *Modern Physics,* July.

——, 1991b. "Some Strategic Questions in Visual Perception." In Gorea, A., et al., eds., *Representations of Vision.* Cambridge: Cambridge University Press.

Kagan, J., 1972. "A Psychologist's Account at Mid-Career." In Krawiec, 1972.

——, 1984. *The Nature of the Child.* New York: Basic Books.

——, 1989. *Unstable Ideas: Temperament, Cognition, and Self.* Cambridge, MA: Harvard University Press.

——, and Havemann, E., 1972. *Psychology: An Introduction.* New York: Harcourt Brace Jovanovich.

——, and Moss, H., 1983. *Birth to Maturity: A Study in Psychological Development*, 2nd ed. New Haven: Yale University Press.

——, et al., 1978. *Infancy: Its Place in Human Development.* Cambridge, MA: Harvard University Press.

Kagitçibaşi, Ç., and Berry, J., 1989. "Cross-Cultural Psychology: Current Research and Trends." *Ann. Rev. Psychol.* 40:493–531.

Kahneman, D., and Tversky, A., 1981. "The Psychology of Preferences." *Scientific American*, January:160–173.

Kandel, E., 2006. "The New Science of Mind." *Scientific American Mind*, April/May.

Kanigel, R., 1984. "An Intricate Edifice: Exploring the Architecture of the Visual Cortex." *Harvard Magazine*, November–December:41–49.

Kant, I., 1900 [1781]. *Critique of Pure Reason.* New York: Colonial Press.

Karasu, T., 1990a. "Toward a Clinical Model of Psychotherapy for Depression, I: Systematic Comparison of Three Psychotherapies." *Amer. J. Psychiatry* 147 (2):133–147.

——, 1990b. "Toward a Clinical Model of Psychotherapy for Depression, II: An Integrative and Selective Treatment Approach." *Amer. J. Psychiatry* 147 (3):269–278.

Karier, C., 1986. *Scientists of the Mind: Intellectual Founders of Modern Psychology.* Urbana, IL: University of Illinois Press.

Karpe, R., 1961. "The Rescue Complex in Anna O's Final Identity." *Psychoanal. Quart.* 30:1–27.

Kassorla, I., 1969. "For Catatonia: Smiles, Praise, and a Food Basket." *Psychology Today*, June:39–41.

Kazdin, A., 1978. *History of Behavior Modification: Experimental Foundations of Contemporary Research.* Baltimore: University Park Press.

——, 1990. "Psychotherapy for Children and Adolescents." *Ann. Rev. Psychol.* 41:21–54.

Kazin, A., 1993. "Love at Harvard." Review of Forrest Robinson's *Love Story Told: A Life of Henry A. Murray. The New York Review of Books*, January 28.

Kellaris, J., and Cox, A., 1989. "The Effects of Background Music in Advertising: A Reassessment." *Jour. Consumer Res.* 16:113–118.

Kelley, H., and Michela, J., 1980. "Attribution Theory and Research." *Ann. Rev. Psychol.* 31:457–501.

Kelly, G., 1955. *The Psychology of Personal Constructs.* New York: W. W. Norton.

Kennedy, S., et al., 1988. "Immunological Consequences of Acute and Chronic Stressors: Mediating Role of Interpersonal Relationships." *Brit. Jour. Medical Psychol.* 61:77–85.

Kennel, J., et al., 1974. "Maternal Behavior One Year after Early and Extended Post-Partum Contact." *Developmental Med. and Child Neurol.* 16:172–179.

Kenny, A., 1963. *Action, Emotion and Will.* London: Routledge and Kegan Paul.

Kessen, W., and Cahan, E., 1986. "A Century of Psychology: From Subject to Object to Agent." *Amer. Scientist* 74:640–649.

Kessler, L., et al., 1987. "Psychiatric Diagnoses of Medical Service Users: Evidence from the Epidemiological Catchment Area Program." *Amer. J. Public Health* 77 (1):18–24.

Kimble, G., and Schlesinger, K., 1985. *Topics in the History of Psychology*, vol. 2. Hillsdale, NJ: Erlbaum.

King, R., 1966. *Readings for an Introduction to Psychology.* New York: McGraw-Hill.

Kinkade, K., 1972. *A Walden Two Experiment.* New York: William Morrow.

Kinsey, A., et al., 1948. *Sexual Behavior in the Human Male.* Philadelphia: W. B. Saunders.

——, 1953. *Sexual Behavior in the Human Female.* Philadelphia: W. B. Saunders.

Kirsch, I., 1985. "Response Expectancy as a Cause of Placebo Effects." Paper presented at meeting of Eastern Psychological Association, Boston.

——, and Council, J. R., 1992. "Situational and Personality Correlates of Hypnotic

834   References

Responsiveness." In Fromm, E., and Nash, M., eds., *Contemporary Hypnosis Research.* New York: Guilford.

Kitchener, R., 1977. "Behavior and Behaviorism." *Behaviorism* 5:11–71.

Kleinmuntz, B., 1980. *Essentials of Abnormal Psychology.* New York: Harper and Row.

Kline, P., 1981. *Fact and Fantasy in Freudian Theory,* 2nd ed. London: Methuen and Company.

——, 1983. *Personality: Measurement and Theory.* New York: St. Martin's Press.

——, 1984. *Psychology and Freudian Theory.* London: Methuen and Company.

Koch, S., ed., 1959, 1962, 1963. *Psychology: A Study of a Science.* 6 vols. New York: McGraw-Hill.

——, 1976. "Language Communities, Search Cells, and the Psychological Studies." In Arnold, W. J., ed., *Nebraska Symposium on Motivation, 1975.* Lincoln: University of Nebraska Press.

——, and Leary, D., eds., 1985. *A Century of Psychology as Science.* New York: McGraw-Hill.

Koenigsberger, L., 1965 [1902]. *Hermann von Helmholtz.* New York: Dover Publications.

Koffka, K., 1922. "Perception, An Introduction to the Gestalt-Theorie." *Psychol. Bull.* 19:531–585.

——, 1924 [1921]. *The Growth of the Mind.* New York: Harcourt Brace.

——, 1963 [1935]. *Principles of Gestalt Psychology.* New York: Harcourt, Brace, and World.

Kohlberg, L., 1969. "Stage and Sequence: The Cognitive-Developmental Approach to Socialization." In Goslin, D. A., ed., *Handbook of Socialization Theory and Research.* Chicago: Rand McNally.

Kohlberg, L., 1984. *The Psychology of Moral Development.* Vol. II of *Essays on Moral Development.* San Francisco: Harper and Row.

Kohler, I., 1962. "Experiments with Goggles." *Scientific American,* May:62–86.

Köhler, W., 1924 [1920]. *Die physischen Gestalten in Ruhe und in stationären Zustand.* Erlangen: Verlag der Philosophischen Akademie.

——, 1925a. "An Aspect of Gestalt Psychology." In Murchison, C., ed., *Psychologies of 1925.* Worcester, MA: Clark University Press.

——, 1925b [1917]. *The Mentality of Apes.* New York: Harcourt Brace.

——, 1929. *Gestalt Psychology.* New York: Horace Liveright.

——, 1948 [1917]. *The Mentality of Apes.* London: Routledge and Kegan Paul. Excerpted in Shipley, 1961.

——, 1955 [1918]. "Simple Structural Functions in the Chimpanzee and in the Chicken." In Ellis, W., 1955.

——, 1957 [1917]. *The Mentality of Apes.* London: Penguin.

——, 1988 [1967]. "Gestalt Psychology." *Psychologische Forschung* 31:xviii–xxx. In Benjamin, 1988.

Korchin, S., 1976. *Modern Clinical Psychology: Principles of Intervention in the Clinic and Community.* New York: Basic Books.

Kozol, H., et al., 1972. "The Diagnosis and Treatment of Dangerousness." *Crime and Delinquency* 19:371–392.

Krantz, D., 1987. "Psychology's Search for Unity." *New Ideas in Psychol.* 5 (3):329–339.

Krawiec, T., ed., 1972–1978. *The Psychologists.* 3 vols. New York: Oxford University Press.

Krebs, D., and Blackman, R., 1988. *Psychology: A First Encounter.* San Diego: Harcourt Brace Jovanovich.

——, and Van Hesteren, F., in press. "The Development of Altruistic Personality." In Oliner, P., et al., eds., *Embracing the Other: Philosophical, Psychological, and Historical Perspectives on Altruism.* New York: New York University Press.

——, et al., 1988. "On the Evolution of Self-Knowledge and Self-Deception." In MacDonald, K., ed., *Sociobiological Perspectives on Human Development.* New York: Springer-Verlag.

——, et al., 1990. "The Corruption of Moral Judgment in Everyday Life." Paper presented at the 15th annual conference of the Association of Moral Education, Notre Dame, Indiana, November 8.

——, et al., in press. "The Structural Flexibility of Moral Judgment." *J. Personality and Soc. Psychol.*

Kretschmer, E., 1925. *Physique and Character.* New York: Harcourt Brace.

Kronlund, A., and Bernstein, D., 2006. "Unscrambling Words Increases Brand Name Recognition and Preference." *J. Applied Cog. Sci.* July.

Kuenne, M., 1946. "Experimental Investigation of the Relation of Language to Transportation Behavior in Young Children." *J. Experimental Psychol.* 36:471–490.

Kuhn, T., 1970. *The Structure of Scientific Revolutions.* Chicago: University of Chicago Press.

Kuijer, A., et al., 2000. "Active Engagement, Protective Buffering, and Overprotection: Three Ways of Giving Support by Intimate Partners of Patients with Cancer." *J. Soc. and Clin. Psychol.* 19:256–275.

Kurtines, W., and Gewirtz, J., 1984. *Morality, Moral Behavior, and Moral Development.* New York: Wiley.

Kushner, M., 1970. "Faradic Aversive Controls in Clinical Practice." In Neuringer, C., and Michael, J., eds., *Behavior Modification in Clinical Psychology.* New York: Appleton-Century-Crofts.

Lackner, J., and Garrett, M., 1973. "Resolving Ambiguity: Effects of Biasing Context in the Unattended Ear." *Cognition* 1:359–372.

Laird, J., 1984. "The Real Role of Facial Response in the Experience of Emotion." *J. Personality and Soc. Psychol.* 47 (4):909–917.

Landis, Carney, 1926. "Studies of Emotional Reactions. V: Severe Emotional Upset." *J. Comparative Psychol.* 6:221–242.

Larrabee, G., and Crook, T., in press. "Neuropsychological Assessment." In Barclay, L., ed., *Clinical Geriatric Neurology.* Malvern, PA: Lea and Febiger.

Lashley, K., 1929. *Brain Mechanisms and Intelligence: A Quantitative Study of Injuries to the Brain.* Chicago: University of Chicago Press.

——, et al., 1951. "An Examination of the Electrical Field Theory of Cerebral Integration. *Psychol. Rev.* 40:175–188.

Latané, B., and Darley, J., 1970. *The Unresponsive Bystander: Why Doesn't He Help?* Englewood Cliffs, NJ: Prentice Hall.

——, and Nida, S., 1981. "Ten Years of Research on Group Size and Helping." *Psychol. Bull.* 89 (2):308–324.

——, et al., 1979. "Many Hands Make Light the Work: The Causes and Consequences of Social Loafing." *J. Personality and Soc. Psychol.* 37:822–832.

Lazar, I., and Darlington, R., 1982. "Lasting Effects of Early Education: A Report from the Consortium for Longitudinal Studies." *Monogr. of the Soc. for Res. in Child Development* 47 (serial no. 195):1–151.

Lazarus, R., 1984. "On the Primacy of Cognition." *Amer. Psychologist* 39 (2):124–129.

——, 1991. "Cognition and Motivation in Emotion." *Amer. Psychologist* 46 (4):352–367.

——, et al., 1965. "The Principle of Short-Circuiting the Threat: Further Evidence." *Psychol. Bull.* 49:293–317.

Leary, D., 1978. "The Philosophic Development of the Concept of Psychology in Germany, 1780–1850." *J. Hist. Behav. Sciences* 14:113–121.

——, 1982. "Immanuel Kant and the Development of Modern Psychology." In Woodward and Ash, 1982.

Lee, D., and Aronson, E., 1974. "Visual Proprioceptive Control of Standing in Human Infants." *Perception and Psychophysics* 15:529–532.

Leibniz, G., *Principles of Nature and Grace: Monadology: New Essays on the Human*

Understanding. In *Selections,* Wiener, P., ed. New York: Charles Scribner's Sons, 1951.

Lepper, M., et al., 1973. "Undermining Children's Intrinsic Interest with Extrinsic Reward: A Test of the Overjustification Hypothesis." *J. Personality and Soc. Psychol.* 28:129–137.

Lerner, R., ed., 1983. *Developmental Psychology: Historical and Philosophical Perspectives.* Hillsdale, NJ: Erlbaum.

Leventhal, G., et al., 1965. "The Effects of Fear and Specificity of Recommendation Upon Attitudes and Behavior." *J. Personality and Social. Psychol.* 2:26–29.

Leventhal, H., and Tomarken, A., 1986. "Emotion: Today's Problems." *Ann. Rev. Psychol.* 7:565–610.

Levine, M., 1975. *Cognitive Theory of Learning: Research on Hypothesis Testing.* Hillsdale, NJ: Erlbaum.

Lewicki, P., 1982. "Social Psychology as Viewed by Its Practitioners: Survey of SESP Members' Opinions." *Personality and Soc. Psychol. Bull.* 8 (3):410–416.

Lewin, K., et al., 1939. "Patterns of Aggressive Behavior in Experimentally Created 'Social Climates.' " *J. Soc. Psychol* 10:271–299.

Lewis, M., et al., 1984. "Predicting Psychopathology in Six-Year-Olds from Early Social Relations." *Child Development* 55:123–136.

——, et al., 1989a. "Deception in 3-Year-Olds." *Developmental Psychol.* 25 (3):439–443.

——, et al., 1989b. "Self Development and Self-Conscious Emotions." *Child Development* 60:146–156.

Lewontin, R., et al., 1984. *Not in Our Genes.* New York: Pantheon Books.

Ley, R., 1990. *A Whisper of Espionage: Wolfgang Köhler and the Apes of Tenerife.* New York: Avery.

Lieberman, P., 1991. *Uniquely Human: The Evolution of Speech, Thought, and Selfless Behavior.* Cambridge, MA: Harvard University Press.

Lilienfeld, S., et al., 2003. *Science and Pseudoscience in Clinical Psychology.* New York: Guilford Press.

Lind, G., 2003. "Empirical Findings on the Cross-Cultural Validity of the Moral Judgment Test (MJT)." Paper presented at the 2003 annual meeting of the American Educational Research Association.

Linden, E., 1988. "Putting Knowledge to Work." *Time,* March 28:60–63.

Lindzey, G., ed., 1980. *A History of Psychology in Autobiography,* vol. 7. San Francisco: W. H. Freeman.

——, 1989. *A History of Psychology in Autobiography,* vol. 8. Stanford: Stanford University Press.

Lindzey, G., and Aronson, E., eds., 1985. *Handbook of Social Psychology,* 3rd ed. 2 vols. New York: Random House.

——, and Hall, C., 1965. *Theories of Personality: Primary Sources and Research.* New York: Wiley.

Livingstone, M., and Hubel, D., 1987. "Psychophysical Evidence for Separate Channels for the Perception of Form, Color, Movement, and Depth." *J. Neuroscience* 7 (11):3416–3468.

——, and Hubel, D., 1988. "Segregation of Form, Color, Movement, and Depth: Anatomy, Physiology, and Perception." *Science* 240:740–749.

Locke, J. *An Essay Concerning Human Understanding.* In Burtt, 1939.

Loeb, J., 1900. *Comparative Physiology of the Brain and Comparative Psychology.* New York: Putnam.

Loehlin, J., 1985. "Fitting Heredity-Environment Models Jointly to Twin and Adoption Data from the California Psychological Inventory." *Behav. Genetics* 15 (3):199–221.

——, 1986. "Heredity, Environment, and the Thurstone Temperament Schedule." *Behav. Genetics* 16 (1):61–73.

——, et al., 1981. "Personality Resemblance in Adoptive Families." *Behav. Genetics* 11 (4):309–330.

——, et al., 1987. "Personality Resemblance in Adoptive Families." *J. Personality and Soc. Psychol.* 53 (5):961–969.

Loevinger, J., 1987. *Paradigms of Personality.* New York: W. H. Freeman.

Loftus, E., 1972. "Nouns, Adjectives, and Semantic Memory." *J. Experimental Psychol.* 96:213–215.

——, 1980. *Memory.* Reading, MA: Addison-Wesley.

Lombardo, T., 1987. The *Reciprocity of Perceiver and Environment: The Evolution of James J. Gibson's Ecological Psychology.* Hillsdale, NJ: Erlbaum.

Lorenz, K., 1937. "The Companion in the Bird's World." *Auk* 54:245–273.

Lowry, R., 1971. *The Evolution of Psychological Theory: 1650 to the Present.* Chicago: Aldine, Atherton.

Luborsky, L., et al., 1975. "Comparative Studies of Psychotherapies: Is It True That 'Everyone Has Won and All Must Have Prizes'?" *Arch. Gen. Psychiatry* 32:995–1008.

——, et al., 1985. "Therapist Success and Its Determinants." *Arch. General Psychi.* 42:602–611.

Luce, R., and Raiffa, H., 1957. *Games and Decisions.* New York: Wiley.

Luchins, A., 1979. "Max Wertheimer." In Sills, 1987.

——, and Luchins, E., 1978. *Revisiting Wertheimer's Seminars.* Vol. 1: *Value, Social Influences, and Power.* Vol. 2: *Problems in Social Psychology.* Lewisburg: Bucknell University Press.

——, and Luchins, E. 1986. "Max Wertheimer: 1919–1929. *Gestalt Theory* 8:4–30.

Lucretius. *On the Nature of Things*, trans. by H. A. J. Munro. London: 1886. Excerpted in Rand, 1912.

Lykken, D., et al., 1990. "The Minnesota Twin Family Registry: Some Initial Findings." *Acta Genet. Med. Gemellol.* 39:35–70.

Maccoby, E., 1980. *Social Development: Psychological Growth and the Parent-Child Relationship.* NY: Harcourt, Brace, Jovanovich.

——, et al., 1974. *The Psychology of Sex Differences.* Stanford: Stanford University Press.

——, et al., 1980. "Sex Differences in Aggression: A Rejoinder and Reprise." *Child Devel.* 51:964–980.

Macfarlane, A., 1977. *The Psychology of Childbirth.* Cambridge, MA: Harvard University Press.

Mader, P., and Hamilton, W., 1966. *Mechanisms of Animal Behavior.* New York: Wiley.

Mandler, G., 1985. *Cognitive Psychology: An Essay in Cognitive Science.* Hillsdale, NJ: Erlbaum.

Mandler, J., and Mandler, G., eds., 1964. *Thinking: From Association to Gestalt.* NY: Wiley.

——, and Mandler, G. 1968. "The Diaspora of Experimental Psychology: The Gestaltists and Others." *Perspectives in American History* 2:371–419. Cambridge; MA: Harvard University Press.

Marcus, G., 2004. *The Birth of the Mind.* New York: Basic Books.

Marr, D., 1982. *Vision: A Computational Investigation into the Human Representation and Processing of Visual Information.* San Francisco: W. H. Freeman.

Marrow, A., 1969. *The Practical Theorist: The Life and Work of Kurt Lewin.* New York: Basic Books.

Maslow, A., 1970. *Motivation and Personality*, 2nd ed. New York: Harper and Row.

Masson, J., 1984. *The Assault on Truth: Freud's Suppression of the Seduction Theory.* New York: Farrar, Straus, and Giroux.

Masters, W., and Johnson, V., 1970. *Human Sexual Inadequacy.* Boston: Little, Brown and Company.

McAdams, D., and Vaillant, G., 1982. "Intimacy Motivation and Psycho-social Adjustment: A Longitudinal Study." *J. Personality Assessment* 46 (6):586–593.

McClelland, J., and Rumelhart, D., 1981. "An Interactive Activation Model of Context Effects in Letter Perception: I. An Account of Basic Findings." *Psychol Rev.* 88:375–407.

McConahay, J., et al., 1977. "The Uses of Social Science in Trials with Political and Racial Overtones: The Trial of Joan Little." *Law and Contemporary Problems* 41:205–229.

McConnell, J., 1974. *Understanding Human Behavior: An Introduction to Psychology.* New York: Holt, Rinehart and Winston.

McCrae, R., 1989. "The Big Five." *Dialogue* (newsletter of the Society for Personality and Social Psychology), Fall.

McDougall, W., 1908. *An Introduction to Social Psychology.* London: Methuen and Company.

McGaugh, J., 1987. "Making Memories." Distinguished Faculty Lecture, 1985. Irvine, CA: Irvine Division of the Academic Senate, University of California.

——, 1990. "Significance and Remembrance: The Role of Neuromodulatary Systems." *Psychol. Science* 1 (I):15–25.

McGraw, M., 1935. *Growth: A Study of Johnny and Jimmy.* New York: Appleton.

McReynolds, P., and Ludwig, K., 1984. "Christian Thomasius and the Origin of Psychological Rating Scales." *Isis* 75:546–553.

——, and Ludwig, K., 1987. "On the History of Rating Scales." *Personality and Indiv. Differences* 8 (2):281–283.

McTear, M., ed., 1988. *Understanding Cognitive Science.* Chichester: Ellis Horwood.

Meredith, N., 1986. "Testing the Talking Cure." *Science* 86, June:31–37.

Merton, R., 1968. *Social Theory and Social Structure.* New York: The Free Press.

——, et al., 1984. "The Kelvin Dictum and Social Science: An Excursion into the History of An Idea." *J. Hist. Behav. Sciences* 20:319–331.

Middlebrooks, J., and Green, D., 1991. "Sound Localization by Human Listeners." *Ann. Rev. Psychol.* 42:135–159.

Milgram, S., 1963. "Behavioral Study of Obedience." *J. Abnormal and Soc. Psych.* 67:371–378.

——, 1965. "Some Conditions of Obedience and Disobedience to Authority." *Human Relations* 18:57–76.

——, 1974. *Obedience to Authority.* New York: Harper and Row.

Mill, J. S., 1889 [1843]. *System of Logic,* 8th ed. London: Longmans, Green.

Miller, G., 1956. "The Magical Number Seven, Plus or Minus Two." *Psychol. Rev.* 63:81–97.

——, 1962. *Psychology: The Science of Mental Life.* New York: Harper and Row.

——, 1989. "George A. Miller." In Lindzey, 1989.

Miller, L., 1988. "The Emotional Brain." *Psychology Today,* February:34–42.

Miller, N., et al., 1976. "Speed of Speech and Persuasion." *J. Personality and Social Psychol.* 34:615–624

Miller, N., et al., 1985. "Cooperative Action in Desegregated Settings: A Laboratory Analogue." *J. Social Issues* 41 (3):63–79.

Miner, B., 2004–2005. "Keeping Public Schools Public." *Rethinking Schools Online,* Winter.

Minton, H., 1998. *Lewis M. Terman: Pioneer in Psychological Testing.* New York: New York University Press.

Mischel, Walter, 1958. "Preference for Delayed Reinforcement: An Experimental Study of a Cultural Observation." *J. Abnormal and Soc. Psychol.* 56:57–61.

——, 1976. *Introduction to Personality,* 2nd ed. New York: Holt, Rinehart and Winston.

——, 1981. "Current Issues and Challenges in Personality." In Benjamin, L., ed., *The G.*

Stanley Hall Lecture Series, vol. 1. Washington, DC: American Psychological Association.

———, 1990. "Personality Dispositions Revisited and Revised: A View After Three Decades." In Pervin, L., ed., *Handbook of Personality.* New York: Guilford Press.

———, and Peake, P., 1983. "Analyzing the Construction of Consistency in Personality." *Nebraska Symposium on Motivation.* M. Page, ed. Lincoln: Nebraska University Press.

———, et al., 1989. "Delay of Gratification in Children. *Science* 244:933–938.

Mitchell, N., 2005. "Neuroethics and the 21st Century Brain." *ABC Radio National Home,* July 30.

Molloy, A., 2002. "Random Samples." *Harvard Public Health Rev.*, Winter.

Monahan, J., 1984. "The Prediction of Violent Behavior: Toward a Second Generation of Theory and Policy." *Amer. Jour. of Psychi.* 141:10–15.

Morgan, C., 1909 [1894]. *An Introduction to Comparative Psychology.* London: Walter Scott.

Morse, S., and Watson, R., eds., 1977. *Psychotherapies: A Comparative Casebook.* New York: Holt, Rinehart, and Winston.

Moskowitz, B., 1978. "The Acquisition of Language." *Scientific American,* November.

Mueller, E., and Lucas, T., 1975. "A Developmental Analysis of Peer Interaction Among Toddlers." In Lewis, M., and Rosenblum, L., eds., *Friendship and Peer Relations.* New York: Wiley.

Münsterberg, H., 1908. *On the Witness Stand.* New York: Clark, Boardman.

———, 1915. *Psychology: General and Applied.* New York: Appleton.

Murchison, C., ed., 1936, 1961. *A History of Psychology in Autobiography.* Worcester: Clark University Press.

———, and Boring, E., eds., 1952. *A History of Psychology in Autobiography,* vol. 4. Worcester: Clark University Press.

Murphy, G., and Kovach, J., 1972. *Historical Introduction to Modern Psychology,* 3rd ed. New York: Harcourt Brace Jovanovich.

———, and Murphy, L., eds., 1969. *Western Psychology: From the Greeks to William James.* New York: Basic Books.

Murphy, J. M., et al. 2000. "A 40-Year Perspective on the Prevalence of Depression." *Archives of General Psych.* 51:208–215.

Murphy, K., and Saal, F., 1990. *Psychology in Organizations: Integrating Science and Practice.* Hillsdale, NJ: Erlbaum.

Murray, D., 1988. *A History of Western Psychology,* 2nd ed. Englewood Cliffs, NJ: Prentice Hall.

Murray, H., 1967. "Henry A. Murray." In Boring and Lindzey, 1967.

———, et al., 1938. *Explorations in Personality.* New York: Oxford University Press.

Murray, L., and Richardson, J., eds., 1989. *Intelligent Systems in a Human Context.* Oxford: Oxford University Press.

Mussen, P., et al., 1979. *Psychological Development: A Life-Span Approach.* New York: Harper and Row.

Myers, B., and Alexopoulos, G., 1988. "Age of Onset and Studies of Late-Life Depression." *Internat. J. Geriatric Psychi.* 3:219–228.

Myers, G., 1986. *William James: His Life and Thought.* New Haven: Yale University Press.

Nagel, T., 1994. "Freud's Permanent Revolution." *The New York Review of Books,* May 12, 34–38.

Napier, A., 2000. "Making a Marriage." In Nichols, W. C., et al., eds. *Handbook of Family Development and Intervention.* New York: Wiley.

Nathan, P., and Gorman, J., eds., 2002. *A Guide to Treatments That Work.* New York: Oxford University Press.

National Academy of Sciences, 1988. *The Behavioral and Social Sciences: Achievements and Opportunities*. Washington, DC: National Academy of Sciences.

National Center for Education Statistics, 1991. *Digest of Education Statistics*. Washington, DC: U.S. Government Printing Office.

National Institute of Mental Health. *Mental Health, United States, 1990*. Manderscheid, R., and Sonnenschein, M., eds. DHHS pub. no. (ADM) 90-1708. Washington, DC: U.S. Government Printing Office.

National Research Council, 1989. *Fairness in Employment Testing: Validity Generalization, Minority Issues, and the General Aptitude Test Battery*, Hartigan, J. and Wigdor, A., eds. Washington, DC: National Academy Press.

National Science Foundation, 1987. *U.S. Scientists and Engineers: 1986*. Washington, DC: National Science Foundation.

——, 1988a. *Characteristics of Doctoral Scientists and Engineers in the United States: 1987*. Washington, DC: National Science Foundation.

——, 1988b. *Profiles—Psychology: Human Resources and Funding* (NSF 88-325). Washington, DC: National Science Foundation.

——, 1990. *Federal Funds for Research, Development, and Other Scientific Activities*. Washington, DC: National Science Foundation.

——, 1991. *Characteristics of Doctoral Scientists and Engineers in the United States: 1989*. Washington, DC: National Science Foundation.

Neisser, U., 1967. *Cognitive Psychology*. Englewood Cliffs, NJ: Prentice Hall.

——, 1976. *Cognition and Reality*. San Francisco: W. H. Freeman.

——, 1988. "Five Kinds of Self Knowledge." Emory Cognition Project Report 14. Atlanta: Emory University.

——, 1991. "Without Perception, There Is No Knowledge: Implications for Artificial Intelligence." Emory Cognition Project Report 18. Atlanta: Emory University.

——, et al., 1966. "Intelligence Knowns and Unknowns." *Amer. Psychol.* 511:77–101.

Nelson, R., 1990. "Mechanisms of Seasonal Cycles of Behavior." *Ann. Rev. Psychol.* 41:81–108.

Newell, A., 1990. *Unified Theories of Cognition*. Cambridge, MA: Harvard University Press.

——, and Simon, H., 1972. *Human Problem Solving*. Englewood Cliffs, NJ: Prentice Hall.

——, et al., 1963. "Empirical Explorations with the Logic Theory Machine: A Case Study in Heuristics." In Feigenbaum, E., and Feldman, J., eds., *Computers and Thought*. New York: McGraw-Hill.

Newman, E. B., 1944. "Max Wertheimer: 1880–1943." *Amer. J. Psychol.* 57:428–435.

Newman, O., 1972. *Defensible Space: Crime Prevention Through Urban Design*. New York: Macmillan.

Niaura, R., et al., 2002. "Hostility, the Metabolic Syndrome, and Incident Coronary Heart Disease." *Health Psychol.* 21:588–593.

Nieuwenhuyse, B., et al., 1987. "Subjective Emotion and Reported Body Experience." *Motivation and Emotion* 11 (2):169–182.

Nisbett, R., and Ross, L., 1980. *Human Inference: Strategies and Shortcomings of Social Judgment*. Englewood Cliffs, NJ: Prentice Hall.

Norcross, J., and Grencavage, L., 1989. "Eclecticism and Integration in Counselling and Psychotherapy: Major Themes and. Obstacles." *Brit. Jour. Guidance and Counselling* 17 (3):227–247.

Norcross, J., et al., 1989. "Clinical Psychologists in the 1980s: II. Theory, Research, and Practice." *Clin. Psychologist* 42 (3):45–53.

Norcross, J., et al., 1992. "The Future of Psychotherapy: Delphi Data and Concluding Observations." *Psychotherapy* 29 (1):150–158.

Norman, D., 1988. *The Psychology of Everyday Things*. New York: Basic Books.

——, 2004. *Emotional Design*. New York: Basic Books.

Observer (anon.), 1978. "Wundt and Experimental Psychology." *Psychol. Record* 28:175–179.

O'Donnell, J., 1985. *The Origins of Behaviorism.* New York: New York University Press.

O'Keefe, D., 1990. *Persuasion: Theory and Research.* Newbury Park, CA: Sage Publications.

Ones, D., et al., 1991. "Meta-Analysis Shows Integrity Tests Are Valid Despite Moderating Influences." Paper presented at 1991 meeting of the American Psychological Society.

Osherson, D., and Hollerbach, J., eds., 1990. *An Invitation to Cognitive Science.* Vol. 2: *Visual Cognition and Action.* Cambridge, MA: MIT Press.

——, and Lasnik, H., eds., 1990. *An Invitation to Cognitive Science.* Vol. 1: *Language.* Cambridge, MA: MIT Press.

——, and Markman, E., 1974–1975. "Language and the Ability to Evaluate Contradictions and Tautologies." *Cognition* 3:213–226.

——, and Smith, E., eds., 1990. *An Invitation to Cognitive Science.* Vol. 3: *Thinking.* Cambridge, MA: MIT Press.

OSS Assessment Staff, 1948. *Assessment of Men: Selection of Personnel for the Office of Strategic Services.* New York: Holt, Rinehart and Winston.

Overmier, J., and Seligman, M., 1967. "Effects of Inescapable Shock upon Subsequent Escape and Avoidance Responding." *J. Compar. and Physiol. Psychol.* 63:28–33.

Packard, V., 1981 [1957]. *The Hidden Persuaders.* New York: Washington Square Press.

Paivio, A., 1978. "Comparison of Mental Clocks." *J. Experimental Psychol.: Perception and Performance* 4:61–71.

Palmer, S., 1987. "PDP: A New Paradigm for Cognitive Theory." *Contemp. Psychol.* 32 (11):925–928.

Palmore, E., 1970. "The Effects of Aging on Activities and Attitudes." In Palmore, E., ed., *Normal Aging: Reports from the Duke Longitudinal Study, 1955–1969.* Durham, NC: Duke University Press.

——, ed., 1981. *Social Patterns in Normal Aging: Findings from the Duke Longitudinal Study.* Durham, NC: Duke University Press.

Panksepp, J., 1990. "Can 'Mind' and Behavior Be Understood Without Understanding the Brain? A Response to Bunge." *New Ideas in Psychol.* 8 (2):139–149.

Papanicolaou, A., 1989. *Emotion: A Reconsideration of the Somatic Theory.* New York: Gordon and Breach.

Papousek, H., 1959. "A Method of Studying Conditioned Food Reflexes in Young Children Up to the Age of Six Months." *Pavlov J. Higher Nervous Activities* 9:136–140.

Parke, R., 1990. "Family-Peer Systems: In Search of Linking Processes." Presidential address, Division 7, presented at the annual meeting of the American Psychological Association, Boston, MA.

Parloff, M., 1984. "Psychotherapy Research and Its Incredible Credibility Crisis." *Clin. Psychol. Rev.* 4:95–109.

——, et al., 1978. "Assessment of Psychosocial Treatment of Mental Health Disorders: Current Status and Prospects." Washington, DC: National Academy of Sciences.

Parsons, I. and Osherson, D., 2001. "New Evidence for Distinct Right and Left Brain Systems for Deductive Versus Probabalistic Reasoning." *Cerebral Cortex* 11:951–965.

Pavlov, I., 1960 [1927]. *Conditioned Reflexes: An Investigation of the Physiological Activity of the Cerebral Cortex.* New York: Dover.

Pearson, K., 1914–1930. *The Life, Letters and Labours of Francis Galton.* 3 vols. Cambridge: Cambridge University Press.

Pellis, S., et al., 1988. "Escalation of Feline Predation Along a Gradient from Avoidance Through 'Play' to Killing." *Behav. Neuroscience* 102 (5):760–777.

Penn: Office of University Communications, 2004. "Your Brain and You," December 17. http://www.upenn.edu/pennnews/article.php?id=727.

Penrose, L., and Penrose, R., 1958. "Impossible Objects: A Special Type of Illusion." *Brit J. Psychol* 49:31.

Perls, F., et al., 1951. *Gestalt Therapy*. New York: Dell.

Perry, R., 1935. *The Thought and Character of William James*. Boston: Little, Brown and Company.

Pervin, L., 1985. "Personality: Current Controversies, Issues, and Directions." *Ann. Rev. Psychol.* 36:83–114.

Petersen, A., 1988. "Adolescent Development." *Ann. Rev. Psychol.* 39:583–607.

Peterson, C., et al., 1977. "Pessimistic Explanatory Style Is a Risk Factor for Physical Illness: A Thirty-five-Year Longitudinal Study." *J. Personality and Soc. Psychol.* 55 (1):23–27.

Peterson, L., 1966. "Short-Term Memory." *Scientific American*, July:90–95.

Peterson, L., and Peterson, M., 1959. "Short-Term Retention of Individual Verbal Items." *J. Experimental Psychol.* 58:193–198.

Petty, R., et al., eds., 1981. *Cognitive Responses in Persuasion*. Hillsdale, NJ: Erlbaum.

Piaget, J., 1948 [1932]. *The Moral Judgment of the Child*. New York: Free Press.

———, 1951. *Play, Dreams, and Imitation in Childhood*. New York: W. W. Norton.

———, 1952a. "Jean Piaget," in Murchison and Boring, 1952.

———, 1952b. *The Origins of Intelligence in Children*. New York: International Universities Press.

———, 1958. *The Growth of Logical Thinking from Childhood to Adolescence*. New York: Basic Books.

———, 1967. *Six Psychological Studies*. New York: Vintage Books.

———, 1969. "Genetic Epistemology." *Columbia Forum* 12(3).

———, and Inhelder, B., 1969. *The Psychology of the Child*. New York: Harper Torchbooks—Basic Books.

Piliavin, J., et al., 1981. *Emergency Intervention*. New York: Academic Press.

Piotrowski, C., 1985. "Clinical Assessment: Attitudes of the Society for Personality Assessment Membership." *Southern Psychologist* 2 (4):80–83.

Piët, S., 1987. "What Motivates Stunt Men?" *Motivation and Emotion* 11 (2):195–213.

Pittman, T., and Heller, J., 1987. "Social Motivation." *Ann. Rev. Psychol.* 38:461–489.

Pitts, E., 1969. "The Biochemistry of Anxiety." *Scientific American*, February:69–75.

Plake, B., ed., 1984. *Social and Technical Issues in Testing: Implications for Test Construction and Usage*. Hillsdale, NJ: Erlbaum.

Plato. *The Works of Plato*, B. Jowett, trans. and ed.; 4 vols. in one. New York: Dial Press, n.d.

———, *Plato's Dialogues*, trans. by J. Wright. New York: A. L. Burt, n.d.

Plomin, R., and Daniels, D., 1987. "Why Are Children in the Same Family So Different from One Another?" *Behav. and Brain Sciences* 10:1–60.

———, and Petrill, S., 1997. "Genetics and Intelligence. What's New?" *Intelligence* 24:53–77.

Plotinus. *The Enneads*. In *Select Works of Plotinus*, trans. by Thomas Taylor. London, 1895.

Plutarch. *The Lives of the Noble Grecians and Romans*, trans. by John Dryden, revised by Arthur Hugh Clough. New York: Modern Library, 1932.

Plutchik, R., 1980. *Emotion: A Psychoevolutionary Synthesis*. New York: Random House.

———, 1984. "Emotions: A General Psychoevolutionary Theory." In Scherer, K., and Ekman, P., eds., *Approaches to Emotion*. Hillsdale, NJ: Erlbaum.

———, 1985. "On Emotion: The Chicken-and-Egg Problem Revisited." *Motivation and Emotion* 9 (2):197–200.

———, 1990. "Emotions and Psychotherapy: A Psychoevolutionary Perspective." In Plutchik, R., and Kellerman, H., eds., *Emotion: Theory, Research, and Experience*, vol. 5. New York: Academic Press.

———, 1991a. Preface to Plutchik, R., *The Emotions*. Lanham, MD: University Press of America.

———, 1991b. "Emotions and Evolution." *Internat. Rev. of Studies on Emotion* 1:37–58.

Pomazal, R., and Clore, G., 1973. "Helping on the Highway: The Effects of Dependency and Sex." *J. Applied Soc. Psychol.* 3 (2):150–164.

Popper, K., 1963. *Conjectures and Refutations*. London: Routledge and Kegan Paul.

Posner, M. I., and Mitchell, R. E., 1967. "Chronometric Analysis of Classification." *Psychol. Rev.* 74:392–409.

Potter, M. C., 1982. "Very Short-Term Memory: In One Eye and Out the Other." Paper presented at the annual meeting of the Psychonomic Society.

Powledge, T., 1983. "The Importance of Being Twins." *Psychology Today*, July:21–27.

Pratkanis, A., and Aronson, E., 1992. *Age of Propaganda*. New York: W. H. Freeman.

Pratt, V., 1987. *Thinking Machines: The Evolution of Artificial Intelligence*. Oxford: Basil Blackwell.

Pyles, R. "Remarks at the 100th Anniversary of *The Interpretation of Dreams*." http://www.apsa.org/pubinfo/pylesremarks.htm.

Pylyshyn, Z., 1978. "Imagery and Artificial Intelligence." In Savage, C., ed., *Perception and Cognition: Minnesota Studies in the Philosophy of Science*, vol. 9. Minneapolis: University of Minnesota Press.

Quinsey, V. L., 1995. "The Prediction and Explanation of Criminal Violence." *Internat. J. of Psychiatry and Law* 18:117–127.

Raley, Y., 2005. "Electric Thoughts?" *Scientific American Mind*, April/May:76–81

Ramachandran, V., and Blakeslee, S., 1998. "Do Martians See Red?" In *Phantoms in the Brain: Probing the Mysteries of the Human Mind*. New York: Quill/William Morrow.

Rand, B., ed., 1966 [1912]. *The Classical Psychologists: Selections Illustrating Psychology from Anaxagoras to Wundt*. Gloucester, MA: Peter Smith.

Rapoport, J., 1989. "The Biology of Obsessions and Compulsions." *Scientific American*, March:83–89.

Reed, E., 1987. "Why Do Things Look As They Do? The Implications of J. J. Gibson's *The Ecological Approach to Visual Perception*. In Costall, A., and Still, A., eds., *Cognitive Psychology in Question*. New York: St. Martin's Press.

———, 1988. *James J. Gibson and the Psychology of Perception*. New Haven: Yale University Press.

Reed, K., et al., 2006. "Haptically Linked Dyads: Are Two Motor-Control Systems Better Than One?" *Psychol. Science* 17 5:365.

Reisman, J., 1976. *A History of Clinical Psychology*. New York: Irvington.

Rennels, G., and Shortliffe, E., 1987. "Advanced Computing for Medicine." *Scientific American*, October:154–161.

Rest, J., 1968. "Developmental Hierarchy in Preference and Comprehension of Moral Judgment." Ph.D. dissertation, University of Chicago, 1968, excerpted in Kohlberg, 1984:49–55.

———, 1986. *Moral Development: Advances in Research and Theory*. New York: Praeger.

Rieff, P., 1961 [1959]. *Freud: The Mind of a Moralist*. New York: Anchor Books, Doubleday.

Rind, B., and Seidel, S., 1991. "Effects of Negative Campaigning on Voter Behavior." Poster presentation, American Psychological Society Convention, Washington, DC.

Rips, L., 1990. "Reasoning." *Ann. Rev. Psychol.* 41:321–353.

Roazen, P., 1976. *Freud and His Followers*. New York: Meridian Books.

Roberts, B., et al., 2006. "Patterns of Mean-Level Change in Personality Traits Across the Life Course: A Meta-Analysis of Longitudinal Studies." *Psychol. Bulletin* 132:1–29.

Robinson, D., 1989. *Aristotle's Psychology*. New York: Columbia University Press.

Rock, I., 1983. *The Logic of Perception*. Cambridge, MA: MIT Press.

———, and Heimer, W., 1957. "The Effect of Retinal and Phenomenal Orientation on the Perception of Form." *Amer. J. Psychol.* 70:493–511.

———, and Palmer, S., 1990. "The Legacy of Gestalt Psychology." *Scientific American*, December:84–90.

Rodin, J., and Salovey, P., 1989. "Health Psychology." *Ann. Rev. Psychol.* 40:533–579.

Roediger, R., 2004. "What Happened to Behaviorism." *APS Observer* 17, March.

Rogers, C., 1947. "The Case of Mary Jane Tilden." In W. Snyder, ed., *Casebook of Non-Directive Counseling*. Boston: Houghton Mifflin.

———, 1951. *Client-Centered Therapy: Its Current Practice, Implications, and Theory*. Boston: Houghton Mifflin.

Rōmer, D., et al., 1986. "A Person-Situation Approach to Altruistic Behavior." *J. Personality and Soc. Psychol.* 51 (5):1001–1012.

Rosen, C., 1987. "The Eerie World of Reunited Twins." *Discover*, September:36–42.

Rosenfeld, A., and Stark, E., 1987. "The Prime of Our Lives." *Psychology Today*, May:62–64.

Rosenhan, D., 1973. "On Being Sane in Insane Places." *Science* 173:250–258.

Rosenman, R. H., et al., 1975. "Coronary Heart Disease in the Western Collaborative Study: Final Follow-up Experience of 8–12 Years." *J. Amer. Med. Assoc.* 233:872–877.

Rosenzweig, S., 1986. *Freud and Experimental Psychology: The Emergence of Idiodynamics*. St. Louis: Rana House.

Ross, L., et al., 1977. "Social Roles, Social Control and Biases in Social-Perception Processes." *J. Personality and Soc. Psychol.* 35:484–494.

Rotter, J., 1954. *Social Learning and Clinical Psychology*. Englewood Cliffs, NJ: Prentice Hall.

———, 1966. "Generalized Expectancies for Internal versus External Control of Reinforcement." *Psychol. Monogr.* 80 (1), whole no. 609.

Rovee-Collier, C., and Lipsitt, L., eds., 1990. *Advances in Infancy Research*, vol. 6. Norwood, NJ: Ablex.

Rowe, D., 1982. "Sources of Variability in Sex-Linked Personality Attributes: A Twin Study." *Developmental Psychol.* 18 (3):431–434.

Royce, J, 1973. "Does Person or Self Imply Dualism?" *Amer. Psychologist* 28 (10):883–886.

———, 1988. "Psychologists and Philosophy: The Birth of Division 24 of the American Psychological Association." *Philosophical Psychol.* 1 (3):371–377.

Rozin, P., and Schiller, D., 1980. "The Nature and Acquisition of a Preference for Chili Pepper by Human Beings." *Motivation and Emotion* 4 (1):77–101.

Rumelhart, D., 1978. "Schemata: The Building Blocks of Cognition." University of California at San Diego, Center for Human Information Processing: CHIP report no. 79.

———, 1989. "The Architecture of Mind: A Connectionist Approach." In Posner, M., ed., *Foundations of Cognitive Science*. Cambridge, MA: MIT Press.

———, et al., 1986. *Parallel Distributed Processing: Explorations in the Microstructure of Cognition*. Vol. 1: *Foundations*. Cambridge, MA: MIT Press.

Russell, B., 1945. *A History of Western Philosophy*. New York: Simon and Schuster.

Russell, D., and Cutrona, C., 1991. "Social Support, Stress, and Depressive Symptoms Among the Elderly: Test of a Process Model." *Psychol. and Aging* 6 (2):190–201.

Russell, D., and Jones, W., 1980. "Reactions to Disconfirmation of Paranormal Beliefs." *Personality and Soc. Psychol. Bull.* 6:83–88.

Ryle, G., 1980. *The Concept of Mind*. London: Hutchinson.

Sachs, J., 1967. "Recognition Memory for Syntactic and Semantic Aspects of Connected Discourse." *Perception and Psychophysics* 2:437–442.

Sagi, A., and Hoffman, M., 1976. "Empathic Distress in the Newborn." *J. Developmental Psychol.* 12 (2):175–176.

Salvendy, J., 1991. "Group Psychotherapy in the Late Twentieth Century: An International Perspective." *Group* 15 (1):3–13.

Samelson, F., 1981. "Struggle for Scientific Authority: The Reception of Watson's Behaviorism, 1913–1920." *J. Hist. Behav. Sciences* 17:399–425.

Sanford, N., 1963. "Personality: Its Place in Psychology." In Koch, 1963.

———, 1970. *Issues in Personality Theory.* San Francisco: Jossey-Bass.

Saxe, Leonard, 1991. "Science and the CQT Polygraph." *Integrative Physiol. and Behav. Science* 26 (3):223–231.

Saxe, L., et al., 1985. "The Validity of Polygraph Testing." *Amer. Psychologist* 40 (3):355–366.

———, and Fine, M., 1981. *Social Experiments: Methods for Design and Evaluation.* Beverly Hills, CA: Sage.

Saxe, R., and Powell, L., 2006. "It's the Thought That Counts: Specific Brain Regions for One Component of Theory of Mind." *Psychol. Science* 17 (8):692–699.

Scarborough, E., and Furumoto, L., 1987. *Untold Lives: The First Generation of American Women Psychologists.* New York: Columbia University Press.

Scarr, S., and McCartney, K., 1983. "How People Make Their Own Environments: A Theory of Genotype-Environment Effects." *Child Development* 54:424–435.

Scarr, S., et al., 1981. "Personality Resemblance among Adolescents and Their Parents in Biologically Related and Adoptive Families." *J. Personality and Soc. Psychol.* 40 (5):885–898.

Schachter, S., 1971. "Some Extraordinary Facts about Obese Human Beings and Rats." *Amer. Psychologist* 26:129–144.

———, 1980. "Non-psychological Explanations of Behavior." In Festinger, 1980.

———, 1989. "Stanley Schachter." In Lindzey, 1989.

———, and Gross, L., 1968. "Manipulated Time and Eating Behavior." *J. Personality and Soc. Psychol.* 10:98–106.

———, and Singer, J., 1962. "Cognitive, Social, and Physiological Determinants of Emotional State." *Physiol. Rev.* 69:379–399.

Scherer, K., and Tannenbaum, P., 1986. "Emotional Experiences in Everyday Life: A Survey Approach." *Motivation and Emotion* 10 (4):295–314.

Schiff, W, 1965. "Perception of Impending Collision." *Psychol. Monogr.* 79:1–26.

Schlenker, B., 1974. "Social Psychology and Science." *J. Personality and Soc. Psych.* 29:1–15.

Schneider, A., and Tarshis, B., 1980. *An Introduction to Physiological Psychology,* 2nd ed. New York: Random House.

Schulz, K., 2006. "Brave Neuro World." *The Nation,* January 9.

Schur, M., 1972. *Freud: Living and Dying.* London: Hogarth Press.

Schwartz, S., and Gottlieb, A., 1980a. "Participants' Postexperimental Reactions and the Ethics of Bystander Research." *J. Experimental Soc. Psychol.* 17:396–407.

———, and Gottlieb, A., 1980b. "Participation in a Bystander Intervention Experiment and Subsequent Everyday Helping: Ethical Considerations." *J. Experimental Soc. Psychol.* 16:161–171.

Scott, T., 1991. "A Personal View of the Future of Psychology Departments." *Amer. Psychologist* 46 (9):975–976.

Scott, W., 1903. *The Theory of Advertising.* Boston: Small and Maynard.

———, 1908. *Psychology of Advertising.* Boston: Small and Maynard.

S.E. (Standard Edition). See: Freud, 1953–1966.

Seagert, S., and Winkel, G., 1990. "Environmental Psychology." *Ann. Rev. Psychol* 41:441–477.

846 References

Searle, J., 1990. "Is the Brain's Mind a Computer Program?" *Scientific American*, January:26–31.

Segal, N., 1990. "The Importance of Twin Studies for Individual Differences Research." *J. Counseling and Development* 68:612–622.

Segall, M., 1986. "Culture and Behavior: Psychology in Global Perspective." *Ann. Rev. Psych.* 37:523–564.

Sekuler, R., and Blake, R., 1985. *Perception.* New York: Knopf.

——, and Ganz, L., 1963. "A New After-Effect of Seen Movement with a Stabilized Retinal Image." *Science* 139:1146–1148.

Seligman, M., 1991. *Learned Optimism.* New York: Knopf.

——, 1993. *What You Can Change and What You Can't.* New York: Knopf.

Serin, R., and Amos, N., 1995. "The Role of Psychopathy in the Assessment of Dangerousness." *Internat. J. of Psychiatry and Law* 18:231–238.

Shaffer, D., 1985. *Developmental Psychology: Theory, Research, and Applications.* Monterey, CA: Brooks/Cole.

Share, D., et al., 1984. "Sources of Individual Differences in Reading Acquisition." *J. Educ. Psychol.* 76 (6):1309–1324.

Shaver, K., 1987. *Principles of Social Psychology*, 3rd ed. Hillsdale, NJ: Erlbaum.

Shaver, P., et al., 1992. "Cross-Cultural Similarities and Differences in Emotion and Its Representation." In Clark, M.. ed., *Review of Personality and Social Psychology*, vol. 13. Newbury Park, CA: Sage.

Shaw, R., and Bransford, J., eds., 1977. *Perceiving, Acting, and Knowing.* Hillsdale, NJ: Erlbaum.

Sheffield, F., 1966. "New Evidence on the Drive-Induction Theory of Reinforcement." In Haber, R. N., ed., *Current Research in Motivation.* New York: Holt, Rinehart and Winston.

Sheldon, W., and Stevens, S., 1942. *The Varieties of Temperament: A Psychology of Constitutional Differences.* New York: Harper and Brothers.

Sheldon, W., et al., 1940. *The Varieties of Human Physique: An Introduction to Constitutional Psychology.* New York: Harper and Brothers.

Shepard, R., and Metzler, J., 1971. "Mental Rotation of Three-Dimensional Objects." *Science* 171:701–703.

Sherif, M., 1935. "A Study of Some Social Factors in Perception." *Arch. Psychol.*, no. 187.

——, 1936. *The Psychology of Social Norms.* New York: Harper and Brothers.

——, et al., 1961. *Intergroup Conflict and Cooperation: The Robbers Cave Experiment.* Norman, OK: Institute of Group Relations, University of Oklahoma.

Sherman, S., et al., 1989. "Social Cognition." *Ann. Rev. Psychol.* 40:281–326.

Shields, M., 1984. "Keeping Psychology Human." *Emory Magazine*, June.

Shipley, T., ed., 1961. *Classics in Psychology.* New York: Philosophical Library.

Shiraev, E., and Levy, D., 2006. *Cross-Cultural Psychology: Critical Thinking and Contemporary Applications*, 3rd ed. Boston: Allyn and Bacon.

Shotland, R., 1985. "When Bystanders Just Stand By." *Psychology Today*, June:50–53.

Shull, R., and Grimes, J., 2006. "Resistance to Extinction Following Variable Interval Reinforcement: Reinforcer Rate and Amount." *J. Experimental Anal. of Behavior* 85:23–39.

Siegler, R., 1989. "Mechanisms of Cognitive Development." *Ann. Rev. Psychol.* 40:353–379.

Sifneos, P., 1987. *Short-Term Dynamic Psychotherapy: Evaluation and Technique.* New York: Plenum.

Silbereisen, R., and Noack, P., 1988. "On the Constructive Role of Problem Behavior in Adolescence." In Bolger, N., et at., eds., *Person and Context: Developmental Processes.* New York: Springer-Verlag.

Sills, D., ed., 1968, 1979. *International Encyclopedia of the Social Sciences.* New York:

Macmillan and The Free Press. (The 1979 item is vol. 18, biographical supplement.)

Simon, H., 1969. *The Sciences of the Artificial.* Cambridge, MA: MIT Press.

———, 1991. *Models of My Life.* New York: Basic Books.

Singer, J., 1984. *The Human Personality.* San Diego: Harcourt Brace Jovanovich.

Skinner, B., 1953. *Science and Human Behavior.* New York: The Free Press.

———, 1956. "A Case History in Scientific Method." *Amer. Psychologist* 11:221–233.

———, 1967. "B. F. Skinner." In Boring and Lindzey, 1967.

———, 1972. *Beyond Freedom and Dignity.* New York: Bantam Books-Vintage Books.

———, 1974. *About Behaviorism.* New York: Random House.

———, 1976. *Particulars of My Life.* New York: Knopf.

———, 1979. *The Shaping of a Behaviorist.* New York: Knopf.

———, 1981. "Pavlov's Influence on Psychology in America?" *Hist. Behav. Sciences* 17:242–245.

———, 1983. *A Matter of Consequences.* New York: Knopf.

Slamecka, N., 1985. "Ebbinghaus: Some Associations." *J. Experimental Psychol.: Learning, Memory, and Cognition* 11 (3):414–435.

Smith, D., 1982. "Trends in Counseling and Psychotherapy." *Amer. Psychologist* 37:802–809.

Smith, M. B., 1972. "Toward Humanizing Social Psychology." In Krawiec, 1972, vol. 1.

Smith, M. L., et al., 1980. *The Benefits of Psychotherapy.* Baltimore: The Johns Hopkins University Press.

Smither, R., 1988. *The Psychology of Work and Human Performance.* New York: Harper and Row.

Snarey, J., 1987. "The Vital Aging of Eriksonian Theory and of Erik H. Erikson." *Contemp. Psychol.* 32:928–930.

Snyderman, M., and Rothman, S., 1988. *The IQ Controversy: The Media and Public Policy.* New Brunswick, NJ: Transaction.

Solms, M., 2004. "Freud Returns." *Scientific American* 290:82–88.

Solomon, D., et al., 1987. "Promoting Prosocial Behavior in Schools: A Second Interim Report on a Five-Year Longitudinal Demonstration Project." San Ramon, CA: Developmental Studies Center.

———, et al., 1985. "A Program to Promote Interpersonal Consideration and Cooperation in Children." In Slavin, R., et al., eds., *Learning to Cooperate, Cooperating to Learn.* New York: Plenum.

———, et al., 1987. "Enhancing Children's Prosocial Behavior in the Classroom." San Ramon, CA: Developmental Studies Center.

Sobel, D., 1982. "A New and Controversial Short-Term Psychotherapy." *New York Times:* June 10.

Spencer, H.; 1977 [1855, 1881]. *The Principles of Psychology.* 2 vols. Longwood Publishing Group.

Sperling, G., 1960. "The Information Available in Brief Visual Presentations." *Psychol. Monographs* 74, whole no. 498.

Sperry, R., 1980. "Mind-Brain Interaction: Mentalism, Yes; Dualism, No." *Neurosciences* 5:195–206.

———, and Miner, N., 1955. "Pattern Perception Following Insertion of Mica Plates into Visual Cortex." *J. Compar. and Physiol. Psychol.* 48:463–469.

Spielberger, C., 1990. "Report of the [APA] Treasurer: 1989." *Amer. Psychologist* 45 (7):807–812.

Spinoza, B., *Ethic[s], Demonstrated in Geometrical Order*, etc., trans. by W. Hale White, as revised by Amelia Hutchison Stirling. 4th ed. Oxford University Press. London: Humphrey Milford, 1923.

Sroufe, L., et al., 1988. *Child Development: Its Nature and Course.* New York: Knopf.

Standing, L., 1973. "Learning 10,000 Pictures." *Quart. J. Experimental Psychol.* 25:207–222.

Staub, E., 1978. *Positive Social Behavior and Morality.* Vol. I: *Social and Personal Influences.* New York: Academic Press.

——, 1979. "Understanding and Predicting Social Behavior—with Emphasis on Prosocial Behavior." In Staub, E., ed., *Personality: Basic Issues and Current Research.* Englewood Cliffs, NJ: Prentice Hall.

Stephan, C., and Stephan, W., 1985. *Two Social Psychologies: An Integrative Approach.* Homewood, IL: Dorsey Press.

Sternberg, R., 1984. *Beyond IQ.* Cambridge, MA: Cambridge University Press.

——, 1988. *The Triarchic Mind: A New Theory of Human Intelligence.* New York: Viking.

——, 1990. *Metaphors of Mind: Conceptions of the Nature of Intelligence.* Cambridge: Cambridge University Press.

——, 1999. "The Theory of Successful Intelligence." *Rev. General Psych.* 3:293–316.

Stevens, G., and Gardner, S., 1982. *The Women of Psychology.* 2 vols. Cambridge, MA: Schenkman.

Stone, A., 1987. "Evidence That Secretary IgA Antibody Is Associated with Daily Mood." *J. Personality and Soc. Psychol.* 52:988–993.

Stratton, G., 1897. "Vision Without Inversion of the Retinal Image." *Psychol. Rev.* 4:341–360.

——, 1917: *Theophrastus and the Greek Physiological Psychology Before Aristotle.* London: George Allen and Unwin.

Suetonius. *Lives of the Twelve Caesars.* London: Loeb Library.

Sullivan, M., et al., 1979. "A Conditioning Analysis of Infant Long-Term Memory." *Child Development* 50:152–162.

Sulloway, F., 1982. "Freud and Biology." In Woodward and Ash, 1982.

——, 1983 [1979]. *Freud, Biologist of the Mind.* NY: Basic Books.

Sundstrom, E., et al., 1980. "Privacy at Work: Architectural Correlates of Job Satisfaction and Job Performance." *Academy of Mgt. Jour.* 23:101–117.

Swets, J., and Bjork, R. 1990. "Enhancing Human Performance: An Evaluation of 'New Age' Techniques Considered by the U.S. Army." *Psychol. Science* 1 (2):85–96.

Szasz, T., 1961. *The Myth of Mental Illness.* New York: Harper and Row.

Tacitus, *Annals.* London: Loeb Library, n.d.

Talmon, M., 1990. *Single-Session Therapy.* San Francisco: Jossey-Bass.

Taube, C., et al., 1984. "Patients of Psychiatrists and Psychologists in Office-Based Practice: 1980." *Amer. Psychologist* 39 (12):1435–1447.

——, et al., 1986. "Estimating the Probability and Level of Ambulatory Mental Health Services Use." *Health Services Res.* 2.1 (2):321–340.

Tellegen, A., et al., 1988. "Personality Similarity in Twins Reared Apart and Together. *J. Personality and Soc. Psychol.* 54 (6):1031–1039.

Terman, L., 1916. *The Measurement of Intelligence.* Boston: Houghton Mifflin.

——, et al., 1923. *Intelligence Tests and School Reorganization.* Yonkers-on-Hudson, NY: World Book.

——, and Miles, C., 1936. *Sex and Personality: Studies in Masculinity and Femininity.* New York: McGraw-Hill.

——, and Oden, M., 1947. *The Gifted Child Grows Up: Twenty-Five Years' Follow-Up of a Superior Group.* Stanford, CA: Stanford University Press.

Tertullian, *De Spectaculis, Ad Uxorem, and De Anima.* In *Ante-Nicene Christian Library,* vol. XV, trans. by Peter Holmes. Edinburgh, 1870.

Thackray, A., and Merton, R., 1972. "On Discipline Building: The Paradoxes of George Sarton." *Isis* 63 (213):473–495.

Thagard, P., 2005. *MIND: Introduction to Cognitive Science.* Cambridge: MIT Press.

Thales. *De Anima.* In Rand, 1966 [1912].

Theophrastus. *On the Senses.* In Stratton, 1917.

Thibaut, J., and Riecken, H., 1955. "Some Determinants and Consequences of the Perception of Social Causality." *J. Personality* 24:113–133.

Thomas, A., et al., 1963. *Behavioral Individuality in Early Childhood.* New York: New York University Press.

Thompson, J., 1988. *The Psychobiology of the Emotions.* New York: Plenum.

Thompson, R., and Madigan, S., 2005. *Memory: The Key to Consciousness.* Washington, DC: Joseph Henry Press.

Thorndike, E., 1898. "Animal Intelligence." *Psychol. Rev. Monogr.*, supplement no. 2. Reprinted in Thorndike, 1911.

——, 1911. *Animal Intelligence.* New York: Macmillan.

——, 1936. "Edward Lee Thorndike," in Murchison, 1936.

——, 1940. *Human Nature and the Social Order.* New York: Macmillan.

Thornton, E. M., 1984. *The Freudian Fallacy.* Garden City, NY: Dial.

Todd, J., and Morris, E., 1986. "The Early Research of John B. Watson: Before the Behavioral Revolution." *Behav. Analyst* 9:71–88.

Tolman, C., and Lemery, C., 1990. "How to Reconcile Theoretical Differences in Psychology." *New Ideas in Psychol.* 8 (3):397–402.

Tolman, E., 1932. *Purposive Behavior in Animals and Men.* New York: Appleton-Century-Crofts.

——, 1938. "The Determiners of Behavior at a Choice Point." *Psychol. Rev.* 45 (1):1–35.

——, 1948. "Cognitive Maps in Rats and Men." *Psychol. Rev.* 55:189–208.

——, and Honzick, C., 1930. " 'Insight' in Rats." *University of Calif. Publications in Psychol.* 4:215–232.

Torrey, E., 1986. *Witchdoctors and Psychiatrists: The Common Roots of Psychotherapy and Its Future.* New York: Harper and Row.

Tractinsky, N., 1997. "Aesthetics and Apparent Usability: Empirically Assessing Cultural and Methodological Issues." CHI 97 Electronic Publications: Papers. http//www.acm.org/sigch97/proceedings/paper/nt.htm.

——, et al., 2000. "What Is Beautiful Is Usable." *Interacting with Computers* 13 (2):127–145.

Treisman, A., 1986. "Features and Objects in Visual Processing." *Scientific American*, November:114.

Trenholm, S., 1989. *Persuasion and Social Influence.* Englewood Cliffs, NJ: Prentice Hall.

Triplett, N., 1897. "The Dynamogenic Factors in Pacemaking and Competition." *Amer. J. Psychol.* 9:507–533.

Trotter, R., 1983. "Baby Face." *Psychology Today*, August:14–20.

——, 1991. "Swimmer Against the Tide." *American Health*, October.

Turing, A., 1950. "Computing Machinery and Intelligence." *Mind* 59:433–460.

Turkheimer, E., and Gottesman, I., 1991. "Individual Differences and the Canalization of Human Behavior." *Developmental Psychol.* 27 (1):18–22.

Turner, J., and Helms, D., 1979. *Life Span Development.* Philadelphia: W. B. Saunders.

Tversky, A., and Kahneman, D., 1981. "The Framing of Decisions and the Psychology of Choice." *Science* 211:453–458.

Underhill, L., 2006. "Biofeedback in Back." MGH brochure on www.healthgate.partners.org/browsing/LearningCenter.asp.

U.S. Congress, Office of Technology Assessment, 1980. *The Implications of Cost-Effectiveness Analysis of Medical Technology. Background Paper 3: The Efficacy and Cost Effectiveness of Psychotherapy.* Washington, DC: U.S. Department of Commerce, National Technical Information Service.

——, 1990. *The Use of Integrity Tests for Pre-Employment Screening.* OTA-SET-442. Washington, DC: U.S. Government Printing Office.

Valins, S., 1966. "Cognitive Effects of False Heart-Rate Feedback." *J. Personality and Soc. Psychol.* 4:400–408.

Van Lankveld, J., et al., 2001. "Cognitive-Behavioral Bibliotherapy for Sexual Dysfunction in Heterosexual Couples: A Randomized Waiting-List Controlled Clinical Trial in the Netherlands." *J. Sex Research*: February.

Walk, R., and Gibson, E., 1961. "A Comparative and Analytical Study of Visual Depth Perception." *Psychol. Monogr.* 75 (15):44.

Wallerstein, R., 1989. "Psychoanalysis and Psychotherapy: An Historical Perspective." *Internat. J. Psycho-Anal.* 70 (4):563–591.

Walrond-Skinner, S., 1986. *A Dictionary of Psychotherapy.* London: Routledge and Kegan Paul.

Walsh, A., 1984. "Johann Christoph Spurzheim: In Memoriam." *Hist. Psychol.* 16 (2):1–6.

Warden, C., ed., 1931. *Animal Motivation: Experimental Studies on the Albino Rat.* New York: Columbia University Press.

Warga, C., 1988. "Profile of Psychologist Albert Ellis." *Psychology Today*, September:54–59.

Watkins, C., et al., 1990. "Personality Assessment Training in Counseling Psychology Programs." *J. Personality Assessment* 55:380–383.

Watson, F., 1915. "The Father of Modern Psychology." *Psychol. Rev.* 22:333–353.

Watson, J., 1913. "Psychology As the Behaviorist Views It." *Psychol. Rev.* 20:158–177.

——, 1916. "The Place of the Conditioned Reflex in Psychology." *Psychol. Rev.* 23:89–116.

——, 1919. *Psychology from the Standpoint of a Behaviorist.* Philadelphia: J. B. Lippincott.

——, 1924, 1930. *Behaviorism*, 1st ed., 2nd ed. Chicago: University of Chicago Press.

——, 1961 [1936]. "John Broadus Watson." In Murchison, 1961.

——, and Rayner, R., 1920. "Conditioned Emotional Reactions." *J. Experimental Psychol.* 3:1–14.

Watson, P., 1978. *War on the Mind: The Military Uses and Abuses of Psychology.* London: Hutchinson.

Watson, R., 1978. *The Great Psychologists*, 4th ed. Philadelphia: J. B. Lippincott.

Wedding, D., and Corsini, R., 1979. *Great Cases in Psychotherapy.* Itasca, IL: F. E. Peacock.

Weinberg, R., et al., 1983. "Effect of Situation Criticality on Tennis Performance of Males and Females." *Newsletter, Society for the Advancement of Soc. Psychol.* 9:8–9.

Weiner, I., and Hess, A., eds., 1987. *Handbook of Forensic Psychology.* New York: Wiley.

Weiss, Jay, 1971a. "Effects of Coping Behavior in Different Warning-Signal Conditions on Stress Pathology in Rats." *J. Compar. and Physiol. Psychol.* 57:270–275.

——, 1971b. "Effects of Coping Behavior with and without a Feedback Signal on Stress Pathology in Rats." *J. Compar. and Physiol. Psychol.* 77:1–13.

Weiss, Jos., 1990. "Unconscious Mental Functioning." *Scientific American*, March:103–109.

Wells, E., 1944. "James McKeen Cattell: 1860–1944." *Amer. J. Psychol.* 77:1–13.

Wertheimer, M., 1955a [1923]. "Investigations of the Doctrine of Gestalt." Reprinted in English in W. Ellis, 1955 [1938].

——, 1955b [1912]. "Numbers and Numerical Concepts in Primitive Peoples." Reprinted in English in W. Ellis, 1955 [1938].

——, 1955c [1925]. "The Syllogism and Productive Thinking." Reprinted in English in W. Ellis, 1955 [1938].

——, 1959 [1945]. *Productive Thinking.* New York: Harper and Row.

——, 1961 [1912]. "Experimental Studies on the Seeing of Motion." In Shipley, 1961; originally in German in *Zeitschrift der Psychol.* 61:161–265.

Wertheimer, M., 1980. "Max Wertheimer, Gestalt Prophet." *Gestalt Theory* 2:3–17.

Whalen, R., and Simon, N., 1984. "Biological Motivation." *Ann. Rev. Psychol.* 35:257–276.

White, R., 1959. "Motivation Reconsidered: The Concept of Competence." *Psychol. Rev.* 66:297–333.

White, S., 1983. "The Idea of Development in Developmental Psychology." In Lerner, 1983.

———, and Buka, S., 1987. "Early Education: Programs, Traditions, and Policies." In Rothkopf, E., ed., *Rev. of Research in Educ.* 14. Washington, DC: American Educational Research Association.

Whorf, B., 1956. *Language, Thought, and Reality.* Cambridge, MA: MIT Press.

Whyte, W., 1980. *The Social Life of Small Urban Spaces.* Washington, DC: Conservation Foundation.

Widiger, T., and Trull, T., 1991. "Diagnosis and Clinical Assessment." *Ann. Rev. Psychol.* 42:109–133.

Wigdor, A., 1990. "Fairness in Employment Testing." *Issues in Science and Technology,* Spring.

Wilson, E., 1975. *Sociobiology: The New Synthesis.* Cambridge, MA: Harvard University Press.

———, 1979. *On Human Nature.* New York: Bantam Books.

Windholz, G., 1983. "Pavlov's Position Toward American Behaviorism." *Jour. Hist. Behav. Sciences* 19:394–407.

Winkler, J., and Bromberg, W., M.D., 1944. *Mind Explorers.* Cleveland: World.

Wise, T., 2002. "Failing the Test of Fairness: Institutional Racism and the SAT." Z, August 15. www.zmag.org.

Wolf, T. H., 1973. *Alfred Binet.* Chicago: University of Chicago Press.

Wolfe, J., ed., 1986. *The Mind's Eye: Readings from Scientific American.* New York: W. H. Freeman.

Wolpe, J., 1958. *Psychotherapy by Reciprocal Inhibition.* Stanford: Stanford University Press.

———, 1969. *The Practice of Behavior Therapy.* New York: Pergamon Press.

Woods, S., and Stricker, E., 1999. "Food Intake and Metabolism." In M. Zigmond et al., eds., *Fundamentals of Neuroscience.* San Diego, CA: Academic Press.

Woodward, W., 1984. "William James's Psychology of Will: Its Revolutionary Impact on American Psychology." In Brozek, 1984.

Woodward, W., and Ash, M., eds., 1982. *The Problematic Science: Psychology in Nineteenth-Century Thought.* New York: Praeger.

Woodworth, R., 1919. *Personal Data Sheet.* Chicago: H. Stoelting, 1919.

———, 1944. "James McKeen Cattell: 1860–1944." *Psychol. Rev.* 51:201–209.

Wundt, Wilhelm, 1862. *Contributions to the Theory of Sensory Perception.* Leipzig, 1862.

———, 1897, 1907. *Outlines of Psychology.* Leipzig: Engelmann.

———, 1908. *Logik.* Leipzig: Engelmann.

———, 1977 [1892, 1919]. *Lectures on Human and Animal Psychology.* Bethesda, MD: University Publications of America.

Yerkes, R., ed., 1921. *Psychological Examining in the United States Army. Memoirs of the Nat. Acad. of Sciences* 15:1–890.

Yerkes, R., and Morgulis, S., 1909. "The Method of Pavlov in Animal Psychology." *Psychol. Bull.* 6 (8):257–273.

Yesavage, J., 1985. "Nonpharmacologic Treatments for Memory Losses With Normal Aging." *Amer. J. Psychi.* 142 (5):600–605.

———, and Sheikh, J., 1988. "Nonpharmacologic Treatment of Age-Associated Memory Impairment." *Comprehensive Therapy* 14 (6):44–46.

Zahn-Waxler, C., et al., eds., 1986. *Altruism and Aggression: Biological and Social Origins.* Cambridge: Cambridge University Press.

———, et al., 1979. "Child Rearing and Children's Prosocial Initiations towards Victims of Distress." *Child Development* 50 (2):319–330.

Zajonc, R. B., 1980. "Feeling and Thinking: Preferences Need No Inferences." *Amer. Psychologist* 35 (2):151–175.

———, 1984. "On the Primacy of Affect." *Amer. Psychologist* 41:862–867.

———, 2001. "Mere Exposure: A Gateway to the Subliminal." *Current Directions in Psychological Science* 10:224–228.

Zaretsky, E., 2004. *Secrets of the Soul.* New York: Knopf.

Zeigarnik, B., 1955 [1927]. "On Finished and Unfinished Tasks." In English translation in W. Ellis, 1955 [1938].

Zeller, E., *Stoics, Epicureans and Sceptics.* London, 1870.

Zigler, E., and Styfco, S., 1994. "Head Start Criticisms in a Constructive Context." *Amer. Psychologist* 49:127–132.

Zihl, J., et al., 1983. "Selective Disturbance of Movement Vision after Bilateral Brain Damage." *Brain* 106:313–340.

Zilbergeld, B., 1986. "Psychabuse." *Science* 86, June.

Zimbardo, P., et al., 1974. "The Psychology of Imprisonment: Privation, Power, and Pathology." In Rubin, Z., ed., *Doing Unto Others.* Englewood Cliffs, NJ: Prentice Hall.

Zuckerman, C., and Wallach, H., 1979. "Wolfgang Kohler." In Sills, 1987.

ACKNOWLEDGMENTS

For this updated edition of *The Story of Psychology*, I received the help of a number of individuals and organizations whom it is my pleasure to thank.

Some deserve special mention: Philip Zimbardo, Donald Norman, and Michael Gazzaniga steered me toward the central issues in the explosive developments in psychology within the fifteen years since the first edition of this book was published. Pamela Wilentz of the APA (American Psychological Association) Public Affairs Office, Jessica Kohout of the APA Office of Research, and Nina Jackson, Membership Coordinator of the APS (Association for Psychological Science) provided me with much essential information, contacts, and other forms of assistance. Donald Cherry, survey statistician, National Center for Health Statistics, Centers for Disease Control, ferreted out answers to a number of difficult statistical questions, Howard Silver, executive director of COSSA (Consortium of Social Science Associations), was an invaluable source of information about political interference with psychological research.

Among the many psychologists and other specialists I spoke to, I owe particular thanks to several for their patient explanations of current developments in their special areas: Martha Farah, director of the Center for Cognitive Neuroscience at the University of Pennsylvania; Donald Norman, co-founder of the Nielsen Norman Group and expert on applied cognitive science; Judith Beck, director of the Beck Institute for Cognitive Therapy and Research; Paul Crits-Christoph, director, Center for Psychotherapy Research, University of Pennsylvania; and Brenda Major, president of SPSP (Society for Personality and Social Psychology).

Other people who were helpful: Heidi and Guy Burgess, co-directors of the University of Colorado Conflict Resolution Consortium; Teddy Fine, of the Office of Communications, SAMHSA (Substance Abuse and Mental Health Services Administration); Harrison Gough; Wray Herbert; Dennis Krebs; Colleen Labbe of NIMH (National Institute of Mental Health) Press; Hani Miletski, chair, Sex Therapy Certification Committee of AASECT (American Association of Sex Educators, Counselors, and Therapists); Mark Olfson; Jennifer Shupinka, Division of Research, APS; and Abe Wolf, president of Division 29 (psychotherapy), APA.

In addition to the organizations already cited, I was assisted in various ways by the American Association for the Advancement of Science, the American Group Psychotherapy Association, the American Psychoanalytic Association, the Cognitive Science Society, the National Association for the Advancement of Psychoanalysis, the National Association of

Social Workers, the Society for the Exploration of Psychotherapy Integration, and the Society for Industrial and Organizational Psychology.

The staff of the Gladwyne Free Library in Gladwyne, Pennsylvania, aided me in gaining access to a number of recondite published works in various public and academic libraries.

Bernice Hunt, my wife, was a multiskilled and tireless helper. Herself a writer, editor, computer buff, and retired psychotherapist, she aided me in many and varied ways, among them editing, proofreading, research assistance, online searching for books I needed, and amanuensis chores. She was not only a female version of Figaro but a Patient Griselda, putting up uncomplainingly with my innumerable requests, obsessive work habits, and fits of grouchiness.

I also want to reiterate my gratitude to the people who helped me with the first edition of *The Story of Psychology.*

Three people deserve my special thanks: Herman Gollob, my editor, who not only conceived of this project but throughout was a writer's dream of what an editor should be; Bernice Hunt, my wife, who painstakingly and excellently line edited the first draft of the entire manuscript; and Frances Apt, who was a superb copy editor. Emily Wolman, my granddaughter, diligently tracked down and identified a number of missing or incomplete references.

My thanks to the psychologists who read chapters about which they have special knowledge and made invaluable corrections and comments: Morton Deutsch, Randy Gobbel, Donald Norman, and Irvin Rock. Bernice Hunt lent her expertise as a psychotherapist and her wide knowledge of that field to a critique of chapter 17.

The following granted me time for lengthy interviews and furnished me with useful data: Raymond D. Fowler, James M. Jones, Lewis P. Lipsitt, and Bryant Welch, all of the APA; Lee Herring of the APS; and Douglas Bray, Linda Gottfredson, Dennis Krebs, Ulric Neisser, Julian Rotter, and Martin E. P. Seligman. I was generously supplied with research materials by the APA, the APS, the National Research Council, the National Science Foundation, the National Institute of Mental Health, the National Institutes of Health, and the Office of Technology Assessment.

Librarians at Long Island University's Southampton College and the main library at the State University of New York, Stony Brook, rendered me invaluable help.

About 250 psychologists and people in other disciplines and professions answered my written and telephoned queries, sent me reprints, and made helpful suggestions. I cannot list them all here but must single out for notice some who extended themselves beyond the bounds of normal collegiality: David W. Arnold, Mitchell G. Ash, Aaron T. Beck, Ludy T. Benjamin, Arthur C. Bohart, Douglas Bray, Timothy C. Brock, Ross Buck, William C. Byham, Paul T. Costa, Kay Deaux, Charles E. Early, Albert Ellis, H. J. Eysenck, Charles R. Gallistel, Harrison G. Gough, Wallace B. Hall, Ann Howard, Karen Hollis, Carroll Izard, Edward E. Jones, Bela Julesz, Sigmund Koch, Ronald W. Mayer, James L. McGaugh, John C. Norcross, J. Bruce Overmier, Robert Plutchik, John A. Popplestone, Irvin Rock, Saul Rosenzweig, Leonard Saxe, Stanley Schachter, Robert S. Siegler, Philip Teitelbaum, Wilse B. Webb, Sheldon H. White, and William R. Woodward.

I acknowledge permission from the following to quote copyrighted text and/or reproduce copyrighted figures as specified:

Allyn and Bacon, figure 9.4, "IQ and Genetic Relationship," from *Psychology and Life,* 17th ed., 2005, by Richard Gerrig and Philip G. Zimbardo (figure 1 in the present work).

American Association for the Advancement of Science and Roger N. Shepard: three figures from "Mental Rotation of Three-Dimensional Objects" by R. N. Shepard, *Science* 171:2/10/11 (figure 36 in the present work).

American Psychological Association: the figure of a cat from "Some Informational Aspects of Visual Perception" by Fred Attneave, *Psychol. Rev.* 61 (1954):183–193 (figure 29 in the present work); American Psychological Association and Jay McClelland: the figure "Network and connectionist representations of concepts relating to birds," from the article "Why there are complementary learning systems and the hippocampus and neocortex," *Psychol. Rev.* 102 (3) (1995):430 (figure 42 in the present work).

The British Psychological Society: two figures of impossible objects from "Impossible Objects: A Special Type of Visual Illusion," *Brit. Jour. of Psychol.* 49 (1958):31–33 (figure 27 in the present work).

Raymond B. Cattell: diagram of three personality profiles from his "Personality Pinned Down," *Psychology Today*, July 1973 (figure 17 in the present work).

Albert Ellis: a passage from his *Growth Through Reason* (Wilshire, 1975), and a passage from his "Self-Direction in Sport and Life," *Rational Living* 17 (1982):27–33.

Elsevier Science Publishers: the logo COGNITION from early 1970s editions of *Cognition* (figure 45 in the present work); figure of Hs and Ss in "Forest Before Trees" by David Navon in *Cognitive Psychology* 9 (3), July, 1977 (figure 14 in the present work).

Lawrence Erlbaum Associates, Inc., and Elizabeth Loftus: figure titled "A piece of the semantic memory network—a later view," from *Cognitive Psychology and Information Processing: An Introduction* (1979), edited by Roy Lachman, Janet L. Lachman, and Earl C. Butterfield (figure 41 in the present work).

H. J. Eysenck: multiplex figure of personality dimensions from *The Causes and Cures of Neurosis* (Knapp, 1965), by H. J. Eysenck and S. Rachman (figure 16 in the present work).

W. H. Freeman and Company, publishers, and Ulric Neisser: figure 1 from Ulric Neisser's *Cognition and Reality*, 1976 (adapted in figure 39 in the present work).

Greenwood Publishing Group: a passage from Wilhelm Wundt's *Lectures on Human and Animal Psychology*, University Publications of America, 1977 [1892, 1919].

Guilford Publications and Aaron T. Beck: two passages from *Cognitive Therapy of Depression*, 1979, by Aaron T. Beck, A. John Rush, et al.

HarperCollins Publishers and James R. Rest: a passage, adapted, from the excerpt of Rest's doctoral dissertation that appears on pp. 49–55 of Lawrence Kohlberg, *Psychology of Moral Development*, vol. II, Harper and Row, 1984.

Hogarth Press, Sigmund Freud Copyrights, and The Institute of Psychoanalysis: passages from *The Standard Edition of the Complete Psychological Works of Sigmund Freud*, 23 vols., 1953–1966, James Strachey, ed.; as follows: three passages from pp. 63, 101–102, and 270 of "Studies in Hysteria," 1893–1895, vol. II of the Standard Edition; two passages from pp. 116–118 of "Fragment of an Analysis of a Case of Hysteria," 1905, vol. VII; a passage from p. 223 of "Formulations on the Two Principles of Mental Functioning," 1911, vol. XII;. and a passage from pp. 94–95 of "Inhibitions, Symptoms and Anxiety," 1926, vol. XX.

Houghton Mifflin Company: a passage from "The Case of Mary Jane Tilden" by Carl Rogers, in *Casebook of Non-Directive Counseling*, 1947, William U. Snyder, ed.; and two passages from *The Origin of Consciousness in the Breakdown of the Bicameral Mind*, 1976, by Julian Jaynes.

Bela Julesz: random-dot stereogram from his *Foundations of Cyclopean Perception*, Chicago University Press, 1971 (figure 34 in the present work).

Dalia S. Kleinmuntz, trustee for the Benjamin Kleinmuntz Trust: four sample Rorschach inkblots with interpretations, from Benjamin Kleinmuntz, *Essentials of Abnormal Psychology*, Harper and Row, 1980 (figure 15 in the present work).

Macmillan Journals, Ltd.: diagram from "Apparent Relative Movement of 'Unsharp' and 'Sharp' Visual Patterns," by E. J. Verheijen, reprinted by permission from *Nature* 29 (1963):160–161 (figure 21 in the present work).

Macmillan Publishing Company: a passage from *Science and Human Behavior* by B. F. Skinner, The Free Press, 1953, and figures 2-14A and 2-14B from *An Introduction to Perception*, 1975, by Irvin Rock (figure 13 in the present work).

Walter Mischel: three sample questions from a personality test, p. 132 of his *Introduction to Personality*, 2nd edition, Holt, Rinehart and Winston, 1976.

The MIT Press: ray figure in D. M. MacKay, "Interactive Processes in Visual Perception," in *Sensory Communication*, 1961, edited by Walter A. Rosenblith (figure 30 in the present work); figure 6-24, p. 160, in *The Logic of Perception*, 1983, by Irvin Rock (figure 32 in the present work); and figure 2, p. 50, from *Parallel Distributed Processing*, vol. 1, *Foundations*, by David E. Rumelhart, James L. McClelland, and the PDP Research Group, 1986 (figure 43 in the present work).

W. W. Norton & Company: from *The Standard Edition of the Complete Psychological Works of Sigmund Freud*, first published in English by Hogarth Press, 23 vols., 1953–1966; passages from "Jokes and Their Relation to the Unconscious," 1905, vol. VIII; "Introductory Lectures on Psychoanalysis," 1916–1917, vol. XVI; "An Autobiographical Study," 1925, vol. XX; "Inhibitions, Symptoms, and Anxiety," 1926, vol. XX; and "New Introductory Lectures," 1933, vol. XXII. Also, three passages from *Pioneers of Psychology*, 1979, by Raymond Fancher.

W. W. Norton & Company, and Michael Gazzaniga: figure 5.20 from *Cognitive Neuroscience: The Biology of the Mind*, 2nd ed., by Michael S. Gazzaniga, Richard B. Ivry, and George R. Mangun, 2002 (figure 31 in the present work); and figure 11.3 from *Psychological Science*, 2nd ed., by Michael S. Gazzaniga and Todd Heatherton, 2006, 2003 (figure 19 in the present work).

Plenum Publishing Corp. and Peter Sifneos: a passage from Sifneos's *Short-Term Dynamic Psychotherapy*, 1987.

Brent Roberts and the APA: fig. 2 from "Patterns of Mean-Level Change in Personality" by Brent Roberts, Kate Walton, and Wolfgang Viechtbauer," *Psychol. Bull.* 132 (figure 18 in the present work).

Julian Rotter and Univ. of Connecticut Psychology and CLAS Academic Services Center: questions 2, 4, 11, and 25 from his monograph "Generalized Expectancies for Internal versus External Control of Reinforcement." *Psychol. Monogr.* 80 (1), whole no. 609 (1966).

Routledge publications: passages from *The Mentality of Apes* by Wolfgang Köhler, 1948 [1917].

Sage Publications, Morton Deutsch, and Bruce M. Russett, editor, *Journal of Conflict Resolution*: map of the "Acme-Bolt Game," from "Studies of Interpersonal Bargaining," by Morton Deutsch and Robert M. Krauss, *Journal of Conflict Resolution* 4 (1962), copyright by Sage Publications, 1962 (figure 20 in the present work).

Roger N. Shepard: top line of figures on p. 107 of "Turning Something Over in the Mind" by Lynn A. Cooper and Roger N. Shepard, *Scientific American*, December 1984 (figure 37 in the present work).

Stanford University Press: a passage from *Psychology by Reciprocal Inhibition* by Joseph Wolpe, 1958.

Wadsworth Publishing Company: figure 7.42, p. 264, in *Sensation and Perception*, 3rd edition, 1989, by E. Bruce Goldstein (figure 35 in the present work).

INDEX

Page numbers in *italics* refer to figures and illustrations.